D0421228

Business Ethics

Decision Ma **Social Responsibility**

for

Business Ethics

Decision Making for Personal Integrity and Social Responsibility

Fourth Edition

Laura P. Hartman
Boston University

Joe DesJardins
College of St. Benedict/ St. John's University

Chris MacDonald
Ryerson University

BUSINESS ETHICS: DECISION MAKING FOR PERSONAL INTEGRITY AND SOCIAL RESPONSIBILITY, FOURTH EDITION

Published by McGraw-Hill Education, 2 Penn Plaza, New York, NY 10121. Copyright © 2018 by McGraw-Hill Education. All rights reserved. Printed in the United States of America. Previous editions © 2014, 2011, and 2008. No part of this publication may be reproduced or distributed in any form or by any means, or stored in a database or retrieval system, without the prior written consent of McGraw-Hill Education, including, but not limited to, in any network or other electronic storage or transmission, or broadcast for distance learning.

Some ancillaries, including electronic and print components, may not be available to customers outside the United States.

This book is printed on acid-free paper.

1 2 3 4 5 6 7 8 9 LCR 21 20 19 18 17

ISBN 978-1-259-41785-6
MHID 1-259-41785-9

Chief Product Officer, SVP Products & Markets: *G. Scott Virkler*
Vice President, Content Production & Technology Services: *Betsy Whalen*
Managing Director: *Susan Gouijnstook*
Director: *Michael Ablassmeir*
Product Developer: *Laura Hurst Spell*
Marketing Manager: *Necco McKinley*
Director, Content Design & Delivery: *Terri Schiesl*
Program Manager: *Mary Conzachi*
Content Project Managers: *Christine A. Vaughan; Keri Johnson*
Buyer: *Susan K. Culbertson*
Design: *Matt Diamond*
Content Licensing Specialist: *Shannon Manderscheid*
Typeface: *10/12 STIX Mathjax Main*
Compositor: *SPi Global*
Printer: *LSC Communications*

All credits appearing on page or at the end of the book are considered to be an extension of the copyright page.

Library of Congress Control Number: 2016043562

The Internet addresses listed in the text were accurate at the time of publication. The inclusion of a website does not indicate an endorsement by the authors or McGraw-Hill Education, and McGraw-Hill Education does not guarantee the accuracy of the information presented at these sites.

www.mheducation.com

To Rachel and Emma.

—Laura Hartman

To Michael and Matthew.

—Joe DesJardins

To Georgia.

—Chris MacDonald

About the Authors

Laura P. Hartman   *Boston University*

Laura Pincus Hartman is director of the Susilo Institute for Ethics in the Global Economy and clinical professor of business ethics in the department of Organizational Behavior at Boston University. For the past 25 years, Hartman was honored to serve in roles at DePaul University, including associate vice president, Vincent de Paul Professor of Business Ethics at DePaul University's Driehaus College of Business, and director of its Institute for Business and Professional Ethics. She has been an invited professor at INSEAD (France), HEC (France), and the Université Paul Cezanne Aix Marseille III, among other European universities, and she previously held the Grainger Chair in Business Ethics at the University of Wisconsin–Madison. Hartman cofounded and currently serves as executive director of a trailblazing trilingual elementary school in Haiti, the School of Choice/l'Ecole de Choix. She also cofounded an online micro-development, finance, and education system for people living in poverty in Haiti, called Zafèn. Previously, Hartman served as director of external partnerships for Zynga.org, the charitable arm of social game developer Zynga. Her other books include *Rising above Sweatshops: Innovative Management Approaches to Global Labor Challenges, Employment Law for Business, Perspectives in Business Ethics,* and *The Legal Environment of Business: Ethical and Public Policy Contexts.* Hartman graduated from Tufts University and received her law degree from the University of Chicago Law School.

Joe DesJardins   *College of St. Benedict/St. John's University*

Joe DesJardins holds the Ralph Gross Chair in Business and the Liberal Arts and is professor of philosophy at the College of St. Benedict and St. John's University in Minnesota. His other books include: *An Introduction to Business Ethics, Environmental Ethics: An Introduction to Environmental Philosophy, Environmental Ethics: Concepts, Policy & Theory, Contemporary Issues in Business Ethics* (coeditor with John McCall), and *Business, Ethics, and the Environment: Imagining a Sustainable Future.* He has served as president and executive director of the Society for Business Ethics, and has published and lectured extensively in the areas of business ethics, environmental ethics, and sustainability. He received his BA from Southern Connecticut State University, and his MA and PhD from the University of Notre Dame.

Chris MacDonald   *Ryerson University*

Chris MacDonald is an associate professor and director of the Ted Rogers Leadership Centre at Ryerson University's Ted Rogers School of Management in Toronto, Canada, and a senior nonresident fellow at Duke University's Kenan Institute for Ethics. His peer-reviewed publications range across business ethics, professional ethics, bioethics, the ethics of technology, and moral philosophy, and he is coauthor of a best-selling textbook called *The Power of Critical Thinking* (4th Canadian Edition, 2016). He is cofounder and coeditor of both the *Business Ethics Journal Review* and the news and commentary aggregator site *Business Ethics Highlights.* He is perhaps best known for his highly respected blog, *The Business Ethics Blog,* which is carried by *Canadian Business* magazine.

Preface

We began writing the first edition of this textbook in 2006, soon after a wave of major corporate scandals had shaken the financial world. Headlines made the companies involved in these ethical scandals household names: Enron, WorldCom, Tyco, Adelphia, HealthSouth, Global Crossing, Arthur Andersen, KPMG, J.P. Morgan, Merrill Lynch, Morgan Stanley, Citigroup, Salomon Smith Barney, and even the New York Stock Exchange itself. At the time, we suggested that, in light of such significant cases of financial fraud, mismanagement, criminality, and deceit, the relevance of business ethics could no longer be questioned.

Sadly, though we are now several editions into the publication, these very same issues are as much alive today as they were a decade ago—and decades prior to our original publication. While our second edition was preceded by the financial meltdown in 2008–2009 and the problems faced by such companies as AIG, Countrywide, Lehman Brothers, Merrill Lynch, and Bear Stearns, and of the financier Bernard Madoff, this current edition continues to witness financial and ethical malfeasance of historic proportions and the inability of market mechanisms, internal governance structures, or government regulation to prevent it.

But the story is not all bad news. While cases of fraud continue to make headlines (think of the recent Volkswagen and Wells Fargo scandals), countless small and large firms provide examples of highly ethical—and profitable—business enterprises. The emergence of benefit corporations (see chapter 5 for examples) is only one instance of corporations dedicated to the common good. In this edition, we aim to tell the stories of both the good and the bad in business.

As we reflect on both the ethical corruption and the ethical success stories of the past decade, the importance of ethics is all too apparent. The questions today are less about whether ethics should be a part of business strategy and, by necessity, the business school curriculum, than about which values and principles should guide business decisions and *how* ethics should be integrated within business and business education.

This textbook provides a comprehensive, yet accessible introduction to the ethical issues arising in business. Students who are unfamiliar with ethics will find that they are as unprepared for careers in business as students who are unfamiliar with accounting and finance. It is fair to say that students will not be fully prepared, even within traditional disciplines such as accounting, finance, human resource management, marketing, and management, unless they are sufficiently knowledgeable about the ethical issues that arise specifically within and across those fields.

Whereas other solid introductory textbooks are available, several significant features make this book distinctive. We emphasize a **decision-making approach** to ethics, and we provide strong **pedagogical support** for both teachers and students throughout the entire book. In addition, we bring both of these strengths to the students through a pragmatic discussion of issues with which they are already often familiar, thus approaching them through subjects that have already generated their interest.

New to the Fourth Edition

While our goal for the fourth edition remains the same as for the first—to provide "a comprehensive yet accessible introduction to the ethical issues arising in business"—readers will notice a few changes. We have retained the same logical structure and chapter organization of previous editions since we have heard from many colleagues and reviewers that this structure works well for a semester-long course in business ethics. But every chapter has been revised to include new and updated material, cases, topics, and readings. Importantly, we continue to provide increased international perspectives, with particular references to Canadian and UK legislation and institutions.

Among the changes to this edition are the following:

New Opening Decision Points for many chapters, including new cases or in-depth discussions on:

- The Olympics
- Executive compensation versus employee pay (at Gravity Payments)
- Benefit corporations
- Digital marketing
- The business of food
- Volkswagen

New cases, Reality Checks, or Decision Points on such topics as:

- Stopping corruption
- Trust in CEOs
- Crony capitalism
- Fooling ourselves
- Stakeholder engagement at Johnson Matthey
- Recognizing the value of stakeholders' trust (at Volkswagen)
- Raising the minimum wage
- Regulating car safety
- Alternative medicine
- Discussion whether all human rights should become legal rights
- What people will say about you when you retire
- Snapchat
- Profits
- Strict products liability and risk management
- GMO food labeling
- Sustainable business
- Triple bottom line
- Zappos' Core Values
- General Motors
- Ethics training programs

- Global culture
- Culture integration
- Timely analyses of the current responses of multinationals to global labor conditions
- Comparison of privacy rights in the United States and Europe

New readings on:

- How bad management leads to bad ethics
- A diverse perspective on culture
- A fresh perspective on Apple's labor conditions in China
- An Asian perspective on sexual harassment
- *Among others*

In addition to this new content, we have updated previous material, including:

- Most cases throughout the text
- Statistics and global applications including the European Union's Data Privacy Accord and the Privacy Shield
- Discussion of culture, including national culture, Hofstede, Jim Collins's more recent work, and the Zappos's management reconfiguration
- Analysis of the recent legal changes on workplace ethics, including the legalization of marijuana in some states and the use by employers of social media investigations during recruitment and selection processes

As always, we reviewed and revised the entire text for accessibility, consistency, and clarity.

Acknowledgments

A textbook should introduce students to the cutting edge of the scholarly research that is occurring within a field. As in any text that is based in part on the work of others, we are deeply indebted to the work of our colleagues who are doing this research. We are especially grateful to those scholars who graciously granted us personal permission to reprint their materials in this or previous editions:

Christine Bader   **Richard Moberly**
Norm Bowie   **Gael O'Brien**
Michael Cranford   **Tara Radin**
Marc Gunther   **Bob Tricker**
Carl Hausman   **Theo Vermaelen**
Avner Levin   **Lindsey Wylie**
Dennis Moberg

Our book is a more effective tool for both students and faculty because of their generosity. In particular, thanks to Ryerson students **Stefania Venneri, Tanya Walia**, and **Daniel Marotta** for their useful suggestions, and to **Katrina Myers** at Boston University and **Summer Brown** at DePaul University for their exceptional research and editing assistance. In addition, we wish to express our deepest gratitude to the reviewers and others whose efforts served to make this manuscript infinitely more effective:

Carolyn Ashe
University of Houston Downtown

Rosemary Hartigan
University of Maryland University College

Jonathan Krabill
Columbus State Community College

Ingemar Patrick Linden
New York University

Patrick Murphy
University of Notre Dame

Cherie Ann Sherman
Ramapo College of New Jersey

Our thanks also go out to the team at McGraw-Hill Education who helped this book come into existence:

Michael Ablassmeir
Director

Laura Hurst Spell
Senior Product Developer

Necco McKinley
Senior Marketing Manager

Christine Vaughan
Lead Content Project Manager

Brief Contents

Table of Contents

Ethics and Business

It takes 20 years to build a reputation and five minutes to ruin it. If you think about that you'll do things differently.

Warren Buffett

Ethics is the new competitive environment.

Peter Robinson, CEO, Mountain Equipment Co-op (2000–2007)

Without commonly shared and widely entrenched moral values and obligations, neither the law, nor democratic government, nor even the market economy will function properly.

Vaclav Havel, 1936–2011

No snowflake in an avalanche ever feels responsible.

Voltaire, 1694–1778

Opening Decision Point[1] *Zika Virus and Olympic Sponsors*

Early in the summer of 2016—just weeks away from the start of the Summer Olympics, scheduled to be held in Rio de Janeiro, Brazil—a group of nearly 200 prominent scientists, physicians, and ethicists signed a letter strongly suggesting that the International Olympic Committee consider moving or postponing the Games. At issue was the ongoing Zika virus epidemic sweeping through parts of Brazil and a couple of dozen other countries, mostly in Latin and South America. Zika virus is carried by mosquitoes (although it can also be spread sexually); it is rarely serious in adults, but pregnant women who are infected can give birth to babies with severe neurological disorders including microcephaly.

The worry, according to these experts, was that the Rio Games would inevitably speed the spread of the virus globally, as some of the anticipated 500,000 athletes and tourists expected to visit Rio during the event would surely become infected and bring the virus home with them.

The letter focused public attention on the International Olympic Committee (IOC) and the advice that the IOC would get in this regard from the World Health Organization (WHO). As the date of the opening ceremonies approached, neither organization seemed moved by the letter.

But the letter addressed to these international organizations failed to mention the role played by another group of powerful organizations, namely the large corporations sponsoring the Games and that effectively make the Olympics possible. For the 2016 Summer Olympics, "Worldwide Olympic Partners" (that is, top-tier sponsors) included Coca-Cola, Bridgestone, McDonald's, General Electric, Visa, and others. Dozens of other companies were listed as "Official Sponsors," "Official Supporters," or "Suppliers." Becoming a top-tier Worldwide Olympic Partner cost each company more than $100 million. That level of financial commitment presumably brings considerable influence. The question was whether, and how, they would use that influence.

Adding to the confusion was the fact that while many experts were worried, the worry was not unanimous. The head of the U.S. Centers for Disease Control and Prevention (CDC), for example, publicly predicted that the Rio Olympics would not be a factor in spreading the Zika virus.

What should the Olympic sponsors have done? What, if anything, should they have done in light of the concerns expressed in the experts' letter? Should they have encouraged the IOC to move or postpone the Games? This would presumably have cost them money: Each sponsor no doubt already had spent millions on marketing linked to the Olympics, and much of it would have been linked directly to the August timing and to Rio. Changing the date or the place would have been very costly. But then, what about the social responsibility to help control an epidemic?

1. How much responsibility do sponsoring corporations bear for the outcomes of things like the Olympic Games? All the sponsors are doing is paying money to have their logos featured at Olympic venues and the right to use the Olympic logo in their advertising. The Rio sponsors wouldn't be *directly* spreading Zika. Does that indirectness matter, ethically?

2. One danger is that the decision would not be based on ethics at all, and that the organizations involved would fall prey to a general "the Olympics must go on!" attitude. It's widely recognized that a "can-do" attitude is what led the National Aeronautics and Space Administration (NASA) to launch the Space Shuttle *Challenger* in January 1986 despite warnings that doing so could be unsafe. Key decision makers believed that as a high-performance organization engaged in an important mission, NASA simply could not fail. The results of that attitude are notorious: *Challenger* exploded 73 seconds into its voyage, killing all seven crew members instantly.

3. Does the lack of full agreement between experts absolve Olympic sponsors of blame if the Rio Olympics ended up contributing to the spread of the Zika virus? Would it be ethically correct of the sponsors to say, after the fact, "We didn't know for sure there would be a problem"?

Source: Adapted from Chris MacDonald, "Should Olympic Sponsors Pull Out over the Danger of Zika Virus?" *Canadian Business* [Blog], June 2, 2016, www.canadianbusiness.com/blogs-and-comment/should-olympic-sponsors-pull-out-over-the-danger-of-zika-virus/ (accessed June 5, 2016).

 Chapter Objectives

After reading this chapter, you will be able to:

1. Explain why ethics is important in the business environment.
2. Explain the nature of business ethics as an academic discipline.
3. Distinguish the ethics of personal integrity from the ethics of social responsibility.
4. Distinguish ethical norms and values from other business-related norms and values.
5. Distinguish legal responsibilities from ethical responsibilities.
6. Explain why ethical responsibilities go beyond legal compliance.
7. Describe ethical decision making as a form of practical reasoning.

Introduction: Making the Case for Business Ethics

Even though years have passed and other scandals have occurred, we still refer to the 2001 Enron Corporation collapse as the landmark event in this century's business ethics news; since that time ethics and values have seldom strayed from the front pages of the press. Recall the 2008 collapse of the investment schemes of former NASDAQ chair Bernie Madoff, the largest fraud of its kind in history with total losses to investors in the billions. When we are referring to scandals such as Canadian publisher Conrad Black's conviction for fraud and obstruction of justice (related to diverting corporate funds for personal use), the list of leaders that have been involved with legal and ethical wrongdoing is, sadly, incredibly long. Reflect for a moment on the businesses that have been involved in scandals or, at least, in flawed decision making since the start of the 21st century: Volkswagen, SNC-Lavalin, Valeant, Siemens, Takata, Enron, Halliburton, AIG, WorldCom, Tyco, Adelphia, Rite Aid, Sunbeam, Waste Management, HealthSouth, Global Crossing, Arthur Andersen, Ernst & Young, ImClone, KPMG, J.P. Morgan, Merrill Lynch, Morgan Stanley, Bear Stearns, Fannie Mae, Countrywide Financial Corp., Citigroup, Salomon Smith Barney, Marsh & McLennan, Credit Suisse, First Boston, Goldman Sachs, AmeriQuest, Deutsche Bank, Bank of America, UBS, Standard & Poor's, Moody's, BP Global, Deep Water Horizon, Johnson & Johnson, Pfizer, Firestone Tire and Rubber Co., and even the New York Stock Exchange. Individuals implicated in ethical scandals include Kenneth Lay, Jeffrey Skilling, Andrew Fastow, Dennis Kozlowski, Bill McGuire, Bob Nardelli, John J. Rigas, Richard M. Scrushy, Martha Stewart, Samuel Waksal, Richard Grasso, Bernard Ebbers, Angelo Mozilo, Kerry Killinger, Stephen Rotella, David Schneider, Vikrim Pandit, and Bernie Madoff. Beyond these well-known scandals, consumer boycotts based on allegations of unethical conduct or alliances have targeted such well-known firms as Nike, McDonald's, Carrefour, Home Depot, Chiquita Brands International, Fisher-Price, Gap, Shell Oil, ExxonMobil, Levi Strauss, Donna Karan, Kmart, Walmart, Nestlé, Nokia, Siemens, BP, H&M, Target, Timberland, Delta Air Lines, and Chick-fil-A.

This chapter will introduce business ethics as a process of responsible decision making. Simply put, the scandals and ruin experienced by all the institutions and every one of the individuals just mentioned were brought about by *ethical failures*. If we do, indeed, reflect on those institutions and individuals, perhaps they should remind us of the often-repeated Santayana warning, "Those who cannot remember the past are condemned to repeat it."[2] This text provides a decision-making model that, we contend, can help individuals understand these failures and avoid future business and personal tragedies. As an introduction to that decision-making model, this chapter reflects on the intersection of ethics and business.

Ethical decision making in business is not at all limited to the type of major corporate decisions with dramatic social consequences listed earlier. At some point, every worker, and certainly everyone in a management role, will be faced with an issue that will require ethical decision making. Not every decision can be covered by economic, legal, or company rules and regulations. More often than not, responsible decision making must rely on the personal values and principles of the individuals involved. Individuals will have to decide for themselves what type of person they want to be.

At other times, decisions will involve significant general policy issues that affect entire organizations, as happened in all the well-known corporate scandals. The managerial role especially involves decision making that establishes organizational precedents and has organizational and social consequences.

Hence, both of these types of situations—the personal and the organizational—are reflected in the title of this book: *Business Ethics: Decision Making for Personal Integrity and Social Responsibility.*

How should we conceive of the relationship between business and market activity, on one hand, and ethical concerns, on the other? This is not a new question, but one that can be found since the very dawn of modern capitalism. Often considered to be the founding father of laissez-faire economics, the 18th-century philosopher Adam Smith is best known for promoting the virtues of self-interest in *The Wealth of Nations.* However, in another of his major works, *The Theory of Moral Sentiments,* Smith suggests that sympathy and benevolence are fundamental human values. The relationship between these two texts has long puzzled scholars and has come to represent the broader issue of the relationship of economic and moral values that is addressed in the study of business ethics. As one commentator writes, "The Adam Smith problem—how to reconcile these two great books—is also the challenge of how to order a society in which competition and ethical sensibility are combined."[3]

As recently as the mid-1990s, articles in such major publications as *The Wall Street Journal, Harvard Business Review,* and *U.S. News and World Report* questioned the legitimacy and value of teaching classes in business ethics. Few disciplines face the type of skepticism that commonly confronted courses in business ethics. Many students believed that the term *business ethics* was a contradiction. Many also viewed ethics as a mixture of sentimentality and personal opinion that would interfere with the efficient functioning of business. After all, who is to identify right and wrong, and, if no law is broken, who will "punish" the "wrongdoers"? However, this approach has left business executives as one of the lowest-ranked professions in terms of trust and honesty, according to a 2011 Gallup poll.[4]

Leaders realize that they can no longer afford this approach in contemporary business. The direct costs of unethical business practice are more visible today than perhaps they have ever been. As discussed earlier, the first decade of the new millennium has been riddled with highly publicized corporate scandals, the effects of which did not escape people of any social or income class. Moreover, we saw the economy take a downward spiral into one of the largest financial crises of the past 80 years, driven significantly by questionable subprime mortgage lending practices at the banks, as well as the widespread trading of risky mortgage-backed securities in the markets. These lending and trading efforts encouraged bad debt to appreciate beyond levels that the market could bear. The inevitable correction caused real estate values in most markets to decline sharply, domestic credit markets to freeze, and the federal government to intervene with a rescue package.

If the key (or not so key) decision makers who contributed to the bubble bursting had acted differently, could these unfortunate consequences have been avoided? It is perhaps enough to point out that it is a bit of a vicious circle. Economic turmoil encourages misconduct; there is a significant bump in observed workplace misconduct during times of economic challenges. Some money-saving strategies deployed by struggling companies, such as compensation/benefit reductions and hiring freezes, have been found to increase misconduct by more than 35 percent,[5] In turn, misconduct based on fraud alone causes an estimated 5 percent loss of annual revenues, equivalent to more than $2.9 trillion of the 2009 gross world product.

Personal retirement accounts, institutional investments like pension funds, government employees' retirement funds, and major insurance companies are heavily invested in corporate stocks and bonds, as well as pooled securities of every size, shape, and order. As a result, the impact of Wall Street failures on Main Street families and businesses become larger and more noticeable by the day.

The questions today are less about *why* or *should* ethics be a part of business; they are about *which* values and principles should guide business decisions and *how* ethics should be integrated within business. (A persuasive case for *why* this shift has occurred can be found in Reading 1-1, "Value Shift," by Lynn Sharp Paine.) Students unfamiliar with the basic concepts and categories of ethics will find themselves as unprepared for careers in business as students who are unfamiliar with accounting and finance. In fact, it is fair to say that students will not be fully prepared, even within fields such as accounting, finance, human resource management, marketing, and management, unless they are familiar with the ethical issues that arise within those specific fields.

Consider the wide range of decisions faced by individuals and teams in the course of carrying out business in the modern economy. Our choices are restricted by law and institutional rules, but only to certain extents. Beyond those limits, we must rely on ethical judgment to reach decisions that fall squarely within the field traditionally described as business-related. Yet, at the same time, our personal ethics also are challenged. While we will return to this tension in Chapter 2, the concept of a personal standard is paramount, and the readings by both MacDonald and Vermaelen examine the potential, for instance, of the MBA Oath as one way to resolve these challenges.

OBJECTIVE

To understand the origins of this shift from *whether* ethics or values should play a role in business decisions to the almost frantic search for *how* most effectively (and quickly!) to do it, consider the range of people who were harmed by Bernie Madoff's pyramid investment scheme. The largest security fraud in history, Madoff's unethical behavior led to cash losses of at least $20 billion for his clients. Though much of the media's initial attention focused on the big banks, wealthy hedge fund managers, and Hollywood celebrities defrauded by Madoff, the impact of his crimes was felt far beyond this small circle. More than 100 nonprofit organizations—including the New York Public Library, the Children's Health Fund, and a neurological research center at the Massachusetts Institute of Technology—had invested assets with Madoff's fund and were forced to reduce or eliminate services as a result of the collapse. The charitable foundation founded by Holocaust survivor and Nobel laureate Elie Wiesel was just one of many nonprofits that were wiped out entirely. The scandal led to the financial devastation of pension funds, hospitals, and universities across the globe, as well as to the bankruptcies of several smaller banks. In each case of economic loss, communities of the investing group or individual were negatively affected by the loss, and the families of those affected suffered hardship. Many of the individuals directly involved in Madoff's fund have since suffered criminal and civil punishment, up to and including prison sentences for some. Indeed, it is hard to imagine anyone who was even loosely affiliated with Madoff who was not harmed as a result of the ethical failings there. Multiply that harm by the dozens of other companies implicated in similar scandals to get a better idea of why ethics is no longer dismissed as irrelevant. The consequences of unethical behavior and unethical business institutions are too serious for too many people to be ignored.

This description of the consequences of the Madoff Ponzi scheme demonstrates the significant impact that business decisions can have on a very wide range of people. Madoff's choices dramatically affected the lives of thousands of people: investors, businesses, schools, nonprofit organizations, retirees, and the communities in which these people live. For better or for worse, the decisions that a business makes will affect many more people than just the decision maker. As we will discuss throughout this text, in order to sustain the firm, ethically responsible business decision making must move beyond a narrow concern with stockholders to consider the impact that decisions will have on a wide range of **stakeholders.** In a general sense, a business *stakeholder* will be anyone who affects or is affected by decisions made within the firm, for better or worse. Failure to consider these additional stakeholders will have a detrimental impact on those stakeholders, on stockholders, specifically, and on the firm's long-term sustainability as a whole. This perspective is articulated effectively by Whole Foods Market's "Declaration of Interdependence."

> Satisfying all of our stakeholders and achieving our standards is our goal. One of the most important responsibilities of Whole Foods Market's leadership *is to make sure the interests, desires and needs of our various stakeholders are kept in balance.* We recognize that this is a dynamic process. It requires participation and communication by all of our stakeholders. It requires listening compassionately, thinking carefully and acting with integrity. Any conflicts must be mediated and win-win solutions found. Creating and nurturing this community of stakeholders is critical to the long-term success of our company. (Emphasis added.)[6]

Whole Foods has maintained this priority structure over nearly 20 years, during which it has performed extremely well for its shareholders. In fiscal year 2015, the company reported sales of approximately $15 billion and more than 430 stores in the United States, Canada, and the United Kingdom.[7]

The Reality Check "How Does the Law Support Ethical Behavior?" describes some legal requirements that have been created since the Enron scandal. Beyond these specific legal obligations, organizational survival relies upon ethical decisions in a great many ways. Unethical behavior not only creates legal risks for a business, it creates financial and marketing risks as well. Managing these risks requires managers and executives to remain vigilant about their company's ethics. It is now clearer than ever that a company can lose in the marketplace, go out of business, and its employees go to jail if no one is paying attention to the ethical standards of the firm.

stakeholder

In a general sense, a stakeholder is anyone who can be affected by decisions made within a business. More specifically, stakeholders are considered to be those people who are necessary for the functioning of a business.

Reality Check *How Does the Law Support Ethical Behavior?*

As we emphasize in this text, ethics and the law are not the same. But law and ethics overlap in many ways. Good laws become law precisely because they promote important ethical values. But in some cases, laws are passed to help support ethical behavior in another way, namely by focusing the attention of corporate leaders on the need to work hard to ensure ethical behavior in their organizations. In 2002, for example, the U.S. Congress passed the Sarbanes-Oxley Act to address the wave of corporate and accounting scandals. Section 406 of that law, "Code of Ethics for Senior Financial Officers," requires that corporations have a code of ethics "applicable to its principal financial officer and comptroller or principal accounting officer, or persons performing similar functions." The code must include standards that promote:

1. Honest and ethical conduct, including the ethical handling of actual or apparent conflicts of interest between personal and professional relationships.

2. Full, fair, accurate, timely, and understandable disclosure in the periodic reports required to be filed by the issuer.

3. Compliance with applicable governmental rules and regulations.

Note: You will see Reality Checks throughout each chapter. Slightly different from Decision Points, these boxes offer practical applications of the concepts discussed during that chapter segment or examples of the ways in which the concepts are implemented in "real" business decision making.

Moreover, given the declining average life expectancy of firms,[8] maintaining an ethical advantage becomes a vital distinction between successful and unsuccessful firms. A firm's ethical reputation can provide a competitive edge in the marketplace with customers, suppliers, and employees. On the positive side, managing ethically can also pay significant dividends in organizational structure and efficiency. Trust, loyalty, commitment, creativity, and initiative are just some of the organizational benefits that are more likely to flourish within ethically stable and credible organizations (see the Reality Check "Why Be Good?"). Research demonstrates that 94 percent of workers consider a firm's ethics critically important in their choice of employers. In fact, 82 percent of employees say they would prefer a position at lower pay in a firm with ethical business practices compared to a higher-paying job at a company with questionable ethics. Further, one-third of U.S. workers have walked off a job on the basis of their ethics.[9] Alternatively, the consumer boycotts of such well-known firms as Nike, McDonald's, Home Depot, Fisher-Price, and Walmart give even the most skeptical business leader reason to pay attention to ethics.

For business students, the need to study ethics should be as clear as the need to study the other subfields of business education. As discussed earlier, without this background, students simply will be unprepared for a career in contemporary business. But even for students who do not anticipate a career in business management or business administration, familiarity with business ethics is just as crucial. After all, it was not only Bernie Madoff who suffered because of his ethical lapses. Our lives as employees, as consumers, and as citizens are affected by decisions made within business institutions; therefore, everyone has good reasons for being concerned with the ethics of those decision makers.

Reality Check   *Why Be Good?*

Ethical Systems, a collaboration of academics and business leaders, takes a thoughtful approach to the question of whether ethics is good for business.

Ethical Systems gives the following list of specific ways in which "ethics pays" for corporations:

- A good reputation is valuable.
- Illegal conduct can be extremely costly.
- Good governance pays off financially.

Source: Ethical Systems, www.ethicalsystems.org/content/ethics-pays (accessed April 16, 2016).

Moreover, as leaders and as emerging leaders, we need to explore how to manage the ethical behavior of others so that we can improve their decisions and encourage them to make ethical, or more ethical, decisions. Certainly, unethical behavior continues to occur within organizations today at all levels, and business decision makers—at all levels—must be equipped with the tools, the knowledge, and the skills to confront that behavior and to respond to it effectively. Just imagine the impact in terms of role modeling of this single statement by Prince Bandar Bin Sultan, in connection with accusations that he received secret and personal "commissions" of approximately $240 million each over a 10-year period in connection with a defense contract between the British government and the Saudi arms manufacturer BAE Systems:

> "The way I answer the corruption charges is this. In the last 30 years, . . . we have implemented a development program that was approximately, close to $400 billion worth. You could not have done all of that for less than, let's say, $350 billion. Now, if you tell me that building this whole country and spending $350 billion out of $400 billion, that we had misused or got corrupted with $50 billion, I'll tell you, 'Yes.' But I'll take that any time.
>
> "But more important, who are you to tell me this? I mean, I see every time all the scandals here, or in England, or in Europe. What I'm trying to tell you is, so what? We did not invent corruption. This happened since Adam and Eve. I mean, Adam and Eve were in heaven and they had hanky-panky and they had to go down to earth. So I mean this is—this is human nature. But we are not as bad as you think!"[10]

In that case, former British Prime Minister Tony Blair had originally allowed the fraud investigation to be dropped. He offered the following statement, in an effort to explain his reasons for the decision: "This investigation, if it had gone ahead, would have involved the most serious allegations in investigations being made into the Saudi royal family. My job is to give advice as to whether that is a sensible thing in circumstances where I don't believe the investigation incidentally would have led anywhere except to the complete wreckage of a vital strategic relationship for our country. . . . Quite apart from the fact that we would have lost thousands, thousands of British jobs."[11]

Some observers may look to the choices made in late 2008 and 2009 by American International Group (AIG), the world's largest insurer, as another example of poor role modeling. One can easily see the impact of those decisions on reputation. In September 2008, AIG was on the brink of bankruptcy. There was a realistic fear that if the company went under, the stability of the U.S. markets may have been in serious jeopardy. Over a five-month period, the U.S. government bailed out AIG to the tune of $152.2 billion (funded by U.S. tax dollars) in order to keep the company afloat because AIG arguably was "too big to fail."

While that consequence alone was unfortunate, it certainly was not unethical. However, in decisions that damaged the reputations of many involved, among other criticisms, one month after AIG received the first round of bailout money, its executives headed to California for a weeklong retreat at an extremely luxurious hotel, with the company covering the nearly half a million dollar tab *with the bailout money*. Six months later, these same executives rewarded themselves with bonuses totaling over $100 million. Although President Obama (some say belatedly) criticized the executives for their legally awarded bonuses, many of the bonuses were paid nevertheless because they had been promised through employee contracts for the purposes of "retaining talent" before AIG had received any bailout money.[12]

Although it did not reach a full congressional hearing, the U.S. House of Representatives even prepared a bill that would impose a 90 percent tax on the bonuses of more than $5 million paid to executives by AIG and other companies that were getting assistance from the government. Instead, the House passed the Grayson-Himes Pay for Performance Act in April 2009 "to amend the executive compensation provisions of the Emergency Economic Stabilization Act of 2008 to prohibit unreasonable and excessive compensation and compensation not based on performance standards."[13] This bill would ban future "unreasonable and excessive" compensation at companies receiving federal bailout money. Treasury Secretary Timothy Geithner would have the power to define what constitutes reasonable compensation and to review how companies give their bonuses.

The case for business ethics is clear and persuasive. Business must take ethics into account and integrate ethics into its organizational structure. Students need to study business ethics. But what does this mean? What is *ethics,* and what is the objective of a class in business ethics?

Business Ethics as Ethical Decision Making

As the title of this book suggests, our approach to business ethics will emphasize **ethical decision making.** No book can magically create ethically responsible people or change behavior in any direct way, and that's certainly not our goal here. But students can learn and practice responsible and accountable ways of thinking and deliberating. We believe that decisions that follow from a process of thoughtful and conscientious reasoning will be more responsible and ethical. In other words, *responsible decision making and deliberation will result in more responsible behavior.*

So what is the point of a business ethics course? On one hand, *ethics* refers to an academic discipline with a centuries-old history; we might expect knowledge about this history to be among the primary goals of a class in ethics. Thus, in an ethics course, students might be expected to learn about the great ethicists of history such as Aristotle, John Stuart Mill, and Immanuel Kant. As in many other courses on other subjects, this approach to ethics would focus on the *informational content* of the class.

Yet, according to some observers, ethical theories and the history of ethics are beside the point. These stakeholders, including some businesses looking to hire college graduates, business students, and even some teachers, expect an ethics class to address ethical *behavior,* not just information and knowledge about ethics. After all, what good is an ethics class if it does not help prevent future Madoffs? For our purposes, **ethics** refers not only to an academic discipline, but also to that arena of human life studied by this academic discipline, namely, *how human beings should properly live their lives.* And we believe the tools provided in this book will better equip students to think clearly about such questions. At very least, after taking a course based on this book, you should be better equipped than the average person to think clearly about ethical issues in business, and to offer a reasoned point of view about those issues. Even if an ethics course does not change your capacity to think, we believe that it could stimulate your choices of what to think *about.*

A caution about influencing behavior within a classroom is appropriate here. Part of the hesitation about teaching ethics involves the potential for abuse; expecting teachers to influence behavior could be viewed as permission for teachers to impose their own views on students. To the contrary, many believe that teachers should remain value-neutral in the classroom and respect a student's own views. Another part of this concern is that the line between motivating students and manipulating students is a narrow one. There are many ways to influence someone's behavior, including threats, guilt, pressure, bullying, and intimidation. Some of the executives involved in the worst of the recent corporate scandals were very good at using some of these methods to motivate the people who worked for them. Presumably, none of these approaches belong in a university classroom, and certainly not in an ethical classroom.

But not all forms of influencing behavior raise such concerns. There is a big difference between manipulating someone and persuading someone, between threatening (unethical) and reasoning (more likely ethical). This textbook resolves the tension between knowledge and behavior by emphasizing ethical judgment, ethical deliberation, and ethical decision making. In line with the Aristotelian notion that "we are what we repeatedly do," we agree with those who believe that an ethics class should attempt to produce more ethical *behavior* among the students who enroll. But we believe that the only academically and ethically legitimate way to achieve this objective is through careful and reasoned decision making. Our fundamental assumption is that a process of rational decision making, a process that involves careful thought and deliberation, can and will result in behavior that is more reasonable, accountable, and ethical.

Perhaps this view is not surprising after all. Consider any course within a business school curriculum. Most people would agree that a management course aims to create better managers. And any finance or accounting course that denied a connection between the course material and financial or accounting practice would likely be counted as a failure. Every course in a business school assumes a connection

OBJECTIVE

ethics
Derived from the Greek word *ethos,* which refers to those values, norms, beliefs, and expectations that determine how people within a culture live and act. Ethics steps back from such standards for how people *do* act, and reflects on the standards by which people *should* live and act. At its most basic level, ethics is concerned with how we act and how we live our lives. Ethics involves what is perhaps the most monumental question any human being can ask: How *should* we live? Following from this original Greek usage, ethics can refer to both the standards by which an individual chooses to live her or his own personal life, and the standards by which individuals live in community with others (see also *morality*). As a branch of philosophy, ethics is the discipline that systematically studies questions of how we ought to live our lives.

between what is taught in the classroom and appropriate business behavior. Classes in management, accounting, finance, and marketing all aim to influence students' behavior. We assume that the knowledge and reasoning skills learned in the classroom will lead to better decision making and, therefore, better behavior within a business context. A business ethics class follows this same approach.

While few teachers think that it is our role to *tell* students the right answers and to *proclaim* what students ought to think and how they ought to live, still fewer think that there should be no connection between knowledge and behavior. Our role should not be to preach our own ethical beliefs to a passive audience, but instead to treat students as active learners and to engage them in an active process of thinking, questioning, and deliberating. Taking Socrates as our model, philosophical ethics rejects the view that passive obedience to authority or the simple acceptance of customary norms is an adequate ethical perspective. Teaching ethics must, in this view, challenge students to *think for themselves.*

Business Ethics as Personal Integrity and Social Responsibility

normative ethics
As a *normative* discipline, ethics deals with norms and standards of appropriate and proper (normal) behavior. Norms establish the guidelines or standards for determining what we should do, how we should act, what type of person we should be. Contrast with *descriptive ethics.*

OBJECTIVE

descriptive ethics
As practiced by many social scientists, provides a descriptive and empirical account of those standards that actually guide behavior, as opposed to those standards that should guide behavior. Contrast with *normative ethics.*

Another element of our environment that affects our ethical decision making and behavior involves the influence of social circumstances. An individual may have carefully thought through a situation and decided what is right, and then may be motivated to act accordingly. But the corporate or social context surrounding the individual may create serious barriers to such behavior. As individuals, we need to recognize that our social environment will greatly influence the range of options that are open to us and can significantly influence our behavior. People who are otherwise quite decent can, under the wrong circumstances, engage in unethical behavior while less ethically motivated individuals can, in the right circumstances, do the "right thing." Business leaders, therefore, have a responsibility for the business environment that they create; we shall later refer to this environment as the "corporate culture." The environment can strongly encourage or discourage ethical behavior. Ethical business leadership is precisely this skill: to create the circumstances within which good people are able to do good, and bad people are prevented from doing bad.

At its most basic level, ethics is concerned with how we act and how we live our lives. Ethics involves what is perhaps the most monumental question any human being can ask: *How should we live?* Ethics is, in this sense, *practical,* having to do with how we act, choose, behave, and do things. Philosophers often emphasize that ethics is **normative,** which means that it deals with our reasoning about how we *should* act. Social sciences, such as psychology and sociology, also examine human decision making and actions; but these sciences are **descriptive** rather than normative. When we say that they are descriptive, we refer to the fact that they provide an account of how and why people *do* act the way they do—they describe; as a normative discipline, ethics seeks an account of how and why people *should* act a certain way, rather than how they *do* act. (For an exploration of some of the relevant factors in such a decision, see the Decision Point, "Management and Ethics.")

morality

Sometimes used to denote the phenomena studied by the field of ethics. This text uses *morality* to refer to those aspects of ethics involving personal, individual decision making. "How should I live my life?" or "What type of person ought I be?" are taken to be the basic questions of morality. Morality can be distinguished from questions of *social justice,* which address issues of how communities and social organizations ought to be structured.

personal integrity

The term *integrity* connotes completeness of a being or thing. Personal integrity, therefore, refers to individuals' completeness within themselves, often derived from the consistency or alignment of actions with deeply held beliefs.

social ethics

The area of ethics that is concerned with how we should live together with others and how social organizations ought to be structured. Social ethics involves questions of political, economic, civic, and cultural norms aimed at promoting human well-being.

How should we live? This fundamental question of ethics can be interpreted in two ways. "We" can mean each one of us individually, or it might mean all of us collectively. In the first sense, this is a question about how I should live my life, how I should act, what I should do, and what kind of person I should be. This meaning of ethics is based on our value structures, defined by our moral systems; and, therefore, it is sometimes referred to as **morality.** It is the aspect of ethics that we refer to by the phrase **"personal integrity."** There will be many times within a business setting where an individual will need to step back and ask: What should I do? How should I act? If morals refer to the underlying values on which our decisions are based, ethics refers to the applications of those morals to the decisions themselves. So, an individual could have a moral value of honesty, which, when applied to her or his decisions, results in a refusal to lie on an expense report. We shall return to this distinction in a moment.

In the second sense, "How should we live?" refers to how we live *together* in a *community.* This is a question about how a society and social institutions, such as corporations, ought to be structured and about how we ought to live together. This area is sometimes referred to as **social ethics** and it raises questions of justice, public policy, law, civic virtues, organizational structure, and political philosophy. In this sense, business ethics is concerned with how business institutions ought to be structured, about whether they have a responsibility to the greater society (corporate social responsibility, or CSR), and about making decisions that will have an impact on many people other than the individual decision maker. This aspect of business ethics asks us to examine business institutions from a social rather than from an individual perspective. We refer to this broader social aspect of ethics as decision making for *social responsibility.*

In essence, managerial decision making will always involve both of these aspects of ethics. Each decision that a business manager makes involves not only a personal decision but also a decision on behalf of, and in the name of, an organization that exists within a particular social, legal, and political environment. Thus, our book's title makes reference to both aspects of business ethics. Within a business setting, individuals will constantly be asked to make decisions affecting both their own personal integrity and their social responsibilities.

Expressed in terms of how we should live, the major reason to study ethics becomes clear. Whether we explicitly *examine* these questions, each and every one of us *answers* them every day through our behaviors in the course of living our lives. Whatever decisions business managers make, they will have taken a stand on ethical issues, at least implicitly. The actions each one of us takes and the lives we lead give very practical and unavoidable answers to fundamental ethical questions. We therefore make a very real choice as to whether we answer them deliberately or unconsciously. Philosophical ethics merely asks us to step back from these implicit everyday decisions to examine and evaluate them. More than 2,000 years ago Socrates gave the philosophical answer to why you should study ethics: "The unexamined life is not worth living."

Imagine that you are examining this chapter's Opening Decision Point in one of your classes on marketing or organizational behavior. What advice would you offer to the Olympics sponsors? What judgment would you make about this case from a financial perspective? Is there any financial risk implied by *encouraging* the IOC to *go ahead* with the Rio Olympics as planned? After offering your analysis and recommendations, reflect on your own thinking and describe what values underlie those recommendations.

- What facts would help you make your decision?
- Does the scenario raise values that are particular to managers?
- What stakeholders should be involved in your advice?
- What values do you rely on in offering your advice?

To distinguish ethics from other practical decisions faced within business, consider two approaches to the Enbridge oil spill scenario in the Decision Point "Ethics after an Oil Spill." This case could just as well be examined in a management, human resource, business law, or organizational behavior class as in an ethics class. The more social-scientific approach common in management or business administration classes would examine the situation and the decision by exploring the factors that led to one decision rather than another or by asking why the manager acted in the way that he did.

A second approach to the Enbridge case, from the perspective of ethics, steps back from the facts of the situation to ask what *should* the manager do? What *rights and responsibilities* are involved? What *good* will come from this situation? Is Enbridge being *fair, just, virtuous, kind, loyal, trustworthy?* This normative approach to business is at the center of business ethics. Ethical decision making involves the basic categories, concepts, and language of ethics: *shoulds, oughts, rights* and *responsibilities, goodness, fairness, justice, virtue, kindness, loyalty, trustworthiness,* and *honesty.*

norms

Those standards or guidelines that establish appropriate and proper behavior. Norms can be established by such diverse perspectives as economics, etiquette, or ethics.

OBJECTIVE

To say that ethics is a *normative* discipline is to say that it deals with **norms:** those standards of appropriate and proper (or "normal") behavior. Norms establish the guidelines or standards for determining what we should do, how we should act, and what type of person we should be. Another way of expressing this point is to say that norms appeal to certain values that would be promoted or attained by acting in a certain way. Normative disciplines presuppose some underlying values.

To say that ethics is a normative discipline is not to say that all normative disciplines involve the study or discipline of ethics. After all, business management and business administration are also normative, are they not? Are there not norms for business managers that presuppose a set of business values? One could add accounting and auditing to this list, as well as economics, finance, politics, and the law. Each of these disciplines appeals to a set of values to establish the norms of appropriate behavior within each field.

Ethics after an Oil Spill[14]

In August 2011, it was reported that an oil pipeline, owned by the energy company Enbridge, had sprung a leak near the tiny, remote town of Wrigley in Canada's Northwest Territories. Not surprisingly, residents were unhappy about the spill, confronting Enbridge with the twin dilemmas of how to clean it up and what to do about the people of Wrigley. More generally, managers at Enbridge had to figure out, in the wake of the leak, what their obligations would be, and to whom those obligations were owed.

Wrigley—slightly farther north than Anchorage, Alaska, but much farther inland—in 2011 had a population of about 165. Most community residents are members of the Canadian aboriginal group known as the Dené. Citizens of the town of Wrigley have very low levels of education—most of the population has received no formal education whatsoever. More than half of the community is unemployed. Poverty and access to the basic amenities of modern life are a serious challenge. At present, there isn't even a year-round road into the town. They maintain a traditional lifestyle based on hunting, fishing, and trapping, one that leaves them almost entirely dependent on the health of local forests and waterways. Environmental protection isn't just a question of principle for the people of Wrigley; it's a matter of survival.

After the spill was discovered, it was estimated that 1,500 barrels of oil had leaked, but company officials said luckily none of the oil had reached the nearby Willowlake River. Locals were skeptical, with some claiming that the water now tasted odd. Immediately after the spill was discovered, the company devised a detailed cleanup plan—a document more than 600 pages long. But locals were not impressed and said the complex technical document was too difficult to understand. When the company offered $5,000 so that the community could hire its own experts to evaluate the plan, locals were offended. How could a rich oil company insult them that way, first polluting their land and then offering such a tiny payment?

For Enbridge, the spill was a significant blow to its ongoing effort to maintain a positive image. Just a year earlier, in the summer of 2010, the company had made headlines when one of its pipelines ruptured in Michigan, spilling more than 20,000 barrels of oil into local rivers. At the time, Enbridge was in the midst of trying to win approval for its proposed Northern Gateway Pipeline project and faced serious opposition from environmental groups and aboriginal communities.

The company faced a number of difficult issues in the wake of the Wrigley spill. The first concern, clearly, would be to clean up the spilled oil. Then there was the issue of remediation—the process of attempting to restore the polluted land back to something like its original state. Further, there was the question of whether and how to compensate the local community for the pollution and loss of use of some of their traditional hunting grounds. All of this was set against a backdrop of controversy surrounding the impact that oil pipelines have on the lands and communities through which they run.

- What do you think motivated the company's decision to offer the community $5,000 to hire its own expert? Why do you think the community was insulted? If you were the company's local manager, what would you have done?
- What facts would be helpful to you, as an outsider, in evaluating the company's behavior after the spill?

(continued)

- What values are involved in this situation? How would Enbridge answer that question internally? How would the people of Wrigley answer that question, if asked?
- Did Enbridge have obligations that went beyond cleaning up the area directly affected by the spill from the company's pipeline? Was it obligated to offer the $5,000? Consider the suggestion made by a member of the community that Enbridge should donate money to build a swimming pool or hockey arena for local kids. Would a donation of this kind help satisfy the company's obligations to the community?

values

Those beliefs that incline us to act or to choose in one way rather than another. We can recognize many different types of values: financial, religious, legal, historical, nutritional, political, scientific, and aesthetic. Ethical values serve the ends of human well-being in impartial, rather than personal or selfish, ways.

These examples suggest that there are many different types of norms and values. Returning to our distinction between values and ethics, we can think of **values** as the underlying beliefs that cause us to act or to decide one way rather than another. Thus, the value that I place on an education *leads me to make the decision* to study this evening, rather than to play video games. I believe that education is more worthy, or valuable, than playing games. I make the decision to spend my money on groceries rather than on a vacation because I value food more than relaxation. A company's core values, for example, are those beliefs that provide the ultimate guide to its decision making.

Understood in this way, many different types of values can be recognized: financial, religious, legal, historical, nutritional, political, scientific, and aesthetic. Individuals can have their own personal values and, importantly, institutions also have values. Talk of a corporation's culture is a way of saying that a corporation has a set of identifiable values that establish the expectations for what is normal within that firm. These norms guide employees, implicitly more often than not, to behave in ways that the firm values and finds worthy. One important implication of this guidance, of course, is that an individual's or a corporation's set of values may lead to either *ethical* or *unethical* results. The corporate culture at Enron, for example, seems to have been committed to pushing the envelope of legality as far as possible in order to get away with as much as possible in pursuit of as much money as possible. Values? Yes. Ethical values? No.

One way to distinguish these various types of values is in terms of the ends or goals they serve. Financial values serve monetary ends; religious values serve spiritual ends; aesthetic values serve the ends of beauty; legal values serve law, order, and justice; and so forth. Different types of values are distinguished by the various ends served by those acts and choices. How are ethical values to be distinguished from these other types of values? What ends do ethics serve?

Values, in general, were earlier described as those beliefs that incline us to act or choose in one way rather than another. Consider again the harms attributed to the ethical failures of Bernie Madoff and those who abetted his fraudulent activity. Thousands of innocent people were hurt by the decisions made by some individuals seeking to boost their own bank accounts or their own egos. This

ethical values
Those properties of life that contribute to human well-being and a life well lived. Ethical values would include such things as happiness, respect, dignity, integrity, freedom, companionship, and health.

example reveals two important elements of **ethical values.** First, ethical values serve the ends of human well-being. Acts and decisions that seek to promote human welfare are acts and decisions based on ethical values. Controversy may arise when we try to define human well-being, but we can start with some general observations. Happiness certainly is a part of it, as are respect, dignity, integrity, and meaning. Freedom and autonomy surely seem to be necessary elements of human well-being, as are companionship and health.

Second, the well-being promoted by ethical values is not a personal and selfish well-being. After all, the Enron and Madoff scandals resulted from many individuals seeking to promote their own well-being. Ethics requires that the promotion of human well-being be done impartially. From the perspective of ethics, no one person's welfare is more worthy than any other's. Ethical acts and choices should be acceptable and reasonable from all relevant points of view. Thus, we can offer an initial characterization of ethics and ethical values: *Ethical values are those values—those decision-guiding beliefs—that impartially promote human well-being.*

Ethics and the Law

OBJECTIVE

Any discussion of norms and standards of proper behavior would be incomplete without considering the law. Deciding what one *should do* in business situations often requires reflection on what the law requires, expects, or permits. The law provides an important guide to ethical decision making, and this text will integrate legal considerations throughout. But legal norms and ethical norms are not identical, nor do they always agree. Some ethical requirements, such as treating one's employees with respect, are not legally required, though they may be ethically justified. On the other hand, some actions that may be legally permitted, such as firing an employee for no reason, would fail many ethical standards.

Some people still hold the view, perhaps more common prior to the scandals of recent years than after, that a business fulfills its social responsibility simply by obeying the law. From this perspective, an ethically responsible business decision is merely one that complies with the law; there is no responsibility to do anything further. Individual businesses may decide to go beyond the legal minimum, such as when a business supports the local arts, but these choices are voluntary. A good deal of management literature on corporate social responsibility centers on this approach, contending that ethics requires obedience to the law; anything beyond that is a matter of corporate philanthropy and charity, something praiseworthy and allowed, but not required.

Over the last decade, many corporations have established ethics programs and have hired ethics officers who are responsible for managing corporate ethics programs. Ethics officers do a great deal of good and effective work, but it is fair to say that much of their work focuses on legal compliance issues. Of course, the environment varies considerably from company to company and industry to industry (see the Reality Check "Business Responsibility to Stop Corruption"). The Sarbanes-Oxley Act created a dramatic and vast new layer of legal compliance issues. But is compliance with the law all that is required to behave ethically? Though we will address this issue in greater detail in Chapter 5, let us briefly explore at this point several persuasive reasons legal compliance is insufficient, in order to move forward to our discussion of ethics as perhaps a more effective guidepost for decision making. See also the Reality Check "Ethics in the Corporate World."

1. Believing that obedience to the law is sufficient to fulfill one's ethical duties raises questions of whether the law, itself, is ethical. Dramatic examples from history, including Nazi Germany and apartheid in South Africa, demonstrate that one's ethical responsibility may run counter to the law. On a more practical level, this question can have significant implications in a global economy in which businesses operate in countries with legal systems different from those of their home country. For instance, some countries permit discrimination on the basis of gender, but businesses that choose to adopt such practices remain ethically accountable to their stakeholders for those decisions. From the perspective of ethics, a business does not avoid its need to consider ethical responsibilities just by obeying the law.

2. Societies that value individual freedom will be reluctant to legally require more than just an ethical minimum. Such liberal societies will seek legally to prohibit the most serious ethical harms, although they will not legally require acts of charity, common decency, and personal integrity that may otherwise constitute the social fabric of a developed culture. The law can be an efficient mechanism to prevent serious harms, but it is not very effective at promoting "goods." Even if it were, the cost in human freedom of legally requiring such things as personal integrity would be extremely high. What would a society be like if it legally required parents to love their children, or even had a law that prohibited lying under all circumstances?

3. On a more practical level, a business acting as if its ethical responsibilities end with obedience to the law is just inviting more legal regulation. Consider the difficulty of trying to create laws to cover each and every possible business challenge; the task would require such specificity that the number of regulated areas would become unmanageable. Additionally, it was the failure of personal ethics among such companies as Enron and WorldCom, after all, that led to the creation of the Sarbanes-Oxley Act and many other legal reforms. If business restricts its ethical responsibilities to obedience to the law, it should not be surprised to find a new wave of government regulations that require what were formerly voluntary actions.

4. The law cannot possibly anticipate every new dilemma that businesses might face, so often there may not be a regulation for the particular dilemma that confronts a business leader. For example, when workplace e-mail was in its infancy, laws regarding who actually owned the e-mail transmissions (the employee or the employer) were not yet in place. As a result, one had no choice but to rely on the ethical decision-making processes of those in power to respect the appropriate boundaries of employee privacy while also adequately managing the workplace (see Chapter 7 for a more complete discussion of the legal implications of workplace monitoring). When new quandaries arise, one must be able to rely on ethics because the law might not yet—or might never—provide a solution.

Reality Check   *Business Responsibility to Stop Corruption*

Transparency International: Putting Corruption out of Business		
Transparency International asked businesses worldwide whether they agreed with this statement: **"My company has an ethical duty to fight corruption."** Responses from selected countries are displayed below.		
Country	**Yes**	**No**
Australia	88%	12%
Brazil	98%	2%
Chile	93%	7%
China	77%	23%
Egypt	57%	43%
Ghana	62%	38%
France	83%	17%
Malaysia	49%	51%
Russia	45%	55%
United States	78%	22%
United Kingdom	81%	19%

NOTES:

To compile this information, Transparency International interviewed more than 3,000 business executives in 30 countries from around the world. The survey was conducted in May 2011.

Source: Data extracted from Transparency International, *Putting Corruption out of Business: Business' Responsibility,* www.transparency.org/research/bps2011.

5. Finally, the perspective that compliance is enough relies on a misleading understanding of law. To say that all a business needs to do is obey the law suggests that laws are clear-cut, unambiguous rules that can be easily applied. This rule model of law is very common, but it is not quite accurate. If the law was clear and unambiguous, there would not be much of a role for lawyers and courts.

OBJECTIVE

Consider one U.S. law that has had a significant impact on business decision making: the Americans with Disabilities Act (ADA). This law requires American employers to make reasonable accommodations for employees with disabilities. (In the United Kingdom, the comparable law is called the Equality Act, 2010. In Canada, where employment law is a provincial matter, there are laws such as the Ontarians with Disabilities Act, 2002, and the Accessibility for Manitobans Act, 2013). But what counts as a disability and what would be considered a "reasonable" accommodation? Over the years, claims have been made that relevant disabilities include obesity, depression, dyslexia, arthritis, hearing loss, high blood pressure, facial scars, and the fear of heights. Whether such conditions are covered under the ADA depends

Reality Check   *Ethics in the Corporate World*

It's no secret that a substantial portion of the public has trouble trusting corporate CEOs. Every time another corporate scandal makes headlines, chatter increases about the fundamental untrustworthiness of business in general, and of business leaders in particular. But just how little does the public trust CEOs? And how does the public's trust in CEOs differ from their trust in members of other occupations and professions? In 2014, the Ted Rogers Leadership Centre at Ryerson University (in Toronto, Canada) conducted a national survey to ask Canadians their perceptions of the ethics of political leadership. One question they asked is: "In general, how much do you trust members of the following professions to behave ethically in their roles—that is, to live up to both public and professional standards in fulfilling their duties?"

Here are the percentages of respondents who indicated that they trust members of the following professions to behave ethically:

Doctors: 78 percent

Judges: 65 percent

Police officers: 60 percent

Public servants: 36 percent

Journalists: 33 percent

Business CEOs: 22 percent

Union leaders: 20 percent

Political staff: 16 percent

Politicians: 13 percent

Lobbyists: 9 percent

Of course, there are important questions about just how to interpret such data. It is worth noting that these numbers suggest a correlation between how much we *trust* various professions and how familiar we are with what they do. Most people know and rely on their family physician, and most people have a pretty good idea of what a judge does. On the other hand, fewer people understand what a CEO does. So what is expressed as a lack of trust *may* just reflect a lack of understanding. Or it might not! But we should always consider a range of explanations in the face of data such as these.

Source: "Public Perceptions of the Ethics of Political Leadership," Ted Rogers Leadership Centre, November 5, 2014, www.ethicssurvey.ca (accessed June 6, 2016). The survey was conducted among a nationally representative sample of n = 1,039 Canadians between October 17 and 22, 2014, using an online panel.

on a number of factors, including the severity of the illness and the effect it has on the employee's ability to work, among others. Imagine that you are a corporate human resource manager and an employee asks you to reasonably accommodate his allergy. How would you decide whether allergies constitute a disability under the ADA?

In fact, the legal answer remains ambiguous. The law offers general rules that find some clarity through cases decided by the courts. Most of the laws that concern business are based on past cases that establish legal precedents. Each precedent applies general rules to the specific circumstances of an individual case. In most business situations, asking, "Is this legal?" is really asking, "Are these circumstances similar enough to past cases that the conclusions reached in those cases will also apply here?" Because there will always be some differences among cases, the question will always remain somewhat open. Thus, there is no unambiguous answer for the conscientious business manager who wishes only to obey the law. There are few situations where a decision maker can simply find the applicable rule, apply it to the situation, and deduce an answer from it.

Without aiming to criticize the legal profession (especially because one of the authors of this text has a legal background!) but merely to demonstrate the preceding ambiguity, it is worth remembering that many of the people involved in the wave of recent corporate scandals were themselves lawyers. In the Enron case, for example, corporate attorneys and accountants were encouraged to "push the envelope" of what was legal. Especially in civil law (as opposed to criminal law), where much of the law is established by past precedent, as described earlier, there is always room for ambiguity in applying the law. Further, in civil law there is a real sense that one has not done anything illegal unless and until a court decides that one has violated a law. This means that if no one files a lawsuit to challenge an action, it is *perceived as* legal.

If moral behavior were simply following rules, we could program a computer to be moral.

Samuel P. Ginder

As some theories of corporate social responsibility suggest, if a corporate manager is told that she has a responsibility to maximize profits within the law, a competent manager will go to her corporate attorneys and tax accountants to ask what the law allows. A responsible attorney or accountant will advise how far the manager can reasonably go before it would obviously be illegal. In this situation, the question is whether a manager has a *responsibility* to "push the envelope" of legality in pursuit of profits.

Most of the cases of corporate scandal mentioned at the start of this chapter involved attorneys and accountants who advised their clients or bosses that what they were doing could be defended in court. The off-book partnerships that were at the heart of the collapse of Enron and Arthur Andersen were designed with the advice of attorneys who thought that, if challenged, they had at least a reasonable chance of winning in court. In the business environment, this strategy falls within the domain of organizational **risk assessment,** defined as "a process . . . to identify potential events that may affect the entity, and manage risk to be within its risk appetite, to provide reasonable assurance regarding the achievement of entity objectives."[15] Accordingly, the decision to "push the envelope" becomes a balance of risk assessment, cost–benefit analysis, and ethics—what is the corporation willing to do, *willing to risk?* Using this model, decision makers might include in their assessment before taking action:

risk assessment
A process to identify potential events that may affect the entity, and manage risk to be within its risk appetite, to provide reasonable assurance regarding the achievement of entity objectives.

- The likelihood of being challenged in court.
- The likelihood of losing the case.
- The likelihood of settling for financial damages.
- A comparison of those costs.
- The financial benefits of taking the action.
- The ethical implication of the options available.

After action is taken, the responsibility of decision makers is not relieved, of course. The U.S. Conference Board suggests that the ongoing assessment and review process might have a greater focus on the final element—the ethical implications—because it could involve:

- Independent monitoring of whistle-blowing or help-line information systems.
- Issuing risk assessment reports.

- Benchmarking for future activities.
- Modifying programs based on experience.[16]

Because the law is often ambiguous—because in many cases it simply is not clear what the law requires—there is little certainty with regard to several of these factors. Therefore, business managers will often face decisions that will challenge their ethical judgments. To suggest otherwise simply presents a false picture of corporate reality. Thus, even those businesspeople who are committed to strictly obeying the law will be confronted on a regular basis by the fundamental ethical questions: What should I do? How should I live?

As suggested earlier, whether we step back and explicitly ask these questions, each of us implicitly answers them every time we make a decision about how to act. Responsible decision making requires that we *do* step back and reflect on them, and then consciously choose the values by which we make decisions. No doubt this is a daunting task, even for experienced, seasoned leaders. Fortunately, we are not alone in meeting this challenge. The history of ethics includes the history of how some of the most insightful human beings have sought to answer these questions. Before turning to the range of ethical challenges awaiting each of us in the world of business, we will review some of the major traditions in ethics. Chapter 3 provides an introductory survey of several major ethical traditions that have much to offer in business settings.

Ethics as Practical Reason

OBJECTIVE

practical reasoning
Involves reasoning about what one ought to do, contrasted with *theoretical reasoning,* which is concerned with what one ought to believe. Ethics is a part of practical reason.

theoretical reasoning
Involves reasoning that is aimed at establishing truth and therefore at what we ought to believe. Contrast with practical reasoning, which aims at determining what is reasonable for us to do.

In a previous section, ethics was described as *practical* and *normative,* having to do with our actions, choices, decisions, and *reasoning* about how we should act. Ethics is therefore a vital element of **practical reasoning**—reasoning about what we should do—and is distinguished from **theoretical reasoning,** which is reasoning about what we should *believe.* This book's perspective on ethical decision making is squarely within this understanding of ethics' role as a part of practical reason.

Theoretical reason is the pursuit of truth, which is the highest standard for what we should believe. According to this tradition, science is the great arbiter of truth. Science provides the methods and procedures for determining what is true. Thus, the scientific method can be thought of as the answer to the fundamental questions of theoretical reason: What should we believe? So the question arises, is there a comparable methodology or procedure for deciding what we should do and how we should act?

The simple answer is that there is no single methodology that can in every situation provide one clear and unequivocal answer to that question. But there are guidelines that can provide direction and criteria for decisions that are more or less reasonable and responsible. We suggest that the traditions and theories of philosophical ethics can be thought of in just this way. Over thousands of years of thinking about the fundamental questions of how human beings should live, philosophers have developed and refined a variety of approaches to these ethical questions. These traditions, or what are often referred to as ethical theories, explain and defend various norms, standards, values, and principles that

Opening Decision Point Revisited
Zika Virus and Olympic Sponsors: No Easy Answers

The question of whether Olympic sponsors should have encouraged the International Olympic Committee (IOC) to move or postpone the Rio Olympics is a complex one. One complexity has to do with the proper role of a sponsoring organization. Is it the sponsor's role even to have an opinion on such things, or should it be a neutral supporter of the IOC and whatever it decides? Would it in fact be wrong for a major multinational to "bully" the IOC into changing its mind?

Another complexity has to do with the relevant science. As noted in the Opening Decision Point, in June 2016 there was some disagreement among well-informed experts. The question that arises—in this and many other cases—is what attitude corporations (and the public, for that matter) should adopt when experts disagree. In some cases, decision makers can afford to say, "let's wait until the experts figure it out." In other cases, such as this one, to wait essentially is to make a decision—namely a decision to go ahead with the Olympics as planned, regardless of the risks.

A third complexity has to do with our obligations in the face of risk and uncertainty. If it were certain that proceeding with the Olympics would spread Zika virus and result in many birth defects, a number of people would likely have considered it ethically imperative to move or postpone the Rio Olympics. But even the experts who called on the IOC to make that decision did not claim that the danger was a certainty, merely that it was a risk. The ethical question here is what attitude we should take in such situations. Should we err on the side of safety? Always? That's a tempting conclusion. But always to err on the side of safety can lead to paralysis, and can itself lead us to take precautions and suffer expenses that prevent us from doing other, ethically important things. For example, moving the Rio Olympics would have had a significant impact on employment opportunities for many people in Rio de Janeiro, and in a city with very high levels of poverty that would be an ethically bad outcome.

Business does not exist in a vacuum. For any company to operate, it must play within the rules of the game. Those rules include not just laws, but also a broader set of social values. As social values evolve, so must businesses. Think of how the menus offered by cafeterias in North America differ from those offered just 20 years ago. Twenty years ago, "light" menu items would have been rare, as would foods drawing on the cultural traditions of places such as India, Korea, and Thailand. Now, all of those things are common: Businesses have adapted to changing values. Any company that finds itself too far out of step with the values of its community faces serious trouble, but any company that fails to change with the times risks becoming obsolete.

Finally, there's a question of responsibility. One factor that might influence sponsors' reasoning—rightly or wrongly—is the potential outcomes for the sponsors themselves. If the Olympic Games were moved or postponed, sponsors presumably would lose money they had spent on things like scheduled advertising. On the other hand, if the Games were to go ahead and if there was a slight increase in cases of Zika around the world, sponsors have a two-pronged defense: first, "you can't prove it's because of the Olympics" (which is probably true), and second, "the CDC and WHO said it was OK" (which they did). So it would be easy for Olympic partners and sponsors to say—and maybe actually believe—that there was no downside to going ahead. Should sponsors think of the situation this way, ethically?

contribute to responsible ethical decision making. Ethical theories are patterns of thinking, or methodologies, to help us decide what to do.

The following chapter will introduce a model for making ethically responsible decisions. This can be considered as a model of practical reasoning in the sense that, if you walk through these steps in making a decision about what to do, you would certainly be making a decision grounded in sound reasoning. In addition, the ethical traditions and theories that we describe in Chapter 3 will help flesh out and elaborate on this decision procedure. Other approaches are possible, and this approach will not guarantee one single and absolute answer to every decision. But this is a helpful beginning in the development of responsible, reasonable, and ethical decision making.

Questions, Projects, and Exercises

1. Questions of ethics and values obviously arise frequently in certain kinds of university courses—particularly in classes on ethics or social responsibility. Are there other courses in your school's curriculum that talk about "the right thing to do," without necessarily using words such as *ethics* or *social responsibility*?

2. Why might legal rules be insufficient for fulfilling one's ethical responsibilities? Can you think of cases in which a businessperson has done something that is legally permitted but ethically wrong? What about the opposite—are there situations in which a businessperson might have acted in a way that was legally wrong but ethically right?

3. What might be some benefits and costs of acting unethically in business? Distinguish between benefits and harms to the individual and benefits and harms to the firm.

4. Review the distinction between personal morality and matters of social ethics. Can you think of cases in which some decisions would be valuable as a matter of social policy but bad as a matter of personal ethics? Something good as a matter of personal ethics and bad as a matter of social policy?

5. As described in this chapter, the Americans with Disabilities Act requires firms to make reasonable accommodations for employees with disabilities. Consider such conditions as obesity, depression, dyslexia, arthritis, hearing loss, high blood pressure, facial scars, mood disorders, allergies, attention deficit disorders, post-traumatic stress syndrome, and the fear of heights. Imagine that you are a business manager and an employee comes to you asking that accommodations be made for these conditions. Under what circumstances might these conditions be serious enough impairments to deserve legal protection under the ADA? What factors would you consider in answering this question? After making these decisions, reflect on whether your decision was more a legal or ethical decision.

6. Do an Internet search for recent news stories about oil spills. Do any of those stories report behaviors that seem especially wise or unwise on the part of the oil companies involved? Do you think that controversies over big pipeline projects like the Keystone pipeline alter how people evaluate the ethics of oil-spill cleanups?

7. Construct a list of all the people who were adversely affected by Bernie Madoff's Ponzi scheme. Who, among these people, would you say had their rights violated? What responsibilities, if any, did Madoff have to each of these constituencies?

8. Do "ethical" behaviors need to be grounded in ethical values in order to be considered ethically *good*? If a business performs a socially beneficial act in order to receive good publicity, or if it creates an ethical culture as a business strategy, has the business

acted in a less-than-ethically praiseworthy way? Is thinking of ethics as "good for business" misleading or just practical?

9. During the recession of 2008–2009, many reputable companies suffered bankruptcies while others struggled to survive. Of those that did remain, some chose to reduce the size of their workforces significantly. Imagine yourself helping run a company during such a recession. Imagine the company that has been doing fairly well, posting profits every quarter and showing a sustainable growth expectation for the future; however, the general uneasiness in the market has caused the company's stock price to fall. In response to this problem, the CEO decides to lay off some of her employees, hoping to cut costs and to improve the bottom line. This action raises investor confidence and, consequently, the stock price goes up. What is your impression of the CEO's decision? Was there any kind of ethical lapse in laying off the employees, or was it a practical decision necessary for the survival of the company?

10. Every year, *Ethisphere Magazine* publishes a list of the world's most ethical companies. Go to its website and find and evaluate its rating methodology and criteria. Then engage in an assessment (that is, provide suggestions for any modifications you might make for a more or less comprehensive list, and so on).

Key Terms

After reading this chapter, you should have a clear understanding of the following key terms. For a complete definition, please see the Glossary.

descriptive ethics, *p. 12*	norms, *p. 14*	stakeholder, *p. 7*
ethical values, *p. 17*	personal integrity, *p. 13*	theoretical reasoning, *p. 22*
ethics, *p. 11*	practical reasoning, *p. 22*	values, *p. 16*
morality, *p. 13*	risk assessment, *p. 21*	
normative ethics, *p. 12*	social ethics, *p. 13*	

Endnotes

1. Decision Points appear throughout each chapter in the text. These challenges are designed to integrate the concepts discussed during that particular segment of the chapter and then to suggest questions or further dilemmas to encourage the reader to explore the challenge from a stakeholder perspective and using the ethical decision-making process. This process will be further described in Chapter 2. Opening Decision Points introduce one of the main themes of the chapters and a conclusion is offered at the end of each chapter.

2. G. Santayana, *Reason in Common Sense,* vol. 1, *The Life of Reason* (New York: C. Scribner's Sons, 1905).

3. D. Willets, "The Invisible Hand That Binds Us All," *Financial Times,* April 24, 2011, www.ft.com/intl/cms/s/2/f3e5965e-6e9a-11e0-a13b-00144feabdc0.html#axzz 1ZFr514r8 (accessed December 1, 2011).

4. J. Jones, "Record 64% Rate Honesty, Ethics of Members of Congress Low," *Gallup Poll,* December 12, 2011, www.gallup.com/poll/151460/Record-Rate-Honesty-Ethics-Members-Congress-Low.aspx (accessed December 14, 2011).

5. Ethics Resource Council, "2009 Business Ethics Survey, Supplemental Research Brief: Saving the Company Comes at a Cost: The Relationship between Belt-Tightening Tactics and Increased Employee Misconduct," February 2010, www.ethics.org/page/nbes-supplemental-research-briefs (accessed November 23, 2011).

6. Whole Foods Market IP, LLP, "Declaration of Independence," www.wholefoodsmarket .com/company/declaration.php, accessed January 15, 2012. *See also* Knowledge @ Wharton, "Building Companies That Leave the World a Better Place," February 28, 2007, p. 2, *excerpting* R. Sisodia, J. Sheth, and D. Wolfe, *Firms of Endearment: How World-Class Companies Profit from Passion and Purpose* (Philadelphia, PA: Wharton Business School Publishing, 2007), ch. 6.

7. "Whole Foods Market Reports Fourth Quarter Results," 2015, http://assets. wholefoodsmarket.com/www/company-info/investor-relations/financial-press-releases/2015/4Q15-Earnings-PR.pdf (accessed April 16, 2016).

8. S. Denning, "What the Sale of NYSE Means: The Decline of Management," *Forbes,* February 15, 2011, www.forbes.com/sites/stevedenning/2011/02/15/what-the-sale-of-nyse-means-the-decline-of-management/ (accessed January 15, 2012).

9. LRN, *Ethics Study: Employee Engagement,* 2007, www.lrn.com (accessed July 20, 2012).

10. L. Bergman and O. Zill de Granados, "Black Money," *Frontline,* April 7, 2009, www. pbs.org/wgbh/pages/frontline/blackmoney/etc/script.html (accessed July 20, 2012).

11. K. Sullivan, "Saudi Reportedly Got $2 Billion for British Arms Deal," *The Washington Post,* June 8, 2007, p. A15, www.washingtonpost.com/wp-dyn/content/article/2007/06/07/AR2007060701301.html (accessed July 20, 2012).

12. D. Goldman and T. Luhby, "AIG: The Bailout That Won't Quit," *CNNMoney. com,* February 27, 2009, http://money.cnn.com/2009/02/27/news/companies/aig_ hailout/ (accessed July 20, 2012); R. Reich, "The Real Scandal of AIG," *Salon. com,* March 16, 2009, www.salon.com/opinion/feature/2009/03/16/reich_aig/ (accessed July 20, 2012); B. Ross and T. Shine, "After Bailout, AIG Execs Head to California Resort," *ABC News,* October 7, 2008, http://abcnews.go.com/Blotter/ story?id=5973452&page=1#.UAnfmUQmzQo (accessed July 20, 2012); E. Strott, "Why AIG Matters," *MSN Money,* September 16, 2008, http://articles.moneycentral. msn.com/Investing/Dispatch/why-aig-matters.aspx (accessed April 13, 2010).

13. The full text of H.R. 1664, "Grayson-Himes Pay for Performance Act of 2009," is available at http://opencongress.org/bill/111-h1664/show (accesssed july 20, 2012)

14. See "Wrigley Residents Voice Pipeline Spill Concerns," *CBC News*, August 12, 2011, www.cbc.ca/news/canada/north/story/2011/08/11/nwt-wrigley-enbridgemeeting .html (accessed July 19, 2012).

15. Committee of Sponsoring Organizations (COSO) of the Treadway Commission, "Executive Summary," *Enterprise Risk Management—Integrated Framework,* September 2004, p. 2.

16. R. Berenbeim, *Universal Conduct: An Ethics and Compliance Benchmarking Survey,* Research Report R-1393-06-RR (New York: The Conference Board, 2006).

Readings

Reading 1-1: "Value Shift," by Lynn Sharp Paine
Reading 1-2: "The MBA Oath"
Reading 1-3: "The Oath Demands a Commitment to Bad Corporate Governance," by Theo Vermaelen
Reading 1-4: "The MBA Oath Helps Remind Graduates of Their Ethical Obligations," by Chris MacDonald

Reading **1-1**

Value Shift

Lynn Sharp Paine

Business has changed dramatically in the past few decades. Advances in technology, increasing globalization, heightened competition, shifting demographics—these have all been documented and written about extensively. Far less notice has been given to another, more subtle, change—one that is just as remarkable as these more visible developments. What I have in mind is the attention being paid to values in many companies today.

When I began doing research and teaching about business ethics in the early 1980s, skepticism about this subject was pervasive. Many people, in business and in academia, saw it as either trivial or altogether irrelevant. Some saw it as a joke. A few were even hostile. The whole enterprise, said critics, was misguided and based on a naïve view of the business world. Indeed, many had learned in their college economics courses that the market is amoral.

Back then, accepted wisdom held that "business ethics" was a contradiction in terms. People joked that an MBA course on this topic would be the shortest course in the curriculum. At that time, bookstores offered up volumes with titles like *The Complete Book of Wall Street Ethics* consisting entirely of blank pages. The most generous view was that business ethics had something to do with corporate philanthropy, a topic that might interest executives *after* their companies became financially successful. But even then, it was only a frill—an indulgence for the wealthy or eccentric.

Today, attitudes are different. Though far from universally embraced—witness the scandals of 2001 and 2002—ethics is increasingly viewed as an important corporate concern. What is our purpose? What do we believe in? What principles should guide our behavior? What do we owe one another and the people we deal with—our employees, our customers, our investors, our communities? Such classic questions of ethics are being taken seriously in many companies around the world, and not just by older executives in large, established firms. Managers of recently privatized firms in transitional economies, and even some farsighted high-technology entrepreneurs, are also asking these questions.

Ethics, or what has sometimes been called "moral science," has been defined in many ways—"the science of values," "the study of norms," "the science of right conduct," "the science of obligation," "the general inquiry into what is good." In all these guises, the subject matter of ethics has made its way onto management's agenda. In fact, a succession of definitions have come to the forefront as a narrow focus on norms of right and wrong has evolved into a much broader interest in organizational values and culture. Increasingly, we hear that values, far from being irrelevant, are a critical success factor in today's business world.

The growing interest in values has manifested itself in a variety of ways. In recent years, many managers have launched ethics programs, values initiatives, and cultural change programs in their companies.

Some have created corporate ethics offices or board-level ethics committees. Some have set up special task forces to address issues such as conflicts of interest, corruption, or electronic data privacy. Others have introduced educational programs to heighten ethical awareness and help employees integrate ethical considerations into their decision processes. Many have devoted time to defining or revising their company's business principles, corporate values, or codes of conduct. Still others have carried out systematic surveys to profile their company's values and chart their evolution over time.

A survey of U.S. employees conducted in late 1999 and early 2000 found that ethics guidelines and training were widespread. About 79 percent of the respondents said their company had a set of written ethics guidelines, and 55 percent said their company offered some type of ethics training, up from 33 percent in 1994. Among those employed by organizations with more than 500 members, the proportion was 68 percent.

Another study—this one of 124 companies in 22 countries—found that corporate boards were becoming more active in setting their companies' ethical standards. More than three-quarters (78 percent) were involved in 1999, compared to 41 percent in 1991 and 21 percent in 1987. Yet another study found that more than 80 percent of the Forbes 500 companies that had adopted values statements, codes of conduct, or corporate credos had created or revised these documents in the 1990s.

During this period, membership in the Ethics Officer Association, the professional organization of corporate ethics officers, grew dramatically. At the beginning of 2002, this group had 780 members, up from 12 at its founding 10 years earlier. In 2002, the association's roster included ethics officers from more than half the Fortune 100.

More companies have also undertaken efforts to strengthen their reputations or become more responsive to the needs and interests of their various constituencies. The list of initiatives seems endless. Among the most prominent have been initiatives on diversity, quality, customer service, health and safety, the environment, legal compliance, professionalism, corporate culture, stakeholder engagement, reputation management, corporate identity, cross-cultural management, work–family balance, sexual harassment, privacy, spirituality, corporate citizenship, cause-related marketing, supplier conduct, community involvement, and human rights. A few companies have even begun to track and report publicly on their performance in some of these areas. For a sampling of these initiatives, see Reading Figure 1.1.

To aid in these efforts, many companies have turned to consultants and advisors, whose numbers have increased accordingly. A few years ago, *BusinessWeek* reported that ethics consulting had become a billion-dollar business. Though perhaps somewhat exaggerated, the estimate covered only a few segments of the industry, mainly misconduct prevention and investigation, and did not include corporate culture and values consulting or consulting focused in areas such as diversity, the environment, or reputation management. Nor did it include the public relations and crisis management consultants who are increasingly called on to help companies handle values-revealing crises and controversies such as product recalls, scandals, labor disputes, and environmental disasters. Thirty or 40 years ago, such consultants were a rare breed, and many of these consulting areas did not exist at all. Today, dozens of firms—perhaps hundreds, if we count law firms and the numerous consultants specializing in specific issue areas—offer companies expertise in handling these matters. Guidance from nonprofits is also widely available.

What's Going On?

A thoughtful observer might well ask, "What's going on?" Why the upsurge of interest in ethics and values? Why have companies become more attentive to their stakeholders and more concerned about the norms that guide their own behavior? In the course of my teaching, research, and consulting over the past two decades, I have interacted with executives and managers from many parts of the world.

READING FIGURE 1.1
Values in Transition

CORPORATE INITIATIVES—A SAMPLER		
COMPREHENSIVE (APPLYING TO ALL ACTIVITIES AND FUNCTIONS)	*Internally Oriented:*	Ethics programs Compliance programs Mission and values initiatives Business principles initiatives Business practices initiatives Culture-building initiatives Cross-cultural management programs Crisis prevention and readiness
	Externally Oriented:	Reputation management programs Corporate identity initiatives Corporate brand-building initiatives Stakeholder engagement activities Societal alignment initiatives Nonfinancial-performance reporting initiatives
FOCUSED (APPLYING TO PARTICULAR ISSUES OR CONSTITUENCIES)	*Employee Oriented:*	Diversity initiatives Sexual harassment programs Work–family initiatives Workplace environment initiatives
	Customer Oriented:	Product and service quality initiatives Customer service initiatives Product safety initiatives Cause-related marketing
	Supplier Oriented:	Supplier conduct initiatives
	Investor Oriented:	Corporate governance initiatives
	Community Oriented:	Environmental initiatives Corporate citizenship initiatives Community involvement initiatives Strategic philanthropy
	Issue Oriented:	Electronic privacy Human rights initiatives Anticorruption programs Biotechnology issues

In discussing these questions with them, I have learned that their motivating concerns are varied:

- An Argentine executive sees ethics as integral to transforming his company into a "world-class organization."

- A group of Thai executives wants to protect their company's reputation for integrity and social responsibility from erosion in the face of intensified competition.

- A U.S. executive believes that high ethical standards are correlated with better financial performance.

- An Indian software company executive sees his company's ethical stance as important for building customer trust and also for attracting and retaining the best employees and software professionals.

- A Chinese executive believes that establishing the right value system and serving society are key components in building a global brand.

- The executives of a U.S. company see their efforts as essential to building a decentralized organization and entrepreneurial culture around the world.

- Two Nigerian entrepreneurs want their company to become a "role model" for Nigerian society.

- A Swiss executive believes the market will increasingly demand "social compatibility."

- An Italian executive wants to make sure his company stays clear of the scandals that have embroiled others.

- A U.S. executive believes that a focus on ethics and values is necessary to allow his company to decentralize responsibility while pursuing aggressive financial goals.

- A U.S. executive answers succinctly and pragmatically, "*60 Minutes.*"

These responses suggest that the turn to values is not a simple phenomenon. Individual executives have their own particular reasons for tackling this difficult and sprawling subject. Even within a single company, the reasons often differ and tend to change over time. A company may launch an ethics initiative in the aftermath of a scandal for purposes of damage control or as part of a legal settlement. Later on, when the initiative is no longer necessary for these reasons, a new rationale may emerge.

This was the pattern at defense contractor Martin Marietta (now Lockheed Martin), which in the mid-1980s became one of the first U.S. companies to establish what would later come to be called an "ethics program." At the time, the entire defense industry was facing harsh criticism for practices collectively referred to as "fraud, waste, and abuse," and Congress was considering new legislation to curb these excesses. The immediate catalyst for Martin Marietta's program, however, was the threat of being barred from government contracting because of improper billing practices in one of its subsidiaries.

According to Tom Young, the company president in 1992, the ethics program began as damage control. "When we went into this program," he explained, "we didn't anticipate the changes it would bring about. . . . Back then, people would have said, 'Do you really need an ethics program to be ethical?' Ethics was something personal, and you either had it or you didn't. Now that's all changed. People recognize the value." By 1992, the ethics effort was no longer legally required, but the program was continued nonetheless. However, by then it had ceased to be a damage control measure and was justified in terms of its business benefits: problem avoidance, cost containment, improved constituency relationships, enhanced work life, and increased competitiveness.

A similar evolution in thinking is reported by Chumpol NaLamlieng, CEO of Thailand's Siam Cement Group. Although Siam Cement's emphasis on ethics originated in a business philosophy rather than as a program of damage control, Chumpol recalls the feeling he had as an MBA student—that "ethics was something to avoid lawsuits and trouble with the public, not something you considered a way of business and self-conduct." Today, he says, "We understand corporate culture and environment and see that good ethics leads to a better company."

Siam Cement, one of the first Thai companies to publish a code of conduct, put its core values into writing in 1987 so they "would be more than just words in the air," as one executive explains. In 1994, shortly after the company was named Asia's "most ethical" in a survey conducted by *Asian Business* magazine, Chumpol called for a thorough review of the published code. The newly appointed CEO wanted to make sure that the document remained an accurate statement of the company's philosophy and also to better understand whether the espoused values were a help or hindrance in the more competitive environment of the

1990s. In 1995, the company reissued the code in a more elaborate form but with its core principles intact. The review had revealed that while adhering to the code did in some cases put the company at a competitive disadvantage, it was on balance a plus. For example, it helped attract strong partners and employees and also positioned the company, whose largest shareholder was the Thai monarchy's investment arm, as a leader in the country.

A very different evolution in thinking is reported by Azim Premji, chairman of Wipro Ltd., one of India's leading exporters of software services and, at the height of the software boom in 2000, the country's largest company in terms of market capitalization. Wipro's reputation for high ethical standards reflects a legacy that began with Premji's father, M.H. Hasham Premji, who founded the company in 1945 to make vegetable oil. The elder Premji's value system was based on little more than personal conviction—his sense of the right way to do things. Certainly it did not come from a careful calculation of business costs and benefits. In fact, his son noted, "It made no commercial sense at the time."

When his father died in 1966, Azim Premji left Stanford University where he was an undergraduate to assume responsibility for the then-family-owned enterprise. As he sought to expand into new lines of business, Premji found himself repeatedly having to explain why the company was so insistent on honesty when it was patently contrary to financial interest. Over time, however, he began to realize that the core values emphasized by his father actually made for good business policy. They imposed a useful discipline on the company's activities while also helping it attract quality employees, minimize transaction costs, and build a good reputation in the marketplace. In 1998, as part of an effort to position Wipro as a leading supplier of software services to global corporations, the company undertook an intensive self-examination and market research exercise. The result was a reaffirmation and rearticulation of the core values and an effort to link them more closely with the company's identity in the marketplace.

Managers' reasons for turning to values often reflect their company's stage of development.

Executives of large, well-established companies typically talk about *protecting* their company's reputation or its brand, whereas entrepreneurs are understandably more likely to talk about *building* a reputation or *establishing* a brand. For skeptics who wonder whether a struggling start-up can afford to worry about values, Scott Cook, the founder of software maker Intuit, has a compelling answer. In his view, seeding a company's culture with the right values is "the most powerful thing you can do." "Ultimately," says Cook, "[the culture] will become more important to the success or failure of your company than you are. The culture you establish will guide and teach all your people in all their decisions."

In addition to company size and developmental stage, societal factors have also played a role in some managers' turn to values. For example, executives in the United States are more likely than those who operate principally in emerging markets to cite reasons related to the law or the media. This is not surprising, considering the strength of these two institutions in American society and their relative weakness in many emerging-markets countries. Since many ethical standards are upheld and reinforced through the legal system, the linkage between ethics and law is a natural one for U.S. executives. In other cases, executives offer reasons that mirror high-profile issues facing their industries or countries at a given time—issues such as labor shortages, demographic change, corruption, environmental problems, and unemployment. Antonio Mosquera, for example, launched a values initiative at Merck Sharp & Dohme Argentina as part of a general improvement program he set in motion after being named managing director in 1995. Mosquera emphasized, however, that promoting corporate ethics was a particular priority for him because corruption was a significant issue in the broader society.

Despite the many ways executives explain their interest in values, we can see in their comments several recurring themes. Seen broadly, their rationales tend to cluster into four main areas:

- Reasons relating to *risk management*.
- Reasons relating to *organizational functioning*.

- Reasons relating to *market positioning*.
- Reasons relating to *civic positioning*.

A fifth theme, somewhat less salient but nevertheless quite important. . . , has to do with the idea simply of "a better way." For some, the rationale lies not in some further benefit or consequence they are seeking to bring about but rather in the inherent worth of the behavior they are trying to encourage. In other words, the value of the behavior resides principally in the behavior itself. For these executives, it is just *better*—full stop—for companies to be honest, trustworthy, innovative, fair, responsible, or good citizens. No further explanation is necessary any more than further explanation is required to justify the pursuit of self-interest or why more money is better than less.

Source: From *Value Shift,* by Lynn Sharp Paine, Copyright © 2004, The McGraw-Hill Companies. Reproduced by permission of the publisher.

Reading **1-2**

The MBA Oath

As a business leader I recognize my role in society.

- My purpose is to lead people and manage resources to create value that no single individual can create alone.
- My decisions affect the well-being of individuals inside and outside my enterprise, today and tomorrow.

Therefore, I promise that:

- I will manage my enterprise with loyalty and care, and will not advance my personal interests at the expense of my enterprise or society.
- I will understand and uphold, in letter and spirit, the laws and contracts governing my conduct and that of my enterprise.
- I will refrain from corruption, unfair competition, or business practices harmful to society.
- I will protect the human rights and dignity of all people affected by my enterprise, and I will oppose discrimination and exploitation.

- I will protect the right of future generations to advance their standard of living and enjoy a healthy planet.
- I will report the performance and risks of my enterprise accurately and honestly.
- I will invest in developing myself and others, helping the management profession continue to advance and create sustainable and inclusive prosperity.

In exercising my professional duties according to these principles, I recognize that my behavior must set an example of integrity, eliciting trust and esteem from those I serve. I will remain accountable to my peers and to society for my actions and for upholding these standards.

This oath I make freely, and upon my honor.

Source: This is the current, revised version of the MBA Oath and makes use of slightly different wording than that referred to by the two commentaries that follow [Readings 1-3 and 1-4]. It is available at MBAoath.com. (The version reproduced here was retrieved August 9, 2012.)

The Oath Demands a Commitment to Bad Corporate Governance

Theo Vermaelen

I don't believe that the MBA oath is a good idea, for three reasons. First, some parts of the pledge are inconsistent with fiduciary duties and ethical standards. Second, the oath is a misplaced response to the financial crisis. Third, I don't believe in pledges as an instrument to guide people's behaviour.

In many countries, board members and, as a consequence, managers have a fiduciary duty to maximize the wealth of shareholders. Even in countries where the corporate governance code insists on promoting maximizing "stakeholder" value, none of these codes would accept that managers promote "social and environmental prosperity worldwide" as the MBA oath requires. Externalities such as the consequences of business decisions for the environment have to be dealt with by the government, unless, of course, a business case can be made that shareholder value is increased by taking care of these externalities.

A second problem is that the oath assumes that the financial crisis was caused by unethical MBAs. For example, in a recent working paper, *The Ethical Roots of The Financial Crisis,* Wharton professor Thomas Donaldson argues that the financial crisis was caused by bad ethics, by bankers who were gambling with other people's money. This accusation ignores the facts.

New research on the crisis shows that banks where the CEO held a lot of stock were also the banks with the biggest losses. So they were not losing other people's money, they lost their own money. They apparently believed in their strategy. Moreover, we know that 81 percent of the mortgage-backed securities purchased by bankers for their own personal accounts were AAA-rated. These securities turned out to be the most mispriced securities: They produced lower returns than the lower-rated tranches.

Finally, my INSEAD colleague, Harald Hau, and his co-author Marcel Thum have shown that the largest bank losses in German banks were experienced by banks with board members who were least educated in finance.

So the evidence is that bankers have made mistakes and board members may have been ignorant, but they are not crooks. They believed rating agencies, which in turn made their forecasts of financial distress based on extrapolating historical data. Rating agencies behaved no differently than climate-change scientists who base their doomsday forecasts of man-made global warming on extrapolation of historical data. If, for example, it turns out that 30 years from now we enter a period of global cooling, will we then accuse climate-change activists of greed and unethical behavior? Presumably not. Forecasting and modeling is a tricky business. So the solution is not more ethics or pledges, but more finance education and better forecasting and risk management models.

The idea that the next crisis will be avoided simply because we sign an oath seems excessively naive. The donkey does not walk because he pledges to walk, but because of the carrot and the stick. Signing the oath doesn't cost anything and is therefore not a credible commitment. Even if Bernie Madoff had signed the HBS oath, he would not have acted any differently. Rather than focusing on pledges, businesses should make sure that managers comply with their fiduciary and ethical responsibility to maximize the wealth of the people who pay their salaries—i.e., the shareholders.

The MBA oath aims to achieve exactly the opposite. It pushes the stakeholder value maximization idea to its extreme by including the whole world as a stakeholder. If this oath indeed would be implemented, then the resulting erosion of shareholder property rights would prevent the development of capital markets and undermine economic growth. As I interpret the oath as a commitment to bad corporate governance, companies that employ those who sign the oath as top executives should disclose this on the first page of their website. In this way, investors are warned that investing in these companies can be "dangerous to your wealth."

If MBA students insist on taking an oath that promotes shareholder-friendly corporate governance, I would propose the following: "I pledge to maximize the wealth of the people who pay my salary— i.e., the shareholders, unless the shareholders tell me in advance that they want me to do something else. I will do my best to learn how to do this by taking the relevant courses."

Source: "The Oath Demands a Commitment to Bad Corporate Governance," *Canadian Business,* October 2010, p. 83.

The MBA Oath Helps Remind Graduates of Their Ethical Obligations

Chris MacDonald

In response to the economic crisis, in 2009 a group of graduating Harvard MBAs proposed that all MBA students sign an oath of professional conduct. It pledges, among other things, to "contribute to the well-being of society" and to "create sustainable economic, social and environmental prosperity worldwide."

The oath has since been taken by students at more than 250 schools around the world, and while it is not a revolutionary thing, not a perfect thing, it is definitely a good thing. Of course, not everyone thinks so. The MBA oath has been assailed by three kinds of critics: ones who say it is too demanding, ones who say it is not demanding enough, and ones who say it shouldn't be necessary in the first place. Each group is, in its own way, badly off-target.

First, consider the critics who say the oath is too demanding. To them, the oath embodies a radical departure from the tenets of economic theory and the requirements of corporate law. There is, after all, a clause under which MBAs promise to protect the planet, and implicitly to do so even when that's not in the best interest of shareholders. But such critics are being perversely literal. Nothing in the MBA oath exhorts MBAs to turn their backs on their fiduciary duties to shareholders, nor even to push in that direction beyond the minimal expectations of decency.

Second, there are critics who say the oath requires too little. Follow the law? Obey contracts? Pay a little attention to the consequences of your actions? Is that all MBAs aspire to? How about a real commitment to social and economic justice? And besides, how much can really be accomplished by a voluntary code, absent any form of enforcement? These critics, too, are off-target. To begin, they ignore the potential impact of getting ethical concerns explicitly onto the business executive's agenda. But perhaps more important, they underestimate the depth of legitimate debate over the way even public-minded MBAs ought to put their values into action when at work. The ethical obligations of business executives are not, despite what the critics say, obvious and easy.

The third group of critics says an oath should not be necessary in the first place. After all, should anyone really need to be told to be ethical? More particularly, shouldn't people who have graduated from an MBA program already know just what is expected of them, ethically, in the environments for which they've been so extensively and expensively trained? Again, the criticism is off-base. For the point of an oath such as this is not to remind the MBA of the details of his or her ethical obligations. It is an affirmation that the MBA intends, in the face of competing pressures, to keep those ethical obligations firmly in mind—something that all available evidence suggests is harder than it sounds. So the MBA who signs the oath signals that, for him or her, ethics wasn't just a compulsory course to pass and then forget about.

None of this is to say that the MBA oath is perfect. It arguably has too little to say about principal agent problems, and about how MBAs ought to handle the conflicts that will inevitably arise between the oath's various injunctions. Note also that the oath insists on the duty to avoid "business practices harmful to society," which is so painfully vague it borders on the vacuous.

But overall, the main problem with the MBA oath isn't really a problem with the oath at all—it's a problem with people's expectations. Dismissive critics say that no oath will solve the deep and abiding moral problems that beset the world of business. That's surely true, but no one could seriously have

thought otherwise. It's trite, but also true, to say that the world of business is increasingly complex. The ethical demands on business are higher than ever. In particular, business executives are called upon with increasing regularity to account for their actions and their policies, and to justify them to an increasing range of stakeholders. Add to that the enormous, lingering cultural rift regarding the proper role of corporations and markets. The MBA oath is of course not going to solve all of the ethical challenges that arise in such a context. Nor is it going to ensure that none of its signatories ever crosses the line into regrettable or disreputable or even disgraceful behaviour. But if given half a chance, the MBA oath might just turn out to play a small but not insignificant role in keeping the discussion alive.

Source: "The MBA Oath Helps Remind Graduates of Their Ethical Obligations," *Canadian Business,* October 2010, p. 82.

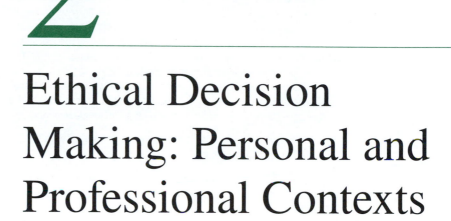

Ethical Decision Making: Personal and Professional Contexts

It is very important to know who you are. To make decisions. To show who you are.
Malala Yousafzai

Nearly all men can stand adversity, but if you want to test a man's character, give him power.
Abraham Lincoln

The time is always right to do what's right.
Martin Luther King Jr.

There are two kinds of people, those who do the work and those who take the credit. Try to be in the first group; there is less competition there.
Indira Gandhi

Imagine that you are the first person to arrive for your business ethics class. As you sit down at your desk, you notice an iPod on the floor underneath the adjacent seat. You pick it up and turn it on. It works just fine, and it even has some of your favorite music listed. Looking around, you realize that you are still the only person in the room and that no one will know if you keep it. A quick check suggests that the iPod's security features have not been activated, so nothing is preventing you from using it.

Not being able to decide immediately, and seeing that other students are beginning to enter the room, you place the iPod on the floor next to your own backpack and books. As the class begins, you realize that you have the full class period to decide what to do.

- What would you think about as you sat there trying to decide what to do?
- What would you do?

Now let us change the scenario. Instead of being the person who finds the iPod, imagine that you are a friend who sits next to that person. As class begins, your friend leans over, tells you what happened, and asks for advice.

The lesson for today's business ethics class is Chapter 2 of your textbook, *Business Ethics: Decision Making for Personal Integrity and Social Responsibility*.

Finally, imagine that you are a student representative on the judicial board of your school. This student decides to keep the iPod and is later accused of stealing. How would you make your decision?

- What are the key facts you should consider before making a decision, as either the person who discovered the iPod, the friend, or a member of a disciplinary panel?
- Is this an ethical issue? What exactly are the ethical aspects involved in your decision?
- Who else is involved, or should be involved, in this decision? Who has a stake in the outcome?
- What alternatives are available to you? What are the consequences of each alternative?
- How would each of your alternatives affect the other people you have identified as having a stake in the outcome?
- Where might you look for additional guidance to assist you in resolving this particular dilemma?

Chapter Objectives

After reading this chapter, you will be able to:

1. Describe a process for ethically responsible decision making.
2. Apply this model to ethical decision points.
3. Explain the reasons why "good" people might engage in unethical behavior.
4. Explore the impact of managerial roles on the nature of our decision making.

Introduction

Chapter 1 introduced our approach to business ethics as a form of practical reasoning, a process for decision making in business. Putting ethics into practice requires not simply decision making, but *accountable* decision making. Chapter 1 also suggested that, even if a person does not consciously think about a decision, her or his own actions will involve making a choice and taking a stand. If you find a lost iPod, you cannot avoid making a decision, whether by act or omission. Whatever you do—or do not do—with the iPod, you will have made a choice that will be evaluated in ethical terms and have ethical implications.

The previous chapter provided a general context for thinking about business ethics; in the current chapter, we begin to bring this topic to a more practical level by examining ethical decision making as it occurs in everyday life and within business contexts. We will examine various elements involved in individual decision making and apply those concepts to the decisions individuals make every day in business. This chapter also examines various ways in which ethical decision making can go wrong, as well as the ways in which business leaders can model the most effective ethical decision making.

A Decision-Making Process for Ethics

OBJECTIVE

ethical decision-making process
Requires a persuasive and rational justification for a decision. Rational justifications are developed through a logical process of decision making that gives proper attention to such things as facts, alternative perspectives, consequences to all stakeholders, and ethical principles.

Let us consider an initial sketch of an **ethical decision-making process.** How would you decide what to do in the iPod case? First, you might wonder how the iPod ended up under the desk. Was it lost? Perhaps someone intentionally discarded the iPod. Would that fact make a significant difference in the ethical judgment that you would make? Or suppose the person who discovered the iPod actually saw it fall from another student's backpack. Would that make a difference in your judgment about that person?

The first step in making decisions that are ethically responsible is to *determine the facts* of the situation. Making an honest effort to understand the situation, to distinguish facts from mere opinion, is essential. **Perceptual differences** surrounding how individuals experience and understand situations can explain many ethical disagreements. Knowing the facts and carefully reviewing the circumstances can go a long way toward resolving disagreements at an early stage.

Let us turn to the iPod case. What facts would be useful to know before making a decision? Suppose you already owned an iPod. Would that make a difference? Suppose you knew who sat at the desk in the previous class. Imagine that the iPod had been in a place not easily seen and you had observed it there over the course of several days. Suppose the iPod did not work and, instead of being discovered underneath a seat, you found it in a wastebasket. How would your decision change as any of these facts changed? Can you imagine a situation in which what looks like an ethical disagreement turns out to be a disagreement over the facts? Considering another technology-based area of challenge, would a situation that involved sharing copyrighted music files over e-mail be an ethical disagreement or a disagreement over the facts?

perceptual differences

Psychologists and philosophers have long recognized that individuals cannot perceive the world independently of their own conceptual framework. Experiences are mediated by and interpreted through our own understanding and concepts. Thus, ethical disagreements can depend as much on a person's conceptual framework as on the facts of the situation. Unpacking our own and others' conceptual schemata plays an important role in making ethically responsible decisions.

Given the general importance of determining the facts, there is a role for science (and critical thinking) in any study of ethics. An ethical judgment made in light of a diligent determination of the facts is a more reasonable ethical judgment than one made without regard for the facts. A person who acts in a way that is based on a careful consideration of the facts has acted in a more ethically responsible way than a person who acts without deliberation. The sciences, and perhaps especially the social sciences, can help us determine the facts surrounding our decisions. For a business example, consider what facts might be relevant for making a decision regarding child labor. Consider how the social sciences of anthropology and economics, for example, might help us understand the facts surrounding employing children in the workplace within a foreign country. Applying this strategy to a business operation would encourage business decision makers to seek out perhaps alternative or somewhat less traditional methods of gathering facts to ensure that she or he has compiled all of the necessary data in processing the most ethical decision.

A second step in responsible ethical decision making requires the ability to recognize a decision or issue as an ethical decision or ethical issue. It is easy to be led astray by a failure to recognize that there is an ethical component to some decisions. *Identifying the ethical issues involved* is the next step in making responsible decisions. Certainly, the first and second steps might arise in reverse order, depending on the circumstances. At times, you have a selection of facts that give rise to a particular ethical dilemma or issue. However, just as likely, there may also be times when you are presented with an issue from the start, say, when a colleague asks you for guidance with a challenging ethical predicament. The issue identification, therefore, becomes the first step, while fact gathering is a necessary second step.

In the iPod case, imagine that the student claims that he simply discovered a lost item and kept it. He denies that this is even an ethical issue because, after all, he did not *steal* the iPod. What is the difference between stealing and finding a lost item? Similarly, in many business situations, what appears to be an ethical issue for one person will be perceived as a simple financial decision by others. How does one determine that a question raises an ethical issue? When does a *business* decision become an *ethical* decision?

First, of course, we need to recognize that "business" or "economic" decisions and ethical decisions are not mutually exclusive. Just because a decision is made on economic grounds does not mean that it does not involve ethical considerations as well. Being sensitive to ethical issues is a vital characteristic that needs to be cultivated in ethically responsible people. Beyond sensitivity, we also need to ask how our decisions will impact the well-being of the people involved—what are the implications for stakeholders?

Consider how ethics and economics intersect in the decision, announced in 2016 by Adidas AG, to resume manufacturing in Germany.[1] Adidas is a German company that makes shoes and sportswear, and for decades it had conducted its manufacturing activities primarily in developing countries. The decision by Adidas to "return" to Germany might have been cause for celebration among

Germans looking for jobs, but there was a catch: The shoes Adidas would be making in Germany would be made by robots. On one hand, a decision regarding what technology to use in manufacturing seems like a purely technical question. And the question of *where* to manufacture seems like a pure question of operational efficiency. But both questions have clear ethical implications. Having shoes made by robots means fewer jobs for people. Having them made in Germany (rather than, say, in Indonesia) means at least some jobs for Germans. But it means no (new) jobs for Indonesians, who on average are much poorer—and hence need jobs much more desperately—than Germans. Whether this decision is better, or worse, than a different decision is not obvious; but what *should* be obvious is that it is a decision with a significant ethical dimension.

As you may recall, Chapter 1 described ethical values as concerned with the *impartial* promotion of human well-being. To the degree that a decision affects the well-being—the happiness, health, dignity, integrity, freedom, respect—of the people involved, it is a decision with ethical implications. Shall we also consider then the environment, animals, future generations? There are often ethical implications for these entities as well. In the end, it is almost impossible to conceive of a decision we might make that does not have at least some impact on the well-being of another. Accordingly, one could suggest that practically all of our decisions have ethical implications.

normative myopia
The tendency to ignore, or the lack of the ability to recognize, ethical issues in decision making.

In business contexts, it can be easy to become so involved in the technical aspects of decisions that one loses sight of the ethical aspects. Perhaps the Adidas board did not contemplate the differential impact its decision would have on various employees and potential employees. Some writers have called this inability to recognize ethical issues **normative myopia,** or shortsightedness about values.[2] Normative myopia does not occur only in business, but in a business context, people may be especially likely to focus on the technical aspects of the task at hand, and thus fail to recognize the ethical aspect. (See the Reality Check "Is There an Ethics of Writing Papers?") Chugh and Bazerman similarly warn of **inattentional blindness,** which they suggest results from focusing failures.[3] If we happen to focus on—or if we are told specifically to pay attention to—a particular element of a decision or event, we are likely to miss all of the surrounding details, no matter how obvious. These focusing failures then result in a moment when we ask ourselves, "How could I have missed that?" You may recall having a conversation with someone while driving and perhaps missing a highway turn-off because your "mind was elsewhere."

inattentional blindness
If we happen to focus on or are told specifically to pay attention to a particular element of a decision or event, we are likely to miss all of the surrounding details, no matter how obvious.

The problem is that when we focus on the wrong thing, or fail to focus, we may fail to see key information that will lead us to success or prevent unethical behavior; we may fail to use the information because we do not know it is relevant; or we may be aware, but we might fail to contribute it to the group. Any of these breakdowns can have disastrous or dangerous consequences. (For more about failures to see relevant information, see the Reality Check, "Fooling Ourselves.")

Reality Check *Is There an Ethics of Writing Papers?*

Perhaps the most common ethical issue that students and teachers confront involves plagiarism. In fact, a 2010 survey of 43,000 high school students showed that one student in three admitted to using the Internet to plagiarize an assignment.[4] From the academic perspective, there is no more serious offense than plagiarizing the work of others. Yet, many students seem honestly surprised to learn that what they believed was research is interpreted as unethical behavior by their teachers.[5]

Many students rely on Internet sources while writing their school papers. It is all too easy to cut and paste sections of an online source into one's own writing assignment, and to neglect to put it inside quotation marks and cite a source. On one particular website, users can post a question that they are struggling with and identify the amount they are willing to pay for an answer. "Tutors" then write a custom lesson that answers the questions posted in order to receive payment. The website claims it does not help the student cheat; instead, it is simply offering an online tutoring service. It contends that all

users, both students and tutors, must agree to the website's academic honesty policy in order to use the website's services.

No doubt, some of this is intentional cheating, such as when a student downloads or purchases an entire paper or answer from a "tutor" or other Internet source. But, in many cases, students seem honestly confused that their teacher treats an unattributed cut-and-pasted passage as cheating. Most teachers can recall situations in which they have had to explain to a student why this practice is unethical.

Such cases are not rare. People often make bad ethical decisions because they fail to understand that there is an ethical issue involved. Typically, they have not thought through the implications of their decision and have not stepped back from their situation to reflect on their choice and to consider their decision from other points of view. Often, they are simply too involved in the immediate situation to think about such things. This is a good example of normative myopia and inattentional blindness.

change blindness
A decision-making omission that occurs when decision makers fail to notice gradual changes over time.

Chugh and Bazerman identify a third means by which ethical issues might go unnoticed: **change blindness.** This omission occurs when decision makers fail to notice gradual changes over time. They offer the example of the Arthur Andersen auditors who did not notice how low Enron had fallen in terms of its unethical decisions. One of the means by which to protect against these decision risks is to ensure that decision makers seek input from others in their decision processes. The researchers report that group input—*any* other input—is almost always a positive factor since individuals collectively can possess and utilize more information than any single person.

The third step involved in ethical decision making involves one of its more critical elements. We are asked to *identify and to consider all of the people affected by a decision, the people often called stakeholders.* "Stakeholders," in this general sense, include all of the groups and/or individuals affected by a decision, policy, or operation of a firm or individual (see Figure 2.1). Examining issues from a variety of perspectives other than one's own, and other than what local conventions suggest, helps make one's decisions more reasonable, accountable, and responsible. And, to the contrary, thinking and reasoning from a narrow and personal point of view virtually guarantees that we will not fully understand the situation. Making decisions from a narrow and personal point of view likewise ensures that we are liable to make a decision that does not give due consideration to other persons and perspectives.

Reality Check *Fooling Ourselves*

"People view themselves as more ethical, fair, and objective than others, yet often act against their moral compass."

  Sezer, Gino, and Bazerman, "Ethical Blind Spots"[6]

  The key factors that these authors say contribute to ethical blind spots include:

- Implicit biases ("Individuals typically fail to recognize the harm that implicit favoritism of in-group members causes to members of social out-groups.")

- Temporal distance (We tend to believe that we will follow our moral compasses "when the time comes," but when the time actually comes, we become more likely to go with our immediate wants.)

- Failure to notice others' unethical behavior (We are less likely to condemn other people's ethical behavior when we benefit from it, or when we have encouraged it.)

One helpful exercise for considering the effects of a decision on others is to shift one's role. Rather than being in the position of the person who discovers the iPod, what would you think of this case if you were the person who lost it? How does that affect your thinking? What would your judgment be if you were the friend who was asked for advice? A long tradition in philosophical ethics argues that a key test of ethical legitimacy is whether a decision would be acceptable from the point of view of all parties involved. If you could accept a decision as legitimate, no matter whose point of view you take, that decision is likely to be fair, impartial, and ethical. If you acknowledge that you would not accept the legitimacy of keeping the iPod if you were the person who lost it rather than the person who found it, then that is a strong indication that the decision to keep it is not a fair or ethical one.

FIGURE 2.1

Stakeholder Map

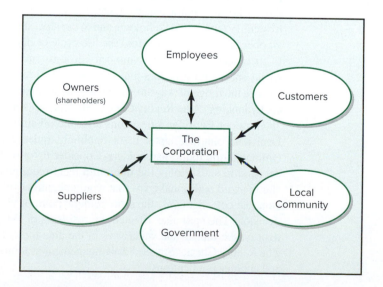

Think back to the Decision Point in the first chapter, "Zika Virus and Olympic Sponsors." One of the key challenges faced by sponsors of the 2016 Olympics was to figure out who their key stakeholders were. To whom does the company owe obligations in the face of a global epidemic? And once the company has identified its stakeholders, then what? Making a list surely is not the end of the hard work.

Consider the relatively easy example of a group that is directly affected: the athletes who will participate in the Olympics. What do the Olympic sponsors owe to this group?

- Should the Olympic sponsors have sought to protect these athletes by advocating moving or postponing the Olympics?
- Should the Olympic sponsors have given priority to stakeholders they can name (such as Olympic athletes) over stakeholders they cannot name (such as the people who might, hypothetically, contract Zika if the Olympics help spread the virus)?
- Should Olympic sponsors have asked any of the relevant stakeholders their opinion? Who should have been included in this discussion?
- If, in the wake of the Rio Olympics, new and unexpected cases of Zika virus turned up in countries that previously had no cases, should Olympic sponsors feel obligated to compensate the victims in some way?

As an example, global mining and extraction company BHP Billiton conducts a comprehensive stakeholder exploration process and then posts the results of this analysis on the Internet in order to demonstrate a commitment to transparency to its stakeholders.[7] It defines its key stakeholders as "people who are adversely or positively impacted by our operations, those who have an interest in what we do, or those who have an influence on what we do"; and then it requires all of its locations to identify their key stakeholders and to consider their expectations and concerns for all operational activities across the life cycle of operations. "Sites are also required to specifically consider any minority groups (such as indigenous groups) and any social and cultural factors that may be critical to stakeholder engagement."[8] You can see the range of ways in which another company engages its various stakeholders by looking at the Reality Check "Stakeholder Engagement at Johnson Matthey."

Consider Enbridge's decisions after the oil spill in Wrigley as described in the Decision Point in Chapter 1. As a publicly traded company, Enbridge has a financial obligation to its shareholders. Considering only this obligation might lead to a decision to satisfy only the minimum legal requirements for cleaning up the spill site to avoid additional costs that would negatively affect profits. However, a decision that considers only the shareholders' point of view would not be a responsible decision. The spill also affected the residents of Wrigley, who are heavily dependent on the forests and waterways in the area for their livelihood and ways of life. The Reality Check "Stakeholder Engagement at Johnson Matthey" further explores stakeholder implications.

Reality Check *Stakeholder Engagement at Johnson Matthey*

The website for British chemicals company Johnson Matthey gives a detailed analysis of who its stakeholders are and the methods the company uses to engage them.

In other words, the company recognizes that it is not enough, ethically, to know who your stakeholders are; you need to engage them in discussion. The company also recognizes that different stakeholders need to be engaged in different ways.

The following table shows the ways in which Johnson Matthey engages just a few of its key stakeholders:

Stakeholder Engagement at Johnson Matthey

Stakeholder*	Ongoing Dialogue	Surveys/ Questionnaires	Regular Meetings	Reviews	Audits	Integrated Annual Report
Employees	Yes	Yes	Yes	Yes		Yes
Shareholders	Yes	Yes	Yes			Yes
Customers	Yes	Yes	Yes		Yes	Yes
Regulatory Bodies	Yes					Yes

*Johnson Matthey also lists, among its stakeholders, institutional investors/analysts, suppliers, NGOs, trade associations, ethical investment markets, and voluntary schemes.

Source: Johnson Matthey, "Our Stakeholders," www.matthey.com/sustainability/sustainability-governance/stakeholders.

The fact that many decisions will involve the interests of multiple stakeholders also helps us understand a major challenge to ethical decision making. The very fact that there are many perspectives and interests at stake means that ethical decisions often involve dilemmas. Each alternative will impose costs on some stakeholders and offer benefits to others. Making a decision that benefits one group often means that other stakeholders will be denied benefits.

Once we have examined the facts, identified the ethical issues involved, and identified the stakeholders, we need to *consider the available alternatives.* Creativity in identifying ethical options—also called **moral imagination**—is one element that distinguishes good people who make ethically responsible decisions from good people who do not.[9] It is important not only to consider the obvious options with regard to a particular dilemma, but also the much subtler ones that might not be evident at first glance.

Consider the case of discovering a lost iPod. One person might decide to keep it because she believes that the chances of discovering the true owner are slim and that, if she does not keep it, the next person to discover it will do so anyway. Another person might be able to think of some alternatives beyond those choices. For example, she could return early for the next class to see who is sitting at the desk, or she could find out who teaches the previous class and ask that teacher for help in identifying the owner. Moral imagination might involve something as

moral imagination
When one is facing an ethical decision, the ability to envision various alternative choices, consequences, resolutions, benefits, and harms.

Reality Check *Recognizing the Value of Stakeholders' Trust*

Statement of Prof. Dr. Martin Winterkorn, CEO of Volkswagen AG (September 20, 2015):

The U.S. Environmental Protection Agency and the California Air Resources Board (EPA and CARB) revealed their findings that while testing diesel cars of the Volkswagen Group they have detected manipulations that violate American environmental standards.

The Board of Management at Volkswagen AG takes these findings very seriously. I personally am deeply sorry that we have broken the trust of our customers and the public. We will cooperate fully with the responsible agencies, with transparency and urgency, to clearly, openly, and completely establish all of the facts of this case.

Volkswagen has ordered an external investigation of this matter.

We do not and will not tolerate violations of any kind of our internal rules or of the law.

The trust of our customers and the public is and continues to be our most important asset. We at Volkswagen will do everything that must be done in order to re-establish the trust that so many people have placed in us, and we will do everything necessary in order to reverse the damage this has caused. This matter has first priority for me, personally, and for our entire Board of Management.

Source: "Statement of Prof. Dr. Martin Winterkorn, CEO of Volkswagen AG," September 20, 2015, www.volkswagenag.com/content/vwcorp/info_center/en/news/2015/09/statement_ceo_of_volkswagen_ag.html (accessed June 17, 2016).

simple as checking in a lost and found department. How would the school community be changed if students went out of their way to return lost items rather than keeping them for their own use?

The next step in the decision-making process is to *compare and weigh the alternatives.* Create a mental spreadsheet (or, if you have time and the situation is complex, create a real one!) that evaluates the impact of each alternative you have devised on each stakeholder you defined. Perhaps the most helpful way to accomplish this task is to try to place oneself in the other person's position, as discussed earlier. Understanding a situation from another's point of view, making an effort to "walk a mile in their shoes," contributes significantly to responsible ethical decision making. Weighing the alternatives will involve predicting the likely, the foreseeable, and the possible consequences to all the relevant stakeholders. A critical element of this evaluation will be the consideration of ways to mitigate, minimize, or compensate for any possible harmful consequences or to increase and promote beneficial consequences.

Ethics experts sometimes ask the decision maker to consider whether he would feel proud or ashamed if *The Wall Street Journal* (or the *Globe and Mail,* or whatever is your relevant daily newspaper) printed this decision as a front-page article, or whether he could explain it to a 10-year-old so the child thinks it is the right decision, or whether it will stand the test of time. Note that, in the iPod case, the student was described as looking around to see if anyone else noticed his discovery. Would your behavior change if other people knew about it? The point of this exercise is to recognize that a fully responsible and ethical decision should be explainable, defensible, and justifiable to the entire range of stakeholders involved. Typically, it is the irresponsible decisions that we wish to keep hidden. (See the Reality Check "Recognizing the Value of Stakeholders' Trust.")

Reality Check *Seeking Guidance?*

It's better to hang out with people better than you. Pick out associates whose behavior is better than yours and you'll drift in that direction.

Warren Buffett

I believe that every right implies a responsibility; every opportunity, an obligation; every possession, a duty.

John D. Rockefeller Jr.

Men of integrity, by their existence, rekindle the belief that as a people we can live above the level of moral squalor. We need that belief; a cynical community is a corrupt community.

John W. Gardner

There is nothing noble about being superior to some other man. The true nobility is in being superior to your previous self.

Hindu Proverb

I hope that my achievements in life shall be these— that I will have fought for what was right and fair, that I will have risked for that which mattered, and that I will have given help to those who were in need, that I will have left the earth a better place for what I've done and who I've been.

C. Hoppe

Laws and principles are not for the times when there is no temptation: they are for such moments as this, when body and soul rise in mutiny against their rigour. . . . If at my convenience I might break them, what would be their worth?

Charlotte Brontë, in Jane Eyre

But consequences or justifications are not the only means for comparing alternatives. Some alternatives might concern matters of principles, rights, or duties that override consequences. Within business settings, individuals may often have specific duties associated with their position. A purchasing manager for a large retail store has a duty associated with her role that directs her to avoid conflicts of interest in dealing with suppliers. Are duties associated with company rules, professional codes of conduct, business roles, or legal duties involved? Perhaps guidance is available in specific circumstances from these sources or others (see the Reality Check "Seeking Guidance?")

One additional factor in comparing and weighing alternatives requires consideration of the effects of a decision on one's own integrity, virtue, and character. Understanding one's own character and values should play a role in decision making. People often make decisions based on an understanding of who they are, and what kind of person they want to be. A responsible person will ask: "What type of person would make this decision? What kind of habits would I be developing by deciding in one way rather than another? What type of corporate culture am I creating and encouraging? How would I, or my family, describe a person who decides in this way? Is this a decision that I am willing to defend in public?" Such questions truly go to the heart of ethical business leadership. An honest person might not even think about keeping the iPod; keeping it for oneself is simply not an option for such a person.

Once you have explored these variables, the next step is to *make a decision*. However, the process is not yet complete. Decisions in business are not typically simple "yes" or "no" decisions; in most cases, making a decision means formulating a plan and carrying it out. Further, to be accountable in our decision making,

Let's give it a try: Should a burger chain—say, McDonald's or Burger King—voluntarily decide to pay its workers the $15 per hour that advocates suggest should be the new, legal minimum wage?

For years, advocates have argued that government should raise the minimum wage substantially—perhaps to as high as $15 per hour. How would *you* make this decision, using the ethical decision-making process provided in this chapter? Let's think through the first few steps.

What facts might be relevant? You would need to consider first what you are currently paying per hour and how many hours per week a typical worker works. You might also consider how the resulting total pay compares to the cost of living. Also relevant would be the pay received in other workplaces, by workers with similar levels of skill. Consider: Who *are* your employees? Are they parents trying to support a family or young people working their first job for a bit of spending cash? Would paying more enable you to attract better workers? If you raise the pay per hour, what will you need to do to offset the additional cost?

What ethical issues does this case raise? To most people, the most significant ethical issue is one of fairness. But fairness can mean many things. One kind of fairness has to do with what counts as fair compensation for a day's work. Another has to do with a fair distribution of benefits among various stakeholders such as employees, customers, and shareholders.

Who are the stakeholders? The most obvious stakeholders are your workers and their families. Also relevant would be more senior frontline workers, who might resent the fact that junior workers now make as much as *they* do after several years of experience. Your customers may also have a stake here, particularly if increased labor costs imply a need to raise your prices. And finally, if your company is a publicly traded one, your shareholders are another obvious stakeholder group.

What alternatives are available? Many options are available. Keeping things just as they are is one option, as is raising pay to the level demanded by activists. Of course, a smaller raise is also an option. A further option would be to reduce the significance of the issue (as some burger joints have done) by hiring fewer minimum-wage employees and installing self-serve kiosks. But don't forget to use your imagination, to go beyond the obvious options. There may be other options that employees would value nearly as much as a raise in pay—things like additional perks, health care benefits, assistance with university or college tuition, and so on.

Complete the process yourself! How would you weigh the alternatives available to a restaurant chain? What decision do you think the restaurant should make, based on this weighing of alternatives? How should the company monitor the outcomes to make sure the appropriate lessons are learned?

Note: At time of writing, the U.S. federal minimum wage is $7.25 per hour. Some states have established higher minimums. In 2014, several U.S. cities (San Francisco, Seattle, and Los Angeles) approved a $15 minimum, to be phased in over time. For comparison, in Canada, where minimum wage is strictly a provincial matter, minimum wage varies from province to province but is generally in the $9 to $12 range.

FIGURE 2.2
An Ethical Decision-Making Process

- Determine the facts.

- Identify the ethical issues involved.

- Identify stakeholders and consider the situation from their point of view.

- Consider the available alternatives—also called using moral imagination.

- Compare and weigh the alternatives, based on:
  - Consequences (for all stakeholders).
  - Duties, rights, principles.
  - Implications for personal integrity and character.

- Make a decision.

- Monitor and learn from the outcomes.

it is not sufficient to deliberate over this process, only to later throw up our hands once the decision is made: "It's out of my hands now!" Instead, we have the ability as humans to learn from our experiences. That ability implies a responsibility to complete the process by proceeding to the final step: evaluate the implications of our decisions, to *monitor and learn from the outcomes,* and to modify our actions accordingly when faced with similar challenges in the future. In institutional terms, this can mean using what is learned to develop a plan for preventing future crises, to institute new practices, and to develop new policies and procedures. The Decision Point "Applying the Decision-Making Model" gives us a chance to put this decision-making process into practice.

OBJECTIVE

The ethical traditions and theories that we describe in the next chapter will help us flesh out and elaborate on this decision process. Other approaches to ethically responsible decision making are possible, and this approach will not guarantee one single and absolute answer to every decision. But it is a helpful beginning in the development of responsible and ethical decision making (see Figure 2.2.).

When Ethical Decision Making Goes Wrong: Why Do "Good" People Engage in "Bad" Acts?

To say that each individual has the ability to follow a similar decision-making process or that each of us has the capacity to make autonomous decisions is not to say that every individual always *does* so. There are many ways in which responsible decision making can go wrong and many ways in which people fail to act in accordance with the ethical judgments they make. Sometimes, of course, people can simply choose to do something unethical. We should not underestimate the real possibility of immoral choices and unethical behavior.

But at other times, even well-intentioned people fail to make ethical choices. What factors determine which companies or individuals engage in ethical behavior and which do not? Why do people we consider to be "good" sometimes do "bad" things? To say that the person who did the bad thing is really a good person does not mean that these unethical decisions or acts are excusable, but that the

Individuals who engage in the unethical behavior may have done so for a variety of reasons that may not immediately be clear to us. As it turns out, there are many stumbling blocks to responsible decision making and behavior. (See Reading 2-1, "When Good People Do Bad Things at Work," by Dennis J. Moberg.)

OBJECTIVE 3

Some stumbling blocks standing in the way of responsible action are cognitive or intellectual. As the model of ethical decision making outlined in this chapter suggests, a certain type of ignorance can account for bad ethical choices. Sometimes that *ignorance* can be almost willful and intentional. After you discover a lost iPod, you might rationalize to yourself that no one will ever know, no one is really going to be hurt, an owner who is so careless deserves to lose the iPod. You might try to justify the decision by convincing yourself that you are only doing what anyone else would do in this circumstance. You might not really believe that, but it's a comforting story to tell yourself. You might even choose not to think about it and try to put any guilty feelings out of your mind.

Another cognitive barrier is that we sometimes *consider only limited alternatives.* When faced with a situation that suggests two clear alternative ways forward, we often consider only those two clear paths, missing the fact that other alternatives might be possible. Upon discovering a lost iPod, you might conclude that if you do not take it, someone else will. Because the original owner will lose out in both cases, it is better that you benefit from the loss than if someone else benefits. Responsible decision making would require that we discipline ourselves to explore additional methods of resolution. If you think carefully about the iPod case, you will likely see that there are quite a few different ways forward. In our ethical decision-making process, we refer to this as the use of moral imagination.

We human beings also generally feel most comfortable with *simplified decision rules.* Having a simple rule to follow can be reassuring to many decision makers. For example, assume you are a business manager who feels the need to terminate a worker in order to cut costs. Of course, your first thought may be to uncover alternative means by which to cut costs instead of firing someone, but assume for the moment that cutting one worker is the only realistic possibility. It may be easiest and most comfortable to terminate the last person you hired, explaining, "I can't help it; it must be done, 'last in/first out,' I have no choice. . . ." Or, in the iPod case, "finders keepers, losers weepers" might be an attractive rule to follow. That is, after all, a rule you've likely heard since kindergarten, and it's a simple rule that likely comes to mind pretty quickly. Using a simple decision rule might appear to relieve us of responsibility for the decision even if it may not be the best possible decision. You did not "make" the decision, you might think; the rule *required* that decision to be made. It's a comforting thought, but it can lead us astray.

We also often select the alternative that satisfies *minimum decision criteria,* otherwise known as satisficing. We select the option that suffices, the one that you and relevant others can live with, even if it might not be the best. Imagine a committee at work that needs to make a decision. They may spend hours arriving at a result and finally reach agreement. At that point, it is unlikely that someone

Reality Check *The Ethics of Cheating*

A 2010 survey of 43,000 American high school students found that a third of boys and a quarter of girls admitted to having stolen from a store within the last year. Almost 60 percent admitted to having cheated on a test in the last year. But almost 90 percent said that it is more important to be a good person than it is to be rich.[10]

As appalling—or disturbing—as those statistics might be, students fare worse when they are categorized by academic discipline. Research has demonstrated that *business* undergraduate students are *the most likely* to have cheated on a test, when compared with prelaw students and the general population.[11] In response to a statement claiming that *not* cheating is the best way to get ahead in the long run, business

students claimed, "You snooze, you lose."[12] Does this mean that, perhaps, there is a failure in ethics in the business arena because the people who go into business already cheat? Or is it that business students are aware that the business arena demands this type of unethical conduct so they prepare themselves for it from the start? Competitiveness might blur the border between ethical and unethical. Either way, as our parents have told us, simply because an environment is replete with a certain type of behavior does not mean that we must follow suit, nor does it relieve us of our responsibility for actions in that environment (thus the common parental question, "If Janie jumps off a bridge, are you going to follow?").

will stand up and say, "Whoa, wait a minute; let's spend another couple of hours and figure out an even *better* answer!" The very fact that a decision was reached by consensus can convince everyone involved that it must be the most reasonable decision, even though it clearly isn't.

Other stumbling blocks are less intellectual or cognitive than they are a question of motivation and willpower. As author John Grisham explained in his novel *Rainmaker,* "Every (lawyer), at least once in every case, feels himself crossing a line he doesn't really mean to cross. It just happens." Sometimes it is simply *easier* to do the wrong thing. After all, who wants to go through all the *trouble* of finding the lost and found office and walking across campus to return the iPod? Consider how you would answer the questions asked in the Reality Check "The Ethics of Cheating."

Unfortunately, we do not always draw the lines for appropriate behavior in advance, and even when we do, they are not always crystal clear. As Grisham suggests, it is often easy to do a little thing that crosses the line, and the next time it is easier, and the next easier still. And then, one day, you find yourself much further over your ethical line than you thought you would ever be.

People also sometimes make decisions they later regret because they *lack the courage* to do otherwise. It is not always easy to make the right decision; you might lose income, your job, or other valuable components of your life. Sherron Watkins was only one of many Enron employees who explained their reluctance to push their concerns by reference to the culture of intimidation and fear that characterized upper management at Enron. Courage is also necessary when responding to significant *peer pressure*. Though we might have believed that we could leave this behind in high school or college, unfortunately, we are subject to it throughout our lives. We tend to give in to peer pressure in our professional environments, both because we want to "fit in" and to achieve success in our organizations, and also because our *actual* thinking is influenced by our peers. We worry that our disagreement means that we might be wrong. Accordingly, we either change our minds to fit our environments, or we simply listen only for the evidence that supports this new way of thinking until our minds slowly change on their own.

Of course, the usual suspects for explaining unethical conduct are still very much apparent in the scandals that make the front pages every day. The shockingly high levels of corporate executive compensation, lack of oversight of corporate executive decisions, significant distance between decision makers and those whose lives they affect, financial challenges, and a set of ethical values that has not yet caught up to technological advances—all of these factors can create an environment rife with ethical challenges and unethical decisions. We can benefit from unethical acts, from gaining something as simple as an iPod to something as significant as a salary package of $180 million. Temptation is often all around us and any person can succumb to it. The questions that are most difficult to answer are often those that are most important to answer in defining who we are. Give it a try in the Decision Point "Ethical Oil: Choose Your Poison."

Making ethically responsible decisions throughout one's life is perhaps the most serious challenge we all face. The easiest thing to do would be to remain passive and simply conform to social and cultural expectations, to "go with the flow." But such passivity is exactly the sort of unexamined life that Socrates claimed was not worth living. To live a meaningful human life, we must step back and reflect on our decisions, taking responsibility as autonomous beings.

Before leaving this discussion, it is worth reflecting on those people who do not succumb to temptations and who seemingly may not even deliberate in the face of an ethical dilemma. In the following chapter, we will describe an ethical tradition that emphasizes ethical character and virtues. For many people, finding a lost iPod would not raise much of a dilemma at all. Many people would not have to *deliberate* about what to do or go through a decision-making process before acting. Many people have developed a certain type of character, a set of ethical habits, that will encourage them, without deliberation, to act ethically. Consider, for example, the issue of executive compensation. In 1980, a senior U.S. corporate executive was paid an average of 40 times more than the typical worker in his or her company; today, the average ratio of highest-to-lowest pay has catapulted to more than 300 to 1 for publicly traded corporations. Such numbers have raised considerable concern, with critics accusing many CEOs of inexcusable greed. In the context of this dramatic rise in executive compensation, Whole Foods CEO John Mackey's decades-long adherence to a publicized pay ratio cap stands out as a remarkable exception to the norm. In 2010, the Whole Foods pay ratio was set at 19 to 1, while Mackey himself has voluntarily set his own salary at $1 per year and receives no stock awards or bonuses.[13] Similarly, the steelmaker Nucor Corp. has not laid off an employee in its 40-year history. Under the stewardship of then-CEO Daniel DiMicco, the company maintained fidelity to its "no layoffs" philosophy through the economic hardship of the late-2000s recessionary period by

In the fall of 2011, a Canadian organization called EthicalOil.org started a public relations campaign aimed at countering criticism of commercial development of Canada's oil sands, a set of oil-extraction sites that require the use of hot water and steam to extract very heavy crude oil from sands buried deep beneath the earth's surface. Critics have aimed harsh criticism at the oil sands development, claiming that this method of extracting oil does immense environmental damage along with posing risks to human health. EthicalOil.org seeks to counter such criticism by pointing out the alternative: Anyone choosing not to buy oil harvested from Canada's oil sands, they argue, is effectively choosing oil produced by certain nondemocratic Middle Eastern countries with very bad records of human rights abuses. Who could be in favor of supporting countries engaged in human rights abuses? Thus, the claim is that Canadian oil, far from being worthy of criticism, is indeed "ethical oil."

Of course, the fact that EthicalOil.org says oil from Canada's oil sands is "ethical oil" does not make it true.

Remember, the gas you put in your car is refined from oil. Imagine you have the choice, as a consumer, between (1) buying gas for your car that comes from a country where oil extraction does vast environmental damage and (2) buying gas from a country where the profits from that oil help support a dictatorship with a history of human rights abuses. Which gas will you buy? Why? Are you willing to pay a bit extra to get oil that is more ethical, whatever that means to you?

Next, imagine that you are responsible for securing a contract to provide gas for your company's fleet of vehicles. If the choice is available to you, will you choose the most environmentally friendly gas? Or the gas least associated with human rights abuses? Or will you just go with the cheapest gas available?

Finally, consider whether the choice between buying gas that harms the environment and gas that contributes to human rights abuses exhausts the alternatives in these scenarios. Are there other courses of action available to the individual car-owning consumer? To the manager responsible for procuring gas for the company fleet?

Source: Adapted from Chris MacDonald, "Ethical Oil: Choose Your Poison," *Canadian Business* [Blog], September 21, 2011, www.canadianbusiness.com/blog/business_ethics/46555 (accessed July 19, 2012).

tightly linking the compensation of all employees—including senior executives—to performance.[14] Developing such habits, inclinations, and character is an important aspect of living an ethical life. (See the Reality Check "Fooling Ourselves" earlier in the chapter.)

Ethical Decision Making in Managerial Roles

In this text, we have already emphasized that individual decision making can be influenced by the social context in which it occurs. Social circumstances can make it easier or more difficult to act in accordance with one's own best judgment. In the world of business, an organization's context sometimes makes it difficult for people to act ethically, even when they really want to. Likewise, the right

Applying our decision-making model to the iPod case, we would first try to determine the facts. Knowing that the iPod functioned perfectly would be good evidence for concluding that it was left behind accidentally rather than intentionally discarded. Knowing the actual cost of the iPod would also be evidence that it is something likely to be highly valued and not something easily abandoned. The cost, as well as your own understanding of private property, makes it clear that this situation raises ethical issues of rights, happiness, personal integrity, and honesty.

Most obviously, this would seem to involve two major stakeholders: the true owner of the iPod and you. But when you think about it, you may also notice that whatever decision you make will have broader implications. People who find out will talk about the stolen iPod or, conversely, the iPod that had been returned; and this hallway chatter could encourage or diminish a campus culture of trust and honesty.

Imagine yourself now in the position of the student who *lost* the iPod, or in the position of the student who might sit in judgment at a campus disciplinary hearing. How does the situation look to you from *that* point of view? Imagining the results of keeping the iPod and then having that fact discovered and publicized is another helpful step. How would you try to justify that decision to others? Considering the number of hours someone might have to work at a minimum-wage job in order to earn enough money to buy another iPod introduces another important perspective. Finally, a concern with personal integrity would encourage you to reflect on the type of person who keeps another's property: Is this who you really are and want to be?

Given all these steps, it would be difficult to imagine that one could ethically justify a decision to keep the iPod.

personal and professional decision making
Individuals within a business setting are often in situations in which they must make decisions both from their own personal point of view and from the perspective of the specific role they fill within an institution. Ethically responsible decisions require an individual to recognize that these perspectives can conflict and that a life of moral integrity must balance the personal values with the professional role-based values and responsibilities.

organizational culture and structure can make it difficult for a dishonest person to act out his or her impulse to behave unethically. Responsibility for the circumstances that can encourage ethical behavior and can discourage unethical behavior falls predominantly to the business management and executive team. Chapter 4 will examine this issue in more detail as we introduce the concepts of corporate culture and ethical leadership, but it is helpful to begin to explore this topic here.

The decision-making model introduced in this chapter starts from the point of view of an individual who finds herself in a particular situation. Personal integrity lies at the heart of such individual decision making: What kind of person am I or do I want to be? What are my values? What do I stand for? Every individual also fills a variety of social roles, and these roles carry with them a range of expectations, responsibilities, and duties. Within a business setting, individuals must consider the ethical implications of both **personal and professional decision making.** Some of our roles are social: friend, son or daughter, spouse, citizen, neighbor. Some roles are institutional: manager, employee, parent, child, professor, president of a student club. Among the major roles and responsibilities that we will examine in this text are those associated with specific professions, including lawyers, accountants, auditors, financial analysts, and others. Decision making in these contexts raises broader questions of social responsibilities and social justice.

OBJECTIVE

Consider how different roles might impact your judgment about the discovery of the iPod. Your judgment about the iPod might differ greatly if you knew that your friend had lost it, if you were a teacher in the class, or if you were a member of the campus disciplinary board.

In a business context, individuals fill roles of employees (including both new hires and "old hands"), managers, senior executives, and board members. Managers, executives, and board members have the ability to create and shape the organizational context in which all employees make decisions. They therefore have a responsibility to promote organizational arrangements that encourage ethical behavior and discourage unethical behavior.

The following three chapters develop these topics. Chapter 3 provides an overview of how some major ethical traditions might offer guidance both to individual decision makers and to those who create and shape social organizations. Chapter 4 examines topics of corporate culture, ethical organizations, and ethical leadership. Chapter 5 looks at corporate social responsibility, the goals toward which ethical organizations and ethical leaders should aim.

Questions, Projects, and Exercises

1. Think about a situation in which you have witnessed someone engaging in unethical behavior but in which you failed to do anything about it. (If you can't think of an example from your own experience, imagine yourself in the position of someone you know about who has witnessed such a situation.) Do you wish you had done something? What would it have taken for you to speak up, either to stop the bad behavior or to report it? How could a person in a position of authority have made it easier for you to take action?

2. Consider your own personal values and explain where they originated. Can you pinpoint their origins? To what degree have you chosen your own values? To what degree are your own values products of your family, your religious or cultural background, or your generation? Does it matter where values come from?

3. What one small *change* do you think would have the biggest impact on the world today? Share it in a brief essay, then convince your reader why it is so important that she or he should also care about that issue to the same extent. It may be effective to use the theories discussed in prior chapters to persuade your reader of the value of your argument.

4. Your CEO recognizes you as having unusually strong skills in decision making and communications, and so she asks for guidance on how to best communicate her plans for an imminent reduction in your company's workforce. What are some of the key strategies you will suggest she employ in reaching such a decision and making the announcement?

5. Describe the qualities you believe are necessary in an "ethical leader." Provide support for your point of view and explain why a leader should display these qualities in order to be considered "ethical." Then identify someone you believe embodies these qualities in her or his leadership and provide examples of relevant behavior. Finally, provide an example of someone whom you believe *does not* possess these qualities and describe that person's leadership.

6. How can a global firm best ensure that it is taking into account the perceptual differences that may exist as a result of diverse cultures, religions, ethnicities, and other factors when creating a worldwide marketing plan?

7. Many people have blamed the global financial crisis of 2008–2009 on a single value or motive, namely, greed. How would you define greed? How common do you think true greed is in the general population? Do you think it is more common on, say, Wall Street than in the general population?

8. As a class exercise, write a brief account of any unethical or ethically questionable experience you have witnessed in a work context. Read and discuss the examples in class, keeping the authors anonymous. Consider how the organization involved allowed or encouraged such behavior and what might have been done to prevent it.

9. Lisa is trying to raise funds to support the creation of a free clinic in a poor neighborhood in her hometown. She has been trying very hard, but she has not been able to raise enough money to get the clinic up and running. One day, she gets a huge check from a high-profile business executive whom she met at a fund-raiser. She is ecstatic and finally sees her dream taking shape. However, after a few days, the person who gave Lisa the money is arrested for fraud, money laundering, and tax evasion. What should Lisa do? Should she still keep the money and look the other way? Does the source of the money matter or does the end justify the means?

10. What values do you think motivated the engineers at Volkswagen who devised the method for falsifying emissions tests? How do you think their motivation may have evolved over the years that the scheme was in play? What do you think they would have said if asked, five years before being caught, to reflect on the values that inspired them in their work?

Key Terms

After reading this chapter, you should have a clear understanding of the following key terms. For a more complete definition, please see the Glossary.

change blindness, *p. 42*	inattentional blindness, *p. 41*	perceptual differences, *p. 39*
ethical decision-making process , *p. 39*	moral imagination, *p. 45*	personal and professional decision making, *p. 54*
	normative myopia, *p. 41*	

Endnotes

1. "Reboot: Adidas to Make Shoes in Germany Again—but Using Robots," *The Guardian,* May 25, 2016, www.theguardian.com/world/2016/may/25/adidas-to-sell-robot-made-shoes-from-2017 (accessed June 8, 2016).

2. The concept of normative myopia as applied to business executives can be found in Diane Swanson, "Toward an Integrative Theory of Business and Society," *Academy of Management Review* 24, no. 3 (July 1999), pp. 506–521.

3. D. Chugh and M. Bazerman, "Bounded Awareness: What You Fail to See Can Hurt You," *Mind & Society* 6 (2007), p. 1.

4. "Installment 2: The Ethics of American Youth: 2010," Josephson Institute: Center for Youth Studies, February 10, 2011, http://charactercounts.org/programs/reportcard/2010/installment02_report-card_honesty-integrity.html (accessed July 17, 2012).

5. For just one website of many that compiles definitions of violations of academic integrity, as well as strategies to maintain academic integrity, see http://academicintegrity.depaul.edu.

6. O. Sezer, F. Gino, and M. H. Bazerman, "Ethical Blind Spots: Explaining Unintentional Unethical Behavior," *Current Opinion in Psychology* 6 (2015), pp. 77–81.

7. See, for example, BHP Billiton, "Our Future: Sustainability Report 2011," www.bhpbilliton.com/home/aboutus/sustainability/Pages/default.aspx (accessed January 20, 2012), pp. 36–37.

8. Ibid., p. 18.

9. For a far more in-depth analysis of moral imagination, please see P. H. Werhane, *Moral Imagination and Management Decision-Making* (New York: Oxford University Press, 1999).

10. "Installment 2: The Ethics of American Youth: 2010," Josephson Institute: Center for Youth Studies, February 10, 2011, http://charactercounts.org/programs/reportcard/2010 /installment02_report-card_honesty-integrity.html (accessed July 17, 2012).

11. Rick Tetzeli, "Business Students Cheat Most," *Fortune,* July 1, 1991, p. 14. See also James Stearns and Shaheen Borna, "A Comparison of the Ethics of Convicted Felons and Graduate Business Students: Implications for Business Practice and Business Ethics Education," *Teaching Business Ethics* 2 (1998), pp. 175–195. This research found that MBA students were more likely to cheat than convicted felons.

12. James Stearns and Shaheen Borna, "A Comparison of the Ethics of Convicted Felons and Graduate Business Students: Implications for Business Practice and Business Ethics Education," *Teaching Business Ethics* 2 (1998), p. 18.

13. Kristin Lin, "Companies Disclose Pay Ratio Before SEC's Final Rule," *The Wall Street Journal,* July 20, 2015, http://blogs.wsj.com/cfo/2015/07/20/companies-disclose-pay-ratio-before-secs-final-rule/ (accessed June 20, 2016).

14. "National Magazine Inducts 10 Manufacturing Leaders into the IW Manufacturing Hall of Fame" [Press Release], *Market Watch,* December 14, 2011, www.marketwatch.com/ story/national-magazine-inducts-10-manufacturing-leaders-into-the-iw-manufacturing-hall-of-fame-2011-12-14 (accessed January 21, 2012); C. Helman, "Test of Mettle," *Forbes,* May 11, 2009, www.forbes.com/forbes/2009/0511/081-executives-companies-business-test-of-mettle.html (accessed January 21, 2012).

Readings

Reading 2-1: "When Good People Do Bad Things at Work: Rote Behavior, Distractions, and Moral Exclusion Stymie Ethical Behavior on the Job," by Dennis J. Moberg

Reading 2-2: "How Bad Management Leads to Bad Ethics: When Scandal Breaks, We Prefer Our Corporate Villains Evil, but the Truth Is Usually More Complicated," by Chris MacDonald

Reading **2-1**

When Good People Do Bad Things at Work: *Rote Behavior, Distractions, and Moral Exclusion Stymie Ethical Behavior on the Job*

Dennis J. Moberg

The news is full of the exploits of corporate villains. We read about how officials at Lincoln Savings and Loan bilked thousands out of their customers' retirement nest eggs. There are stories of the lies Brown and Williamson Tobacco executives told about the addictive nature of cigarettes and the company's subsequent campaign to destroy whistle-blower Jeffrey Wigant. Also in the news are the top managers at Time Warner who looked the other way rather than forgo millions from the sale of rap music with lyrics that advocated violence directed at women and the police. Such acts are hard to forgive. Scoundrels such as these seem either incredibly weak or dangerously flawed.

Yet not all corporate misdeeds are committed by bad people. In fact, a significant number of unethical acts in business are the likely result of foibles and failings rather than selfishness and greed. Put in certain kinds of situations, good people inadvertently do bad things.

For those of us concerned about ethical actions and not just good intentions, the problem is clear. We must identify the situational factors that keep people from doing their best and eliminate them whenever we can.

Problem No. 1: Scripts

One factor is something psychologists call scripts. This term refers to the procedures that experience tells us to use in specific situations. When we brush our teeth or congratulate a friend on the arrival of a new grandchild, we probably use scripts.

Unlike other forms of experience, scripts are stored in memory in a mechanical or rote fashion. When we encounter a very familiar situation, rather than actively think about it, we reserve our mental energy for other purposes and behave as though we are cruising on automatic pilot.

In a classic psychological experiment, people approached someone at an office machine making copies and asked, "May I please make just one copy because. . . ." The person at the machine generally complied with this request, but the really interesting finding was that the likelihood of compliance was totally independent of the reasons stated. In fact, superfluous reasons such as "because I need to make a copy" were just as successful as good reasons such as "because my boss told me she needed these right away." Apparently, we have all experienced this situation so often that we don't give the reasons our full attention, not to mention our careful consideration.

One ethical lapse clearly attributable to scripts was Ford Motor Co.'s failure to recall the Pinto in the 1970s. The Pinto was an automobile with an undetected design flaw that made the gas tank burst into flames on impact, resulting in the death and disfigurement of scores of victims. Dennis Gioia, the Ford recall coordinator at the time, reviewed hundreds of accident reports to detect whether a design flaw was implicated. Later, he recalled,

> When I was dealing with the first trickling-in of field reports that might have suggested a significant problem with the Pinto, the reports were essentially similar to many others that I was dealing with (and dismissing) all the time. . . . I was making this kind of decision automatically every day. I had trained myself to respond to prototypical cues, and these didn't fit the relevant prototype for crisis cases.

Situations like this occur frequently in the work world. Repetitive jobs requiring vigilance to prevent ethical lapses can be found in quality control, customer service, and manufacturing. In this respect, consider what happened when a nurse with a script that called for literal obedience to a doctor's written orders misread the directions to place ear drops in a patient's right ear as "place in Rear." Good people can inadvertently do very bad things.

Scripts may also be at work when we come face-to-face with those who are suffering. In situations where we observe the pain of those in need, scripts permit us to steel ourselves against feelings of empathy. Most of us have been approached by the homeless on the street, exposed to horrific images on the television news, and asked for donations on behalf of the victims of natural disasters.

According to research at the University of Kansas, scripts allow people to avoid responsibility for the suffering of others in situations when providing help appears costly. In work contexts, this might explain why businesspeople do not always respond philanthropically to documented cases of human suffering. What appears to be calculated indifference may actually not be calculated at all.

Whenever there is repetition, there are likely to be scripts. Accordingly, the best way to eliminate the potential of scripts to result in unethical behavior is to keep people out of highly repetitive situations. Technology can and has been used to eliminate highly routine tasks, but job rotation is also an option. For example, the *Daily Oklahoman* newspaper of Oklahoma City cross-trains most of its editors and schedules them to switch roles often. This helps keep the editors mentally sharp.

One editor who often switches roles from night to night commented: "You're fresh when you come to a particular job. Like last night I did inside [design], and it was a long and torturous night because of the large paper. But then again I turn around and do something thoroughly different tonight, so I don't feel like I'm trudging back to the same old rut again."

Daily Oklahoman News Editor Ed Sargent thinks editing quality has improved because those who switch roles are exposed to the different approaches their colleagues take to the job. "Every editor has different opinions, obviously, about what's a big error and what's a little error," he said. Although the original intent of the role switching was to distribute stress more evenly, a side effect is that the paper is probably less prone to ethical lapses.

Problem No. 2: Distractions

Scripts are cognitive shortcuts that take the place of careful thinking. A similar human tendency is our mindless treatment of distractions. Think for a moment about the last time you drove to a very important meeting. Once there, were you able to recall any details of your journey? Most of us cannot, which demonstrates that when concentrating on completing an involving task, we don't deal well with distractions.

This inattention to what is happening on the periphery can get us into trouble with our spouses and significant others, and it can also result in ethical lapses. In one very telling experiment, divinity students were told that they had to deliver a lecture from prepared notes in a classroom across campus. Half the students were told they had to hurry to be on time, and the other half were told they had more than ample time.

On the way, the students came across a person in distress (actually an actor), who sat slumped motionless in a doorway, coughing and groaning. Shockingly, only 16 of the 40 divinity students stopped to help, most of them from the group that had ample time. To those in a hurry, the man was

a distraction, a threat to their focus on giving a lecture. Ironically enough, half of them had been asked to discuss the parable of "The Good Samaritan."

Mindlessness about distractions at work is most pronounced when employees, with limited means of gaining perspective, are encouraged to be focused and driven. The best way to combat this tendency is for senior managers to model the virtue of temperance. If the president of a company is a workaholic, it is difficult to convince employees to be open to problems on the outskirts of their commitments. In contrast, an organizational culture that facilitates work–family balance or encourages employee involvement in the community may move experiences that should not be seen as mere distractions onto the center stage of consciousness.

Problem No. 3: Moral Exclusion

A final problem that brings out the worst in good people is the very human tendency to morally exclude certain persons. This occurs when individuals or groups are perceived as outside the boundary in which moral values and considerations of fairness apply. The most striking example occurs during warfare when the citizens of a country readily perceive their enemies in demonic terms. This tendency to discount the moral standing of others results in us discounting all kinds of people, some of them as close as coworkers and valued customers.

Greater awareness and extensive training have reduced some of the exclusion women and people of color have historically experienced. More work needs to be done in this area, as well as in other equally insidious forms of exclusion.

One way such exclusion shows up is in our use of pronouns. If *we* are in marketing and *they* are in production, the chances are that the distance may be great enough for us to be morally indifferent to what happens to them. Similarly, if we use stereotypic terms like *bean counter* or sneer when we say *management,* then it is clear that people in these categories don't count.

Not surprisingly, one way to expand the scope of justice is to promote direct contact with individuals who have been morally excluded, One company that applied this notion in an intriguing way is Eisai, a Japanese pharmaceutical firm. In the late 1980s, Haruo Naito had recently become CEO, and his closest advisors expressed concern that his managers and employees lacked an understanding of the end users of Eisai's products.

Hearing this, Naito decided to shift the focus of attention from the customers of his company's products—doctors and pharmacists—to *their* customers—patients and their families. Eisai managers, he decided, needed to identify better with end users and then infuse the insights from this sense of inclusion throughout the organization. This was a revolutionary idea for this company of 4,500 employees, but Naito believed his employees needed a more vivid reason to care deeply about their work.

"It's not enough to tell employees that if they do something, the company will grow this much or their salary will increase this much. That's just not enough incentive," says Naito. "You have to show them how what they are doing is connected to society, or exactly how it will help a patient." Accordingly, Naito decided to send 100 managers to a seven-day seminar: three days of nursing-home training and four days of medical care observation.

These managers were then sent to diverse regions throughout Japan, where they had to deal with different people, many of whom were in critical condition. They met patients with both physical and emotional problems; some of the patients they came in contact with died during their internships.

This pilot program grew to include more than 1,000 Eisai employees. Pretty soon, even laboratory support personnel had to leave their benches and desks and meet regularly with pharmacists and hospital people.

"Getting them out of the office was a way to activate human relationships," says Naito. Another way was to institute hotlines, which have generated product ideas. As a consequence, many new Eisai drugs were produced, including some that have promise in dealing with Alzheimer's disease. Clearly, moral inclusion was stimulated at Eisai, at least insofar as the end users of its products are concerned.

Failing to Bother

Jesuit scholar James F. Keenan reminds us that "sinners in the New Testament are known not for what they did, but for what they failed to do—for failing to bother." We are all prone to this failure, but not necessarily because we are sinners. Repetition, distractions, and our natural tendency to exclude those unfamiliar to us cloud our best thinking and forestall the expression of our virtues. We owe it to ourselves to resist these pernicious influences, and we owe it to those in our work communities to help them to do the same.

Source: *Issues in Ethics* 10, no. 2 (Fall 1999), Markkula Center for Applied Ethics (www.scu.edu/ethics/publications /iie/v10n2/peopleatwork.html). Reprinted by permission of the author. All rights reserved.

How Bad Management Leads to Bad Ethics: *When Scandal Breaks, We Prefer Our Corporate Villains Evil, but the Truth Is Usually More Complicated*

Chris MacDonald

What's the connection between ethics and competence in business? What part was played in Volkswagen's wrongdoing by the fact that the company's engineers were apparently technically incapable of making good on the promises their marketing department was apparently intent on making?

I've written before about my hypothesis that cheating is often a way of covering up for your lack of talent. This hypothesis suggests that executives cook the books to hide the failure of their strategies. Companies offer bribes because they know their product or service isn't good enough to compete otherwise. Salespeople fudge their sales numbers because they're not as good at their jobs as they need to be.

A year or so ago I heard a presentation by someone who worked in compliance at a global company that had, some years ago, been embroiled in a bribery scandal. One of the most shocking things the speaker said is that, during the years in which the bribery scandal took place, it was not uncommon for *hundreds of thousands of dollars* to go missing from the books—not "missing" in the metaphorical sense ("That money is—wink, wink!—*missing*"), but missing in the literal "we don't know where the money *went*" sense. The very strong suggestion here was that bribery on a large scale went hand in hand with very loose and unprofessional accounting standards. The managers at this company simply literally did not have a good sense of where their money was, a situation that easily enabled ethical lapses.

Consider also the case of the prosecution of Glaxo-SmithKline, a few years ago, for selling adulterated drugs. The problem again was incompetence. Some of the pills manufactured at the company's Cidra facility, in Puerto Rico, had been mislabeled. Others had been found to contain more (much more!), or less, of their active ingredient than they were supposed to. Still others contained metal particles, the result apparently of machinery having broken and then been repaired in an amateurish way that resulted in metal parts rubbing together. Through and through, the story is one of general incompetence—frontline work being done badly, managers ignoring problems,

and *senior* managers failing to institute remedies once serious deficiencies in manufacturing practices were brought to their attention.

These anecdotes suggest at least several different connections between failures of ethics and plain business incompetence.

One connection involves resorting to unethical behavior to cover up for mistakes or poor performance. Once you've found out that sloppy work has led to a poor product, you can either face up to it (but that's inconvenient and painful and maybe expensive) or you can unethically (and maybe dangerously) sweep the problem under the carpet.

Another connection is that in some cases poor management makes unethical behavior easier to get away with. This might involve sloppy accounting, but it could just as easily involve poor training, poor oversight, and unclear lines of accountability.

And then (perhaps more commonly) there are more complex cases, in which lack of business skill (say, at providing high-quality service) results in a desire by some employees to engage in compensatory wrongdoing, and that wrongdoing is made easier by ongoing incompetent accounting.

We all prefer simple stories, ones with clear villains. And, to paraphrase Homer Simpson, we like our beer cold, our TV's loud, and our corporate villains *evil*. So it's hard to accept that sometimes the truth is both more complex and less dramatic. But we'll do better at understanding, and avoiding, corporate wrongdoing if we come to grips with the messier truth.

Source: "How Bad Management Leads to Bad Ethics," *Canadian Business,* October 28, 2015, www.canadianbusiness.com/blogs-and-comment/how-bad-management-leads-to-bad-ethics/ (accessed June 8, 2016).

Chapter 3

Philosophical Ethics and Business

Integrity without knowledge is weak and useless, and knowledge without integrity is dangerous and dreadful.

Samuel Johnson, 1709–1784

It's better to hang out with people better than you. Pick out associates whose behavior is better than yours and you'll drift in that direction.

Warren Buffett

A man does what he must—in spite of personal consequences, in spite of obstacles and dangers and pressures—and that is the basis of all human morality.

John F. Kennedy

Opening Decision Point

Are CEOs Paid Too Much, Compared to Their Employees?

In April 2015, CEO Dan Price of Gravity Payments made a shocking announcement. Price, who is also founder and co-owner of Gravity, decided to cut his own salary by 93 percent, and then to use that money—along with a big chunk of corporate profits—to ensure that every single one of his employees makes a minimum of $70,000.[1]

The news was certainly welcomed by Gravity's employees. (For the lowest-paid employees, the raise to $70k meant a doubling of their salaries.) And Price was widely applauded by commentators and on social media.

Price's move was especially noteworthy in an era in which many CEOs have been criticized for accepting astronomically high levels of pay. In a 2015 article on executive compensation, *Bloomberg.com* reported,[2] for example, that Elon Musk, the entrepreneurial CEO of Tesla Motors Inc., earned just over $100 million in 2014. But that's far from the high end of executive compensation: The same article noted that Nicholas Woodman, CEO of GoPro Inc., had earned a whopping $285 million that year. Criticism of CEO pay has not focused solely on the absolute amount earned, but also on the ratio of CEO pay to what those CEOs' employees are paid. According to the *Bloomberg* article, "The CEOs of 350 Standard & Poor's 500 companies made 331 times more than their employees in 2013."

Some people defend high levels of pay for CEOs, pointing out that the highest levels of compensation are achieved through stock options, which means that CEOs do well only when the value of the company's stock goes up, a sign that the CEO is actually doing a good job. Others, however, are skeptical. As the *Bloomberg* article points out, "Stock options, once believed to align executives with shareholders because they appreciate when the stock price rises, are now derided for encouraging short-term financial engineering at the expense of long-term planning." In other words, stock options encourage CEOs to find short-term ways to boost stock prices (such as reducing costs by cutting employees), even if those moves aren't in the long-term interests of the company and its shareholders.

Let's turn back to Price's decision. Different people had different reactions to the decision. Some applauded it as a move toward justice or fairness in compensation. Others thought it was a savvy business move, aimed at producing better outcomes for Gravity Payments by motivating employees and gaining free publicity for the company. Still others thought it spoke well of Price's character; to them, Price looked like what a good CEO ought to look like, in comparison to the greedy CEOs of so many other companies.

- Do you think Dan Price is a hero? Why or why not?
- Are there any further facts that you would want to know before making a judgment about this case?
- Gravity Payments is privately owned by Dan Price and his brother. If Gravity were a publicly traded company with thousands of shareholders, would that change your view about the ethics of his decision? If so, in what way?
- If you were an employee at Gravity Payments, already making $70,000, how would you feel about employees who made half what you make suddenly making the same amount as you?

Chapter Objectives

After reading this chapter, you will be able to:

1. Explain the ethical framework of utilitarianism.
2. Describe how utilitarian thinking underlies economic and business decision making.
3. Explain how the free market is thought to serve the utilitarian goal of maximizing the overall good.
4. Explain some challenges to utilitarian decision making.
5. Explain the principle-based, or rights-based, framework of ethics.
6. Explain the concept of human rights and how they are relevant to business.
7. Distinguish moral rights from legal rights.
8. Explain several challenges to principle-based ethics.
9. Describe and explain virtue-based framework for thinking about ethical character.

Introduction: Ethical Frameworks—Consequences, Principles, Character

Consider the reasons that you or others offered to defend or criticize Dan Price's decision to equalize his own salary with that of his employees. Upon reflection, these reasons fall into three general categories. Some reasons appeal to the *consequences* of this move: they either will or will not provide incentives for producing good work and beneficial future consequences. Other reasons appeal to certain principles: "no one's work is worth 14 times what someone else's work is worth," or "everyone deserves to be paid a living wage." Other reasons cite matters of *personal character*: accepting millions in compensation while others can barely pay the rent is greedy, or distasteful. Giving employees a raise when you've got the ability to do that is just what a good and decent boss would do.

As it turns out, the three major traditions of ethical framework that we will rely on in this text are represented by these three categories. This should be no surprise because ethical traditions in philosophy reflect common ways to think and reason about how we should live, what we should do. Ethics of consequences, ethics of principles, and ethics of personal character are the three traditions that will be introduced in this chapter.

Chapters 1 and 2 introduced ethics as a form of practical reasoning in support of decision making about how we should live our lives. Ethics involves what is perhaps the most significant question any human being can ask: How *should* we live our lives? But, of course, this question is not new; every major philosophical, cultural, political, and religious tradition in human history has grappled with it. In light of this, it would be unwise to ignore these traditions as we begin to examine ethical issues in business.

Nevertheless, many students think that discussions of philosophical ethics are too abstract to be of much help in business. Discussion of ethical "frameworks" often seems to be too *theoretical* to be of much relevance to business. Throughout this chapter, we hope to suggest a more accessible and pragmatic understanding of ethics, one that will shed some light on the practical and pragmatic application of these frameworks to actual problems faced by businesspeople. (For an examination of the pragmatic application, see Reading 3-3, "It Seems Right in Theory but Does It Work in Practice?," by Norman E. Bowie at the end of this chapter.)

An ethical framework is nothing more than an attempt to provide a systematic answer to the fundamental ethical question: How should human beings live their lives? In many ways, this is a simple question that we ask, at least implicitly, every day. What am I going to do today, and why? Ethics can be understood as the practice of examining these decisions and thinking about answers to the question: Why?

Ethics attempts to answer the question of how we should live, but it also gives *reasons* to support the answers. Ethics seeks to provide a rational justification for why *we* should act and decide in a particular prescribed way. Anyone can offer prescriptions for what you should do and how you should act, but a *philosophical* and reasoned ethics must answer the "why?" question as well.

Why does the question "why?" matter so much? At least two reasons can be offered. First, "why" matters because without offering reasons, all we are doing is giving an opinion. An opinion, on its own, is not terribly useful. You may think your company should fire a particular employee, but if you're to convince the *boss,* your mere opinion won't do much. In order to convince the boss, you'll need to offer opinions. In business, there is just about *always* someone you need to convince, whether it's your boss or your employees or your teammates.

Second, the question "why?" matters because superficial agreement can mask underlying *dis*agreement. Imagine that a three-person management team agrees on the need to fire a particular employee named Tahmina. Should you be comforted by the fact that you all agree? What if, unbeknownst to all of you, one of you thinks Tahmina should be fired because he (wrongly) believes that Tahmina has not performed well as an employee; another thinks she should be fired because you need to cut costs; and the third thinks Tahmina should be fired because of her sexual orientation? What looks like agreement, here, actually masks deep and important *dis*agreements, ones that need to be sorted out before any action is taken.

Many people and cultures across the world would answer this "why" question in religious terms and base their normative judgments on religious foundations. "You ought to live your life in a certain way because God commands it." Or: "You ought to behave as commanded in our holy book!" The biggest practical problem with this approach, of course, is that people differ widely about their religious beliefs, and are dedicated to different holy books or to none at all. If ethics is based on religion, and if different cultures have widely divergent religious beliefs,

Decision Point

Who Is to Say What Is Right or Wrong?

Are you an ethical relativist? **Ethical relativism** holds that ethical values are relative to particular people, cultures, or times. Relativism denies that there can be any rationally justified or objective ethical judgments. When there are ethical disagreements between people or cultures, the ethical relativist concludes that there is no way to resolve that dispute and prove one side is right or more reasonable than the other.

Often, people describe behavior they don't approve of as "distasteful." Ordinarily, we think of matters of taste as personal, subjective things. You enjoy spicy Indian food, while I prefer a simple burger and fries. It is all a matter of personal taste. You might think sky-high executive salaries are distasteful, but others find them well deserved. Ethical relativists believe that ethical values are much like tastes in food; it all depends on, or it is all relative to, one's own background, culture, and personal opinions.

Ethical relativism is generally not thought by ethicists to be a credible point of view, but many people still find it tempting.

Do *you* believe that there is no way to decide what is ethically right or wrong? Imagine a teacher returns an assignment to you with a grade of F. When you ask for an explanation, you are told that, frankly, the teacher does not believe that people "like you" (e.g., men, Christians, African Americans) are capable of doing good work in this field (e.g., science, engineering, math, finance). When you object that this is unfair and wrong, the teacher offers a relativist explanation. "Fairness is a matter of personal opinion," the professor explains. "Who determines what is fair or unfair?" you ask. Your teacher claims that his view of what is fair is as valid as any other. Because everyone is entitled to his or her own personal opinion, the professor is entitled to fail you because, in his personal opinion, you do not deserve to succeed.

- Would you accept this explanation and be content with your failing grade? If not, how would you defend your own opposing view?
- Are there any relevant facts on which you would rely to support your claim?
- What values are involved in this dispute?
- What alternatives are available to you?
- Besides you and your teacher, are there any other stakeholders—people who are or should be involved in this situation?
- What reasons would you offer to the dean in an appeal to have the grade changed?
- What consequences would this professor's practice have on education?
- If reasoning and logical persuasion do not work, how else could this dispute be resolved?

then it would seem that ethics cannot escape the predicament of relativism. (See the Decision Point "Who Is to Say What Is Right or Wrong" for more on ethical relativism.)

Unlike religious ethics that explains human well-being in religious terms, philosophical ethics provides justifications that must be applicable to all people

utilitarianism
An ethical theory that tells us that we can determine the ethical significance of any action by looking to the consequences of that act. Utilitarianism is typically identified with the policy of "maximizing the overall good" or, in a slightly different version, of producing "the greatest good for the greatest number."

regardless of their religious starting points. The justifications of philosophical ethics tend to connect the "oughts" and "shoulds" of ethics to some underlying account of human well-being. Thus, for example, "you should contribute to disaster relief because it will reduce human suffering" is a philosophical justification for an ethical judgment, whereas "you should contribute to disaster relief because God commands it, or because it will bring you heavenly rewards" are religious rather than philosophical justifications.

Ethics is not comprised of a single principle or framework. Different ethical frameworks have evolved over time and have been refined and developed by many different thinkers. The insights of an ethical framework prove to be lasting if they truly do pick out some important elements of human experience. To emphasize this fact, this chapter will refer to these theories more commonly as ethical "traditions." These traditions have their origins in the works of specific philosophers, but they are ways of thinking that have been widely influential in our culture, in our literature, and in our legal thinking.

This chapter will introduce three ethical frameworks that have proven influential in the development of business ethics and that have a very practical relevance in evaluating ethical issues in modern business. **Utilitarianism** is an ethical tradition that directs us to decide based on overall consequences of our acts. The **principle-based framework** directs us to act on the basis of moral principles such as respecting human rights. **Virtue ethics** tells us to consider the *moral character* of individuals and how various character traits can contribute to, or obstruct, a happy and meaningful human life. Reading 3-2, "The Caux Principles for Responsible Business," by the Caux Round Table (CRT) provides an interesting blend of utilitarian, principled, and virtue-based guidelines for business.

Utilitarianism: Making Decisions Based on Ethical Consequences

OBJECTIVE

consequentialist theories
Ethical theories, such as utilitarianism, that determine right and wrong by calculating the consequences of actions.

The first ethical tradition that we shall examine, utilitarianism, has its roots in 18th- and 19th-century social and political philosophy, but its core idea is just as relevant in the 21st century. Utilitarianism's fundamental insight is that outcomes matter, and so we should decide what to do by considering the overall *consequences* of our actions. In this sense, utilitarianism has been called a **consequentialist** approach to ethics and social policy: We should act in ways that produce better consequences than the alternatives we are considering. Much more needs to be said to turn this simple insight into an adequate approach to ethics. The first, and most obvious, question is: What is meant by "better consequences"?

In a business context, a temptation is to answer in terms of financial consequences: The right decision is one that produces the best financial returns. But this answer would reduce ethics to economics by identifying ethically best as economically best. A more useful answer to this question can be given in terms of the ethical values described in the previous chapters. "Better consequences" are those that promote human well-being: the happiness, health, dignity, integrity, freedom,

principle-based framework

A framework for ethics that grounds decision making in fundamental principles such as justice, liberty, autonomy, and fairness. Principle-based ethics typically assert that individual rights and duties are fundamental and thus can also be referred to as a rights-based or duty-based (deontological) approach to ethics. Often distinguished from consequentialist frameworks, which determine ethical decisions based on the consequences of our acts.

virtue ethics

An approach to ethics that studies the character traits or habits that constitute a good human life, a life worth living. The virtues provide answers to the basic ethical question "What kind of person should I be?"

and respect of all the people affected. If these elements are basic human values, then an action that promotes more of them than the alternative action does is more reasonable from an ethical point of view. A decision that promotes the greatest amount of these values for the greatest number of people is the most reasonable decision from an ethical point of view.

Utilitarianism is commonly identified with the rule of producing "the greatest good for the greatest number." The ultimate ethical goal, according to utilitarians, is to attempt to produce the best consequences overall, taking into account all parties affected by the decisions. Decisions that accomplish this goal are the right decisions to make ethically; those that do not are ethically wrong.

The emphasis on producing the greatest good for the greatest number makes utilitarianism a social philosophy that opposes policies that aim to benefit only a small social, economic, or political minority. Historically, utilitarianism has provided strong support for democratic institutions and policies. Government and all social institutions exist for the well-being of all, not to further the interests of the monarch, the nobility, or some small group of the elite. Likewise, the economy and economic institutions exist to provide the highest standard of living for the greatest number of people, not to create wealth for a few.

As another business-related example, consider the case of child labor, discussed in further detail in chapter 6. Utilitarian thinking would advise us to consider all the likely consequences of a practice of employing young children in factories. Obviously, there are some harmful consequences: children suffer physical and psychological harms, they are denied opportunities for education, their low pay is not enough to escape a life of poverty, and so forth. Many of the human values previously described are diminished by child labor. But these consequences must be compared to the consequences of alternative decisions. What are the consequences if children in poor regions are denied factory jobs? These children would still be denied opportunities for education; they would be in worse poverty; and they would have less money for food and family support. In many cases, the only alternatives for obtaining any income available to young children who are prohibited from joining the workforce might include crime, drugs, or prostitution. Further, we should consider not only the consequences to the children themselves, but to the entire society. Child labor can have beneficial results for bringing foreign investment and money into a poor country. In the opinion of some observers, allowing children to work for pennies a day under sweatshop conditions produces better overall consequences than the available alternatives. Thus, one might argue on utilitarian grounds that such labor practices are ethically permissible because they produce better overall consequences than the alternatives.

This example highlights several important aspects of utilitarian reasoning. Because utilitarians decide strictly on the basis of consequences, and because the consequences of our actions will depend on the specific facts of each situation, utilitarians tend to be very pragmatic thinkers. No type of act is ever absolutely right or wrong in all cases in every situation; it will always depend on the consequences. For example, lying is neither right nor wrong in itself, according to utilitarians. There might be situations in which lying will produce greater overall

Reality Check *Everyone Matters*

While the obligation to maximize pleasure or happiness sounds selfish and egoistic, utilitarianism differs from **egoism** in important ways. Egoism is also a consequentialist theory, but it focuses exclusively on the happiness of the individual making the decision. In other words, instead of determining the "greatest good for the greatest number," egoism seeks "the greatest good for me!"

Utilitarianism judges actions by their consequences for the general and overall good. Consistent with the utilitarian commitment to democratic equality, however, the general good must take into consideration the well-being of each and every individual affected by the action. In this way utilitarianism serves the ultimate goal of ethics: the impartial promotion of human well-being. It is impartial in that it considers the consequences for everyone, not just for the individual. People who act in ways to maximize only their own happiness or the happiness of their company are not utilitarians, they are egoists.

egoism
As a psychological theory, egoism holds that all people act only from self-interest. Empirical evidence strongly suggests that this is a mistaken account of human motivation. As an ethical theory, egoism holds that humans ought to act for their own self-interest. Ethical egoists typically distinguish between one's perceived best interests and one's true best interests.

good than telling the truth. In such a situation, it would be ethically justified to tell a lie.

The example of child labor also highlights the fact that utilitarian reasoning usually acknowledges some support for competing available alternatives—that is, ban child labor as harmful to the overall good or allow child labor as contributing to the overall good. Utilitarianism realistically admits that there may be conflicting evidence in favor of different options. Deciding on the ethical legitimacy of alternative decisions requires that we make judgments about the likely consequences of our actions. How do we do this? Within the utilitarian tradition, there is a strong inclination to turn to social science for help in making such predictions. After all, social science studies the causes and consequences of individual and social actions. Who is better situated than a social scientist to help us predict the social consequences of our decisions? Consider the fields to which one might turn in order to determine the likely consequences of child labor. Economics, anthropology, political science, sociology, public policy, psychology, and medical and health sciences are some of the fields that could help determine the likely consequences of such practices in a particular culture.

In general, the utilitarian position is that happiness is the ultimate good, the only thing that is and can be valued for its own sake. Happiness is the best and most reasonable interpretation of human well-being. (After all, does it sound plausible to you to claim that *un*happiness is good and happiness is bad?) The goal of ethics, both individually and as a matter of public policy, should be to maximize the overall happiness. (See the Reality Check "Everyone Matters.")

Utilitarianism and Business

OBJECTIVE

We previously claimed that studying ethical theories had a practical relevance for business ethics. In fact, perhaps utilitarianism's greatest contribution to philosophical thought has come through its influence in economics. With roots in Adam Smith, the ethical view that underlies much of 20th-century economics—essentially what we think of as the free market—is decidedly utilitarian. In this way, utilitarianism continues to have a very strong impact on business and business ethics.

Utilitarianism answers the fundamental questions of ethics—for example, What should we do?—by reference to a very simple rule: maximize the overall good. This rule might remind you of the financial practice of conducting a cost–benefit analysis and making a decision based on maximizing net benefits over costs. But even if we agree that maximizing the overall good is the right goal, another question remains to be answered: *How* do we achieve this goal? What is the best means for attaining the utilitarian goal of maximizing the overall good? Two answers prove especially relevant in business and business ethics.

OBJECTIVE

One movement within utilitarian thought points to the line of thinking that originated with Adam Smith, and claims that free and competitive markets are the best means for attaining utilitarian goals. The argument here is that voluntary transactions make people better off, and so a *system* of such transactions—a free market—is going to maximize benefit overall. This version of utilitarianism would promote policies that deregulate private industry, protect property rights, allow for free exchanges, and encourage competition. In such situations decisions of rationally self-interested individuals will result, as if lead by an "invisible hand," in Adam Smith's terms, to the maximum satisfaction of individual happiness.

In classic free-market economics, economic activity aims to satisfy consumer demand. People are made happy—human welfare or well-being increases—when they get what they desire. Overall human happiness is increased, therefore, when the overall satisfaction of consumer demand increases. The law of supply and demand tells us that economies should, and healthy economies do, produce (supply) those goods and services that consumers most want (demand). Because scarcity and competition prevent everyone from getting all that they want, the goal of free-market economics is to optimally satisfy wants and thus maximize happiness. Free markets accomplish this goal most efficiently, according to defenders, by allowing individuals to decide for themselves what they most want and then bargain for these goods in a free and competitive marketplace. This process will, over time and under the right conditions, guarantee the optimal satisfaction of wants, which this tradition equates with maximizing overall happiness.

Given this utilitarian goal, current free-market economics advises us that the most efficient means to attain that goal is to structure our economy according to the principles of free-market capitalism. This requires that business managers, in turn, seek to maximize profits. This idea is central to one common perspective on corporate social responsibility. By pursuing profits, business ensures that scarce resources are going to those who most value them and thereby ensures that resources will provide optimal satisfaction. Thus, competitive markets are seen as the most efficient means to the utilitarian end of maximizing happiness.

A second influential version of utilitarian thought turns to policy experts who have insight into the outcome of various policies and design and implement policies that will attain utilitarian ends. Because utilitarian reasoning determines what to do on the basis of consequences, reasonable judgments must take into account the likely consequences of our actions. But predicting consequences of human action can be studied and improved by careful observation. Experts in

Reality Check *Utilitarian Experts in Practice*

Consider how central banks (such as the U.S. Federal Reserve Board or the Bank of England) set interest rates. There is an established goal, a public policy "good," that the central bank takes to be the greatest good for the country. (This goal is something like the highest sustainable rate of economic growth compatible with minimal inflation.) The central bank examines the relevant economic data and makes a judgment about the present and future state of the economy. If economic activity seems to be slowing down, the central bank might decide to lower interest rates as a means for stimulating economic growth. If the economy seems to be growing too fast and the inflation rate is increasing, it might choose to raise interest rates. Lowering or raising interest rates, in and of itself, is neither good nor bad; the rightness of the act depends on the consequences. The role of public servants is to use their expertise to judge the likely consequences and make the decision that is most likely to produce the best result for the public as a whole.

predicting such consequences, usually trained in the social sciences such as economics, political science, and public policy, are familiar with the specifics of how society works and they therefore are in a position to determine which policy will maximize the overall good. (See the Reality Check "Utilitarian Experts in Practice.")

This approach to public policy underlies one theory of the entire administrative and bureaucratic side of government and organizations. Consider, for example, the American political system. From this view, the legislative body (from Congress to local city councils) establishes the public goals that they believe will maximize overall happiness. The administrative side (presidents, governors, mayors) executes (administers) policies to fulfill these goals. The people working within the administration know how the social and political system works and use this knowledge to carry out the mandate of the legislature. Governments are filled with such people, typically trained in fields such as economics, law, social science, public policy, and political science. This utilitarian approach, for example, would be sympathetic to government regulation of business on the grounds that such regulation will ensure that business activities do contribute to the overall good.

It is important to see that these two approaches to policy are both grounded in utilitarianism. They both seek to implement policies that will tend to maximize good outcomes overall; but they differ strongly in the approach that they believe will achieve that outcome.

The dispute between these two versions of utilitarian policy, what we might call the "market" and the "administrative" versions of utilitarianism, characterize many disputes in business ethics. One clear example concerns regulation of workplace health and safety. (Similar disputes might arise over product safety, environmental protection, regulation of advertising, and almost every other example of government regulation of business.) One side argues that questions of safety and appropriate levels of risk should be determined by experts who then establish standards that business is required to meet. Government regulators are then expected to enforce safety standards. (See the Decision Point "Is Regulation Making Cars Too Safe?")

Decision Point

Is Regulation Making Cars Too Safe?

The North American auto industry is heavily regulated. Fuel efficiency is of course regulated (by the Environmental Protection Agency in the United States, and by Transport Canada in Canada) as are tailpipe emissions. But even more significant are the safety regulations to which the modern North American vehicle is subject. Safety standards cover everything from the design of seat belts to the performance of braking systems, the presence and functioning of air bags, and the ability of front and rear bumpers to survive low-speed collisions. All of these things have made the cars driven by North Americans (and Europeans) vastly safer—both under "normal" driving conditions and during emergencies—than they were, say, 50 years ago.

Economist and blogger Alex Tabarrok points out that in order to fully evaluate the outcomes of safety regulations, we need to look at how those regulations affect people's decisions.[3] One way they affect consumer decision making is through their impact on prices. Safety features have inevitably driven up the price of cars. This has made cars unaffordable to some consumers, with some consumers instead opting to drive motorcycles. Motorcycles, after all, are much less expensive. As just one example, in North America a basic Honda motorcycle costs less than one-third as much as Honda's cheapest model of car, the Honda Fit.

But motorcycles are not only less expensive than cars—they are *less safe,* too. (The U.S. National Highway Traffic Safety Administration says that per mile traveled, motorcycles are 26 times more deadly than cars.[4]) As we all know, air bags have made cars safer, but also more expensive. And as Tabarrok points out, motorcycles don't have air bags. So what is the net effect of regulations that increase the safety of car drivers, but that also push some drivers to buy motorcycles instead? It's not clear that anyone knows the answer to that.

- *If* careful study showed that more people were being killed by automotive safety requirements than saved, would you be in favor of regulations that allowed manufacturers to make at least some cars that are less safe?
- If a single potential car buyer opts to buy a motorcycle because cars are now too expensive for her, and if she dies or is injured in a motorcycle accident, should we blame regulators?
- If regulators didn't force car makers to install safety equipment, would consumer demand be enough to get car makers to do so anyway? Or would car makers abuse the fact that most consumers don't know which safety features are really most worth paying for?

Source: Inspired by "When Are Safer Cars a Bad Idea?," *Business Ethics Highlights* (May 23, 2016), https://businessethicshighlights.com/2016/05/23/when-are-safer-cars-a-bad-idea/ (accessed June 26, 2016).

The other side argues that the best judges of acceptable risk and safety are workers themselves. A free and competitive labor market will ensure that workers get the level of safety that they want. Individuals calculate for themselves what risks they wish to take and what trade-offs they are willing to make in order to attain safety. Workers willing to take risks likely will be paid more for their labor than workers who demand safer and less risky employment. The very basic economic concept of efficiency can be understood as a placeholder for the utilitarian goal of maximum overall happiness. Thus, according to this view, market-based solutions will be best at optimally satisfying these various and competing interests and will thereby serve the overall good.

Challenges to Utilitarian Ethics

OBJECTIVE

While the utilitarian tradition contributes much to responsible ethical decision making, it is not without problems. A review of some general challenges to utilitarianism can guide us in evaluating later applications of utilitarian decision making.

A first set of problems concerns the need for utilitarian reasoning to count, measure, compare, and quantify consequences. If utilitarianism advises that we make decisions by comparing the consequences of alternative actions, then we must have a method for making such comparisons. In practice, however, some comparisons and measurements are very difficult.

For example, in principle, utilitarianism tells us that the interests of all stakeholders who will be affected by a decision ought to be included in calculating the consequences of a decision. But there simply is no consensus among utilitarians on how to measure and determine the overall good. Many business ethics issues highlight how difficult this could be. Consider the consequences of using nonrenewable energy sources and burning fossil fuels for energy. Imagine trying to calculate the consequences of a decision to invest in construction of a nuclear power plant whose wastes remain toxic for tens of thousands of years. Consider how difficult it would be to calculate all the consequences of the decision faced by members of Congress to provide hundreds of billions of dollars to bail out companies that are "too big to fail."

A second challenge goes directly to the core of utilitarianism. The essence of utilitarianism is its reliance on consequences. Ethical and unethical acts are determined by their consequences. In short, for utilitarians the end justifies the means. But this seems to deny one of the earliest ethical principles that many of have learned: the end does *not* always justify the means.

This challenge can be explained in terms of ethical principles. When we say that "the ends do not justify the means" what we are saying is that there are certain things we must do, certain rules we should follow, no matter what the consequences. The ends (or goals) of our actions are not all that matters; it also matters how we *achieve* those ends (i.e., the means we use). Put another way, we have certain duties or responsibilities that we ought to obey even when doing so does not produce a net increase in overall happiness. Examples of such duties are those required by such principles as justice, loyalty, and respect, as well as the responsibilities that flow from our roles as a parent, spouse, friend, citizen, or professional.

Several examples can be used to explain why this is a serious criticism of utilitarian reasoning. Because utilitarianism focuses on the overall consequences, utilitarianism seems willing to sacrifice the good of some individuals for the greater overall good. So, for example, it might turn out that the overall happiness would be increased if children were held as slave labor. Utilitarians would object to child labor, not as a matter of principle, but only if and to the degree that it detracts from the overall good. If it turns out that slavery and child labor increase the net overall happiness, utilitarianism would have to support these practices. In the judgment of many people, such a decision would violate fundamental ethical principles of justice, equality, and respect.

The ethical tradition that we will turn to in the next section argues that individuals possess certain basic rights that should not be violated even if doing so would increase the overall social happiness. Rights function to protect individuals from being sacrificed for the greater overall happiness. Thus, for example, it is often argued that child labor is ethically wrong in principle even if it contributes to the overall social good because it violates the rights of young children.

A similar example cites those principles that arise from commitments that we all make in our daily lives and the duties that flow from them. For example, as parents we love our children and have certain duties to them. Violating such commitments and duties in order to maximize utility for some larger group would require individuals to sacrifice their own integrity for the common good.

Such commitments and duties play a large role in business life. Contracts and promises are commitments that one ought to honor, even if the consequences turn out to be unfavorable. The duties that one takes on as part of a professional role function in a similar way. Arthur Andersen's auditors should not have violated their professional duties simply to produce what they saw as greater overall beneficial consequences. Lawyers have a duty not to help their clients find ways to violate the law, even if they are offered a high salary to do so. Teachers should not violate their professional duties by failing students whom they do not like. Similarly, a boss might argue for deciding not to lay off workers during a recession: she might point out that although this risks bad overall consequences, she must remain loyal to her employees as a matter of principle. We will consider similar themes, concerning professional commitments, and duties when later chapters examine the role of professional responsibilities within business institutions.

Despite these challenges, utilitarian reasoning does contribute to an ethically responsible decision in important ways. First, and most obviously, we are reminded that responsible decision making requires that we consider the consequences of our acts. But it is equally important to remember that utilitarian reasoning does not exhaust the range of ethical concerns. Consequences are only part of the ethical landscape. Responsible ethical decision making also involves matters of duties, principles, and personal integrity. We turn to such factors in the following sections.

An Ethics of Principles and Rights

OBJECTIVE

Consideration of the likely consequences of the available options certainly should be part of responsible ethical decision making. But this approach must be enriched with the recognition that some decisions should be a matter of principle, not consequences. As noted earlier, the ends do not always justify the means.

But how do we know what principles we should follow and how do we decide when a principle should outweigh our desire to produce beneficial consequences? Principle-based ethical frameworks work out the details of such questions.

Consider as an example the relationship between the legislative and judicial branches of government found in constitutional democracies. The legislative role can be thought of as pursuing the utilitarian goal of creating policies to produce the greatest good for the greatest number, while the judiciary's role is to enforce basic principles of justice and fairness. The essential insight of constitutional democracies is that majority-rule decisions that seek the greatest overall happiness should be restricted by constitutional limits that reflect fundamental principles of human rights. This political example reflects the idea that a utilitarian framework should be supplemented by a framework that also accounts for fundamental ethical principles. In other words, utilitarian ends do not justify any and all means to those ends.

The second ethical framework that will prove crucial for business ethics begins with the insight that we should make some ethical decisions as a matter of principle rather than consequences. Ethical principles can be thought of as a type of rule, and this approach to ethics tells us that there are some rules that we ought to follow even if doing so prevents good consequences from happening or even if it results in some bad consequences. **Principles** are ethical rules that put values into action. We may *value* honesty, but disagree as to how to put that into action. It is only once we have stated a principle—"never lie," or "never lie except to prevent great harm," for example—that we know what valuing honesty means in practical terms.

It is also worth noting that principles (e.g., "obey the law," "keep your promises," "uphold your contracts") create ethical **duties** that bind us to act or decide in certain ways. For example, there is an ethical rule prohibiting slave labor, even if this practice would have beneficial economic consequences for society.

What principles or rules should guide our decisions? Legal rules, obviously, are one major set of rules that we ought to follow. We have a duty to pay our taxes, even if we think the money might be more efficiently spent on our children's college education. I ought to stop at a red light, even if no cars are coming and I could get to my destination a little sooner by going straight through the light. I ought not to steal my neighbor's property, even if he will never miss it and I will gain many benefits from it. Decision making within a business context will involve many situations in which one ought to obey legal rules even when the consequences, economic and otherwise, seem to be undesirable.

Other rules are derived from various institutions in which we participate, or from various social roles that we fill. As a teacher, I ought to read each student's assignment carefully and diligently, even if they will never know the difference and their final grade will not be affected. In my role as teacher and university faculty member, I have taken on certain responsibilities that cannot be abandoned whenever it is convenient for me to do so. As the referee in a sporting event, I have the duty to enforce the rules fairly, even when it would be easier not to do so. Similar rule-based duties follow from our roles as friends ("do not gossip

principles
Ethical rules that put values into action.

duties
Those obligations that one is bound to perform, regardless of consequences. Duties might be derived from basic ethical principles, from the law, or from one's institutional or professional role.

Reality Check *Ethical Principles and the United Nations Global Compact*

Ethical principles and duties can often be found in corporate and professional codes of conduct. One example of such a code that has had worldwide impact is the UN Global Compact's Ten Principles. The United Nations launched the UN Global Compact in 2000 as a means to encourage businesses throughout the world to commit to ethical business practices. Businesses joining the Global Compact commit to following 10 universal principles in the areas of human rights, labor, the environment, and anti-corruption. The UN Global Compact Ten Principles are as follows:

Human Rights

Principle 1: Businesses should support and respect the protection of internationally proclaimed human rights; and

Principle 2: make sure that they are not complicit in human rights abuses.

Labour Standards

Principle 3: Businesses should uphold the freedom of association and the effective recognition of the right to collective bargaining;

Principle 4: the elimination of all forms of forced and compulsory labour;

Principle 5: the effective abolition of child labour; and

Principle 6: the elimination of discrimination in respect of employment and occupation.

Environment

Principle 7: Businesses should support a precautionary approach to environmental challenges;

Principle 8: undertake initiatives to promote greater environmental responsibility; and

Principle 9: encourage the development and diffusion of environmentally friendly technologies.

Anti-Corruption

Principle 10: Businesses should work against corruption in all its forms, including extortion and bribery.

Source: United Nations Global Compact, "The Ten Principles," www.unglobalcompact.org/what-is-gc/mission/principles. Reprinted with permission of United Nations Global Compact.

---

about your friends"), family members ("do your chores at home"), students ("do not plagiarize"), church members ("contribute to the church's upkeep"), citizens ("inform yourself about the issues"), and good neighbors ("do not operate your lawn mower before 8 A.M.").

There will be many occasions in which such role-based duties arise in business. As an employee, one takes on a certain role that creates duties. Every business will have a set of rules that employees are expected to follow. Sometimes these rules are explicitly stated in a code of conduct, other times in employee handbooks, whereas still others are simply stated by managers. (See the Reality Check "Ethical Principles and the United Nations Global Compact.") Likewise, as a business manager there are many rules one ought to follow in respect to stockholders, employees, suppliers, and other stakeholders.

Perhaps the most dramatic example of role-based duties concerns the work of professionals within business. Lawyers, accountants, auditors, financial analysts, and bankers have important roles to play within political and economic institutions. Many of these roles, often described as "gatekeeper functions," ensure the integrity and proper functioning of the economic, legal, or financial system. Chapter 2 introduced the idea of professional responsibilities within the workplace and this theme will be developed further in chapter 10.

Reality Check *Alternative Medicine and the Risks of Consequence-Based Reasoning*

Homeopathy and other "alternative" therapies (such as Reiki and Traditional Chinese Medicine) continue to be controversial. Scientists tell us, with a high degree of confidence, that homeopathy in particular absolutely cannot have any therapeutic value; homeopathic remedies contain no active ingredients, and the principles according to which they are supposed to work conflict with all kinds of well-established science. Other alternative therapies (including some herbal remedies) may have some physical effects, but often such effects are poorly established and in some cases manufacturing standards are quite low, leading to products of highly variable quality. But many pharmacies continue to sell homeopathy and other alternative treatments nonetheless. The U.S. National Center for Complementary and Integrative Health estimates that Americans spend over $33 billion on such treatments every year.[5] But this presents a puzzle. Pharmacies are generally overseen by pharmacists, who are health professionals with scientific training that enables them to understand the damning evidence against the effectiveness of alternative medicines. How can scientifically trained professionals sell scientifically doubtful or even disproven products?

One hypothesis, of course, is greed. Such products are *profitable*. But other, less cynical reasons are available. Some pharmacists are comfortable with selling homeopathy, for example, because they see little harm. There are, after all, absolutely no side effects (recall that homeopathy has no active ingredients!), and for minor ailments, a "placebo" may bring patients psychological comfort. But on the other hand, if a very sick patient makes use of a homeopathic remedy instead of seeking an effective medicine prescribed by a physician, the outcome could be very bad indeed. Then again, if the patient really *wants and believes in* homeopathy, the pharmacist might well alienate the patient entirely if she refuses to discuss or sell a homeopathic remedy. This might lead to mistrust, and lead the patient even farther from scientifically proven medicines. So the full consequences of selling (or refusing to sell) homeopathic remedies may be hard to see,[6] and a pharmacist (or pharmacy owner) may naturally tend to see only the positive consequences of selling such a profitable product, and to downplay the negative ones.

The risks of consequence-based reasoning in such contexts is why many pharmacists promote a simpler, principle-based form of ethical reasoning, which includes this central principle: *Pharmacists should never sell a product that they do not believe to be supported by sound scientific evidence.*

The Enron and Arthur Andersen case provides a helpful example for understanding professional duties. While examining Enron's financial reports, the auditors at Arthur Andersen knew that diligent application of strict auditing standards required one particular decision, but also that the consequences of this diligent application would be harmful to Arthur Andersen's business interests. A fair analysis of this aspect of the Enron–Arthur Andersen scandal would point out that Andersen's auditors failed their ethical duties precisely because they did not follow the rules governing their professional responsibilities and allowed beneficial consequences to override their professional principles.

So far we have mentioned legal rules, organizational rules, role-based rules, and professional rules. We can think of these rules as part of a very broad social agreement, or social "contract," that functions to organize and ease relations between individuals. No group could function if members were free at all times to decide for themselves what to do and how to act. By definition, any cooperative activity requires cooperation, that is, requires rules that each member follows.

In the view of many philosophers, there are ethical duties that are more fundamental and that bind us in a stricter way than the way we are bound by contracts or by professional duties. You should not be able to "quit" ethical duties and walk away from them in quite the way that one can dissolve a contract or walk away from professional duties by quitting the profession. In the language of many philosophers, ethical duties should be **categorical imperatives** rather than hypothetical. Hypothetical duties would be like a professional code of conduct that binds you *only if* you are a member of the profession. Categorical duties do not contain this "if" clause. I *should* or *must* (an imperative) obey a fundamental ethical rule *no matter what* (a categorical).

Human Rights and Duties

OBJECTIVE

categorical imperative
An imperative is a command or duty; "categorical" means that it is without exception. Thus a categorical imperative is an overriding principle of ethics. Philosopher Immanuel Kant offered several formulations of the categorical imperative: act so as the maxim implicit in your acts could be willed to be a universal law; treat persons as ends and never as means only; treat others as subjects, not objects.

Are there *any* such fundamental or "categorical" duties? Are there any rules we should follow, decisions we should make, no matter what the consequences and no matter who we are or what we desire? Many ethical traditions have answered these questions in terms of a fundamental respect owed to each human being. These traditions agree that each and every human being possess an intrinsic value, or essential dignity, that should never be violated. Some religious traditions, for example, see this inherent dignity as something "endowed by the creator" or that stems from being created in the image and likeness of God.

A common way of expressing this insight is to say that each and every human being possesses a fundamental human right to be treated with respect, and that this right creates duties on the part of every human to respect the rights of others. Eighteenth-century philosopher Immanuel Kant expressed this as the fundamental duty we all have to treat each person as an end in themselves and never only as means to our own ends. In other words, our fundamental duty is to treat people as subjects capable of living their own lives and not as mere objects that exist for our purposes. To use the familiar subject/object categories from grammar, humans are subjects because they make decisions and perform actions rather than being objects that are acted upon. Humans have their own ends and purposes and therefore should not be treated simply as a means to the ends of others. Persons, in other words, must never be treated as mere tools.

Such human rights, or moral rights, have played a central role in the development of modern democratic political systems. The U.S. Declaration of Independence speaks of "inalienable rights" that cannot be taken away by government. Other democracies have similar rights embedded in their constitutions, such as in the Canadian Charter of Rights and Freedoms or France's Declaration of the Rights of Man and of the Citizen. Following World War II, the United Nations created the UN's Declaration of Human Rights as a means for holding all governments to fundamental standards of ethics.

To return to an earlier example, this rights-based framework of ethics would object to child labor because such practices violate our duty to treat children with respect. We violate the rights of children when we treat them as mere means to the ends of production and economic growth. We are treating them merely as means because, as children, they have not rationally and freely chosen their own ends. We are simply using them as tools or objects. Thus, even if child labor produced beneficial consequences, it would be ethically wrong because it violates a fundamental human right.

In this way, the concept of a human or moral right is central to the principle-based ethical tradition. The inherent dignity of each individual means that we cannot do whatever we choose to another person. Human rights protect individuals from being treated in ways that would violate their dignity and that would treat them as mere objects or means. Rights imply that some acts and some decisions are "off-limits." Accordingly, our fundamental moral duty (the categorical imperative) is to respect the fundamental human rights of others. Our rights establish limits on the decisions and authority of others.

Consider how rights function relative to the utilitarian goal of maximizing the overall good. Suppose that you owned a local business and your local government decided that your property would make a great location for a city park. Imagine that you are the only person who disagrees. On utilitarian grounds, it might seem that your land would best serve the overall good by being used for a park. However, your property rights prevent the community from taking your land (at least without fair compensation) to serve the public.

A similar point could be made by considering the case of the hackers who in 2014 hacked the iCloud file-storage accounts of a number of celebrities.[7] The hackers then stole and posted online a number of private photos, many of them containing nudity. Some might be tempted to argue, on utilitarian grounds, that this was a good thing to do. After all, while posting the photos caused embarrassment to the celebrities who were targeted, a very large number of people enjoyed having access to the photos. It is possible, then, that the hackers had caused more happiness overall by posting the photos than had they left the celebrities' iCloud accounts alone. But such an analysis ignores the celebrities' right to privacy. The photos may have been enjoyed by a large number of people, but those people didn't own them. They were the private property of the celebrities involved. And surely the celebrities involved would argue that their rights should not have been violated simply to produce happiness for other people.

In summary, we can say that human rights are meant to offer protection of certain central human interests, prohibiting the sacrifice of these interests merely to provide a net increase in the overall happiness. The standard account of human rights offered through the Western ethical tradition connects basic human rights to some theory of a basic human nature. The Kantian tradition claims that our fundamental human rights, and the duties that follow from them, are derived from our nature as free and rational beings. Humans do not act only out of instinct and conditioning; they make free choices about how they live their lives, about their own goals. In this sense, humans are said to have a fundamental human right of **autonomy**, or "self-rule."

autonomy
From the Greek for "self-ruled," autonomy is the capacity to make free and deliberate choices. The capacity for autonomous action is what explains the inherent dignity and intrinsic value of individual human beings.

Human Rights and Social Justice

From these origins, we can see how two related rights have emerged as fundamental components of social justice. If autonomy, or self-rule, is a fundamental characteristic of human nature, then the liberty to make our own choices deserves special protection as a basic right. But, because all humans possess this fundamental characteristic, equal treatment and equal consideration must also be fundamental rights. Liberty and equality are, according to much of this tradition, "natural rights" that are more fundamental and persistent than the legal rights created by governments and communities. (See the Reality Check "Are Fundamental Human Rights Universally Accepted?")

Reality Check *Are Fundamental Human Rights Universally Accepted?*

In 1948—just three years after the end of the Second World War—the United Nations adopted a Universal Declaration of Human Rights. Since that time, this Declaration has been translated into more than 300 languages and dialects. The Declaration contains 30 articles outlining basic human rights. In part the Declaration includes the following:

PREAMBLE

Recognition of the inherent dignity and of the equal and inalienable rights of all members of the human family is the foundation of freedom, justice and peace in the world.

Article 1.

All human beings are born free and equal in dignity and rights. They are endowed with reason and conscience and should act towards one another in a spirit of brotherhood.

Article 2.

Everyone is entitled to all the rights and freedoms set forth in this Declaration, without distinction of any kind, such as race, colour, sex, language, religion, political or other opinion, national or social origin, property, birth or other status.

Article 3.

Everyone has the right to life, liberty and security of person.

Article 4.

No one shall be held in slavery or servitude; slavery and the slave trade shall be prohibited in all their forms.

Article 5.

No one shall be subjected to torture or to cruel, inhuman or degrading treatment or punishment.

Article 9.

No one shall be subjected to arbitrary arrest, detention or exile.

Article 10.

Everyone is entitled in full equality to a fair and public hearing by an independent and impartial tribunal, in the determination of his rights and obligations and of any criminal charge against him.

Article 18.

Everyone has the right to freedom of thought, conscience and religion; this right includes freedom to change his religion or belief, and freedom, either alone or in community with others and in public or private, to manifest his religion or belief in teaching practice, worship and observance.

Article 19.

Everyone has the right to freedom of opinion and expression; this right includes freedom to hold opinions without interference and to seek, receive and impart information and ideas through any media and regardless of frontiers.

Article 23.

(1) Everyone has the right to work, to free choice of employment, to just and favourable conditions of work and to protection against unemployment.

(2) Everyone, without any discrimination, has the right to equal pay for equal work.

(3) Everyone who works has the right to just and favourable remuneration ensuring for himself and his family an existence worthy of human dignity, and supplemented, if necessary, by other means of social protection.

(4) Everyone has the right to form and to join trade unions for the protection of his interests.

Article 25.

(1) Everyone has the right to a standard of living adequate for the health and well-being of himself and of his family, including food, clothing, housing and medical care and necessary social services, and the right to security in the event of unemployment, sickness, disability, widowhood, old age or other lack of livelihood in circumstances beyond his control.

Article 26.

(1) Everyone has the right to education.

Liberty and equality are also the core elements of most modern conceptions of social justice. They are in particular fundamental to theories of social justice upon which democratic societies and capitalist economies have been built and, thus, are crucial to an understanding of business ethics.

Libertarian understandings of social justice argue that individual liberty—freedom from coercion by others—is the most central element of social justice. This means that a just society is one in which individuals are free from governmental intrusion as long as they are not harming others. Political perspectives that seek to reduce the size of government and limit government regulation of the market typically cite individual liberty as their primary ethical justification.

If we acknowledge liberty as the most basic human right, it would be easy to generate an argument for a more laissez-faire, free-market economic system. As long as individuals are not harming others, they should be free to engage in any voluntary economic exchange. Government's only role, in such a system, is to ensure that there is free and open competition and that economic transactions are free from coercion, fraud, and deception.

From this libertarian perspective, businesses should be free to pursue profit in any voluntary and nondeceptive manner. An ethical business is one that pursues profit within the law. Unethical business practices would include fraud, deception, and anticompetitive behavior. Government regulation aimed at preventing such behaviors, as well as government activity to enforce contracts and compensate for harms, would be just. All other government regulation would be seen as unjust interference in the market.

Egalitarian versions of justice, on the other hand, argue that equality is the most central element of social justice. *Socialist* egalitarian theories argue that equal distribution of basic economic goods and services is at the heart of social justice. Other egalitarian theories argue that equal opportunity, more than equality of outcome, is crucial. Egalitarian theories of social justice typically support greater governmental responsibility in the economy as a necessary means to guarantee equality.

Human Rights and Legal Rights

OBJECTIVE

human rights
Those moral rights that individuals have simply in virtue of being a human being. Also called *natural rights* or *moral rights*.

It will be helpful at this point to distinguish between **human rights** and legal rights. To illustrate this distinction, let us take employee rights as an example. Three kinds of employee rights are common in business. First, there are those *legal* rights granted to employees on the basis of legislation or judicial rulings. For example, employees have a right to a minimum wage, equal opportunity, to bargain collectively as part of a union, to be free from sexual harassment, and so forth. Second, employees have rights to those goods that they are entitled to on the basis of contractual agreements with employers. In this sense, a particular employee might have a right to a specific health care package, a certain number of paid holidays, pension funds, and the like. Finally, employees have rights grounded in moral entitlements to which employees have a claim independently of any particular legal or contractual factors. Examples of such rights include the right not to be bullied, the right not to be lied to, and the right not to be

Decision Point

Should All Human Rights Become Legal Rights?

Employees have both human rights (as persons) and legal rights (as employees). Some rights—such as the right to be treated equally regardless of sexual identity—have only quite recently been recognized as legal rights. For example, in 2015 the U.S. Equal Employment Opportunity Commission ruled that workplace discrimination based on sexual orientation is a form of sex discrimination, and is hence illegal under the the 1964 Civil Rights Act.[8] And yet many would argue that freedom from such discrimination is a human right. That is, they would argue that all employees had a right not to be discriminated against all along. From an ethical point of view, that right didn't just appear with the recent *legal* recognition of it—the right was there all along. This raises an interesting question: Should all human rights be entrenched in law, such that they become legal rights? Why or why not? Why might some rights be recognized as human rights and yet not turned into legal rights?

sexually harassed. Such rights would originate with the respect owed to them as human beings.

It is worth considering how legal and contractual rights interact. In general, both parties to an employment agreement bargain over the conditions of work. Employers offer certain wages, benefits, and working conditions and in return seek worker productivity. Employees offer skills and abilities and seek wages and benefits in return. Thus, employment rights emerge from contractual promises. However, certain goods are legally exempt from such negotiation. An employer cannot make a willingness to submit to sexual harassment or acceptance of a wage below the minimum established by law a part of the employment agreement. In effect, legal rights place certain issues outside the realm of the employment contract. Such legal rights set the basic legal framework within which business operates. They are established by the legal system and, in this sense, are part of the price of doing business.

So, too, human rights lie outside of the bargaining that occurs between employers and employees. Unlike the minimum wage, moral rights are established and justified by moral, rather than legal, considerations. Moral rights establish the basic moral framework for the legal environment itself, and more specifically for any contracts that are negotiated within business. Thus, as described in the U.S. Declaration of Independence and in the Canadian Charter of Rights and Freedoms, governments and laws are created in order to secure more fundamental natural moral rights. The rights outlined earlier in the excerpt from the United Nations fit this conception of fundamental moral rights.

Challenges to an Ethics of Rights and Duties

OBJECTIVE

So what rights do we have and what does that mean for the duties of others? In the U.S. Declaration of Independence, Thomas Jefferson claimed that we have "inalienable rights" to life, liberty, and the pursuit of happiness. Jefferson was influenced by the British philosopher John Locke, who spoke of "natural rights" to life, health, liberty, and possessions. The UN Universal Declaration of Human Rights (see again the Reality Check "Are Fundamental Human Rights Universally Accepted?") lists more than 26 human rights that it says are universal.

Acknowledging this diversity of rights makes it easy to understand the two biggest challenges to this ethical tradition. There appears to be much disagreement about what rights truly are basic human rights and, given the multiplicity of views about this, it is unclear how to apply this approach to practical situations, especially in cases where rights appear to conflict.

Take, for example, a possible right to health care. During debates over health care reform in the U.S. Congress in 2009, many claimed that humans have a right to health care. Other societies would seem to agree in that many countries have instituted national health plans to provide citizens with at least minimal health care. The UN Declaration would seem to agree, claiming that humans have a right "to a standard of living adequate for the health and well-being" and that this right includes medical care. But many disagree and point out that such a right would carry significant costs for others. If every human has a right to health care, who has the duty to provide it and at what costs? Does this mean that doctors and nurses can be required to provide free medical care? Does this right entail a right to the best treatment possible? To elective surgeries? To wellness care or nursing homes? To cosmetic surgery?

Critics charge that unless there is a specific person or institution that has a duty to provide the goods identified as "rights," talk of rights amounts to little more than a wish list of things that people want. What are identified as "rights" often are nothing more than good things that most people desire. But, if every human truly does have a right to a standard of living adequate for all the goods mentioned in Article 25 of the UN Declaration, who has the duty to provide them?

More relevant to business is the Declaration's Article 23 that everyone has a "right to work, to free choice of employment." What would this mean to a business? Is it helpful to say that an employee's human rights are violated if they are laid off during a recession? Who has the duty to provide jobs to every unemployed person? This same article refers to a "right to just and favourable remuneration." But what is a just wage and who gets to decide?

The first major challenge to an ethics based on rights is that there is no agreement about the scope and range of such rights. Which good things qualify as rights, and which are merely things that people want? Critics charge that there is no way to answer this. Yet, unless there is some clear way to distinguish the two, the list of rights will only grow to unreasonable lengths and the corresponding duties will unreasonably burden everyone.

A second challenge also points to practical problems in applying a theory of rights to real-life situations. With a long list of human rights, all of which are claimed to be basic and fundamental, how would we decide between one individual's right to medical care and the physician's right to just remuneration of her work? Suppose the person needing medical care could not afford to pay a just fee for the care?

Perhaps the most important rights-related conflict in a business setting would occur when an employer's rights to property come into conflict with an employee's alleged rights to work, just wages, and health care. While the UN Declaration does not mention a right to property as a basic human right, many philosophers in the Western tradition agree with John Locke and include it among our natural rights. Granting economic rights to employees would seem to create numerous conflicts with the property rights of employers. Critics point out that the ethical tradition of rights and duties has been unable to provide a persuasive and systematic account for how such conflicts are to be resolved.

Virtue Ethics: Making Decisions Based on Integrity and Character

OBJECTIVE 9

For the most part, utilitarian and principle-based frameworks focus on rules that we might follow in deciding what we should do, both as individuals and as citizens. These approaches conceive of practical reason in terms of deciding how to act and what to do. Chapter 1 pointed out, however, that ethics also involves questions about the type of person one should become. Virtue ethics is a tradition within philosophical ethics that seeks a full and detailed description of those character traits, or virtues, that would constitute a good and full human life.

Virtues can be understood as those character traits that would constitute parts of a good and meaningful human life. Being friendly and cheerful; having integrity; being honest, forthright, and truthful; having modest wants; and being tolerant are some of the characteristics that are typically thought of as being part of a good and meaningful human life. (For additional qualities, see the Reality Check "Virtues in Everyday Language.") One can see virtue ethics at play in everyday situations: we all know people we look up to because we respect them for their character, and we all know people whom we describe as being people of integrity. Perhaps the best place to see the ethics of virtue is in the goal of every good parent who hopes to raise happy and decent children.

To understand how virtue ethics differs from utilitarian and principle-based frameworks, consider the problem of egoism. As mentioned previously, egoism is a view that holds that people act only out of self-interest. Many economists, for example, seem to assume that all individuals always act out of self-interest; indeed, many seem to assume that rationality itself should be defined in terms of acting out of self-interest. The biggest challenge posed by egoism and, according to some, the biggest challenge to ethics is the apparent gap between self-interest and altruism, or between motivation that is "self-regarding" and motivation that is "other-regarding." Ethics requires us, at least at times, to act for the well-being of others. Yet, those who believe in egoism would claim that this is not possible.

An ethics of virtue shifts the focus from questions about what a person should *do,* to a focus on who that person *is.* This shift requires not only a different view of ethics but, at least as important, a different view of ourselves. Implicit in this distinction is the recognition that our identity as individuals is constituted in part by our wants, beliefs, values, and attitudes. A person's **character**—those dispositions, relationships, attitudes, values, and beliefs that popularly might be called a "personality"—is not some feature that remains independent of that person's

character
The sum of relatively set traits, dispositions, and habits of an individual. Along with rational deliberation and choice, a person's character accounts for how she or he makes decisions and acts. Training and developing character so that it is disposed to act ethically is the goal of virtue ethics.

The language of "virtues" and "vices" may seem old-fashioned or quaint for modern readers, but this was a dominant perspective on ethics in the Western world for centuries. Go ahead and develop a short list of adjectives that describe a good person's character, and you will find that the language of virtues and vices is not as outdated as it may seem.

The ancient Greeks identified four primary virtues: courage, moderation, wisdom, and justice. Early Christians described the three cardinal virtues of faith, hope, and charity. Boys Scouts pledge to be trustworthy, loyal, helpful, friendly, courteous, kind, obedient, cheerful, thrifty, brave, clean, and reverent.

According to ancient and medieval philosophers the virtues represented a balanced midpoint, the "golden mean," between two extremes, both of which would be considered vices. Thus, for example, a brave person finds the balance between too little courage, which is cowardice, and too much courage, which is reckless and foolhardy.

The virtues are those character traits or habits that would produce a good, happy, and meaningful life. To practice such virtues and habits and acting in accord with one's own character is to live a life of integrity.

When you stop to think about it, you'll find that talking about ethics in terms of character traits comes quite naturally. Can you think of examples of how we express appreciation of someone's character in everyday conversation with friends? Or how such appreciation is expressed in military contexts? Or in action movies? Or even in rap music?

identity. Character is not like a suit of clothes that you step into and out of at will. Rather, the self is identical to a person's most fundamental and enduring dispositions, attitudes, values, and beliefs.

Note how this shift changes the nature of justification in ethics. If, as seems true for many people, justification of some act requires that it be tied to self-interest, we should not be surprised to find that this justification often fails. Ethical controversies often involve a conflict between self-interest and ethical values. Why should I do the ethical thing if it would require me to give up a lot of money? To a person whose personality does not already include a disposition to be modest, the only avenue open for justification would involve showing how such a disposition serves some other interest that person has, such as her own profit. Why should an executive turn down a multi-million-dollar bonus? The only way to answer this question appears to be to show how it would be in her self-interest to do so. But, this is at times unlikely.

On the other hand, for the person already characterized by modest, down-to-earth desires, the question of justifying smaller salaries is less relevant. If I am the type of person who has moderate and restrained desires for money, then there is no temptation to be unethical for the sake of a large bonus. For many people, the "self" of self-interest is a caring, modest, authentic, altruistic self. For these people, there simply is no conflict between *self*-interest and altruism.

The degree to which we are capable of acting for the well-being of others therefore seems to depend on a variety of factors such as our desires, our beliefs, our dispositions, and our values; in short, it depends on our character or the type of person we are. If people are caring, empathetic, charitable, and sympathetic, then the challenge of selfishness and egoism is simply not a factor in their decision making.

Virtue ethics recognizes that our motivations—our interests, wants, desires—are not the sorts of things that each of us chooses anew each morning. Instead, human beings act according to who they are, according to their character. By adulthood, these character traits typically are deeply ingrained and conditioned within us. Given that our character plays such a key role in our behavior, and given the realization that our character can be shaped by factors that are controllable (by conscious individual decisions, by how we are raised, by the social institutions in which we live, work, and learn), virtue ethics seeks to understand how those traits are formed and which traits are conducive to and which ones undermine a meaningful, worthwhile, and satisfying human life.

Virtue ethics can offer us a more fully textured understanding of life within business. Rather than simply describing people's behavior as good or bad, and decisions as right or wrong, an ethics of virtue encourages a fuller description of persons as a whole. For example, we might describe a whistle-blower as heroic and courageous. We might describe a boss like Dan Price as a man of integrity, who sympathizes with employees and cares about their well-being. Other executives might be described as greedy or ruthless, proud or competitive. Faced with a difficult dilemma, we might ask not, What should I do? but, What would a person with *integrity* do? What would an *honest* person say? Do I have the *courage* of my convictions? In other words, you might think of (or imagine) someone you believe to be especially virtuous and ask yourself what that person would do in this situation. What would a virtuous person do?

Besides connecting the virtues to a conception of a fuller human life, virtue ethics also reminds us to examine how character traits are formed and conditioned. By the time we are adults, much of our character is formed by such factors as our parents, schools, church, friends, and society. But powerful social institutions such as business and especially our own places of employment and our particular roles within them (e.g., manager, professional, and trainee) have a profound influence on shaping our character. Consider an accounting firm that hires a group of trainees fully expecting that fewer than half will be retained after one year and where only a very small group will make partner. That corporate environment encourages motivations and behavior very different from a firm that hires fewer people but gives them all a greater chance at long-term success. A company that sets unrealistic sales goals will find it creates a different sales force than one that understands sales more as customer service. Virtue ethics reminds us to look to the actual practices we find in the business world and to ask what types of people are being created by these practices. Many individual moral dilemmas that arise within business ethics can best be understood as arising from a tension between the type of person we seek to be and the type of person business expects us to be. (See the Reality Check "Where Do Virtues Come From?")

Consider an example described by someone (whom the authors of this textbook know) who has conducted empirical studies of the values found within marketing firms and advertising agencies. This person reported that, on several occasions, advertising agents told her that they would never allow their own children to watch the very television shows and advertisements that their own firms

Reality Check   *Where Do Virtues Come From?*

Where do virtues come from? How do we become good people?

Plato's famous dialogue the *Meno* opens with the title character asking Socrates this basic question: Can virtue be taught? If ethics involves developing the right sort of character traits and habits, as the virtue theorist holds, then the acquisition of those traits becomes a fundamental question for ethics. Can we teach people to be honest, trustworthy, loyal, courteous, moderate, respectful, and compassionate?

Meno (the title character of the dialogue) initially cast the question in terms of two alternatives: either virtue is taught or it is acquired naturally. In modern terms, this is the question of nurture or nature, environment or genetics. Socrates's answer is more complicated. Virtue cannot simply be taught by others, nor is it acquired automatically through nature. Each individual has the natural potential to become virtuous, and learning from one's surroundings is a part of this process But, ultimately, virtues must be developed by each individual through a complex process of personal reflection, reasoning, practice, and

observation as well as social reinforcement and conditioning. Virtues are habits, and acquiring any habit is a subtle and complex process.

Parents confront this question every day. I know my children will lead happier and more meaningful lives if they are honest, respectful, cheerful, moderate and not greedy, envious, gloomy, arrogant, or selfish. Yet simply telling my children to be honest and to avoid greed is insufficient; nor can I remain passive and assume that these traits will develop naturally. Instilling these character traits and habits is a long-term process that develops over time.

Business institutions also have come to recognize that character formation is both difficult and unavoidable. Employees come to business with certain character traits and habits, and these can get shaped and reinforced in the workplace. Hire a person with the wrong character traits, and there will be trouble ahead. Designing a workplace, or creating a corporate culture to reinforce good character traits and discourage bad ones is one of the greatest challenges for an ethical manager.

were producing. By their own admission, the ads for such shows aim to manipulate children into buying, or getting their parents to buy, products that had little or no real value. In some cases, the ads promoted beer drinking and the advertisers themselves admitted, as their "dirty little secret," that they were intended to target the teenage market. Further, their own research evidenced the success of their ads in increasing sales.

Independent of the ethical questions we might ask about advertising aimed at children, a virtue ethics approach would look at the type of individuals who are so able to disassociate themselves and their own values from their work and the social institutions and practices that encourage it. What kind of people are willing to subject others' children to marketing practices that they are unwilling to accept for their own children? Such individuals seem to lack even the most elementary form of personal integrity. What kind of organization encourages people to treat children in ways that they willingly admit are indecent? What kind of people do they become working in such an organization?

Finally, the virtue ethics focus on character formation should lead us to ask questions about the choices we make and how those choices affect our character. This can happen in two ways. First, note that each decision you make has a subtle but meaningful impact on subsequent decisions. Each lie, as the saying goes, makes it easier to tell the next lie. Indeed, each small lie makes it easier for

One useful way to think about character is to ask yourself this question: When you retire, likely many years from now, what will people say about you at your retirement party? Certainly they will congratulate you, and point to your various achievements, and to the important milestones of your career. But they will likely also talk about who you *are*. What will they say about the kind of person you are—about your character?

More to the point, what do you *want* them to say about you? Do you want them to say that throughout your career you were "a tough-minded businessperson" or "a

kind and generous co-worker?" Do you aspire to being remembered as a "watchful boss" or as a "supportive mentor"? Do you hope they will describe you as "dedicated to your job" or as "devoted to friends and family"? What other character traits do you hope, looking forward, they will use to describe you and your career?

Finally, ask yourself: What can I do between now and then to make that wish come true? How should I behave over the coming decades to make myself into the kind of person who will earn the kinds of words I hope they'll use to describe me when I retire?

you to tell bigger and bigger lies. This suggests that there is a reciprocal relationship between character and action: Our character affects how we act, but how we act ends up affecting our character. (For more about the way our choices affect the person we eventually become, see the Reality Check "What Will They Say When You Retire?") The second way in which our choices affect our character is through the people we choose to associate with and the organizations we choose to become part of. If you spend time with patient, gentle people, you are liable to become more like them. If you spend time with mean, belligerent people, you are likely to become more like *them*. This has important implications for the companies we choose to work for. As we will discuss further in chapter 4, the organizational cultures that we become part of will inevitably change who we are as persons. So it is best to choose carefully.

A Decision-Making Model for Business Ethics Revisited

This chapter provided an introduction to three historically and philosophically important ethical frameworks. While some of the material covered in this chapter might appear esoteric and too abstract for a business ethics class, all of it has a very practical aim. Understanding the philosophical basis of ethics will enable you to become more aware of ethical issues, better able to recognize the significance of your decisions, and more likely to make better informed and more reasonable decisions. In addition, the theories allow us to better and more articulately explain ourselves when we are asked why we have made or intend to make a particular decision. Whereas a statement such as "we should do this because it is the right thing to do" will often be seen as vague or unpersuasive, an alternative explanation such as "we should do this because more people will be better off than will be harmed if we do so" could be much more effective and convincing. When a key stakeholder asks you why you support or oppose a specific proposal, your response now has comprehensive substance behind it and will therefore be more sophisticated, credible, and convincing.

Over the course of the year following Dan Price's April 2015 announcement, he was embroiled in a legal battle with his brother Lucas, co-owner of Gravity Payments.[9] Lucas Price sued Dan, claiming that his brother had violated the 2008 agreement governing the ownership and management of the company. Under the terms of that agreement, Dan owned 67.5 percent of the company, and Lucas stepped away from what had previously been his day-to-day involvement in the company. Lucas sued, in part, because he says his brother had failed to involve him even in very major decisions—including the decision to change how much Gravity workers were paid. The lawsuit also claimed that Dan was paying himself too much. Court documents showed that Dan had tried to get his own total compensation raised to $5.5 million, which amounted to more than half of the company's total revenue. At the time of writing, the judge in the case had agreed to the two brothers' request to be allowed to attempt to resolve their problems out-of-court, through mediation.

- Dan Price's decision to pay Gravity employees more required spending some of the company's profits. Did this violate the rights of his brother, Lucas, given that Lucas wasn't consulted first?

- Dan Price's announcement that he would himself be taking a substantial cut in pay (to pay for *part* of the raise his employees would be getting) came just two weeks after he learned that his brother was suing him. Does that change your assessment of the ethics of his decision to shift most of his own compensation to his employees?

- Using the vocabulary of virtue ethics, how would you describe your original impression of Dan Price? How would you describe him in light of the information on this page?

These ethical theories and traditions also provide important ways in which to develop the decision-making model introduced in chapter 2. These ethical theories, after all, provide systematic and sophisticated ways to think and reason about ethical questions. We now can offer a more detailed version of our decision-making model, one in which ethical theories are integrated into an explicit decision procedure. The decision-making process introduced here aims, above all else, to help you make ethically responsible business decisions. To summarize, we now review that decision-making process in more detail.

1. **Determine the facts.** Gather all of the relevant facts. It is critical at this stage that we do not unintentionally bias our later decision by gathering only those facts in support of one particular outcome.

2. **Identify the ethical issues involved.** What is the ethical dimension? What is the ethical issue? Often we do not even notice the ethical dilemma. Avoid normative myopia.

3. **Identify stakeholders.** Who will be affected by this decision? What are their relationships, to me, and what is their power over my decision or results? Who

has a stake in the outcome? Do not limit your inquiry only to those stakeholders to whom you believe you owe a duty; sometimes a duty becomes clear only once the impact on a stakeholder is assessed. For instance, you might not necessarily first consider your competitors as stakeholders; however, once you understand the impact of your decision on those competitors, an ethical duty may arise.

4. **Consider the available alternatives.** Exercise "moral imagination." Are there creative ways to resolve conflicts? Explore not only the obvious choices, but also those that are less obvious and that require some creative thinking or thinking "outside the box."

5. **Compare and weigh the alternatives.** Take the point of view of other people involved. How is each stakeholder affected by my decision? Compare and weigh the alternatives: ethical theories and traditions can help here.

   a. Consequences
      i. Beneficial and harmful consequences
   b. Duties, rights, principles
      i. What does the law say?
      ii. Are there professional duties involved?
      iii. Which principles are most obligatory?
      iv. Are people being treated fairly, with respect for their autonomy and equality?
   c. Implications for personal integrity and character
      i. What type of person am I becoming through this decision?
      ii. What are my own principles and purposes?
      iii. Can I live with public disclosure of this decision?

6. **Make a Decision.** Is this a point-in-time decision, or something that will be carried out over time? What is your plan, and how are you going to implement it? What will you do if something unexpected happens as a result?

7. **Monitor and Learn.** Have you built in mechanisms for assessment of your decision and possible modifications? Make sure that you learn from each decision and move forward with that increased knowledge; you may face similar decisions in the future or find it necessary to make changes to your current situation. Do policies or procedures need to be revised as a result of this situation or its resolution?

Questions, Projects, and Exercises

1. Not all ethical norms get entrenched in law. In which philosophical tradition—consequences, rights, or virtue—are we most likely to find norms that have ended up becoming laws?

2. What makes a decision or issue an *ethical* one? How would you explain the differences between ethical/nonethical, on one hand, and ethical/unethical, on the other?

3. What ethical disputes or dilemmas have you experienced in your own workplace? What about in a club or student group you belong to? How were these disputes or dilemmas resolved?

4. Do an Internet search on international human rights and/or fundamental moral rights. Can you find any moral rights that seem to be universally acknowledged across all cultures?

5. Why might economic growth be considered a utilitarian goal?

6. Some political philosophers understand the ethical foundations of legislatures to be utilitarian, while the ethical foundation of the judiciary is deontological. How would you explain this distinction?

7. If the right to *autonomy* is the right to make your own free and deliberate choices, what limits do you think there must be on that right? Does the right to autonomy literally allow us to do anything we want?

8. The right of private property is often described as a "bundle" of rights. What rights are involved in ownership of property? Given this understanding, should shareholders be considered owners of corporations?

9. Can such character traits as honesty, loyalty, trustworthiness, compassion, and humility be taught? Do people learn to be selfish, greedy, or aggressive, or do these traits come naturally?

10. Do professionals such as physicians, accountants, and lawyers have duties and obligations that other people do not? Where would such duties come from?

Key Terms

After reading this chapter, you should have a clear understanding of the following key terms. For a complete definition, please see the Glossary.

autonomy, *p. 80*
categorical imperative, *p. 79*
character, *p. 85*
consequentialist theories, *p. 68*

duties, *p. 76*
egoism, *p. 70*
ethical relativism, *p. 67*
human rights, *p. 82*
principle-based framework, *p. 68*

principles, *p. 76*
utilitarianism, *p. 68*
virtue ethics, *p. 68*

Endnotes

1. Patricia Cohen, "One Company's New Minimum Wage: $70,000 a Year," *The New York Times,* April 13, 2015, www.nytimes.com/2015/04/14/business/owner-of-gravity-payments-a-credit-card-processor-is-setting-a-new-minimum-wage-70000-a-year.html (accessed June 26, 2016).

2. Caleb Melby, "Executive Pay: Valuing CEOs," *Bloomberg.com* (March 15, 2015) www.bloomberg.com/quicktake/executive-pay (accessed June 26, 2016).

3. Alex Tabarrok, "Unsafe Cars Can Save Lives," *Marginal Revolution* (May 23, 2016), http://marginalrevolution.com/marginalrevolution/2016/05/safety-is-relative.html (accessed June 28, 2016)

4. Insurance Institute for Highway Safety, Highway Loss Data Institute, "Motorcycles," www.iihs.org/iihs/topics/t/motorcycles/fatalityfacts/motorcycles (accessed June 28, 2016).

5. National Center for Complementary and Integrative Health, "The Use of Complementary and Alternative Medicine in the United States: Cost Data," https://nccih.nih.gov/news/camstats/costs/costdatafs.htm (accessed July 2, 2016).

6. For more on the ethics of selling alternative medicines, see Chris MacDonald and Scott Gavura, "Alternative Medicine and the Ethics of Commerce," *Bioethics* 30, no. 2 (2016), pp. 77–84.

7. See "iCloud Leaks of Celebrity Photos," *Wikipedia,* https://en.wikipedia.org/wiki/ICloud_leaks_of_celebrity_photos (accessed July 3, 2016).

8. Dale Carpenter, "Anti-gay Discrimination Is Sex Discrimination, Says the EEOC," *The Washington Post* (July 16, 2015), www.washingtonpost.com/news/volokh-conspiracy/wp/2015/07/16/anti-gay-discrimination-is-sex-discrimination-says-the-eeoc/ (accessed July 3, 2016).

9. Rachel Lerman, "Gravity Payments brothers square off in court" *Seattle Times*, May 31, 2016. http://www.seattletimes.com/business/technology/brothers-square-off-in-court-over-company-paying-employees-70k-a-year/.

Readings

Reading 3-1: "The U.N. Guiding Principles on Business and Human Rights: Analysis and Implementation," by Kenan Institute for Ethics, Duke University

Reading 3-2: "The Caux Principles for Responsible Business," by the Caux Round Table

Reading 3-3: "It Seems Right in Theory but Does It Work in Practice?," by Norman E. Bowie

Reading 3-4: "Business Decisions Should Not Violate the Humanity of a Person," by Norman E. Bowie

Reading **3-1**

The U.N. Guiding Principles on Business and Human Rights:
Analysis and Implementation

Kenan Institute for Ethics, Duke University

Background

History

The modern international human rights framework was created by governments, for governments. Its foundational document, the Universal Declaration of Human Rights, was created in the wake of World War II to articulate a set of rights and freedoms that *states* would commit to protecting and fulfilling.

But business has grown in scale and scope since the Universal Declaration was created in 1948. While companies have delivered innovations and efficiencies that have dramatically raised standards of living and lifted millions of people out of poverty, they have also caused and contributed to human rights abuses around the world.

Consequently, there have been a number of initiatives to develop codes of conduct for business: by multi-lateral agencies like the Organisation for Economic Co-operation and Development (OECD), which issued the first version of its Guidelines for Multi-national Enterprises in 1976; or for particular sectors: The Fair Labor Association to improve working conditions in factories was incorporated in 1999; the Voluntary Principles on Security and Human Rights for extractive companies were announced in 2000.

But efforts to establish an authoritative and universal set of principles at the United Nations failed:

The U.N. Commission on Transnational Corporations was established in 1973 to draft a corporate code of conduct, but after many drafts was dissolved in 1994.

From Norms to Guiding Principles

In 2003, the U.N. Commission on Human Rights received from one of its subsidiary bodies a proposed code of conduct for transnational corporations for its approval: "Norms on the Responsibilities of Transnational Corporations and Other Business Enterprises with Regard to Human Rights" (the Norms).

The 2003 Norms asserted that business has "the obligation to promote, secure the fulfillment of, respect, ensure respect of, and protect human rights recognized in international as well as national law." The Norms provoked a strong negative reaction from the International Organization of Employers and the International Chamber of Commerce, who asserted that the Norms were a "counterproductive" attempt to shift responsibilities to companies for "what are and should remain government responsibilities and functions." In part because of that opposition, a number of states lined up to oppose the Norms. The fact that the Sub-Commission that drafted the Norms involved few states or companies in the process may have also contributed to the lack of support.

Some NGOs such as Amnesty International supported the Norms. But such support wasn't enough for the Commission on Human Rights, which declined to consider the Norms, saying they had some helpful elements but no legal standing.

In 2005, the Commission requested that the Secretary-General appoint a Special Representative to "identify and clarify standards of corporate responsibility and accountability for transnational corporations and other business enterprises with regard to human rights." Then-Secretary-General Kofi Annan appointed Harvard Kennedy School professor John Ruggie.

In 2008, Ruggie presented to the Human Rights Council (which replaced the Commission in 2006) the "Protect, Respect and Remedy" framework, which he described as the "conceptual and policy framework to anchor the business and human rights debate, and to help guide all relevant actors." The Council passed a resolution welcoming the framework and gave Ruggie a new three-year mandate to develop more practical guidance.

Ruggie followed that instruction by developing a set of Guiding Principles. In presenting the Guiding Principles to the Council in June 2011, Ruggie stated that "[t]he Guiding Principles' normative contribution lies not in the creation of new international law obligations but in elaborating the implications of existing standards and practices for States and businesses; integrating them within a single, logically coherent and comprehensive template; and identifying where the current regime falls short and how it should be improved."

Two weeks after Ruggie's presentation, the Council passed without a vote a resolution endorsing the Guiding Principles. It is highly unusual for an intergovernmental body to endorse a text they did not themselves negotiate, a testament to the engagement of states by Ruggie throughout his mandate. The Council also established a Working Group to "promote the effective and comprehensive dissemination and implementation of the Guiding Principles."

The Council gives limited support to Special Procedures, but throughout his mandate Ruggie raised money from governments to hire staff, visit stakeholders and sites, and hold meetings around the world, many of which were organized in partnership with civil society organizations. He held large regional multistakeholder consultations in Bangkok, Bogota, Buenos Aires, Johannesburg, Moscow, and New Delhi; separate business and NGO consultations; small expert gatherings on subjects including corporate law and investment; numerous meetings with government representatives in Geneva and in their home capitals, and an online forum that attracted hundreds of comments and thousands of viewers.

An Emerging Consensus

After years of lively and sometimes contentious debate, involving everyone from indigenous peoples' representatives to Wall Street lawyers, uptake of Ruggie's recommendations was widespread, as the many stakeholders who participated in the mandate's consultations felt ownership over its outcomes. Ruggie also collaborated with other standard-setting bodies, such as the International Finance Corporation, the International Standards Organisation (ISO), and the OECD to embed his work into their own.

To understand the success of the Special Representative's mandate, it is also worth considering the Guiding Principles in the context of the historical moment in which they were created: the financial crisis bringing scrutiny to corporate practices and state failures; growing economic power from non-Western countries, with companies serving as their *de facto* ambassadors; heightened transparency through technology and social media; debates over global governance within institutions like the United Nations and the G20, and over transnational issues like climate change and financial regulation.

Among those involved in the mandate over its six years, there was a palpable sense of relief at the Council's endorsement of the Guiding Principles" affirmation that consensus has been achieved from a truly global set of stakeholders representing all sectors of society. Yet there is acknowledgment that the Guiding Principles will not solve the world's problems; that there is fragility around this new-born set of standards, whose formal custody was transferred shortly after its birth with the new guardian yet to begin its work; and that the Special Representative's mandate was one phase—albeit a significant one—in a much longer journey.

The Guiding Principles

The Guiding Principles are organized by the three pillars of the "Protect, Respect and Remedy" framework that preceded them:

- The **State Duty to Protect** against human rights abuses by third parties, including business enterprises, through appropriate policies, regulation, and adjudication;
- The **Corporate Responsibility to Respect** human rights, which means that business enterprises

should act with due diligence to avoid infringing on the rights of others and to address adverse impacts with which they are involved;

- The need for greater **Access to Remedy** by victims of corporate-related abuse, both judicial and non-judicial.

The three-pillar framework emphasizes the multistakeholder nature of the issue and avoids the failed attempt of the Norms to impose an expansive array of state responsibilities onto business. This approach was welcomed by business, which felt that the Norms and the corporate social responsibility field more generally absolved governments of their responsibilities; by human rights advocates, who saw both governments and companies as equally important players; and by states, some of whom had questioned the implied suggestion of the Norms that companies assume some of their responsibilities.

The State Duty to Protect

The State Duty to Protect section of the Guiding Principles affirms states' existing obligations under international human rights law to protect people within their territory and/or jurisdiction from human rights abuses, including by non-state actors; recommends that states enforce relevant laws, provide guidance to companies, and address the common lack of policy coherence across government agencies; and emphasizes the necessity of proactive measures by states where a business receives some form of government support, and in conflict-affected areas.

Extraterritorial jurisdiction—what powers and duties governments have when companies domiciled in their countries commit or contribute to human rights abuses abroad—was the most complex and controversial issue within the State Duty to Protect pillar, as it cuts to the heart of issues of national sovereignty and the very nature of multinational business.

After much engagement with governments, legal experts, and other stakeholders, Ruggie chose to focus on the fact that states can take a number of steps with extraterritorial effect that clearly fall within the current permissible scope of their jurisdiction. In taking such an approach of clarification, Ruggie managed to avoid controversy that could have threatened overall support of his mandate, while helpfully dispelling misperceptions about the concept that had come from many corners.

The Corporate Responsibility to Respect

Ruggie defined the Corporate Responsibility to Respect as the responsibility for business not to infringe on the rights of others and address negative impacts with which they are involved. This second pillar of the Guiding Principles outlines a process for companies to "know and show" that they are meeting their responsibility to respect human rights: Companies should have a human rights policy; conduct human rights due diligence, which includes assessing actual and potential impacts, integrating human rights throughout their operations, and tracking and reporting outcomes; and remediate any adverse impacts that they have caused or contributed to.

According to the Guiding Principles, the human rights that companies must respect at a minimum are those outlined in the International Bill of Human Rights and ILO core conventions (as opposed to the limited subset of rights that the Norms named). Ruggie was careful to point out that international human rights law generally does not currently impose direct legal obligations on business enterprises (which some stakeholders disputed), although it is enshrined in domestic jurisdictions in numerous ways, such as legislation on labor standards, privacy, or land use. Rather, the "responsibility to respect human rights is a global standard of expected conduct for all business enterprises wherever they operate." While grounding a foundational principle in social norms might seem unstable, it was as clever as it was irrefutable: What company would stand up and say it *doesn't* have a responsibility not to hurt people?

On the other hand, some argued that "respect" is too *low* a bar, that companies should have so-called "positive" obligations as well including to fulfill or realize rights. Ruggie responded that the responsibility to respect is indeed "not merely a passive responsibility for firms"; and that "[t]here may be situations in which companies have additional responsibilities. But the responsibility to respect is the baseline norm for all companies in all situations." The commentary for the first Guiding Principle under this pillar states, "Addressing adverse human rights impacts requires taking adequate measures for their prevention, mitigation and, where appropriate, remediation."

Other issues debated during the development of the Corporate Responsibility to Respect principles and addressed to varying extents in the final product included the applicability of the Guiding Principles to small- and medium-sized enterprises; whether financial institutions merit special attention; and the extent of a company's responsibility for impacts occurring in its value chain.

Access to Remedy

The Access to Remedy pillar of the framework addressed both state responsibilities to provide access to effective judicial and non-judicial mechanisms, and the corporate responsibility to prevent and remediate any negative impacts that they cause or contribute to.

One subtopic within this pillar that captured broad attention for breaking new ground was the criteria for effective company-based grievance mechanisms. Such criteria were piloted by companies in different sectors and regions, and made the subject of a separate online resource.

One of the most-debated topics was the status and enforcement of the principles themselves. Business and NGO concerns alike wondered whether the Guiding Principles would be yet another voluntary code of conduct, or whether they would be enforced. Ruggie tried to move the debate beyond this voluntary-versus mandatory dichotomy: Saying that "no single silver bullet can resolve the business and human rights challenge" became a common refrain, as he tried to avoid the ill-fated Norms debate that focused on one international instrument. In his 2007 report that mapped the spectrum of ways in which corporations are held accountable for human rights abuses, he emphasized that many voluntary initiatives have accountability mechanisms. He worked to embed the Guiding Principles into other standards that have their own enforcement mechanisms, like the OECD Guidelines for Multinational Enterprises. And he emphasized that his role was to not to create international law, but to provide policy recommendations to the Council, whose member states would then be responsible for implementing his recommendations should they be adopted.

But some NGOs continued to lament the lack of an overarching accountability mechanism in the Guiding Principles themselves. At the same time, some business concerns fretted that "non-binding U.N. guidelines could inform binding common law. Or a non-binding U.N. report could inspire binding statutory law, which is after all one of the report's goals."

The Guiding Principles had to be general enough to apply to all kinds of companies in all industrial sectors and win the support of a broad range of Human Rights Council member states. As such, they are hardly an operational manual to be downloaded and implemented. As Ruggie said in his final presentation to the Human Rights Council in June, invoking Winston Churchill, "I am under no illusion that the conclusion of my mandate will bring all business and human rights challenges to an end. But Council endorsement of the Guiding Principles will mark the end of the beginning."

Workshop Summary

Workshop participants agreed that the Guiding Principles were a noteworthy development for multiple domains: for the ongoing evolution of the human rights regime; for the study of norms development; and for globalization, regulation, corporate and international law.

Today there is both excitement and apprehension about what lies ahead. The previous six years were about bringing diverse stakeholders together to converge on a set of principles; now a very different set of issues lie in wait. Participants in the workshop framed those issues in terms of 1) **defining questions,** clarifying the fundamental nature of the Guiding Principles enterprise; 2) practical questions about **implementing** the Guiding Principles; and 3) **opportunities** in the current moment, as we move from the development of the Guiding Principles into their implementation.

Defining Questions

In the workshop, participants raised a number of questions and issues on which they held divergent views. The debate made it clear that those issues need to be tackled head on—whether by the new U.N. Working Group, other actors in the field, or some combination—if the Guiding Principles are to succeed and corporate-related human rights abuses are to be prevented and addressed.

Principles versus Architecture

One fundamental question is whether the **application of human rights to business** is a natural extension of the human rights movement and architecture, or new language for describing the complex effects of globalization. This question is important for a number of reasons.

First, rights-based **discourse** is not always obviously applicable to companies—the foundational human rights instruments were written primarily by and for states—and as such can be inappropriate or constraining when applied to multinational business. More important, human rights is not just a set of vocabulary or principles, but a system that comes with its own **architecture** and enforcement mechanisms. Some human rights advocates expressed disappointment with the Guiding Principles because they thought they neither added to nor fit within that architecture: Part of the strength of human rights instruments is the potential for their enforcement, even if that potential is often not realized.

It's unclear how existing U.N. human rights mechanisms—or even a new one—could enforce the Guiding Principles, particularly those aimed at companies, which live outside of the purview of the U.N. system. Participants from all stakeholder groups suggested that if the Guiding Principles do not find their link to the U.N. architecture, they risk becoming yet another voluntary code of conduct—which would disappoint both NGOs, who want accountability, and companies, who face myriad standards and want to know which one is authoritative. Does lack of infrastructure fundamentally undermine the Guiding Principles, or is it beside the point?

Practical versus Aspirational

From the advocate point of view, another perceived weakness of the Guiding Principles is that they read as **more practical than aspirational**—not the sort of document that mobilizes citizens, as the human rights community aims to do. On the other hand, companies suggest that fully implementing a human rights due diligence system is indeed ambitious and aspirational; similarly for states to thoroughly meet their "duty to protect" as outlined in the Guiding Principles. Whether the Guiding Principles are aspirational or practical is more than just an intellectual debate, because it speaks to whether states and companies should be held accountable for their intent or their specific actions and outcomes.

Process versus Outcomes

Related to that question of what parties should be held accountable for is whether the choice of a **process-based standard** is helpful or not. Participants agreed that a process-based standard is useful from a practical perspective, for instructing companies on what to do and others on what to look for, but examples abound of good processes with poor outcomes; processes are necessary but insufficient on their own.

If companies and states are to be held accountable for outcomes rather than "just" processes, how should those outcomes be measured? The lack of **data and metrics** for the human rights impacts of business—and the dearth of requirements to **disclose** that information—was cited as a barrier to getting mainstream investors to ask the right questions and getting companies to evaluate and improve their performance.

Implementation

In discussing implementation of the Guiding Principles, the discussion ranged between the theoretical and the practical, and gravitated towards the agenda and working methods of the new U.N. Working Group on business and human rights—though many of the questions for the Working Group apply to other actors in the field as well.

There is clearly concern about where **authoritative interpretation** of the Guiding Principles will come from, to avoid the sort of "lethal mutations" that one participant warned of from other domains. The Working Group seems the obvious source, but will need to develop its own resources and credibility in order to put forth opinions that are widely accepted.

The questions that the Working Group will need to tackle will not just be about the Guiding Principles, but the serious **dilemmas** and challenges that have vexed the human rights community for decades: e.g., when rights conflict with each other, or when governments are part of the problem, for example in this context by coercing companies to violate human rights or undermining investor protection.

Due to the Working Group's limited resources and timeframe, there was discussion as to whether its focus should be on **breadth or depth** (i.e., promoting awareness of the Guiding Principles, particularly in emerging markets, or working with a smaller group of companies who are ready to delve deeply into the challenges of implementation). In either case, there was general agreement that the Working Group should continue in the mode of the Special Representative on business and human rights, who received research support from a wide variety of academics and organizations rather than conducting all of the work within his small team.

There was a great deal of discussion on what the **strategic leverage points** might be for the Working Group, i.e., what stakeholders, issues, or ways of operating would have the greatest multiplier effects: big marquee companies in select countries and the finance and technology sectors were given as possible examples.

But some expressed concern that such an approach might be too opportunistic, and avoid the necessary challenge of getting to the root causes of corporate-related abuse. For example, there is currently a great deal of focus on how multinational companies can push the Guiding Principles down through their supply chains. Is that a distraction from ensuring that governments enforce their own labor laws? The group had some debate over whether the root cause of corporate-related abuses was **states or companies,** and how much an individual's or organization's answer to that question informs strategy and tactics; but others believed the question was irrelevant since addressing the roles of both players is clearly critical.

Such questions could also be asked of other organizations, which need to work out their own **theories of change** and where they can have the greatest impact. A number of participants spoke of the need to draw upon existing research on how change occurs within organizations, and within companies in particular; and on what causes governments to change policies and behaviors, individually and collectively. Company participants spoke of their challenges working out what issues and functions are most relevant to human rights, while those involved with civil society organizations spoke of their need to effectively allocate their scarce resources—for example whether to focus on companies or states, and in those relationships how to balance advocacy versus partnership.

Related to the question of the theory of change is the question of what the right **analogy** is for business and human rights: Is it health and safety, or compliance and ethics, where activity is largely company-led and compliance-based, with culture and regulation being important components? Or is it the environment, where progress has come from convergence of the interests of companies and their investors, advocates, and (some) policymakers? Or is the right analogy the movement against child labor, where there was a clear business case for the "wrong" position, but society pushed for regulation? Numerous **legal** questions follow, such as whether safe harbor provisions might be instituted for companies that undertake human rights due diligence, as has been the case in other domains.

Participants saw all of these issues and questions related to implementation as important for both the U.N. Working Group and other stakeholders to address if the Guiding Principles are to succeed— both in terms of their status as an authoritative global standard, and for having their desired impact on the ground.

Opportunities

Despite all of the challenging questions that remain, there was a great deal of excitement among participants about what lies ahead, with the recognition that the field now moves into a very different phase. The six years that led to the Guiding Principles were about the convergence of positions into a single authoritative foundation. Now, **different skills and coalitions** will be needed for this next phase of dissemination and implementation.

Some participants expressed the belief that the prolonged debate over the Guiding Principles and associated accountability distracted the global community from the effects that companies are having on communities and individuals every day. But others countered that the Guiding Principles developed quickly compared to other instruments and norms, and that the convergence phase was absolutely critical to implementation going forward. In any case, there was hope that even with the fundamental questions that remain, the emphasis could be on **more practical** aspects of the issue going forward.

Participants thought that most of the tangible progress in the field to date had been made by a small number of multinational companies, which presented both a challenge and an opportunity in terms of creating space for **government leadership.** Participants wondered about the feasibility of a Government Leaders Initiative on Business and Human Rights, similar to business-led initiatives such as the Business Leaders Initiative on Human Rights and Global Business Initiative on Human Rights.

There was also a hope that the debate would move beyond where it has largely been focused, i.e., on extractives and manufacturing, and those impacts at the early stages of products and services. **Technology, finance, and product use** were seen as critical to bring into the debate more prominently.

There were high hopes that the U.N. Working Group would become a focal point and a catalyst for **convening** on business and human rights, for example through its Annual Forum, and for **research** on the wide range of topics that will be needed for progress going forward. Whether or not that comes to fruition, participants emphasized the need for ongoing **expert multistakeholder dialogue,** for example in the form of this workshop.

Source: Kenan Institute for Ethics, *The U.N. Guiding Principles on Business and Human Rights: Analysis and Implementation* (2012), http://kenan.ethics.duke.edu /wp-content/uploads/2012/07/UN-Guiding-Principles- on-Business-and-Human-Rights-Analysis-and- Implementation.pdf.

Note: Notes and references were removed for publication here, but are available on the book website at www.mhhe. com/busethics4e.

Reading **3-2**

The Caux Principles for Responsible Business

The Caux Round Table (March 2009)

Introduction

The Caux Round Table (CRT) Principles for Responsible Business set forth ethical norms for acceptable businesses behavior.

Trust and confidence sustain free markets and ethical business practices provide the basis for such trust and confidence. But lapses in business integrity, whether among the few or the many, compromise such trust and hence the ability of business to serve humanity's needs.

Events like the 2009 global financial crisis have highlighted the necessity of sound ethical practices across the business world. Such failures of governance and ethics cannot be tolerated as they seriously tarnish the positive contributions of responsible business to higher standards of living and the empowerment of individuals around the world.

The self-interested pursuit of profit, with no concern for other stakeholders, will ultimately lead to business failure and, at times, to counterproductive regulation. Consequently, business leaders must always assert ethical leadership so as to protect the foundations of sustainable prosperity.

It is equally clear that if capitalism is to be respected, and so sustain itself for global prosperity, it must be both responsible and moral. Business therefore needs a moral compass in addition to its practical reliance on measures of profit and loss.

The CRT Principles

The Caux Round Table's approach to responsible business consists of seven core principles as detailed below. The principles recognize that while laws and market forces are necessary, they are insufficient guides for responsible business conduct.

The principles are rooted in three ethical foundations for responsible business and for a fair and functioning society more generally, namely: responsible stewardship; living and working for mutual advantage; and the respect and protection of human dignity.

The principles also have a risk management foundation—because good ethics is good risk management. And they balance the interests of business with the aspirations of society to ensure sustainable and mutual prosperity for all.

The CRT Principles for Responsible Business are supported by more detailed Stakeholder Management Guidelines covering each key dimension of business success: customers, employees, shareholders, suppliers, competitors, and communities.

Principle 1—Respect Stakeholders Beyond Shareholders

- A responsible business acknowledges its duty to contribute value to society through the wealth and employment it creates and the products and services it provides to consumers.

- A responsible business maintains its economic health and viability not just for shareholders, but also for other stakeholders.

- A responsible business respects the interests of, and acts with honesty and fairness towards, its customers, employees, suppliers, competitors, and the broader community.

Principle 2—Contribute to Economic, Social and Environmental Development

- A responsible business recognizes that business cannot sustainably prosper in societies that are failing or lacking in economic development.

- A responsible business therefore contributes to the economic, social and environmental development of the communities in which it operates, in order to sustain its essential 'operating' capital—financial, social, environmental, and all forms of goodwill.

- A responsible business enhances society through effective and prudent use of resources, free and fair competition, and innovation in technology and business practices.

Principle 3—Respect the Letter and the Spirit of the Law

- A responsible business recognizes that some business behaviors, although legal, can nevertheless have adverse consequences for stakeholders.

- A responsible business therefore adheres to the spirit and intent behind the law, as well as the letter of the law, which requires conduct that goes beyond minimum legal obligations.

- A responsible business always operates with candor, truthfulness, and transparency, and keeps its promises.

Principle 4—Respect Rules and Conventions

- A responsible business respects the local cultures and traditions in the communities in which

it operates, consistent with fundamental principles of fairness and equality.

- A responsible business, everywhere it operates, respects all applicable national and international laws, regulations and conventions, while trading fairly and competitively.

Principle 5—Support Responsible Globalization

- A responsible business, as a participant in the global marketplace, supports open and fair multilateral trade.

- A responsible business supports reform of domestic rules and regulations where they unreasonably hinder global commerce.

Principle 6—Respect the Environment

- A responsible business protects and, where possible, improves the environment, and avoids wasteful use of resources.

- A responsible business ensures that its operations comply with best environmental management practices consistent with meeting the needs of today without compromising the needs of future generations.

Principle 7—Avoid Illicit Activities

- A responsible business does not participate in, or condone, corrupt practices, bribery, money laundering, or other illicit activities.

- A responsible business does not participate in or facilitate transactions linked to or supporting terrorist activities, drug trafficking or any other illicit activity.

- A responsible business actively supports the reduction and prevention of all such illegal and illicit activities.

Source: The Caux Round Table, www.cauxroundtable.org/ index.cfm?&menuid=8 (March 2009).

Reading **3-3**

It Seems Right in Theory but Does It Work in Practice?

Norman E. Bowie

It is not uncommon for business people, including business executives, to find the conclusions of an ethical framework as it applies to a case in business to be persuasive, but nonetheless not accept the conclusions because to do so would be impractical from a business point of view. Thus it might be right in theory but it is not practical in business. There are three great traditions in ethical framework, the virtue theory of Aristotle, the duty theory of Immanuel Kant, and the utilitarianism of Jeremy Bentham and John Stuart Mill. In recent times these traditions have been supplemented by other theories such as feminist ethics. It seems to me that if ethical framework is to serve as a foundation for business ethics, it must be the case that these traditional theories are not only persuasive as theories but also can be applied practically to actual business practice. In this essay, I will try to show how the fundamental principles of Kant's ethical framework are both theoretically persuasive and practical in a business context.

Before proceeding it is important to note that the question I am addressing is not strictly an ethical question. After all under our starting assumption business people have already agreed that as a matter of ethical framework, they are persuaded by the answer the ethical framework gives to the case at hand. They just don't think that doing what the ethical framework requires is possible in a business context. What the business person seems to want is for an answer that is both ethically justified and prudent from a business perspective. For Kant showing that something is ethically required is sufficient since morality always trumps prudence. Although Kantians may accept the moral answer as definitive for action, business people will not. If acting morally undermines my business, why should I be moral? That is the question that a business person is like to ask.

Framing the issue as ethics vs. business is an example of what R. Edward Freeman calls "the

separation thesis." By the separation thesis he means the thesis that ethical concerns and business concerns are in two separate realms. Freeman argues that business and ethics are always intertwined in business activity. A manager should strive to make business decisions that are both ethically sound and sound in business terms. In what follows I will show how Kant's theory enables managers to make decisions that are sound from both an ethical and a business point of view.

Business Decisions Should Not Be Self-Defeating

Kant's fundamental moral principle is the categorical imperative. Kant's moral imperative is categorical because it always holds—there are no "ifs, and, or buts." The classic statement of the categorical imperative is "One must always act on that maxim that one can will to be a universal law." What does Kant mean here? An illustration regarding stealing should help. Why is stealing even when one is in difficult financial circumstances wrong? Suppose one is in financial difficult circumstances and is tempted to steal? If one should decide to steal what is the principle (maxim) for such an action? It must be that "it is morally permissible for me to steal when I am in financial difficulty." Kant now requires that on the basis of rational consistency we must make my maxim "it is ok for me to steal when I am in financial difficulty" into a universal principle, "it is morally permissible for any person in financial difficulty to steal." After all what applies in one case must apply in all similar cases. However, the universal maxim that would permit stealing is self-defeating. An important point of a system of property rights is that it assumes that property rights are morally protected even if others might need the property more. To accept a maxim that permits stealing is to undermine the very system of property rights—the very property rights that the thief must presuppose in order to be a thief.

If this seems too abstract consider the rule of lining up. Suppose one is in a hurry and wonders if it would be morally permissible to cut in line? The maxim for that action would be "it is morally permissible to cut in line when one is in a hurry." However, the universal version of that maxim is that "It is morally permissible for anyone to cut in line when he or she is in a hurry." But that maxim is self-defeating. If anyone could cut in line when he or she was in a hurry, the very notion of lining up would make no sense. A similar argument shows that lying or the breaking of contracts is wrong.

Kant's reasoning shows why free riding is wrong. A free rider benefits when others follow the rule, but the free rider does not. If everyone behaved as the free rider (if the free riding maxim were made universal), there could be no free riding because you would no longer have the rule. Universal free riding on a rule makes the rule nugatory. Put it another way, the free rider is not making a contribution to the institution that relies on the contributions of those participating in the institution—a contribution the free rider agreed to make when he or she participated in the institution. Now if a maxim permitting free riding were universalized, the institution itself would be undermined.

Kant's reasoning here is highly practical in business. After the collapse of the communist economic system in Russia, one of the tasks Russia had was to establish a stock market. However, the companies that were listed on the stock market did not give out accurate financial information. In other words these companies were not transparent and there was no regulatory apparatus in place to make them transparent. But a stock market can only exist if there is a reasonable amount of transparency regarding the financials of the listed companies. Thus the initial attempts at a stock market fell short; the stock market in Russia only came into existence when a number of companies were able to establish themselves as truth tellers about their financial condition.

Poland had a similar difficulty in establishing a national banking system. The first attempt to establish a national bank failed because people did not pay back their loans. If enough people fail to pay their loans, the bank cannot stay in business.

Kant's reasoning is also relevant when one examines the string of financial scandals in the United States culminating in the subprime lending crisis of 2007–2008. The categorical imperative shows why breaking a promise is wrong. If a maxim that permitted promise breaking were made universal, then promises would have no point. A promise breaker can only succeed if most people keep their promises. If anyone could break his or her promise whenever it was convenient, then no one would make promises. The breaking of contracts is also wrong for the same reason.

Financial markets work best when there is maximum transparency. The greater the amount of knowledge, the easier it is to assign risk. Increasing transparency makes markets more efficient. Thus participants in the financial markets support rules that increase transparency. What contributed to the Enron debacle was the fact that off balance sheet entities were created that hid Enron's risks. Once the risks came to light, Enron collapsed very quickly. Something similar happened in the subprime mortgage crisis. Mortgages with varying degrees of risk were bundled together in ways that made in very difficult to determine the underlying value of the assets behind the mortgages. Once the housing market turned and prices began to fall, investors began to worry about the risk but were unable to determine what their risks were. What amounted to a run on the bank occurred with the firm Bear Stearns. It was widely rumored that Lehman Brothers and even Merrill Lynch might go under. Only action by the Federal Reserve provided sufficient capital to prevent a financial collapse. Nonetheless financial institutions lost hundreds of billions of dollars. Financial markets require transparency. Universalizing actions that undermine transparency undermine financial markets. When a tipping point is reached, financial markets freeze up and cease to function. Participants in markets are morally required to support transparency.

Both academics and practitioners concerned with corporate strategy have discovered the role of trust as a significant element of competitive advantage.

Let us define a trusting relationship as one where those in the relationship will not take undue advantage of opportunistic situations. In business, relationships built on trust provide competitive advantage in two basic ways. First, within a firm, trusting relationships make the firm more efficient. For example, when there is trust between employers and employees, there is less monitoring, some behavior may not need to be monitored at all and there is less need for detailed information. The relation between an employer and an employee can be a mentoring relationship rather than simply a monitored relationship. As a result teamwork is more easily achieved. All of this creates a competitive advantage for those companies that pursue enlightened human resource management based on trust.

Another way of illustrating the competitive advantage of trust relationships is to look at a common management problem. With a commission system, sales people are given incentives to sell as much of a product as they can without regard to the ability of the manufacturing unit of the business to manufacture the product in a timely manner. If a manager wants to build a cooperative relation between sales and manufacturing, then he or she must think carefully about the use of commissions as a way to reward sales. Yet another illustration is provided by a long-standing tradition in American business to separate the design process from manufacturing. Thus engineers create prototypes that are then given to manufacturing to produce. However, since there was no communication between design and manufacturing, inevitably there are "bugs" that need to

be worked out. Working out the bugs is an unnecessary transaction cost that could be greatly mitigated or even avoided if engineering and manufacturing worked together through both the design and the manufacturing stage. The Japanese auto manufacturers learned this early and the efficiencies that resulted helped Japan seize extensive market share at the expense of American automobile manufacturers.

It may seem that these arguments are purely consequentialist. They are consequentialist but not purely so. Consider the following argument that shows the power of Kant's categorical imperative here.

1. A business that fails to be competitive will go out of business.
2. A person or group of persons who start a business and invest in it, do not want it to go out of business.
3. Building relationships of trust are necessary if the business is to be competitive.
4. Therefore intentional actions that fail to develop these trust relationships involve the business people in self-defeating actions. The actors both want the business to survive and by consciously failing to take the actions necessary for it to survive, they show that they do not want it to survive and that is surely self-defeating behavior.

Thus Kant's categorical imperative shows that trusting relationships are required on both utilitarian grounds and on Kantian grounds as well.

Source: The ideas in the essay are adapted from my book *Business Ethics: A Kantian Perspective,* Blackwell Publishers, 1999.

Reading **3-4**

Business Decisions Should Not Violate the Humanity of a Person

Norman E. Bowie

Kant's ethical framework involves more than a formal test that ethical decisions should not be self-defeating. After all, suppose that treating employees simply as a cost and thus as interchangeable with capital and machinery gave business a

competitive advantage. Using an argument similar to the one I used for trusting relationships I could show that such treatment of people would be morally required. But, according to Kant, treating employees in that way would be immoral.

Kant has a second formulation of the categorical imperative which says, "Act so that you treat humanity, whether in your own person or in that of another, always as an end and never as a means merely." To act in accord with this formulation of the categorical imperative, one must treat persons with respect. Why? Because persons have a dignity that Kant said was beyond price. That is why Kant would not permit employers to treat employees as if they were simply on a par with capital or machinery—as if they were mere factors of production.

Kant argued that only human beings were free and that as a result of being free, they could act rationally, by which Kant meant that could act according to laws of their own making. As free and rational creatures, they could also be held responsible for their actions. Since persons can be held responsible, they can be held subject to moral law. It is the fact that persons are free, rational, responsible beings capable of acting morally that gives them the dignity that is beyond price.

Kant believed that each of us recognizes that we have dignity that is entitled to respect. Indeed, in contemporary society, failure to respect a person can easily result in the disrespected person acting angrily or even violently against those who show disrespect. Since each of us feels entitled to respect and is justified in this feeling, then as a matter of logic each of us must respect those who are like us, namely we must respect other persons. Since the obligation of respect is a matter of consistency, the first and second formulations of the categorical imperative are linked.

The obligation to respect persons has direct application to business and business ethics. Management actions that coerce people or deceive them do not treat employees with respect. Coercion is a direct denial of autonomy and deception also robs a person of his or her freedom since alternatives that would be available to a person are kept off the table. The courts have recognized that coercion is a serious violation of ethics. In the classic case of *Henningsen vs. Bloomfield Motors* the court voided standardized warranties that limited liability in the light of injury from defective automobiles. The court said, "The warranty before us is a standardized form designed for mass use. It is imposed on the automobile consumer. He takes it or leaves it. No bargaining is engaged in with respect to it."

The court must have reasoned that the take it or leave it alternative is analogous to the demand of the armed robber, "your money or your life." Although there is a choice here, it is a coerced choice.

Certain business practices support respecting the humanity of a person. Open book management is a technique that in effect turns everyone in the business into a chief finance officer (CFO). Under this technique all employees receive all the numbers that are relevant to the business. In this way they understand the business and are better able to act for the longer term success of the business. Open book management has a number of devotees and is increasingly adopted. Open book management in conjunction with other enlightened management practices empowers employees and empowerment is one way of showing that the employee is respected. Another way to show respect for employees is to provide them with meaningful work. Empowerment is one of the characteristics of meaningful work. A complete list of the characteristics of meaningful work is beyond the scope of this essay, but suffice it to say, if employees believed their work was meaningful, some popular phrases or references would not be so ubiquitous. There would not be as many references to TGIF or to Monday as blue Monday or Wednesday as hump day (halfway to TGIF). Empowered employees who believe they are making a contribution to the public good through their work are highly motivated and contribute mightily to the success of the business enterprise. What is right in ethical framework in this case contributes to successful business practice.

Business Should Be Seen as a Moral as Well as an Economic Community

If employees deserve a kind of respect that capital and machinery does not, then what should a business look like from the point of view of a Kantian? Kant's third formulation of the categorical imperative helps us understand what such a business should look like. Kant says that we should act as if we were a member of an ideal kingdom of ends in which we were both subject and sovereign at the same time. Substitute "moral organization" for "ideal kingdom of ends." How should such an organization be run? Well, if the rules for running the organization are to be morally justified, they would have to be rules that everyone in the organization could accept. In that way each person would be both subject and sovereign with respect to the rules.

Kant's ideas here are a moral challenge to hierarchical theories of management—a challenge to a management philosophy that says to the employee, "Yours is not to question why, but simply do or die." Kant's moral theory is also a challenge to the pervasive doctrine of employment at will—a doctrine which says that you can be fired for any reason, good, bad, or morally unjustifiable reason. For Kant unjustifiable actions cannot be moral actions. What Kant's third formulation requires is that employees have a say in the organization's rules and procedures. The work of psychologists has shown that Kant's moral demands are sound from a practical point of view. Some of the pioneering work here has been done by Chris Argyris, one of the most consistent critics of hierarchical management. Employees who are given a say are more highly motivated employees and highly motivated employees contribute to the bottom line of the business. Also, teamwork and cooperation, which are so highly valued in today's organization, require that members of the organization have a voice in how the organization is run and in the decisions it makes.

Also, a Kantian who views the organization from the perspective of an ideal kingdom of ends will not treat the organization as a mere instrument for their own personal use. If the individuals in an organization view it purely instrumentally, these individuals are predisposed to behave in ways that harm organizational integrity. The insight of the contemporary Kantian John Rawls that organizations are social unions constituted by certain norms is useful here. Organizations are not mere instruments for achieving individual goals. To develop this notion of a social union, Rawls contrasts two views of how human society is held together: In the private view human beings form social institutions after calculating that it would be advantageous to do so; in the social view human beings form social institutions because they share final ends and value common institutions and activities as intrinsically good. In a social union, cooperation is a key element of success because each individual in a social union knows that he cannot achieve his interests within the group by himself. The cooperation of others is necessary as it provides stability to the organization, enables it to endure, and enables individuals both to realize their potential and to see the qualities of others that lead to organizational success. Rawls's notion of a social union has much in common with Kant's ideal kingdom of ends.

This analysis can be applied directly to the issue of excessive executive compensation and to the endless chain of corporate scandals from 2001 to the 2007–2008 sub-prime mess. Many have reacted to the recent wave of corporate scandals by saying that executives are overly greedy: a character flaw. But why have some executives become greedy? The explanation is in the distinction between viewing an organization as merely an instrument to satisfying one's individual needs and seeing an organization as a social union. If the organization is seen as a means to personal enrichment and not seen as a cooperative enterprise of all those in the organization, it should come as no surprise that the executives of such an organization feel entitled to the rewards. Psychological theorists have shown that people tend to take credit when things go well and blame bad luck or circumstances beyond one's control when things go badly. Thus a CEO takes all the credit when an organization performs well but blames the general economy or other factors when things go poorly. This human tendency is predictable when executives look at organizations instrumentally.

Conclusion

This essay provides a brief tour through Kantian ethical framework and shows how it is both theoretically sound and practical. At least with Kantian ethics there need be no divergence between good theory and sound practice.

Source: The ideas in the essay are adapted from my book *Business Ethics: A Kantian Perspective,* Blackwell Publishers, 1999.

Chapter 4

The Corporate Culture—Impact and Implications

Although gold dust is precious, when it gets in your eyes it obstructs your vision.

Hsi-Tang Chih Tsang, renowned Zen master

Our plans miscarry because they have no aim. When a person does not know what harbor he [or she] is making for, no wind is the right wind.

Seneca

There is nothing more difficult to carry out, nor more doubtful of success, nor more dangerous to handle, than to initiate a new order of things.

Machiavelli

Creating an Ethics Program

Imagine that you work in the Human Resources department of your company. Your CEO has asked the HR department to develop an ethics program for the firm, and you have been assigned responsibility for creating it. You have been asked to report back to your CEO in two weeks with a draft version of a code of ethics for the company, a summary of other elements that the ethics program will include, and a proposal for how you will be able to assess whether the program is working. Your CEO also asks that you come prepared to explain what role she can play in promoting ethics and to ensure the success of the ethics program.

You begin your research and quickly find that there are a number of potentially desirable and somewhat overlapping outcomes of effective ethics programs:

1. Discovery of unethical/illegal behavior and reduction of meltdowns, resulting in avoidance or reduction of fines/criminal charges (also applies to several of the items included below):
2. Awareness of ethical and legal issues.
3. A resource for guidance and advice.
4. Accurate reports of wrongdoing.
5. Greater customer loyalty, resulting in increased sales and better reputation.
6. Incorporation of values in decision processes.
7. Greater employee commitment and loyalty to the organization, resulting in higher productivity.
8. Satisfaction of external and internal stakeholder needs (all resulting in more effective financial performance).

Play the role of this HR person in several different types of businesses: a fast-food restaurant, an automobile dealership, a retail store selling consumer electronics, a government agency, and a large international corporation.[1]

- List the issues you think should be addressed in a code of ethics.
- Other than a code of ethics, what other elements would you include in an ethics program?
- How will you define "success"? Are there any facts that you will need to gather to make this judgment?
- How would you measure success along the way? How will you measure whether your ethics program is "working" before you reach any end objective?
- Whom will you define as your primary stakeholders?
- What are the interests of your stakeholders in your program and what are the impacts of your program on each stakeholder? How might the measurement of the program's success influence the type of people attracted to the firm or people who are most motivated within your organization?
- How will you answer the CEO's questions about her own role in promoting ethics?

✳ Chapter Objectives

After reading this chapter, you will be able to:

1. Define corporate culture.
2. Explain how corporate culture impacts ethical decision making.
3. Discuss the differences between a compliance-based culture and a values-based culture.
4. Discuss the role of corporate leadership in establishing the culture.
5. Explain the difference between effective leaders and ethical leaders.
6. Discuss the role of mission statements and codes in creating an ethical corporate culture.
7. Explain how various reporting mechanisms such as ethics hotlines and ombudspersons can help integrate ethics within a firm.
8. Discuss the role of assessing, monitoring, and auditing the culture and ethics program.
9. Explain how culture can be enforced via governmental regulation.

What Is Corporate Culture?

This chapter examines the ways in which corporations develop ethical cultures. Cultures in organizations encourage and support individuals in making ethically responsible decisions—or they do not! The ethical decision-making model emphasizes the individual responsibility for the decisions they make in business. These decisions impact your personal integrity and also have consequences for many stakeholders with whom business organizations interact.

But, personal decision making does not exist in a vacuum. Decision making within a firm is influenced, limited, shaped, and, in some cases, virtually determined by the corporate culture of the firm. Individuals can be helped—or hindered—in making the "right" or "wrong" decision (according to their own values) by the expectations, values, and structure of the organization in which they live and work. We will explore in this chapter some of the major issues surrounding the development, influence, and management of a corporate culture, as well as the role of business leaders in creating, enhancing, and preserving cultures that support ethical behavior.

Even in this age of decentralized corporations and other institutions, there remains a sense of culture in organizations. This is especially true in small local firms, but it is just as true of major global corporations such as Google or BMW. Despite the fact that corporations have many locations, with diverse employee groups and management styles, an individual working for a large global firm in one country will share various aspects of her or his working culture with someone working for the same firm halfway around the world. This is not to say that their working environments cannot be wholly different in many regards; the corporate culture, however, survives the distance and differences.

FIGURE 4.1

OBJECTIVE

culture
A shared pattern of beliefs, expectations, and meanings that influences and guides the thinking and behaviors of the members of a particular group.

What do we mean by *corporate culture*? Every organization has a **culture** fashioned by a shared pattern of beliefs, expectations, and meanings that influences and guides the thinking and behaviors of the members of that organization. While culture shapes the people who are members of the organization, it is also shaped by the people who make up that organization. (See Figure 4.1.) Consider how your own company or organization or school, dormitory, or fraternity/sorority differs from a similar one. Is there a "type" of person who is stereotypical of your organization, dormitory, or fraternity/sorority? Are there unspoken but still persuasive standards and expectations that shape students at your school or workplace? How would you be different if you had chosen a different university, joined a different fraternity or sorority, or had participated in a different organization? (See the Reality Check "Built to Last.")

If culture involved a shared pattern of beliefs, expectations, and meanings, then we will find it at different levels including:

- religious, ethnic, linguistic affiliation
- generation
- gender
- social class
- organization/corporate
- family

The cultural elements might then be illustrated by various characteristics such as language, the use of space, perceptions of time, the interpretation of nonverbal behaviors, the importance of hierarchy, the definition of gender roles and criteria for success, among many others. The most well-known scholar in national culture research is Geert Hofstede. Though somewhat controversial, he organized national cultures into six "dimensions" or categories of predispositions.

1. *Power distance:* The distance between individuals at different levels of a hierarchy (more equal = low power distance).
2. *Individualism vs. collectivism:* The degree to which people prefer to act individually or in groups.

3. *Uncertainty avoidance:* The extent to which people are comfortable with uncertainty, ambiguity, change, and risks.

4. *Time and order orientation:* A high long-term orientation (LTO) suggests a comfort with long-term commitments, traditions, and rewards linked to hard work, strong relationships, and status. A low LTO indicates that change may occur more rapidly.

5. *Masculinity vs. femininity:* A low masculinity score indicates greater equality, stronger maintenance of warm personal relationships, service, care for the weak, solidarity. A high masculinity score suggests a strong culture of assertiveness, success, and competition.

6. *Indulgent vs. restrained:* The extent to which people try to control their desires and impulses.

Hofstede validated his country scores across over 400 measures from other sources. However, critics contend that his resulting culture divisions remain based on generalizations, if not outright stereotypes. Further, while our national cultures certainly are important to our understanding of international business and each other, it does not explain everything that is different from one place and people to another. Hofstede focused his work during a single period of time, they argue, and a particular global firm (IBM). However, to be fair his results have been replicated many times since. Critics continue their challenges, explaining that his perspective is biased by his Western views and limited number of countries included. Take all of these challenges into account as you consider his conclusions and read Dr. Geetanee Napal's account of her experiences living and working in Mauritius in Reading 4-1, "When Ethical Issues Derive from Cultural Thinking," at the end of this chapter.

Just as there are national cultures, businesses also have unspoken, yet influential standards and expectations. IBM was once famous for a culture in which highly starched white shirts and ties were part of the required dress code. To the contrary, many software and technology companies today have reputations for cultures of informality and playfulness. Some companies have a straight nine-to-five work schedule; others expect employees to work long hours and on weekends. A person who joins the second type of firm with a "nine-to-five attitude," intending to leave as the clock strikes five, might not "fit" and is likely not to last long. The same might hold true for a firm's values. If you join a firm with a culture that supports values other than those with which you are comfortable, there will be values conflicts—for better or worse.

No culture, in business or elsewhere, is static. Cultures change; but modifying culture—indeed, having any impact on it at all—is a bit like moving an iceberg. The iceberg is always moving and if you ignore it the iceberg will continue to float with whatever currents hold sway at the moment. One person cannot alter its course alone; but strong leaders—sometimes from within, but often at the top—can have a significant impact on a culture. A strong business leader can certainly have a significant impact on a corporate culture.

A firm's culture can be its sustaining value, offering it direction and stability during challenging times, or it can prevent a firm from responding to challenges in creative and timely ways. For example, some point to Toyota's culture—embodied in "The 14 Principles of the Toyota Way"—as the basis for its high quality and consistent customer satisfaction.[2] Others suggest that the "Toyota Way" prevented the company from responding to reports of unintended acceleration in many of its vehicles in a responsible, swift, effective, and transparent way. Some even argue that this is due to a cultural barrier in translating the traditional Japanese components of the "Toyota Way" to Western employees, thus causing further mishaps.[3]

"Since Toyota's founding, we have adhered to the core principle of contributing to society through the practice of manufacturing high-quality products and services. Our business practices and activities based on this core principle created values, beliefs and business methods that over the years have become a source of competitive advantage. These are the managerial values and business methods that are known collectively as the Toyota Way," explains Fujio Cho, then-president of Toyota (from *The Toyota Way;* see the Reality Check "Walk This Way: The Toyota Way").

The stability that a corporate culture provides can be a benefit at one time and a barrier to success at another time. Review the 14 Principles of the Toyota Way in the Reality Check "Walk This Way: The Toyota Way" and reflect on which might have contributed to a culture of high-quality products and which might have contributed to a culture of defensiveness, secrecy, and denial.

While some corporate cultures are defined from the top-down, others are developed by the employees themselves. At Zappos, the employees persuaded CEO Tony Hsieh to establish a code of ethics. He did so by e-mailing all employees in the company to ask them what they thought were the core values of Zappos. His e-mail resulted in 10 "Core Values," which represent a strong emphasis on employee and customer satisfaction.[4] Take a look at the Reality Check "Living Our Core Values" and consider how those values may have been influenced by employee input. What values do you think you might have emphasized as an employee responding to your CEO?

In 2010, Zappos demonstrated the power of its Core Values when a computer glitch emerged on 6pm.com, a Zappos-owned bargain retailer. A flaw in the website caused the price of every product on the site to be listed as $49.95 (this was not the correct price, of course). Within six hours of discovering the error, Zappos's employees had fixed the glitch. But the company agreed to honor every transaction that occurred during those six hours, costing Zappos over $1.6 million! Zappos lived its core values, both continuing to build open and honest relationships with communication by honoring its communication during those six hours, and also delivering WOW through its reliable service.[5]

Defining the specific culture within an organization is not an easy task since it is partially based on each participant's perception of the culture. In fact, perception may actually impact the culture in a circular way—a culture exists, we perceive it to be a certain type of culture, we respond to the culture on the basis

Reality Check *Built to Last*

Does a corporate culture matter? James Collins and Jerry Porras, authors of the best-selling book *Built to Last: Successful Habits of Visionary Companies,* researched dozens of very successful companies looking for common practices that might explain their success. These companies not only have outperformed their competitors in financial terms; they have outperformed their competition financially *over the long term.* On average, the companies Collins and Porras studied were more than 100 years old. Among their key findings was the fact that the truly exceptional and sustainable companies all placed great emphasis on a set of core values. These core values are described as the "essential and enduring tenets" that help define the company and are "not to be compromised for financial gain or short-term expediency."[6]

Collins and Porras cite numerous examples of core values that were articulated and promoted by the founders and CEOs of such companies as IBM, Johnson & Johnson, Hewlett-Packard, Procter & Gamble, Walmart, Merck, Motorola, Sony, Walt Disney, General Electric, and Philip Morris (now called Altria). Some companies made "a commitment to customers" their core value, while others focused on employees, their products, innovation, or even risk-taking. The common theme was that core values and a clear corporate purpose, which together are described as the organization's core ideology, were essential elements of sustainable and financially successful companies.

More recently, in his book *How the Mighty Fall: And Why Some Companies Never Give In,* Collins emphasized the importance of core values in staving off corporate decline. His research reveals that key clues to corporate decline include when people cannot easily articulate what the organization stands for, where core values have eroded to the point of irrelevance, and when the organization has become "just another place to work." It is at this point where employees lose faith in their ability to triumph and prevail. Instead of passionately believing in the organization's core values and purpose, employees become distrustful, regarding visions and values as little more than PR and rhetoric.[7]

Discussing a corporation's "culture" is a way of saying that a corporation has a set of identifiable values. All of the companies that Collins and Porras described are known for having strong corporate cultures and a clear set of values. In more recent research, Harvard professors Jim Heskett and Earl Sasser, along with coauthor Joe Wheeler,

strongly support the conclusions reached by Collins and Porras. In their 2008 book *The Ownership Quotient* they connect strong, adaptive cultures to the valuable corporate outcomes of innovation, productivity, and a sense of ownership among employees and customers. By analyzing traits that the authors found common to these organizations, we can learn much about what sustains them.

1. Leadership is critical in codifying and maintaining an organizational purpose, values, and vision. Leaders must set the example by living the elements of culture.

2. Like anything worthwhile, culture is something in which you invest.

3. Employees at all levels in an organization notice and validate the elements of culture.

4. Organizations with clearly codified cultures enjoy labor cost advantages.

5. Organizations with clearly codified and enforced cultures enjoy great employee and customer loyalty.

6. An operating strategy based on a strong, effective culture is selective of prospective customers.

7. The result of these cultural elements is "the best serving the best."

8. This operating strategy becomes a self-reinforcing source of operating leverage, which must be managed carefully to make sure that it does not result in the development of dogmatic cults with little capacity for change.

9. Organizations with strong and adaptive cultures foster effective succession in the leadership ranks.

10. Cultures can sour.[8]

Not only does a strong corporate culture create a sense of ownership among employees, but it also results in measurable financial returns. Haskett argues in his 2011 book, *The Culture Cycle: How to Shape the Unseen Force That Transforms Performance,* that an effective culture can account for a 20 to 30 percent differential in financial performance over companies without strong cultures! Haskett used what he calls a **"Four R Economic Model"** to measure a culture's impact on the bottom line. The Four Rs include Referrals, Retention, Returns to labor, and Relationships with customers. These variables prove how important a strong corporate culture can be to the ultimate financial performance of a successful organization.[9]

Reality Check *Walk This Way: The Toyota Way*

The 14 Principles of the Toyota Way constitute Toyota's system of continuous improvement in production and management.

1. Base your management decisions on a long-term philosophy, even at the expense of short-term financial goals.
2. Create a continuous process flow to bring problems to the surface.
3. Use "pull" systems to avoid overproduction.
4. Level out the workload (*heijunka*). (Work like the tortoise, not the hare.)
5. Build a culture of stopping to fix problems, to get quality right the first time.
6. Standardized tasks and processes are the foundation for continuous improvement and employee empowerment.
7. Use visual control so no problems are hidden.
8. Use only reliable, thoroughly tested technology that serves your people and processes.
9. Grow leaders who thoroughly understand the work, live the philosophy, and teach it to others.
10. Develop exceptional people and teams who follow your company's philosophy.
11. Respect your extended network of partners and suppliers by challenging them and helping them improve.
12. Go and see for yourself to thoroughly understand the situation (*genchi genbutsu*).
13. Make decisions slowly by consensus, thoroughly considering all options; implement decisions rapidly (*nemawashi*).
14. Become a learning organization through relentless reflection (*hansei*) and continuous improvement (*kaizen*).

Source: Jeffrey K. Liker, *The Toyota Way: 14 Management Principles from the World's Greatest Manufacturer* (New York: McGraw-Hill, 2004).

Reality Check *Living Our Core Values*

Zappos's Core Values emphasize its commitment to its customers and also to its employees through integrity and honesty, based on input received from its employees.

ZAPPOS CORE VALUES

1) Deliver WOW Through Service.
2) Embrace and Drive Change.
3) Create Fun and a Little Weirdness.
4) Be Adventurous, Creative, and Open-Minded.
5) Pursue Growth and Learning.
6) Build Open and Honest Relationships With Communication.
7) Build a Positive Team and Family Spirit.
8) Do More With Less.
9) Be Passionate and Determined.
10) Be Humble.

Source: Zappos.com, Inc., *Code of Business Conduct and Ethics* (May 1, 2010), www.zappos.com/c/code-of-conduct (accessed August 2, 2014).

of our perception, and we thereby impact others' experience of the culture. Several of the elements that are easiest to perceive, such as attitudes and behaviors, are only a small fraction of the elements that comprise the culture. In addition, culture is present in and can be determined by exploring any of the following, among others:

- tempo of work
- the organization's approach to humor

FIGURE 4.2

- methods of problem solving
- the competitive environment
- incentives
- individual autonomy
- hierarchical structure

Even with this list of cultural elements, it can be difficult for individuals in a firm to identify the specific characteristics of the culture within which they work. That phenomenon is best illustrated by the cartoon in Figure 4.2. Culture becomes so much a part of the environment that participants do not even notice its existence. Consider the culture you experience within your family. Often, it is only when you first move away from your family (when you go off to college, for example) that you can recognize that your family has its own culture. As you delve into the quirky particularities of your family's relationships, choices, preferences, communication styles, even gift-giving practices, you will notice that each family has a culture that is distinct and self-perpetuating. It is the same with business.

Culture and Ethics

OBJECTIVE

How, exactly, does the notion of culture connect with ethics? More specifically, what role does corporate culture play in business ethics? We can answer these questions by reflecting on several topics introduced previously.

In chapter 1, we considered the law's limitations in ensuring ethical compliance. For example, U.S. law requires a business to make reasonable accommodations for employees with disabilities. But the law can be ambiguous in determining whether a business should make a reasonable accommodation for an employee with allergies, depression, dyslexia, arthritis, hearing loss, or high blood pressure.

In situations where the law provides an incomplete answer for ethical decision making, the business culture is likely to be the determining factor in the decision. Ethical businesses must find ways to encourage, to shape, and to allow ethically responsible decisions.

Each of the factors in the decision-making model we introduced in chapter 2, from fact gathering through moral imagination to assessment, can be supported or discouraged by the environment in which the decision is made. An ethical environment, or culture, would be one in which employees are empowered and expected to act in ethically responsible ways, even when the law does not require it. Later in this chapter, we will examine types of cultures and various ways in which a corporation can create or maintain a culture that encourages ethical action. But to understand that cultures can influence some types of behaviors and discourage others, consider as an example two organizational approaches to the relief efforts following Hurricane Katrina in September 2005, and then how FEMA learned from its mistakes in connection with Hurricane Sandy in 2012.

The Federal Emergency Management Agency (FEMA) was charged with overall responsibility for the government's response to Hurricane Katrina in 2005. FEMA was created in 1979 when several governmental agencies, ranging from fire prevention, to insurance, to civil defense, were merged into one larger agency. FEMA itself was later subsumed into the federal Department of Homeland Security. By all accounts at the time of the hurricane, FEMA was an enormous, bureaucratic, hierarchical organization with a ton of rules and procedures that were required for every decision; and almost all of them needed approval from people in authority. At one point, emergency personnel were delayed in reaching the hurricane area for days because FEMA rules required that they first attend mandatory training sessions on preventing sexual harassment in the workplace— unquestionably important, of course, but perhaps that training might have taken place after this particular *emergency* situation.

Despite years of preparation and planning, the magnitude of the hurricane and resultant flooding overwhelmed FEMA's ability to respond and FEMA's bureaucracy seemed incapable of acting with any discretion. Temporary homes and supplies, despite being stored nearby, were not moved into the area for months after the storm because those in authority had not yet given approval. Days after the hurricane, while television reports showed thousands of people stranded at the New Orleans convention center, FEMA director Michael Brown claimed that he had learned of these survivors only from a reporter's question. The organization seemed unable to move information up to decision makers; and lower-level managers lacked authority to decide for themselves.

Analyzed according to the theories from chapter 3, the culture lacked ethical justification as well. Explored from a utilitarian perspective, it certainly was not a culture that revolved around the consequences of its decision-making process. While the ultimate decision might have incorporated this type of consideration, the culture itself did not place great weight on the impact of its process on its stakeholders. Human well-being, especially the health and dignity of the people affected by the tragedy, was not given the highest priority. Given this omission, one might look at whether some overarching universal principle or right was protected by the hierarchical decision-making process enforced during the time following the hurricane. Surely, FEMA would point to its strict adherence to the law; but those who might otherwise have made decisions in a more autonomous manner would have pointed instead to the "higher" values of health and human dignity, along with FEMA's ultimate duty to serve its mission.

In comparison to FEMA, the U.S. Coast Guard is an organization with similar responsibilities for search and rescue during emergency situations. In fact, FEMA director Michael Brown was eventually removed from his position and replaced by a Coast Guard admiral. The Coast Guard has a reputation for being a less bureaucratic organization and its unofficial motto is "rescue first, and get permission later," reflecting a far more utilitarian perspective to its mission. The Coast Guard empowers frontline individuals to solve problems without waiting for superiors to make decisions or to give directions. Imagine how the same person working in either of these organizations would approach a decision—and whom that person might perceive to be her or his primary stakeholders—and you will have some idea of the importance of organizational culture.

It is fair to say that FEMA and the Coast Guard are two very similar organizations with similar missions, rules, and legal regulations, but they have significantly different cultures. The decisions made throughout both organizations reflect the culture of each. The attitudes, expectations, and habits encouraged and reinforced in the two agencies reflect the differences of culture.

FEMA took to heart its failures—both actual and perceived—during Hurricane Katrina and made substantial changes to its organizational culture in order to better respond to future disasters. Nowhere is this better seen than its response to Hurricane Sandy, which blasted the Eastern Seaboard of the United States during fall 2012. As a result of legislation, FEMA reorganized prior to Sandy in order to reduce the bureaucratic red tape that delayed an immediate response during prior disasters.[10] In contrast to its efforts during Katrina, FEMA was better able during Sandy to stockpile and place supplies strategically in advance, plus it initialized the flow of federal money well before the hurricane hit shore. FEMA officials also established better relationships with local authorities and allowed them to make immediate decisions on the ground.[11] Many of these effective changes came from a new leader, now required by legislation to have at least five years of disaster response experience.[12] These changes demonstrate many of the key components to creating an effective organizational culture: strong, focused leadership, being proactive rather than reactive, and creating habits that place stakeholder satisfaction at the heart of the organization's mission.

The notion of expectations and habits is linked closely to a topic raised in our discussion of the philosophical foundations of ethics. Chapter 3 introduced the ethics of virtue and described the virtues as character traits and habits. The cultivation of habits, including the cultivation of ethical virtue, is greatly shaped by the culture in which one lives. When we talk about decision making, it is easy to think in terms of a rational, deliberative process in which a person consciously deliberates about and weighs each alternative before acting. But the virtue ethics tradition reminds us that our decisions and our actions are very often less deliberate than that. We are as likely to act out of habit and based on character as we are to act after careful deliberations. So the question of where we get our habits and character is all-important.

Part of the answer surely is that we can choose to develop some habits rather than others. But, it is also clear that our habits are shaped and formed by education and training—by culture. This education takes place in every social environment, ranging from our families and religions, to entire societies and cultures. It also takes place in the workplace, where individuals quickly learn behaviors that are appropriate and expected and through which they get rewarded and promoted. Intentionally or not, business institutions provide an environment in which habits are formed and virtues, or vices, are created.

The effect of this workplace culture on decision making cannot be overemphasized. The Ethics Resource Center (ERC) reports that "by every measure, strong ethics programs and strong ethics cultures produce substantially better outcomes—less pressure, less misconduct, higher reporting, and less retaliation—than in weaker ethical environments."[13] It is not difficult to see, therefore, that an ethical culture can have a direct and practical impact on the bottom line. Research supports this impact; when indexed together, the publicly traded businesses on the Ethisphere Institute's World's Most Ethical Companies list regularly outperforms other major indices, including the S&P 500.[14] If attended to and supported, a strong ethical culture can serve as a deterrent to stakeholder damage and improve bottom-line sustainability. Alex Brigham, executive director of the Ethisphere Institute, also states that "many companies promote [their 'World's Most Ethical Company' designation] in their recruitment materials, as studies show that employees increasingly want to work for an organization that aligns with their own personal values. They are more loyal to such organizations."[15] If ignored, the culture could instead reinforce a perception that "anything goes," and "any way to a better bottom line is acceptable," destroying long-term sustainability in both financial performance and employee retention/recruitment. See, also, how the devastating impact is not limited to a single industry or type of business, as is demonstrated by the Reality Check "Ignore at Your Peril!"

Chris MacDonald suggests in Reading 4-5, "Greg Smith, Goldman Sachs, and the Importance of Corporate Culture," that perhaps Goldman allowed its attention to drift away from its culture, and it suffered as a result. Though MacDonald acknowledges that Smith's account of his personal experiences at Goldman are simply that—the account of *one professional's* experiences within an organization—he also recounts that there have been other stories of challenging circumstances involving the organization. Maybe corporate culture is one example that proves the adage "where there's smoke, there's fire" because the perception is more important than the reality with regard to influencing decision making. MacDonald highlights why attention to these issues is so vital.

Responsibility for creating and sustaining such ethical corporate cultures rests on business leaders. In fact, former Johnson & Johnson CEO and chair Ralph

Consider the costs involved in the following examples of unethical behavior:

- **HSBC:** Fined $470 million for "abusive mortgage practices" in connection with the 2007–2009 housing crisis. This sanction follows a 2013 fine for $2.46 billion for violating federal securities laws, *after* having paid $1.9 billion in 2012 for poor anti–money laundering controls and violating sanctions laws![16]

- **Walmart:** Spent over $738 million in FCPA and compliance-related expenses since the 2013 fiscal year; this number is expected to grow to approximately $850 million.[17]

- **JPMorgan Chase & Co.:** Paid $267 million in SEC fines and was required to "admit wrongdoing to settle charges that they failed to disclose conflicts of interest to clients."[18]

- **Credit Suisse:** Paid $2.6 billion in penalties to the U.S. government for helping American citizens hide their money from the IRS in Swiss bank accounts.[19]

---

compliance-based culture
A corporate culture in which obedience to laws and regulations is the prevailing model for ethical behavior.

Larsen sets the leadership example by affirming that at J&J its "credo is all about personal responsibility."

Collins and Porras's book *Built to Last: Successful Habits of Visionary Companies* explains the power of a corporate culture to shape the individuals who work within it. While it may be true that individuals can shape an organization, and perhaps charismatic leaders can do this especially well, it is equally true, if not more so, that organizations shape individuals. Imagine spending a 20-, 30-, or even 40-year career in the same organization. The person you become, your attitudes, values, expectations, mindset, and habits, will be significantly determined by the culture of the organization in which you work. (See also the earlier Reality Check "Built to Last.")

Compliance and Values-Based Cultures

OBJECTIVE

values-based culture
A corporate culture in which conformity to a statement of values and principles rather than simple obedience to laws and regulations is the prevailing model for ethical behavior.

In the 1990s, a distinction came to be recognized in types of corporate culture: some firms were classified as **compliance-based cultures** (the traditional approach) while others were considered to be integrity-based or **values-based cultures.** These latter cultures are perceived to be more flexible and far-sighted corporate environments. The distinction between compliance-based and values-based cultures perhaps is most evident in accounting and auditing situations, but it can also be used more generally to understand wider corporate cultures. See Table 4.1 for an analysis of the differences between the traditional, compliance-based culture and the more progressive-style cultures that have evolved.

As the name suggests, a compliance-based culture emphasizes obedience to the rules as the primary responsibility of ethics. A compliance-based culture will empower legal counsel and audit offices to mandate and to monitor compliance with the law and with internal codes. A values-based culture is one that reinforces a particular set of *values* rather than a particular set of *rules*. Certainly, these firms may have codes of conduct; but those codes are predicated on a statement

TABLE 4.1

The Evolution of Compliance Programs into Values-Based Programs

Source: From Paul Lindow and Hill Race, "Beyond Traditional Audit Techniques," *Journal of Accountancy Online,* July 2002. Copyright 2002 American Institute of Certified Public Accountants, Inc. All rights reserved. Used with permission.

Traditional	Progressive (Best Practices)
Audit focus	Business focus
Transaction-based	Process-based
Financial account focus	Customer focus
Compliance objective	Risk identification, process improvement objective
Policies and procedures focus	Risk management focus
Multiyear audit coverage	Continual risk-reassessment coverage
Policy adherence	Change facilitator
Budgeted cost center	Accountability for performance improvement results
Career auditors	Opportunities for other management positions
Methodology: Focus on policies, transactions, and compliance	Methodology: Focus on goals, strategies, and risk management processes

of values and it is presumed that the code includes mere examples of the values' application. Integrating these values into the firm's culture encourages a decision-making process that uses the values as underlying principles to guide employee decisions rather than as hard-and-fast rules.

The argument in favor of a values-based culture is that a compliance culture is only as strong and as precise as the rules with which workers are expected to comply. A firm can have only a certain number of rules and the rules can never unambiguously apply to every conceivable situation. A values-based culture recognizes that where a rule does not apply, the firm must rely on the personal integrity of its workforce when decisions need to be made. (See the Reality Check "Compliance versus Values.")

This is not to say that values-based organizations do not include a compliance structure. The relationship between ethical culture and strong ethics and compliance programs is often symbiotic. In 2013, the Ethics Resource Center (ERC) reported that "companies' commitment to standards and good conduct, i.e. their ethics cultures" can be influenced profoundly by a "robust and well-implemented ethics and compliance program." Businesses recognize this strong relationship, as the ERC study points out: "by almost every measure, companies are working harder to build strong cultures and further develop their ethics and compliance programs. . . . [For example,] the percentage of companies providing ethics training rose from 74 percent to 81 percent from 2011 [to] 2013." Given this rise in the ethics training nationwide, "the percentage of companies with 'strong' or 'strong-leaning' ethics cultures climbed to 66 percent in 2013."[20]

The goals of a traditional compliance-oriented program may include meeting legal and regulatory requirements, minimizing risks of litigation and indictment, and improving accountability mechanisms. The goals of a more evolved and inclusive ethics program may entail a broader and more expansive application to the firm, including maintaining brand and reputation, recruiting and retaining desirable employees, helping unify a firm's global operations, creating a better working environment for employees, and doing the right thing in addition to

---

Reality Check *Compliance versus Values*

The master said, govern the people by regulations, keep order among them by chastisements, and they will flee from you, and lose all self-respect. Govern them by moral force, keep order among them by ritual, and they will keep their self-respect and come to you of their own accord.

The Analects of Confucius

---

doing things right. You should notice the more comprehensive implications of the latter list for the firm, its sustainability, and its long-term bottom line.

If a firm were to decide that it prefers the benefits and structure of a values-based orientation to its ethics program, the next question is how to integrate ethics into the compliance environment to most effectively prevent these common dilemmas and to create a "culture" of ethics. That question is addressed in the next section.

Ethical Leadership and Corporate Culture

If the goal of corporate culture is to cultivate values, expectations, beliefs, and patterns of behavior that best and most effectively support ethical decision making, it becomes the primary responsibility of corporate leadership to steward this effort. Leaders are charged with this duty in part because stakeholders throughout the organization are guided to a large extent by the "tone at the top." This is not at all to relieve leaders throughout an organization from their responsibilities as role models, but instead to suggest the pinnacle position that the executive leader plays in setting the direction of the culture. In fact, neither can be successful independent of the other; there must be a consistent *tone* throughout the firm. Unfortunately, according to one study published in 2013, senior leaders are more likely than lower-level employees to break rules, and 60 percent of misconduct reported is attributed to managers.[21] This is an alarming trend that should be considered by businesses as they develop their ethics and compliance training programs. Ralph Larsen, past chair and CEO of Johnson & Johnson, explains: "Being bound together around the values . . . around our credo . . . being bound together around values is like the trim tab for leadership at Johnson & Johnson."[22]

TIAA-CREF's CEO, Roger Ferguson, further elaborates: "The tone is truly set at the top. Companies can have the most extensive processes and procedures, but if they have the wrong people in positions of leadership or, if those people do not behave with transparency and integrity, they won't necessarily have a culture that promotes doing the right thing."[23] If a leader is perceived to be shirking her or his duties, misusing corporate assets, misrepresenting the firm's capabilities, or engaging in other inappropriate behavior, stakeholders receive the message that this type of behavior is not only acceptable, but perhaps expected and certainly the way to get ahead in that organization! Consider the responsibilities of leaders, both for their own actions and also for the decisions and actions of the leaders that precede them. Mary Barra, CEO of General Motors, had to answer for the prior wrongs of her predecessor (see the Decision Point "A Leader Takes Responsibility").

Today's GM will do the right thing. That begins with my sincere apologies to everyone who has been affected by this recall, especially the families and friends [of those] who lost their lives or were injured. I am deeply sorry.

> *Mary Barra, CEO of General Motors, apologizing for a botched recall of 2.6 million GM vehicles that contained dangerous and deadly ignition switch defects*

Mary Barra, CEO of General Motors, appeared before Congress in April 2014 to apologize publicly for 13 deaths that GM says were caused by a faulty ignition switch, as well as for GM's 10-year delay in issuing a recall for the vehicles containing this dangerous defect.

Barra faced serious questions from the U.S. House of Representatives about why GM waited almost 10 years when internal documents demonstrated that the company knew about the defect as early as 2005, but decided that the $0.57 modification was too costly. The House of Representatives asked Barra what had changed at GM to ensure this same process of decision making does not occur in the future.

Barra had stepped into the CEO role at GM only three months prior to her congressional appearance, in January 2014. The defect was made known to the public in February 2014. Therefore, much of Barra's testimony reiterated that the decisions—and culture—that caused this ethical lapse in judgment came before her time and knowledge. However, she emphasized that her primary focus was to change GM from a "cost culture" to a "customer culture." She explained to Congress that she had recently established a new position specifically responsible for global vehicle safety in order to encourage interdepartment communication, and she assured the Congressional members that GM was doing a full investigation of the issue. She also hired a high-profile compensation consultant to consider appropriate compensation for victims' families. However, House members did report that no engineer or manager was fired for their culpability in the incident.

1. Do you think it is fair for Barra to be held responsible for mistakes made under prior CEOs? If not, then how do we hold organizations responsible once a leader departs?

2. Barra was criticized for spending a significant portion of her congressional testimony responding that she just "didn't know." From what you read here, do you think that she made effective decisions on her arrival at GM to address the problem?

3. What additional facts might you need to uncover, if any, to respond to this particular issue?

4. Do you see any additional ways to respond to the issue(s) facing Barra? If you were Barra, what else might you do at GM to (1) respond to this particular issue and (2) modify the culture?

5. Who are Barra's primary stakeholders in her most pressing decisions right now?

6. What would you suggest might be Barra's most effective ethical strategy for decision making at present?

Sources: C. Isidore and K. Lobosco, "GM CEO Barra: 'I Am Deeply Sorry,' " *CNN Money.com* (April 1, 2014), http://money.cnn.com/2014/04/01/news/companies/barra-congress-testimony/ (accessed February 23, 2016).

Instead, if a leader is clearly placing her or his own ethical behavior above any other consideration, stakeholders are guided to follow that role model and to emulate that priority scheme. Ethical leaders say no to conduct that would be inconsistent with their organization's and their own personal values. If they demonstrate this courage, they are sending the message that this is the way to succeed in this culture. They also expect others to say no to them. Clearly, one of a leader's primary responsibilities, therefore, is to be a role model by setting a good example, by keeping promises and commitments, by maintaining their own standards, and by supporting others in doing so. Employees are often looking to leaders/supervisors for guidance on how to act. (See the Reality Check "The Effect of Ethics Training.")

OBJECTIVE

Beyond personal behavior, leadership sets the tone through other mechanisms such as the dedication of resources. Ethical business leaders not only talk about ethics and act ethically on a personal level, but they also allocate corporate resources to support and to promote ethical behavior. There is a long-standing credo of management: "budgeting is all about values." More common versions are "put your money where your mouth is" and "walk the talk."

ethics officers
Individuals within an organization charged with managerial oversight of ethical compliance and enforcement within the organization.

For example, when **ethics officers** were first introduced to the corporate structure in the early 1990s, the extent to which they were supported financially indicated their relevance and influence within the organization. Ethics was not a priority if the general counsel served as the ethics officer in her "spare time," and no additional resources were allocated to that activity. Ethics holds a different position in the firm if a highly skilled individual is hired into an exclusive position as ethics officer and is given a staff and a budget to support the work required. Similarly, if a firm mandates ethical decision making from its workers through the implementation of a code of conduct, extending the same standard for its vendors, suppliers, and other contractors, then trains all of these stakeholders with regard to these expectations and refers to the code and this process on a regular basis, these efforts demonstrate how seriously the firm takes the code.

When firms are effective in enacting ethics programs, employees are more likely to see themselves as participants in an ethical workplace culture. In a nationwide survey completed in 2013, almost three-quarters of workers who reported receiving positive feedback from a supervisor for engaging in ethical conduct also reported unethical conduct when they observed it in their workplace. Only half of those who were not praised for their own ethical conduct reported misconduct when they observed it. Note that the survey involved workers who did, in fact, observe

Reality Check *The Effect of Ethics Training*

Even when companies offer ethics and compliance training programs, employees continue to share concerns surrounding ethics, culture, and ethical leadership within their workplaces.

NAVEX Global evaluated ethics and compliance programs around the world. Despite the fact that 75 percent of respondents either "agreed" or "strongly agreed" that "each employee receives the ethics and compliance training they need to safeguard our people, reputation and bottom line," they still had significant concerns about the amount of training supervisors or leaders were receiving based on their current conduct. Additional findings were as follows:

Area of Concern Employees Had Surrounding Their Supervisors	Percentage of Respondents Who Considered It to Be a Significant or Moderate Concern
Not receiving adequate training to help avoid missteps	95%
Mishandling or downplaying complaints or reports from employees	87%
Exhibiting attitudes or conduct that undermines our commitment to ethics and compliance	88%
Exerting or giving in to pressure to compromise standards to achieve business results	85%
Retaliating (mistreating or taking action against an employee after a report is made)	81%
Failing to strongly back ethics and compliance by senior leaders	67%
Employing discriminatory hiring, firing, or performance management decisions	79%

Source: NAVEX Global, *NAVEX Global's 2014 Ethics and Compliance Training Benchmark Report*, www.navexglobal.com/sites/default/files/uploads/NAVEXGlobal_2014_Training_Benchmark_Report_US_07.01.pdf (accessed February 24, 2016). Table created by authors.

misconduct; it simply found more workers reported it if they previously had been commended for their own good acts.[24]

Creating a shared company culture is a key responsibility of leaders, if they wish to prioritize ethics in their respective companies. One way in which leaders create that shared culture was explored in a study of the nature of ethical leadership that emphasized the importance of being *perceived* as a people-oriented leader, as well as the importance of leaders engaging in *visible ethical action*. Beyond people orientation, traits that were important also included receptivity, listening, and openness in addition to the more traditionally considered traits of integrity, honesty, and trustworthiness. Finally, being perceived as having a broad ethical awareness, showing concern for multiple stakeholders (a responsibility *to* stakeholders, rather than *for* them), and using ethical decision processes are also important.[25] Those perceived as ethical leaders do many of the things "traditional leaders" do (e.g., reinforce the conduct they are looking for, create standards for

Reality Check *Perception of Leadership Qualities*

A 2014 study conducted by Zenger and Folkman evaluated the effectiveness of women as business leaders. The scholars collected data from 16,000 business leaders comprised of two-thirds men and one-third women.

Overall, 54.5 percent of participants perceived women to be *more effective leaders* than men. Women ranked higher than men in 12 of the 16 listed leadership competencies, including:

- Takes initiative
- Displays high integrity and honesty
- Drives for results
- Practices self-development
- Develops others
- Inspires and motivates others
- Builds relationships
- Utilizes collaboration and teamwork
- Champions change
- Establishes stretch goals

Men ranked higher than women on the following four qualities:

- Solves problems and analyzes issues
- Communicates powerfully and prolifically
- Connects the group to the outside world
- Innovates

The researchers asked the woman participants why they thought that women came out ahead as effective leaders. The most common response was "in order to get the same recognition and rewards, I need to do twice as much, never make a mistake and constantly demonstrate my competence."

Source: Adapted from K. Sherwin, "Why Women Are More Effective Leaders Than Men," *Business Insider* (January 24, 2014), www.businessinsider.com/study-women-are-better-leaders-2014-1 (accessed February 24, 2016).

behavior, and so on), but they do that within the context of an ethics agenda. People perceive that the ethical leader's goal is not simply job performance, but performance that is consistent with a set of ethical values and principles. Finally, ethical leaders demonstrate caring for people (employees and external stakeholders) in the process.

However, as mentioned earlier all of these traits and behaviors must be visible. If an executive is "quietly ethical" within the confines of the top management team, but more distant employees do not know about her or his ethical stance, they are not likely to be perceived as an ethical leader. Traits and behaviors must be socially visible and understood in order to be noticed and influence perceptions.[26] Take a look at the importance of that visibility in the Reality Check "Perception of Leadership Qualities." People notice when an executive walks the talk and acts on concerns for the common good and society as a whole, and long-term business prospers. Executives are expected to be focused on the financial bottom line and the short-term demands of stock analysts, but it is noteworthy when they focus on these broader and longer-term concerns.

The impact of ethical leadership is significant, which is why in this chapter we have focused on the issue of ethical leadership. We have discussed how leaders have the opportunity to influence the tone of a culture because research shows how a culture can influence employees' level of commitment to their work and also whether they intend to leave.[27] Average annual employee turnover has hovered in the mid-teens throughout this decade (15.7 percent in 2014)[28] and the cost of turnover can surpass 250 percent of the employee's annual salary for management and sales positions.[29] Therefore, maintaining employee satisfaction with the culture is a high priority!

Effective Leadership and Ethical, Effective Leadership

As we have discussed, being perceived as a leader plays an important role in a leader's ability to create and transform an ethical corporate culture. Key executives have the capability of transforming a business culture, for better or for worse. If the corporate culture has a significant impact on ethical decision making within the firm, leaders have the responsibility for shaping that environment so that ethical decision making can flourish. But what is the difference between the effective leader and the *ethical,* effective leader?

OBJECTIVE

This distinction is clearly critical since there are many effective leaders; are they all ethical? What do we mean by an "ethical" leader? Since leaders guide, direct, and escort others toward a destination, an effective leader is someone who does this successfully and, presumably, efficiently. Effective leaders are able to get followers to their common destination. But not every effective leader is an ethical leader.

One key difference lies with the means used to motivate others and achieve one's goals. Effective leaders might be able to achieve their goals through threats, intimidation, harassment, and coercion. They can also lead using more amenable interpersonal means such as modeling ethical behavior, persuasion, or using the impact of their institutional role.

Some of the discussions in the literature on leadership suggest that ethical leadership is determined solely by the *methods* used in leading. Promoters of certain styles of leadership suggest that their style is a superior style of leadership. Consequently, they tend to identify a method of leading with "true" leadership in an ethical sense. Along this line of thinking, for example, Robert Greenleaf's "Servant Leadership" suggests that the best leaders are individuals who lead by the example of serving others, in a nonhierarchical style. Other discussions similarly suggest that "transformative" or "transactional" leaders employ methods that empower subordinates to take the initiative and to solve problems for themselves, and that this constitutes the best in ethical leadership.

Certainly, ethically appropriate methods of leadership are central to becoming an ethical leader. Creating a corporate culture in which employees are empowered and expected to make ethically responsible decisions is a necessary part of being an ethical business leader. But, while some means may be ethically more appropriate than others (e.g., persuasion rather than coercion), it is not the method alone that establishes a leader as ethical. The other element of ethical leadership involves the *end* or *objective* toward which the leader leads. Recalling our discussion of ethical theory from chapter 3, this distinction should sound reminiscent of the emphasis on means in the deontological theory of universalism or the focus on ends or results in utilitarianism. Ethical leadership seems to embody both elements. If we judge a leader solely by the results produced—the utilitarian greatest good for the greatest number—we may ignore the mistreatment of workers that was necessary to achieve that end. Alternatively, if we look only to the working conditions protected by universalism, we may not appropriately account for a failure to produce a marketable product or one sufficient to reap a profit necessary to support the working conditions provided in a sustainable manner.

Similarly, in the business context, productivity, efficiency, and profitability are minimal goals in order to be sustainable. A business executive who leads a firm into bankruptcy is unlikely to qualify as an effective or successful leader. An executive who transforms a business into a productive, efficient, and profitable business, to the contrary, likely will be judged as a successful business leader. One who succeeds in a manner that respects subordinates and/or empowers them to become creative and successful in themselves is, at least at first glance, both an effective and ethical leader. But are profitability and efficiency accomplished through ethical means alone enough to make a business leader an ethical leader?

Imagine a business leader who empowers her or his subordinates, respects their autonomy by consulting and listening, but who leads a business that publishes child pornography or pollutes the environment or sells weapons to radical organizations. Would the *method* of leading alone determine the ethical standing of such a leader? Beyond the goal of profitability, other socially responsible goals might be necessary before we conclude that the leader is fully ethical. Chapter 5 will pick up on this theme as we examine corporate social responsibility.

Building a Values-Based Corporate Culture

Recall the iceberg example we discussed earlier; we explained that modifying culture alone seems about as tough as moving an iceberg. Each individual in an organization has an impact on the corporate culture, although no one individual can build or change the culture alone. Culture derives from leadership, integration, assessment, and monitoring.

Mission Statements, Credos, Codes of Conduct, and Statements of Values

One of the key manifestations of ethical leadership is the articulation of values for the organization. Of course, this articulation may evolve after an inclusive process of values identification; it need not simply mimic the particular values of one chief executive. However, it is that leader's responsibility to ensure that the firm is guided by some set of organizing principles that can guide employees in their decision-making processes. But do codes make a difference? Consider the Reality Check "Do Codes Make a Difference?" which seeks to respond to that

Reality Check *Do Codes Make a Difference?*

As a result of its quick and effective handling of its experience with tainted Tylenol in both 1982 and 1986, Johnson & Johnson has often been viewed as one of the most admired firms in the world. J&J had sales of $71.3 billion in 2013. It has had 30 consecutive years of earnings increases and 51 consecutive years of dividend increases. All of these data demonstrate that a firm that lives according to its strong values and a culture that supports those values can not only survive but sustain a profit over the long term.[30] Former CEO Ralph Larsen credits these successes directly to the J&J Credo: "it's the glue that holds our decentralized company together. . . . For us, the credo is our expression of managing the multiple bottom lines of products, people, planet and profits. It's the way we conceptualize our total impact on society."[31]

Of course, no code on its own can preclude all problems. In 2013, J&J agreed to pay $2.2 billion to settle civil and criminal claims against it for allegedly bribing doctors and pharmacies to prescribe its products to elderly people, to children, and to individuals with disabilities despite health risks or a lack of scientific evidence showing any benefits to patients.[32] Still, J&J's Credo is widely regarded as a leading example of how an ethics statement can be woven into a corporation's culture and form part of its mission.

The Johnson & Johnson Credo

The values that guide our decision making are spelled out in Our Credo. Put simply, Our Credo challenges us to put the needs and well-being of the people we serve first.

Robert Wood Johnson, former chairman from 1932 to 1963 and a member of the Company's founding family, crafted Our Credo himself in 1943, just before Johnson & Johnson became a publicly traded company. This was long before anyone ever heard the term "corporate social responsibility." Our Credo is more than just a moral compass. We believe it's a recipe for business success. The fact that Johnson & Johnson is one of only a handful of companies that have flourished through more than a century of change is proof of that.[33]

Our Credo

We believe our first responsibility is to the doctors, nurses and patients, to mothers and fathers and all others who use our products and services. In meeting their needs everything we do must be of high quality. We must constantly strive to reduce our costs in order to maintain reasonable prices. Customers' orders must be serviced promptly and accurately. Our suppliers and distributors must have an opportunity to make a fair profit.

We are responsible to our employees, the men and women who work with us throughout the world. Everyone must be considered as an individual. We must respect their dignity and recognize their merit. They must have a sense of security in their jobs. Compensation must be fair and adequate, and working conditions clean, orderly and safe. We must be mindful of ways to help our employees fulfill their family responsibilities. Employees must feel free to make suggestions and complaints. There must be equal opportunity for employment, development and advancement for those qualified. We must provide competent management, and their actions must be just and ethical.

We are responsible to the communities in which we live and work and to the world community as well. We must be good citizens—support good works and charities and bear our fair share of taxes. We must encourage civic improvements and better health and education We must maintain in good order the property we are privileged to use, protecting the environment and natural resources.

Our final responsibility is to our stockholders. Business must make a sound profit. We must experiment with new ideas. Research must be carried on, innovative programs developed and mistakes paid for. New equipment must be purchased, new facilities provided and new products launched Reserves must be created to provide for adverse times. When we operate according to these principles, the stockholders should realize a fair return.[34]

Source: Courtesy of Johnson & Johnson, www.jnj.com.

code of conduct
A set of behavioral guidelines and expectations that govern all members of a business firm.

mission statement
A formal summary statement that describes the goals, values, and institutional aim of an organization.

question by exploring Johnson & Johnson's experience as one of the first firms to have a code.[35]

Before impacting the culture through a **code of conduct** or statement of values, a firm must first *determine its mission* so that decision makers have direction when faced with dilemmas. In the absence of other values, the only value is profit—at any cost. Consequently, without additional guidance from the top, a firm is sending a clear message that a worker should do whatever it takes to reap profits. A code of conduct, therefore, may more specifically delineate this foundation both for internal stakeholders, such as employees, and for external stakeholders, such as customers. In so doing, the code has the potential to both enhance corporate reputation and to provide concrete guidance for internal decision making, thus creating a built-in risk management system.

The mission can be inspiring—indeed it *should be* inspiring. For instance, the corporate mission of Southwest Airlines emphasizes the importance of treating employees, as well as customers, with respect and dignity. Founder and former CEO Herb Kelleher explains, "It began by us thinking about what is the right thing to do in a business context. We said we want to really take care of these people, we want to honor them and we love them as individuals. Now that induces the kind of reciprocal trust and diligence that made us successful."[36] By establishing (especially through a participatory process) the core tenets on which a company is built, corporate leadership is effectively laying down the law with regard to the basis and objectives for all future decisions. In fact, the **mission statement** or corporate credo serves as an articulation of the fundamental principles at the heart of the organization and those that should guide all decisions, without abridgment.[37] From a universalist perspective, while many decisions might be made with the end in mind (utilitarian), none should ever breach the underlying mission as an *ultimate dictate*.

Developing the Mission and Code

The past two decades brought a proliferation of corporate codes of conduct and mission statements as part of the corporate response to the Federal Sentencing Guidelines for Organizations and the Sarbanes-Oxley Act (see later in this chapter). The success of these codes depends in large part on the process by which they are conceived and written, as well as their implementation. As with the construction of a personal code or mission, it is critical to first ask yourself what you stand for or what the company stands for. Why does the firm exist? What are its purposes? How will it implement these objectives? Once you make these determinations, how will you share them and encourage a commitment to them among your colleagues and subordinates? (See Table 4.2.)

The second step in the development of guiding principles for the firm is the articulation of a *clear vision* regarding the firm's direction. Why have a code? Bobby Kipp, PricewaterhouseCoopers's global ethics leader, explains: "We felt it was important for all our clients, our people and other stakeholders to understand exactly what we stand for and how they can expect us to conduct ourselves. . . . The code doesn't change the basic nature of the business we undertake, but instead it articulates the way we strive to conduct ourselves. The code shows how we apply our values to our daily business practices."[38]

The third step in this process is to identify *clear steps* as to how this cultural shift will occur. You have a code, but you cannot simply "print, post and pray," as Ethics Resource Center past president Stuart Gilman has referred to Enron's experience. Do you just post a sign on the wall that says, "Let's make more money!" Of course not. You need to have processes and procedures in place that support and then sustain that vision. Put in a different way, "a world-class code is no guarantee of world-class conduct," caution four other scholars in a *Harvard Business Review* article on benchmarking codes. "A code is only a tool, and like any tool, it can be used well or poorly—or left on the shelf to be admired or to rust."[39]

Finally, to have an effective code that will successfully impact culture there must be a belief throughout the organization that this culture is actually possible and achievable. If conflicts remain that will prevent certain components from being realized, or if key leadership is not on board, no one will have faith in the changes articulated. See Table 4.2 for Ethics Resource Center guidelines on writing an effective ethics code.

It should be noted that, although many organizations have individual codes of conduct, industries and/or professions might also publish codes of conduct that apply to firms or people who do business in those arenas. While adherence to some codes is prerequisite to participation in a profession, such as the legal community's Code of Professional Responsibility, many codes are produced by professional associations and are voluntary in nature. For example, certified public accountants, the defense industry, the direct marketing industry, and some faculty associations all have codes.[40] One might presume that implementation would be effective in all areas based on the industry-wide approach; however, research shows that the key elements of success are specific goals; performance measures oriented to outcomes; monitoring by independent, external groups to verify compliance; and fully transparent disclosure to the public.[41]

TABLE 4.2
Ethics Code Guidelines

Source: Ethics Resource Center, "Code Construction and Content," www.ethics.org/eci/research/free-toolkit/code-construction." Reprinted with permission of Ethics Resource Center.

The Ethics Resource Center provides the following guidelines for writing an ethics code:
1. Be clear about the objectives the code is intended to accomplish.
2. Get support and ideas for the code from all levels of the organization.
3. Be aware of the latest developments in the laws and regulations that affect your industry.
4. Write as simply and clearly as possible. Avoid legal jargon and empty generalities.
5. Respond to real-life questions and situations.
6. Provide resources for further information and guidance.
7. In all its forms, make it user-friendly because ultimately a code fails if it is not used.

You are a corporate vice president of one of the largest units in your organization. Unfortunately, you have noticed over the past few years that your unit has developed a singular focus on profits, since employees' performance appraisals and resulting compensation increases are based in significant part on "making the numbers." Though the unit has done well in this regard, you have noticed that people have been known to cut corners, to treat others less respectfully than you would like, and to generally disregard other values in favor of the bottom line. While this might be beneficial to the firm in the short run, you have grave concerns about the long-term sustainability of this approach.

- What are the ethical issues involved in striving to define or impact the culture of a unit?
- How might you go about defining the culture of your unit so that employees might be able to understand your concerns?
- What will be the most effective means by which to alter this culture?
- What stakeholders would be involved in your suggestion in response to the previous question? How might the different stakeholder groups be impacted by your decision on this process?
- How can you act in order to ensure the most positive results? How will you measure those results or determine your success? Will you measure inputs or outcomes, responsibilities, and rights?

Culture Integration: Ethics Hotlines, Ombudspersons, and Reporting

OBJECTIVE

Recalling Gilman's warning not to "print, post and pray," many business firms must have mechanisms in place that allow employees to come forward with questions, concerns, and information about unethical behavior. Integrating an ethical culture throughout a firm and providing means for enforcement is vitally critical both to the success of any cultural shift and to the impact on all stakeholders. Integration can take a number of different forms, depending both on the organizational culture and the ultimate goals of the process.

One of the most decisive elements of integration is communication because without it there is no clarity of purpose, priorities, or process. Communication of culture must be incorporated into the firm's vocabulary, habits, and attitudes to become an essential element in the corporate life, decision making, and determination of success. In the end, the Ethics & Policy Integration Centre contends that communication patterns describe the organization far better than organization charts! The Decision Point "Short Term versus Long Term" challenges you to create some of those integrative mechanisms, while the Reality Check "Examples of Culture Integration" demonstrates how two firms have imaginatively responded to this very challenge.

Reality Check *Examples of Culture Integration*

- Walmart's Integrity in Action Award recognizes associates who demonstrate integrity through consistent actions and words, and who inspire other associates always to do the right thing. The award is based on voluntary nominations received from associates, and global votes determine an award recipient from each country for the most inspiring associate.[42]

- Lockheed Martin offers an Ethics Awareness Training for its employees, based on Dr. Mary Gentile's book *Giving Voice to Values*. The annual training equips employees with the knowledge and skills to recognize and react to situations that may require ethical decision making. The training engages every member across the company's organizational structure, starting from its chair, president, and CEO, by empowering managers to train their respective teams.[43]

- Merck & Co., Inc., one of the largest pharmaceutical companies in the world, offers ethics and compliance training to ensure that all employees act in compliance with its Code of Conduct and policies. To enhance transparency, the company also "discloses information through a variety of mechanisms, including financial and corporate responsibility reporting, through the media, and through one-on-one stakeholder discussions." From 2011 to 2014, the percentage of employees trained in its Code of Conduct increased from 90 to 99 percent. At that same time, reported concerns regarding privacy practices, breaches of privacy, and losses of personal data dropped from 68 to 18 percent.[44]

- Dell uses a game developed by LRN called the Honesty Project to reinforce the important lessons of ethics and compliance by allowing employees to describe the damage corruption and bribery causes, recognize red flags that may indicate corruption or bribery, and identify the appropriate contact when confronted with a solicitation to pay a bribe or when witnessing a bribe being paid.[45]

- Best Buy goes about things in a very different, very modern way. Best Buy's chief ethics officer, Kathleen Edmond, writes a blog that often gives details of ethical dilemmas faced by Best Buy employees and sometimes (anonymized) details of her investigations of various ethical infractions within the company. Her blog can be found at www.kathleenedmond.com/.

To explore the effectiveness of a corporation's integration process, consider whether incentives are in the right place to encourage ethical decision making and whether ethical behavior is evaluated during a worker's performance review. It is difficult to reward people for doing the right thing, such as correctly filing an expense report, but as the Lockheed Martin Chairman's Award shows, incentives such as appropriate honors and positive appraisals are possible. Are employees comfortable raising questions relating to unethical behavior? Are multiple and varied reporting mechanisms in place? Do employees believe their reports will be free from retaliation? What can be done to ensure that employees who violate the company code are disciplined appropriately, even if they are good performers?

How does communication about ethical matters occur? The fact of the matter is that reporting ethically suspect behavior is a difficult thing to do. Childhood memories of "tattletales" or "snitches," along with a general social prohibition against informing on others, create barriers to reporting unethical behavior. More ominously, individuals often pay a real cost when they report on unethical behavior (such as retaliation), especially if workplace superiors are involved in the report of wrongdoing.

Whistle-blowing is one of the classic issues in business ethics. Whistle-blowing refers to situations where an employee discloses unethical or illegal activities to

whistle-blowing
A practice in which an individual within an organization reports organizational wrongdoing to the public or to others in position of authority.

someone who is in a position to take action to prevent or punish the wrongdoing. Whistle-blowing can expose and end unethical activities. But it can also seem disloyal; it can harm the business and sometimes it can exact significant costs on the whistle-blower.

Whistle-blowing can occur both internally and externally. One of the most highly visible cases of internal whistle-blowing cases occurred when Sherron Watkins reported her concerns about Enron's accounting practices to Ken Lay. It also can occur when a whistle-blower shares her or his concerns with external agencies, such as when Jeffrey Wigand (portrayed in the movie *The Insider*) reported to *60 Minutes* Brown & Williamson's deceptive activities involving the dangers of cigarettes. Not only did Wigand have evidence that B&W concealed and knowingly misled the public about the harmful effects of cigarettes, but he also could demonstrate that they used additives that increased the potential for their harm. Whistle-blowing also can occur externally when employees or other stakeholders report wrongdoing to legal authorities, such as when private fraud investigator Harry Markopolos repeatedly tried to alert the Securities and Exchange Commission about Bernie Madoff's Ponzi scheme.

Because whistle-blowing to external groups, such as the press and the legal authorities, can be so harmful to both the whistle-blower and to the firm itself, internal mechanisms for reporting wrongdoing are preferable for all concerned. But the internal mechanisms must be effective; must allow confidentiality, if not anonymity; and must strive to protect the rights of the accused party. In addition to or as part of ethics and compliance officers' responsibilities, many firms have created ethics ombudspersons and internal or external ethics hotlines. These mechanisms allow employees to report wrongdoing and to create mechanisms for follow-up and enforcement.

To encourage a different, more positive image for the concept of whistle-blowing (as opposed to reporting on one's peers), some firms call their systems "speak-up" programs. Vocabulary has an impact and could inspire workers to feel a sense of empowerment from their contribution to the corporate culture in contrast to the origins of the phrase *blowing the whistle* on a peer.

While these reporting systems might seem evident, reasonable, and commonplace, many organizations do not have them in place for a variety of reasons. In addition, even when they are in place, people who observe threats to the organization might choose not to report the threat or possible wrongdoing.

Consider the *Columbia* space shuttle disaster, which is reviewed by the *Columbia* Accident Investigation Board in Reading 4-2, "Assessment and Plan for Organizational Culture Change at NASA." On February 1, 2003, the *Columbia* space shuttle lost a piece of its insulating foam while the shuttle reentered Earth's atmosphere. The damage resulted in the death of seven astronauts, one of NASA's most serious tragedies. The foam had dislodged during the original launch, which then damaged one of the shuttle's wings, causing the accident a few weeks later on reentry. When the foam dislodged, no one could assess the true extent of the damage. No one could "see around the corner," so to speak. The engineers could see the foam strike the wing but, because of a poor angle of sight and the fact that foam strikes had not caused major accidents in the past, senior managers downplayed the threat.

Was this an operations failure, a failure in judgment; pressure from above to complete the shuttle mission; the cavalier, cowboy culture of NASA to keep moving forward *at any cost*? *Columbia*'s engineers worked in a data-driven culture. No one made a move without data to support it; unless there were data to prove that the vehicle was unsafe with the current "proven" technology, they could not justify the extra cost of scheduling a moonwalk to investigate.

Is this a crisis of culture or a failure in a whistle-blowing system? Some analysts consider it instead a "natural, albeit unfortunate, pattern of behavior . . . a prime example of an ambiguous threat—a signal that may or may not portend future harm."[46]

One of the challenges with reporting systems is that they do not make the values of the organization clear, what is or is not accepted within its culture. Therefore, while massive threats might give rise to quite evident responses, "the most dangerous situations arise when a warning sign is ambiguous and the event's potential for causing a company harm is unclear. In these cases, managers tend to actively ignore or discount the risk and take a wait-and-see attitude."[47] There are methods by which firms might actively curtail these negative influences, as follows:

- Leaders should *model* the act of reporting wrongdoing, in an obvious manner, so that everyone throughout the organization can see that reporting is the highest priority—not covering up malfeasance.

- Leaders can explain the process of decision making that led to their conclusion.

- While "crisis management" teams or plans are often unsuccessful (since they are so seldom used, there is no habit formed at all), *practicing* reports is a valuable exercise. Running drills or rehearsals of challenging events will allow for much greater comfort and generate a level of expectation among workers that might not otherwise exist.

- In addition, a culture that allows sufficient time for reflection in order to reach responsible decisions is most likely to encourage consideration of appropriate implications.

- Finally, the most effective way to ensure clarity and thereby ensure a successful reporting scheme is to consistently and continuously communicate the organization's values and expectations to all stakeholders, and to reinforce these values through the firm's compensation and reward structure.

See Reading 4-4, "Whistleblower Policies in United States Corporate Codes of Ethics" by Richard Moberly and Lindsey E. Wylie, for a review of the status of whistle-blower provisions and codes of ethics today. Moberly and Wylie explain that while corporations' codes might provide significant protection—sometimes greater than U.S. statutory and tort law—unfortunately the concept of employment at will, which diminishes an employee's right to a position without a contract, prevents an employee from enforcing many, if not most, of these provisions.

Beyond the question of cultural differences in reporting sensitivities and processes, a firm must consider the bare logistical questions in global implementation of its code of conduct and ethics and compliance program. How will the code and accompanying program align with local standards of practice, laws, and customs? Will there be just one version of the code for world operations, or multiple versions for each local base of operations, and not simply in the local language but modified in order to be sensitive to these local standards and customs? How "deep" will your code reach into your supply chain? The codes of some firms apply only to their employee base while others apply to all vendors, suppliers, and other contracting parties. Must you consult with (or even seek approval from) labor representatives, unions, and/or works councils prior to implementing the code or program in any of the countries in which you operate? Finally, be aware that the standard acknowledgment form that many employees are asked to sign upon receipt of a code of conduct in the United States may be presumed to be coerced in other environments, given the unequal bargaining positions of the parties. While you might opt to dispense with that requirement, how will you serve the purpose of demonstrating acceptance and understanding?

OBJECTIVE

Assessing and Monitoring the Corporate Culture: Audits

Unfortunately, if one does not measure something, people often perceive a decline in its importance. The same result occurs with regard to culture. If we cannot or do not measure, assess, or monitor culture, it is difficult to encourage others throughout the organization to pay attention to it. Alternatively, monitoring and an ongoing ethics audit allow organizations to uncover silent vulnerabilities that could pose challenges later to the firm, thus serving as a vital element in risk assessment and prevention. By engaging in an ongoing assessment, organizations are better able to spot these areas before other stakeholders (both internal and external) spot them.

Beyond uncovering vulnerabilities, an effective monitoring process may include other significantly positive objectives. These may include an evaluation of appropriate resource allocation, whether the program is keeping pace with organizational growth, whether all of the program's positive results are being accurately measured and reported, whether the firm's compensation structure is adequately rewarding ethical behavior, and whether the "tone at the top" is being disseminated effectively.

Identifying positive results might be a familiar process. But, how do you detect a potentially damaging or ethically challenged corporate culture—sometimes referred to as a "toxic" culture? The first clear sign would be a lack of any generally accepted fundamental values for the organization, as discussed earlier. In addition, warning signs can occur in the various component areas of the organization. How does the firm treat its customers, suppliers, clients, and workers? The management of its internal and external relationships is critical evidence of its values. How does the firm manage its finances? Of course, a firm can be in a state of financial disaster without engaging in even one unethical act (and vice versa); but the manner in which it manages and communicates its financial environment is telling.

Consulting firm LRN suggests myriad options by which to measure the impact of efforts to change a culture. The first is to determine whether employee perception of the culture or working conditions has changed. Surveys of employee job satisfaction in general or about specific elements of the culture may return interesting data, though sometimes employees will tell the firm what they believe the organization wishes to hear. Alternatively, leaders may opt for an audit by an independent organization in order to determine the employee perception or to assess the firm's vulnerabilities or risks. The external auditor will also be able to provide information relating to benchmarking data in connection with the firm's code, training program, or other education or integration components, as well as the evaluation of those programs if they are offered. Data surrounding the help line or hotline are also noteworthy in terms of both the quantity and quality of the calls and responses. As with any element of the working environment, any feedback or other communication from employees, whether at the beginning of employment, throughout, or subsequent to employment, should be gathered and analyzed for valuable input regarding the culture.[48] Information is available everywhere—take a look at Reading 4-3, "Does the Company Get It—20 Questions to Ask Regarding Compliance, Ethics, and Risk Management," by OCEG at the end of the chapter.

Mandating and Enforcing Culture: The Federal Sentencing Guidelines for Organizations

OBJECTIVE

United States Sentencing Commission (USSC)
An independent agency in the United States judiciary created in 1984 to regulate sentencing policy in the federal court system.

When internal mechanisms for creating ethical corporate cultures prove inadequate, the business community can expect governmental regulation to fill the void. The **United States Sentencing Commission (USSC),** an independent agency in the United States Judiciary, was created in 1984 to regulate sentencing policy in the federal court system. Prior to that time, differences in sentencing, arbitrary punishments, and crime control had been enormous issues before Congress. By using the USSC to mandate sentencing procedures and make recommendations for terms, Congress has been able to incorporate the original purposes of sentencing in federal court procedures, bringing some of these challenges and variations under control.

Beginning in 1987, the USSC prescribed mandatory **Federal Sentencing Guidelines for Organizations (FSGO)** that apply to individual and organizational defendants in the federal system, bringing some amount of uniformity and fairness to the system. These prescriptions, based on the severity of the offense, assign most federal crimes to one of 43 "offense levels." Each offender also is placed into a criminal history category based on the extent and recency of past misconduct. The court then inputs this information in a sentencing grid and determines the offender's sentence guideline range (ranges are either in six-month intervals or 25 percent of the sentence, whichever is greater), and is subject to adjustments.

In its 2005 decision in *U.S. v. Booker,* however, the Supreme Court separated the "mandatory" element of the guidelines from their advisory role, holding that their mandatory nature violated the Sixth Amendment right to a jury trial. Accordingly, though no longer mandatory, a sentencing court is still required

Federal Sentencing Guidelines for Organizations (FSGO)
Developed by the United States Sentencing Commission and implemented in 1991, originally as mandatory parameters for judges to use during organizational sentencing cases. By connecting punishment to prior business practices, the guidelines establish legal norms for ethical business behavior. However, since a 2005 Supreme Court decision, the FSG are now considered to be discretionary in nature and offer some specifics for organizations about ways to mitigate eventual fines and sentences by integrating bona fide ethics and compliance programs throughout their organizations.

to consider guideline ranges. The court is also permitted to individually tailor a sentence in light of other statutory concerns. You can imagine that this modification from mandatory to "required to consider" has not come without a bit of confusion. "Since Booker, the courts have drifted farther from guideline-based sentences, with many courts applying the guidelines less than half the time," says white-collar enforcement and compliance attorney Matthew Miner, who served as a prosecutor and senior counsel to U.S. Senate committees for over a decade.[49]

The relevance of these guidelines to our exploration of ethics and, in particular, to our discussion of the proactive corporate efforts to create an ethical workplace is that the USSC strived to use the guidelines to create both a legal *and an ethical* corporate environment. (See Figure 4.3.) This effort was supported by the Sarbanes-Oxley Act, which subsequently directed the USSC to consider and to review its guidelines for fraud relating to securities and accounting, as well as to obstruction of justice, and specifically asked for severe and aggressive deterrents in sentencing recommendations. Further, the Sarbanes-Oxley Act required public companies to establish a code of conduct for top executives and, if they did not have one, to explain why it did not exist. Several stock exchanges followed suit and also required codes of business conduct and ethics from its publicly held companies.

In recognition of the significant impact of corporate culture on ethical decision making, the USSC updated the guidelines in 2004 to include references not only to compliance programs but also to "ethics and compliance" programs and, further, required that organizations promote "an organizational culture that encourages ethical conduct and commitment to compliance with the law." The revision also includes a requirement that organizations assess areas of risk for ethics and compliance, and periodically measure the effectiveness of their programs. In addition, the criteria for an effective program, which used to be outlined just in the guidelines's commentary, are now found in a separate specific guideline.

The guidelines seek to encourage corporations to create or maintain effective ethics and compliance programs. Those companies that can demonstrate that they have these programs, but find themselves in court as a result of a bad apple or two, either will not be penalized or the recommended penalty will be reduced (called a "mitigated" penalty). On the other hand, firms that do not have effective ethics

FIGURE 4.3
Sources of Culture

> **Review: Culture Derives from Leadership, Integration, and Assessment/Monitoring**
>
> 1. **Leadership** (and maintenance) of the control environment
>   - Through high-level commitment and management responsibility, leaders set the standard and the tone
> 2. **Control activities, information, and communication**
>   - Statements, policies, operating procedures, communications and training
>   - Constant/consistent integration into business practices
> 3. **Review, assessment, ongoing monitoring**
>   - Monitoring, evaluation, historical accountability

and compliance systems will be sentenced to an additional term of probation and ordered to develop a program during that time (called an "aggravated" penalty).

The USSC notes that organizations shall "exercise due diligence to prevent and detect criminal conduct; and otherwise promote an organizational culture that encourages ethical conduct and a commitment to compliance with the law." The guidelines identify those specific acts of an organization that can serve as due diligence in preventing crime and the *minimal* requirements for an effective compliance and ethics program. These include the following actions:[50]

1. **Standards and Procedures.** The organization shall establish standards and procedures to prevent and detect criminal conduct.

2. **Responsibility of Board and Other Executives; Adequate Resources and Authority.**

   (A) The organization's board shall be knowledgeable about the compliance and ethics program and shall exercise reasonable oversight with respect to its implementation and effectiveness.

   (B) High-level personnel must be assigned to have responsibility for the program and must then ensure its effectiveness.

   (C) Specific individual(s) within the organization shall be delegated day-to-day operational responsibility for the program and shall report periodically to these high-level personnel and, as appropriate, to the governing authority, or an appropriate subgroup of the governing authority, on the effectiveness of the compliance and ethics program. They shall also be given adequate resources, appropriate authority, and direct access to the governing authority.

3. **Preclusion from Authority: Prior Misconduct.** The organization shall avoid placing people in charge of the program who have previously engaged in illegal activities or other conduct inconsistent with an effective compliance and ethics program.

4. **Communication and Training.** The organization shall communicate its standards and procedures to all members of the organization through training or other means appropriate to such individuals' respective roles and responsibilities.

5. **Monitoring, Evaluation, Reporting Processes.** The organization shall take reasonable steps:

   (A) to ensure that the organization's compliance and ethics program is followed, including monitoring and auditing to detect criminal conduct;

   (B) to evaluate periodically the effectiveness of the organization's compliance and ethics program; and

   (C) to have and publicize a system, which may include mechanisms that allow for anonymity or confidentiality, whereby the organization's employees and agents may report or seek guidance regarding potential or actual criminal conduct without fear of retaliation.

6. **Incentive and Disciplinary Structures.** The organization's compliance and ethics program shall be promoted and enforced consistently throughout the organization through

(A) appropriate incentives to perform in accordance with the compliance and ethics program; and

(B) appropriate disciplinary measures for engaging in criminal conduct and for failing to take reasonable steps to prevent or detect criminal conduct.

7. **Response and Modification Mechanisms.** After criminal conduct has been detected, the organization shall take reasonable steps to respond appropriately to the criminal conduct and to prevent further similar criminal conduct, including making any necessary modifications to the organization's compliance and ethics program.

In connection with item number one on the list, imagine the challenges faced by companies seeking to ensure compliance in a variety of distinct cultures throughout the world.

The Reality Check "The Global Culture for Corporations" explores some of those obstacles with regard to Chile. Chile was chosen simply to provide a window into the array of issues for which companies need to be prepared today.

Item number two on the USSC list above mandates that the organization's governing body (usually, a board of directors) has the duty to act prudently, to be knowledgeable about the content and operation of the compliance and ethics program, and must undergo ongoing and consistent training. The content could include instruction surrounding the nature of board fiduciary duties, personal liability, stock exchange regulations, insider trading, confidentiality, intellectual property, and business secrets. A 2010 RAND symposium brought together "thought leaders" who serve on corporate boards, corporate executives, ethics and compliance officers, scholars, and policymakers to examine ethics issues from the perspective of corporate boards of directors. The symposium participants noted that "a tension sometimes exists around bringing an ethics perspective and a C&E [compliance and ethics] focus to the boardroom." They also shared the observation that "directors are far less likely to seek outside guidance on their C&E responsibilities, for example, than they are on more traditional questions concerning governance and strategy."[51] The results of a 2009 survey of 1,600 in-house corporate attorneys support these observations; only half of the respondents reported that they had provided their boards with compliance or ethics training.[52] (*More recent figures were not available.*)

In 2010, the USSC adopted amendments to the Federal Sentencing Guidelines for Organizations (FSGO) to lower the penalties for compliance violations if the organization meets the following four conditions:

1. The individual or individuals with operational responsibility for the compliance and ethics program have direct reporting obligations to the governing authority or an appropriate subgroup thereof (e.g., an audit committee of the board of directors).

2. The compliance and ethics program detected the offense before discovery outside the organization or before such discovery was reasonably likely.

Reality Check   *The Global Culture for Corporations—Guidance from Ethisphere: Chile*

While by no means one of South America's largest countries when measured by population or geography, Chile nonetheless distinguishes itself as the poster child of Latin American economic growth and development. Although Chile represents the 60th largest population and 44th largest economy (as ranked by total gross domestic product [GDP]) in the world, Chile has a sustained history of market-friendly reforms and—aside from Agusto Pinochet's 16 1/2-year dictatorial regime—a long history of stable governance. As a sign of the stability of Chile's economy, the country was the first in South America to join the Organization for Economic Cooperation and Development (OECD).

There are more than 17 million people living in Chile, with almost a third of them in the country's capital city, Santiago, which is the largest city and located near the center of Chile's sliver-shaped boundaries. The official language of Chile is Spanish, and the next most common languages are Mapudungun (a language local to the country), German, and English. The majority of the people practice Roman Catholicism, according to the CIA *World Factbook,* followed by Evangelical Christians.

The government of Chile is a presidential republic, and the current president is Sebastián Piñera, the fifth elected president since Pinochet ran the country. Chile's elections are generally considered fair by third-party observers. Probably the most well-known ruler of Chile around the world is Augusto Pinochet, who ran the country as a dictator until 1990. Pinochet took control in the early 1970s, after rising to general chief of staff of the army and later commander-in-chief of the Chilean Army, a position he received by then-president Salvador Allende. Pinochet later participated in a coup d'état which led him to take charge of the country.

Chile is exceptionally rich geographically and the country boasts of an amazingly diverse climate—from the eastern and southern alpine tundra and glaciers; to subtropical Easter Island; to central Chile's Mediterranean climate; to Atacama, the world's driest desert found in northern Chile. Chile's largest border is shared by Argentina to the east, and the country also borders Bolivia to the northeast and Peru to the north. The west coast of Chile touches the Pacific Ocean. The climate of the country is varied as the north is primarily desert, and cools down with frequent rainfall in the south.

Thanks to the incredibly dry Atacama, Chile is rich in mineral resources, most prevalently copper. While certainly not without its inherent challenges to foreign investors, Chile is undoubtedly South America's most advanced economy, and is a truly open, free-market economy.

A number of compliance challenges exist in Chile and include intellectual property protection and civil unrest within certain parts of the country.

FIVE COMPLIANCE AND ETHICAL ISSUES TO CONSIDER, AND HOW TO DEAL WITH THEM

Bureaucracy

While Chile is committed to being an open business and trade partner, and remains the most open-market country in the region, there are certainly bureaucratic challenges. Perhaps due to the country's relatively small size and sustained growth over an extended period of time, there is a markedly conservative approach toward regulatory change. Indeed, foreign companies need be patient in their efforts to do business in Chile, as there can be cumbersome delays in processing paperwork and obtaining approvals.

Deal with It

In order to adequately deal with the unique delays associated with doing successful business in Chile, it's important to find an in-country partner that can help overcome regulatory hurdles. Indeed, finding a good partner already operating in Chile can afford an international investor both business and social connections that can help mitigate cultural, language, and regulatory barriers. It's important to keep in mind that there are a relatively small number of actors in control of most sectors of Chilean business. Finding a well-connected partner can open important doors throughout the Chilean business world.

Intellectual Property Protection

Although Chile is extremely advanced in many areas of legislature, the country continues to face significant challenges in the area of intellectual property. While there have been legislative efforts made to enhance IP protection laws, major challenges remain, both in hard goods and Internet privacy. This is a monumental hurdle for many businesses, especially given that Chile is undergoing a major push to market itself as a haven for high-technology manufacturing and research and development foreign direct investment (FDI).

Deal with It

While the issue of intellectual property rights is certainly a major concern for many foreign investors, the good news is that the government is taking strides to mitigate the issue. Former president Michelle Bachelet was a proponent for legislative reform, and supported various initiatives to improve IP protection. However, many hurdles remain before an acceptable level of protection can be expected. Until then, companies can help protect proprietary knowledge and technology in a couple of ways. First, they must be well-aware of existing legislature. Second, they can develop relationships with organizations such as the International Intellectual Property Alliance in order to become better aware of existing IP laws in Chile and how to best handle their deficiencies.

Socioeconomic Disparity

Chile has performed admirably in its attempts to increase its economic standing, both within the region and in the world. In many ways, these attempts have resulted in unprecedented success. However, in one area this is not the case. Chile continues to struggle mightily with great economic disparity throughout the populace. In some aspects, Chile can argue that its developmental state is shifting from "emerging" to "developed."

Deal with It

At first glance, the issue of economic disparity may not be of major concern to international investors. However, this viewpoint can quickly shift when one considers the significant security implications inherent to economic inequality. The wider the gap between the poor and the members of the economic elite, the more significant the potential challenge to a foreign investor. In order to help mitigate the possible unrest presented by economic inequality, investors may want to consider increasing support of social programs meant to help develop lesser-developed sectors of the economy.

Civil Unrest

In comparison to many other countries in the region, Chile's struggles with civil unrest may appear somewhat insignificant. Nonetheless, they can present hurdles to effective and profitable business operations. In the decades following the Pinochet regime, Chile has done an excellent job ensuring

civil liberties, such as freedom of speech. This is obviously a positive indicator of development. However, there have been cases where protests and political rallies have become violent, such as the education reform rallies organized by university students over the last couple years.

Deal with It

The best thing companies can do when political rallies or protests begin to take shape is to remain as uninvolved and far-removed as possible from the situation. Protests and rallies are typically announced prior to when they actually take place, so it's important for companies and their in-country representatives to be aware of these types of developing situations. Once it becomes apparent that a potentially combustible situation is developing, it's imperative that companies and their representatives stay far away from them in order to ensure no connection is made to the organization and to make sure that employee safety remains uncompromised.

Corporate Taxation

Thanks to the devastating earthquakes that rocked the country in February 2010, President Piñera enacted an emergency hike on royalties for mining companies and corporate taxes—from 17 to 20 percent—in order to assist in the rebuilding of affected areas. [**Update:** Chile instituted further increases in 2014, raising the corporate tax rate to 27 percent by 2017 and up to 35 percent thereafter.[53]] This could certainly make life difficult for many current and potential foreign investors, and could open the door for companies to attempt to subvert the new tax structure in unethical ways.

Deal with It

A 3 percent tax increase is certainly not insignificant. However, at the same time, even at 20 percent Chile's corporate tax rate does not even come close to being among some of the world's highest. Indeed, the United States boasts the highest in the world, coming in at 39.2 percent. While Chile's rate increase is certainly meaningful, it still remains far below what U.S. companies are paying in their home market.

FIVE ETIQUETTE TIPS YOU SHOULD KNOW BEFORE YOU GO

Greetings

Chile has a generally very warm and open culture, and this extends to business interactions. While it is common to see individuals accompanying greetings or farewells with a kiss on the right cheek, in business dealings it is generally expected that you greet counterparts with a firm handshake. If meeting a woman, common courtesy is to wait for her to extend her hand first. Initial introductions typically dictate that greetings are formal, referring to counterparts either by title, or the formal *Señor* or *Señora*. One should be careful when using common American hand gestures, as they may carry vastly different meanings in other countries.

Business Meetings

The concept of time is definitely more fluid in Chile than in the United States. Do not be offended if counterparts are slightly late for meetings, as this is not uncommon. However, as the guest, it's important that you always be punctual. Chileans rely heavily on perception and personal interaction in business dealings. While business plans and related research are important as they are in any country, and will be considered, personal connection will be the most compelling factor in successful interactions. Similarly, expect many business dealings to take place over lunch or after-work drinks, and for these interactions to begin and end with lengthy personal discussions. Indeed, business lunches are extremely common, and can be expected to last at least two hours. The ability to build a personal connection with the host will be integral to subsequent successful negotiations.

Business Cards

The exchanging of business cards is very common in Chile. As in many Latin American cultures, advanced degrees are extremely well-regarded, and should thus be included on business cards. Further, business cards should also include a Spanish translation on one side.

Gift Giving

The exchanging of gifts is not generally expected in Chilean business culture. However, it's quite acceptable to bring a small token, such as a pen engraved with your company name, for your host. Further, if you're invited to have dinner with your host, it is appropriate to bring a bottle of wine or alcohol for the occasion. Additionally, if invited to the host's home for any occasion, it's polite to bring a small gift for the host and his or her spouse.

Dinner and Social Events

As stated previously, relationship building is extremely important in Chilean business culture. It is not uncommon to be invited to dinner with one's host, either with other work colleagues or with the host's family. Dress at these events is usually business formal. Formal etiquette is also very important. For example, be sure to refrain from speaking with food in one's mouth, use the proper utensils when eating (such as using the knife rather than a fork for cutting), and keep elbows off the table when eating.

It is also important to steer clear of combustible subject matter in conversations, such as politics and regional conflicts. Safe subjects to highlight include fútbol, pisco sour (the national drink), Chilean history, art and literature, and U.S. culture.

Source: Adapted from Jamey Long, "Global Compliance: Chile," *Ethisphere* (June 4, 2013), http://ethisphere.com/magazine-articles/global-compliance-chile/. Reprinted with permission from *Ethisphere*.

---

3. The organization promptly reported the offense to appropriate governmental authorities.

4. No individual with operational responsibility for the compliance and ethics program participated in, condoned, or was willfully ignorant of the offense. [54]

The first condition is designed to reward companies that ensure that personnel who implement an organization's compliance and ethics programs have reporting access to boards of directors. In order to qualify for eased penalties under the first condition, compliance and ethics personnel must be authorized explicitly to *communicate to the board of directors "promptly on any matter involving criminal conduct or potential criminal conduct," and "no less than annually on the implementation and effectiveness of the compliance and ethics program."*[55] The other three conditions also seek to encourage reporting by providing incentives to detect and report misconduct and to discourage weak, ineffectual, or corrupt compliance and ethics programs.

Protecting confidentiality is one of the most effective tools in creating a corporate culture in which illegal and unethical behavior can be uncovered. Corporate ethics officers, ombudspersons, and ethics hotlines typically guarantee that any reports of illegal or unethical behavior will be held in strictest confidence. Ethics officers promise anonymity to whistle-blowers, and those who report wrongdoing trust that this promise of confidentiality will be upheld.

However, Federal Sentencing Guidelines can create real ethical dilemmas for corporations that promise anonymity and confidentiality. The guidelines call for significantly reduced punishment for firms that immediately report potential wrongdoing to government authorities. Failure to report evidence of wrongdoing can mean the difference between a significant penalty and exoneration. Of course, failure to promise confidentiality can also be evidence of an ineffective ethics and compliance system, itself a potential risk for receiving stiffer legal penalties.

- Should ethics officers guarantee confidentiality to those who report wrongdoing, and should they violate that confidence to protect the firm from prosecution?
- What facts would you want to know before making this decision?
- Can you imagine any creative way out of this dilemma?
- To whom does the ethics officer owe duties? Who are the stakeholders?
- What are the likely consequences of either decision? What fundamental rights or principles are involved?

Though these steps are likely to lead to an effective program, a report by the Ethics Resource Center on the occasion of the 20th anniversary of the enactment of the FSGO highlights the challenge posed to business managers by the lack of clarity in some portions of the guidelines. "On the one hand," the ERC report points out, "FSGO criteria are principles-based, which provides organizations with valuable flexibility in tailoring an approach that best fits their circumstances and avoids a 'one-size-fits-all' standard for compliance." On the other hand, "the benefits of flexibility and innovation notwithstanding, the principles-based nature of the FSGO criteria means that reasonable minds can disagree on what certain high-level principles mean."[56] For instance, the guidelines require an investigation in response to a report of wrongdoing; but they also seem to require more than that. A firm must learn from its mistakes and take steps to prevent recurrences such as follow-up investigation and program enhancements. The USSC also mandates consideration of the size of the organization, the number and nature of its business risks, and the prior history of the organization; mitigating factors such as self-reporting of violations, cooperation with authorities, and acceptance of responsibility; and aggravating factors such as its involvement in or tolerance of criminal activity, a violation of a prior order, or its obstruction of justice. These standards are to be judged against applicable industry standards; however, this requires that each firm benchmark against comparable companies. Consider the challenges involved in developing an airtight system and process in the Decision Point "Legal Pressure to Violate Confidentiality."

You have developed and implemented an ethics program. But how do you know whether the ethics program is "working"? How will you define "success"? Whom do you define as your primary stakeholders? What are their interests in your program and what are the impacts of your program on each stakeholder? How could you modify your program to ensure even greater success?

This Decision Point asks you to define the "success" of an ethics program, an extraordinary challenge even for those in this business for many years. One way to look at the inquiry would be to consider the measures by which you might be willing to be evaluated, since this is your project. Overall, you will need to explore whether there are pressures in your environment that encourage worker misconduct. You will need to consider whether there are systematic problems that encourage bad decisions. Have you identified all the major legal, ethical, and reputational risks that your organization faces, and have you determined the means by which to remediate those risks?

Because you will encourage the performance that you plan to measure, it is important to determine whether you will be most concerned with the end results or consequences or with the protection of particular values articulated by your program or codes. If you measure outcomes alone, you will have a singular focus on the achievement of those outcomes by decision makers. If you measure the protection of rights alone, you may be failing to consider the long-range implications of decisions in terms of their costs and benefits to the firm.

According to the Ethics Resource Center, the Federal Sentencing Guidelines are rarely applied to large corporations today. Those guidelines apply only to decisions by courts, and it is more common for cases against large corporations to be settled by means of Deferred Prosecution Agreements or Non-Prosecution Agreements.[57] On the other hand, ethics programs seem to be having an effect internally. A 2013 study found that corporate employees in the United States are witnessing record-low levels of wrongdoing; and these levels have continued to drop since 2007. However, while employees' willingness to report wrongdoing has declined, some of that decline is due, in part, to high retaliation rates that discourage reporting.[58]

To provide some context to this exploration, consider which offenses are most likely to lead to a fine for an organization. In 2014, the USSC received information on 162 organizations sentenced. Of those, 25.9 percent had been charged with fraud; 13 percent were charged with environmental offenses related specifically to water; 13 percent were charged with import/export offenses. Approximately 71 percent were required to pay a fine (or a fine plus restitution), and another 17.9 percent were required to pay restitution only. The average restitution payment imposed was almost $1.2 million, and the average fine imposed was more than $27.5 million. The average fine for cases involving fraud was more than $46.5 million, while the average fine in public corruption cases was $41.7 million, and in antitrust cases, the average was $65.6 million.[59]

Questions, Projects, and Exercises

1. To help understand an organizational culture, think about some organization to which you belong. Does your company, school, or fraternity/sorority have its own culture? How would you describe it? How does it influence individual decision making and action? Would you be a different person had you attended a different school or joined a different fraternity/sorority? How would you go about changing your organization's culture?

2. Consider how you evaluate whether a firm is "one of the good guys" or not. What are some of the factors you use to make this determination? Do you actually know the facts behind each of those elements, or has your judgment been shaped by the firm's reputation? Identify one firm you believe to be decent or ethical and make a note of the basis for that conclusion. Next, identify a second firm that you do not believe to be ethical or that you think has questionable values and write down the basis for that alternate conclusion. Now, using the Internet and other relevant sources, explore the firms' cultures and decisions, checking the results of your research against your original impressions of the firms. Try to evaluate the cultures and decisions of each firm as if you had no idea whether they were ethical. Were your impressions accurate or do they need to be modified slightly?

3. You will need to draft a memorandum to your chief executive identifying the value of a triple-bottom-line approach, which would represent an enormous shift from the firm's current orientation. What are three key points that you could make and how would you best support this argument?

4. Now that you have an understanding of corporate culture and the variables that impact it, how would you characterize an ethically effective culture, one that would effectively lead to profitable and valuable long-term sustainability for the firm?

5. One element that surely impacts a firm's culture is its employee population. While a corporate culture can shape an employee's attitudes and habits, it will do so more easily if people who have already developed those attitudes and habits are hired in the first place. How would you develop a recruitment and selection process that would most successfully allow you to hire the best workers for your particular culture? Should you get rid of employees who do not share the corporate culture? If so, how would you do that?

6. What are some of the greatest benefits and hazardous costs of compliance-based cultures?

7. Assume you have a number of suppliers for your global apparel business. You have in place a code of conduct both for your workplace and for your suppliers. Each time you visit a particular supplier, even on unannounced visits, it seems as if that supplier is in compliance with your code. However, you have received communications from that supplier's employees that there are violations. What should you do?

8. You are aware of inappropriate behavior and violations of your firm's code of conduct throughout your operation. In an effort to support a collegial and supportive atmosphere, however, you do not encourage co-workers to report on their peers. Unfortunately, you believe that you must make a shift in that policy and institute a mandatory reporting structure. How would you design the structure and how would you implement the new program in such a way that the collegiality that exists is not destroyed?

9. *Wasta* is the term used in the United Arab Emirates (UAE) for favoritism. In the UAE it is a highly valued element of the culture. In fact, while nepotism might be kept under wraps or discussed in hushed tones in an American firm, *wasta* is more likely to be

worn on one's sleeve among UAE professionals. It is precisely who you know that often dictates the position you might get in many companies or how fast you might get approved for certain processes. If you were assigned to build and then lead a team based in the UAE that would be comprised of both UAE nationals (called "Emiratis") as well as U.S. expatriates (expats), how might you most effectively respond to this culture of historical and embedded preferential treatment, reflecting the local realities, while at the same time respecting your own or your home country's value structure, *if different?*

10. A large U.S.-based corporation has decided to develop a mission statement and then conduct training on a new ethics program. It engages you to assist in these endeavors. What activities would you need to conduct in order to complete this project? What are some of the concerns you should be sure to consider?

11. Put yourself in the position of someone who is establishing an organization from the ground up. What type of leader would you want to be? How would you create that image or perception? Do you create a mission statement for the firm and/or a code of conduct? What process would you use to do so? Would you create an ethics and/ or compliance program and how would you then integrate the mission statement and program throughout your organization? What do you anticipate might be your successes and challenges?

12. With regard to employee recognition in the workplace, what effects would a program like "employee of the month" have on the corporate culture, and what factors might lead you to recommend it as a motivational program for your company?

13. Identify an industry in which you would like to work, and choose a company for whom you would like to work, ideally. Use the company's website to learn about its core values and culture in order to find your best fit and then explain your choice. Next, identify a company at which you would *not* like to work based on its core values and culture. Explain your reasons.

Key Terms

After reading this chapter, you should have a clear understanding of the following key terms. For a complete definition, please see the Glossary.

code of conduct, *p. 129*
compliance-based culture, *p. 119*
culture, *p. 110*
ethics officers, *p. 123*

Federal Sentencing Guidelines for Organizations (FSGO), *p. 136*
mission statement, *p. 129*

United States Sentencing Commission (USSC), *p. 136*
values-based culture, *p. 119*
whistle-blowing, *p. 132*

Endnotes

1. Adapted from EPIC, "Measuring Organizational Integrity and the Bottom Line Results One Can Expect," www.epic-online.net/quest_7.html (accessed July 24, 2012).

2. J. Liker, *Toyota Culture; The Heart and Soul of the Toyota Way* (Burr Ridge, IL: McGraw-Hill, 2007).

3. Martin Fackler, "The 'Toyota Way' Is Translated for a New Generation of Foreign Managers," *The New York Times* (February 15, 2007), www.nytimes.com/2007/02/15 /business/worldbusiness/15toyota.html?pagewanted=all (accessed February 23, 2016).

4. Max Chafkin, "The Zappos Way of Managing," *Inc.* (May 1, 2009), www.inc.com /magazine/20090501/the-zappos-way-of-managing.html#ixzz39pzykw7s (accessed February 23, 2016); Tony Hsieh, *Delivering Happiness: A Path to Profits, Passion and Purpose* (New York: Business Plus, 2010).

5. Chloe Albanesius, "Zappos-Owned 6pm.com Glitch Prices Everything at $50," *PC Magazine,* May 24, 2010.

6. James Collins and Jerry Porras, *Built to Last: Successful Habits of Visionary Companies* (New York: HarperCollins, 1994), p. 73.

7. James C. Collins, *How the Mighty Fall: And Why Some Companies Never Give In* (New York: HarperCollins, 2009).

8. Adapted from Jim Heskett, Earl Sasser, and Joe Wheeler, *The Ownership Quotient: Putting the Service Profit Chain to Work for Unbeatable Competitive Advantage* (Boston: Harvard Business Publishing, 2008).

9. James L. Heskett, *The Culture Cycle: How to Shape the Unseen Force That Transforms Performance* (Upper Saddle River, NJ: FT Press, 2012).

10. Tim Starks, "Katrina's Lessons Seen in Response to Sandy," *Congressional Quarterly* (December 29, 2012), http://public.cq.com/docs/weeklyreport/weeklyreport-0000004197197.html (accessed February 23, 2016).

11. Brian Naylor, "Lessons from Katrina Boost FEMA's Sandy Response," NPR (November 12, 2012), www.npr.org/2012/11/03/164224394/lessons-from-katrina-boost-femas-sandy-response (accessed February 23, 2016).

12. Tim Starks, "Katrina's Lessons Seen in Response to Sandy," *Congressional Quarterly* (December 29, 2012), http://public.cq.com/docs/weeklyreport/weeklyreport-0000004197197.html (accessed February 23, 2016).

13. Ethics Resource Center, *National Business Ethics Survey* (2011).

14. Sara Marzec, "Leaders Engaged and Outspoken," *Ethisphere* (April 22, 2014), http://ethisphere.com/magazine-articles/leaders-engaged-and-outspoken/#sthash.jNNqTw4F.dpuf (accessed August 16, 2014).

15. Jacquelyn Smith, "The World's Most Ethical Companies," *Forbes* (March 6, 2013), www.forbes.com/sites/jacquelynsmith/2013/03/06/the-worlds-most-ethical-companies-in-2013/ (accessed February 23, 2016).

16. Rupert Neate, "HSBC Fined $470m for 'Abusive Mortgage Practices' during 2008 Crisis," *The Guardian* (February 5, 2016), www.theguardian.com/business/2016/feb/05/hsbc-fined-morgage-practices-financial-crisis (accessed March 7, 2016); Associated Press, "HSBC Unit to Pay 2.5 Billion in Fraud Case," *USA Today* (October 18, 2013), www.usatoday.com/story/money/business/2013/10/18/hsbc-unit-fined-securities-fraud-lawsuit/3007199/ (accessed February 5, 2016); Aruna Viswanatha and Brett Wolf, "HSBC to Pay $1.9 Billion U.S. Fine in Money-Laundering Case," *Reuters.com* (December 11, 2012), www.reuters.com/article/2012/12/11/us-hsbc-probe-idUSBRE8BA05M20121211 (accessed February 5, 2016).

17. "Wal-Mart's FCPA and Compliance-Related Expenses Stand at $738 Million— Expected to Grow to Approximately $850 Million," *FCPA Professor* (February 23, 2016), http://fcpaprofessor.com/wal-marts-fcpa-and-compliance-related-expenses-stand-at-738-million-expected-to-grow-to-approximately-850-million/ (accessed March 7, 2016).

18. U.S. Securities and Exchange Commission, "J.P. Morgan to Pay $267 Million for Disclosure Failures" (December 18, 2015), www.sec.gov/news/pressrelease/2015-283.html (accessed March 8, 2016).

19. J. Anderson, "Credit Suisse Loses $779 Million after Settling Tax Evasion Case," *The New York Times* (July 22, 2014), p. B4, http://dealbook.nytimes.com/2014/07/22/credit-suisse-posts-largest-loss-since-2008-after-u-s-fine/ (accessed February 23, 2016).

20. Ethics Resource Center, "National Business Ethics Survey of the U.S. Workforce" (2013), www.ethics.org/downloads/2013NBESFinalWeb.pdf (accessed August 18, 2014).

21. Ethics Resource Center, "National Business Ethics Survey of the U.S. Workforce" (2013), www.ethics.org/downloads/2013NBESFinalWeb.pdf (accessed February 23, 2016).

22. R. Larsen, "Leadership in a Values-Based Organization," Sears Lectureship in Business Ethics, Bentley College, Waltham, MA (February 7, 2002).

23. R. Ferguson, "Business Ethics and the Financial Services Sector: The Way Forward," *Raytheon Lectureship in Business Ethics* (April 2, 2013).

24. Ethics Resource Center, "National Business Ethics Survey of the U.S. Workforce" (2013), www.ethics.org/downloads/2013NBESFinalWeb.pdf (accessed August 18, 2014).

25. L. Trevino, M. Brown, and L. Hartman, "A Qualitative Investigation of Perceived Executive Ethical Leadership: Perceptions from Inside and Outside the Executive Suite," *Human Relations* 56, no. 1 (January 2003), pp. 5–37.

26. Ibid.

27. O. Demirtas and A. A. Akdogan, "The Effect of Ethical Leadership Behavior on Ethical Climate, Turnover Intention, and Affective Commitment," *Journal of Business Ethics Online* (May 11, 2014). doi:10.1007/s10551-014-2196-6.

28. Compensation Force, "2014 Turnover Rates by Industry" (March 2015), www.compensationforce.com/2015/03/2014-turnover-rates-by-industry.html (accessed February 24, 2016).

29. W. G. Bliss, "Cost of Employee Turnover," *The Advisor* (June 17, 2014), www.isquare.com/turnover.cfm (accessed February 24, 2016).

30. Johnson & Johnson, "Investor Fact Sheet" (2011), www.investor.jnj.com/investor-facts.cfm (accessed July 24, 2012); "Johnson & Johnson at a Glance," *Forbes* (n.d.), http://finapps.forbes.com/finapps/jsp/finance/compinfo/CIAtAGlance.jsp?tkr=JNJ (accessed July 24, 2012).

31. R. Larsen, "Leadership in a Values-Based Organization," *Sears Lectureship in Business Ethics,* Bentley College Waltham, MA (February 7, 2002).

32. D. Ingram and R. Krasny, "Johnson & Johnson to Pay $2.2 Billion to End U.S. Drug Probes," *Reuters.com* (November 4, 2014), www.reuters.com/article/2013/11/04/us-jnj-settlement-idUSBRE9A30MM20131104 (accessed February 24, 2016).

33. Johnson & Johnson, "Our Credo Values" (August 29, 2014), www.jnj.com/about-jnj/jnj-credo.

34. Courtesy of Johnson & Johnson, www.jnj.com/our_company/our_credo_history/index.htm (accessed April 4, 2010); www.jnj.com/connect/about-jnj/jnjcredo/ (accessed July 24, 2012).

35. www.jnj.com/our_company/our_credo_history/index.htm (accessed July 24, 2012).

36. Quoted in E. G. Flamholtz and Y. Randle, *Corporate Culture: The Ultimate Strategic Asset* (Stanford, CA: Stanford University Press, 2011), p. 101.

37. For an exceptional analysis of the distinction between four types of ethics statements (values statements, corporate credos, codes of ethics, and Internet privacy policies) see P. E. Murphy, "Developing, Communicating and Promoting Corporate

Ethics Statements: A Longitudinal Analysis," *Journal of Business Ethics* 62 (2005), pp. 183–189.

38. PricewaterhouseCoopers, "Why Have a Code?," www.pwc.com/extweb/newcoatwork .nsf/docid/BCC554487E1C3BC680256C2B003115D5 (accessed July 24, 2012).

39. L. S. Paine, R. Deshpande, J. D. Margolis, and K. E. Bettcher, "Up to Code: Does Your Company's Conduct Meet World-Class Standards?," *Harvard Business Review* (December 2005).

40. American Institute of Certified Public Accountants, www.aicpa.org/RESEARCH /STANDARDS/CODEOFCONDUCT/Pages/default.aspx; Defense Industry Initiative on Business Ethics and Conduct, www.defenseethics.org/; Direct Marketing Association, www.the-dma.org/nonprofitfederation/EthicsGuidelines103007.pdf; Academy of Management, www.aomonline.org/aom.asp?ID5257 (accessed July 24, 2012).

41. S. Prakesh Sethi, *Globalization and Self-Regulation: The Crucial Role That Corporate Codes of Conduct Play in Global Business* (New York: Macmillan, 2011), pp. 11–12.

42. Walmart, "Ethics & Integrity," http://corporate.walmart.com/our-story/ethics-integrity (accessed February 11, 2016).

43. Lockheed Martin, "Ethics Awareness Training" (2016), www.lockheedmartin.com /us/who-we-are/ethics/training.html com (accessed March 6, 2016).

44. Merck & Co., Inc., "2014 Corporate Responsibility Report" (2014), www.merck responsibility.com/ethics-transparency/ (accessed March 8, 2016).

45. Ben DiPietro, "Turning Employees into Ethics Believers," *The Wall Street Journal* [Blog] (September 26, 2014), http://blogs.wsj.com/riskandcompliance/2014/ 09/26/turning-employees-into-ethics-and-compliance-believers/ (accessed March 6, 2016).

46. M. Roberto, R. Bohmer, and A. Edmondson, "Facing Ambiguous Threats," *Harvard Business Review* (November 2006), pp. 106–113; http://hbr.org/2006/11/facing-ambiguous-threats/ar/1 (accessed July 24, 2012).

47. Ibid.

48. LRN, *The Impact of Codes of Conduct on Corporate Culture* (Los Angeles, CA: LRN, 2006).

49. Matthew Miner, "It's Time to Fix Our Sentencing Laws," *National Law Journal* 34, no. 4 (September 26, 2011), p. 43.

50. USSC, *Guidelines Manual,* sec. 8B2.1, "Effective Compliance and Ethics Program" (2011), www.ussc.gov/Guidelines/2011_Guidelines/Manual_HTML/8b2_1.htm (accessed July 16, 2012).

51. Michael D. Greenberg, "Directors as Guardians of Compliance and Ethics within the Corporate Citadel: What the Policy Community Should Know," *Conference Proceedings, RAND Center for Corporate Ethics and Governance* (2010), pp. 15–16, www.rand.org/pubs/conf_proceedings/CF277.html (accessed August 10, 2012).

52. Ibid., p. 8.

53. W. McBride, "Corporate Tax Hike Signals End of Chilean Miracle," Tax Foundation (September 30, 2014), http://taxfoundation.org/blog/corporate-tax-hike-signals-end-chilean-miracle (accessed August 23, 2016).

54. USSC, § 8C2.5(3).

55. Ibid., note 11.

56. Ethics Resource Center, "The Federal Sentencing Guidelines for Organizations at Twenty Years: A Call to Action for More Effective Promotion and Recognition of Effective Compliance and Ethics Programs," Discussion Draft for Public Comment (2011), www.ethics.org/fsgo (accessed August 10, 2012).

57. Ethics Resource Center, "Federal Sentencing Guidelines for Corporations" (2011), www.ethics.org/fsgo (accessed August 1, 2012).

58. Ethics Resource Center, "2013 National Business Ethics Survey" (2013), www.ibe.org.uk/userassets/surveys/nbes2013.pdf (accessed February 11, 2016).

59. U.S. Sentencing Commission, *2014 Sourcebook of Federal Sentencing Statistics* (2014), www.ussc.gov/research-and-publications/annual-reports-sourcebooks/2014/sourcebook-2014 (accessed February 11, 2016).

Readings

Reading **4-1**

When Ethical Issues Derive from Cultural Thinking

Geetanee Napal

I am a professor of business ethics who has been "working toward justice" in Mauritius for over 15 years. The purpose of this discussion is to share some of the ethical problems that prevail in an emerging nation where ethics is very slowly evolving.

In 2001, after more than four years' negotiation, I was permitted to introduce a business ethics module in our undergraduate Management program at my university. In 1997, I was told that "ethics [wasn't] important . . . [because] we shouldn't aspire to produce overly ethical managers." I never heard of such a thing as an "overly ethical manager." In 2001, things got better as a new Dean with a law background took office.In the years that followed, I was able to introduce ethics modules in other management, finance and law programs, including a "Business Ethics & CSR" module in the Masters of Business Administration program, an "Ethics in Organizational Management" module in a program for the Mauritius Police Force and a Corporate Ethics module for an online MBA program. Being the only full-time staff to teach ethics, I face a fair bit of pressure as the workload increases over the years.

However, changing people's thinking is no easy task considering the culturally accepted unethical business practices that I face on a recurring basis. The individualist culture that is prevalent in Mauritius tends to tempt decision-makers to put relationships before duty and invites "easy money," sacrificing goodwill and sustainability in the process. Most people in more economically developed parts of the world may have an idealized or romanticized vision of what it means to act "ethically" in a developing economy. Certainly, if you are a large business, such as Shell Oil, you might be able to enter that environment and assert that you will not pay bribes or you will only engage in business according to a pre-conceived set of values. However, most of us are not Shell Oil. Therefore, for many or most in these economies, simply to "make do," one must make decisions every day about which values are more important. Some of us have the privilege of small compromises. However, for many in this world who live in extreme poverty or under undue duress, those compromises are much more severe. While we all have choices, some of us often adopt courses of action that deviate from the ethical route.

Let me tell you a bit about the culture in which I work and live.

Mauritius is a developing island nation in the Indian Ocean, independent in its government since 1968. The country has a working constitution and a competitive multi-party system. Civil liberties remain fairly secure amidst open and forceful partisan politics and a fairly autonomous judiciary. The political culture of the country remains democratic, socially cohesive and ethnically tolerant. Mauritius experienced 360 years of Dutch, French, and British colonial rule and became independent from Britain in 1968. Since then, the country has been one of the most successful democracies in the developing world.

However, in spite of having a relatively autonomous investigative body, a more-or-less independent judiciary and good laws, corruption remains a serious problem across various sectors of the economy. Below are some examples of "malpractice" that the business sector experienced over the last decade.

In 2001, the national aviation company Air Mauritius faced a major fraud scandal following revelations of its financial malpractice. Senior officials made unauthorized payments from a "secret fund" and then distributed free air tickets to politicians and journalists (Hamel, 2001; Scandales Financiers, 2003). A sum of Rs 85 million (over €2 million) was embezzled from the company (Affaire Air Mauritius, 2003) while a significant amount of "black money" was allegedly channelled to political parties and used to fund the overseas trips of eminent figures (Affaire Air Mauritius, 2003; Questions, 2003; Scandales Financiers, 2003).

An equally shocking scandal is the case of the Royal Mint, the British institution that mints coins for the United Kingdom. The Royal Mint originated over 1,100 years ago and has since then been involved in the production of coins for Great Britain and other countries around the world. In 2004, the Serious Fraud Office of Great Britain denounced a number of illicit transactions effected by the Royal Mint. The Royal Mint was accused of making illegal payments to both specific financial institutions and also to high-profile personalities including the former governor of the Bank of Mauritius (Un Paiement Suspect, 2003). These payments were linked to at least twelve contracts by the Royal Mint to supply coinage to the Bank of Mauritius. The former bank governor had negotiated and was paid secret, illicit commissions on those contracts (Affaire Royal Mint, 2003; Royal Mint Saga, 2004). Evidently, the abuse of power runs through the very highest echelons of Mauritian financial institutions. Mauritius has effective laws on its books; the problem lies in their implementation (Napal, 2008).

Considering the prevalence and severity of corruption:

1. How does one handle the abuse of power as a main contributing factor? Is it different when it is in business and in government?
2. Can stricter laws help control the excessive use of power where culture seems to permit or even condone unethical decisions in business?
3. What do you think might have motivated the governor of the Bank of Mauritius to sacrifice his reputation and to negotiate payments of what appears to be relatively nominal amounts of returns?
4. In connection with the Air Mauritius case, it was reported that members of the Mauritius cabinet were aware of the existence of the illegal fund all along (Affaire Air Mauritius, 2003; Hamel, 2001). How might we explain the decision-making processes of those institutions that are accountable to the State? What motivations could have been at play?

As a Mauritius citizen, observing these circumstances over and over again, it is my perception that those in developing economies passively accept the abuse of power that accounts predominantly for corrupt behavior (Affaire Royal Mint, 2003; Alleged Corruption, 2004; L'Événement, 2004; L'Événement L'ICAC, 2004; Napal, 2012; Un Paiement Suspect, 2003). Revelations of situations like Air Mauritius or the Royal Mint—large-scale corruption in a small-island economy—undoubtedly shock outsiders such as business students and practitioners who have an expectation of ethics in their workplace.

Yet, in a national culture where these behaviors are not simply accepted but expected, consider the following questions:

1. How could ethical leadership contribute to impact existing norms and values in a way that could guide corporate behavior and decision-making?
2. What contribution do mission statements and ethics codes have in creating a more effective ethical corporate culture?
3. Do you have any faith in the roles that devices like ethics help lines might have in the corporate cultures of firms like Air Mauritius or the Royal Mint?
4. Can governmental regulation have an impact on corporate cultures?
5. What do you think might motivate a high-profile individual, such as a bank governor, to "throw everything away" for a relatively small financial gain?

References

Affaire Air Mauritius: Tyack Autorisé à Faire un Retrait Mensuel de Rs 75000, Retrieved June 8, 2011, from http://www.lexpress.mu [October 18, 2003].

Affaire Royal Mint: Sir Indur Ramphul Interrogé de Nouveau, Retrieved June 15, 2011, from http://www.lexpress.mu [June 14, 2003].

Alleged Corruption: Damning Testimony Against ICAC Boss, Retrieved June 10, 2011, from http://www.lexpress.mu [May 18, 2004].

"Building an Island of Integrity: Proceedings of a Workshop on National Integrity Systems in Mauritius," Presented by the Office of the Attorney General, 1998.

Hamel, I. Caisse noire d'Air Mauritius à Genève, Retrieved December 7, 2015, from http://www.swissinfo.ch [October 18, 2001].

L'Événement: Beekarry Indispose le Gouvernement, Retrieved June 9, 2011, from http://www.lexpress.mu [April 25, 2004].

L'Événement: L'ICAC en Pleine Tempête, Retrieved June 9, 2011, from http://www.lexpress.mu [January 11, 2004].

Napal G. 2005. An Assessment of Power Abuse under Ethics Philosophies, *Electronic Journal of Business Ethics and Organizational Studies,* 10, 1: 29–34.

Napal G. 2008. "Anti-Corruption Reform: Where Do We Go Wrong in Mauritius?," presented at The 2nd World Business Ethics Forum: Rethinking the Value of Business Ethics, Hong Kong Baptist University, 11–12 December 2008.

Napal G. 2012. *Ethical Issues at the Independent Commission against Corruption* in "Contemporary Challenges in Corporate Governance," RossiSmith Academic Publishing.

Questions à Ramanooj Gopalsingh, Commissaire de Police: Nos Succès ne Nous Endormiront Pas, Retrieved August 13, 2011, from http://www.lexpress.mu [August 11, 2003].

Report of the Select Committee on Fraud and Corruption, 2001.

Royal Mint Saga. L'Affaire Indur Ramphul: Enquête Élargie en Vue, Retrieved June 15, 2011, from http://www.lemauricien.mu [29 February 2004].

Scandales Financiers: Pleins Feux sur les Enquêtes à Sensation, Retrieved August 12, 2011, from http://www.lexpress.mu [August 3, 2003].

Un Paiement Suspect du Royal Mint Découvert: Le Serious Fraud Office Britannique Veut Savoir si un Paiement a été Effectue en 1993 par un Fabricant de Pieces de Monnaie à Sir Indur Ramphul, ex-Gouverneur de la Banque Centrale, Retrieved June 15, 2011, from http://www.lexpress.mu [February 24, 2003].

Source: Permission granted by the author.

Reading 4-2

Assessment and Plan for Organizational Culture Change at NASA

The *Columbia* Accident Investigation Board

Editors' note: Following the accident that destroyed the Space Shuttle *Columbia* in 2003, the National Aeronautics and Space Administration (NASA) appointed the *Columbia* Accident Investigation Board (CAIB) to investigate the causes of the accident. The loss of *Columbia* came eighteen years after the Space Shuttle *Challenger* exploded during take-off. The CAIB report identified the organizational culture at NASA as having "as much to do with the accident as the External Tank foam." Following the CAIB report, NASA hired an outside consulting firm, Behavioral Science Technology (BST), to recommend changes in the organization. This reading is taken from the BST report of their investigation. As was the case following the *Challenger* disaster, responsibility for the accident was attributed as much to the culture and practices of NASA as it was to physical or mechanical causes.

Executive Summary

On February 1, 2003, the Space Shuttle *Columbia* and its crew of seven were lost during return to Earth. A group of distinguished experts was appointed to comprise the *Columbia* Accident Investigation Board (CAIB), and this group spent six months conducting a thorough investigation of the cause of the accident. The CAIB found that NASA's history and culture contributed as much to the *Columbia* accident as any technical failure.

As a result of the CAIB and related activities, NASA established the objective of completely transforming its organizational and safety culture.

BST was selected to assist NASA in the development and implementation of a plan for changing the safety climate and culture Agency-wide. The scope of this effort is to develop and deploy an organizational culture change initiative within NASA, with an emphasis on safety climate and culture.

The first task assigned to BST was to conduct an assessment of the current status and develop an implementation plan, both to be completed within 30 days. This report summarizes the assessment findings and the recommended implementation plan.

This assessment concluded that there are many positive aspects to the NASA culture. The NASA culture reflects a long legacy of technical excellence, a spirit of teamwork and pride, and a can-do approach to task achievement. In particular, culture attributes related to work group functioning at the peer level are among the strongest we have seen. These characteristics are consistent with NASA's rating in the 2003 Office of Personnel Management Survey at the top of the Best Places to Work in the Federal Government.

Despite these positive attributes, there are some important needs for improvement. The present NASA culture does not yet fully reflect the Agency's espoused core values of Safety, People, Excellence, and Integrity. The culture reflects an organization in transition, with many ongoing initiatives and lack of a clear sense at working levels of "how it all fits together."

- **Safety** is something to which NASA personnel are strongly committed in concept, but NASA has not yet created a culture that is fully supportive of safety. Open communication is not yet the norm and people do not feel fully comfortable raising safety concerns to management.

- **People** do not feel respected or appreciated by the organization. As a result, the strong commitment people feel to their technical work does not transfer to a strong commitment to the organization.

- **Excellence** is a treasured value when it comes to technical work, but is not seen by many NASA personnel as an imperative for other aspects of the organization's functioning (such as management skills, supporting administrative functions, and creating an environment that encourages excellence in communications).

- **Integrity** is generally understood and manifested in people's work. However, there appear to be pockets where the management chain has (possibly unintentionally) sent signals that the raising of issues is not welcome. This is inconsistent with an organization that truly values integrity.

There is an opportunity and need to become an organization whose espoused values are fully integrated into its culture—an organization that "lives the values" by fostering cultural integrity. We recommend an initiative with that as its theme.

The recommended initiative should address working through existing leaders to instill behaviors consistent with the Agency's values and the desired culture, while also establishing the foundation for developing future leaders who will sustain that culture and individual contributors who reflect the desired culture in their actions. A long-term (three year) plan is identified with a specific series of actions identified in the first five months to launch this effort.

BST's first efforts were to understand the current culture and climate at NASA in order to identify focus areas for improvement. We approached this task with the belief that there was much that was positive about NASA's culture. Our challenge was to build from positive aspects of the existing culture, strengthening the culture and at the same time addressing the issue raised in the CAIB report.

By culture we mean the shared values and beliefs of an organization—commonly described as "the way we do things here." The culture can also be thought of as the shared norms for the behavior in the organization, often motivated by unstated assumptions.

Where organizational culture comprises unstated assumptions that govern how we do things within an organization, climate describes the prevailing influences on a particular area of functioning (such as safety) at a particular time. Thus, the culture is something that is more deeply embedded and long-term, taking longer to change and influencing organizational performance across many areas of functioning. Climate, on the other hand, changes faster and more immediately reflects the attention of leadership.

Culture influences behavior in that the group's shared norms and beliefs will influence what people do. However, leaders' behavior is an important influence on culture. Through the examples they set, the messages they send, and the consequences they provide, leaders influence the behaviors of others, as well as their beliefs about what is acceptable and what is valuable to the organization.

The CAIB had produced a detailed report on the causes of the *Columbia* accident, and explicitly addressed "organizational causes" as the critical contributor. Specifically, the CAIB identified the following organizational cause of the *Columbia* accident:

> The organizational causes of this accident are rooted in the Space Shuttle Program's history and culture, including the original compromises that were required to gain approval for the Shuttle Program, subsequent years of resource constraints, fluctuating priorities, schedule pressures, mischaracterizations of the Shuttle

as operational rather than developmental, and lack of an agreed national vision. Cultural traits and organizational practices detrimental to safety and reliability were allowed to develop, including: reliance on past success as a substitute for sound engineering practices (such as testing to understand why systems were not performing in accordance with requirements/specifications); organizational barriers which prevented effective communication of critical safety information and stifled professional differences of opinion; lack of integrated management across program elements; and the evolution of an informal chain of command and decision making processes that operated outside the organization's rules. In the Board's view, NASA's organizational culture and structure had as much to do with this accident as the External Tank foam. Organizational culture refers to the values, norms, beliefs, and practices that govern how an institution functions. At the most basic level, organizational culture defines the assumptions that employees make as they carry out their work. It is a powerful force that can persist through reorganizations and the reassignment of key personnel.

Source: The full *Columbia* Accident Investigation Board report is available at www.nasa.gov/columbia/home/CAIB_Vol1.html.

Reading 4-3

Does the Company Get It?—20 Questions to Ask Regarding Compliance, Ethics, and Risk Management

OCEG

This OCEG questionnaire has been designed as a tool that can be used to determine whether a company has an effective process and culture in place to control and mitigate compliance and ethics related risks.

Questions 1 through 3 address organizational culture to determine if a company is taking the formal steps necessary to address the subject of compliance and ethics—and whether management, the

Board of Directors and the employees really believe that compliance and ethics are an integral part of the company's corporate culture. A stakeholder should evaluate whether the company has seriously considered all of the enterprise risks of non-compliance or unethical conduct, has established its own goals and objectives, and has communicated its behavioral expectations effectively throughout the organization.

Questions 4 and 5 consider scope and strategy of the compliance and ethics program, assessing how thoroughly it can address potential risks. Most important is the integration of that process with overall enterprise risk management. The Securities & Exchange Commission expects compliance and ethics issues to be considered even when fast-paced decisions must be made. Stakeholders in publicly traded companies must be able to determine whether the compliance and ethics program is sufficiently broad in scope and well enough planned to address this need.

Questions 6 through 8 identify the structure and resources dedicated to the ethics and compliance program, judging the seriousness of commitment to effective management of the program. It is the audit committee's responsibility to ensure that a structural process is in place that encourages both top-down communication and bottom-up feedback, and that issues are dealt with quickly and completely. If the proper resources are not funded and in place to prevent the audit committee from becoming a "choke point," the program will be judged a failure, and the blame for inadequately addressing enterprise risk will be placed on upper management.

Questions 9 through 14 evaluate management of policies and training, and further address program adequacy by looking at the mechanics of the processes in place. These questions evaluate how Codes of Conduct and other policies are distributed, tracked and kept up to date, and under what circumstances they can be waived or overridden. They also address how employees and other stakeholders are trained to understand and apply established policies and procedures, and how information is communicated to them.

Questions 15 through 18 focus on internal enforcement, assessing whether the company appropriately and consistently deals with violations of established policies and procedures. If individuals are allowed to ignore, disobey or even mock the objectives and requirements of the compliance and ethics program, stakeholders can conclude that management is not fully committed to ensuring ethical conduct.

Questions 19 and 20 assess evaluation and continual improvement efforts in the compliance and ethics program. Without processes to judge program elements and implement necessary improvements, any compliance and ethics program will have difficulty staying efficient, effective and up to date. Well-developed routine monitoring and periodic assessment processes, with clear paths for communication of recommended changes, may be the best sign of a mature and effective management system.

Culture

1. **What does your organization say about compliance, ethics, and values in its formal mission and vision statement?**

Why Ask This Question?

Review of the formal mission and vision statement gives the investor some insight into the organization's compliance and ethics values and commitments. An investor should look at the scope of this statement to see if the organization addresses some or all of the following constituencies: employees, customers, suppliers, shareholders, and the community/society at large.

Potential Answers

- There is a separate formal compliance and ethics mission and vision statement.

- There is no formal mission and vision statement but there is a general Code of Conduct.

- Mission and vision for compliance and ethics is part of the overall organizational mission and vision statement.

Red Flags

- The absence of a formal statement may indicate that management is not taking a necessary first step regarding compliance and ethics management. In addition, this may violate

Sarbanes-Oxley provisions and listing requirements (if publicly traded).

- A boilerplate or unspecific mission statement indicates lack of thought, and possibly commitment, to an effective compliance and ethics function.

2. **How does your Board, and management, set the "tone at the top" and communicate compliance and ethics values, mission, and vision?**

Why Ask This Question?

An organization that can articulate the formal and informal processes that it uses to communicate mission, vision, and values exhibits a clear understanding of the need for leadership in compliance and ethics and the benefit of strong communication of Board and management commitment.

Potential Answers

- Distribute a Code of Conduct.
- Email all employees regularly.
- Communicate responsibilities in annual/quarterly meeting.
- Discussion of mission, vision and values in staff meetings and at presentations by leadership.

Red Flags

- If top leadership does not periodically or continuously communicate the values, mission, and vision (which represent the expectations of the organization), employees and other stakeholders may believe the formal statements lack credibility and executive backing.
- Passive or canned communications are often ignored by employees. More active forms of communicating expectations (e.g., inclusion of compliance and ethics criteria in performance reviews and compensation structures/decisions) send a clearer message.

3. **How do you know if your employees and other stakeholders are "convinced" that the organization is serious about its compliance and ethics responsibilities?**

Why Ask This Question?

When an organization can answer this question, indicating that its leadership and management at least tries to measure stakeholder beliefs, it evidences a strong commitment to follow through and support for its values, mission and vision. In addition, the answer to this question will help to measure whether the communications are understood and whether or not the actual mission, vision and values are embraced by employees.

Potential Answers

- Annual survey.
- Focus groups or interviews.
- Collect data during annual reviews.
- Exit interviews.
- Informal conversations.

Red Flags

- No effort is made to collect or determine employee and other stakeholder perceptions—This may indicate management is passively or affirmatively ignorant of the perceptions on the "shop floor." It may also mean that leadership views its job as done when a mission statement is issued.
- Company says it is "too expensive" to poll employees—There are inexpensive means of polling employee perceptions. Leadership and management should have some interest in knowing if their message is heard and believed.
- Company says it doubts the value of poll results in determining true employee beliefs—This may indicate that even the leadership does not believe that its mission and values are taken seriously, and that it knows that "practice" does not follow the company's stated "principles."

Scope/Strategy

4. **What is the scope of your compliance and ethics program and how does it integrate with your overall business strategy?**

Why Ask This Question?

If an organization understands its domestic risks, but has little understanding of its international risks, problems may arise. Similarly, the company may deal with compliance and ethics risks in functional "Domains" of Financial Assurance, Employment, Environmental, etc. with little coordination between them, and may effectively address certain areas of concern but fail to address others. Coordination of the compliance and ethics function with larger business strategy and goals is also essential.

Potential Answers

- We address compliance and ethics globally/locally.
- We address compliance and ethics issues in each function separately.
- Reactive or proactive consideration of business strategy in development or management of compliance and ethics functions.

Red Flags

- Inability to articulate a meaningful program—This may indicate a well developed and managed program does not exist, or that management is unaware of the program's operations. In either case, severe legal risk exists.
- Inability to articulate relationship between program and larger business strategy—This may indicate low level consideration by management to compliance and ethics functions.

5. **How do you assess compliance and ethics risks and how does this process integrate with enterprise risk management (ERM)?**

Why Ask This Question?

The more detailed and routine the risk assessment process, the more likely it is effective. In addition, understanding of ERM (e.g., COSO ERM) and integration with enterprise-wide analysis of risk may indicate a higher level of leadership and management concern for compliance and ethics functions.

Potential Answers

- Compliance and ethics risks are considered as part of our quarterly/annual risk management process.
- We deal with compliance and ethics risks in our compliance department (or legal of ce). They tell us what we need to do.

Red Flags

- Inability to articulate how legal and ethical risks are considered as part of ERM—This may indicate that management does not fully consider and analyze where legal and ethical risks are present. It may also indicate that legal and ethical risk management is not appropriately funded.
- Inability to understand ERM—This may indicate management does not have a comprehensive understanding of risks that may impede the organization from reaching its objectives.

Structure/Resources

6. **What position in the organization provides oversight and leadership in the compliance/ethics function and where does this position fall in the organizational chart?**

Why Ask This Question?

It is vital to know where responsibility for the compliance and ethics function falls in order to determine the level of influence and independence held by the person or people in such management positions. The identification of a chief compliance/ethics officer, the chain of authority this person (or people) reports within, the level of access to the Board, and which Board committee has oversight all serve as indicators of the strength and value attributed to the compliance and ethics function. In addition, it is valuable to know if compliance and ethics responsibilities are separated within the entity or combined. If separated, it is vital to learn how they coordinate.

Potential Answers

- Full-time chief compliance and ethics officer/ Part-time chief compliance and ethics officer.

- Chief ethics officer and separate lower level compliance managers within functional areas.

- Reports to the CEO/general counsel/dotted-line to the audit committee, etc.

Red Flags

- Independence is questionable—Without sufficient independence, the chief compliance and ethics officer may not be objective when viewing the activities of senior executives.

- Lack of senior level oversight—Federal Sentencing Guidelines indicate that a sufficiently senior level executive should provide program oversight.

- Lack of adequate coordination between "ethics" and "compliance" management.

7. **What is the organizational structure of your compliance and ethics management team?**

Why Ask This Question?

Different organizational structures are appropriate for different organizations and the answer to this question allows analysis of the appropriateness of structure and the actual commitment of resources to compliance and ethics.

Potential Answers

- Centralized vs. Decentralized. Dedicated Team vs. Shared or "Virtual" Team where compliance and ethics management responsibilities are part of other job roles.

Red Flags

- Structure does not match larger organization— An investor should be careful to note if the structure makes sense given the nature of the organization. For example, a centralized team of 3 people is probably inconsistent with a global conglomerate of 50,000 employees.

- A team that relies solely on part-time managers with other duties may not have adequately dedicated resources.

8. **How are resources allocated for compliance and ethics management activities, both routinely and to address significant issues that arise?**

Why Ask This Question?

How an organization determines to spend money and time on compliance and ethics matters is a good indication of the seriousness with which it takes these commitments and obligations.

Potential Answers

- Unified budget.

- Part of several department budgets.

- Funds identified for potential issues that risk analysis indicates may arise in a given budget cycle.

Red Flags

- No budget or unclear articulation of the budget may indicate the organization has seriously underfunded compliance and ethics management activities.

- Disconnected budget—If the budget is not directed by the chief compliance and ethics officer, it may indicate that there is a lack of coordinated strategy.

- Short term budget determinations without long range budgets to address anticipated future needs may indicate lack of adequate planning and analysis.

Policies

9. **What does your Code of Conduct address and who receives it?**

Why Ask This Question?

SOX and the Exchanges require a Code of Conduct for publicly traded companies. Beyond these requirements, a comprehensive Code of Conduct (or collection of policies) addressing all legal and regulatory requirements, expectations of employee/management behavior, ethical business conduct and social responsibility indicates an organization which has evaluated its values and decided how to articulate them.

Potential Answers

- The organization should be able to furnish its Code of Conduct and other policies, and identify the audience to whom they are distributed.

- The leadership and management should know the scope and content of the Code of Conduct and, in general, other policies.

Red Flags

- No Code of Conduct—This is such a widely accepted practice that it should be considered a basic requirement.

- Code is "canned"—If the Code of Conduct looks and feels like a generic policy, it may indicate that the organization has not thoughtfully addressed its unique compliance and ethics risk areas. As well, employees will most likely believe it is simple "window dressing" rather than a real guidepost for conduct.

- A Code of Conduct that does not adequately address all risk areas of the organization or clearly enunciate company values and expectations for behavior.

10. **How do you distribute your Code of Conduct and confirm that employees both receive and understand the Code and other policies?**

Why Ask This Question?

This gives insight into whether or not the Code is simply a piece of paper that is signed by each employee and filed for legal purposes—or if some confirmation of "understanding" is sought; a clear indication of leadership's seriousness

in demanding compliance with the Code and policies.

Potential Answers

- Distribute paper Code with new hire training and have employees sign it.

- Distribute the Code electronically each year with a multiple choice test.

- Present the Code of Conduct in live or electronic training sessions with opportunity for questions and discussion.

Red Flags

- No confirmation of receipt—This may indicate that, although it exists, the code is not being properly sent to employees.

- Weak confirmation of understanding—In addition to distributing the Code of Conduct, the organization should strive to ensure that the Code is understood by employees and other stakeholders.

- Too expensive—If an organization says that it is cost prohibitive to distribute the Code of Conduct to all employees with confirmation of receipt, it is probably unaware of many low cost and free tools. It also most likely indicates a low level of leadership commitment to the Code.

11. **What is your process for updating policies/procedures?**

Why Ask This Question?

Evidence of an established process for updating policies and procedures indicates a well managed component of the compliance and ethics program. Absence of such may indicate inadequate resources or lack of commitment to the program.

Potential Answers

- Annual review, quarterly review, etc.

- Notification from trade associations or outside counsel/consultants of changes in law/regulations.

Red Flags

- No process or infrequent updates—This may indicate that the organization is "out of date" with regard to its compliance and ethics risks.

- Sole reliance on periodic and non-routine updates from outside counsel/associations.

- No consideration of changes in organizational activities/locales, etc.

12. **Can any requirements established by the Code of Conduct and other policies be waived or overridden and, if so, what is the process for doing so?**

Why Ask This Question?

It is not inappropriate to provide for override of Code and policy requirements in certain circumstances, but it is important to know when and how they can be waived, and to ensure that a transparent process for doing so is in place.

Potential Answers

- All waivers must be approved by the Board and included in Board minutes.

- There is no formal process, but waiver decisions are made on a case-by-case basis by the Board, or management, or counsel.

Red Flags

- No process or a very loose case-by-case process.

- Lack of transparency/no waivers are disclosed.

Communication and Training

13. **How often, and by what methods, does your management communicate the values, mission, and vision of the compliance and ethics program to employees and other stakeholders?**

Why Ask This Question?

Having a mission statement is not enough—it is important to know that it is regularly and effectively communicated to employees and stakeholders

so that they know the organization's values and believe that the organization's leadership is serious about acting on those values.

Potential Answers

- Annual meeting for employees.

- Annual report for shareholders.

- Each master supplier agreement contains a statement regarding our Code of Conduct.

- Regular and routine reference to the Code of Conduct in all presentations by leadership about the organization's activities, plans and future.

- Regular and routine informal reference to values and mission by all levels of management.

Red Flags

- Lack of formal communication.

- 100% of communication is formal—While formal communications are important, most research confirms that employees gain much from informal communications from senior executives and managers about compliance and ethics responsibilities.

14. **Do you provide comprehensive training and conduct performance evaluations for each job role to ensure compliance and ethics responsibilities are understood and followed, and that necessary skills are learned and employed?**

Why Ask This Question?

Effective processes for ensuring employees have and use the information and skills needed to fulfill their compliance and ethics responsibilities is a critical component of an effective program. "Policies" do not necessarily equal "Performance."

Potential Answers

- For each role, we have a compliance and ethics curriculum.

- We embed some compliance and ethics training in each of our courses.

- We embed compliance and ethics criteria into our job evaluations.

Red Flags

- No help contribution line mechanism for immediate reporting of critical issues.

- New hire "dunk"—When all new employees are "dunked" into the same new hire program, regardless of job role, it may indicate that the organization has not clearly identified compliance and ethics risks as the apply to each job. As well, this may be viewed by DOJ and the courts as a lack of effort on the part of the organization (see Ad Hoc Committee on Federal Sentencing Guidelines for Organizations).

- Training only upon initial hiring—research shows training must be repeated for adequate learning. As well, the Federal Sentencing Guidelines for Organizations appear to head in the direction of increased training (see Ad Hoc Committee on Federal Sentencing Guidelines for Organizations).

- No consideration of compliant or ethical behavior in performance reviews or, even worse, positive evaluation or rewards even in the face of noncompliant behavior.

Issue Management

15. **How do employees, agents and other stakeholders raise issues regarding compliance and ethics-related matters?**

Why Ask This Question?

Providing effective avenues to raise issues without fear of retribution is a critical component of an effective program. It is important to know how employees and other stakeholders can raise issues and to confirm that they not only know how to do so, but also feel safe and comfortable in doing so or are even encouraged and rewarded.

Potential Answers

- Telephone helpline staffed by internal/external personnel.

- Web-based format.

- Email program.

- In person to supervisor or designated person.

Red Flags

- No help contribution line mechanism for immediate reporting of critical issues.

- No possibility of anonymous reporting

- Lack of access for stakeholders who are not employees.

- Lack of consistent call-handling or report of issue management.

- Inability to certify that stakeholders are aware of the mechanism—This may indicate that the organization is not in compliance with Sarbanes-Oxley section 301.

16. **How do you handle compliance and ethics issues that arise and scrutinize the sources of compliance failures?**

Why Ask This Question?

It is not enough that a mechanism exists to report issues—Management must have effective and consistent methods for managing and resolving issues and the source of recurrent problems.

Potential Answers

- Consistent process for all issues that can be fully explained and demonstrated.

- Consistent process for issues within a particular Domain (employment, financial, environmental, etc.), but not for all relevant Domains.

- Case by case basis.

Red Flags

- Lack of consistency.

- Lack of independent processing.

- Lack of scrutiny of sources of repeat problems.

17. **How consistently, and in what way, have you taken action against violators of the Code and Program?**

Why Ask This Question?

This gives insight into whether the organization has put some real "teeth" in the compliance and ethics program by disciplining violators.

Potential Answers

- Each organization should be able to provide examples of past actions taken.

Red Flags

- Termination of employment should be a possible outcome for failing to meet compliance or ethics requirements. Without this potential, employees and other stakeholder may not believe there are "teeth" to the program.

- Lack of consistency—If noncompliant or unethical behavior is tolerated, the program has no credibility.

18. **What is the process for determining which issues are escalated to the Board and for informing the Board when issues are resolved?**

Why Ask This Question?

This gives insight into the process for escalating and reporting compliance and ethics issues to the Board—and whether or not the Board is actually involved in the process and resolution of issues when appropriate.

Potential Answers

- Quarterly report to the audit committee regarding "significant" financial issues.

- Annual report to the Board regarding "significant" issues in all Domains (financial, employment, environmental, etc.).

- Report to Board, through legal counsel, of material risks presented by issues that arise.

- Board notification and involvement only in financial assurance areas or issues directly related to Board or Senior Management actions.

Red Flags

- No escalation criteria.

- No follow-up by Board.

Evaluation

19. **What ongoing processes are in place to monitor the effectiveness of the compliance and ethics program?**

Why Ask This Question?

This gives insight into whether the organization monitors efficacy and relative performance of its program against peers. Right now, true benchmarking is difficult due to inconsistent approaches, etc. Initiatives such as OCEG should help to solve this problem.

Potential Answers

- We perform annual internal audit of compliance and ethics controls.

- We perform periodic benchmarking with industry peers.

- We retain outside consultants to perform external audit of controls in some or all functional areas.

- We measure and keep records of compliance and ethics issues over time for use in improving controls.

Red Flags

- No process.

- Process lacks independence.

- Process has no ongoing, day to day component— only widely spaced periodic audits.

- Audits only determine that controls are followed, not that they are effective.

20. **Does the organization engage an external law firm or consultant to audit compliance and ethics program elements?**

Why Ask This Question?

While some organizations view external audits as a negative policing of employees, there is value in an independent external analysis of the effectiveness of selected controls and level of compliance with those controls. External assessors can also bring new ideas and tools to the attention of management.

Potential Answers

- We use our outside counsel.

- We use our external auditor/some other auditor.

- We use an outside risk management or ethics consultant.

Red Flags

- Process lacks independence.

- Process only judges compliance with selected controls and does not evaluate the appropriateness of the controls or their effectiveness in achieving compliance and ethical behavior.

Source: Adapted from EPIC, "Measuring Organizational Integrity and the Bottom Line Results One Can Expect," www .epic-online.net/quest_7.html (accessed July 24, 2012).

Reading **4-4**

Whistleblower Policies in United States Corporate Codes of Ethics

Richard Moberly and Lindsey E. Wylie

Introduction

Companies have issued Codes of Ethics (also called Codes of Conduct) for decades, and these Codes increasingly have contained provisions related to whistleblowing. For example, Codes often encourage or even require corporate employees to report incidents of misconduct they witness. Code provisions describe the types of misconduct employees should report and provide numerous ways for employees to make reports. Moreover, companies use Codes to promise employees that they will not retaliate against whistleblowers. Indeed, because these whistleblowing provisions have become an important part of a corporation's internal control and risk management systems, they merit closer examination to determine exactly what they require and promise. . . .

Methodology

This study used content analysis to examine the types of protections provided by U.S. corporate Codes of Ethics now that these substantial changes have had time to take effect. It differs from previous studies of Codes of Ethics in two important ways. First, most other studies of Codes catalog various provisions contained in Codes of Ethics generally. This study focuses discretely on a Code's whistleblower provisions. . . .

* * *

The current study . . . used public documents to obtain Codes from a randomly-selected sample of thirty publicly-traded companies from each of the three largest U.S. stock exchanges, the NYSE, the NASDAQ, and the AmEx, providing a sample of ninety companies. The random sample was obtained from a list generated by searches of annual SEC filings for the calendar year 2007. The searches were run on 10kwizard.com, a fee-based subscription service that collects corporate filings. We found the company Codes in each company's annual filing (called the Form 10-K or 10-KSB, collectively the "Form 10s") or on the company's website.

* * *

Discussion

. . . This section will highlight two of the more interesting findings from the study.

An Emerging Consensus

First, the results indicate that U.S. corporations have developed a consensus regarding the contents and scope of whistleblower provisions in corporate Codes. This consensus has emerged despite the facts that U.S. statutory and regulatory law provides little guidance regarding the Codes' contents, and that the listing agencies differ widely on the requirements they impose upon corporations.

Who Do the Codes Cover?

As noted above, Sarbanes-Oxley, the SEC regulations, and the stock exchange listing requirements all contain slightly different mandates on who should be covered by a company's Code of Ethics. Sarbanes-Oxley mentions only senior financial officers, the SEC regulations add principal executive officers, and all three stock exchanges require the Code to cover "all directors, officers, and employees." The majority of Codes comply with the stock exchanges' broad requirements: 98.9% cover all employees, 78.7% cover officers and senior management, and 82.0% cover directors. Interestingly, only 22.5% of the Codes specifically cover "financial officers," the one group mentioned by both Sarbanes-Oxley and the SEC regulations. About a quarter of the Codes (25.8%) permit contractors (i.e., people who are not "employees" but provide work for the company, such as self-employed consultants) to report wrongdoing and over half (53.9%) explicitly mention that the Code covers subsidiary corporations or the entire corporate family of companies.

Is Reporting Required or Encouraged?

Although some exceptions exist, the law rarely *requires* employees (or any individual) to report illegal behavior. The SEC follows this norm and only mandates that companies "promote" internal reporting of misconduct. U.S. corporations, however, have responded to this regulatory mandate by going beyond merely "promoting" whistleblowing. Instead, corporations *require* employees to report misconduct: 96.6% of these Codes make whistleblowing a duty of employment. Thirty-six percent also "encourage" employees to report misconduct. In other words, U.S. companies recognize the importance of whistleblowing to their own internal control mechanisms by demanding that every employee become a whistleblower if the employee witnesses misconduct.

What Violations Matter to the Companies?

Whistleblowers must always determine whether the misconduct they witness is the type of wrongdoing the company wants reported and whether the company will protect them for disclosing. To resolve the question of what violations should be reported, the SEC and the listing standards provide a variety of suggestions. The SEC states that "violations of the code" should be reported—no other types of misconduct, such as illegal or unethical behavior, are mentioned. As for the listing standards, the NYSE requires companies to encourage reports of "violations of laws, rules, regulations or the Code of business conduct" and the NASDAQ encourages reports of "questionable behavior." The AmEx simply adopts the SEC regulation approach by addressing only reports of Code violations.

A large percentage of companies (93.3%) follow the SEC regulations precisely and indicate that the misconduct to be reported are violations of the Code itself. However, many companies expand this basic requirement and require employees to report a broader range of wrongdoing. For example, 76.4% broaden the reporting requirement to include violations of the law or regulations and more than half (52.8%) mandate reporting "unethical" or "improper" conduct. Taken together, the Codes' requirement that employees report violations of the Code, illegal conduct, and unethical behavior indicate that companies want employees to report an extremely broad range of potential misconduct. . . .

Interestingly, many corporations went beyond these general instructions to point out specific types of misconduct that should be reported. These categories may shed some light on the type of misconduct corporations truly think will be beneficial to have reported. Indeed, from one perspective, the Codes identify specific areas to be reported that align with the corporation's self-interest. For example, the most frequently identified misconduct to be reported was conflicts of interest—either one's own conflict or the conflict of others—by 79.8% of the Codes. This outcome was followed by requests that employees report "financial reporting problems, including accounting, internal controls or auditing problems"—by 65.2% of the Codes—and fraud (36.0%). By contrast, Codes did not identify areas that might have broad societal benefits nearly as frequently. Health and safety issues were the highest (29.2%), but other areas were remarkably low, such as environmental issues (7.9%), criminal offenses (3.4%), insider trading, bribery, and money laundering (9.0%).

Only 21.3% of the Codes identified harassment and discrimination as problems that should be reported. This result seems low, because a pair of 1998 U.S. Supreme Court cases gave companies who implement internal reporting mechanisms for complaints about harassment an affirmative defense in cases in which harassment has been alleged. (*Burlington Indus. Inc. v. Ellerth* 1998, *Faragher v. City of Boca Raton* 1998) The conventional wisdom after those cases was that companies would implement complaint channels in order to utilize the affirmative defense. According to the results of this study, although companies utilize complaint channels, only about 1 in 5 specifically identify harassment as one of the problems that should be reported. One explanation may be that procedures for harassment complaints are identified more thoroughly in other documents, such as an employee handbook.

Who Should Receive Reports of Misconduct?

The SEC regulations and the AmEx listing standards are vague on who should receive reports of misconduct. Both state that reports should be made to "an appropriate person . . . identified in the code." The NASDAQ standard does not identify a person to receive reports, while the NYSE states that reporting should be to "supervisors, managers, or other appropriate personnel." Given this variety among different regulatory regimes, the study examined who Codes said should receive a whistleblower's disclosure of wrongdoing.

Contrary to the vagueness of the SEC Regulations, as well as the AmEx and NASDAQ listing standards, many Codes listed several possible recipients of whistleblower reports, either as a primary contact for whistleblowers or a secondary option. By far the most popular person identified as a potential recipient is the employee's supervisor, who was listed in 75.3% of the Codes. This result seems to indicate that corporations, by and large, would still prefer that employees make whistleblower reports through the chain of command. . . .

Two types of recipients were listed by almost half of the Codes: the corporate audit committee (55.1%) and an employee hotline (47.2%). The popularity of these options may be a reflection of Sarbanes-Oxley's requirement that publicly-traded companies provide a disclosure channel directly to the company's audit committee. (Sarbanes-Oxley Act of 2002, § 301) On the other hand, a 1999 study of *Fortune* 1000 companies found that 51% of those companies had an ethics hotline for employees to report misconduct *before* Sarbanes-Oxley was passed in 2002.

. . . [H]otlines have received mixed reception from actual employee whistleblowers. . . . Regardless, clearly some corporations have adopted this approach and begun advertising their hotlines through their Codes of Ethics. Indeed, some scholars have indicated that companies have responded to Sarbanes-Oxley's requirement by contracting with an independent, third-party hotline to receive employee reports. This study confirms that view in part, as many (36.7%) of the companies that indicated a hotline should receive an employee report also indicated that the hotline was managed by a third-party. That said, more than half (57.1%) of the companies that mentioned a hotline did not provide any contact details for the hotline, which seems to undermine the company's reliance on this channel to receive valuable information.

We also examined whether companies listed recipients of whistleblowing reports as "primary" or "secondary" options, because often companies mention that reports should first be made to a particular recipient, but then could also be made to others. In fact, 98.9% of the companies mention a secondary contact. However, about 2/3 of the companies did not provide any reason for reporting to a secondary contact.

Of the remaining companies, we examined when companies told their employees a secondary contact should be used. The most frequent response was if the whistleblower felt "uncomfortable" or wanted "anonymity" (58.6%). Other reasons, in descending order of frequency were:

- if the whistleblower thought that after reporting to the primary contact, the report was not handled "properly" or if the whistleblower was not "satisfied" with the response from the primary contact (48.3%);

- if the primary contact was not "appropriate" or if there were difficulties with "communication" (34.5%);

- the absence of a primary contact (for example, if the committee does not exist) (10.3%);

- if the report contains a serious violation of the law (3.4%).

Not surprisingly, all of the Codes focused almost exclusively on internal recipients. (Only two of the 89 Codes mentioned an external recipient, such as a regulatory authority or Congress.) Although scholars debate whether whistleblowers should report internally or externally, it clearly is in a corporation's best interest to encourage internal reports. Corporations can address wrongdoing at an earlier stage and perhaps avoid negative publicity that can surround disclosure of illegal behavior. Additionally, by providing employees with direction on how to report internally, companies may avoid employees going externally in the first place. . . . Moreover, studies demonstrate that employees typically are better off reporting internally because internal whistleblowers experience less retaliation than external whistleblowers.

The results also indicate that perhaps employees receive confusing message on who should receive a whistleblowing report. Over two-thirds of the Codes provide different recipients for reports depending on a variety of factors. Over half (56.2%) vary the recipient by the type of misconduct being reported. For example, 49.4% of the companies identify a special contact for reporting financial problems specifically. Some vary by who is engaging in misconduct (14.6%), while others vary because of who is doing the reporting (18.0%). That said, some variability is beneficial. For example, as noted above, numerous companies provided a secondary contact to whom a whistleblower could report if the whistleblower was not comfortable with the primary person identified or the whistleblower was not satisfied with the response from the primary option. . . .

Do Companies Promise Not to Retaliate Against Whistleblowers?

Almost all (91.0%) of the companies either promise that the company will not retaliate against an employee whistleblower or affirmatively prohibit retaliation against whistleblowers. Almost one-third (30.3%) also state that the company will punish anyone who retaliates against a whistleblower. These promises go well beyond anything required by Sarbanes-Oxley or the SEC, neither of which require any sort of corporate promise regarding retaliation. Of the stock exchanges examined by the study, the NYSE and the NASDAQ explicitly mention that Codes of Conduct should include protection from retaliation.

None of the legal sources, however, give much guidance on the type of reports that will receive protection. Only the NYSE states that reports should be made in "good faith"—no other listing exchange makes any other requirement. In that vacuum, companies seem to be incorporating several consistent practices. Over three-fourths of the companies (76.4%) adopt the NYSE "good faith" requirement, while only 11.2% use the more rigorous "reasonable belief" standard found in many whistleblower statutes. Companies claim to protect reports of "suspected" violations (68.5%) as well. In addition to these carrots, companies use the stick as well: 21.3% state that they will punish false or malicious reports.

Are Confidentiality or Anonymity Guaranteed?

Neither Sarbanes-Oxley, the SEC regulations, nor the stock exchange listing requirements address whether Codes need to ensure confidentiality or anonymity for whistleblower reports generally. Despite this lack of guidance, a majority of the company Codes claim that *all* reports made by whistleblowers will be kept confidential (59.6%) and that *all* violations can be reported anonymously (56.2%). That said, a quarter of the companies do not address confidentiality (25.8%) or anonymity (27.0%). Another group of Codes only permit confidentiality and anonymity in some cases—14.6% and 16.9%, respectively. Indeed, 76.4% of the Codes state affirmatively that the company will investigate whistleblower reports, and 27.0% state that they expect employees to cooperate with the investigation. Perhaps the desire to investigate explains why 13.5% of the companies actually discourage anonymity in reporting.

The trend in the law seems to be to promote anonymity in order to encourage whistleblowers. The primary example of this trend is Sarbanes-Oxley's requirement that U.S. publicly-traded corporations must provide a channel for employees to report financial fraud to the board of directors anonymously. (15 U.S.C. § 78f(m)(4)) Companies clearly have responded to this requirement by instituting ways in which employees can make anonymous and confidential reports.

In sum, despite little direction from U.S. statutory or regulatory law, companies in this study seem to have developed whistleblower provisions for their Codes of Ethics that have remarkable consistency. The provisions generally apply to all company employees, and seem to require employees to report a broad range of misconduct to the company. The Codes identify numerous potential recipients of a whistleblower's report, including primary and secondary contacts. In return, the Code provisions promise protection from retaliation for employees who report violations of the code itself, the law, or even ethical violations. Additionally, companies consistently permit whistleblowers to remain anonymous or keep their disclosures confidential.

* * *

Conclusion

. . . The research described in this chapter provides an initial view of the ways in which the private sector in the United States attempts to manage whistleblowing. We found that, on paper at least, U.S. corporations have similar ways in which to encourage employees to report misconduct. Companies make whistleblowing a duty of employment and provide detailed instructions on how to blow the whistle internally. Numerous people in the organization can receive employee reports. And, perhaps most importantly, companies promise to protect whistleblowers from retaliation.

However, because of the strength of the at-will rule in the United States, employees will have a difficult time enforcing these promises, particularly if companies continue to include disclaimers in their Code of Ethics. These disclaimers essentially negate the companies' promise to protect whistleblowers from retaliation. This result seems counter-productive and ultimately, simply unfair. As the study shows, corporate Codes of Ethics make reporting a duty—a requirement of employment. In fact, this requirement is one of the most consistent provisions of these codes across the board: 96.6% tell their employees that they *must* report misconduct. Protecting employees from retaliation—enforcing the promise made by almost all corporations—is a simple matter of fairness. Companies should not be able to make whistleblowing a job requirement, and then be permitted to retaliate when the employee does exactly what the employee is told to do.

Further research is needed to examine how companies actually implement these policies.

Employees may have difficulty enforcing promises not to retaliate *legally,* but the *practical* effects of such promises are still understudied. Now that we know the content and scope of private sector whistleblower policies, attention needs to turn to how companies implement these policies and whether they effectively encourage whistleblowing and reduce misconduct.

Source: Richard Moberly and Lindsey E. Wylie, "An Empirical Study of Whistleblower Policies in United States Corporate Codes of Ethics" (August 26, 2011). *Whistleblowing and Democratic Values,* Forthcoming. Available at SSRN: http://ssrn.com/abstract=1961651.

Note: Notes and references have been removed for publication here. The full version with notes and references can be found online at http://ssrn.com/abstract=1961651.

Reading **4-5**

Greg Smith, Goldman Sachs, and the Importance of Corporate Culture

Chris MacDonald

Why I Am Leaving Goldman Sachs
Greg Smith

Today is my last day at Goldman Sachs. After almost 12 years at the firm—first as a summer intern while at Stanford, then in New York for 10 years, and now in London—I believe I have worked here long enough to understand the trajectory of its culture, its people and its identity. And I can honestly say that the environment now is as toxic and destructive as I have ever seen it.

To put the problem in the simplest terms, the interests of the client continue to be sidelined in the way the firm operates and thinks about making money. Goldman Sachs is one of the world's largest and most important investment banks and it is too integral to global finance to continue to act this way. The firm has veered so far from the place I joined right out of college that I can no longer in good conscience say that I identify with what it stands for.

It might sound surprising to a skeptical public, but culture was always a vital part of Goldman Sachs's success. It revolved around teamwork, integrity, a spirit of humility, and always doing right by our clients. The culture was the secret sauce that made this place great and allowed us to earn our clients' trust for 143 years. It wasn't just about making money; this alone will not sustain a firm for so long. It had something to do

with pride and belief in the organization. I am sad to say that I look around today and see virtually no trace of the culture that made me love working for this firm for many years. I no longer have the pride, or the belief.

But this was not always the case. For more than a decade I recruited and mentored candidates through our grueling interview process. I was selected as one of 10 people (out of a firm of more than 30,000) to appear on our recruiting video, which is played on every college campus we visit around the world. In 2006 I managed the summer intern program in sales and trading in New York for the 80 college students who made the cut, out of the thousands who applied.

I knew it was time to leave when I realized I could no longer look students in the eye and tell them what a great place this was to work.

When the history books are written about Goldman Sachs, they may reflect that the current chief executive officer, Lloyd C. Blankfein, and the president, Gary D. Cohn, lost hold of the firm's culture on their watch. I truly believe that this decline in the firm's moral fiber represents the single most serious threat to its long-run survival.

Over the course of my career I have had the privilege of advising two of the largest hedge funds on the planet, five of the largest asset managers in the United States, and three of the most prominent sovereign wealth funds in the Middle East and Asia. My clients have a total asset base of more than a trillion dollars. I have always taken a lot of pride in advising my clients to do what I believe is right for them, even if it means less money for the firm. This view is becoming increasingly unpopular at Goldman Sachs. Another sign that it was time to leave.

How did we get here? The firm changed the way it thought about leadership. Leadership used to be about ideas, setting an example and doing the right thing. Today, if you make enough money for the firm (and are not currently an ax murderer) you will be promoted into a position of influence.

What are three quick ways to become a leader? a) Execute on the firm's "axes," which is Goldman-speak for persuading your clients to invest in the stocks or other products that we are trying to get rid of because they are not seen as having a lot of potential profit. b) "Hunt Elephants." In English: get your clients—some of whom are sophisticated, and some of whom aren't—to trade whatever will bring the biggest profit to Goldman. Call me old-fashioned, but I don't like selling my clients a product that is wrong for them. c) Find yourself sitting in a seat where your job is to trade any illiquid, opaque product with a three-letter acronym.

Today, many of these leaders display a Goldman Sachs culture quotient of exactly zero percent. I attend derivatives sales meetings where not one single minute is spent asking questions about how we can help clients. It's purely about how we can make the most possible money off of them. If you were an alien from Mars and sat in on one of these meetings, you would believe that a client's success or progress was not part of the thought process at all.

It makes me ill how callously people talk about ripping their clients off. Over the last 12 months I have seen five different managing directors refer to their own clients as "muppets," sometimes over internal e-mail. Even after the S.E.C., Fabulous Fab, Abacus, God's work, Carl Levin, Vampire Squids? No humility? I mean, come on. Integrity? It is eroding. I don't know of any illegal behavior, but will people push

the envelope and pitch lucrative and complicated products to clients even if they are not the simplest investments or the ones most directly aligned with the client's goals? Absolutely. Every day, in fact.

It astounds me how little senior management gets a basic truth: If clients don't trust you they will eventually stop doing business with you. It doesn't matter how smart you are.

These days, the most common question I get from junior analysts about derivatives is, "How much money did we make off the client?" It bothers me every time I hear it, because it is a clear reflection of what they are observing from their leaders about the way they should behave. Now project 10 years into the future: You don't have to be a rocket scientist to figure out that the junior analyst sitting quietly in the corner of the room hearing about "muppets," "ripping eyeballs out" and "getting paid" doesn't exactly turn into a model citizen.

When I was a first-year analyst I didn't know where the bathroom was, or how to tie my shoelaces. I was taught to be concerned with learning the ropes, finding out what a derivative was, understanding finance, getting to know our clients and what motivated them, learning how they defined success and what we could do to help them get there.

My proudest moments in life—getting a full scholarship to go from South Africa to Stanford University, being selected as a Rhodes Scholar national finalist, winning a bronze medal for table tennis at the Maccabiah Games in Israel, known as the Jewish Olympics—have all come through hard work, with no shortcuts. Goldman Sachs today has become too much about shortcuts and not enough about achievement. It just doesn't feel right to me anymore.

I hope this can be a wake-up call to the board of directors. Make the client the focal point of your business again. Without clients you will not make money. In fact, you will not exist. Weed out the morally bankrupt people, no matter how much money they make for the firm. And get the culture right again, so people want to work here for the right reasons. People who care only about making money will not sustain this firm—or the trust of its clients—for very much longer.

In early March of 2012, *The New York Times* published a letter from Greg Smith, a mid-level executive at investment bank Goldman Sachs. The letter was actually Smith's letter of resignation, addressed to his bosses at Goldman. The letter outlined Smith's reasons for leaving, citing in particular the firm's "toxic and destructive" work environment. Not surprisingly, the letter's publication caused an uproar—it was yet another blow to a firm, and an industry, that had already seen its share of troubles in recent years.

Goldman, like other big financial institutions today, is seen by many as the corporate embodiment of evil, and so people were bound to be fascinated by an insider's repudiation of the firm—especially accompanied, as it was, by a good dollop of juicy details. But there's more to it than that, and the "more" here is instructive.

I think the key to understanding why Smith's letter caused such an uproar is the fact that Greg Smith's letter taps into a deep, dark fear that every consumer has, namely the fear that, somewhere out there, someone who is supposed to be looking out for us is instead trying to screw us.

Smith's letter basically said that *that* is exactly what is going on at Goldman, these days: the employees charged with advising clients about an array of complex financial decisions are, according to Smith, generally more focused on making money than they are on serving clients. At Goldman, according to Smith's letter, "the interests of the client" are "sidelined in the way the firm operates and thinks about making money."

Now, a couple of words about the letter. It goes without saying that we should take such a letter with a grain of salt. It's just one man's word, after all, which is pretty far from conclusive evidence about a firm as large and complex as Goldman. Now that doesn't make Smith's account of the tone at Goldman implausible. He's certainly not the first to suggest that there's something wonky at Goldman. It just means that we should balance his testimony against other evidence, including for example the kinds of large-scale surveys of Goldman employees that the company's own

response[1] to Smith's letter cites. According to the company's press release, Smith's letter fails to represent "how the vast majority of people at Goldman Sachs think about the firm." The press release, penned by CEO and Chairman Lloyd C. Blankfein and President and Chief Operating Officer Gary D. Cohn, noted that internal surveys suggest that nearly 90% of the company's employees feel that the firm "provides exceptional service" to customers. Then again, such surveys are themselves highly imperfect devices. Either way: when it comes to these competing claims, buyer beware.

But it's worth noting that there is one group that *must* take this stuff seriously, namely Goldman's Board of Directors. A loyal employee taking a risk like Smith has is *not* a good sign, and so his story deserves to be investigated thoroughly by the Board. You and I can largely afford to be agnostic about Smith's claims and Blankfein and Cohn's rebuttal. But the Board has an obligation to get to the bottom of this.

OK, but you and I aren't on the Board. So let's bracket the reliability of Smith's account, and ask—*if* it does accurately reflect the tone at Goldman—why that *matters*.

The reason Smith's account matters has to do with this awkward fact: in many cases, in business, all that stands between you the customer and getting ripped off is a mysterious, amorphous thing called "corporate culture." Now, corporate culture matters in lots of ways. But from a customer's point of view, corporate culture plays a very specific role in fostering trust. Most of us, after all, are susceptible to being ripped off in all kinds of ways by the businesses we interact with. That's true whether the business in question is my local coffee shop (is that coffee *really* Fair Trade?) or a financial institution trying to get me to invest in some new-fangled asset-backed security. My best hope in such cases is that the business in question fosters a corporate culture within which employees are expected to tell me the truth and help me get the products I really want.

Now, corporate culture is a notoriously hard thing to define, and harder still to manage. Culture is sometimes explained as "a shared set of practices" or "the way things are done" or "the glue that holds a company together."

Why does culture matter? It matters because, other things being equal, the people who work for a company won't *automatically* feel inspired to spend their day doing things that benefit either the company or the company's clients. People have their own ambitions and desires, and those ambitions and desires don't automatically line up with anyone else's. So employees may need to be *convinced* to provide loyal service. In part, such loyalty can be ensured through a combination of rewards and penalties and surveillance. *Work hard, and you'll earn a bonus.* And, *Treat our customers well, or your fired.* And so on.

But sticks and carrots will only get you so far. Far better if you can get employees to adopt the right behaviours voluntarily, to internalize a set of rules about loyal service and fair treatment. An employee who thinks that diligence and fair treatment just go with the turf is a lot more valuable than one who needs constantly to be monitored and cajoled. And, humans being the social animals that we are, getting employees to adopt and internalize a set of rules is a lot easier if you make it part of the ethos of a group of comrades. Once you've got the group ethos right, employees are much less likely act badly. Because, well, *that's just not the sort of thing we do around here!* In the terminology used by economists and management theorists, culture helps solve "agency problems." Whatever it is that you want employees to be focusing their energies on, corporate culture is the key.

Of course, there's still the problem of what exactly employees *should* be focusing their energies on. Should they be taking direct aim at maximizing profit? Or should they be serving customers well, on the assumption that good service will result in profits in the long run? In any reasonably sane market, one without "Too Big Too Fail" financial institutions, the latter strategy would be the way to go, practically every time. You don't want every employee aiming at profits any more than you want every player on a football team trying to carry the ball into the end zone. Every player has a specific task, and if they all perform the task properly, the result should be a team that performs well at its overall objective. So for the most part, a services company like Goldman ought to want employees to focus on providing excellent service, because that's the route to long-term success. And that fact is precisely what makes large-scale commerce practical. Consumers enjoy an enormous amount of protection from everyday wrongdoing due to the simple fact that most businesses have an interest in promoting basic honesty and decency on the part of their employees.

Unfortunately, it's far from clear that Goldman operates in a sane market. So it is entirely plausible that the company could have allowed its corporate culture to drift away from seeing customers as partners in long-term value creation, toward seeing them as sources of short-term revenue. I don't know whether Greg Smith's tale is true and representative of the culture at Goldman Sachs. But if it is, that means not just that Goldman isn't serving its clients well. It means that Goldman embodies a set of values with the potential to undermine the market itself.

Sources: Greg Smith, "Why I Am Leaving Goldman Sachs," *The New York Times* (March 14, 2012), www.nytimes.com/2012/03/14/opinion/why-i-am-leaving-goldman-sachs.html (accessed August 8, 2012); Chris MacDonald, "Greg Smith, Goldman Sachs, and the Importance of Corporate Culture," *Canadian Business* [Blog] (March 15, 2012), www.canadianbusiness.com/blog/business_ethics/75701 (accessed August 8, 2012).

Endnote

1. Lloyd C. Blankfein and Gary D. Cohn, "Goldman Sachs Response to March 14, 2012, *The New York Times* Op-Ed," Press Release, March 14, 2012. http://www.goldmansachs.com/media-relations/comments-and-responses/current/nyt-op-ed-response.html (accessed August 8, 2012).

Chapter 5

Corporate Social Responsibility

Business has to take account of its responsibilities to society in coming to its decisions, but society has to accept its responsibilities for setting the standards against which those decisions are made.[1]

Sir Adrian Cadbury

We are not in business to make maximum profit for our shareholders. We are in business . . . to serve society. Profit is our reward for doing it well. If business does not serve society, society will not long tolerate our profits or even our existence.[2]

Kenneth Dayton, former chair of the Dayton–Hudson Corporation

Make the World a Better Place

Ben and Jerry's corporate mission statement

Corporations are people.

Mitt Romney, former governor of Massachusetts and U.S. presidential candidate

A corporation is an organization created by law and treated as a legal entity, literally a legal "person," that is separate from and independent of the individuals who are involved in it. As a legal person, a corporation has legal rights and duties that are primarily determined by the laws of the state in which the organization is incorporated. Forming a corporation has several benefits, including limiting legal liability, protecting personal assets, providing tax advantages, and ensuring organizational continuation beyond the life or involvement of individuals.

Traditionally, the state of Delaware has incorporation laws that provide very generous terms for shareholders. Over 50 percent of U.S. corporations and over 60 percent of the *Fortune* 500 corporations are incorporated in Delaware. Among the benefits provided by Delaware law are strong legal protections for the interests of corporate stockholders. In the words of the chief justice of the Delaware Supreme Court, "American corporate law makes corporate managers accountable to only one constituency—the stockholders."[3]

This framework underlies what R. Edward Freeman (see Reading 5-2, "Managing for Stakeholders") has called the "dominant model" of managerial capitalism. Under that model, business managers act as agents of corporate stockholders and, thus, their primary responsibility is to serve stockholders by maximizing profits. This view was famously summarized in the title of a 1970 *New York Times* article by economist Milton Friedman: "The Social Responsibility of Business Is to Increase Its Profits."

Framed in this way, there is an inherent tension between the legal responsibility of business managers and the call for greater corporate social responsibility. Pursuing general goals of social responsibility would violate the primary legal responsibility of business managers to pursue profits. But what if the stockholders themselves choose socially responsible goals in addition to, and perhaps even superior to, profit maximization? Benefit corporations, a new legal model created by more than 20 states (including Delaware), aim to do just this.

Like any corporation, a benefit corporation is a legal entity with legal rights and duties created to achieve the general benefits of any corporation: limiting liability, protecting owner assets, achieving tax advantages, and so on. Importantly, benefit corporations are not nonprofits; they are for-profit businesses that create value for their stockholders as a by-product of creating values for a wide range of other stakeholders. Benefit corporations differ from traditional corporations in that their boards and managers are given the legal authority to pursue social and environmental goals in addition to the financial goals that corporations generally pursue. This means that benefit corporations are free to make social and environmental goals part of the very mission and identity of the corporation and therefore make the boards and managers accountable to wider social goals. The profit sought by stockholders thus becomes one among other equally legitimate goals sought by a range of corporate stakeholders. The tension that is thought to exist between social ends and profit disappears in the benefit corporation model.

One estimate is that there were over 2,000 active benefit corporations in the United States in 2015.[4] Some of the best-known companies include King Arthur Flour, Patagonia, Kickstarter, Seventh Generation, and Plum Organics. These for-profit businesses recognize that without profitability they will neither remain in business nor attract the investment needed to grow. But profit is recognized as a means, not an end in itself. Profits serve socially responsible ends by making the business financially sustainable so that it can pursue social ends.

A number of advantages are claimed for benefit corporations besides the normal financial benefits of any incorporation. Perhaps the most important is that the benefit corporation model allows corporations with socially responsible missions to protect that mission by giving both managers and boards the legal ability to prioritize mission over profits. Especially at a time when corporations and their managers are judged by short-term, quarterly earnings reports, normal corporate charters can create pressures on managers to back away from social missions in order to increase short-term profit. Recognizing that there can be different paths to profitability, benefit corporations hold management accountable for finding a path that also achieves socially responsible mission goals.

Advocates also claim that benefit corporations have the advantage of attracting employees, especially among a younger generation that is concerned as much with workplace quality as with such traditional benefits as salary and status. One study reported that businesses with a clear social mission and a reputation for creating social benefits were more successful in attracting and retaining millennial employees.[5]

Benefit corporations are also better positioned to attract socially motivated customers and investors. There is a growing market among socially conscious consumers for businesses that serve the common good. There is also a growing capital market among institutional and individual investors seeking socially responsible investments. Pursuit of socially responsible ends is part of the legal charter of benefits corporations and not something done simply as a public relations ploy.

As in any good business practice, benefit corporations have stimulated a movement to measure, assess, and certify businesses engaged as benefit corporations. Some choose to take an additional step and become certified as "B-Corps" by working with an independent nonprofit group, B-Labs, to assess the effectiveness of their strategy in serving socially responsible goals. Becoming a certified B-Corp provides a means for assuring consumers, investors, employees, and the general public that the company is successful in its mission. It is also possible for traditional corporations to meet the criteria established by B-Labs and become certified as a B-Corps without having the underlying legal structure of the benefit corporation.

Ben and Jerry's was among the first and best-known corporations that adopted a strong socially responsible mission. From its earliest years in the 1980s, Ben and Jerry's made its social responsibility goals part of its corporate mission. Although legally not a benefit corporation (the legal designation did not exist when the company was incorporated in 1984), its founding owners Ben Cohen and Jerry Greenfield committed the company to a range of social and environmental causes.

Ben and Jerry's famously identified three fundamental goals as its corporate mission: to make the world's best ice cream, to run a financially successful company, and to "make the world a better place." It also started a foundation that was funded from 7.5 percent of the pretax earnings of the company. However, as a publicly traded corporation the fiduciary responsibility of Ben and Jerry's management and board remained primarily a financial duty.

These issues came to a head in 2000 when Unilever, the multinational food and consumer product corporation, offered to buy Ben and Jerry's for $43 per share, more than double its recent trading value of $17. Corporate buyouts by outside groups typically happen when the outsiders judge that the company is worth more than what is reflected by its share price. In this sense, the outside groups believe that the company is underperforming and worth more than how it is presently valued by the market. Both Ben Cohen and Jerry Greenfield opposed selling the company to Unilever. They feared that a corporate takeover would jeopardize the social mission of Ben and Jerry's. But the corporate board had an independent duty to the stockholders.

- Does the Ben and Jerry's board of directors have an ethical duty to sell the company to the highest bidder, even if this risks a change in the corporate mission?
- Should the fact that Unilever has a reputation as a socially progressive and responsible business influence that decision? Would the decision be different if Unilever planned to change the nature of Ben and Jerry's mission?
- If things had been different and Ben and Jerry's had been incorporated as a benefit corporation, would an offer at more than twice the present value be enough to change the company mission?
- How do benefit corporations fit into the model of private property, free-market capitalism?
- Suppose shareholders objected not to the mission to "make the world a better place," but to the mission to "make the world's best ice cream" and claimed that Ben and Jerry's could maximize profits by making mediocre ice cream. Should shareholder desire override that aspect of the corporate mission?

 ## Chapter Objectives

After reading this chapter, you will be able to:

1. Define corporate social responsibility.
2. Describe and evaluate the economic model of corporate social responsibility.
3. Distinguish key components of the term *responsibility*.
4. Describe and evaluate the economic model of corporate social responsibility.
5. Describe and evaluate the stakeholder model of corporate social responsibility.
6. Describe and evaluate the integrative model of corporate social responsibility.
7. Explain the role of reputation management as motivation behind CSR.
8. Evaluate the claims that CSR is "good" for business.

Introduction

This chapter addresses the nature of corporate social responsibility (CSR) and how firms opt to meet this perceived responsibility. No one denies that business has *some* social responsibilities. At a minimum, it is indisputable that business has a social responsibility to obey the law. A large part of this legal responsibility includes the responsibility to fulfill the terms of contract with employees, customers, suppliers, lenders, accounting firms, and so forth. Legal responsibilities also include responsibilities to avoid negligence and other liabilities under tort law. Economists might also say that business has a social responsibility to produce the goods and services that society demands. If a firm fails to meet society's interests and demands, it will fail. But beyond these legal and economic responsibilities, controversies abound.

As Chris MacDonald explains in Reading 5-1, "BP and Corporate Social Responsibility," there are ambiguities involved in each of the three terms *corporate, social,* and *responsibilities.* In general terms, we can say that the primary question of CSR is the extent to which business organizations and the managers who run them have ethical responsibilities that go *beyond* producing needed goods and services within the law. There are a range of answers to this question and it will be helpful to clarify some initial concepts before turning to competing models of CSR.

Ethics and Social Responsibility

OBJECTIVE 1

As a first step toward a better understanding, we should recognize that the words *responsible* and *responsibility* are used in several different ways. One meaning involves attributing something as a cause for an event or action. For example, poor lending practices were *responsible* for (i.e., the cause of) the collapse of many banks during the 2008 economic crisis; and the location of the gas tank was *responsible* for fires in the Ford Pinto. Being responsible in this causal sense does not carry any ethical attribution; it merely describes events. So, for example, we might say that the wind was *responsible* for the damage to a house or a particular gene is *responsible* for blue eyes.

In a second sense, to be responsible does carry an ethical connotation. When we say that business is responsible *to* someone or *for* something, we are referring to what a business ethically ought or should do. Ethical responsibilities establish limits to our decisions and actions. To say, for example, that a business has a responsibility to its employees is to say that there are ethical limits to how a business should treat its employees.

Laws regarding product safety and liability involve these various meanings of being responsible. When a consumer is injured, for instance, a first question to ask is whether the product was responsible for the injury, in the sense of having caused the injury. Several years ago a controversy developed over the drug Vioxx, produced by the pharmaceutical company Merck. Evidence suggested that Vioxx was responsible for causing heart attacks in some users. In the debates that followed, two questions required answers: Was Vioxx the *cause* of the heart attacks, and was Merck ethically responsible (i.e., should it be held legally liable for the heart attacks)? Once the causal question is settled, we then go on to ask if the manufacturer is responsible in the sense of doing what was expected ethically.

When we speak of corporate social responsibility, we are referring to the ethical expectations that society has for business. Ethical responsibilities are those things that we ought, or should, do, even if sometimes we would rather not. We are ethically expected to fulfill our responsibilities; and we will be held account-able if we do not. Thus, to talk about corporate social responsibility is to be concerned with society's interests that should restrict or limit business's behavior. Social responsibility is what a business should or ought to do for the sake of society, even if this comes with an economic cost.

Philosophers often distinguish between three different levels of responsibilities on a scale from less to more obligatory. First, there are ethical responsibilities to do good. Volunteering and charitable work are typical examples of responsibilities in this sense. While doing a good thing is ethically responsible and something that ethics encourages, we normally do not fault someone for choosing not to contribute to charity. To call an act volunteer work is precisely to suggest that it is optional; one does not have a duty to do it, but it is still a good thing to do. Examples of corporate philanthropy, as when a business sponsors a charity event or contributes to a school project, fit this sense of social responsibility. Ethical considerations would encourage business to support charities or the arts, but it is not something ethically mandatory or required.

A second, more obligatory sense of ethical responsibility is the responsibility to prevent harm. What are often referred to as Good Samaritan cases are examples of people acting to prevent harm, even though they have no strict duty or obligation to do so. Thus, for example, we might say that a company has a responsibility to use renewable energy, even though its actions alone are not causing harm and fossil fuels are legal to use.

The most demanding sense of responsibility is the responsibility not to cause harm to others. Often called a duty or an obligation to indicate that they oblige us in the strictest sense, responsibilities in this sense bind, or compel, or require us to act in certain ways. Society expects fulfillment of these responsibilities and uses the full force of social sanctioning, including the law and legal punishment to enforce them. Thus, a business ought not to sell a product that causes harm to consumers, even if there would be a profit in doing so.

Is there a duty for business not to cause harm? Let us consider how each of these three types of responsibilities might be seen in business. The strongest sense of responsibility is the duty not to cause harm. Even when not explicitly prohibited by law, ethics would demand that we not cause avoidable harm. If a business causes harm to someone and, if that harm could have been avoided by exercising due care or proper planning, then both the law and ethics would say that business should be held liable for violating its responsibilities. By all accounts, this ethical duty not to cause harm overrides business's pursuit of profit.

In practice, this ethical requirement is the type of responsibility established by the precedents of tort law. When it is discovered that a product causes harm, then business can appropriately be prevented from marketing that product and can be held liable for harms caused by it. So, in the classic case of cigarettes, tobacco companies can be restricted in marketing products that have been proven to cause cancer even if this prevents them from maximizing profits for shareholders.

Is there a responsibility for business to prevent harm? There are also cases in which business is not causing harm, but could easily prevent harm from occurring.

A more inclusive understanding of corporate social responsibility would hold that business has a responsibility to prevent harm. Consider the actions taken by the pharmaceutical firm Merck & Co. with its drug Mectizan. Mectizan is a Merck drug that prevents river blindness, a disease prevalent in tropical nations. River blindness infects between 40 and 100 million people annually, causing severe rashes, itching, and loss of sight. A single tablet of Mectizan administered once a year can relieve the symptoms and prevent the disease from progressing—quite an easy and effective means to prevent a horrendous consequence.

On the surface, Mectizan would not be a very profitable drug to bring to market. The once-a-year dosage limits the demand for the drug among those people who require it. Further, the individuals most at risk for this disease are among the poorest people living in the poorest regions of Africa, Asia, Central America, and South America. However, in 1987 Merck began a program that provides Mectizan free of charge to people at risk for river blindness and pledged to "give it away free, forever." Cooperating with the World Health Organization, UNICEF, and the World Bank, Merck's program has donated billions of doses of Mectizan to tens of millions of people since 1987. The program has also resulted in the development of a health care system, necessary to support and administer the program, in some of the poorest regions of the world. Merck's actions were explained by reference to part of its corporate identity statement: "We are in the business of preserving and improving human life."[6]

Clearly Merck was not at all responsible for causing river blindness and, therefore, according to the narrow model of CSR discussed earlier, Merck had no social responsibility in this case. The drug was not profitable and Merck had no legal obligation to provide it. In fact, the narrow economic model of corporate social responsibility might well fault Merck's management for failing to maximize shareholder value. But, Merck's management saw the issue differently. Given the company's core business purpose and values, its managers concluded that they did have a social responsibility to prevent a disease easily controlled by their patented drug. George Merck, grandson of Merck's founder, explains, "We try never to forget that medicine is for the people. It is not for the profits. The profits follow and, if we have remembered that, they have never failed to appear. The better we have remembered it, the larger they have been."

Is there a responsibility to do good? The third, and perhaps the most wide-ranging, standard of CSR would hold that business has a social responsibility to do good things and to make society a better place. Corporate philanthropy would be the most obvious case in which business takes on a responsibility to do good. Corporate giving programs to support community projects in the arts, education, and culture are clear examples. Some corporations have a charitable foundation or office that deals with such philanthropic programs. (See the Reality Check "Corporate Philanthropy: How Much Do Corporations Give?") Small-business owners in every town across America can tell stories of how often they are approached to give donations to support local charitable and cultural activities.

Some people argue that, like all cases of charity, philanthropy is something that deserves praise and admiration; but it is not something that every business *ought* to do. Philosophers sometimes distinguish between obligations and responsibilities

Reality Check *Corporate Philanthropy. How Much Do Corporations Give?*

In 2011, total charitable giving in the United States was estimated to be almost $300 billion. Individual contributions totaled more than $200 billion. Corporate giving totaled $14.5 billion, or 5 percent of the total giving rate that has remained flat over the past 40 years.

Source: "2012 Giving USA: The Annual Report on Philanthropy for the Year 2011/Executive Summary" (June 18, 2012), www.givingusareports.org/.

precisely in order to make this point. A responsible person is charitable, but donating to charity is not an obligation. Others argue that business does have an obligation to support good causes and to "give back" to the community. This sense of responsibility is more akin to a debt of gratitude and thankfulness—something less binding than a legal or contractual obligation perhaps, but more than a simple act of charity. Perhaps a clear way to understand the distinction is to compare it to your obligation to write a thank-you note for a birthday gift. You might not have a legal requirement to send the note, but nevertheless you have a responsibility to do so.

These considerations suggest that there are competing understandings of corporate social responsibility and management's role in fulfilling these responsibilities. What we will call the narrow *economic model* of CSR directs managers to maximize profit and shareholder wealth and recognizes only legal limitations on the pursuit of profit. A variation of this model acknowledges that philanthropy is an ethically good thing that can indirectly contribute to profit by improving reputation and brand recognition.

Another model recognizes that there is a wide range of ethical responsibilities and duties that are owed to others and that management must balance these responsibilities against the responsibility to shareholders. What we will call the *stakeholder model* asserts that neither a business nor the individuals who work for it are exempt from the ordinary ethical responsibilities that everyone has to cause no harm, to prevent harm, and to sometimes do good.

Finally, some businesses might choose to make social responsibility part of its very purpose and mission. In what we will call the *integrative* model of CSR, part of the managerial responsibility to shareholders is to serve the social good. These three models are summarized in Figure 5.1.

Economic Model of CSR

OBJECTIVE

Most involved in the business would accept the general definition of the term **corporate social responsibility (CSR)** as referring to the ethical responsibilities that a business has to the society in which it operates. From a narrow economic perspective, a business is an institution that exists to benefit society by producing goods and services and, by doing this, creates jobs and wealth that provide further social benefits.

FIGURE 5.1
Models of Corporate Social Responsibility

The law has created a form of business called a *corporation,* which promotes these economic ends by limiting the liability of individuals for the risks involved in these activities. Legislatures thought that businesses could be more efficient in raising the capital necessary for producing goods, services, jobs, and wealth if investors were protected from undue personal risks. This fact reminds us that business organizations in general, and corporations specifically, are social institutions created by society to serve human ends.

OBJECTIVE

economic model of CSR

Limits a firm's social responsibility to the minimal economic responsibility of producing goods and services and maximizing profits within the law.

What we shall refer to as the **economic model of CSR** holds that businesses' sole social responsibility is to fulfill the economic functions they were designed to serve. This general model has direct implications for the proper role of business management. Corporations are understood to be a particular legal form of property which the owners get to use for their own ends. Managers are employees, or agents, of those owners and must work to further the owners' interests. In Reading 5-2, "Managing for Stakeholders," as discussed at the beginning of this chapter, R. Edward Freeman identifies this perspective as the dominant model of CSR and refers to it as "managerial capitalism."

This economic model of CSR places shareholders at the center of the corporation and, from this point of view, the ethical responsibility of management is to serve those shareholders. Specifically, managers have a primary responsibility to pursue profit within the law. Because profit is assumed to be an indication that business is efficiently and successfully producing the goods and services that society demands, profit is a direct measure of how well a business firm is meeting society's expectations.

corporate social responsibility (CSR)
The responsibilities that businesses have to the societies within which they operate. In various contexts, it may also refer to the voluntary actions that companies undertake to address economic, social, and environmental impacts of their business operations and the concerns of their principal stakeholders. The European Commission defines CSR as "a concept whereby companies decide voluntarily to contribute to a better society and a cleaner environment." Specifically, CSR suggests that a business identify its stakeholder groups and incorporate its needs and values within its strategic and operational decision-making process.

Because corporations are created by society and require a stable political and economic infrastructure in which to conduct business, like all other social institutions, they are expected to obey the legal mandates established by the society. The economic model of CSR denies that business has any social responsibilities beyond the economic and legal ends for which it was created.

Nobel Prize–winning economist Milton Friedman's classic 1970 *New York Times* article, "The Social Responsibility of Business Is to Increase Its Profits," is perhaps best known as an argument for the economic model of CSR. Contrary to popular belief, Friedman does not ignore ethical responsibility in his analysis; he simply suggests that managers fulfill their ethical responsibility by increasing shareholder wealth and pursuing profit. Friedman explains that a corporate executive has a

> responsibility to conduct business in accordance with [his or her employer's] desires, which generally will be to make as much money as possible while conforming to the basic rules of society, *both those embodied in law and those embodied in ethical custom* (emphasis added).

This common view of corporate social responsibility has its roots in the utilitarian tradition and in neoclassical economics (as discussed in the section on utilitarianism in chapter 3). As agents of business owners, the contention is that managers do have social responsibilities, but their primary responsibility is to serve shareholders. By maximizing profits, a business manager will allocate resources to their most efficient uses. Consumers who most value a resource will be willing to pay the most for it; so profit is the measure of optimal allocation of resources. Over time, the pursuit of maximum profit will continuously work toward the optimal satisfaction of consumer demand which, in one interpretation of utilitarianism, is equivalent to maximizing the overall good.

But even within this dominant economic model, there is room to pursue social responsibilities. What we might identify as a philanthropic offshoot of the economic model holds that, like individuals, business is free to contribute to social causes as a matter of philanthropy. From this perspective, business has no strict obligation to contribute to social causes, but it can be a good thing when it does so. Just as individuals have no ethical *obligation* to contribute to charity or to do volunteer work in their community, business has no strict ethical responsibility to serve wider social goods. But, just as charity is a good thing and something that we all want to encourage, business should be encouraged to contribute to society in ways that go beyond the narrow obligations of law and economics. This approach is especially common with small, privately owned businesses where the owners also often play a prominent leadership role within their local community.

Within the philanthropy offshoot there are occasions in which charity work is done because it brings the firm good public relations, provides a helpful tax deduction, and builds goodwill and/or a good reputation within the community. (See the Reality Check "Putting Your Money Where Your Mouth Is?") Many corporate sponsorships in sports or the arts, or contributions to community events,

Reality Check *Profits: Pursue, Increase, or Maximize?*

Two important assumptions underlie much of the controversy surrounding corporate social responsibility. First, many people assume that the competition between profit and other social goals is a zero-sum game and that if a business manager pursues one she must sacrifice the other. The second assumption is that stockholders always desire the highest possible rate of return on their investment. But once again, this is an area where careful thinking can go a long way toward resolving some of the controversies.

The tension between social responsibility and profit will vary significantly whether we are focused on *pursuing profit, increasing profit,* or *maximizing profit.* The goal of *pursuing profit* simply recognizes that to keep a business operating, management must maintain profitability. But there is nothing inherently contradictory about pursuing profit and social goals at the same time. The Opening Decision Point in this chapter provides Ben and Jerry's as a case of a business that did just that. Ben and Jerry's was profitable for many years while also vigorously pursuing, and attaining, social goals.

To *increase profits* suggests that business should be looking for ways to grow and improve profitability. Consistent with a utilitarian justification of market economics, this prescription advises managers to continue to increase profits because, in an ideal market, this would ensure increasing efficiency in the allocation of resources. This approach is reflected in the title of the Milton Friedman article quoted earlier: "The Social Responsibility of Business Is to Increase Its Profits." But once again, there is no inherent contradiction between increasing profit and pursuing some social agenda. Ben and Jerry's increased its profits annually while pursuing its social agenda.

The only time that the pursuit of social goals does cause conflicts is when one assumes that the business goal should be to *maximize,* or *optimize, profit* and assumes that a social agenda cannot be a means to that goal. The dominant economic model makes both of these

assumptions. In this case, any corporate resource that is used for a social goal instead of being retained for profit violates managerial responsibility to "make as much money as possible" (in Friedman's words) for shareholders. But why should we assume that business always ought to aim to *maximize* profit?

The most common answer is that this is what shareholders (or "owners" as Friedman describes them) desire. But is this answer true? In one sense, it seems to be. Every investor presumably prefers more rather than less return on his or her investment. However, two important and related variables should cause us to be cautious in assuming that every investor wants to maximize profits.

First, as we learn in finance and economics, increasing profits typically come with increasing risks. Many investors, particularly institutional investors such as mutual funds, pension plans, and insurance companies, much prefer less risk and steady profit than higher risk for the possibility of higher profit. Second, the desire for maximum profits also depends on the time frame involved. Short-term investors, perhaps better described as traders rather than as owners, may well prefer that managers use all the corporate resources to maximize profits. But short-term profit poses greater risks, especially to those investors seeking stable long-term returns on their investments. Managing quarterly earnings reports to demonstrate maximum profit over the short term can greatly increase the risk to long-term profitability.

Thus, we should be careful when using general terms like *shareholders* or *stockholders.* Corporate shares are owned by individuals and institutions who have a variety of purposes. Asserting that the primary responsibility of management is to maximize profit can give those who seek short-term maximum profit a priority over other shareholders that is unjustified. Whenever one hears the claim that business should maximize profit, one should immediately ask: "Over what time period?" and "For whom?"

benefit businesses in this way. Peruse the program you receive when entering a local art gallery, museum, theater, or school event and you will likely see a list of local businesses that serve as donors or sponsors that have contributed to the event. In these cases, businesses have engaged in supporting these activities, and they have received some benefit in return.

Reality Check *Putting Your Money Where Your Mouth Is?*

Do you make purchases based on a company's social contributions? Are you more or less likely to buy something if you know that a company supports causes that are (or are not) important to you? Philanthropic CSR suggests that businesses contribute to society in the hopes that this will have beneficial reputational payoffs.

According to a 2011 global survey conducted by Cone Communications, consumers in general do care about corporate responsibility. For instance, 94 percent of respondents worldwide indicated that where price and quality are the same, they would be likely to switch brands to one associated with a worthwhile cause. And 93 percent of consumers indicated that they would boycott a company that they felt had conducted itself irresponsibly. In addition, 65 percent said that they had, within the last 12 months, bought a product associated with a cause.

Interestingly, consumers were less focused on expressing their opinions to companies directly: Only a third of consumers indicated that they had actually given feedback about social responsibility to a company within the last 12 months.

The same survey suggested interesting international differences: 95 percent of Chinese respondents said they were likely to believe a company's statements about its social and environmental impact, whereas only 39 percent of French respondents and 42 percent of Russian respondents said the same.

Source: Cone Communications, *2011 Cone/Echo Global CR Opportunity Study* (Boston, MA: Cone), www.coneinc.com/globalCRstudy.

You might notice that cases where a business supports a social cause for the purpose of receiving good public relations, or other business benefits, are not much different from the economic view of CSR. In these situations, a business manager exercises managerial discretion in judging that the social contribution will have economic benefits. In these cases, the social contribution is as much an investment as it is a contribution. Certainly, proponents of the economic model of CSR would support social responsibility from this perspective. Thus, there is a great deal of overlap between decision makers who engage in the economic model for reputational reasons and those who follow the economic view of business's social responsibilities.

But, there are also those cases in which a business might contribute to a social cause or event without seeking any reputational benefit. Some firms contribute to charity anonymously. Some support causes that have little or no business or financial payoff as a matter of giving back to their communities. In such cases, one might contend that corporate support for these social causes is not done for potential business benefits, but instead because the business manager or owner decides that it is simply a good and right thing to do. Others could suggest that the contributor has concluded that the society in which the firm does business is a stronger or better one if this particular activity exists.

The economic model in which business support for a social cause is done simply because it is the right thing to do differs from the reputational version only in terms of the underlying motivation. To some, this seems a trivial difference. In one case, the social good is done as a means to economic ends; in the other, it is done as an end in itself. Yet, this different motivation is, in the opinion of others, precisely what makes one action ethically responsible and the other not. From the perspective of the economic model of CSR, only philanthropy done for reputational reasons and financial ends is ethically responsible. Because business managers are the agents of owners, they have no right to use corporate resources except to earn owners greater returns on their investment. (Milton Friedman called such acts a "tax" on owners being levied by managers.)

Stakeholder Model of CSR

OBJECTIVE

stakeholder model of CSR
The view that business exists within a web of social relationships. The stakeholder model views business as a citizen of the society in which it operates and, like all members of a society, business must conform to the normal range of ethical duties and obligations that all citizens face.

A second perspective on CSR is called the **stakeholder model of CSR.** The stakeholder model understands that business exists within a web of social and ethical relationships. The stakeholder model holds that businesses exist to create value for a range of stakeholders, including employees, customers, suppliers, and local communities as well as investors and stockholders. Business managers have responsibilities to all those who have a stake in the success or failure of the company, not only to those who have invested financially.

Philosopher Norman Bowie has defended one version of CSR that expands the economic model in this direction (see Reading 3-3, "It Seems Right in Theory but Does it Work in Practice?" and Reading 3-4. "Business Decisions Should Not Violate the Humanity of a Person"). Bowie argues that, beyond the economic model's duty to obey the law, business has an equally important ethical duty to respect human rights. Respecting human rights is the "moral minimum" that we expect of every person, whether they are acting as individuals or within corporate institutions. To explain this notion of a "moral minimum," Bowie appeals to the framework for distinguishing responsibilities that was described earlier and that is derived from the principle-based traditional ethics described in chapter 3.

Bowie identifies his approach as a "Kantian" theory of business ethics. In simple terms, he begins with the distinction described previously between the ethical imperatives to cause no harm, to prevent harm, and to do good. People have a strong ethical duty to cause no harm, and only a *prima facie* duty to prevent harm or to do good. The obligation to cause no harm, in Bowie's view, overrides other ethical considerations. The pursuit of profit legitimately can be constrained by this ethical duty. On the other hand, Bowie accepts the economic view that managers are the agents of stockholder-owners and thus they also have a duty (derived from the contract between them) to further the interests of stockholders. Thus, while it is ethically good for managers to *prevent harm* or *to do good,* their duty to stockholders overrides these concerns. As long as managers comply with the moral minimum and cause no harm, they have a responsibility to maximize profits.

Thus, Bowie would argue that business has a social responsibility to respect the rights of its employees, even when not specified or required by law. Such rights might include the right to safe and healthy workplaces, right to privacy, and right to due process. Bowie would also argue that business has an ethical duty to respect the rights of consumers to such things as safe products and truthful advertising, even when not specified in law. But, the contractual duty that managers have to stockholder-owners overrides the responsibility to prevent harm or to do (philanthropic) good.

stakeholder theory

A model of corporate social responsibility that holds that business managers have ethical responsibilities to a range of stakeholders that go beyond a narrow view that the primary or only responsibility of managers is to stockholders.

Perhaps the most influential version of **stakeholder theory** was introduced by R. Edward Freeman (see Reading 5-2, "Managing for Stakeholders"). Stakeholder theory begins with the recognition that every business decision affects a wide variety of people, benefiting some and imposing costs on others. Think of the best-known business ethics cases—Volkswagen, Walmart, Enron, and Arthur Andersen; AIDS drugs in Africa; executive compensation; AIG; Merck and river blindness—and recognize that decisions made by business managers produce far-ranging consequences to a wide variety of people. Remember, as well, the economic lesson about opportunity costs. Every decision involves the imposition of costs, in the sense that every decision also involves opportunities foregone, choices given up.

Stakeholder theory recognizes that every business decision imposes costs on someone and mandates that those costs be acknowledged. A manager who seeks to maximize profit is imposing costs on employees, consumers, and suppliers. The dominant economic model argues that these costs are justified because managers owe an ethical duty to shareholders. The stakeholder model simply acknowledges this principle and points out that other ethical duties have an equal claim on managerial decision making. Any theory of corporate social responsibility must explain and defend answers to the questions: For whose benefit and at whose costs should the business be managed?

The economic model argues that the firm should be managed for the sole benefit of stockholders. This view is justified by appeal to the rights of owners, the fiduciary duty of managers, and the social benefits that follow from this arrangement. The stakeholder theory argues, on factual, legal, economic, and ethical grounds, that this is an inadequate understanding of business. Let us examine who are the stakeholders, what reasons can be offered to justify the legitimacy of their claims on management, and what are the practical implications of this view for business managers.

R. Edward Freeman offers a defense of the stakeholder model in Reading 5-2, "Managing for Stakeholders." He describes both a narrow and a wider understanding of the concept of a "stakeholder." In a narrow sense, a stakeholder includes anyone who is vital to the survival and success of the corporation. More widely, a stakeholder could be "any group or individual who can affect or be affected by the corporation."

Stakeholder theory argues that the narrow economic model fails both as an accurate descriptive and as a reasonable normative account of business management. As a descriptive account of business, the classical model ignores over a century of legal precedent arising from both case law and legislative enactments. While it might have been true over a century ago that management had an overriding obligation to stockholders, the law now recognizes a wide range of managerial obligations to such stakeholders as consumers, employees, competitors, the environment, and individuals with disabilities. Thus, as a matter of law it is false to claim that management can ignore duties to everyone but stockholders.

We also need to recognize that these legal precedents did not simply fall from the sky. It is the considered judgment of the most fundamental institutions of a democratic society, the courts, and legislatures that corporate management must limit their fiduciary duty to stockholders in the name of the rights and interests of various constituencies affected by corporate decisions.

Factual, economic considerations also diminish the plausibility of the economic model. The wide variety of market failures recognized by economists show that, even when managers pursue profits, there are no guarantees that they will serve the interests of either stockholders or the public. When markets fail to attain their goals, society has no reason to sanction the primacy of the fiduciary obligation to stockholders.

But perhaps the most important argument in favor of the stakeholder theory rests in ethical considerations. The economic model appeals to two fundamental ethical norms for its justification: utilitarian considerations of social well-being and individual rights. On each of these normative accounts, however, due consideration must be given to all affected parties. Essential to any utilitarian theory is the commitment to balance the interests of all concerned and to give to each (arguably, equal) consideration. The stakeholder theory simply acknowledges this fact by requiring management to balance the ethical interests of all affected parties. Sometimes, as the classical model would hold, balancing will require management to maximize stockholder interests, but sometimes not. Utilitarianism requires management to consider the consequences of its decisions for the well-being of all affected groups. Stakeholder theory requires the same.

Likewise, any theory of moral rights is committed to equal rights for all. According to the rights-based ethical framework, the overriding moral imperative is to treat all people as ends and never as means only. Corporate managers who fail to give due consideration to the rights of employees and other concerned groups in the pursuit of profit are treating these groups as means to the ends of stockholders. This, in the rights-based ethical framework, is unjust. (Of course, ignoring the interests of stockholders is equally unjust.)

Thus, the stakeholder theory argues that on the very same grounds that are used to justify the classical model, a wider "stakeholder" theory of corporate social responsibility is proven ethically superior. Freeman argues that "the stakeholder theory does not give primacy to one stakeholder group over another, though there will be times when one group will benefit at the expense of others. In general, however, management must keep the relationships among stakeholders in balance."[7]

Firms exist in a web of relationships with many stakeholders and these relationships can create a variety of responsibilities. As we have seen in several of the cases and examples mentioned previously, it may not be possible to satisfy the needs of each and every stakeholder in a situation. But, stakeholder theory also recognizes that some stakeholders have different power and impact on decisions than others; that organizations have distinct missions, priorities, and values affecting the final decisions. Therefore, social responsibility would require decisions to prioritize competing and conflicting responsibilities.

Integrative Model of CSR

Most discussions about CSR are framed in terms of a debate: Should business be expected to sacrifice profits for social ends? Much of the CSR literature assumes a tension between the pursuit of profit and social responsibility. But, of course, there have always been organizations that turn this tension around, organizations that pursue social ends as the very core of their mission. Nonprofits—such as hospitals, nongovernmental organizations (NGOs), foundations, professional organizations, schools, colleges, and government agencies—have social goals at the center of their operations. The knowledge and skills taught in business schools, from management and marketing to human resources and accounting, are just as relevant in nonprofits as they are in for-profit organizations. For this reason alone, students in these various subdisciplines of a business school curriculum should be familiar with nonprofit business models.

But there is a growing recognition that some for-profit organizations also have social goals as a central part of the strategic mission of the organization. Within the growing benefit corporation movement, many for-profit businesses are placing social responsibility at the core of their strategic mission and corporate purpose. (For more details of such a business model, see the Opening Decision Point "Benefit Corporations" and the Reality Check "Browsing for Social Good.")

integrative model of CSR

For some business firms, social responsibility is fully integrated with the firm's mission or strategic plan.

Because these firms fully integrate economic and social goals by bringing social responsibilities into the core of their business model, we refer to this as the **integrative model of CSR**. At first glance, firms that adopt the integrative model raise no particular ethical issues. Even advocates of the narrow economic model of CSR such as Milton Friedman would agree that owners of a firm are free to make the pursuit of social goals a part of their business model. They would just disagree that these social goals should be part of *every* business's mission.

No one claims that every business should adopt the principles of benefit corporations and devote all their activities to service of social goals. There are clearly other needs that businesses are designed to address. At best, benefit corporations demonstrate that profit is not incompatible with doing good, and therefore that one can do good profitably. (See the Reality Check "Fairness in a Cup of Coffee: Example of the Integrative Model.") On the other hand, there are some who would argue that the ethical responsibilities associated with sustainability are relevant to every business concern. In some ways, sustainability offers a model of CSR that suggests that ethical goals should be at the heart of every corporate mission. There are reasons to think that sustainability promises to be a concept of growing importance in discussions of CSR.

The Implications of Sustainability in the Integrative Model of CSR

Sustainability, and specifically its definition, will be discussed in greater detail in chapter 9; but as a topic within CSR, sustainability holds that a firm's financial goals must be balanced against, and perhaps even overridden by, environmental considerations. Defenders of this approach point out that all economic

Reality Check *Browsing for Social Good*

The popular web browser Firefox and e-mail program Thunderbird are products of Mozilla Corporation, a for-profit subsidiary of Mozilla Foundation, a nonprofit organization. Mozilla Corporation had revenues of more than $120 million and over 400 million users of its Firefox browser in 2010. Mozilla is described on its website as follows:

WHAT IS MOZILLA?

We're a global community of thousands who sincerely believe in the power of technology to enrich people's lives.

We're a public benefit organization dedicated not to making money but to improving the way people everywhere experience the Internet.

The common thread that runs throughout Mozilla is our belief that, as the most significant social and technological development of our time, the Internet is a public resource that must remain open and accessible to all. With this in mind, our efforts are ultimately driven by our mission of encouraging choice, innovation and opportunity online.

To achieve these goals, we use a highly transparent, extremely collaborative process that brings together thousands of dedicated volunteers around the world with our small staff of employees to coordinate the creation of products like the Firefox web browser. This process is supported by the Mozilla Corporation, which is a wholly-owned subsidiary of the nonprofit Mozilla Foundation.

In the end, the Mozilla community, organization and technology is all focused on a single goal: **making the Internet better for everyone.**

Source: Mozilla Foundation, *The State of Mozilla: Annual Report* (2010), www.mozilla.org/en-US/foundation/annual-report/2010/faq/ (accessed July 27, 2012).

activity exists within a biosphere that supports all life. They argue that the present model of economics, and especially the macroeconomic goal of economic growth, is already running up against the limits of the biosphere's capacity to sustain life. Fundamental human needs for goods such as clean air, water, nutritious food, and a moderate climate are threatened by the present dominant model of economic activity.

From this perspective, the success of a business must be judged not only against the financial bottom line of profitability, but also against the ecological and social bottoms lines of sustainability. A business or industry that is financially profitable, but that uses resources (e.g., fossil fuels) at unsustainable rates and that creates wastes (e.g., carbon dioxide) at rates that exceed the earth's capacity to absorb them, is a business or industry that is failing its fundamental social responsibility. Importantly, a firm that is environmentally unsustainable is also a firm that is, in the long-term, financially unsustainable. (To learn more about how firms are sharing the results of their sustainability efforts, see the Reality Check "Will Sustainability Reports Replace the Annual Financial Reports?")

The sustainability version of CSR suggests that the long-term financial well-being of every firm is directly tied to questions of how the firm both affects and is affected by the natural environment. A business model that ignores the biophysical and ecological context of its activities is a business model doomed to failure.

Reality Check *Fairness in a Cup of Coffee: Example of the Integrative Model*

The integrative model of CSR is evidenced in a company called Equal Exchange (www.equalexchange.com), which is a worker-owned and governed business committed to Fair Trade with small-scale coffee, tea, and cocoa farmers. Its "Vision of Fairness to Farmers" explains its model:

A VISION OF FAIRNESS TO FARMERS

Fairness to farmers. A closer connection between people and the farmers we all rely on. This was the essence of the vision that the three Equal Exchange founders—Rink Dickinson, Michael Rozyne, and Jonathan Rosenthal—held in their minds and hearts as they stood together on a metaphorical cliff back in 1986.

The three, who had met each other as managers at a New England food co-op, were part of a movement to transform the relationship between the public and food producers. At the time, however, these efforts didn't extend to farmers outside of the U.S.

The founders decided to meet once a week—and did so for three years—to discuss how best to change the way food is grown, bought, and sold around the world. At the end of this time they had a plan for a new organization called Equal Exchange that would be:

- *A social change organization that would help farmers and their families gain more control over their economic futures.*

- *A group that would educate consumers about trade issues affecting farmers.*

- *A provider of high-quality foods that would nourish the body and the soul.*

- *A company that would be controlled by the people who did the actual work.*

- *A community of dedicated individuals who believed that honesty, respect, and mutual benefit are integral to any worthwhile endeavor.*

No Turning Back

It was a grand vision—with a somewhat shaky grounding in reality. But Rink, Michael, and Jonathan understood that significant change only happens when you're open to taking big risks. So they cried "¡Adelante!" (rough translation from the Spanish: "No turning back!") and took a running leap off the cliff. They left their jobs. They invested their own money. And they turned to their families and friends for start-up funds and let them know there was a good chance they would never see that money again.

The core group of folks believed in their cause and decided to invest. Their checks provided the $100,000 needed to start the new company. With this modest financing in hand, Rink, Michael, and Jonathan headed into the great unknown. At best, the project, which coupled a for-profit business model with a nonprofit mission, was viewed as utopian; at worst it was regarded as foolish. For the first three years Equal Exchange struggled and, like many new ventures, lost money. But the founders hung on and persevered. By the third year they began to break even.

Source: From www.equalexchange.coop/story. Reprinted with permission.

Exploring Enlightened Self-Interest: Does "Good Ethics" Mean "Good Business"?

OBJECTIVE

In one of the quotations that opened this chapter, the former chair of the Dayton–Hudson Corporation, Kenneth Dayton, explained that "If business does not serve society, society will no long tolerate our profits or even our existence." This logic suggests that CSR not only provides benefits to society, but it can also benefit an organization by securing its place within a society. Are there other reasons besides self-interest and economics for a business to engage in socially

Reality Check   *Will Sustainability Reports Replace the Annual Financial Reports?*

Various laws and regulations require corporations to file an annual report that provides a comprehensive accounting of a business's activities in the preceding year. The report is intended to provide shareholders and the public with information about the financial performance of the company in which they have invested. While varied information is contained in an annual report, it is primarily a financial report and will include an auditor's report and summary of revenues and expenses.

As corporations move to more fully integrate social responsibilities into their corporate mission, a different type of reporting and assessment mechanism will be required. Within the last decade, thousands of companies have supplemented this financial annual report with a **corporate sustainability report**, which provides an overview of the firm's performance on environmental and social, as well as financial, grounds. In some cases, sustainability reports are replacing financial reports by integrating assessment of financial, environmental, and social performance into one comprehensive report.

Global Reporting Initiative, a nonprofit organization that was instrumental in creating a widely accepted sustainability reporting framework, defined sustainability reporting as follows:

> Sustainability reporting is a process for publicly disclosing an organization's economic, environmental, and social performance. Many organizations find that financial reporting alone no longer satisfies the needs of shareholders, customers, communities, and other stakeholders for information about overall organizational performance. The term "sustainability reporting" is synonymous with citizenship reporting, social reporting, triple-bottom line reporting and other terms that encompass the economic, environmental, and social aspects of an organization's performance.

Source: www.globalreporting.org.

---

corporate sustainability report
Provides all stakeholders with financial and other information regarding a firm's economic, environmental, and social performance.

responsible activities? Can we make a "business case" for CSR, such as the reputational value we discussed earlier?

Perhaps the most obvious answer is the one we touched on earlier with regard to the impact that CSR can have on a firm's reputation within a community. CSR-related activities can improve profitability by enhancing a company's standing among its stakeholders, including consumers and employees. For example, some evidence suggests that employees who are well treated in their work environments may prove more loyal, more effective, and more productive in their work. Liz Bankowski, director of social missions at Ben & Jerry's Homemade Ice Cream Company, claims that 80 to 90 percent of Ben & Jerry's employees work there because "they feel they are part of a greater good."[8] The positive impact on the bottom line, therefore, stems not only from customer preference but also from employee preference.

The problem with a focus on reputation, however, is that social responsibility then can become merely social marketing. That is, a firm may use the image of social responsibility to garner customer support or employee loyalty while the facts do not evidence a true commitment. Paul Hawken, cofounder of Smith & Hawken gardening stores and an advocate of business social responsibility, reminds us that

> you see tobacco companies subsidizing the arts, then later you find out that there are internal memos showing that they wanted to specifically target the minorities in the arts because they want to get minorities to smoke. That's not socially

responsible. It's using social perception as a way to aggrandize or further one's own interests exclusively.[9]

Of course, the gap between perception and reality can work in the opposite direction as well. Consider Procter & Gamble Co., which was harshly criticized by respondents to a survey seeking to rank firms on the basis of their corporate philanthropy. Respondents contended that P&G did "absolutely nothing to help" after the September 11 tragedy in New York City.[10] However, in truth P&G provided more than $2.5 million in cash and products, but it simply did not publicize that contribution. The same held true for Honda Motor Co., which donated cash, all-terrain vehicles, and generators for use at the World Trade Center site during the same time period. Perhaps unaware of these efforts, respondents instead believed these companies to lack compassion for their failure to (publicly) support America.

reputation management

The practice of caring for the "image" of a firm.

The practice of attending to the "image" of a firm is sometimes referred to as **reputation management.** There is nothing inherently wrong with managing a firm's reputation, and in fact the failure to do so might be a poor business decision, but observers could challenge firms for engaging in CSR activities *solely* for the purpose of affecting their reputations. The challenge is based on the fact that reputation management often *works!* Figure 5.2 shows the elements that Harris Interactive considers critical to the construction of a reputation and the resulting benefits that attention to these elements can produce. If a firm creates a good self-image, it builds a type of trust bank — consumers or other stakeholders seem to give it some slack if they then hear something negative about the firm. Similarly, if a firm has a negative image, that image may stick, regardless of what good the corporation

FIGURE 5.2

The Construction of Corporate Reputation

Source: Copyright © Harris Interactive Research. Reprinted by permission from www.harrisinteractive.com/services/reputation.asp.

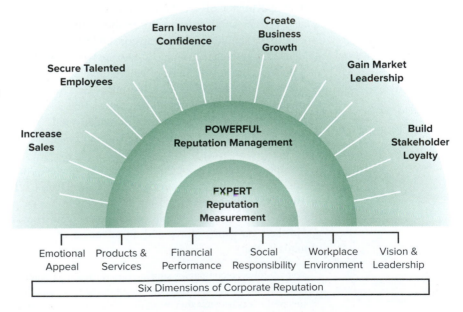

Reality Check *Enron and BP as Most Admired?*

Would you rather be an unethical firm with a good reputation or an ethical firm with a reputation for injustice? Some very high-profile firms have reaped enormous praise, while at the same time conducting themselves in a manner that would soon lead to scandal. Enron and BP are good examples.

Enron included the following accomplishments in its 2000 Corporate Responsibility Annual Report. The list drives home the challenges incumbent in any awards mechanism that strives to reward a trait such as "most innovative" or "all-star, most admired" rather than an enduring, measurable element of the corporate environment. On the other hand, awards such as those listed here can serve as influential motivating factors in corporate financial decisions, so many executives in fields affected by these honors would prefer they remain.

AS REPORTED IN ENRON'S 2000 CORPORATE RESPONSIBILITY ANNUAL REPORT:

The Most Innovative Company in America

—*Fortune* magazine for six consecutive years

100 Best Companies to Work for in America

—*Fortune* magazine for three consecutive years, ranked number 22 in 2000

All-Star List of Global Most Admired Companies

—*Fortune* magazine, ranked number 25 in 2000

100 Fastest Growing Companies

—*Fortune* magazine, ranked number 29 in 2000

THE CALM BEFORE THE STORM

In April 2010, a tragic oil spill that polluted the Gulf Coast made BP into one of the most despised corporations in the world. The name *BP* became widely associated with unethical, irresponsible corporate behavior. But prior to that, BP had enjoyed a strong reputation. In 2005, for example, BP was named one of the 100 Most Sustainable Companies. BP was also among the top 10 companies listed on *Fortune* magazine's Accountability Rating for 2006, 2007, and 2008. In 2007, it was ranked number one on that list.

Sources: 2000 Enron Corporate Responsibility Annual Report (2001), pp. 2–3; 2005 Global 100 List, www.global100.org/annual-lists/2005-global-100-list.html; The Accountability Rating, www.accountabilityrating.com/past_results.asp.

may do. Plato explored this issue when he asked whether one would rather be an unethical person with a good reputation or an ethical person with a reputation for injustice. You may find that, if given the choice between the two, companies are far more likely to survive under the first conception than under the second. On the issue of reputation management and the impact of a variety of stakeholders on a firm's reputation, see the Reality Check "Enron and BP as Most Admired?" and examine the perspectives of various consumer and advocacy groups in connection with well-known businesses at any of the following websites:

- www.ethicalconsumer.org/boycotts/boycottslist.aspx
- www.cokespotlight.org
- www.ihatestarbucks.com
- www.noamazon.com
- www.starbucked.com
- www.walmartsurvivor.com

In some ways, reputation may often be more forceful than reality, as with the P&G and Honda cases mentioned earlier. Shell Oil has publicized its efforts toward good citizenship in Nigeria; but it has an unfortunate record in terms of the timing of its responsiveness to spills, and its community development projects have created community rifts in areas around oilfields. Similarly, British American Tobacco heavily and consistently promotes its high health and safety standards; but it receives ongoing reports from contract farmers in Brazil and Kenya about ill health as a result of tobacco cultivation. Which image would you expect to be more publicized and, therefore, more likely to remain in stakeholders' consciousness?

A larger question involves the possible correlation between profits and ethics. Is good ethics also good business? One important justification offered for CSR, what is often called *enlightened self-interest,* presumes that it is, or at least it can be. A great deal of research has concentrated on examining this connection. In fact, theorists continue to dispute whether ethical decisions lead to more significant profits than unethical decisions. While we are all familiar with examples of unethical decisions leading to high profits, there is general agreement that, in the long run, ethics pays off. However, it is the measurement of that payoff that is the challenge. In Figure 5.2, Harris Interactive juxtaposes indicators of performance in the CSR arena with those traditionally used in the financial environment to provide some guidance in this area. Though executives responsible for organizational measurement and risk assessment might be less familiar with the processes for assessing the elements included on the right side of the chart, those elements are by no means less measurable. Often, however, the long-term value is not as evident or obvious.

OBJECTIVE

Though there are many justifications for ethics in business, often the discussion returns to, well, *returns*—is there a business case for a return on investment from ethics? There is evidence that good ethics is good business; yet the dominant thinking is that, if it cannot be measured, it is not important. As a result, efforts have been made to measure the bottom-line impact of ethical decision making.

Measurement is critical because the business case is not without its detractors. David Vogel, a political science professor at Berkeley, contends that although there is a market for firms with strong CSR missions, it is a niche market and one that therefore caters to only a small group of consumers or investors.[11] He argues that, contrary to a global shift in the business environment, CSR instead should be perceived as just one option for a business strategy that might be appropriate for certain types of firms under certain conditions, such as those with well-known brand names and reputations that are subject to threats by activists. He warns of the exposure a firm might suffer if it then does not live up to its CSR promises. He also cautions against investing in CSR when consumers are not willing to pay higher prices to support that investment. Though this perspective is persuasive, a review of the scholarly research on the subject suggests the contrary on numerous counts, most predominantly the overall return on investment to the corporation.

Persuasive evidence of impact comes from a study titled "Developing Value: The Business Case for Sustainability in Emerging Markets," based on a study produced jointly by SustainAbility, the Ethos Institute, and the International

Reality Check *So They Say*

Whether at the World Trade Organization, or at the OECD, or at the United Nations, an irrefutable case can be made that a universal acceptance of the rule of law, the outlawing of corrupt practices, respect for workers' rights, high health and safety standards, sensitivity to the environment, support for education and the protection and nurturing of children are not only justifiable against the criteria of morality and justice. The simple truth is that these are good for business and most business people recognize this.[12]

Thomas d'Aquino, CEO of Canada's Business Council on National Issues

We all pay for poverty and unemployment and illiteracy. If a large percentage of society falls into a disadvantaged class, investors will find it hard to source skilled and alert workers; manufacturers will have a limited market for their products; criminality will scare away foreign investments, and internal migrants to limited areas of opportunities will strain basic services and lead to urban blight. Under these conditions, no country can move forward economically and sustain development. . . . It therefore makes business sense for corporations to complement the efforts of government in contributing to social development.[13]

J. Ayala II

Our findings, both cross-sectional and longitudinal, indicate that there are indeed systematic linkages among community involvement, employee morale, and business performance in business enterprises. To the best of our knowledge, this is the first time that such linkages have been demonstrated empirically. Moreover, the weight of the evidence produced here indicates that community involvement is positively associated with business performance, employee morale is positively associated with business performance, and the interaction of community involvement—external involvement—with employee morale—internal involvement—is even more strongly associated with business performance than is either "involvement" measure alone.[14]

Report of a study by UCLA graduate school of business professor David Lewin and J. M. Sabater (formerly IBM director of corporate community relations) in 1989 and 1991 involving in-depth, statistical research surveys of over 150 U.S.-based companies to determine whether there is a verifiable connection between a company's community involvement and its business performance

Finance Corporation. The research found that in emerging markets cost savings, productivity improvement, revenue growth, and access to markets were the most important business benefits of sustainability activities. Environmental process improvements and human resource management were the most significant areas of sustainability action. The report concludes that it does pay for businesses in emerging markets to pursue a wider role in environmental and social issues, citing cost reductions, productivity, revenue growth, and market access as areas of greatest return for multinational enterprises (MNEs).

In addition, studies have found that there are a number of expected—and measurable—outcomes to ethics programs in organizations. Some people look to the end results of firms that have placed ethics and social responsibility at the forefront of their activities, while others look to those firms that have been successful and determine the role that ethics might have played. (For additional areas of measurement see the Reality Check "So They Say.") With regard to the former, consider Johnson & Johnson, known for its quick and effective handling of its experience with tainted Tylenol. As highlighted in the Reality Check "Do Codes Make a Difference" in chapter 4, Johnson

In April 2000, the board of directors of Ben and Jerry's accepted Unilever's offer and agreed to sell Ben and Jerry's for $326 million. At least two other offers were made, one by a group that included Ben Cohen with plans to take the company private so that its social mission could be protected. At the time, one of the competing buyers was quoted as saying, "The board felt they had no choice but to let all three groups put their best offers on the table yesterday. We think it's horrible that a company has no choice but to sell to the highest bidder or get sued." [15]

But as part of the sale, Ben and Jerry's board negotiated a number of unusual conditions aimed at maintaining the company's social mission. Unilever agreed to establish an independent board of directors and operate Ben and Jerry's as an autonomous subsidiary of the parent corporation. Unilever agreed that Ben and Jerry's independent board of directors would operate free from control by the Unilever board, would maintain the right to sue that board, and would exist in perpetuity. Unilever also agreed to sustain the 7.5 percent contribution to the Ben and Jerry Foundation, add an additional $5 million to that foundation, make additional contributions to socially responsible initiatives, and maintain jobs. It also agreed to work with Ben Cohen to find ways to improve Unilever's own social and environmental work. From Unilever's perspective, a large part of what it was buying was the Ben and Jerry's brand, and that brand was strongly identified with progressive social causes. Unilever claimed that it only made sense to continue the original mission.

There were some challenges during the early years after the purchase, however. Unilever closed some operations and eliminated some jobs, something that Ben and Jerry's never had done. But by 2015, the record seemed to show that the relationship had succeeded and Ben and Jerry's continued to operate in ways identical to its original operating plans. In 2012, Ben and Jerry's received certification as an official B-Corp, the first wholly owned corporate subsidiary to receive that designation. Unilever itself, due in part to the influence of Ben and Jerry's, has continued to evolve into one of the world's most progressive and socially responsible corporations and has been exploring the possibility of becoming a B-Corp. [16]

& Johnson has had more than seven decades of consecutive sales increases, two decades of double-digit earnings increases, and four decades of dividend increases. Each of these quantifiable measurements can perhaps serve as proxies for success, to some extent, or at least would be unlikely to occur in a company permeated by ethical lapses.

Moreover, a landmark study by Professors Stephen Erfle and Michael Frantantuono found that firms that were ranked highest in terms of their records on a variety of social issues (including charitable contributions, community outreach programs, environmental performance, advancement of women, and promotion of minorities) had greater financial performance as well. Financial performance was better in terms of operating income growth, sales-to-assets ratios, sales growth, return on equity, earnings-to-asset growth, return on investment, return on assets, and asset growth.[17] The Reality Check "So They Say" demonstrates that these perspectives are gaining traction worldwide.

Another study by Verschoor and Murphy reports that the overall financial performance of the 2001 *Business Ethics* magazine Best Corporate Citizens was significantly better than that of the remaining companies in the S&P 500 index, based on the 2001 *BusinessWeek* ranking of total financial performance.[18]

In addition, the researchers found that these same firms had a significantly better reputation among corporate directors, security analysts, and senior executives. The same result was found in a 2001 *Fortune* survey of most admired companies. The UK-based Institute of Business Ethics did a follow-up study to validate these findings and found that, from the perspectives of economic value added, market value added, and the price/earnings ratio, those companies that had a code of conduct outperformed those that did not over a five-year period.[19] The higher performance translated into significantly more economic value added, a less volatile price/earnings ratio (making the firm, perhaps, a more secure investment), and 18 percent higher profit/turnover ratios. The research concluded:

> This study gives credence to the assertion that "you do business ethically because it pays." However, the most effective driver for maintaining a high level of integrity throughout the business is because it is seen by the board, employees and other stakeholders to be a core value and therefore the right thing to do. . . . [A] sustainable business is one which is well managed and which takes business ethics seriously. Leaders of this type of business do not need any assurance that their approach to the way they do business will also enhance their profitability, because they know it to be true.[20]

This chapter sought to answer the question of whether there exists a social responsibility of business. Several sources of that responsibility were proposed. The responsibility may be based in a concept of good corporate citizenship, a social contract, or enlightened self-interest. Notwithstanding its origins, we then explored the challenge of how an inanimate entity like a corporation could actually have a responsibility to others and discussed the extent of that obligation, both in law and ethics.

No matter how one answers the several questions posed by this chapter, however, one thing is certain: It is impossible to engage in business today without encountering and addressing CSR. Despite substantial differences among companies, research demonstrates that almost all companies will confront CSR issues from stakeholders at some point in the near future.[21]

Questions, Projects, and Exercises

1. What is your overall perspective on CSR after reviewing this chapter? If market forces do not encourage responsibility for social causes, should a firm engage in this behavior? Does social responsibility apply only to firms, or do consumers have a responsibility as well to support firms that take socially responsible action and withhold our support from firms that fail to exhibit socially responsible behavior? If we stand by and allow irresponsible actions to take place using profits made on our purchases, do we bear any responsibility?

   - How did you reach your decision? What key facts do you need to know in order to judge a firm's actions or your complicity in them by supporting a firm with your purchases or other choices?
   - How do you determine responsibility? Do you pay attention to these issues in your purchases and other choices?
   - Would you be more likely to support a company by purchasing its products or services if the company (a) donated a portion of the proceeds to a cause that was important to you; (b) paid its workers a "fair" wage (however you would define that concept); or (c) was a good investment for its stockholders? Which consequence is more influential to you? On the contrary, would you refrain from purchasing from a firm that failed in any of those areas?
   - How do the alternatives compare? Do you believe different purchasing decisions by consumers could really make a difference?

2. Which of the three models of CSR is most persuasive to you and why? Which do you believe is most prevalent among companies that engage in CSR efforts?

3. This chapter has asked in several ways whether the social responsibility of the companies you patronize has ever made any difference to your purchasing decisions. Will it make any difference in the future as a result of what you have learned? Consider your last three largest purchases. Go to the websites of the companies that manufacture the products you bought and explore those firms' social responsibility efforts. Are they more or less than what you expected? Do your findings make a difference to you in terms of how you feel about these firms, your purchases, and/or the amount of money you spent on these items?

4. One of the leading figures in the Enron debacle was company founder Kenneth Lay, who died in 2006 after his conviction for fraud and conspiracy but before he began serving his sentence. Prior to the events that led to the trial and conviction, Lay was viewed in Houston as one of its "genuine heroes" and Enron was a "shining beacon" according to a professor at Rice University in Houston. The Houston Astros's field was named after Enron when the company gave the Astros a large grant. Enron also gave money to local organizations such as the ballet and national organizations based in Houston such as United Way. The Lays individually supported Houston's opera and ballet, its Holocaust Museum, the University of Texas MD Anderson Cancer Center, and other charitable organizations. If you were on the jury, would *any* of this information be relevant to your decision about Kenneth Lay's guilt or innocence? If your jury had determined that Lay was guilty, would *any* of this information be relevant to your decision about the sentence you would then impose? Defend your decision from an ethical perspective.

5. In 2005, Nestlé S.A. CEO Peter Braeck-Letmathe explained, "Companies shouldn't feel obligated to 'give back' to communities because they haven't taken anything away. Companies should only pursue charitable endeavors with the underlying intention of

making money. It is not our money we're handing out but our investors.' A company's obligation is simply to create jobs and make products. What the hell have we taken away from society by being a successful company that employs people?"[22] Which model of CSR would the Nestlé CEO advocate, and do you agree with his assessment?

6. Supermodel Kate Moss appeared in photos in a number of tabloid magazines and elsewhere using illegal drugs. Subsequent to the appearance of the photographs, several of her clients, including Chanel, H&M, and Burberry, canceled their contracts (some only temporarily) with her or determined that they would not renew them when they became eligible for renewal. Other clients opted to retain her services, preferring to "stand by her" during this ordeal. Moss issued a statement that she had checked herself into a rehabilitation center for assistance with her drug use. Assume that you are the marketing vice president for a major global fashion label that is a client of Moss at the time of these events. Use the ethical decision-making process to evaluate how to respond to the situation. What is your decision on what to do?

7. What kind of organization would you like to work for? What would be the best? What would be the most realistic? Think about its structure, physical environment, lines of communication, treatment of employees, recruitment and promotion practices, policies toward the community, and so on. Consider also, however, what you lose because of some of these benefits (for example, if the company contributes in the community or offers more benefits for employees, there might be less money for raises).

8. Take another look at the quote earlier in this chapter by Paul Hawken. He seems to be saying that it is not acceptable to use social perception as a way to further one's own interests (exclusively). Now find the Smith & Hawken site on the web and any additional information you can locate regarding Smith & Hawken or Paul Hawken and CSR. Would you identify Smith & Hawken as a firm interested in CSR? Would you identify Paul Hawken as an individual interested in CSR or personal social responsibility? Which model of CSR would you suggest that Paul Hawken supports?

9. Given the significant financial power that a retailer and sponsor like Nike can have in the sports world, does it have any obligation to use that power to do good in connection with its particular industry? A 2006 *New York Times* article[23] suggested that "more than television packages, more than attendance at the gate, track and field is driven by shoe company dough. Nike could, if it chose, threaten to pull its financial support from the coaches and trainers of athletes who are barred for doping violations. For years, the caretakers of the athletes have also been suspected as the doping pushers. Curiously, Nike hasn't fallen in line with everyone else calling for strict liability among coaches, trainers and athletes." The article instead suggests that Nike does not benefit when a star falls from glory so it tends to shy away from this area of oversight. In fact, it goes so far as to say that "Nike is the doping society's enabler." Can you make the argument that Nike has an obligation to intervene? Or, if you do not agree with an argument for its responsibility to do good, could you instead make an economic argument in favor of intervention?

10. Make a list of the five products on which you have spent the most money over the past three years. Using the Internet, find corporate sustainability reports for the companies that produced those products or that had some responsibility in their production. Are you able to find a sustainability report for each company? What can you determine about the company's sustainability efforts by reviewing these reports? Can you determine anything about their sincerity? Do you perceive that the company is undergoing a fundamental transformation in its efforts to sustainability, or does it seem more a matter of window-dressing (or, in other words, for the *sole* purpose of reputation)?

Key Terms

After reading this chapter, you should have a clear understanding of the following key terms. For a complete definition, please see the Glossary.

corporate social responsibility (CSR), *p. 182*

corporate sustainability report, *p. 191*

economic model of CSR, *p. 181*

integrative model of CSR, *p. 188*

reputation management, *p. 192*

stakeholder model of CSR, *p. 185*

stakeholder theory, *p. 186*

End Notes

1. Sir Adrian Cadbury, "Ethical Managers Make Their Own Rules," *Harvard Business Review* (September/October 1987).

2. Stakeholder Alliance, www.stakeholderalliance.org/Buzz.html (accessed April 11, 2010).

3. Leo Strine, "Making It Easier for Directors to 'Do the Right Thing,' " *Harvard Business Law Review* 4 (2014), p. 241.

4. Ellen Berrey, "How Many Benefit Corporations Are There?" (May 5, 2015), http://ssrn.com/abstract=2602781.

5. Deloitte Millennial Survey (January 2014), www2.deloitte.com/content/dam/Deloitte/global/Documents/About-Deloitte/gx-dttl-2014-millennial-survey-report.pdf (accessed April 14, 2015).

6. "Mission Statement: Our Values," www.merck.com/about/mission.html (accessed April 11, 2010).

7. William Evan and R. Edward Freeman, "A Stakeholder Theory of the Modern Corporation: Kantian Capitalism," in *Contemporary Issues in Business Ethics,* 4th ed., ed Joseph R. DesJardins and John McCall (Belmont, CA: Wadsworth Publishing 2000), p. 89.

8. Joel Makower, *Beyond the Bottom Line* (New York: Simon & Schuster, 1994), p. 68.

9. Ibid., p. 15.

10. Ronald Alsop, "For a Company, Charitable Works Are Best Carried out Discreetly," *The Wall Street Journal,* January 16, 2002, Marketplace Section, p. 1.

11. David Vogel, *The Market for Virtue: The Potential and Limits of Corporate Social Responsibility* (Washington, DC: Brookings Institution, 2005).

12. Quoted in C. Forcese, "Profiting from Misfortune? The Role of Business Corporations in Promoting and Protecting International Human Rights" (MA thesis, Norman Paterson School of International Affairs, Carleton University, Ottawa 1997), referred to in C. Forcese, "Putting Conscience into Commerce: Strategies for Making Human Rights Business as Usual" (Montréal International Centre for Human Rights and Democratic Development, 1997).

13. J. Ayala II, "Philanthropy Makes Business Sense," *Ayala Foundation Inc. Quarterly* 4, no. 2 (July–September, October–November 1995), p. 3.

14. D. Lewin and J. M. Sabater, "Corporate Philanthropy and Business Performance," *Philanthropy at the Crossroads* (Bloomington: University of Indiana Press, 1996), pp. 105–126.

15. Constance L. Hays, "Ben & Jerry's to Unilever, with Attitude," *The New York Times* (April 13, 2000), www.nytimes.com/2000/04/13/business/ben-jerry-s-to-unilever-with-attitude.html (accessed April 15, 2016).

16. David Gelles, "How the Social Mission of Ben & Jerry's Survived Being Gobbled Up," *The New York Times* (August 21, 2015), www.nytimes.com/2015/08/23/business/how-ben-jerrys-social-mission-survived-being-gobbled-up.html?_r=2 (accessed April 15, 2016).

17. Joel Makower, *Beyond the Bottom Line* (New York: Simon & Schuster, 1994), pp. 70–71.

18. Curtis Verschoor and Elizabeth Murphy, "The Financial Performance of Large Firms and Those with Global Prominence: How Do the Best Corporations Rate?," *Business & Society Review* 107, no. 3 (2002), pp. 371–380. See also Elizabeth Murphy and Curtis Verschoor, "Best Corporate Citizens Have Better Financial Performance," *Strategic Finance* 83, no. 7 (January 2002), p. 20.

19. Simon Webley and Elise More, *Does Business Ethics Pay?* (London: Institute of Business Ethics, 2003), p. 9.

20. Simon Webley and Elise More, *Does Business Ethics Pay?* (London: Institute of Business Ethics, 2003), p. 9.

21. Margot Lobbezoo, "Social Responsibilities of Business," unpublished manuscript available from the author.

22. Jennifer Heldt Powell, "Nestlé Chief Rejects the Need to 'Give Back' to Communities," *Boston Herald* (March 9, 2005), p. 33, www.bc.edu/schools/csom/cga/executives/events/brabeck/; www.babymilkaction.org/press/press22march05.html (accessed April 11, 2010).

23. Selena Roberts, "Coaches like Graham Still Have Their Sponsors," *The New York Times* (August 2, 2006), http://select.nytimes.com/2006/08/02/sports/othersports/02roberts.html?_r=1 (accessed April 11, 2010).

Readings

Reading 5-1: "BP and Corporate Social Responsibility," by Chris MacDonald

Reading 5-2: "Managing for Stakeholders," by R. Edward Freeman

Reading 5-3: What's Wrong—and What's Right—with Stakeholder Management," by John R. Boatright

Reading **5-1**

BP and Corporate Social Responsibility

Chris MacDonald

I've long been critical of the term "CSR," or Corporate Social Responsibility. In particular, I've argued that all three parts of the term—"corporate" and "social" and "responsibility"—are misleading, at least if the term CSR is thought of, as it often is, as referring to the full range of ethical issues in business. After all, many businesses, including some very large and important ones, are not corporations. So the word "corporate" is out of place there. And many important ethical issues are not "social" issues. An employee's right to a safe workplace, for example, results in his or her employer having an obligation to him or her as an individual; it is not in any clear way a "social" obligation. And the word "responsibility" does not come close to summing up all the ethical questions that apply to individuals and organizations in the world of business: we are interested in questions not just about responsibilities, but also about rights, duties, entitlements, permissions, and actions that are ethically good but not required. If we think about how business should behave purely in terms of "responsibility," we are leaving a lot out.

But for a lot of people, the word "CSR" is virtually a synonym for the much broader term, "Business Ethics." And that's a mistake. Of course, social responsibility is still an important topic. It is good for corporations to think about what their social responsibilities are, and to try hard to live up to them. But the term "CSR" often leads such thinking astray.

The BP *Deepwater Horizon* explosion and oil spill of 2010 serves as a good example to illustrate this problem. The ethical problems associated with that catastrophic event demonstrate nicely the distinction between those ethical issues that do fit nicely under the heading of "CSR," and those that clearly do not. In particular, that oil spill illustrates the terrain carved out by the "S," or "Social," aspect of CSR. Too many people use the term "CSR" when they actually want to talk about basic business ethics issues like honesty or product safety or workplace health and safety—things that are not, in any clear way at least, matters of a company's *social* responsibilities. But the BP oil spill raises genuine CSR questions—it's very much a question of corporate, *social,* responsibility.

Let's take a look at the range of ethical obligations that fall to a company like BP. BP—the company formerly known as British Petroleum—is in the business of finding crude oil, refining it, and selling the refined gasoline and various by-products that result. In the course of doing business, BP interacts with a huge range of individuals and organizations, and those interactions bring with them an enormous range of ethical obligations.

A short list of the very *basic* ethical obligations that fall to such a business would include things like:

a. the obligation to provide customers with the product they're expecting—rather than one adulterated with water, for example;

b. the obligation to deal honestly with suppliers;

c. the obligation to ensure reasonable levels of workplace health and safety;

d. the obligation to make an honest effort to build long-term share value;

e. the obligation to comply with environmental laws and industry best practices;

. . . and so on.

It is important to recognize that most of those obligations are obligations to identifiable individuals— to individual customers, employees, shareholders, and so on. There's nothing really "social" about any of those obligations, if we take the word "social" seriously as implying something to do with society as a whole. The possible exception is the obligation to comply with the law, which probably is best thought of as a social obligation.

And it is entirely possible that BP, in the weeks leading up to the spill, met most of ethical obligations on that list. In other words, the company may well have lived up to its ethical obligations to most of the individuals and groups it dealt with. The exception, of course, involves the company's obligations regarding workplace health and safety— eleven workers were killed in the *Deepwater Horizon* blowout, likely indicating failures within the company to give safety the level of attention it deserves. But even had no one been killed or hurt during the blowout, and if we could thus conclude that the company had met literally all of its ethical obligations to all the individuals it dealt with, that would certainly not mean that BP had acted ethically. A question of social responsibility would remain. That is why the *Deepwater Horizon* spill makes it especially appropriate to talk about CSR.

So, what makes the oil spill a matter of social responsibility? Precisely the fact that the risks of BP's deep-water drilling operations, and the eventual devastating consequences of those operations, were borne by society at large, rather than just by specific individuals. The spill resulted in enormous negative externalities—negative effects on people who weren't involved economically with BP, and who didn't consent (at least not directly) to bear the risks of the company's operations. The fishing industry up and down the gulf coast was brought to a standstill. The tourism industry in affected regions ground to a virtual halt. The resulting unemployment meant huge costs for various elements of the tax-supported social safety net. And the massive cleanup effort undertaken in the wake of the spill required very substantial participation by a range of government agencies, all of which implied significant costs. In other words, BP imposed risks, and eventually costs, on American society as a whole. The company seems to have failed in its social responsibilities.

Now, all (yes all!) production processes involve externalities. All businesses emit some pollution (either directly, or indirectly via the things they consume) and all businesses impose at least some risks on non-consenting third parties. So the question of CSR really has to do with the magnitude of those risks, and the extent to which a company is morally responsible for those effects, and maybe the extent to which companies have an obligation not just to avoid social harms (or risks) but also an obligation to contribute socially—that is, to contribute socially beyond making a product people value.

From a CSR point of view, then, the question with regard to BP is whether the risks taken were reasonable ones. Most people are likely tempted to say "no." But then most of us still want plentiful cheap gas. So if we are to avoid hypocrisy, most of us need to consent to the risks involved in the basic process of oil exploration and extraction. Our economy would literally come to a standstill without the massive quantities of fossil fuels currently provided by petroleum companies like BP. The risks implied by those basic exploration and extraction practices are ones that society implicitly consents to, and so those risks can't plausibly be seen as violating BP's basic social responsibilities. The risks implied by the specific behaviours of BP and its employees—the behaviours that were directly responsible for the explosion and resulting oil spill—are another matter altogether. There is little doubt that those actions pushed the level of risk beyond what is socially acceptable.

We can only understand the ethical significance of the BP oil spill of 2010 by thinking of it specifically from a social point of view. The company's ethical failures have important social dimensions, in addition to the ways in which the company failed specific individuals such as employees. Thus the BP oil spill provides an excellent way to illustrate the way we should understand the scope of the term "corporate social responsibility," and how to keep that term narrow enough for it to retain some real meaning.

Source: This essay is based in part on: Chris MacDonald, "BP and CSR," *Business Ethics Blog,* September 1, 2010, http://businessethicsblog.com/2010/09/01/bp-and-csr/; and Chris MacDonald, "CSR Is Not C-S-R," *Business Ethics Blog,* August 10, 2009, http://businessethicsblog.com/2009/08/10/csr-is-not-c-s-r/.

Reading **5-2**

Managing for Stakeholders[1]

R. Edward Freeman

I. Introduction

The purpose of this essay is to outline an emerging view of business that we shall call "managing for stakeholders."[2] This view has emerged over the past thirty years from a group of scholars in a diverse set of disciplines, from finance to philosophy.[3] The basic idea is that businesses, and the executives who manage them, actually do and should create value for customers, suppliers, employees, communities, and financiers (or share-holders). And, that we need to pay careful attention to how these relationships are managed and how value gets created for these stakeholders. We contrast this idea with the dominant model of business activity; namely, that businesses are to be managed solely for the benefit of shareholders. Any other benefits (or harms) that are created are incidental.[4]

Simple ideas create complex questions, and we proceed as follows. In the next section we examine why the dominant story or model of business that is deeply embedded in our culture is no longer workable. It is resistant to change, not consistent with the law, and for the most part, simply ignores matters of ethics. Each of these flaws is fatal in business world of the 21st Century.

We then proceed to define the basic ideas of "managing for stakeholders" and why it solves some of the problems of the dominant model. In particular we pay attention to how using "stakeholder" as a basic unit of analysis makes it more difficult to ignore matters of ethics. We argue that the primary responsibility of the executive is to create as much value for stakeholders as possible, and that no stakeholder interest is viable in isolation of the other stakeholders. We sketch three primary arguments from ethical theory for adopting "managing for stakeholders." We conclude by outlining a fourth "pragmatist argument" that suggests we see managing for stakeholders as a new narrative about business that lets us improve the way we currently create value for each other. Capitalism is in this view a system of social cooperation and collaboration, rather than primarily a system of competition.

II. The Dominant Story: Managerial Capitalism with Shareholders at the Center

The modern business corporation has emerged during the 20th Century as one of the most important innovations in human history. Yet the changes that we are now experiencing call for its reinvention. Before we suggest what this revision, "managing for stakeholders" or "stakeholder capitalism," is, first we need to understand how the dominant story came to be told.

Somewhere in the past, organizations were quite simple and "doing business" consisted of buying raw materials from suppliers, converting it to products, and selling it to customers. For the most part owner-entrepreneurs founded such simple businesses and worked at the business along with members of their families. The development of new production processes, such as the assembly line, meant that jobs could be specialized and more work could be accomplished. New technologies and sources of power became readily available. These and other social and political forces combined to require larger amounts of capital, well beyond the scope of most individual owner-manager-employees. Additionally, "workers" or non-family members began to dominate the firm and were the rule rather than the exception.

Ownership of the business became more dispersed, as capital was raised from banks, stockholders, and other institutions. Indeed, the management of the firm became separated from the ownership of the firm. And, in order to be successful, the top managers of the business had to simultaneously satisfy the owners, the employees and their unions, suppliers and customers. This system of organization of businesses along the lines set forth here was known as managerial capitalism or laissez faire capitalism, or more recently, shareholder capitalism.[5]

As businesses grew, managers developed a means of control via the divisionalized firm. Led by Alfred Sloan at General Motors, the divisionalized firm with a central headquarters staff was widely adapted.[6] The dominant model for managerial authority was the military and civil service bureaucracy. By creating rational structures and processes, the orderly progress of business growth could be well-managed.

Thus, managerialism, hierarchy, stability, and predictability all evolved together, in the United States and Europe, to form the most powerful economic system in the history of humanity. The rise of bureaucracy and managerialism was so strong, that the economist Joseph Schumpeter predicted that it would wipe out the creative force of capitalism, stifling innovation in its drive for predictability and stability.

During the last 50 years this "Managerial Model" has put "shareholders" at the center of the firm as the most important group for managers to worry about. This mindset has dealt with the increasing complexity of the business world by focusing more intensely on "shareholders" and "creating value for shareholders." It has become common wisdom to "increase shareholder value," and many companies have instituted complex incentive compensation plans aimed at aligning the interests of executives with the interests of shareholders. These incentive plans are often tied to the price of a company's stock which is affected by many factors not the least of which is the expectations of Wall Street analysts about earnings per share each quarter. Meeting Wall Street targets, and forming a stable and predictable base of quarter over quarter increases in earnings per share has become the standard for measuring company performance. Indeed all of the recent scandals at Enron, Worldcom, Tyco, Arthur Anderson and others are in part due to executives trying to increase shareholder value, sometimes in opposition to accounting rules and law. Unfortunately, the world has changed so that the stability and predictability required by the shareholder approach can no longer be assured.

The Dominant Model Is Resistant to Change

The Managerial View of business with shareholders at the center is inherently resistant to change. It puts shareholders' interests over and above the interests of customers, suppliers, employees, and others, as if these interests must conflict with each other. It understands a business as an essentially hierarchical organization fastened together with authority to act in the shareholders' interests. Executives often speak in the language of hierarchy as "working for shareholders," "shareholders are the boss," and "you have to do what the shareholders want." On this interpretation, change should

occur only when the shareholders are unhappy, and as long as executives can produce a series of incrementally better financial results there is no problem. According to this view the only change that counts is change oriented toward shareholder value. If customers are unhappy, if accounting rules have been compromised, if product quality is bad, if environmental disaster looms, even if competitive forces threaten, the only interesting questions are whether and how these forces for change affect shareholder value, measured by the price of the stock every day. Unfortunately in today's world there is just too much uncertainty and complexity to rely on such a single criterion. Business in the 21st Century is global and multi-faceted, and shareholder value may not capture that dynamism. Or, if it does, as the theory suggests it must eventually, it will be too late for executives to do anything about it. The dominant story may work for how things turn out in the long run on Wall Street, but managers have to act with an eye to Main Street as well, to anticipate change to try and take advantage of the dynamism of business.[7]

The Dominant Model Is Not Consistent with the Law

In actual fact the clarity of putting shareholders' interests first, above that of customers, suppliers, employees, and communities, flies in the face of the reality the law. The law has evolved to put constraints on the kinds of tradeoffs that can be made. In fact the law of corporations gives a less clear answer to the question of in whose interest and for whose benefit the corporation should be governed. The law has evolved over the years to give *de facto* standing to the claims of groups other than stockholders. It has, in effect, required that the claims of customers, suppliers, local communities, and employees be taken into consideration.

For instance, the doctrine of "privity of contract," as articulated in *Winterbottom v. Wright* in 1842, has been eroded by recent developments in products liability law. *Greenman v. Yuba Power* gives the manufacturer strict liability for damage caused by its products, even though the seller has exercised all possible care in the preparation and sale of the product and the consumer has not bought the product from nor entered into any contractual arrangement with the manufacturer. *Caveat emptor* has been replaced in large part, with *caveat venditor.* The Consumer Product Safety Commission has the power to enact product recalls, essentially leading to an increase in the number of voluntary product recalls by companies seeking to mitigate legal damage awards. Some industries are required to provide information to customers about a product's ingredients, whether or not the customers want and are willing to pay for this information. Thus, companies must take the interests of customers into account, by law.

A similar story can be told about the evolution of the law forcing management to take the interests of employees into account. The National Labor Relations Act gave employees the right to unionize and to bargain in good faith. It set up the National Labor Relations Board to enforce these rights with management. The Equal Pay Act of 1963 and Title VII of the Civil Rights Act of 1964 constrain management from discrimination in hiring practices; these have been followed with the Age Discrimination in Employment Act of 1967, and recent extensions affecting people with disabilities. The emergence of a body of administrative case law arising from labor-management disputes and the historic settling of discrimination claims with large employers have caused the emergence of a body of management practice that is consistent with the legal guarantee of the rights of employees.

The law has also evolved to try and protect the interests of local communities. The Clean Air Act and Clean Water Act, and various amendments to these classic pieces of legislation, have constrained management from "spoiling the commons." In an historic case, *Marsh v. Alabama,* the Supreme Court ruled that a company-owned town was subject to the provisions of the U.S. Constitution, thereby guaranteeing the rights of local citizens and negating the "property rights" of the firm. Current issues center around protecting local businesses, forcing companies to pay the health care costs of

their employees, increases in minimum wages, environmental standards, and the effects of business development on the lives of local community members. These issues fill the local political landscapes and executives and their companies must take account of them.

Some may argue that the constraints of the law, at least in the U.S., have become increasingly irrelevant in a world where business is global in nature. However, globalization simply makes this argument stronger. The laws that are relevant to business have evolved differently around the world, but they have evolved nonetheless to take into account the interests of groups other than just shareholders. Each state in India has a different set of regulations that affect how a company can do business. In China the law has evolved to give business some property rights but it is far from exclusive. And, in most of the European Union, laws around "civil society" and the role of "employees" are much more complex than even U.S. law.

"Laissez faire capitalism" is simply a myth. The idea that business is about "maximizing value for stockholders regardless of the consequences to others" is one that has outlived its usefulness. The dominant model simply does not describe how business operates. Another way to see this is that if executives always have to qualify "maximize shareholder value" with exceptions of law, or even good practice, then the dominant story isn't very useful anymore. There are just too many exceptions. The dominant story could be saved by arguing that it describes a normative view about how business should operate, despite how actual businesses have evolved.[8] So we need to look more closely at some of the conceptual and normative problems that the dominant model raises.

The Dominant Model Is Not Consistent with Basic Ethics

Previously we have argued that most theories of business rely on separating "business" decisions from "ethical" decisions.[9] This is seen most clearly in the popular joke about "business ethics as an oxymoron." More formally we might suggest that we define:

The Separation Fallacy

It is useful to believe that sentences like, "x is a business decision" have no ethical content or any implicit ethical point of view. And, it is useful to believe that sentences like "x is an ethical decision, the best thing to do all things considered" have no content or implicit view about value creation and trade (business).

This fallacy underlies much of the dominant story about business, as well as in other areas in society. There are two implications of rejecting the Separation Fallacy. The first is that almost any business decision has some ethical content. To see that this is true one need only ask whether the following questions make sense for virtually any business decision.

The Open Question Argument

1. If this decision is made for whom is value created and destroyed?
2. Who is harmed and/or benefited by this decision?
3. Whose rights are enabled and whose values are realized by this decision (and whose are not)?
4. What kind of person will I (we) become if we make this decision?

Since these questions are always open for most business decisions, it is reasonable to give up the Separation Fallacy, which would have us believe that these questions aren't relevant for making business decisions, or that they could never be answered. We need a theory about business that builds in answers to the "Open Question Argument" above. One such answer would be "Only value to shareholders counts," but such an answer would have to be enmeshed in the language of ethics as well as business. Milton Friedman, unlike most of his expositors, may actually give such a morally rich answer. He claims that the responsibility of the executive is to make profits subject to law and ethical custom. Depending on how "law and ethical custom" is interpreted, the key difference with the stakeholder approach may well be that we disagree

about how the world works. In order to create value we believe that it is better to focus on integrating business and ethics within a complex set of stakeholder relationships rather than treating ethics as a side constraint on making profits. In short we need a theory that has as its basis what we might call:

The Integration Thesis

Most business decisions or sentences about business have some ethical content, or implicit ethical view. Most ethical decisions or sentences about ethics have some business content or implicit view about business.[10]

One of the most pressing challenges facing business scholars is to tell compelling narratives that have the Integration Thesis at its heart. This is essentially the task that a group of scholars, "business ethicists" and "stakeholder theorists," have begun over the last 30 years. We need to go back to the very basics of ethics. Ethics is about the rules, principles, consequences, matters of character, etc. that we use to live together. These ideas give us a set of open questions that we are constantly searching for better ways to answer in reasonably complete ways.[11] One might define "ethics" as a conversation about how we can reason together and solve our differences, recognize where our interests are joined and need development, so that we can all flourish without resorting to coercion and violence. Some may disagree with such a definition, and we do not intend to privilege definitions, but such a pragmatist approach to ethics entails that we reason and talk together to try and create a better world for all of us.

If our critiques of the dominant model are correct then we need to start over by re-conceptualizing the very language that we use to understand how business operates. We want to suggest that something like the following principle is implicit in most reasonably comprehensive views about ethics.

The Responsibility Principle[12]

Most people, most of the time, want to, actually do, and should accept responsibility for the effects of their actions on others.

Clearly the Responsibility Principle is incompatible with the Separation Fallacy. If business is separated from ethics, there is no question of moral responsibility for business decisions; hence, the joke is that "business ethics" is an oxymoron. More clearly still, without something like the Responsibility Principle it is difficult to see how ethics gets off the ground. "Responsibility" may well be a difficult and multi-faceted idea. There are surely many different ways to understand it. But, if we are not willing to accept the responsibility for our own actions (as limited as that may be due to complicated issues of causality and the like), then ethics, understood as how we reason together so we can all flourish, is likely an exercise in bad faith.

If we want to give up the separation fallacy and adopt the integration thesis, if the open question argument makes sense, and if something like the responsibility thesis is necessary, then we need a new model for business. And, this new story must be able to explain how value creation at once deals with economics and ethics, and how it takes account of all of the effects of business action on others. Such a model exists, and has been developing over the last 30 years by management researchers and ethics scholars, and there are many businesses who have adopted this "stakeholder framework" for their businesses.

III. Managing for Stakeholders

The basic idea of "managing for stakeholders" is quite simple. Business can be understood as a set of relationships among groups which have a stake in the activities that make up the business. Business is about how customers, suppliers, employees, financiers (stockholders, bondholders, banks, etc.), communities and managers interact and create value. To understand a business is to know how these relationships work. And, the executive's or entrepreneur's job is to manage and shape these relationships, hence the title, "managing for stakeholders."

Reading figure 2.1 depicts the idea of "managing for stakeholders" in a variation of the classic "wheel and spoke" diagram.[13] However, it is important to note that the stakeholder idea is perfectly general. Corporations are not the center of the universe, and there are many possible pictures. One might put customers in the center to signal that a company puts customers as the key priority. Another might put employees in the center and link them to customers and shareholders. We prefer the generic diagram because it suggests, pictorially, that "managing for stakeholders" is a theory about management and business; hence, managers and companies in the center. But, there is no larger metaphysical claim here.

Stakeholders and Stakes

Owners or financiers (a better term) clearly have a financial stake in the business in the form of stocks, bonds, and so on, and they expect some kind of financial return from them. Of course, the stakes of financiers will differ by type of owner, preferences for money, moral preferences, and so on, as well as by type of firm. The shareholders of Google may well want returns as well as be supportive of Google's articulated purpose of "Do No Evil." To the extent that it makes sense to talk about the financiers "owning the firm," they have a concomitant responsibility for the uses of their property.

Employees have their jobs and usually their livelihood at stake; they often have specialized skills for which there is usually no perfectly elastic market. In return for their labor, they expect security, wages, benefits and meaningful work. Often, employees are expected to participate in the decision making of the organization, and if the employees are management or senior executives we see them as shouldering a great deal of responsibility for the conduct of the organization as a whole. And, employees are sometimes financiers as well, since many companies have stock ownership plans, and loyal employees who believe in the future of their companies often voluntarily invest. One way to think about the employee relationship is in terms of contracts. Customers and suppliers exchange resources for the products and services of the firm and in return receive the benefits of the products and services. As with financiers and

READING FIGURE 2.1

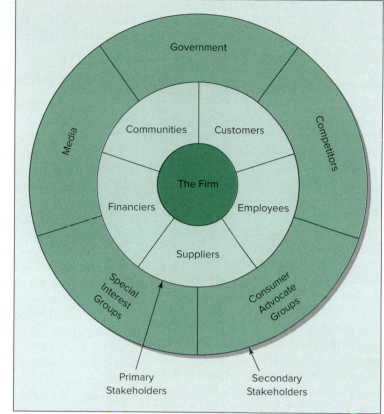

employees, the customer and supplier relationships are enmeshed in ethics. Companies make promises to customers via their advertising, and when products or services don't deliver on these promises then management has a responsibility to rectify the situation. It is also important to have suppliers who are committed to making a company better. If suppliers find a better, faster, and cheaper way of making critical parts or services, then both supplier and company can win. Of course, some suppliers simply compete on price, but even so, there is a moral element of fairness and transparency to the supplier relationship.

Finally, the local community grants the firm the right to build facilities, and in turn, it benefits from the tax base and economic and social contributions of the firm. Companies have a real impact

on communities, and being located in a welcoming community helps a company create value for its other stakeholders. In return for the provision of local services, companies are expected to be good citizens, as is any individual person. It should not expose the community to unreasonable hazards in the form of pollution, toxic waste, etc. It should keep whatever commitments it makes to the community, and operate in a transparent manner as far as possible. Of course, companies don't have perfect knowledge, but when management discovers some danger or runs afoul of new competition, it is expected to inform and work with local communities to mitigate any negative effects, as far as possible.

While any business must consist of financiers, customers, suppliers, employees, and communities, it is possible to think about other stakeholders as well. We can define "stakeholder" in a number of ways. First of all we could define the term fairly narrowly to capture the idea that any business, large or small, is about creating value for "those groups without whose support, the business would cease to be viable." The inner circle of Reading figure 2.1 depicts this view. Almost every business is concerned at some level with relationships among financiers, customers, suppliers, employees, and communities. We might call these groups "primary" or "definitional." However, it should be noted that as a business starts up, sometimes one particular stakeholder is more important than another. In a new business start up, sometimes there are no suppliers, and paying lots of attention to one or two key customers, as well as to the venture capitalist (financier) is the right approach.

There is also a somewhat broader definition that captures the idea that if a group or individual can affect a business, then the executives must take that group into consideration in thinking about how to create value. Or, a stakeholder is any group or individual that can affect or be affected by the realization of an organization's purpose. At a minimum some groups affect primary stakeholders and we might see these as stakeholders in the outer ring of Reading figure 2.1 and call them "secondary" or "instrumental."

There are other definitions that have emerged during the last 30 years, some based on risks and rewards, some based on mutuality of interests. And, the debate over finding the one "true definition" of "stakeholder" is not likely to end. We prefer a more pragmatist approach of being clear of the purpose of using any of the proposed definitions. Business is a fascinating field of study. There are very few principles and definitions that apply to all businesses all over the world. Furthermore, there are many different ways to run a successful business, or if you like, many different flavors of "managing for stakeholders." We see limited usefulness in trying to define one model of business, either based on the shareholder or stakeholder view that works for all businesses everywhere. We see

much value to be gained in examining how the stakes work in the value creation process, and the role of the executive.

IV. The Responsibility of the Executive in Managing for Stakeholders

Executives play a special role in the activity of the business enterprise. On the one hand, they have a stake like every other employee in terms of an actual or implied employment contract. And, that stake is linked to the stakes of financiers, customers, suppliers, communities, and other employees. In addition, executives are expected to look after the health of the overall enterprise, to keep the varied stakes moving in roughly the same direction, and to keep them in balance.[14] No stakeholder stands alone in the process of value creation. The stakes of each stakeholder group are multi-faceted, and inherently connected to each other. How could a bondholder recognize any returns without management paying attention to the stakes of customers or employees? How could customers get the products and services they need without employees and suppliers? How could employees have a decent place to live without communities? Many thinkers see the dominant problem of "managing for stakeholders" as how to solve the priority problem, or "which stakeholders are more important," or "how do we make tradeoffs among stakeholders." We see this as a secondary issue.

First and foremost, we need to see stakeholder interests as joint, as inherently tied together. Seeing stakeholder interests as "joint" rather than opposed is difficult. It is not always easy to find a way to accommodate all stakeholder interests. It is easier to trade off one versus another. Why not delay spending on new products for customers in order to keep earnings a bit higher? Why not cut employee medical benefits in order to invest in a new inventory control system?

Managing for stakeholders suggests that executives try to reframe the questions. How can we invest in new products and create higher earnings? How can we be sure our employees are healthy and happy and are able to work creatively so that we can capture the benefits of new information technology such as inventory control systems? In a recent book reflecting on his experience as CEO of Medtronic, Bill George summarized the managing for stakeholders mindset:[15]

> Serving all your stakeholders is the best way to produce long term results and create a growing; prosperous company. . . . Let me be very clear about this: there is no conflict between serving all your stakeholders and providing excellent returns for shareholders. In the long term it is impossible to have one without the other. However, serving all these stakeholder groups requires discipline, vision, and committed leadership.

The primary responsibility of the executive is to create as much value as possible for stakeholders.[16] Where stakeholder interests conflict, the executive must find a way to rethink the problems so that these interests can go together, so that even more value can be created for each. If tradeoffs have to be made, as often happens in the real world, then the executive must figure out how to make the tradeoffs, and immediately begin improving the tradeoffs for all sides. Managing for stakeholders is about creating as much value as possible for stakeholders, without resorting to tradeoffs.

We believe that this task is more easily accomplished when a business has a sense of purpose. Furthermore, there are few limits on the kinds of purpose that can drive a business. Wal-Mart may stand for "everyday low price." Merck can stand for "alleviating human suffering." The point is that if an entrepreneur or an executive can find a purpose that speaks to the hearts and minds of key stakeholders, it is more likely that there will be sustained success.

Purpose is complex and inspirational. The Grameen Bank wants to eliminate poverty. Fannie Mae wants to make housing affordable to every income level in society. Tastings (a local restaurant) wants to bring the taste of really good food and wine to lots of people in the community. And, all of these organizations have to generate profits, or else they cannot pursue their purposes. Capitalism works because we can pursue our purpose with others. When we coalesce around a big idea, or a joint purpose evolves from our day to day activities with each other, then great things can happen. To create value for stakeholders, executives must understand that business is fully situated in the realm of humanity. Businesses are human institutions populated by real live complex human beings. Stakeholders have names and faces and children. They are not mere placeholders for social roles. As such, matters of ethics are routine when one takes a managing for stakeholders approach. Of course this should go without saying, but a part of the dominant story about business is that business people are only in it for their own narrowly defined self interest. One main assumption of the managerial view with shareholders at the center is that shareholders only care about returns, and therefore their agents, managers, should only care about returns. However, this does not fit either our experiences or our aspirations. In the words of one CEO, "The only assets I manage go up and down the elevators everyday."

Most human beings are complicated. Most of us do what we do because we are self-interested and interested in others. Business works in part because of our urge to create things with others and for others. Working on a team, or creating a new product or delivery mechanism that makes customers lives better or happier or more pleasurable all can be contributing factors to why we go to work each day. And, this is not to deny the economic incentive of getting a pay check. The assumption of narrow self-interest is extremely limiting, and can be self-reinforcing—people can begin to act in a narrow self-interested way if they believe that is what is expected of them, as some of the scandals such as Enron, have shown. We need to be open to a more complex psychology—one any parent finds familiar as they have shepherded the growth and development of their children.

V. Some Arguments for Managing for Stakeholders

Once you say stakeholders are persons then the ideas of ethics are automatically applicable. However you interpret the idea of "stakeholders," you must pay attention to the effects of your actions on others. And, something like the Responsibility Principle suggests that this is a cornerstone of any adequate ethical theory. There are at least three main arguments for adopting a managing for stakeholders approach. Philosophers will see these as connected to the three main approaches to ethical theory that have developed historically. We shall briefly set forth sketches of these arguments, and then suggest that there is a more powerful fourth argument.[17]

The Argument from Consequences

A number of theorists have argued that the main reason that the dominant model of managing for shareholders is a good idea is that it leads to the best consequences for all. Typically these arguments invoke Adam Smith's idea of the invisible hand, whereby each business actor pursues her own self interest and the greatest good of all actually emerges. The problem with this argument is that we now know with modern general equilibrium economics that the argument only works under very specialized conditions that seldom describe the real world. And further, we know that if the economic conditions get very close to those needed to produce the greatest good, there is no guarantee that the greatest good will actually result.

Managing for stakeholders may actually produce better consequences for all stakeholders because it recognizes that stakeholder interests are joint. If one stakeholder pursues its interests at the expense of all the others, then the others will either withdraw their support, or look to create another network of stakeholder value creation. This is not to say that there are not times when one stakeholder will benefit at the expense of others, but if this happens continuously over time, then in a relatively free society, stakeholders will either: (1) exit to form a new stakeholder network that satisfies their needs; (2) use the political process to constrain the offending stakeholder; or, (3) invent some other form of activity to satisfy their particular needs.[18]

Alternatively, if we think about stakeholders engaged in a series of bargains among themselves, then we would expect that as individual stakeholders recognized their joint interests, and made good decisions based on these interests, better consequences would result, than if they each narrowly pursued their individual self interests.[19]

Now it may be objected that such an approach ignores "social consequences" or "consequences to society," and hence, that we need a concept of "corporate social responsibility" to mitigate these effects. This objection is a vestigial limb of the dominant model. Since the only effects, on that view, were economic effects, then we need to think about "social consequences" or "corporate social responsibility." However, if stakeholder relationships are understood to be fully embedded in morality, then there is no need for an idea like corporate social responsibility. We can replace it with "corporate stakeholder responsibility" which is a dominant feature of managing for stakeholders.

The Argument from Rights

The dominant story gives property rights in the corporation exclusively to shareholders, and the natural question arises about the rights of other stakeholders who are affected. One way to understand managing for stakeholders is that it takes this question of rights, seriously. If you believe that rights make sense, and further that if one person has a right to X then all persons have a right to X, it is just much easier to think about these issues using a stakeholder approach. For instance, while shareholders may well have property rights, these rights are not absolute, and should not be seen as such. Shareholders may not use their property to abridge the rights of others. For instance, shareholders and their agents, managers, may not use corporate property to violate the right to life of others. One way to understand managing for stakeholders is that it assumes that stakeholders have some rights. Now it is notoriously difficult to parse the idea of "rights." But, if executives take managing for stakeholders seriously, they will automatically think about what is owed to customers, suppliers, employees, financiers and communities, in virtue of their stake, and in virtue of their basic humanity.

The Argument from Character

One of the strongest arguments for managing for stakeholders is that it asks executives and entrepreneurs to consider the question of what kind of company they want to create and build. The answer to this question will be in large part an issue of character. Aspiration matters. The business virtues of efficiency, fairness, respect, integrity, keeping commitments, and others are all critical in being successful at creating value for stakeholders. These virtues are simply absent when we think only about the dominant model and its sole reliance on a narrow economic logic.

If we frame the central question of management as "how do we create value for shareholders" then the only virtue that emerges is one of loyalty to the interests of shareholders. However if we frame the central question more broadly as "how do we create and sustain the creation of value for stakeholders" or "how do we get stakeholder interests all going in the same direction," then it is easy to see how many of the other virtues are relevant. Taking a stakeholder approach helps people decide how companies can contribute to their well-being and kinds of lives they want to lead. By making ethics explicit and building it into the basic way we think about business, we avoid a situation of bad faith and self deception.

The Pragmatist's Argument

The previous three arguments point out important reasons for adopting a new story about business. Pragmatists want to know how we can live better, how we can create both ourselves and our communities in ways where values such as freedom and solidarity are present in our everyday lives to the maximal extent. While it is sometimes useful to think about consequences, rights, and character in isolation, in reality our lives are richer if we can have a conversation about how to live together better. There is a long tradition of pragmatist ethics dating to philosophers such as William James and John Dewey. More recently philosopher Richard Rorty has expressed the pragmatist ideal:[20]

> . . . pragmatists . . . hope instead that human beings will come to enjoy more money, more free time, and greater social equality, and also that they will develop more empathy, more ability to put themselves in the shoes of others. We hope that human beings will behave more decently toward another as their standard of living improves.

By building into the very conceptual framework we use to think about business a concern with freedom, equality, consequences, decency, shared purpose, and paying attention to all of the effects of how we create value for each other, we can make business a human institution, and perhaps remake it in a way that sustains us.

For the pragmatist, business (and capitalism) has evolved as a social practice, an important one that we use to create value and trade with each other. In this view, first and foremost, business is about collaboration. Of course, in a free society, stakeholders are free to form competing networks. But, the fuel for capitalism is our desire to create something of value, and to create it for ourselves and others. The spirit of capitalism is the spirit of individual achievement together with the spirit of accomplishing great tasks in collaboration with others. Managing for stakeholders makes this plain so that we can get about the business of creating better selves and better communities.

Endnotes

1. The ideas in this paper have had a long development time. The ideas here have been reworked from: R. Edward Freeman, *Strategic Management: A Stakeholder Approach* [Boston: Pitman, 1984]; R. Edward Freeman, "A Stakeholder Theory of the Modern Corporation,

in T. Beauchamp and N. Bowie (eds.), *Ethical Theory and Business* [Englewood Cliffs: Prentice Hall, 7th edition, 2005], also in earlier editions co-authored with William Evan; Andrew Wicks, R. Edward Freeman, Patricia Werhane, and Kirsten Martin, *Business Ethics: A Managerial Approach* [Englewood Cliffs: Prentice Hall, 2008]; and, R. Edward Freeman, Jeffrey Harrison, and Andrew Wicks, *Managing for Stakeholders* [New Haven: Yale University Press, 2007]. I am grateful to editors and coauthors for permission to rework these ideas here.

2. It has been called a variety of things from "stakeholder management," "stakeholder capitalism," "a stakeholder theory of the modern corporation," etc. Our reasons for choosing "managing for stakeholders" will become clearer as we proceed. Many others have worked on these ideas, and should not be held accountable for the rather idiosyncratic view outlined here.

3. For a stylized history of the idea see R. Edward Freeman, "The Development of Stakeholder Theory: An Idiosyncratic Approach," in K. Smith and M. Hitt (eds.), *Great Minds in Management,* Oxford: Oxford University Press, 2005.

4. One doesn't manage "for" these benefits (and harms).

5. The difference between managerial and shareholder capitalism is large. However, the existence of agency theory lets us treat the two identically for our purposes here. Both agree on the view that the modern firm is characterized by the separation of decision making and residual risk bearing. The resulting agency problem is the subject of a vast literature.

6. Alfred Chandler's brilliant book, *Strategy and Structure,* Boston: MIT Press, 1970, chronicles the rise of the divisionalized corporation. For a not so flattering account of General Motors during the same time period see Peter Drucker's classic work, *The Concept of the Corporation,* New York: Transaction Publishers, Reprint Edition, 1993.

7. Executives can take little comfort in the nostrum that in the long run things work out and the most efficient companies survive. Some market theorists suggest that finance theory acts like "universal acid" cutting through every possible management decision, whether or not actual managers are aware of it. Perhaps the real difference between the dominant model and the "managing for stakeholders" model proposed here is that they are simply "about" different things. The dominant model is about the strict and narrow economic logic of markets, and the "managing for stakeholders" model is about how human beings create value for each other.

8. Often the flavor of the response of finance theorists sounds like this. The world would be better of if, despite all of the imperfections, executives tried to maximize shareholder value. It is difficult to see how any rational being could accept such a view in the face of the recent scandals, where it could be argued that the worst offenders were the most ideologically pure, and the result was the actual destruction of shareholder value (see *Breaking the Short Term Cycle,* Charlottesville, VA: Business Roundtable Institute for Corporate Ethics/CFA Center for Financial Market Integrity, 2006). Perhaps we have a version of Aristotle's idea that happiness is not a result of trying to be happy, or Mill's idea that it does not maximize utility to try and maximize utility. Collins and Porras have suggested that even if executives want to maximize shareholder value, they should focus on purpose instead, that trying to maximize shareholder value does not lead to maximum value (see J. Collins and J. Porras, *Built To Last,* New York: Harper Collins, 2002).

9. See R. Edward Freeman, "The Politics of Stakeholder Theory: Some Future Directions," *Business Ethics Quarterly,* 4, 409–422.

10. The second part of the integration thesis is left for another occasion. Philosophers who read this essay may note the radical departure from standard accounts of political philosophy. Suppose we began the inquiry into political philosophy with the question of "how is value creation and trade sustainable over time" and suppose that the traditional beginning question, "how is the state justified" was a subsidiary one. We might discover or create some very different answers from the standard accounts of most political theory. See R. Edward Freeman and Robert Phillips, "Stakeholder Theory: A Libertarian Defense," *Business Ethics Quarterly,* Vol. 12, No. 3, 2002, pp. 331f.

11. Here we roughly follow the logic of John Rawls in *Political Liberalism,* (New York: Columbia University Press, 1995).

12. There are many statements of this principle. Our argument is that whatever the particular conception of responsibility there is some underlying concept that is captured, like our willingness or our need, to justify our lives to others. Note the answer that the dominant view of business must give to questions about responsibility. "Executives are responsible only for the effects of their actions on shareholders, or only in so far as their actions create or destroy shareholder value."

13. The spirit of this diagram is from R. Phillips, *Stakeholder Theory and Organizational Ethics* two styles in these notes (San Francisco: Berret-Koehler Publishers, 2003).

14. In earlier versions of this essay in this volume we suggested that the notion of a fiduciary duty to stockholders be extended to "fiduciary duty to stakeholders." We believe that such a move cannot be defended without doing damage to the notion of "fiduciary." The idea of having a special duty to either one or a few stakeholders is not helpful.

15. Bill George, *Authentic Leadership,* San Francisco: Jossey Bass, Inc., 2004.

16. This is at least as clear as the directive given by the dominant model: Create as much value as possible for shareholders.

17. Some philosophers have argued that the stakeholder approach is in need of a "normative justification." To the extent that this phrase has any meaning, we take it as a call to connect the logic of managing for stakeholders with more traditional ethical theory. As pragmatists we eschew the "descriptive vs. normative vs. instrumental" distinction that so many business thinkers (and stakeholder theorists) have adopted. Managing for stakeholders is inherently a narrative or story that is at once: *descriptive* of how some businesses do act; *aspirational* and *normative* about how they could and should act; *instrumental* in terms of what means lead to what ends; and *managerial* in that it must be coherent on all of these dimensions and actually guide executive action.

18. See S. Venkataraman, "Stakeholder Value Equilibration and the Entrepreneurial Process," *Ethics and Entrepreneurship,* The Rufffin Series, 3: 45–57, 2002; S. R. Velamuri, "Entrepreneurship, Altruism, and the Good Society," *Ethics and Entrepreneurship,* The Ruffin Series, 3: 125–143, 2002; and, T. Harting, S. Harmeling, and S. Venkataraman, "Innovative Stakeholder Relations: When 'Ethics Pays' (and When It Doesn't)," *Business Ethics Quarterly,* 16: 43–68, 2006.

19. Sometimes there are tradeoffs and situations that economists would call "prisoner's dilemma" but these are not the paradigmatic cases, or if they are, we seem to solve them routinely, as Russell Hardin has suggested in *Morality within the Limits of Reason,* Chicago: University of Chicago Press, 1998.

20. E. Mendieta (ed.), *Take Care of Freedom and Truth Will Take Care of Itself: Interviews with Richard Rorty* (Stanford: Stanford University Press, 2006), p. 68.

Reading **5-3**

What's Wrong—and What's Right—with Stakeholder Management

John R. Boatright

The concept of a stakeholder is one of the more prominent contributions of recent business ethics. Since the introduction of this concept by R. Edward Freemen in *Strategic Management: A Stakeholder Approach* (Freeman, 1984), a concern for the interests of all stakeholder groups has become a widely recognized feature, if not the defining feature, of ethical management.

Although the stakeholder concept has been developed in various ways, it has been expressed most often in the moral prescription that managers, in making decisions, ought to consider the interests of all stakeholders. The list of stakeholders is commonly taken to include employees, customers, suppliers, and the community, as well as shareholders and other investors. This obligation to serve all stakeholder interests, which is often called "stakeholder management," is generally contrasted with the standard form of corporate governance, in which shareholder interests are primary. This latter view—which might be called "stockholder management"—is regarded by advocates of stakeholder management as morally unjustified. To focus attention on only one stakeholder, they allege, is to ignore other important groups whose interests a business organization ought to serve.

Advocates of stakeholder management get one point right: the modern for-profit corporation should serve the interests of all stakeholder groups. On this point, however, there is no conflict with the argument for the current system of corporate governance. Where stakeholder management goes wrong is in failing to recognize that a business organization in which managers act in the interest of the shareholders can also be one that, at the same time, benefits all stakeholder groups. This failure is due to a second mistake on the part of those who advocate stakeholder management. It is the simple fallacy of passing from the true premise that corporations ought to serve the interests of every stakeholder group to the false conclusion that this is a task for *management*. Stakeholder management assumes that management decision making is the main means by which the benefits of corporate wealth creation are distributed among stakeholders, but these benefits can also be obtained by groups interacting with a corporation in other ways, most notably through the market. Insofar as the market is able to provide the desired benefits to the various stakeholder groups, they have no need for management to explicitly consider their interests in making decisions.

At bottom, the dispute between stockholder and stakeholder management revolves around the question of how best to enable each stakeholder group or corporate constituency to benefit from the wealth-creating activity of business. Stakeholder management goes wrong by (1) failing to appreciate the extent to which the prevailing system of corporate governance, marked by shareholder primacy, serves the interests of all stakeholders, and (2) assuming that all stakeholder interests are best served by making this the task of management rather than using other means. Stakeholder management is right, however, to stress the moral requirement that every stakeholder group benefit from corporate activity and to make managers aware of their responsibility to create wealth for the benefit of everyone.

Two Forms of Stakeholder Management

It is important at the outset to distinguish two forms of stakeholder management. The main point of difference is whether stakeholder management is incompatible with and an alternative to the prevailing form of corporate governance, or whether it is a managerial guide that can be followed within corporations as they are currently legally structured.

First, it is a simple fact that a corporation has stakeholders in the sense of "groups who can affect, or who are affected by, the activities of the firm" (Freeman, 1984). And any successful corporation must manage its relations with all stakeholder groups, if for no other reason than to benefit the shareholders. To manage stakeholder relations is not necessarily to serve each group's interest (although this might be the effect) but to consider their interests sufficiently to gain their cooperation. The manager's role is not merely to coordinate the contribution of the various stakeholders but to inspire them to put forth their best efforts in a joint effort to create valuable products and services. Any firm that neglects its stakeholders or, worse, alienates them is doomed to failure.

Second, managers also have obligations to treat each stakeholder group in accord with accepted ethical standards. These obligations include not only those that are owed to everyone, such as honesty and respect, but also the obligations to abide by agreements or contracts made with a firm. In most countries, basic moral obligations concerning the treatment of employees, customers, and other parties as well as agreements and contracts are codified in laws that constitute the legal framework of business. Treating all stakeholders ethically is a requirement of any form of business organization, although differences may exist about what ethics requires.

This version of stakeholder management, which is roughly what Donaldson and Preston (1995) call *instrumental,* does not constitute a system of corporate governance. Another form of stakeholder management, however, goes beyond the necessity of managing stakeholder relations and the obligations that are owed to stakeholder groups to the question of *how* stakeholder interests ought to be considered. Indeed, most advocates of stakeholder management hold that stakeholder interests should

be central to the operation of a corporation in much the same way that shareholder interests dominate in the conventional shareholder-controlled firm. In general, they contend that in making key decisions, managers ought to consider all interests, those of shareholders and non-shareholders alike, and balance them in some way.

This form of stakeholder management, which corresponds more or less to Donaldson and Preston's *normative* stakeholder theory, does have implications for corporate governance. More specifically, the prevailing system of corporate governance may be expressed in three related propositions: (1) that shareholders ought to have control; (2) that managers have a fiduciary duty to serve shareholder interests alone; and (3) that the objective of the firm ought to be the maximization of shareholder wealth. The main theses of stakeholder management can then be stated by modifying each of these propositions as follows: (1) all stakeholders have a right to participate in corporate decisions that affect them; (2) managers have a fiduciary duty to serve the interests of all stakeholder groups; and (3) the objective of the firm ought to be the promotion of all interests and not those of shareholders alone.

The issues in these two sets of propositions—who has control or the right to make decisions, who is the beneficiary of management's fiduciary duty, and whose interests ought to be the objective of a firm—are at the heart of corporate governance. Consequently, stockholder management and this form of stakeholder management constitute two competing models of how corporations ought to be governed. Stakeholder management goes wrong when it is developed as an alternative system of corporate governance. As a prescription for corporate governance, stakeholder management not only is inferior to the prevailing system but involves several crucial mistakes. Stakeholder management as a guide for managers, on the other hand, contains much that is helpful to managers and constitutes a valuable corrective to some common misunderstandings of the argument for stockholder management.

An Economic Approach to Corporate Governance

The prevailing stockholder model of corporate governance is founded on an economic approach that conceives a firm as a nexus of contracts between a legal entity called the firm and its various constituencies, which include employees, customers, suppliers, investors, and other groups. This approach begins with the assumptions that in a market, all individuals with economic assets—such as employees with skills, suppliers with raw materials, customers and investors with money, and so on—would trade with each other in order to obtain a greater return, and that the greatest return will often be obtained by combining individual assets in joint production. That is, individuals will frequently realize a greater economic return by cooperating with others in productive activity than by participating in a market alone.

* * *

The Role of Governance

A firm requires many *inputs*. Economists classify these as land, labor, and capital, although they also recognize the need for managerial expertise to coordinate these inputs. Traditional stakeholder groups interact with a business organization or firm as *input providers*—employees providing labor, suppliers providing raw materials, and so on. Each input brings a return such as employees' wages, suppliers' payments, and investors' interest and dividends. It is necessary in a firm for each input provider to *secure* their return, that is, to employ some means for ensuring that wages are paid, supplier payments are made, and so on. Generally, this security can be obtained by contracts or legal rules that obligate a firm to provide the return due to each corporate constituency.

Governance can be understood as *the contractual agreements and legal rules that secure each input provider's claim for the return due on that input provider's contribution to the productive activity of a firm.* Accordingly, every asset contributed to joint production will be accompanied by a governance structure of some kind, which may vary depending on the features of the asset provided. That is, the governance structure for securing employees' wages and other benefits may be different from those protecting suppliers, and similarly for other input providers.

When the protection for each group's input can be provided by fully specified contracts or precise legal rules, the governance structure is relatively uncomplicated. Customers, for example, are adequately protected, for the most part, by sales contracts, warranties, and the like. The market also provides some protection. Thus, customers are protected by the opportunity to switch from one seller to another. The greatest problems of governance occur for *firm-specific* assets, which are assets that cannot easily be removed from production. When assets are firm specific, the providers become "locked in."

For example, employees, who ordinarily assume little risk when they can easily move from one firm to another, are at greater risk when they develop skills that are of value only to their current employer. When their skills are firm specific, a move to another firm usually results in lower pay. Similarly, a supplier who invests in special equipment to manufacture goods used by only one customer is providing a firm-specific asset. In both cases, the input provider becomes "locked in" and thus has a greater need for protection than, say, customers.

Developing governance structures to protect input providers is also more complicated when contracts and legal rules cannot be developed easily due to *complexity* and *uncertainty*. Contracts and legal rules provide protection only when the situations likely to be encountered can be anticipated and the ways of proceeding in each situation can be specified. When planning is difficult because of the complexity and uncertainty of the situations that might arise, other means must be found to protect stakeholder interests.

Despite the three problems of lock-in, complexity, and uncertainty, governance structures for the assets of each input provider are relatively easy to provide for each stakeholder group except one, namely shareholders, the providers of equity capital.

Shareholder Governance

Although shareholders are commonly called the owners of a corporation, this sense of ownership is different from its ordinary use. Shareholders do not "own" General Motors in the same way that a person owns a car or a house. Rather, shareholders have a certain bundle of rights that includes the right of control and the right to the profits of a firm. . . .

Equity capital is money provided to a firm in return for a claim on profits—or, more precisely, for a claim on residual revenues, which are the revenues that remain after all debts and other legal obligations are paid. Just as customers buy a company's products, equity capital providers "buy" the future profits of a firm; or, alternatively, in order to raise capital, a company "sells" its future profits to investors. In addition, since future profits are risky, investors not only provide capital but also assume much of the risk of a firm. The willingness of shareholders to bear this *residual risk*—which is the risk that results from having a claim on residual revenues rather a fixed claim—benefits all other input providers. As long as a firm in solvent—which is to say that it can pay all its fixed obligations, such as employee wages, suppliers' payments, and so on—then the claims of these groups are secure.

The remaining question, then, is why equity capital providers, who in effect "buy" the future profits of a firm and "sell" their risk bearing services, should also have control and thus the right to have the firm run in their interest. The answer is very simple: control is the most suitable protection for their firm-specific asset. If their return on the asset they provide, namely capital, is the residual earnings or profit of a firm, then this return is very insecure unless they can ensure that the firm is

operated for maximum profit. By contrast, the right of control is of little value to other input providers or stakeholder groups because their return is secure as long as a firm is solvent, not maximally profitable. In addition, the return on the firm-specific contribution of other, non-shareholder groups is better protected by other means.

That equity capital providers have control is in the best interests of the other stakeholder groups. First, everyone benefits when business organizations are maximally profitable because of the greater wealth creation. If firms were controlled by groups whose interests are served only by firms that are solvent, not maximally profitable, then they would create less wealth. Second, every non-shareholder group benefits when shareholders assume much of the risk of an enterprise because their return is all the more secure. Shareholders are willing to assume this risk—in return for some compensation, of course—because they are better able to diversify their risks among a large number of companies. Employees, by contrast, are very undiversified inasmuch as their fortunes depend wholly upon the employing firm. Third, without the right of control, equity capital providers would require a greater return to compensate for the increased risk to their investment. This in turn would drive up the price of capital, thus increasing the cost of production for everyone.

Firms can be owned by groups other than equity capital providers. Some corporations are employee owned, and others are owned by customers or suppliers (these are usually called cooperatives). Mutual insurance companies are owned by the policy holders. These forms of ownership are not common, however, because of their relative inefficiency. It is only under certain economic conditions that they would be preferred by the corporate constituencies involved.

The bottom line is that equity capital providers are usually (but not always) the shareholders of a firm, the group with control, because control rights are the best means for protecting their particular firm-specific asset. Each group has the opportunity to seek the best protections or safeguards for their own interests, which is to say the return on the firm-specific assets that they provide to a firm. Usually, non-shareholder groups are better served by safeguards other than control, which is left to shareholders. This outcome is not only efficient but also morally justified because it best serves the interest of all stakeholder groups and results from voluntary agreements or contracts made by all the relevant groups.

* * *

Comparing Stockholder and Stakeholder Management

Viewed in terms of an economic approach to the firm, stakeholder management offers managerial decision making as a means for protecting and advancing stakeholder interests. Insofar as it proposes that managers have a fiduciary duty to serve the interests of all stakeholders and that maximizing all stakeholder interests be the objective of the firm, it seeks to extend the means used to safeguard shareholders to benefit all stakeholders. In short, stakeholder management proposes that all stakeholders be treated like shareholders.

The fundamental mistake of stakeholder management is a failure to see that the needs of each stakeholder group, including shareholders, are different and that different means best meet these needs. The protection that shareholders derive from being the beneficiaries of management's fiduciary duty and having their interests be the objective of the firm fit their particular situation as residual claimants with difficult contracting problems, but employees, customers, suppliers, and other investors (such as bondholders, who provide debt that rather than equity) are better served by other means, which include contractual agreements and various legal rules. Management decision making is a relatively ineffective means for protecting the interests of non-shareholder stakeholders. In any event, the choice of means for protecting each stakeholder

group's interest is mainly an empirical one about what works best in practice, and the evidence tends to support the prevailing stockholder-centered system of corporate governance.

Finally, insofar as stakeholder management assigns to managers the task of ensuring that the wealth created by a firm is distributed in a fair way that departs from the distribution that results from purely market forces, this task, too, is better done by other means, most notably through the political process. Managers lack both the ability and the legitimacy that are required to fulfill this task, and, in any event, the attempt to address pressing social problems by making changes in corporate governance is ill-conceived. Corporate governance, which is designed to solve specific problems of economic organization, is simply the wrong tool, like using a screwdriver to hammer a nail.

What's Right with Stakeholder Management

Despite this generally negative appraisal of stakeholder management, it is still an important, constructive development in business ethics. Its positive contributions are obscured to some extent by those who present it as an alternative form of corporate governance and thus create a false choice between stakeholder and stockholder management. Stakeholder management can be understood in a way that complements rather than challenges the prevailing system of corporate governance.

First, stakeholder theory rightly insists that the purpose of a firm is to benefit every corporate constituency or stakeholder group. The prevailing system of corporate governance may obscure this purpose by failing to emphasize that management's fiduciary duty to shareholders and the objective of shareholder wealth maximization are merely means to an end. These benefits result from the agreements that a firm makes with one input provider, namely shareholders. However, a firm also makes agreements or contracts with other constituencies, including employees, customers, suppliers, and other investors, all for mutual advantage. When the assets contributed by these parties are firm-specific, they are accompanied by safeguards that constitute forms of governance. The agreements between these groups and a firm create both moral and legal obligations that are every bit as binding as those owed to shareholders. In addition, each stakeholder group, including managers, has an obligation to treat all others in accord with accepted ethical standards.

Although stockholder and stakeholder management are agreed on the purpose of a firm—to conduct economic activity in ways that benefit everyone—there is disagreement on how this is done. In particular, the stakeholder view makes it a task of *management* to ensure that this outcome occurs, whereas on the economic approach, mutual benefit is a result of the opportunity each group has to make mutually advantageous agreements. That is, a firm works like a market in creating mutual benefit from the opportunity to trade. Just as a market achieves this result without any person directing it, so, too, does a firm—in theory!

In practice, though, some stakeholders fail to benefit as they should from a firm's activity. This may occur for a variety of reasons including management's willful violation of agreements, market failures, and externalities or third-party effects. For example, a company might fail to make expected contributions to a pension plan, sell a product to consumers with undisclosed defects, or operate a polluting factory. In general, it is the responsibility of government to prevent or correct for these possibilities, but managers, especially those at the top of a business organization, might also be held to have some responsibility. Stakeholder management asks managers to recognize that a firm should benefit all stakeholders, to be aware when it fails to do so, and to take some responsibility for correcting the problems that lead to this failure. Just as we all have a responsibility to make sure that markets work as they should to produce a benefit for all, so, too, do we all, including managers, have a responsibility for ensuring the proper functioning of firms.

Second, corporate governance is concerned with how business organizations should be legally structured and controlled. The provisions that management has a fiduciary duty to serve shareholder interests and that shareholder wealth maximization should be the objective of the firm dictate how decisions about major investment decisions and overall strategy should be made. They tell us very little about how managers should actually go about their task of managing a firm so as to create wealth for shareholders or anyone else. Everyone can benefit from the productive activity of a firm only if there is a vision for a creating a valuable product or service as well as a strategy for achieving this vision. . . .

Freeman and his colleagues (Freeman, Wicks, and Parmar, 2004, p. 364) describe stakeholder management as addressing this matter of what managers and other need to do to create wealth. They write,

> Economic value is created by people who voluntarily come together and cooperate to improve everyone's circumstances. Managers must develop relationships, inspire their stakeholders, and create communities where everyone strives to give their best to deliver the value the firm promises.

The first sentence expresses the fundamental principle that firms exist to benefit all those who take part in them, which is shared with the economic approach. The second sentence is concerned with how managers should actually carry out their role. Left unaddressed, though, is who should have control of a firm and in whose interest a firm should be run. If, as the economic approach holds, the answer is the shareholders, then stakeholder management is not only compatible with stockholder management but an essential complement.

Stakeholder management, then, as a guide for managers rather than a form of corporate governance, provides a valuable corrective to managers who fail to appreciate how shareholder primacy benefits all stakeholders and use it a reason for disregarding other stakeholders. Such managers commit a mistake of their own by confusing how a corporation should be *governed* with how it should be *managed*. There is no reason why managers who act in the interests of shareholders and seek maximum shareholder wealth cannot also run firms that provide the greatest benefit for everyone. Indeed, a manager who fails to benefit every

stakeholder group is not achieving the full potential of a firm.

Source: John R. Boatright, "What's Wrong—and What's Right—with Stakeholder Management," *Journal of Private Enterprise* 21, no. 2 (2006).

Note: References have been removed from publication here, but are available on the book website at www.mhhe.com/busethics4e.

6

Ethical Decision Making: Employer Responsibilities and Employee Rights

It is to the real advantage of every producer, every manufacturer, and every merchant to cooperate in the improvement of working conditions, because the best customer of American industry is the well-paid worker.

Franklin D. Roosevelt

There are now more slaves on the planet than at any time in human history. True abolition will elude us until we admit the massive scope of the problem, attack it in all its forms, and empower slaves to help free themselves.

E. Benjamin Skinner, "A World Enslaved"[1]

Arguably, the clothing company American Apparel (AA) evolved through the personality and vision of its former CEO and creator Dov Charney. Promoted by Charney as "sweatshop-free," AA is known for providing its mostly Latino factory workers with high wages, health insurance, and on-site English classes; for keeping its clothing production within the United States—rare in an industry in which upwards of 95 percent of goods are imported; and for provocative, no-frills advertising campaigns that feature "real women," many of them company employees. AA's racy ads, all created in-house and many photographed by Charney himself, along with its generous worker benefit policies, have contributed to the brand's popularity with young consumers.

However, after years of allegations of illegal and unethical conduct, plus more recent lackluster financial performance by AA, its board of directors fired Charney.[2]

Here is a timeline of some of the incidents leading up to this decision by the board:

- 2005–2006: Four former employees filled sexual harassment lawsuits against AA, charging that they were subjected to an unsafe working environment in which female employees faced sexual misconduct and innuendo. Two of the cases have been settled; the third is pending in private negotiations. Regarding the fourth case, the Equal Employment Opportunity Commission (EEOC) determined that AA had discriminated against "women, as a class, on the basis of their female gender, by subjecting them to sexual harassment."

- 2008: A former employee sued AA, asserting that he had been wrongfully terminated after refusing to pad inventory reports. The company denies wrongdoing.

- 2009: An immigration investigation found that many of AA's 5,600 factory employees were not properly documented. Charney was forced to lay off more than a quarter of his production workforce.

- 2009: AA paid filmmaker Woody Allen $5 million to settle a lawsuit charging that the company illegally used Allen's image in an advertisement without permission.

- 2009: An AA advertisement featuring a partially dressed model who appears to be under 16 was banned in the UK.

- 2010: A popular blog claimed that AA requires job applicants for retail positions to submit a full-body photograph that must be approved by executives before hiring and charged that only model-thin white or Asian applicants tend to make the cut.

- In 2011, five more female employees filled sexual harassment charges against Charney. Allegations included a charge that Charney pressured some of them to perform sex acts against their will.

- In 2013, AA posted a loss of $106 million and its stock price plunged to just $0.47 from its high in prior years of $15 a share. AA also lost some of its high-level, talented executives because of Charney's "relentlessly controlling" management style.[3]

- In 2014, information emerged about another long-running lawsuit by a former employee who claimed that Charney called the employee a homophobic slur and also assaulted him by choking him and rubbing dirt in his face because Charney was displeased by the store's condition.[4]

- AA's board finally removed Charney as CEO in June 2014 and eventually removed all of his remaining authority with the company in December 2014.

- Immediately thereafter the company issued a revised code of ethics that was designed to "clarify, update, or enhance the descriptions of the standards of conduct that were expected of all directors, officers and employees of the company." The new code apparently strengthens AA's rules preventing sexual harassment among its employees and prohibits discriminatory slurs against employees.[5]

- In April 2015, the Securities and Exchange Commission opened an investigation into the circumstances surrounding Charney's exit; and AA shares took a tumble. At that point, AA had not seen a profit at that point for over six years.[6]

AA requires all employees to sign an agreement that states that the employee promises to use closed-door arbitration in connection with all conflicts he or she might have with the company. Therefore, many of the details of the claims against Charney were not fully known to the board or to the public, and they led to numerous monetary settlements with the claimants in exchange for silence on the matter. Further, rather than alter his advertising approach (or change his behavior), Charney denied all wrongdoing and established an employee contract clause (which is still in effect!) that states:

> American Apparel is in the business of designing and manufacturing sexually charged T-shirts and intimate apparel, and uses sexually charged visual and oral communications in its marketing and sales activities. Employees working in the design, sales, marketing and other creative areas of the company will come into contact with sexually charged language and visual images. This is a part of the job for employees working in these areas.[7]

In 2010, Charney was pictured in an AA advertisement in bed with two female employees. "If you're offended by sexual innuendo or masturbation or sexual coloring books—if you're offended by any of these, then don't work here," Charney said. He has spoken openly in interviews about having sexual relations with employees.[8] The steady stream of lawsuits and the forced production layoffs took a heavy financial toll on AA, which teetered on the brink of bankruptcy in early 2011. As stated, the company posted heavy losses in the last two years and investors became increasingly "skittish" about Charney's reputation. This cocktail of variables led the board to fire Dov Charney in June 2014.

- Do you see a connection between the subject of the lawsuits discussed here and the choices made by the popular retailer?

- Do you feel that Charney did anything wrong by promoting his personal vision in corporate decisions, from advertising and production to hiring and corporate culture? What are the key facts relevant to your determination?

- Are there ethical issues involved in your decision? Please identify.

(continued)

- Who are the stakeholders in this scenario? Are any stakeholders' rights abridged by Charney's decisions? In what way?

- Even if you answered no to the first question, evidently certain stakeholders believed that American Apparel acted inappropriately. Was there any way to have prevented the negative publicity from happening in the first place, without undercutting American Apparel's reputation as an anticorporate, provocative brand? What alternatives were originally available to the retailer? How would each of these new alternatives have affected each of the stakeholders you have identified?

- Do you feel that the AA board made its decision to fire Charney based on his alleged unethical and/or illegal conduct, or because of the financial performance of the company? Imagine if AA did not post losses, but in fact had demonstrated fantastic financial performance. Do you believe the board would have a fiduciary duty to protect a leader's position despite his unethical behavior, if the leader is considered to be the singular "creative force" and visionary for the company?

- As it moves forward from this point, what alternatives now exist for American Apparel to heal relationships with its stakeholders? What recommendations would you offer to American Apparel?

- In July 2014, one month after he was fired, Dov Charney was rehired by AA to serve as a strategic consultant to the company, during the time a board committee planned to review the accusations against him. At the conclusion of the investigation, the committee would then determine whether it would be appropriate for Charney to serve as CEO, an officer, or an employee of American Apparel. At that time, five of the seven board members voluntarily stepped down from the board.[9] What is your reaction to AA's change of position regarding Charney's future and the board's future? What are the ethical issues involved in a board committee investigating Charney's alleged offenses?

- In December 2014, Paula Schneider was officially named CEO. For the next year, Charney continued to try to retrieve control of the company, but was unsuccessful. In October 2015, admitting continuing cash-flow problems, AA declared bankruptcy. As of press time, the company is out of bankruptcy and Schneider remains in control of the company.[10] How would you evaluate AA's handling of this situation?

Chapter Objectives

After reading this chapter, you will be able to:

1. Discuss the two distinct perspectives on the ethics of workplace relationships.
2. Explain the concept of due process in the workplace.
3. Define employment at will (EAW) and its ethical rationale.
4. Describe the costs of an EAW environment.
5. Explain how due process relates to performance appraisals.

6. Discuss whether it is possible to downsize in an ethical manner.

7. Explain the difference between intrinsic and instrumental value in terms of health and safety.

8. Describe the "acceptable risk" approach to health and safety in the workplace.

9. Describe the nature of an employer's responsibility with regard to employee health and safety and why the market is not the most effective arbiter of this responsibility.

10. Explain the basic arguments for and against regulation of the global labor environment.

11. Describe the argument for a market-based resolution to workplace discrimination.

12. Define diversity as it applies to the workplace.

13. Explain the benefits and challenges of diversity for the workplace.

14. Define affirmative action and explain the three ways in which affirmative action may be legally permissible.

15. Articulate the basic guidelines for affirmative action programs.

Introduction

Ethics in the employment context is perhaps the most universal topic in business ethics because nearly every person will have the experience of being employed or employing someone else. While legislators and the courts have addressed many aspects of the working environment, countless ethical issues remain that these regulatory and judicial bodies have left unresolved. The law provides guidance for thinking about ethical issues in the workplace, but these issues go well beyond legal considerations!

This chapter explores those areas of ethical decision making in the workplace where the law remains relatively fluid and where answers are not easily found by simply calling the company lawyer. Issues may also arise where the law does seem clear but, for one reason or another, it is insufficient to protect the interests of all stakeholders. We will examine various ethical challenges that face the nature of employer responsibilities and the employee, whether that employee is a worker on an assembly line, the manager of a restaurant, or the CEO of a large corporation. Although individual perspectives may change, similar conflicts and stakeholders present themselves across business settings.

As you examine each issue raised in this chapter, consider how you might employ the ethical decision-making process we have discussed to reach the best possible conclusion for the stakeholders involved. Severe time constraints, limited information, and pressure usually accompany these challenging business decisions. Though using the ethical decision-making process may seem cumbersome at the outset, once the process becomes embedded in the professional landscape and culture, its effectiveness and efficiency in resolving these issues will become apparent. In fact, utilizing an ethical decision-making process will avoid later hurdles, thus removing barriers to progress and momentum. Let us consider the issues that exist in the current workplace environment to test the effectiveness of the ethical decision-making process.

Ethical Issues in the Workplace: The Current Environment

We all have decisions to make about how we will treat others in the workplace and how we will ask to be treated. Ethics at work and in human resource management is about our relationships with others and with our organizations. Research demonstrates that companies that place employees at the core of their strategies produce higher long-term returns to shareholders than do industry peers—more than double![11]

The same holds true for interpersonal relationships. Notwithstanding these truths, 54 percent of U.S. workers feel a very strong sense of loyalty to their employer.[12] When asked about the greatest influence on their commitment, workers responded that the most important factor is fairness at work, followed by care and concern for employees—all key components of an ethical working environment. These influences play out in practical ways for businesses because research shows that 41 percent of U.S. workers have observed misconduct in the workplace during the previous 12 months.[13] Seventy-eight percent of employees who have experienced unethical or uncivil behavior at work report that their commitment to the organization declined, and 66 percent report that their performance declined.[14] These challenges are compounded by the fact that misconduct rates increase, while misconduct reporting decreases, when employees do not perceive a positive ethical culture in the workplace.[15]

OBJECTIVE

These observations call attention to the fact that there are two very distinct, and sometimes competing, perspectives on the ethics of workplace relationships. On one hand, employers might decide to treat employees well as a means to produce greater workplace harmony and productivity, and as a 2010 study has demonstrated, higher levels of innovation.[16] (This approach, focusing on end results, could be reminiscent of the utilitarian ethics discussed in chapter 3 if couched in terms of the creation of a better workplace for all. On the other hand, it also raises a question about moral motivation and instrumentalist, self-interested reasons for doing good that is similar to our discussion of corporate social responsibility in chapter 5.) While no one is claiming that employees have some universal right to a "happy" workplace,[17] a comprehensive review of research by Jeffrey Pfeffer suggests that effective firms are characterized by a set of common practices, all of which involve treating employees in humane and respectful ways.[18]

As an example of these concerns, consider the role of emotion in the workplace. Studies suggest that managers can have a significant impact on the emotions of their workers, and this impact can greatly affect productivity and loyalty, as well as perceptions of fairness, care, and concern. Scholar Neal Ashkanasy and colleagues suggest that managers should pay attention to the emotional impact of various jobs within their workplace and model a positive emotional environment.[19]

Reality Check   *Protecting Employee Rights through Unions*

In 1960, about one-third of the American workforce was represented by unions. Today, that figure is 11 percent. This compares to 17 percent in Australia, 18 percent in Japan, 26 percent in the United Kingdom, 27 percent in Canada, and nearly 68 percent in Sweden.[20] Not surprisingly, federal and state regulations governing work practices have exploded as union membership has declined. The variety of protections is prodigious: antidiscrimination laws, wage and hour laws, worker safety laws, unemployment compensation, workers' compensation, and social security, to name a few.

Five states—North Carolina, South Carolina, Virginia, Texas (excluding firefighters and police officers), and Georgia (excluding firefighters)—prohibit collective bargaining with public employees.[21] In the wake of the 2008 economic downturn, almost every state proposed legislation changes to public-sector unions.[22] These legislative proposals have been met with strong resistance by public employees and their supporters.

In 2011, large protests flared up between public-sector unions and legislatures in several states, led by demonstrations of up to 100,000 marchers in Wisconsin. Much of the legislation that led to the protests made its way through the federal courts with various outcomes (most typically ended with a compromise position). Noteworthy is a 2014 U.S. Supreme Court decision that restricted the definition of *public employee* in order to uphold the First Amendment rights of certain workers (who did not wish to join or support a union) not to have public union dues automatically deducted from their paychecks.[23]

Rewards and compensation structures can clearly impact the emotions of workers, as can the composition of teams or the power relationships within a workplace. When employees see that a firm values their emotions, as well as exhibits values such as honesty, respect, and trust, they feel less pressure, more valued as employees, and more satisfied with their organizations. Because reporting to external stakeholders has become such a key issue in recent scandals, one might also want to consider whether a more satisfied employee is more or less likely to report misconduct to outside parties.

On the other hand, of course, employers might treat employees well out of a sense of duty and rights (reminiscent of Kant), regardless of the either utilitarian or self-interested productivity consequences. This deontological approach emphasizes the rights and duties of all employees, and treating employees well simply because "it is the right thing to do." Defenders of employee rights argue that rights should protect important employee interests from being constantly subjected to utilitarian and financial calculations. This sense of duty might stem from the law, professional codes of conduct, corporate codes of conduct, or such moral principles as fairness, justice, or human rights on the part of the organization's leadership. (See the Reality Check "Protecting Employee Rights through Unions.")

Defining the Parameters of the Employment Relationship

The following section will explore the legal and ethical boundaries that will help us define the employment relationship based on some of the principles discussed earlier. "Employment" per se implicates ethical issues because of the very nature of the relationship it implies. Consider the situation in which an individual agrees to work for another individual. This arrangement raises issues of power, obligation, responsibility, fair treatment, and expectations. In many circumstances, the livelihoods of both parties rely on each other's contributions to the relationship. Though legal requirements might serve to protect some interests, they can only go so far and cover so many bases. We will begin by looking to the ethics underlying the concepts of due process and fairness that help determine what is or is not acceptable behavior in the workplace. We will discover some of the ways in which employers might be able to remain true to these principles, even when specifically challenged by vexing circumstances such as a reduction in force. The relationship is further defined by the application of these principles to working conditions such as health and safety, both in domestic operations and abroad.

Note that the issues in the following sections are predominantly settled from an ethical perspective by their *justification*. In other words, people of goodwill would be likely to agree that an employee has a right to a safe and healthy workplace. Disagreements do remain in discussions surrounding the implementation, interpretation, or extent of that right. In contrast, the second section of this chapter explores several issues that are not perceived as settled from either a legal or ethical point of view. Reasonable minds may differ not only as to whether the means to achieve the ends are justified but whether the ends themselves are just, fair, or ethical. An example of this latter issue would be affirmative action, a thorny matter for courts, managers, and philosophers, alike.

Due Process and Just Cause

OBJECTIVE

Employment security—getting and keeping a job—is perhaps the most significant aspect of work from the employee's ethical perspective. Fundamental questions of justice arise because employees are subject to considerable harms from a lack of security in their jobs and do not have much power to create security. But should employers' rights and ability to hire, fire, or discipline employees therefore be restricted in order to prevent injustices? Are there any other means by which to protect against unethical behavior or unjust results?

Philosophically, the right of **due process** is the right to be protected against the arbitrary use of authority. In legal contexts, *due process* refers to the procedures that police and courts must follow in exercising their authority over citizens. Few dispute that the state, through its police and courts, has the authority to punish citizens. This authority creates a safe and orderly society in which we all can live, work, and do business. But that authority is not unlimited; it can be exercised only in certain ways and under certain conditions. Due process rights specify these conditions.

Similarly, due process in the workplace acknowledges an employer's authority over employees. Employers can tell employees what to do, and when, and how to do it. They can exercise such control because they retain the ability to discipline or fire an employee who does not comply with their authority. Because of the immense value that work holds for most people, the threat of losing one's job is a powerful motivation to comply. However, basic fairness—implemented through due process—demands that this power be used *justly*. It is the definition of basic

due process
The right to be protected against the arbitrary use of authority. In legal contexts, due process refers to the procedures that police and courts must follow in exercising their authority over citizens. In the employment context, due process specifies the conditions for basic fairness within the scope of the employer's authority over its employees.

Reality Check *Protests in Support of Employment Security in Europe*

As discussed in this chapter, a number of states maintain employment "at will" for employees. The term *employment at will* means that, unless an agreement specifies otherwise, employers are free to fire an employee at any time and for any reason, except for a reason prohibited by case law or statute *(see the following text discussing Learning Objective 3)*. However, this is not the case in some other countries. In Europe, for instance, there is no concept of at-will employment. Employment in European countries is structured by formal contracts that place a variety of restrictions on employee dismissal and impose legal obligations on employers when termination occurs. Varying from country to country, termination laws may require long periods of prior notification, government approval for dismissal, or legal recourse for unfair dismissal, or they may include other mechanisms that limit the capacity of companies to dismiss workers at will.

Spanish employment law, for example, creates barriers to termination by requiring a significant amount of severance pay in order for employers to fire employees.

In response to the global economic recession, which began in 2008, countries across Europe enacted austerity measures to encourage economic growth. While some countries, such as Spain, faced up to 20 to 25 percent unemployment rates, governments looked for ways to provide companies with greater flexibility in hiring and firing, increased the retirement age, and generally reduced strong European labor laws. In response, protests immediately flared.

In the years that followed, while most of Europe experienced a modest recovery from the recession, many of the southern European countries such as Italy, Spain, and Greece continued to report high unemployment. In 2014, new protests of up to 65,000 people occurred in both Italy and Spain, challenging the continued labor reform.[24]

fairness that remains the challenge. Review, for instance, the conflicting versions of fair labor standards between Europe and the United States, discussed in the Reality Check "Protests in Support of Employment Security in Europe."

Unfortunately, there is evidence to suggest that this acknowledged authority of employers over employees, or simply managers over subordinates, is not always exercised in a just or fair manner—and it is not only the worker who suffers the consequence. In a 2014 survey, 27 percent of workers reported that they had experienced workplace "bullying" firsthand, defined as "the repeated, malicious, health-endangering mistreatment of one employee . . . by one or more employees."[25] The mistreatment need not be physically threatening, of course, but might simply involve a boss who is constantly yelling dictates at workers, or a co-worker who spreads rumors about another in order to sabotage his or her position.

These behaviors lead not only to emotional abuse but also to a complete loss of personal dignity, intimidation, and fear. Moreover, others in the workplace suffer vicariously with these same sensations; evidence demonstrates that the employer has significant bottom-line expenses from workers' compensation claims based on stress and other emotional stimuli, and there are increased costs related to potential litigation arising from claims of abusive work situations. There is also the indirect impact on employee morale, and certainly the negative effects that occur when one would prefer not to be at the workplace: turnover, absenteeism, poor customer relationships, and acts of sabotage. (Please see Decision Point: Bullying in the Workplace?")

The issue of workplace bullying is one that we hear about more and more, especially in economies based on strong service sectors. There have been

Should states enact anti-bullying laws that would enable victims of workplace bullying to sue their harassers and also to hold their employers accountable? Surveys show that at least 48 percent of U.S. workers have experienced bullying in their place of employment or have seen others experience bullying.[26] Advocates of anti-bullying laws argue that the extent of the problem—when considered alongside evidence that bullying causes significant physical, emotional, and economic harm to its victims—calls for a legislative response. On the other hand, critics worry that anti-bullying legislation would lead to a spike in employee lawsuits and point to the difficulty of determining whether abusive bullying has taken place, particularly in high-pressure work environments.[27]

Since 2003, 26 states and 2 territories have introduced workplace bullying legislation that would allow workers to sue for harassment without requiring any evidence of discrimination.[28] New Hampshire, for example, began considering a bill in 2013 that defines bullying broadly and would include "the repeated use of derogatory remarks, insults, and epithets, as well as conduct that a 'reasonable person' would find threatening, intimidating or humiliating." The bill passed both the New Hampshire House and Senate, only to be vetoed by the governor.[29] As of 2014, only one state—Tennessee—has passed an anti-bullying statute into law.[30]

- How would you define "bullying" if you were to design an anti-bullying law? What stakeholder groups should be considered in crafting your definition?
- As a manager, what steps might you take to prevent bullying behavior in your company?
- Do you believe that legislation is needed to respond to the problem of workplace bullying? Why or why not?
- A 2014 study revealed that the majority of workplace bullying is same-gender harassment, with 77 percent of targets being bullied by perpetrators of the same gender.[31] Unless another protected class (such as race or religion) is involved, or the harassment reaches the level of criminal violence, same-gender bullying is not illegal. Do these data affect your views about anti-bullying legislation? Why or why not?

countless newspaper articles, business journals, academic journals, conferences, and even television news programs devoted to the subject in recent years.[32] It is more predominant in the service sector because that work relies significantly on interpersonal relationships and interaction. "Frequent, ongoing personal interaction between workers often becomes a basic element of a job, especially in work arrangements between supervisors and subordinates. The more people interact, the more likely it is that personalities will clash," says scholar and bullying expert David Yamada.[33] Add to those interactions the personal threats that people sense from pressures during a downturn in the economy, and one can only imagine the boiling points that might ensure. A 2014 study found that downsizing is a particularly powerful trigger of abusive supervision, since it enhances the vulnerability of already submissive employees and ignites reactions in overburdened supervisors.[34]

employment at will (EAW)

The legal doctrine that holds that, absent a particular contractual or other legal obligation that specifies the length or conditions of employ-ment, all employees are employed "at will." Unless an agreement specifies otherwise, employers are free to fire an employee at any time and for any reason. In the same manner, an EAW worker may opt to leave a job at any time for any reason, without offering any notice at all; so the freedom is *theoretically* mutual.

just cause

A standard for termina-tions or discipline that requires the employer to have sufficient and fair cause before reaching a decision against an employee.

Ironically, while basic fairness may demand that employer power be used justly, the law has not always clearly supported this mandate of justice. Much employment law within the United States instead evolved in a context of a legal doctrine known as **employment at will (EAW).** Employment at will holds that, in the absence of a particular contractual or other legal obligation that specifies the length or conditions of employment, all employees are employed "at will." (See the Reality Check "Employing 'Employees.'") This means that, unless an agreement specifies otherwise, employers are free to fire an employee at any time and for any reason. In the words of an early court decision, "all may dismiss their employee at will, be they many or few, for good cause, for no cause, or even for cause morally wrong."[35] In the same manner, an EAW worker may opt to leave a job at any time for any reason, without offering any notice at all; so the freedom is *theoretically* mutual.

The ethical rationale for EAW, both historically and among contemporary defenders, has both utilitarian and deontological elements. EAW was thought to be an important management tool. Total discretion over employment gives man-agers the ability to make efficient decisions that should contribute to the greater overall good. It was thought that the manager would be in the best position to know what was best for the firm and that the law should not interfere with those decisions. Another basis for EAW was the rights of private property owners to control their property by controlling who works for them.

Both legal and ethical analyses of these claims, however, demonstrate that there are good reasons to limit EAW. Even if EAW proved to be an effective management tool, justice demands that such tools not be used to harm other people. Further, even if private property rights grant managers authority over employees, the right of private property itself is limited by other rights and duties. Also, though the freedom to terminate the relationship is theoretically mutual, the employer is often responsible for the employee's livelihood, while the opposite is unlikely to be true; the differential creates an unbalanced power relationship between the two parties.

Considerations such as these have led many courts and legislatures to create exceptions to the EAW rule (see Table 6.1). Civil rights laws, for example, pro-hibit firing someone on the basis of membership in certain prohibited classes such as race, sex, disability, age, national origin, religion, or ethnic background. Labor laws prevent employers from firing someone for union activities. When the employer is the government, constitutional limitations on government authority are extended into the workplace to protect employees.

A crucial element to recognize with these exceptions, however, is the fact that EAW has priority unless the employee can prove that her or his case falls under one of the exceptions. That is, EAW is the default position on which courts will rely until and unless an exception can be demonstrated. The burden of proof lies with the dismissed employee to show that she or he was unjustly or illegally fired. Due process and **just cause,** whether instituted as part of internal corporate pol-icy or through legislation, would reverse this burden of proof and require employ-ers to show cause to justify the dismissal of an employee.

Reality Check *Employing "Employees"*

Because the status of employment at will depends on the determination of whether someone is employed at all, the definition of *employee* becomes critical. The employment relationship brings with it a plethora of benefits and responsibilities, which means that either party might be in a position to argue in its favor, or against. However, most often it is the worker who is arguing for employee status.

There are several tests that courts use in order to determine a worker's status as an employee or, to the contrary, an "independent contractor," (i.e., one who works for another, according to her or his own methods, and who is not under the other's control regarding the physical details of the work). These tests include the common-law test of agency, which focuses on the right of control, the Internal Revenue Service (IRS) 20-factor analysis, and the economic realities analysis. Several courts also use a hybrid approach, using one test that combines factors from other tests.

Under the **common-law agency test,** a persuasive indicator of independent contractor status is the ability to control the manner in which the work is performed. Under the common-law agency approach, the employer need not actually control the work, but must merely *have the right or ability* to control the work for a worker to be classified an employee.

In two landmark 2014 cases heard by the Ninth Circuit Court of Appeals, the federal court evaluated whether Federal Express ground package drivers in California and Oregon (a total of over 2,500 drivers) were employees entitled to reimbursement for work-related expenses (for uniforms, specific trucks, and so on), overtime pay and other federal benefits. The court applied the common-law test and found that they were, in fact, employees. The court explained that FedEx had a broad right to "control the manner in which the drivers perform their work" because "the drivers must wear FedEx uniforms, drive FedEx-approved vehicles, and groom themselves according to FedEx's appearance standards. . . . FedEx tells its drivers what packages to deliver, on what days, and at what times."[36]

Not all courts or circuits agree with the Ninth Circuit on this issue, however. The same issue has been litigated in 40 states and some of the other courts have found in favor of FedEx, holding that the workers' ability to hire their own employees, manage multiple routes, and sell those routes without FedEx's permission "as well as the parties' intent expressed in the contract, argues strongly in favor of independent contractor statutes." Evidently, it is not a black-and-white issue![37]

The second test is the **IRS 20-factor analysis,** a list of 20 factors to which the IRS looks to determine whether someone is an employee or an independent contractor. The IRS compiled this list from the results of judgments of the courts relating to this issue. Finally, under the **economic realities test,** courts consider whether the worker is economically dependent on the business or, as a matter of economic fact, is in business for himself or herself.

Some employers hire individuals as employees rather than independent contractors as a matter of principle. Phyllis Apelbaum, CEO of Arrow Messenger Service in Chicago, explains that her guiding philosophy in terms of her workers is to "hire hard working, friendly messengers; compensate them fairly including benefits and treat them as your greatest asset!" Her employees make a strong contribution to the culture and values of the firm. When Apelbaum considered using independent contractors instead of employees about 15 years ago, she explained, "I wouldn't be able to sleep at night and thought, it'll never work. Well, it has worked for 15 years for other companies. Because of that ethical decision, we have not grown to be the biggest in the city. We've grown nicely, no question about it. But we battle everyday that company that has independent contractors. Because, if you have employees, you've got about a 28 percent bottom number there. So, if the two of us walk in the door, and he charges you a dollar, I'm going to have to charge you $1.28. I'm always fighting that. The ethical decision to go in that direction meant that we had to work harder at our vision to provide better service. Otherwise, why should you be willing to pay 28 cents more? Why? There would be no reason for it."[38]

TABLE 6.1
Exceptions to the Doctrine of Employment at Will

States vary in terms of their recognition of the following exceptions to the doctrine of employment at will. Some states recognize one or more exceptions, while others might recognize none at all. In addition, the definition of these exceptions may vary from state to state.

- Bad faith, malicious or retaliatory termination in violation of *public policy.*
- Termination in breach of the *implied covenant of good faith and fair dealing.*
- Termination in breach of some other *implied contract term,* such as those that might be created by employee handbook provisions (in certain jurisdictions).
- Termination in violation of the doctrine of *promissory estoppel* (where the employee reasonably relied on an employer's promise, to the employee's detriment).
- Other exceptions as determined by *statutes* (such as the Worker Adjustment and Retraining Notification Act [WARN] or the Family and Medical Leave Act [FMLA]).

IRS 20-factor analysis
A list of 20 factors to which the IRS looks to determine whether someone is an employee or an independent contractor.

5

OBJECTIVE

common-law agency test
A persuasive indicator of independent contractor status that provides the employer the ability to control the manner in which the work is performed. Under the common-law agency approach, the employer need not actually control the work, but must merely have the right or ability to control the work for a worker to be classified an employee.

economic realities test
A test by which courts consider whether the worker is economically dependent on the business or, as a matter of economic fact, is in business for himself or herself.

Due process issues arise in other employment contexts as well. Employees are constantly supervised and evaluated in the workplace, and such benefits as salary, work conditions, and promotions can also be used to motivate or sanction employees. Thus, being treated fairly in the workplace also involves fairness in such things as promotions, salary, benefits, and so forth. Because these decisions are typically made on the basis of performance appraisals, due process rights should also extend to this aspect of the workplace.

The ethical questions that remain in this EAW environment, therefore, are whether this atmosphere is one that is fairest and most just for all stakeholders, whether it leads to the most effective employment outcomes, and whether it satisfactorily guards the rights and interests of both employers and employees. Relevant inquiries in reaching a conclusion on these matters will include those that comprise our decision-making framework. Consider the key facts relevant to issues of due process and fairness. What are the ethical issues involved in your decision and implementation? Who are the stakeholders involved in your decision? What alternatives are available to you? Might there be a way to safeguard the rights of the stakeholders involved while also protecting the interests of the decision makers? If you are, for instance, striving to serve the autonomy of the employer, could you perhaps serve the due process interests of the employee by offering additional notice of termination or more information about alternatives?

Recall that due process is the right to be protected against the *arbitrary* use of authority. It is your role as decision maker to ensure protection against those arbitrary decisions. Employers should be fair in their implementation of judgments and just in their implementation of process in order to serve the preceding principles. The overarching obligation here is to make sure that decisions are made in light of reasons that can be defended from an ethical perspective.

Downsizing

One of the most emotional issues for both employees and corporate decision makers is the challenge not only of a single termination but firing many employees

downsize
The reduction of human resources at an organization through terminations, retirements, corporate divestments, or other means.

when a firm makes a decision to **downsize.** Terminating workers—whether 1 or 100—is not necessarily an unethical decision! However, the decision itself raises ethical quandaries because alternatives may be available to an organization in financial difficulty. Making the choice between firing someone or cutting costs through some other method poses the ethical dilemma—which answer is truer to your values and those of your firm, and which will pose the greatest strategic benefit in the long run? In addition, because a number of negative consequences may result, it is important to consider the impact of each alternative from the perspective of all stakeholders involved.

These negative outcomes may include poor recommendations of the firm by former employees, a decline in customer service by surviving employees, an increase in errors or even dangerous behavior by employees, or merely a bad attitude by staff who fear that they might be the next to be cut. The impact may extend to perceptions related to your corporate social responsibility or strategy as well. A 2013 study reported that the more responsibility given to leadership for the downsizing, the more likely that stakeholders also will have a negative perception of a firm's commitment to corporate social responsibility—everything is connected, whether you see a connection or not.[39]

OBJECTIVE 6

Accordingly, the question of whether to resort to widespread terminations based on financial challenges in place of other options that may be available does not always lead to a clear answer. Once the decision has been made, are there ways in which an organization can act more ethically in the process of downsizing? How might our earlier discussion of due process and fairness offer some guidance and/or define limitations in a downsizing environment?

Professor José Luis Illueca García-Labrado argues, "people affected by the restructuring process must be treated with the same respect and interest that was shown when hiring them. . . . When they were hired, they were important to the success of the company; now they are equally important to the company's survival as they leave." Ethics, therefore, must be central to the design and management of layoff policies.[40] In fact, our decision-making model offers significant guidance in a situation such as a downsizing.

First, the decision regarding downsizing should be made by a representative group so that all stakeholder interests can be considered and to earn the trust of those who will be impacted. The facts should be collected and issues should be determined. Because employees should be kept aware of business conditions, the need for a downsizing effort should not come as a great surprise. However, the question of notice is debatable.

It can be argued that a firm should give notice of an intent to downsize as soon as the need is determined, and let those who will be impacted know who will be let go as soon as that list is devised. Leadership IQ, a leadership research and training company, conducted a large-scale survey of more than 4,000 workers who remained in more than 300 companies that engaged in layoffs. The survey found that productivity and quality were more than two-thirds less likely to suffer when managers exhibited visibility, approachability, and candor.[41] On the other hand, the uncertainty and rumors that are sure to develop between the announcement

Reality Check   *Is It Really "Inevitable"?*

As inevitable as downsizing may seem during downturns in the economy, some firms have survived decade after decade without any layoffs. How do they do it? While many firms became quite creative during the economic crisis that began during the second half of 2008, other firms have maintained these innovations for years. For instance, Hypertherm Inc., a manufacturer of metal-cutting equipment, has gone for its almost 50-year history without ever laying off a permanent employee. When the 2008 economic crisis hit, it opted instead to eliminate overtime, cut temporary staff, and delay a facility expansion, citing an ongoing "social contract" with its employees as the root of its strategy.[42]

Another company, Nucor Corporation, has not laid off a worker for over 30 years. However, it maintains a "pay for performance" policy. When the plant has large contracts and everyone is busy, workers earn up to $24 per hour. But when business is slow, the company reduces wages to $12 per hour.[43] Other firms have entered into agreements with their workers under which the firm promises not to terminate workers for reasons of the economy as long as the workers agree to lower wages

or decreased hours during tough periods. For instance, Marvin Windows and Doors, a privately held Minnesota company employing more than 4,000 workers, upheld its vow to avoid terminations by cutting pay, reducing benefits, and suspending profit-sharing payments to both employees and owners during the worst of the recession.

Company president Susan Marvin said that her no-layoff policy was "as much a business wager as an act of benevolence." Taking the long-term view, Marvin believed that maintaining the company's skilled workforce would benefit the company over time despite short-term losses. This view proved true, as the company began distributing profit sharing checks again in December 2012.[44]

Other options to stave off terminations can include the obvious decision to freeze hiring, to offer attractive voluntary retirement packages that provide an overall financial benefit to the firm, to reduce hours for all rather than fewer positions, to lower salaries, or to reduce or delay giving raises. Finally, some employers have chosen to cut benefits for which they would normally pay, such as bonuses, employer contributions to retirement plans, training, or education allocations.

of downsizing and the decision about who will be terminated may outweigh the benefits gained in early notification. In addition, allowing a worker to remain in a position for a period of time once she or he has been notified of impending termination might not be the best option. Workers may interpret early notice as an effort to get the most out of them before departure rather than an effort to allow them time to come to grips with the loss of their jobs.

These costs and benefits must be weighed in any communication decision and certainly considered in managing and interacting with employees following a lay-off. "Managers need to be highly visible to their staff, approachable even when they don't have anything new to say, and candid about the state of things in order to build their trust and credibility. If your company has to conduct a layoff, it is imperative that you train your managers how to both manage that process and deal with the highly debilitating aftermath. Otherwise you will waste any potential cost savings from the layoff on lost productivity, quality problems and service breakdowns," says Mark Murphy, chair of Leadership IQ.[45]

Once the stakeholders are identified, it will be vital to enumerate any and all possible options with regard to the downsizing efforts and to catalog the impact of each option on each group of stakeholders. (See the Reality Check "Is It Really 'Inevitable'?" for a discussion of options.) When a firm decides to downsize, as with any other termination, it is critical to lessen the impact as much as possible and to allow the terminated employees to depart with dignity (for example, unless there is some other reason for the decision, having a security guard follow terminated employees until they leave the building might not be the best option). Above all, during a time when relationships might be strained, it is critical to be honest and forthright and to be sensitive to the experiences of those who will be affected.

From a legal perspective, the decision about whom to include in a downsizing effort must be carefully planned. If the firm's decision is based on some criterion that seems to be neutral on its face, such as seniority, but the plan results in a different impact on one group than another, the decision may be suspect. For example, assume the firm does make termination decisions based on longevity with the organization. Also assume that those workers who are most senior are almost entirely male because women entered this industry only in recent years. If the firm moves forward with this process, the majority of those fired will be women and the majority of those remaining will be men. In this case, the effort may violate Title VII's prohibition against discrimination based on gender because the termination policy has a more significant—and negative—impact on women.

To avoid this result, firms should review both the fairness of their decision-making process and the consequence of that process on those terminated and the resulting composition of the workforce. One of the most effective philosophical theories to employ in downsizing decisions is John Rawls's theory of justice presented in chapter 3. Under his formulation, you would consider what decision you would make—whether to downsize or how to downsize—if you did not know what role you would be playing following the decision. In other words, you might be the corporate executive with the secure position; you might be a terminated employee with years of seniority who was close to retirement; or you might be a worker who survives the termination slips. If you do not know which role you would be playing, Rawls contends that you are more likely to reach a decision that is relatively fairest to all impacted. Consider what facts might shift your decision in one way or another based on this formulation.

Perhaps the most important consideration in the event of a downsizing or layoff is the fact that there are people who will be impacted by the decisions involved—countless stakeholders. Ralph Larsen, past chair and CEO of Johnson & Johnson, explains the angst he experienced when he made a decision to close approximately 50 small plants around the world.

> I was responsible to our employees in those plants, but I was also responsible to the patients who needed our products to keep them affordable. And I was responsible to all of our other employees around the world to keep the company healthy and growing. The harsh reality was that a great many more would be hurt down the road if I failed to act and we became less and less competitive.

> In addition to our employees, I was also responsible to the tens of thousands of stockholders (individuals, retired folks, pension plans, and mutual funds) who owned our stock. The facts were clear. . . . I knew what had to be done, and we did it as thoughtfully and sensitively as possible. But the decision was hard, because it was personal.[46]

Health and Safety

The previous sections addressed ethics in the creation or termination of the employment relationship. The following discussion explores one particular responsibility within that relationship—the employer's role in protecting the employees' health and safety while at work. Within the United States and throughout many other countries with developed economies, there is a broad consensus that employees have a fundamental right to a safe and healthy workplace. However, in some other regions employees lack even the most basic health and safety protections, such as in working environments that are often termed *sweatshops* (that term and the concepts behind it are discussed later in this chapter). Even within the United States, this issue becomes quite complicated upon closer examination. Not only is the very extent of an employer's responsibility for workplace health and safety in dispute, there is also significant disagreement concerning the best policies to protect worker health and safety.

Like work itself, health and safety are "goods" that are valued both as a means for attaining other valuable ends and as ends in themselves. Whatever else we desire out of life, being healthy and safe makes it much more likely that we will be capable of attaining our goals. In this sense, health and safety have a very high instrumental value because part of their value derives from the fact that we use them to attain other things of value. Insurance therefore seeks to compensate workers for injuries they incur by paying the employees for the wages they lose as a result of being unable to work.

OBJECTIVE

Yet health and safety are also valuable in and of themselves. They have intrinsic value in addition to their instrumental value. To understand this distinction, consider how one might respond to the question of how much her or his life is worth. The life of one who dies in a workplace accident has instrumental value that can be measured, in part, by the lost wages that would have been earned had that person lived. But these lost wages do not measure the *intrinsic* value of the life, something that financial compensation simply cannot replace. The Decision Point "Measuring Our Worth" explores the measurement of intrinsic value.

What is the value of health and what does it mean to be healthy? When is a workplace safe? When is it unsafe? If "healthy" is taken to mean a state of flawless physical and psychological well-being, arguably no one is perfectly healthy. If "safe" means completely free from risk, certainly no workplace is perfectly safe. If health and safety are interpreted as ideals that are impossible to realize, then it would be unreasonable to claim that employees have a right to a healthy and safe workplace.

Health and Safety as Acceptable Risk

OBJECTIVE

Employers cannot be responsible for providing a completely safe and healthy workplace. Instead, discussions in ethics about employee health and safety will tend to focus on the *relative* risks workers face and the level of *acceptable* workplace risk. In this discussion, "risks" can be defined as the probability of harm, and we determine "relative risks" by comparing the probabilities of harm

How do we measure the intrinsic value of a life, in addition to the instrumental value? Though perhaps an interesting mental exercise in which to engage, it is also a critical component of some business decisions and dilemmas. The following decision, though decades old, continues to teach us the hazards of considering only the instrumental value of a life. Though the instrumental calculation seems to make sense, and presumably it did at the time to those involved, you will see in hindsight that the "human element" seems to be missing.

In 1968, Ford Motor Company made a historic decision regarding the Ford Pinto, which was engineered with a rear gas tank assembly that had a tendency to explode in accidents that involved some rear-end collisions. The company allowed the Pinto to remain on the market after it determined that it would be more costly to engage in a recall effort than to pay out the costs of liability for injuries and deaths incurred. In an infamous memo, Ford's senior management calculated what the company would likely have to pay per life lost. It is noteworthy that these estimates were not Ford's alone but were based instead on figures from the National Highway Traffic Safety Administration.

Expected Costs of Producing the Pinto *with* Fuel Tank Modifications:

- Expected unit sales: 11 million vehicles (includes utility vehicles built on same chassis)
- Modification costs per unit: $11
- **Total Cost: $121 million [11 million vehicles x $11 per unit]**

Expected Costs of Producing the Pinto *without* Fuel Tank Modifications:

- Expected accident results (assuming 2,100 accidents):
  180 burn deaths
  180 serious burn injuries
  2,100 burned out vehicles

- Unit costs of accident results (assuming out of court settlements):
  $200,000 per burn death
  $67,000 per serious injury
  $700 per burned out vehicle
- **Total Costs: $49.53 million** [= (180 deaths × $200k) + (180 injuries × $67k) + (2,100 vehicles × $700 per vehicle)]

Using these figures, the costs for recalling and modifying the Pinto were $121 million, while the costs for settling cases in which injuries were expected to occur would reach only $50 million.

If you were responsible for deciding whether to engage in the recall, how would you conduct the decision-making process? How would you account for the *intrinsic* as well as the *instrumental* value of a human life? Returning to the question that opened this Decision Point, consider how you would measure your own worth or the value of someone close to you. Who are your stakeholders and what is your value to each of them? How will you measure it—*financially*? Would any of the following questions offer you a guidepost?

- How much would your stakeholders suffer if they lost you?
- How much do you currently contribute to society and what would society lose if you were not here?
- How much would society benefit if you continued to survive?

Businesses have reasons to consider these issues, though extraordinarily difficult; how would you prefer that they reach conclusions in these areas?

involved in various activities. Therefore, scientists who compile and measure data can determine both risks and relative risks (see Figure 6.1). It is an easy step from these calculations to certain conclusions about acceptable risks. If it can be determined that the probability of harm involved in a specific work activity is equal to or less than the probability of harm of some more common activity, then we can conclude that this activity faces an "acceptable level of risk." From this perspective, *a workplace is safe if the risks are acceptable.*

Imagine if we generalize this conclusion and determine all workplace health and safety standards in this manner. Such an approach would place the responsibility for workplace safety solely on management. A business would hire safety engineers and other experts to determine the risks within their workplace. These experts would know the risk levels that are otherwise accepted throughout the society. These might involve the risks involved in driving a car, eating high-fat food, smoking, jogging, and so forth. Comparing these to the risks faced in the workplace, safety experts could perform a risk assessment and determine the relative risks of work. If the workplace were less risky than other common activities, management could conclude that they have fulfilled their responsibility to provide a healthy and safe workplace.

FIGURE 6.1
Calculating Acceptable Level of Risk

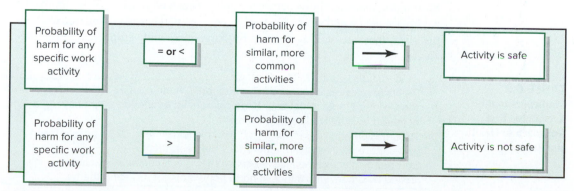

However, such an approach to workplace health and safety issues has several problems. First, this approach treats employees disrespectfully by ignoring their input as stakeholders. Such paternalistic decision making effectively treats employees like children and makes crucial decisions for them, ignoring their role in the decision-making process. Second, in making this decision we assume that health and safety are mere preferences that can be traded off against competing values, ignoring the fundamental deontological right an employee might have to a safe and healthy working environment. Third, it assumes an equivalency between workplace risks and other types of risks when there are actually significant differences between them. Unlike many daily risks, the risks faced in the workplace may not be freely chosen, nor are the risks faced in the workplace within the control of workers. Fourth, it disregards the utilitarian concern for the consequences of an unsafe working environment on the social fabric, the resulting product or service created, the morale of the workforce, and the community, as well as other large-scale results of an unhealthy workplace.

Perhaps most important, unlike some daily risks each of us freely undertakes, the risks faced at work could be controlled by others, particularly by others who might stand to benefit by *not* reducing the risks. For instance, making the workplace safe may pose substantial costs to employers. Relative to the risks one might face by smoking, for example, working in a mill and inhaling cotton dust may not seem as risky. But, in the former case, the smoker chooses to take the risk and could take steps to minimize or eliminate them by herself or himself. In the latter case, the mill worker cannot avoid the risks as long as she or he wants to keep a job. Often someone else can minimize or eliminate these risks, but this other party also has a financial incentive not to do so. In one case, smoking, the decision maker freely chooses to take the risk, knowing that she or he can control it. In the other case, the worker's choices and control are limited. The challenges involved in the acceptable risk approach to workplace health and safety are summarized in Table 6.2.

Health and Safety as Market Controlled

Perhaps we can leave health and safety standards to the market. Defenders of the free market and the classical model of corporate social responsibility would favor individual bargaining between employers and employees as the approach to workplace health and safety. On this account, employees would be free to choose the risks they are willing to face by bargaining with employers. Employees

TABLE 6.2
Challenges to the Acceptable Risk Approach to Health and Safety

- Treats employees disrespectfully by ignoring their input as stakeholders.
- Ignores the fundamental deontological right an employee might have to a safe and healthy working environment.
- Assumes an equivalency between workplace risks and other types of risks when there are significant differences between them.
- Improperly places incentives because the risks faced at work could be controlled by others who might stand to benefit by *not* reducing them.

If one follows the market-based recommendation to allocate workplace risks on the basis of an optimal distribution of risks and benefits, one would conclude that, from a business perspective, dangerous jobs ought to be exported to those areas where wages are low and where workers are more willing to accept risky working conditions. The harms done by dangerous jobs, in terms of forgone earnings, are lower in regions with low wages and lower life expectancies. The benefits of providing jobs in regions with high unemployment would also outweigh the benefits of sending those jobs to regions with low unemployment. (See also the discussion of global labor markets, later in this chapter.)

Following this market-based logic, many U.S.-based pharmaceutical companies seeking to test new medications conduct pharmaceutical trials abroad—and China and India are their fastest-growing locations. Clinical trials in developing economies tend to be subject to far fewer regulations than trials in the United States and, therefore, are significantly less costly.[47] In 2014, over 50 percent of all clinical trials took place outside the United States, with almost 20,000 of those trials taking place in India and China.[48]

- What facts would you want to know before deciding whether the practice of exporting clinical trials was fair and responsible?
- What alternatives to exporting clinical trials exist for a pharmaceutical company?
- Who are the stakeholders of your decision? What is the impact of each alternative mentioned here on each stakeholder you have identified?
- Should local legal regulations govern the situation or the legal regulations in the pharmaceutical company's home country?
- What are the consequences of such a decision? What rights and duties are involved? If the consequences are effective and valuable to the majority but fundamental rights are implicated, how will you decide what to do?

would balance their preferences for risk against their demand for wages and decide how much risk they are willing to take for various wages. Those who demand higher safety standards and healthier conditions presumably would have to settle for lower wages; those willing to take higher risks presumably would demand higher wages.

In a competitive and free labor market, such individual bargaining would result in the optimal distribution of safety and income. Of course, the market approach can also support compensation to injured workers when it can be shown that employers were responsible for causing the harms. So an employer who fails to install firefighting equipment in the workplace can be held liable for burns an employee suffers during a workplace fire. The threat of compensation also acts as an incentive for employers to maintain a reasonably safe and healthy workplace. The Decision Point "Should Clinical Trials for New Drugs Be Exported?" considers whether it is therefore ethical for a pharmaceutical company to outsource its medical trials to countries with fewer health and safety regulations than the United States and a population willing to accept lower pay for participation in trials.

OBJECTIVE

This free-market approach has a number of serious problems. First, labor markets are not perfectly competitive and free. Employees do not have the kinds of free choices that the free-market theory would require in order to attain optimal satisfactions. Though enlightened self-interest would be a valuable theory to introduce and apply in this environment, it is unrealistic to presume employees always have the choices available to them that make it possible. For example, risky jobs are often also the lowest-paying jobs, and people with the fewest employment choices hold them. Individuals are forced to accept the jobs because they have no choice but to accept; they are not actually "balancing their preferences for risk against their demand for wages" because they do not have options. Second, employees seldom, if ever, possess the kind of complete information efficient markets require. If employees do not know the risks involved in a job, they will not be in a position to freely bargain for appropriate wages and therefore they will not be in a position to effectively protect their rights or ensure the most ethical consequences. This is a particular concern when we recognize that many workplace risks are in no sense obvious. An employee may understand the dangers of heavy machinery or a blast furnace; but few employees can know the toxicity or exposure levels of workplace chemicals or airborne contaminants.

Such market failures can have deadly consequences when they involve workplace health and safety issues. Of course, market defenders argue that over time markets will compensate for such failures, employers will find it difficult to attract workers to dangerous jobs, and employees will learn about the risks of every workplace. But this raises what we call a "first-generation" problem. The market gathers information by observing the harms done to the first generation exposed to imperfect market transactions. Thus, workers learn that exposure to lead is dangerous when some female workers exposed to lead suffer miscarriages or when others have children who are born with serious birth defects. We learn that workplace exposure to asbestos or cotton dust is dangerous when workers subsequently die from lung disease. In effect, markets sacrifice the first generation in order to gain information about safety and health risks. These questions of public policy, questions that after all will affect human lives, would never even be asked by an individual facing the choice of working at a risky job. To the degree that these are important questions that ought to be asked, individual bargaining will fail as an ethical public policy approach to worker health and safety. Table 6.3 summarizes the challenges inherent in the free-market approach to health and safety.

TABLE 6.3
Challenges with the Free-Market Approach to Health and Safety

- Labor markets are not perfectly competitive and free.
- Employees seldom, if ever, possess the kind of perfect information markets require.
- We ignore important questions of social justice and public policy if we approach questions solely from the point of view of an individual.

Health and Safety as Government-Regulated Ethics

In response to such concerns, government regulation of workplace health and safety appears more appropriate from an ethical perspective. Mandatory government standards address most of the problems raised against market strategies. Standards can be set according to the best available scientific knowledge and thus overcome market failures that result from insufficient information. Standards prevent employees from having to face the fundamentally coercive choice between job and safety. Standards also address the first-generation problem by focusing on prevention rather than compensation after the fact. Finally, standards are fundamentally a social approach that can address public policy questions ignored by markets.

Occupational Safety and Health Administration (OSHA)
The United States Occupational Safety and Health Administration, an agency of the federal government that publishes and enforces safety and health regulations for U.S. businesses.

In 1970, the U.S. Congress established the **Occupational Safety and Health Administration (OSHA)** and charged it with establishing workplace health and safety standards. Since that time the major debates concerning workplace health and safety have focused on how such public standards ought to be set. The dominant question concerns the appropriateness of using cost–benefit analysis to set health and safety standards.

When OSHA was first established, regulations were aimed at achieving the safest *feasible* standards. This "feasibility" approach allows OSHA to make trade-offs between health and economics, but it is prejudiced in favor of health and safety by placing the burden of proof on industry to show that high standards are not economically feasible. Health and safety standards are not required, no matter the cost; however, an industry is required to meet the highest standards attainable within technological and economic reason.

Some critics charge that this approach does not go far enough and unjustly sacrifices employee health and safety. From that perspective, industries that cannot operate without harming the health and safety of its employees should be closed. But the more influential business criticism has argued that these standards go too far. Critics in both industry and government have argued that OSHA should be required to use cost–benefit analysis in establishing such standards. From this perspective, even if a standard is technologically and economically feasible, it would still be unreasonable and unfair if the benefits did not outweigh the costs. These critics argue that OSHA should aim to achieve the optimal, rather than highest feasible, level of safety.

Using a cost–benefit analysis to set standards in effect returns us to the goals of the market-based, individual bargaining approach. Like that market approach, this use of cost–benefit analysis faces serious ethical challenges. We should note, however, that rejecting cost–benefit analysis in setting standards is not the same as rejecting cost-effective strategies in implementing those standards. A commitment to cost-effectiveness would require that, once the standards are set, we adopt the least expensive and most efficient means available for achieving those standards. Cost–benefit analysis, in contrast, uses economic criteria in setting the standards in the first place. It is cost–benefit, not cost-effectiveness, analysis that is ethically problematic. (See the Reality Check "Do Health and Safety Programs

Reality Check *Do Health and Safety Programs Cost Too Much?*

Evidence collected by the Occupational Safety and Health Administration suggests just the opposite: Safety and health programs *add* value and *reduce* costs. Workplaces can reduce injuries 20 to 40 percent by establishing safety and health programs. Several studies have estimated that safety and health programs save $3 to $6 for every dollar invested. These savings result from a decrease in employee injuries and illnesses, lower workers' compensation costs, decreased medical costs, reduced absenteeism, lower turnover, higher productivity, and increased morale. Employers are finding that disease prevention and wellness programs are important tools in the battle to reduce rising medical costs.[49]

According to World Economic Forum statistics, companies that have implemented proactive wellness programs have saved an average $700 per year, per employee. Plus, employees are more attracted to and value a business that appreciates them; so companies with an employee wellness program have lower turnover. A 2013 study shows that workplace wellness programs have emerged as a common employer-sponsored benefit that is now available at about half of U.S. employers with 50 or more employees—that covers three-quarters of the U.S. workforce!

Sources: "Safety and Health Add Value," OSHA Publication 3180 (n.d.), www.osha.gov/Publications/safety-health-addvalue. html (accessed February 21, 2016); World Economic Forum, "The Workplace Wellness Alliance—Making the Right Investment: Employee Health and the Power of Metrics" (January 31, 2013), www3.weforum.org/docs/WEF_HE_WorkplaceWellnessAlliance_ Report_2013.pdf (accessed February 21, 2016); Soeren Mattke, Hangsheng Liu, John P. Caloyeras, et al., "Workplace Wellness Programs Study" (2013), United States Department of Labor, Employment Benefits Security Administration, www.dol.gov/ebsa/ pdf/workplacewellnessstudyfinal.pdf (accessed February 21, 2016).

Cost Too Much?" as well as the Decision Point "How Much Is Enough?" for an application of cost–benefit analysis.)

The use of cost–benefit analysis in setting workplace health and safety standards commits us to treating worker health and safety as just another commodity, another individual preference, to be traded off against competing commodities. It treats health and safety merely as an instrumental value and denies its intrinsic value. Cost–benefit analysis requires that an economic value be placed on one's life and bodily integrity. Typically, this would follow the model used by the insurance industry (where it is used in wrongful death settlements, for example) in which one's life is valued in terms of one's earning potential. Perhaps the most offensive aspect of this approach is the fact that because, in feasibility analysis, health and safety are already traded off against the economic viability of the industry, a shift to cost–benefit analysis entails trading off health and safety against profit margin.

The policies that have emerged by consensus within the United States seem to be most defensible. Employees have a legitimate ethical claim on mandatory health and safety standards within the workplace. To say that employees have a right to workplace health and safety implies that they should not be expected to make trade-offs between health and safety standards and job security or wages. Further, recognizing that most mandatory standards reduce rather than eliminate risks, employees should also have the right to be informed about workplace risks. If the risks have been reduced to the lowest feasible level and employees are fully aware of them, then a society that respects its citizens as autonomous decision makers has done its duty.

While there is a cost associated with workplace health and safety violations, some argue that this cost is not sufficiently high to deter violations. In other words, they advocate higher fines in order to deter violations or to encourage employers to provide safer conditions. In one case, OSHA imposed a fine of $87.5 million on British Petroleum (BP), the largest fine in OSHA's history.[50] OSHA had found more than 400 new safety violations at the company's Texas City refinery. The violations were considered egregious because they were discovered in 2009, four years after a deadly explosion at the refinery (15 deaths, 170 injured) had led BP to sign an OSHA agreement promising to improve safety conditions.

If you were on the OSHA Commission to review the amounts of fines imposed, how would you reach a decision as to how much is enough? What factors would you consider?

- Who are the stakeholders involved in your decision?
- What do you foresee will be the impact of your decision on the stakeholders involved?
- How might ethical theory assist you in reaching this particular decision?
- Once you have reached your decision, which constituencies do you anticipate will be most supportive and which will be most against your decision, and why?

Global Applications: The Global Workforce and Global Challenges

As you consider the issues of due process, fairness, and health and safety raised thus far in the chapter, note that the application of the law discussed here is limited to workers who are employed in the United States. Workers outside the United States may be subject to some U.S. laws if they work for an American-based organization, though enforcement is scattered. In some cases, workers in other countries are often protected by even more stringent laws than those in the United States. Many countries in the European Union, for example, have strong laws protecting workers' rights to due process and participation. But in many other cases, especially in certain developing countries, workers find themselves subject to conditions that U.S.-based workers would find appalling. While those of us who work in the United States may benefit from battles fought in years past for occupational safety and health, workers in certain Southeast Asian countries, for instance, are simply arguing for at-will bathroom breaks.

OBJECTIVE

The response to this stark contrast is not a simple one. Though few people, if any, would argue for the continuation of the circumstances described earlier, economists and others do not agree about a solution. Some contend that the exploitation of cheap labor allows developing countries to expand export activities and to improve their economies. This economic growth brings more jobs, which will cause the labor market to tighten, which in turn will force companies to improve conditions in order to attract workers (see Figure 6.2). In fact, several commentators argue that encouraging greater global production will create additional opportunities for expansion domestically, providing a positive impact

FIGURE 6.2

The Case *for* Sweatshops

Source: D. Arnold and L. Hartman, "Worker Rights and Low Wage Industrialization: How to Avoid Sweatshops," *Human Rights Quarterly* 28, no. 3 (August 2006), pp. 676–700.

sweatshops
A term that remains subject to debate. Some might suggest that all workplaces with conditions that are below standards in more developed countries are sweatshops because all humans have a right to equally decent working conditions. (See the discussion in chapter 6 and D. Arnold and L. Hartman, "Beyond Sweatshops: Positive Deviancy and Global Labor Practices," *Business Ethics: A European Review* 14, no. 3 [July 2005].) In this text we use the following definition: any workplace in which workers are typically subject to two or more of the following conditions: systematic forced overtime, systematic health and safety risks that stem from negligence or the willful disregard of employee welfare, coercion, systematic deception that places workers at risk, underpayment of earnings, and income for a 48-hour workweek less than the overall poverty rate for that country (one who suffers from overall poverty lacks the income necessary to satisfy one's basic nonfood needs such as shelter and basic health care).

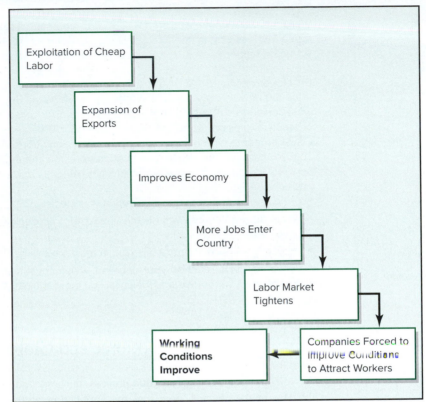

on more stakeholders.[51] Though it is an unpopular sentiment with the general consuming public, many economists argue that the maintenance of **sweatshops** is therefore supported by economic theory. Indeed, even the term *sweatshop* remains open to debate.

Philosophers Benjamin Powell and Matthew Zwolinski explore the issue from a slightly different perspective in a seminal article titled "The Ethical and Economic Case against Sweatshop Labor: A Critical Assessment." They defend the moral legitimacy of sweatshops and respond to the question of whether a worker under these conditions can actually consent to them or be considered to be working "voluntarily" at all. They conclude that a worker actually *is able* to give consent. Therefore, the moral imperative of supporting sweatshops "is the welfare of the least advantaged—sweatshop workers, potential sweatshop workers, and future generations of workers and potential workers who deal with the economic aftermath of today's economic and political decisions."[52] They argue that workers see the extreme dangers sometimes associated with working in sweatshops, but the workers make the decision that working in a sweatshop will give them economic power that they have not accessed previously. Choice, within a severely limited set of options, is still a choice. Thus, they conclude, "genuine respect for workers' dignity requires recognizing their freedom decide for themselves issues of central importance to their lives."[53]

On the other hand, opponents to this perspective argue that allowing sweat-shops to continue will not necessarily lead to the anticipated result, just as vol-untarily improving legal compliance, wages, and working conditions will not inevitably lead to the negative consequences the free market advocates threaten. Reading 6-1, "Confessions of a Sweatshop Inspector," by T. A. Frank offers a perspective somewhat in opposition to Powell and Zwolinski's. Frank discusses a sign observed in large characters on a factory's wall, "If you don't work hard today, look hard for work tomorrow." The author might take issue with Zwolinski's claim of worker consent to conditions where few alternatives exist. From a unique point of view, Frank shares the experience of inspecting, serving as an indepen-dent monitor of overseas suppliers to multinational retailers.

One of Frank's key clues to whether a client "cared" about working conditions was the nature of its relationships with its suppliers. "Long-term commitments are what motivate both parties to behave: the supplier wants to preserve the rela-tionship, and the customer wants to preserve its reputation." An interesting and high-profile case unfolded in early 2012 when the public realized—through the aid of the media—that their iPhones and other Apple devices were largely created in China by suppliers under conditions that might not be deemed ethically accept-able in the United States and that certainly violated internal standards issued by Apple and local Chinese labor laws.

Apple responded immediately after the media attention, but some say the response was significantly tardy because some violations went back for several years. Reading 6-2, "Polishing Apple: Fair Labor Association Gives Foxconn and Apple Undue Credit for Labor Rights Progress, by Scott Nova and Isaac Shapiro makes more significant claims, suggesting that the Fair Labor Association "gives Foxconn and Apple undue credit for labor rights progress." After reading the five bases for their conclusion, ask yourself how you might have responded if had you been appointed chief ethics officer for Apple at the moment the issues hit the front pages! What would have been the *most ethical response possible*?

Consider Aristotle's statement "we are what we do" as you orient your per-spective on Apple's decision making. Is it relevant that Apple is a company that relies heavily on consumers' positive opinion? In turn, Foxconn relies heavily on its relationship with Apple; and both Apple and Foxconn reap their profits from stable, long-term relationships. Have a look at the Reality Check "Making Better Mistakes Tomorrow" and Reading 6-4, "A Tale of Two Agreements," by Chris MacDonald to learn about the impact the market can have—both after Apple's experience, and then after a significant tragedy in the marketplace, one of the worst in manufacturing history.

Of course, the Apple/Foxconn scenario took place across global boundaries, between the United States and China. Often, as we examine the ethical issues that arise in our workplaces, it is both vital and helpful to consider the global dimen-sions of our ethically responsible workplaces.

As we examine ethical issues in the workplace, a helpful exercise is to con-sider the global dimension of an ethically responsible workplace. Certainly it is arguable that some minimum standards might apply and multinationals may have

Reality Check *Making Better Mistakes Tomorrow*

Those who cannot remember the past are condemned to repeat it.

> Santayana, *The Life of Reason*, 1905

Just one year following the public attention to the Apple case discussed in the text, a large factory considered a sweatshop in Bangladesh called Raza Plaza collapsed in 2013 due to shoddy building materials and overused facilities. The tragedy killed over 1,100 workers and injured over 2,500. It is considered the deadliest garment-factory accident in history, as well as the deadliest accidental structural failure in modern human history.

Major global retailers, including Benetton, the Children's Place, Joe Fresh, and Walmart, produced goods using this facility and faced an international outcry both to compensate the victims' families and also to make changes in their use of what was considered to be sweatshop labor.

Under pressure to avoid future tragedies, many of the companies that purchased apparel from (any) Bangladeshi factories formed organizations to improve safety and working conditions at those factories. A group of 17 major North American retailers, including Walmart, The Gap, Target, and Macy's (several of whom were not directly connected to the factory that collapsed, but to other locations), announced a plan to improve factory safety in Bangladesh. Unfortunately and unlike a separate accord joined mainly by European retailers (such as H&M), the North American plan lacked legally binding commitments to pay for those improvements.

Academic (and coauthor of this text) Chris Mac-Donald explains the conflict between the initial accord and the later agreement in Reading 6-4. One year later, an international watchdog group did find that many of the nation's garment factories were indeed being upgraded, monitoring of safety conditions improved, and new labor laws were making it easier for workers there to organize. Alliance signatories also have committed $42 million to victims' compensation. Of course, Bangladeshi working conditions remain a far cry from those in developed nations.

Sources: Claire O'Connor, "These Retailers Involved in Bangladesh Factory Disaster Have Yet to Compensate Victims," *Forbes* (April 26, 2014), www.forbes.com/sites/clareoconnor/2014/04/26/these-retailers-involved-in-bangladesh-factory-disaster-have-yet-to-compensate-victims/ (accessed February 21, 2016); Bruce Kennedy, "The Bangladesh Factory Collapse One Year Later," *CBS News* (April 23, 2014), www.cbsnews.com/news/the-bangladesh-factory-collapse-one-year-later/ (accessed February 21, 2016).

some core ethical obligations to employees, just as Foxconn owes its employees a commitment both to local Chinese labor laws as well as to Apple's minimum core values. But, in the absence of some specific guidance, how do we determine what those might be? Should the best employment practices in the United States set the standard for the global economy? That would mean concluding that the standards of one particular country are appropriate for all countries and cultures of the world, not necessarily the optimal conclusion.

Instead, some scholars have argued that Kantian universal principles should govern the employment relationship and that the ethical obligation of respect for persons should guide the employment interactions. "To fully respect a person, one must actively treat his or her humanity as an end, and not merely as a means to an end. This means that it is impermissible to treat persons like disposable tools."[54] Though different ethical theories may yield conflicting responses, it is arguable that a fundamental moral minimum set of standards exists that should be guaranteed to workers in all countries notwithstanding culture, stage of economic development, or availability of resources. Philosophers Denis Arnold and Norman E. Bowie contend that multinationals "must ensure the physical well-being of employees and refrain from undermining the development of their rational and moral capacities. . . . [R]especting workers in global factories requires that factories of multinational corporations (MNCs), including contract factories, adhere to local labor laws, refrain from the use of coercion, provide decent working conditions, and provide wages above the overall poverty line for a 48-hour work week."[55] Others contend the list should also include a minimum age for child labor, nondiscrimination requirements (including the right to equal pay for equal work), and free association including the right to organize and to bargain collectively in contract negotiations.[56]

Even defining a "living wage" is problematic. In a world that cannot seem to agree on the number of people living in poverty,[57] figuring out how much is sufficient to offer a subsistence quality of life represents hurdles. A number of companies have implemented living wage policies in their global operations. For example, more than 65 companies (including Burberry, Gap Inc., and The Body Shop International) have joined the Ethical Trade Initiative (ETI), an alliance of corporations, trade unions, and voluntary organizations dedicated to improving the conditions of workers.[58] The ETI has established a "Base Code" of ethical standards that all signatories commit to uphold. The portion of the Base Code addressing living wages states the following:

- Wages and benefits paid for a standard working week meet, at a minimum, national legal standards or industry benchmark standards, whichever is higher. In any event, wages should always be enough to meet basic needs and to provide some discretionary income.

- All workers shall be provided with written and understandable information about their employment conditions with respect to wages before they enter employment and about the particulars of their wages for the pay period concerned each time that they are paid.

- Deductions from wages as a disciplinary measure shall not be permitted nor shall any deductions from wages not provided for by national law be permitted without the expressed permission of the worker concerned. All disciplinary measures should be recorded.

Non-wage benefits are an important and neglected aspect of the debate over global sweatshops. In many instances such benefits can provide an advantage to both the worker and the employer. For example, an MNC factory that provides free health checkups and basic health care services to workers through a factory clinic will typically have a healthier and more productive workforce than factories that lack such benefits. Levi Strauss & Company provides medical services to employees, their families, and members of the surrounding communities. Since 1999, the company's factories have sponsored vaccination, nutrition, and mental health campaigns. Since 2007, Levi Strauss & Co. has participated in HERproject, a partnership of global corporations and local networks that uses peer education to improve existing factory clinic resources by providing low-wage women workers with access to critical health information and services.[59]

Because public health care in the locations where the Levi Strauss factories are located is generally poor, particularly in smaller cities and remote rural areas, companies play a vital role in providing additional assistance. Levi Strauss is not the only company to provide a medical clinic, but one of the few to see the business value of investing in women's health as a pathway to strengthening whole communities.

International nongovernmental organizations have also attempted to step into this fray to suggest voluntary standards to which possible signatory countries or organizations could commit. For instance, the International Labour Office has promulgated its Tripartite Declaration of Principles Concerning Multinational Enterprises and Social Policy, which offers guidelines for employment, training, conditions of work and life, and industrial relations. The "Tripartite" part of the title refers to the critical cooperation necessary from governments, employers' and workers' organizations, and the multinational enterprises involved.

As mentioned earlier, the discussion of legal and ethical expectations and boundaries in this chapter is based on the law in the United States. However, awareness of the limitations of this analysis and sensitivity to the challenges of global implementation are critical in today's multinational business operations. We will revisit the quandary of varying ethical standards as applied to diverse economic and social environments in the next section with regard to the issue of child labor.

The Case of Child Labor

One of the key issues facing business in today's globalized economy is the potential for cultural or legal conflicts in connection with worldwide labor management. Though the issues stir our consciences, their resolution is not so clear. Let us consider, for example, the case of **child labor.** As we begin to understand the circumstances facing children worldwide, we can see that a simple prohibition might not offer us the best possible solution. But what options exist? (For a general inquiry, see the Decision Point "What to Do about Child Labor.")

According to International Labour Office estimates, more than 168 million children between 5 and 17 years old currently work in developing countries, with 85 million of these children performing "hazardous work." The category of hazardous work developed by the ILO includes all forms of labor that adversely affect children's safety, health, or moral development. However, this category is also considered a proxy for the worst forms of child labor for which data are difficult to secure, such as forced and bonded labor, child soldiering, and commercial sexual exploitation.[60] Because work takes children out of school, nation-specific studies show that high levels of child labor are associated with low literacy levels.[61] In addition, regions with a high prevalence of child labor are also characterized by high levels of childhood morbidity associated with HIV/AIDS, non-HIV infectious diseases, and malaria. The harmful effects are not limited to child laborers themselves; because children who work are more likely to earn low wages as adults, the risk that poverty and child labor will be passed to the next generation increases.[62]

child labor
Though the term literally signifies children who work, it has taken on the meaning of exploitative work that involves some harm to a child who is not of an age to justify his or her presence in the workplace. The elements of that definition—harm, age of the child, justification to be in the workplace relative to other options—remain open to social and economic debate. UNICEF's 1997 State of the World's Children Report explains, "Children's work needs to be seen as happening along a continuum, with destructive or exploitative work at one end and beneficial work—promoting or enhancing children's development without interfering with their schooling, recreation and rest—at the other. And between these two poles are vast areas of work that need not negatively affect a child's development."

As you explore the question of child labor that follows, consider the many stakeholders involved and the power each one holds (or lack thereof), the options available to the multinational corporations, and the options consumers have in determining from whom they will buy, what rights might be implicated and the consequences of protecting them, and how you would respond if you were a labor advocate seeking to determine the best next steps in the debate.

- What are the key facts relevant to your decision regarding child labor?
- What are the ethical issues involved in child labor? What incentives might be in place that would actively support or pose challenges to your response?
- Who are the stakeholders in connection with child labor?
- What alternative responses might you suggest?
- How would each of your alternatives affect each of the stakeholders you have identified?
- Is there any guidance available from global organizations to assist you in resolving this particular dilemma?

Of course, employers in many economically developed countries currently use children as laborers, albeit with restrictions (for instance, children are employed in roles on television and in movies, all of the time!); so one should carefully review the social and economic structure within which the labor exists. While the easy answer may be to rid all factories of all workers under 18 years of age, that is often not the best answer for the children or the families involved, depending on the economy in question. Prospects for working children in developing countries are often bleak. Children may begin work as young as three years old. They not only may work in unhealthy conditions; they may also live in unhealthy conditions. The labor opportunities that exist almost always require children to work full time, thereby precluding them from obtaining an education. However, if children are not working, their options are not as optimistic as those of children in developed economies. Sophisticated education systems or public schools are not always available. Often children who do not work in the manufacturing industry are forced to work in less hospitable "underground" professions, such as drug dealing or prostitution, simply to earn their own food each day.[63]

Moreover, even if educational alternatives are available in some environments, recommending removal of the child from the workplace completely ignores the financial impact of the child leaving his or her job. The income the youth worker generates may, at the very least, assist in supporting his or her fundamental needs (food, clothing, and shelter); at the most, it may be critical in supporting the entire family.

Recently, Bolivia became the first country to legalize child labor from the age of 10. While this may seem unconscionable to certain readers throughout the world, lawmakers argue that this law is meant to protect children who are going to be in the workplace—whether it is legal or not. Further, research suggests that legalizing child labor actually may *lower* the number of children who work. Scholars explain that, in environments where child labor is illegal, employers who choose to hire children anyway pay them lower wages because they factor in the cost of the risk of fines for their illegal labor when determining wages. As a result, families often have to send more children to work to make up for that lower wage.

As one article on child labor in Bolivia states, "we would all like, of course, for there to be less child labour, greater safety at work and for all to have greater leisure. But it's necessary for there to be sufficient economic wealth to allow such things before the regulations and legislation happen."[64]

Rights and Responsibilities in Conflict: Discrimination, Diversity, and Affirmative Action

In preceding sections, we explored the ethical environment of several elements of the employment relationship. As explained earlier, the ethical issues discussed in the first section of this chapter are, for the most part, settled. Though our discussion addressed particular areas of outstanding contention, the underlying rights have been established.

In the following section, we consider several matters that scholars, jurists, and corporate leaders continue to debate. The focus is on those subtle areas where the law may not yet be completely settled, where it remains open to diverse cultural interpretations, strong minority opinions, and value judgments. Though the courts have been forced to render judgment in these areas, their decisions might not be unanimous or might reverse a strong lower-court opinion representing a contrary perspective.

From a Kantian, deontological perspective, agreement on the fundamental rights implied by the following issues and on their appropriate prioritization is not yet universal. From a utilitarian viewpoint, reasonable minds engaged in these ethical issues do not always agree on which resolution might lead toward the greatest common good, or even what that good should ultimately be. Distributive justice does not provide a clear-cut solution as each camp can often make an argument for fairness. Our purpose here is to articulate and apply the ethical decision-making process to the challenges presented, provide a cross section of the arguments advocates involved make, and explore the insights that ethical theory might supply.

Discrimination

The courts have carefully construed legal precedent in the decades since Title VII of the United States Civil Rights Act was passed in 1964 and created the prohibited classes of discrimination. Although several specific areas of delicate and subtle quandaries remain, many of the original legal and ethical debates have been fought, offering business decision makers arguably clear guidance on appropriate behavior in the workplace. For instance, while the advent of sexual harassment as a basis for a legal complaint was new to the court system during the last century, seldom does a new recruit begin employment at a large company today without standard sexual harassment training. When the issue was first raised in U.S. workplaces, employees were at a loss about what was or was not acceptable. Today the Equal Employment Opportunity Commission (EEOC),[65] as well as a host of other sources, provides explicit guides and resources detailing appropriate behavior as well as offering legal direction and parameters for both employees and employers. However, perceptions and definitions may continue to vary from culture to culture. (See Reading 6-5, "Sexual Harassment: An Asian Perspective," by G. Chan and G. Shenoy.)

As we have stated throughout this text, the law can only go so far. While it is not our purpose to explore in detail the law relating to workplace discrimination, suffice it to say that the law allows employers to make decisions on *any basis* other than those prohibited by the Constitution, precedent, and several statutes (such as age, religion, race, disability, gender, national origin, color, and, depending on the jurisdiction, sexual orientation). Some commentators would contend that this broad mandate allows employers enormous autonomy in their employment decisions while many employers still bemoan any regulation of their workplaces.

Widespread disagreement on a global basis remains about the rights of employees with regard to discrimination, the extent of protected classes, and the more specific subtopics such as diversity and affirmative action that we will examine shortly. Even in the United States, the concept of discrimination remains one of the most intensely debated issues today. Employers continue to advocate for their rights to manage the workplace and to be permitted to hire, retain, and terminate employees without external influence or control. Employees fear unfair treatment and a loss of power based on reasons completely outside their control. Judge Richard Posner argues in the Decision Point "Who Needs Ethics? Can the Market 'Fix' Discrimination?" how the market might be able to relieve employees of some of these fears—*at least in theory*. The Reality Check "When in Rome . . ." identifies the current application of Judge Posner's theory.

OBJECTIVE

Without diminishing the impact of overt acts of discrimination or their continuation in the workplace, covert forms of discrimination are also widely prevalent, though they often go unnoticed. For instance, University of Chicago scholars Marianne Bertrand and Sendhil Millainathan found that there remains discrimination simply on the basis of one's name.[66] In order to determine the extent of discrimination in the labor market on the basis of the racial sound of a name, these researchers answered help-wanted ads in Boston and Chicago newspapers by submitting résumés that were exactly the same in their substance, but that used different names. The number of callbacks for each résumé differed significantly. Names that were traditionally associated with Caucasians (such as Jill, Allison, Neil, and Brad) drew 50 percent more callbacks than did those traditionally associated with African Americans (such as Aisha, Ebony, Tremayne, and Leroy). Even when the researchers increased the quality of the résumés, higher-quality résumés from candidates who sounded African American received no more callbacks than the original résumé. The only bright spot in the research was the

One approach toward discrimination in employment calls for no corporate or governmental intervention. Defenders of the market argue that if the market were left to its own devices, we could expect discrimination to fall by the wayside. That is, if a firm hires its employees on the basis of prejudices and discriminatory views (such as that women cannot do a certain job), then it is limiting its pool of possible employees. Another firm that does not discriminate can choose from the larger pool and is more likely to obtain the *most* qualified individual for the job. There is therefore an opportunity cost to discrimination. Labor is clearly a factor of production; when we leave productive resources unused, the entire economy suffers. The human capital of women and minorities is lost when we deny them opportunities in the economy. Judge Richard Posner explains the economic impact of this theory in terms of race discrimination as follows:

> In a market of many sellers, the intensity of the prejudice against blacks will vary considerably. Some sellers will have only a mild prejudice against them. These sellers will not forgo as many advantageous transactions with blacks as their more prejudiced competitors (unless the law interferes). Their costs will therefore be lower, and this will enable them to increase their share of the market. The least prejudiced sellers will come to dominate the market in much the same way as people who are least afraid of heights come to dominate occupations that require working at heights: they demand a smaller premium.[67]

Should corporate policymakers and government leave such issues to the market? Should employees' fears or concerns about workplace discrimination be relieved on understanding Judge Posner's theory? Why or why not?

- What key facts do you need to determine whether the market can solve this challenge? Under what circumstances would Posner's argument fail? What market failures might prevent economic forces from efficiently ending discrimination?

- What are some of the other ethical issues that come to mind when you consider this proposed "solution"? What is the effect of regulation such as Title VII on Posner's argument? Even if the market could work against discrimination, is this matter sufficiently important from an ethical perspective that society should address it more actively through legislation?

- Who are the stakeholders involved in this particular issue?

- What alternative responses could you propose? Are you more comfortable with management through legislation or a free market? Consider the implications if the discriminating firm held a monopoly on its good or service.

- How would each of your alternatives affect each of the stakeholders you have identified?

- Where might you look for additional guidance to assist you in resolving this particular dilemma?

- Finally, the United States has more significant antidiscrimination provisions than some other countries, such as those in the Middle East. Is this information in support of or contrary to the judge's proposition?

Reality Check *When in Rome . . .*

In 2011, Delta Air Lines's announcement of an alliance agreement with Saudi Arabian Airlines was received with considerable controversy. Critics raised concerns that the alliance would require Delta to enforce discriminatory Saudi visa requirements, particularly regarding Jewish passengers. The Saudi government prohibits the public practice of any religion but Islam, and the public display of non-Islamic religious items is not permitted. Foreign travelers to Saudi Arabia must be granted a visa by the state to enter the country, and applicants are asked to state their religious affiliation. Visa applicants who hold Israeli passports are barred entry by formal policy. Informally, the U.S. State Department warns that U.S. citizens have reported being denied a Saudi visa "because their passports reflected travel to Israel or indicated that they were born in Israel."[68] Unconfirmed assertions about foreigners being refused entry to the country because they are Jewish were reported in blog postings and news stories critical of the Delta alliance, leading a U.S. senator to call for an investigation to determine if Delta had denied U.S. citizens their right to fly on the sole basis of their religion.[69]

In response to the controversy, Delta released a statement declaring that the airline "does not discriminate nor . . . condone discrimination against any of our customers in regards to age, race, nationality, religion, or gender." However, the statement also included a reminder that all international airlines, including Delta, "are required to comply with all applicable laws governing entry into every country we serve."[70] In light of the possibility that the Saudi visa policy (in practice, if not formally) might discriminate against Jewish and Israeli-affiliated visa applicants, which laws should be of greater ethical and legal concern to Delta—U.S. laws prohibiting discrimination on the basis of religion or Saudi laws that prohibit non-visa holders from entering the country?

Based on circumstances such as these, Congress amended Title VII by the Civil Rights Act of 1991 to include a foreign laws exception. Specifically, the exception permits a U.S. employer to make decisions that would otherwise be discriminatory if it does so in order to avoid violating the laws of a foreign country where a U.S. employee works.[71] The exception applies to Title VII, the Americans with Disabilities Act and the Age Discrimination in Employment Act, thus covering discrimination based on race, national origin, color, religion, pregnancy, gender, age, and disability. Therefore, for instance, requiring a pilot to convert to Islam as a condition of employment, though a clear violation of Title VII in the United States, would be permitted in Saudi Arabia because the local law provides that non-Muslim employees caught flying in Mecca are to be beheaded.[72] To the contrary, a mere preference for males over females in certain positions is not sufficient to warrant the practice.

Where does that leave Delta, if it is faced with the choice of enforcing a discriminatory visa policy or obeying U.S. laws barring discrimination on the basis of religion? In response to criticism, Delta declared that it never will request that its customers disclose their religious affiliation, nor seek such information on behalf of any partner.[73] However, under U.S. law, Delta would likely be permitted to bar a Jewish passenger from a flight to Saudi Arabia *if the passenger's visa had been denied for any reason*—including religious belief, or (to cite another example of Saudi visa policy that conflicts with U.S. law) age (applicants for work visas who are over the age of 50 will be denied). In such situations, Delta would be discriminating, intentionally and legally, on the basis of prohibited categories. In order to do business in this country, what additional options might Delta have? Does it make a difference that Israel also bans those holding Saudi passports from entering the country? If you owned a company that sought to do business in Saudi Arabia, how might you negotiate a conflict between this country's visa policies and the nondiscrimination laws of the United States?

finding that Chicago employers in African American neighborhoods discriminated less than those in other communities.

Discrimination in the United States persists not only with regard to race, but also in connection with gender. Women often face challenges that are distinct from those faced by men. For instance, women and men are both subject to gender stereotyping, but suffer from different expectations in that regard.

Marianne Cooper, sociologist and lead researcher for the *New York Times* best-selling book *Lean In: Women, Work and the Will to Lead* (written by Facebook COO Sheryl Sandburg), explains that success and likability do not go together for women. Often women are "applauded for delivering results at work but then reprimanded for being 'too aggressive,' 'out for herself,' 'difficult,' and 'abrasive.'"[74]

Oddly, a similar catch-22 does not exist for men. Less emotional men are viewed in positive terms— going after what they want, and not letting anything get in their way—and men who demonstrate a bit of emotion are praised for having a softer side and understanding the women's perspective. Cooper uses the example of a former executive editor of the *New York Times,* Jill Abramson. Abramson was described by certain staffers as "impossible to work with," and "not approachable"; yet, the paper won four Pulitzer Prizes under her leadership—the third highest number ever received by the newspaper. There was also speculation that Abramson pushed for pay and pension benefits equal to her predecessor, a man, after discovering the discrepancy. While the pay gap was closed after she complained, the lingering tension with her management was speculated as a major reason for her ultimate termination—a suspect scenario for a company that was once sued by female employees for discriminatory practices.[75]

A study of the effects of gender stereotyping on communication styles adds support to the experiences reported by powerful women.[76] The study found that women who believed that they were being stereotyped on the basis of their gender tended to adopt a more masculine style of communication. However, other test subjects rated these women as less likable and were less likely to follow their leadership.

Diversity

The U.S. workforce today is significantly more diverse than ever before and all data suggest that this will continue. Efforts toward eliminating discrimination in employment over the past 30 years are partially responsible for this change. But a changing population is also a major factor in the increasingly diverse workplace.

Diversity refers to the presence of differing cultures, languages, ethnicities, races, affinity orientations, genders, religious sects, abilities, social classes, ages, and national origins of the individuals in a firm. Eighty percent of employees in U.S. businesses believe they work in a diverse workplace, with 50 percent finding their workplaces to be "very" diverse and 30 percent finding their places of work to be "somewhat" diverse.[77] This is not surprising because the pool of eligible and interested workers is becoming more and more diverse as well. In 2016, only 35.8 percent of the workforce was comprised of white men over 20.[78]

A few European countries have outpaced the United States in terms of diversity efforts and, in particular, in connection with board representation. While the average representation of women on European boards is around 20 percent (a significant increase from 15 percent in 2012), Norway (38.9 percent), Finland (32.1 percent), and France (28.5 percent) are well above that average.[79] One reason for Norway's leadership is a federal law that required companies to fill

diversity
Diversity refers to the presence of differing cultures, languages, ethnicities, races, affinity orientations, genders, religious sects, abilities, social classes, ages, and national origins of the individuals in a firm. When used in connection with the corporate environment, it often encompasses the values of respect, tolerance, inclusion, and acceptance.

OBJECTIVE

Reality Check   *Diversity = Less Risk?*

As you recall from our opening scenario, American Apparel experienced some challenges in connection with sexual harassment allegations against its now departed CEO Dov Charney, among other issues.

Perhaps as a consequence, the firm chose in 2014 to add a woman to its board of directors. Research demonstrates that even *a single woman* has a significant impact on decision making by boards of directors. Scholars who examined decisions and performance of more than 2,000 companies between 1998 and 2011 found that firms that brought on just one woman to a previously all-male board of directors were more risk-averse, spent less on capital expenditure, research and development, and acquisitions; and demonstrated lower volatility in their stock returns.

This research suggests that the addition of a woman, therefore, is not simply a public relations move

but, in addition, can mean a larger financial return for shareholders. One of the coauthors of the study, Ya-wen Yang, explains that diverse boards experience "greater challenges in communicating and accepting one shared decision," so they may not reach consensus as quickly as a homogeneous board. They are therefore more likely to shy away from risks. While these boards may miss a risky venture that could provide benefits in the end, they also could reduce severely unwarranted risks, thereby providing an effective balancing mechanism.

Source: Michael Casey, "Study Finds a Diverse Corporate Boards Rein In Risk, Good for Shareholders," *Fortune* (July 30, 2014), fortune.com/2014/07/30/study-finds-a-diverse-corporate-boards-rein-in-risk-good-for-shareholders (accessed March 8, 2016).

40 percent of corporate board seats with women by 2008; failure to comply would result in a complete shutdown of operations.

Other countries have also set up quotas, including India where, as of 2013, only 4.7 percent of corporate directors were women. In India, a 2013 law requires that any public company with five or more directors must have at least one female board member. Germany passed a law requiring boards to give 30 percent of their supervisory seats to women beginning in 2016; France requires 40 percent of board positions in public companies to be held by women by 2017 (private companies have until 2020); they are joined by Spain, Iceland, Italy, the UK, and Belgium. The United Arab Emirates, with only 1.2 percent female corporate directors as of 2013, now requires that all companies have at least one woman on the board, although there is no deadline for compliance.[80]

The United States does not have any similar requirement and the S&P 500 has 19 percent female representation on its boards (and more than two-thirds have no women of color at all).[81] The business case for gender diversity is strong. One 2014 Credit Suisse study of 28,000 senior managers at over 3,000 companies found that "greater diversity in boards and management is empirically associated with higher returns on equity, higher price / book valuations and superior stock price performance. . . . The average return on equity (ROE) for companies with at least one woman on the board over the [evaluation period] was 16%, four percentage points higher than that of companies with no women on their boards (12%)."[82] The Reality Check "Diversity = Less Risk?" further details how gender diversity can make companies more risk averse, contributing to the bottom line.

Diversity has brought benefits to the workplace, but diversity efforts have also created new conflicts. Recall the definition of diversity given earlier: Diversity

OBJECTIVE

refers to the presence of differing cultures, languages, ethnicities, races, affinity orientations, genders, religious sects, abilities, social classes, ages, and national origins of the individuals in a firm. When a firm brings together individuals with these (or other) differences—often exposing these individuals to such differences for the first time—areas of tension and anxiety may emerge. In addition, the organization is likely to ask its employees to work together toward common goals, on teams, in supervisory or subordinate roles, and in power relationships, all requests that might lead to conflicts or tension even without additional stressors such as cultural challenges.

Diversity can potentially increase several areas of values tension. Where differences are new or strong, *and* where negative stereotypes previously ruled interactions between particular groups, sensitivity to the potential for conflict is necessary.

Another concern involves integrating diverse viewpoints with a preexisting corporate culture. There seems nothing inappropriate about seeking to ensure that workers will support the particular values of a firm, but it might be difficult to do this while also encouraging diversity. Diversity, which might be the source of positive gains for the organization, might also be the source of fundamental differences in values that must be balanced. Some scholars suggest that job applicants be screened with regard to their values, but how can employers do so? Hiring is not an area to be taken lightly, but most firms go with a "gut" instinct about whether or not a job applicant will "fit in." In the same way that you might apply the "can you sleep at night" test to an ethical dilemma after considering all the implications of a decision, you might trust an employment choice to the same test.

It is not discriminatory to refuse to hire someone about whom you simply have a "bad feeling," unless that bad feeling is based on their difference in race or gender. On the other hand, it is vital to be wary of prejudgments based solely on differences in interpretations of culturally based standards. While variance in fundamental standards might justify a sense of a "bad fit" between a potential employer and employee, divergence in culturally based standards such as attire, hairstyles, or manner of speaking might instead be treated differently. Efforts at understanding **multiculturalism** such as acknowledging and promoting diversity through celebration and appreciation of various cultures in the workplace, can serve both to educate and to encourage the benefits linked to diversity efforts.

Honoring diversity or promoting freedoms of expression can certainly be taken to an extreme and go too far. One might imagine the "bad fit," mentioned earlier, where a divergence of cultures between a potential employee and one's clientele will render the hire ineffective. Though the law is slow to catch up to social mores, it does eventually come apace, so these characteristics of diversity are often resolved by statute or other codification. On the other hand, a few gray areas remain.

In considering the American Apparel situation from the opening scenario, you will recall that there is a blurred line between corporate culture, freedom of expression, and the law surrounding sexual harassment. While AA's former CEO,

multiculturalism
Similar to diversity, refers to the principle of tolerance and inclusion that supports the co-existence of multiple cultures, while encouraging each to retain that which is unique or individual about that particular culture.

Dov Charney, contended that his "tone at the top" was simply a philosophy that permeated the company—a sexual energy that was vital to the creativity of the brand—plaintiffs in lawsuits against him and AA offer a different perspective and instead contend that he used his power to exploit. Charney ultimately did lose his CEO position, but one month later was hired back as a "strategic consultant" to AA, while a board committee reviewed the accusations against him to determine whether he could be rehired. As a result, the strong statement against his behavior issued by his termination was substantially reduced through subsequent actions of the AA board.

On the other hand, the cost of ignoring diversity is high, not only in terms of losses of productivity, creativity, and other performance-based measures, but also in terms of legal liability. Though seemingly an old tale, Texaco's experience with what insiders refer to simply as "the crisis" in 1996 offers an instructive lesson. The company was required to pay $175 million to settle a racial discrimination lawsuit that was brought based on taped conversations of executives using racist language—referring to some of their workers as "black jelly beans"—as well as documented compensation below the minimum salary for minorities in a number of positions.

A firm often reaches its depths before it emerges anew, and Texaco's numbers subsequent to the lawsuit tell a much different story. Six years after the settlement, minority hires accounted for 46 percent of all new employees, including some key senior executives, and more than 20 percent of promotions and 34 percent of new hires were women. Texaco pledged to spend at least $1 million with minority and women contractors within five years of the settlement and, of course, diversity training is now mandated for all workers, with management compensation tied to the attainment of success in implementing new initiatives.

These types of cases cross industry lines as well. A group of black financial advisors filed a lawsuit in 2005 against Merrill Lynch alleging that their bosses systematically steered the most profitable business to white employees. They also were able to show that white workers made salaries averaging 43 percent more than black employees at the firm. Eight years later, in 2013, Merrill Lynch agreed to pay $160 million, to be distributed among all black investment brokers and trainees who worked at the firm from mid-2001 to that time (around 1,200 people).

At the time of the suit, black traders made up so few of the firm's staff that Merrill branches in more than half of U.S. states did not even have a single black broker. The suit claimed that Merrill Lynch sometimes relied on stereotypes, once allegedly suggesting that its managers encourage black brokers to "learn to play golf or other activities designed to learn how business gets done in manners (they) might not be familiar with." They also found that, beginning in the first month of the training program for new hires, the company gave more and larger accounts from new customers or retiring brokers to the white trainees. Merrill Lynch has a history of discrimination issues, settling gender discrimination suits in the 1970s and 1990s, plus an ongoing suit over a company training course recommending women employees read a book called *Seducing the Boys Club: Uncensored Tactics from a Woman at the Top.*[83]

There have been no published reports on the impact of the 2013 judgment on the Merrill culture. But, Merrill did agree to take part in a three-year program designed to improve conditions for African American workers. The firm said that the program "will enhance opportunities for financial advisers in the future." The firm was not to distribute accounts to trainees in their first year and committed to placing extra emphasis on the clients trainees bring in on their own. The firm said it would hire two coaches to work with black brokers and two experts, one chosen by the plaintiffs and one by Merrill Lynch, to study the impact of team selection. Finally, all the settlement efforts would be overseen by a council of black brokers. The firm also created new minority recruitment incentives, added an Office of Diversity to the duties of the unit's operating chief, and went on a hiring spree that, for a period, more than doubled the number of black financial advisers.[84] See the Decision Point "Women's Economic Development Programs" for a discussion of Walmart's efforts to respond to its own diversity challenges, and the Reality Check "Bias Interrupters" for other ideas on how to respond to these challenges.

Affirmative Action

affirmative action
A policy or a program that strives to redress past discrimination through the implementation of proactive measures to ensure equal opportunity. In other words, affirmative action is the intentional inclusion of previously excluded groups. Affirmative action efforts can take place in employment environments, education, or other arenas.

reverse discrimination
Decisions made or actions taken against those individuals who are traditionally considered to be in power or the majority, such as white men, or in favor of a historically non-dominant group.

Throughout this chapter, we have discussed the means by which to protect employer interests and employee rights. With regard to the latter, we have focused on employee rights to fair treatment and due process in the workplace. A question arises, however, when we consider balancing those rights with competing employee rights, as may occur in the case of **affirmative action.** The question regarding affirmative action is not necessarily whether a person has a right to fair process in connection with employment but instead whether one has a right to the job in the first place. Does one person deserve a position *more* than another person? For instance, efforts to encourage greater diversity may also be seen as a form of **reverse discrimination:** discrimination against those traditionally considered to be in power or the majority, such as white men. A business that intentionally seeks to hire a candidate from an underrepresented group might be seen as discriminating against white males, for example.

The arguments on both sides of this issue have a tendency toward emotional persuasion. Imagine you are hiring a social worker to serve an overwhelmingly African American community that is currently facing issues, among others, of teen pregnancy. Not only might you argue that you want to hire someone who is African American; you might also want a female social worker who might be better able to speak with the teenage women in that community. On the other hand, in front of you is a 40-year-old white male with a master's degree from an extraordinarily valuable program. He has years of experience in the field and in fact has an adopted African American daughter himself. He claims he can handle the job. In fact, he claims he *deserves* the job. Does he? Does it matter whether he deserves it? Does he have a *right* to the job? Assume you still want the younger African American woman you know is next on your interview list. What is the fairest decision? Fair to whom? Fairest to the young women of your community, to the applicants you are interviewing, or to other stakeholders? How should you decide? What will be the consequences of your decision?

Women's Economic Development Programs

In September 2011, Wal-Mart Stores Inc. announced its Global Women's Economic Power Initiative and planned to invest billions in new programs aimed at women, including a commitment to double its purchases from women-owned businesses by 2016, provide support for training women in factories and farms that supply its stores, and donate $100 million to organizations that foster women's economic development. "We're stepping up our efforts to help educate, source from and open markets for women around the world," said Walmart CEO Mike Duke.

As of 2014, Walmart's women's empowerment work has involved several major collaborations, including partnering with Dress for Success and Goodwill Industries, among others. In total, the Walmart Foundation says that it has contributed a total of $45 million in grants for women's empowerment efforts since it launched its initiative in 2011.

Three months prior to the creation of the initiative, the U.S. Supreme Court dismissed a class-action suit, first filed by six employees in 2001, that alleged systematic gender discrimination in pay and promotion decisions at Walmart, the nation's largest private employer. Representing 1.6 million female Walmart employees and a potential for losses in the billions for the corporation, the case was the biggest sex discrimination class action in history. Although Walmart was victorious in defeating the class-action suit, the Supreme Court decision allows individual employees to file civil actions. In addition, the company faced negative publicity from the high-profile case.

Corporate spokespersons denied any connection between the gender discrimination charges and the launch of the new women's programs. However, some charged that the initiative represents a public relations attempt by Walmart to improve its reputation and, as a Wall Street strategy analyst proposed, "get out in front of any potential future lawsuits."

- What do you believe was Walmart's motivation for the initiative discussed here?
- Who are its key stakeholders for this launch announcement—and for the programs themselves?
- With the current level of giving and the collaborations established, do you think that Walmart is living up to its commitment? What do you believe would be the key components to make this program successful?
- One of the key goals for Walmart's Initiative is "creating the building blocks of success and self-sufficiency for women," and much of its funding goes to highly practical efforts to help women help themselves. Some argue that this objective is in line with Walmart's conservative stance on economic opportunity and demonstrates no acknowledgment or empathy for other economic forces that undermine earning power for low-skilled workers (e.g., race, poverty). Do you think this critique is justified?

Sources: Walmart, "Supplier Diversity," corporate.walmart.com/suppliers/supplier-diversity/ (accessed February 21, 2016); S. Clifford and S. Strom, "Wal-Mart to Announce Women-Friendly Plans," *The New York Times* (September 14, 2011), www.nytimes.com/2011/09/14/business/wal-mart-to-announce-women-friendly-plans.html (accessed February 21, 2016); A. Lutz and M. Boyle, "Wal-Mart Announces Multi-Billion Women's Initiative," *Bloomberg News* (September 14, 2011), www.bloomberg.com/photo/wal-mart-to-announce-multibillion-dollar-women-sinitiative-/101977.html (accessed February 21, 2016); J. Shipps "Teach a Woman to Fish: The Walmart Foundation and Women's Empowerment," *Inside Philanthropy* (October 16, 2014), www.insidephilanthropy.com/home/2014/10/16/teach-a-woman-to-fish-the-walmart-foundation-and-womens-empo.html (accessed February 21, 2016).

Reality Check *Bias Interrupters*

What do you think that companies can do to make work-places fairer, more diverse, and more inclusive? Joan C. Williams, a professor of law at the University of California–Hastings offers three "bias interrupters," basic interventions that can stop bias in its tracks in the workplace.

Williams suggests that companies examine areas of possible bias within their cultures; identify key metrics for tracking the results of interventions; and implement these interrupters on an ongoing basis.

EXAMPLES OF BIAS INTERRUPTERS

Interventions may be as simple as rewriting help-wanted advertisements to remove traditionally masculine words.

Williams offers the example of Google, which redesigned the process by which people receive promotions. Google found that men received promotions far more often than women. The company uncovered one of the reasons: Google had a system that required employees to nominate themselves for promotions and, traditionally, this is

not something that women are socialized to do. In fact, Google found that men routinely nominated themselves at far higher rates than women did.

What did Google do? It changed the culture. Google asked every employee who met promotion requirements to nominate herself or himself and then also asked managers to follow the same model. Also, Google nurtured role models among female senior leaders. It asked these senior women to speak at meetings and also within the women's "employee resource group" to highlight the value and benefits of self-promotion. These efforts created a culture where self-promotion became expected and desirable for everyone. As a result, the difference between male and female promotions diminished.

Source: Katherine Reynolds Lewis, "How to Make Your Company Less Sexist and Racist," *The Atlantic* (March 31, 2015), www.theatlantic.com/business/archive/2015/03/how-to-make-your-company-less-sexist-and-racist/388931/ (accessed February 21, 2016).

Diversity issues raise other less apparent problems. For example, consider a report by the U.S. Commission on Civil Rights that addresses the unique predicament of Asian Americans. The report contends that the typical Asian stereotype of being hardworking, intelligent, and successful is actually a detriment to Asian Americans. This stereotype results in the problems of overlooking poor Asians and preventing successful Asian Americans from becoming more successful. In an article highlighting the report, *Fortune* magazine contends that the problem is really that the commission is "being driven crazy by the fact that Asian Americans have been succeeding essentially *without the benefit of affirmative action.*"[85] Some theorists argue that formal affirmative action measures have often served to create a greater divide rather than to draw people closer.

OBJECTIVE

Let us take a closer look at affirmative action to explore the ethical issues it raises. The term *affirmative action* refers to a policy or a program that tries to respond to instances of past discrimination by implementing proactive measures to ensure equal opportunity today. It may take the form of intentional inclusion of previously excluded groups in employment, education, or other environments.

The use of affirmative action policies in both business and universities has been controversial for decades. In its first discussion of affirmative action in employment, the U.S. Supreme Court found that employers could intentionally include minorities (and thereby exclude others) in order to redress past wrongs. However, the holding was not without restrictions, which have caused confusion. Even today, the law is not clear and we must turn to values systems to provide direction, which we will discuss shortly.

Affirmative action arises in the workplace in three ways. The first way is through legal requirements. Much of the law relating to affirmative action applies only to about 20 percent of the workforce; however, those employees of federal contractors with 50 or more employees are subject to Executive Order 11246, which requires affirmative action efforts to ensure equal opportunity. Second, where Executive Order 11246 does not apply, courts may require "judicial affirmative action" in order to remedy a finding of past discrimination. A third form of affirmative action involves voluntary affirmative action plans, which are plans that employers undertake in order to overcome barriers to equal opportunity. These might include training plans and programs, focused recruiting activity, or the elimination of discrimination that might be caused by hiring criteria that exclude a particular group. A demonstrated underrepresentation of a particular group or a finding of past discrimination is required to justify affirmative action efforts under either of these latter two options.

OBJECTIVE

After a number of legal opinions, employers are left with some basic guidelines for creating these programs and policies. Consider how the following *legal* constraints to an affirmative action program are in line with deontological and teleological frameworks that also support ethical decision making:

1. The affirmative action efforts or policy may not unnecessarily infringe upon the majority employees' rights or create an absolute bar to their advancement.

2. The affirmative action effort or policy may not set aside any positions for women or minorities and may not be construed as quotas to be met.

3. It should unsettle no legitimate, firmly rooted expectation of employees.

4. It should be only temporary in that it is for the purpose of attaining, not maintaining, a balanced workforce.

5. It should represent a minimal intrusion into the legitimate, settled expectations of other employees.

Opponents to affirmative action contend that the efforts do more harm than good, that affirmative action creates ill will and poor morale among workforces. They argue that it translates into current punishment of past wrongs and therefore is inappropriately placed because those who "pay" for the wrongs are unfairly burdened and should not bear the responsibility for the acts of others. Not only white males make this claim. Supreme Court Justice Clarence Thomas writes in his autobiography that the affirmative action program at Yale Law School was responsible for the difficulties he faced in finding a job after graduation. In his view, prospective employees doubted that he was as intelligent as his grades at the Ivy League law school indicated, due to their presumption that he had been favored as an African American student. His Yale law degree was basically worthless, Justice Thomas wrote, because it bore "the taint of racial preference."[86]

In its first ruling on this issue in more than a decade, the Supreme Court addressed affirmative action again through a case of "reverse discrimination" in 2003. While this particular case involved university admissions, American business was a stakeholder in the case as well. The University of Michigan Law School relied on an admissions policy that took into account the ability of each applicant to contribute to the school's social and intellectual life. As part of this criterion, the school considered the applicant's race on the assumption that a diverse student body would contribute to the goals of the law school and that a critical mass of minority students was required to accomplish that goal. Thus, although scores from LSAT tests, undergraduate college grades, letters of recommendation, and other traditional factors were primarily used to grant admission, an applicant's race was also a factor. Two white females who were denied admission brought the lawsuit, arguing that admission of minority students with lower grades and test scores violated their rights to equal treatment.

General Motors Corporation filed an *amicus curiae* ("friend of the court") brief in support of the law school's admission policy. By doing so, GM went out of its way at great expense to identify itself as a business stakeholder and argue publicly in support of affirmative action. In its brief, GM claimed that the need to ensure a racially and ethnically diverse student body was a compelling reason to support affirmative action policies. GM claimed that "the future of American business and, in some measure, of the American economy depends on it." In its own business experience, "only a well educated, diverse workforce, comprising people who have learned to work productively and creatively with individuals from a multitude of races and ethnic, religious, and cultural backgrounds, can maintain America's competitiveness in the increasingly diverse and interconnected world economy." Prohibiting affirmative action likely "would reduce racial and ethnic diversity in the pool of employment candidates from which the nation's businesses can draw their future leaders, impeding businesses' own efforts to achieve and obtain the manifold benefits of diversity in the managerial levels of their work forces."[87]

The court seemed to agree.

> Diminishing the force of such stereotypes is both a crucial part of the Law School's mission, and one that it cannot accomplish with only token numbers of minority students. Just as growing up in a particular region or having particular professional experiences is likely to affect an individual's views, so too is one's own, unique experience of being a racial minority in a society, like our own, in which race unfortunately still matters. The Law School has determined, based on its experience and expertise, that a "critical mass" of underrepresented minorities is necessary to further its compelling interest in securing the educational benefits of a diverse student body.[88]

In a case challenging the admissions policies of the University of Texas in 2013, the U.S. Supreme Court upheld the idea that race-conscious selection can be constitutionally permissible in states that wish to use it. However, in 2014 the Supreme Court upheld a Michigan constitutional amendment that bans affirmative action in admissions to the state's public universities (an amendment that passed as a result of its prior 2013 decision). This decision opened the door to similar amendments in seven other states. As a result, states that forbid affirmative action in higher education, such as Florida and California as well as Michigan, have seen

Opening Decision Point Revisited
American Apparel: Image Consciousness?

American Apparel is not the only company criticized for using controversial, sexualized imagery to sell its products. British advertising regulators have censored others for appearing to sexualize underage girls in their ads, including Coca-Cola's Oasis brand beverage company and designer Marc Jacobs. In the 1990s, Calvin Klein ads were charged with glamorizing "heroin chic" with its use of very thin models depicted in gritty, urban settings. More recently, a Calvin Klein billboard in Manhattan drew controversy when it appeared to show three seminude teens in the midst of a sexual encounter. Such ad campaigns are often criticized for pushing the envelope of cultural norms, but they are sometimes—as in the case of American Apparel—successful in securing a brand's identification with young, urban trend-setters. Nor is Dov Charney, the company's founder, alone in using perceived physical beauty as a factor in hiring decisions. Studies have shown that both employers, when hiring, and consumers, when purchasing from salespeople, display a bias toward those seen as more physically attractive.[89] While American Apparel may have gone further than other companies in its provocative advertising and promotion of its CEO's personal tastes, Charney's risqué ad campaigns and provocative, highly visible lifestyle were largely responsible for the company's earlier financial and reputational success but also are at the root of the company's current problems. Analysts are charging that many factors that brought the company success are responsible for its current struggles.

When one explores the impact of American Apparel's corporate culture, it is interesting to consider both sides of the stakeholder opinions. Charney's critics accused him of creating a brand and retail image that borders on the pornographic, inappropriately sexualizing young women—with several plaintiffs alleging that the advertisements mirror a highly sexualized corporate culture in which misconduct was rampant. However, Charney and his defenders felt that employees who sought jobs at AA should understand that the culture of the company reflected the style of the brand, a style that, while controversial, attracted young, trend-conscious consumers. One of the values in a diverse workforce is the ability to weigh varying stakeholder perspectives. While one group or individual might consider a marketing campaign or a sexualized corporate environment to be "pushing the envelope" in a cutting-edge fashion, another might be brutally pained by the imagery or find such a working environment to be hostile. A greater diversity among decision makers certainly does not guarantee that all perspectives are represented, but it does ensure that a broader range of opinions might be considered.

Now that Charney is no longer with AA, it might benefit from a broader range of opinions on a variety of matters. Efforts by AA to appeal to a more diverse audience of women in order to repair its public reputation have met with mixed results. An online, audience-judged, plus-sized modeling contest on the company's website garnered more than 1,000 submissions. However, online voters selected a plus-sized blogger who mocked AA for running what she perceived as an offensive marketing campaign that tried "to use one fat girl as a symbol of apology and acceptance to a demographic it had long insisted on ignoring, while simultaneously having that girl (and a thousand other girls) shill their product."[90] AA chose not to hire the winner for its campaign, a decision that led to further negative publicity.

a significant drop in the enrollment of black and Hispanic students in their most selective colleges and universities.[91]

Do you believe that a diverse student body contributes to the ability of a school to accomplish its educational mission? Should the law prohibit, allow, or require affirmative action programs? Would General Motors be ethically correct in adopting a similar affirmative action hiring policy? Can you think of cases in which an employee's race or ethnic background would be a qualification—or a disqualification—for employment? Given the most recent cases discussed, do you think the Court effectively has dismissed affirmative action as an option for college admissions committees?

Questions, Projects, and Exercises

1. Maya confides in her friend and colleague, Alicia, "My husband Gene is very sick. I haven't shared this with anyone else at work because I didn't want them to think I couldn't manage my responsibilities. He was diagnosed last year with progressive Parkinson's and I thought it would move slowly, and that I could handle everything. Believe me, I am trying to keep everything under control, but our home life is just overwhelming me already. You couldn't imagine how hard this is—physically and emotionally—plus there's the added pressure of keeping it under wraps at work. You know they'll start diminishing my role on those larger projects if they knew my attention might be diverted, and Gene and I just can't risk the financial instability that it might cause. I really appreciate being able to talk to you. I had to get this off my chest, and I knew I could trust you." Alicia offered her shoulder and told Maya that she could count on her to cover for her, if need be, or to support her in any way she needed. Three weeks later, Alicia and Maya are separately called into the president's office and told that they are both being considered for a more senior-level position. This new position would require a great commitment of both time and energy and would involve taking on a large number of subordinates for mentoring and development. Both women express a strong interest in the position and are told that they will learn of the president's decision within two weeks. What should Alicia do with the information Maya gave her, if anything? Notwithstanding your response to the previous question, if Alicia chooses to inform the president of Maya's current situation, would you consider that action to be wrong, unethical? If you were the president in this current scenario, what could you do to impact the corporate culture to ensure that your preferred result in this dilemma occurred in the future?

2. Review the earlier discussion regarding global labor challenges. Choose a specific issue, such as child labor or sweatshop labor. Go online and find a news story about a particular company accused of employing child labor or sweatshop labor. How did the company involved defend itself against the accusations? Did it deny involvement in those practices or, rather, defend the practices themselves? Do you find the company's defense convincing? Why or why not? Would a different defense be more plausible?

3. We can distinguish due process from just cause in the following way: Imagine a company wanted to abandon the arbitrary nature of employment at will and ensure that its employees were treated fairly in any termination decision. Can you imagine how the employment environment in that firm might be different than in other firms? One

approach would be to specify the acceptable reasons for terminating an employee. Obvious candidates would include absenteeism, incompetent job performance, theft, fraud, and economic necessity. This approach might also identify unacceptable reasons for dismissal. Such a policy would be identified as a "just cause" practice because it defines the factors that would justify dismissing an employee for cause. But creating such a list could be a challenge in that one would have to know beforehand all possible reasons for firing someone. As the common law clearly shows, one cannot anticipate all future ways in which something unjust could occur. As a result, a due process policy might be created to complement, or substitute for, a just cause policy. A policy guaranteeing due process, for example, would outline procedures that must be followed before an employee can be dismissed. The process itself is what determines a just dismissal. If an employer followed the process, the decision would be considered just; if the process was violated, then dismissal would be considered unjust. Such procedures might include regular written performance appraisals, prior warnings, documentation, probationary periods, rights to appeal, or response to accusations. Can you imagine other ways in which this hypothetical firm might change standard processes to ensure fairness?

- What are the key facts relevant to issues of due process and fairness?
- What are the ethical issues involved in your decision and implementation?
- Who are the stakeholders involved in your decision?
- What alternatives are available to you?
- How would each of your alternatives affect each of the stakeholders you have identified?
- Where might you look for additional guidance to assist you in resolving this particular dilemma?

4. What is the difference in your mind and in your common usage, between a perception, a generalization, and a stereotype? Can you give an example of each? After doing so, go to the web and find dictionary-equivalent definitions of the terms to determine whether your common understanding is the correct one. Are each or all consistently unethical judgments or are they sometimes or always ethically justified in their use and implementation? Under what conditions?

5. A particular research study provides some evidence that those born between 1979 and 1994 are perceived as "impatient, self-serving, disloyal, unable to delay gratification and, in short, feeling that they are entitled to everything without working for it." The study dubs this group the "entitlement generation." Do you know people born during those years? Is this true generally or would you consider the perception instead a stereotype? From where do you think it stems?

6. As a result of rising health care costs and the challenge to contain them, companies are trying to encourage employees to take better care of themselves, and some are even penalizing employees if they do not. In 2012, Wal-Mart Inc. started charging tobacco-using employees higher health care premiums, but also offered free smoking cessation programs to all employees. While the Patient Protection and Affordable Care Act (passed in 2012) prohibits health insurers from rejecting people with preexisting conditions, it still allows insurers to charge higher premiums based on risk factors such as age, location, family composition, and tobacco use. Tobacco use carries the heaviest penalties, allowing insurers to charge premium rates as much as 50 percent higher for smokers than nonsmokers under the law. A survey conducted by a consulting firm

and the National Business Group on Health reports that about 40 percent of American employers reward or penalize employees based on tobacco use (smoke and smokeless). In addition, a growing number of companies are refusing to hire smokers. What do you think of businesses attempts to decrease health care costs by helping employees become healthier? What are the ethical issues associated with a firms choice to cut health care costs by eliminating people who are unhealthy? What rights, duties, responsibilities, and consequences does this strategy imply? Do you think people who don't take care of themselves should be responsible for their increased health care costs? How would you feel personally if your past health conditions and current health practices were part of an employment application?

7. You run a small consulting business that serves a relatively diverse community and have 24 employees in professional positions. You are not subject to Executive Order 11246. You are concerned that, of the employees in professional positions, your workplace has only 1 African American, no other employees of color, and 3 women. At this time, your upper-level management—the top 6 executives and you—are all white males. On the other hand, you have 15 support staff (secretaries and other clerical workers), of whom 14 are women and 11 are either African American or Latino.

   You would very much like to better represent the community in which you do business and you believe a diverse workforce has significant business benefits. You therefore decide to institute a program that will increase the numbers of minorities and women in professional positions as soon as possible. Is this permissible? Do you have all the relevant facts you will need to answer this question? What steps will you undertake in your plan to increase these proportions and what pitfalls must you avoid?

8. You are a senior global human resource manager for a large apparel retailer that purchases goods from all over the world. The media have focused a great deal of attention on the conditions of your suppliers workplaces and, for myriad reasons including a strong commitment to your values-based mission as well as a concern for your reputation, you are paying close attention to the wages paid to the workers who construct your clothing. Your suppliers in several locations have agreed to talk with you about developing a policy that would apply throughout your operations—now and in the future, wherever you plan to do business—and would impose a minimum wage requirement for all factory workers. You begin to explore some of the resources publicly available to you, such as www.globalexchange.org, www.workersrights.org, www.fairlabor.org, and www.ethicaltrade.org/, to find out what other firms are doing and what labor advocates recommend in terms of language for policies such as these. You explore Nike's website at www.nikeinc.com, www.adidas-group.com, and others. Now it is time to begin constructing your own policy. What will you include, how specific will you make this policy, how will you determine what will be the "living wage" in each region, and what elements will it contain? Please draft a policy for your company on implementing a living wage worldwide.

9. As a project manager, Kelly is leading a team on an international business trip where she is scheduled to do a presentation on its project and to negotiate a deal. Just a few days before the trip, Kelly gets a call asking whether she is willing to let a male member of her team do all the talking because the managers at the company with whom they were planning to do business feel more comfortable dealing with men. Kelly is told that she would still be in charge and that this would never happen again. If this deal works out, it would prove very profitable for the company as well as for Kelly's career. Kelly thinks about the situation in which she finds herself; she has worked very hard on this

project and, if the deal is successful, she is bound to get a promotion. On the other hand, she feels discriminated against based on the fact that she is a woman. She has the choice of acting on her principles and calling off the deal, or going ahead with this modification on a "one-time basis" and getting a promotion. After contemplating the issue for a while, she decides to go ahead with the deal and let someone else do all the talking. When they get back she is promoted and everybody is happy. What do you think of Kelly's decision? Could this situation be prevented all together? If you were in a similar situation what would you choose to do, and why?

10. *Fortune* magazine compiles a "Best Companies to Work For" list every year. Go to its website, http://fortune.com/best-companies/, and review the full list. See if you can spot trends or similarities, if any, among the listed companies and find policies or programs that you think may help attract employees.

Key Terms

After reading this chapter, you should have a clear understanding of the following key terms. For a complete definition, please see the Glossary.

affirmative action, *p. 262*
child labor, *p. 252*
common-law agency test, *p. 234*
diversity, *p. 258*
downsize, *p. 236*
due process, *p. 230*

economic realities test, *p. 234*
employment at will (EAW), *p. 233*
IRS 20-factor analysis, *p. 234*
just cause, *p. 233*

multiculturalism, *p. 260*
Occupational Safety and Health Administration (OSHA), *p. 245*
reverse discrimination, *p. 262*
sweatshops, *p. 248*

Endnotes

1. E. Benjamin Skinner, "A World Enslaved," *Foreign Policy* (March/April 2008), www.foreignpolicy.com/story/cms.php?story_id=4173 (accessed August 11, 2011).

2. Elizabeth Harris and Steven Greenhouse, "The Road to Dov Charney's Ouster at American Apparel," *The New York Times* (June 26, 2014), www.nytimes.com/2014/06/27/business/road-to-dov-charneys-ouster-at-american-apparel.html (accessed February 20, 2016).

3. Elizabeth Harris and Steven Greenhouse, "The Road to Dov Charney's Ouster at American Apparel," *The New York Times* (June 26, 2014), www.nytimes.com/2014/06/27/business/road-to-dov-charneys-ouster-at-american-apparel.html (accessed February 21, 2016).

4. Ibid.

5. The text of the revised code of ethics can be seen here: http://files.shareholder.com/downloads/APP/3734914605x0x169419/1a4a6647-1fe0-4570-8a2d-314af2a955f8/AA__Code_of_Ethics.pdf (accessed February 21, 2016); see also J. Kell, "American Apparel Updates Its Ethics Code after Ousting Charney," *Fortune* (January 6, 2015), http://fortune.com/2015/01/06/american-apparel-new-ethics-code/ (accessed January 7, 2015); M. Townsend, "American Apparel Adds Sex-Harassment Rules after Firing CEO," *Bloomberg News* (January 6, 2015), www.bloomberg.com/news/2015-01-06/american-apparel-bolsters-harassment-rules-after-firing-charney.html (accessed January 7, 2015).

6. H. Tabuchi, "SEC Is Investigating Dov Charney's Departure," *The New York Times* (March 25, 2015), p. B2, www.nytimes.com/2015/03/26/business/dov-charney-in-sec-investigation-american-apparel-says.html?_r=0 (accessed February 21, 2016).

7. J. Wolfe, "And You Thought Abercrombie & Fitch Were Pushing It?," *The New York Times* (April 23, 2006), www.nytimes.com/2006/04/23/magazine/23apparel. html?pagewanted 51 (accessed August 11, 2012).

8. N. Casey, "American Apparel Bares All," *The Wall Street Journal* (April 12, 2008), http://online.wsj.com/article/SB120796037535209509.html?mod5googlewsj (accessed August 11, 2012).

9. Susanna Kim, "American Apparel Re-Hires Fired Founder as Consultant," *ABC News* (July 10, 2014), http://abcnews.go.com/Business/american-apparel-hires-fired-founder-contractor/story?id=24510118 (accessed February 21, 2016).

10. Kai Ryssdal and Bridget Bodnar, "A New CEO and New Strategy for American Apparel," *Marketplace* (February 17, 2016), www.marketplace.org/2016/02/17 /business/new-ceo-and-new-strategy-american-apparel (accessed March 9, 2016).

11. A. Edmans, "Does the Stock Market Fully Value Intangibles? Employee Satisfaction and Equity Prices" (December 30, 2008), http://papers.ssrn.com/sol3/papers.cfm?abstract_ id5985735 (accessed August 11, 2012); see also Purdue University News, "Purdue Research Links Employee Satisfaction, Profits" (September 14, 2004), www.purdue. edu/uns/html4ever/2004/040913.Oakley.sat.html (accessed October 12, 2011).

12. Metlife, "9th Annual Study of Employee Benefits Trends" (2011), www.metlife.com /business/insights-and-tools/industry-knowledge/employee-benefits-trends-study /index.html#highlights (accessed October 14, 2011).

13. Ethics Resource Center, "2013 National Business Ethics Survey" (2013), www.ethics .org/nbes (accessed February 22, 2016).

14. Ethics Resource Center, "2013 National Business Ethics Survey" (2013), www .ethics.org/nbes (accessed February 21, 2016); Christine, Porath, and Christine Pearson, "The Price of Incivility," *Harvard Business Review* 91, no. 1/2 (2013), pp. 114–121.

15. Ethics Resource Center, "2009 National Business Ethics Survey: Supplemental Research Brief: Reporting" (2009), www.ethics.org/page/nbes-supplemental-research-briefs (accessed October 17, 2011).

16. Chen Chen, Yangyang Chen, and Edward J. Podolski, "Does Employee Treatment Facilitate Corporate Innovative Success? Evidence from Patent Data" (June 30, 2014), available at SSRN: http://ssrn.com/abstract=2461021 (accessed September 7, 2014); Sun Young Sung and Jin Nam Choi, "Workforce Diversity in Manufacturing Companies and Organizational Performance: The Role of Status-Relatedness and Internal Processes," UCLA: The Institute for Research on Labor and Employment (2013), http://escholarship.org/uc/item/9r68v14v (accessed September 21, 2015).

17. For a curious legal case on this question, see *Sampath v. Concurrent Tech.,* No. 08-2370 (3d Cir. November 14, 2008), www.ca3.uscourts.gov/opinarch/082370np. pdf (accessed August 11, 2012) ["Title VII does not 'mandate a happy workplace.'"]; and *Jensen v. Potter,* 435 F.3d 444, 451 (3d Cir. 2006), overruled in part on other grounds by *Burlington N. & Santa Fe Ry. Co. v. White,* 548 U.S. 53 (2006).

18. Jeffrey Pfeffer, "Shareholders First? Not So Fast . . . ," *Harvard Business Review* 87 no. 7/8 (2009); see also Jeffrey Pfeffer, *The Human Equation: Building Profits by Putting People First* (Boston: Harvard University Press, 1998).

19. Neal M. Ashkanasy, W. J. Zerbe, and Charmine E. J. Härtel, *Emotions and the Organizational Fabric* (Bingley, UK: Emerald, 2014), www.emeraldinsight. com/1746-9791/10 (accessed February 21, 2016).

20. Organization for Economic Cooperation and Development, "Trade Union Density," http://stats.oecd.org/Index.aspx?DatasetCode5UN_DEN (accessed August 11, 2012).

21. Milla Sanes and John Schmitt, "Regulation of Public Sector Collective Bargaining in the States," Center for Economic and Policy Research (March, 2014), www.cepr.net /documents/state-public-cb-2014-03.pdf (accessed February 21, 2016).

22. Julia Edwards, "Union Protests Spread across the U.S." *NationalJournal.com* (April 8, 2011), www.nationaljournal.com/union-protests-spread-across-the-u-s-20110408 (accessed February 21, 2016).

23. *Harris v. Quinn,* 134 S. Ct. 2618 (2014); see also www.scotusblog.com/case-files /cases/harris-v-quinn/ (accessed February 21, 2016).

24. "Timeline: Tracking Europe's Debt Crisis," *CBC News* (October 2, 2013), www .cbc.ca/news2/interactives/europe-debt-crisis-timeline/ (accessed September 19, 2015); "Anti-austerity Protest in Italy Turns Violent," *Al Jazeera* (April 13, 2014), www.aljazeera.com/news/europe/2014/04/anti-austerity-protest-italy-turns-violent-20144122357869885.html (accessed September 19, 2015); "Anti-austerity Protesters March in Spain," *Al Jazeera* (March 23, 2014), www.aljazeera.com/news /europe/2014/03/anti-austerity-protesters-march-spain-2014322192956618925.html (accessed September 19, 2015).

25. "2014 WBI Workplace Bullying Survey," Workplace Bullying Institute (2014), www .workplacebullying.org/wbiresearch/wbi-2014-us-survey/ (accessed February 24, 2016).

26. "2014 WBI Workplace Bullying Survey," Workplace Bullying Institute (2014), www .workplacebullying.org/wbiresearch/wbi-2014-us-survey/ (accessed September 13, 2014).

27. Roy Maurer, "Workplace-Bullying Laws on the Horizon?" (July 16, 2013), Society for Human Resource Management, www.shrm.org/hrdisciplines/safetysecurity/articles /pages/workplace-bullying-laws.aspx (accessed September 19, 2014).

28. The Healthy Workplace Bill (September 18, 2014), http://healthyworkplacebill.org/ (accessed February 24, 2016).

29. Kathleen Ronayne, "NH Gov. Veto of Partial Workplace Bullying Bill Holds," *The Boston Globe* (September 18, 2014), www.bostonglobe.com/metro/2014/09/17 /lawmakers-uphold-veto-workplace-bullying-bill/9HZdQ8Lu7iAIzF6NfqWR6H /story.html (accessed February 24, 2016).

30. Adam Rubenfire, "First State Workplace Bullying Law Has Few Fans," *The Wall Street Journal* Online Blog (June 20, 2014), http://blogs.wsj.com/atwork/2014/06/20 /first-state-workplace-bullying-law-has-few-fans/ (accessed February 24, 2016).

31. "2014 WBI Workplace Bullying Survey," Workplace Bullying Institute (2014), www .workplacebullying.org/wbiresearch/wbi-2014-us-survey/ (accessed September 19, 2015).

32. V. J. Roscigno, S. H. Lopez, and R. Hodson, "Supervisory Bullying, Status Inequalities and Organizational Context," *Social Forces* 87, no. 3 (2009); F. Bulutlar and E. Ü. Öz, "The Effects of Ethical Climates on Bullying Behaviour in the Workplace," *Journal of Business Ethics* 86, no. 3 (2009); M. Harvey, D. Treadway, J. T. Heames, and A. Duke, "Bullying in the 21st Century Global Organization: An Ethical Perspective," *Journal of Business Ethics* 85, no. 1 (2009); D. Nishi, "What to Do If Your Boss Is the Problem," *The Wall Street Journal* (April 20, 2010); T. Parker-Pope, "When the

Bully Sits in the Next Cubicle," *The New York Times* (March 25, 2008); C, Tuna, "Lawyers and Employers Take the Fight to 'Workplace Bullies,'" *The Wall Street Journal* (August 4, 2008).

33. D. Yamada, "Workplace Bullying and Ethical Leadership," *Legal Studies Research Paper Series, 08-37* (November 14, 2008), http://ssrn.com/abstract=1301554 (accessed February 21, 2016).

34. Pedro Neves, "Taking It out on Survivors: Submissive Employees, Downsizing, and Abusive Supervision," *Journal of Occupational and Organizational Psychology* 87, no. 3 (2014), pp. 507–534.

35. *Payne v. Western & A.A.R. Co.,* 81 Tenn. 507 (1884).

36. *Slayman v. FedEx,* Nos. 12-35525 and 12-35559, http://cdn.ca9.uscourts.gov /datastore/opinions/2014/08/27/12-35525.pdf; *Alexander v. FedEx,* Nos. 12-17458 and 12-17509, 9th Cir.; 2014 U.S. App. LEXIS 16585, http://cdn.ca9.uscourts.gov /datastore/opinions/2014/08/27/12-17458.pdf.

37. *FedEx Home Delivery v. NLRB,* 563 F.3d 492 (D.C. Cir. 2009).

38. P. H. Werhane et al., *Women in Business: The Changing Face of Leadership* (New York: Greenwood Publishing, 2007).

39. C. Lakshman, A. Ramaswami, R. Alas, J. F. Kabongo, and J. R. Pandian, "Ethics Trumps Culture? A Cross-National Study of Business Leader Responsibility for Downsizing and CSR Perceptions," *Journal of Business Ethics Online* (October 4, 2013), http://link.springer.com/article/10.1007%2Fs10551-013-1907-8.

40. José Luis Illueca García-Labrado, "Ethics and Restructuring: Promising Match or Marriage of Convenience?," *IESE Business School: Business Ethics Blog* (January 24, 2014), http://blog.iese.edu/ethics/2014/01/24/ethics-and-restructuring-promising-match-or-marriage-of-convenience/ (accessed February 21, 2016).

41. Leadership IQ, "Don't Expect Layoff Survivors to Be Grateful" (December 10, 2008), available at *PRWeb,* www.prweb.com/releases/Leadership_IQ/Layofs/prweb1754974 .htm (accessed February 21, 2016).

42. C. Tuna, "Some Firms Cut Costs without Resorting to Layoffs," *The Wall Street Journal* (December 15, 2008), http://online.wsj.com/article/SB122929306421405071. html (accessed February 21, 2016); see also Hypertherm, Inc. Company Fact Sheet, www.hypertherm.com/en-us/About_us/News_and_media/company_fact_sheet.jsp (accessed February 21, 2016).

43. R. Barrett, "No Lay Offs at Nucor, Despite Bad Economy," *Milwaukee Journal Sentinel* (May 22, 2010), www.jsonline.com/business/93960929.html (accessed February 21, 2016); see also Nucor Corporation, "Benefits," www.nucor.com/careers /benefits/(accessed February 21, 2016).

44. Andrew Martin, "No Lay-Off Company Now Writes Profit Sharing Checks," *The New York Times* (December 21, 2012), www.nytimes.com/2012/12/22/business/marvin-windows-and-doors-offers-workers-profit-sharing-checks.html (accessed February 21, 2016); Andrew Martin, "Housing Slump Forces Cuts at Small Town Company," *The New York Times* (September 11, 2011), www.nytimes.com/2011/09/25/business/economy /housing-slump-forces-cuts-at-a-small-town-company.html?pagewanted=all (accessed February 21, 2016).

45. Leadership IQ, "Don't Expect Layoff Survivors to Be Grateful" (December 10, 2008), www.prweb.com/releases/Leadership_IQ/Layoffs/prweb1754974.htm (accessed February 21, 2016).

46. R. S. Larsen, "Leadership in a Values-Based Organization," *The Sears Lectureship in Business Ethics at Bentley College* (February 7, 2002).

47. B. Wilson, "Clinical Studies Conducted Outside of the United States and Their Role in the FDA's Drug Marketing Approval Process," *University of Pennsylvania Journal of International Law* 34, no. 3 (August 2013); Latham & Watkins, "FDA Offers New Guidance on Acceptance of Foreign Clinical Trials," *Client Alert* #1325 (April 23, 2012); D. L. Barnett and J. B. Steele, "Deadly Medicine," *Vanity Fair* (January 2011), www.vanityfair.com/politics/features/2011/01/deadly-medicine-201101 (accessed February 21, 2016).

48. U.S. National Institutes of Health, "Map of All Studies in ClinicalTrials.gov," ClinicalTrials.gov, http://clinicaltrials.gov/ct2/search/map (accessed February 21, 2016).

49. "Safety and Health Add Value," OSHA Publication 3180 (n.d.), www.osha.gov/dcsp /products/topics/businesscase/benefits.html (accessed February 24, 2016); K. Baicker, D. Cutler, and Z. Song, "Workplace Wellness Programs Can Generate Savings," *Health Affairs* 29, no. 2 (2010). doi: 10.1377/hlthaff.2009.0626.

50. U.S. Department of Labor, "News Release: OSHA Issues Record-Breaking Fines to BP" (2009), www.osha.gov/pls/oshaweb/owadisp.show_document?p_table 5NEWS_ RELEASES&p_id516674 (accessed February 21, 2016).

51. Craig Karmin, "Off-shoring Can Generate Jobs in the U.S.," *The Wall Street Journal,* March 16, 2004; Nicholas Kristof, "Where Sweatshops Are a Dream," *The New York Times* (January 15, 2009), www.nytimes.com/2009/01/15/opinion/15kristof.html (accessed October 22, 2011).

52. Benjamin Powell and Matt Zwolinski, "The Ethical and Economic Case against Sweatshop Labor: A Critical Assessment," *Journal of Business Ethics* 107, no. 4 (2012), pp. 449–472.

53. Ibid.

54. D. Arnold and L. Hartman, "Worker Rights and Low Wage Industrialization: How to Avoid Sweatshops," *Human Rights Quarterly* 28, no. 3 (August 2006), pp. 676–700.

55. Denis G. Arnold and Norman E. Bowie, "Sweatshops and Respect for Persons," *Business Ethics Quarterly* 221 (2003), pp. 223–224.

56. L. Hartman, B. Shaw, and R. Stevenson, "Exploring the Ethics and Economics of Global Labor Standards: A Challenge to Integrated Social Contract Theory," *Business Ethics Quarterly* 13, no. 2 (2003), pp. 193–220.

57. P. Werhane, S. Kelley, L. Hartman, and D. Moberg, *Alleviating Poverty Through Profitable Partnerships: Globalization, Markets and Economic Well-Being* (New York: Routledge/Taylor & Francis, 2009), chap. 1.

58. Ethical Trade Initiative, "About ETI," "Members," and "What Companies Sign Up To," www.ethicaltrade.org (accessed February 21, 2016).

59. "HERProject: Investing in Women for a Better World" (2010), http://herproject.org/ (accessed October 5, 2015).

60. International Labour Organization, "Marking Progress against Child Labour: Global Estimates and Trends 2000–2012" (2013), www.ilo.org (accessed March 2, 2016).

61. P. Dorman, "Child Labour, Education and Health: A Review of the Literature" (2008), International Labour Office, www.ilo.org (accessed October 5, 2015).

62. P. Roggero, V. Mangiaterra, F. Bustreo, and F. Rosati, "The Health Impact of Child Labor in Developing Countries: Evidence from Cross-Country Data," *American Journal of Public Health* 97, no. 2 (2007). doi: 10.2105/AJPH.2005.066829.

63. However, some advocacy groups fail to consider all perspectives. For example, the Global Reporting Initiative's discussion on its Child Labour Indicators fails to take into account the impact of the termination of children beyond their removal from the workplace.

64. Tim Worstall, "Bolivia Legalises Child Labour and Child Labour Might Decline in Bolivia," *Forbes* (July 21, 2014), www.forbes.com/sites/timworstall/2014/07/21/bolivia-legalises-child-labour-and-child-labour-might-decline-in-bolivia/ (accessed February 21, 2016).

65. EEOC, "Sexual Harassment" (n.d.), www.eeoc.gov/laws/types/sexual_harassment.cfm (accessed November 7, 2011).

66. Marianne Bertrand and Sendhil Millainathan, "Are Emily and Brendan More Employable Than Lakisha and Jamal?," *American Economic Review* 94 (2002). doi:10.1257/0002828042002561.

67. Richard A. Posner, *Economic Analysis of Law* (New York: Aspen, 2002), p. 616.

68. "Saudi Arabia: Country Specific Information," Travel.State.Gov: A Service of the Bureau of Consular Affairs (n.d.), http://travel.state.gov/travel/cis_pa_tw/cis/cis_1012.html#safety (accessed November 5, 2011).

69. H. Sampson, "Delta, Saudis Deny Accusations of Discrimination," *Miami Herald* (June 27, 2011), www.miamiherald.com/2011/06/25/2287492/delta-saudis-deny-accusations.html (accessed November 5, 2011); H. L. Krieger, "Senator Urges Probe of Delta–Saudi Airline Discrimination," *Jerusalem Post* (June 25, 2011), www.jpost.com/JewishWorld/JewishNews/Article.aspx?id5226480 (accessed November 5, 2011); J. Freed, "Delta Criticized over Visas to Saudi Arabia," *ABC News*/Associated Press (June 25, 2011), http://abcnews.go.com/Business/wireStory?id513926018#.TrWuAXFD2tcn (accessed November 5, 2011).

70. H. Sampson, "Delta, Saudis Deny Accusations of Discrimination," *Miami Herald* (June 27, 2011), www.miamiherald.com/2011/06/25/2287492/delta-saudis-deny-accusations.html (accessed November 5, 2011).

71. 42 U.S.C. §§ 2000e-1(b), 12112(c)(1); 29 U.S.C. § 630(f)(1). See also EEOC Enforcement Guidance, N-915.002.

72. *Kern v. Dynalectron Corp.,* 577 F. Supp. 1196, 1200-01 (N.D. Tex. 1983).

73. Simon Wiesenthal Center, "Delta Air/Saudi Controversy: After Meeting at SWC, Delta Formally Declares: 'We Will Not Request . . . Religious Affiliation'" (August 22, 2011), www.wiesenthal.com/site/apps/nlnet/content2.aspx?c=lsKWLbPJLnF&b=4441467&ct=11195715#.VD7uJPk7uSo (accessed February 21, 2016).

74. Marianne Cooper, "For Women Leaders, Likability and Success Hardly Go Hand-in-Hand," *Harvard Business Review,* HBR Blog Network (April 30, 2013), http://blogs.hbr.org/2013/04/for-women-leaders-likability-a/ (accessed February 21, 2016).

75. Ken Auletta, "Why Jill Abramson Was Fired," *The New Yorker* (May 14, 2014), www
     .newyorker.com/business/currency/why-jill-abramson-was-fired (accessed February
     21, 2016).

76. C. von Hippel, C. Wiryakusuma, J. Bowden, and M. Shochet, "Stereotype Threat
     and Female Communication Styles," *Personal Social Psychology Bulletin* 37, no. 10
     (2011). doi: 10.1177/0146167211410439.

77. Rebecca R. Hastings, "Poll: Many Employees Don't Embrace Diversity" (November 15,
     2012), www.shrm.org/hrdisciplines/diversity/articles/pages/employees-dont-embrace-
     diversity.aspx (accessed February 21, 2016).

78. U.S. Bureau of Labor Statistics, "Employment Status of the Civilian Noninstitutional
     Population by Sex, Age, and Race" (February 10, 2016), www.bls.gov/cps/cpsaat05.
     htm (accessed February 22, 2016).

79. Egon Zehnder, "2014 Egon Zehnder European Board Diversity Analysis" (2014), www
     .egonzehnder.com/files/2014_egon_zehnder_european_board_diversity_analysis.pdf
     (accessed February 21, 2016). [This study examined companies with market capital
     over 4 billon euro. Where countries did not have five companies with market capital
     over 4 billion euro, the top five companies by market capital were included.]

80. Ernst & Young, "Point of View: Women on Boards: Global Approaches to Advancing
     Diversity" (July 2014), www.womenonboards.co.uk/resource-centre/reports/diversity
     /2014-ey-diversity-global-approach-wob-who-is-doing.pdf (accessed February 21, 2016).

81. Carol Cain Miller, "Women on Boards," *The New York Times* (March 10, 2015),
     www.nytimes.com/2015/03/11/upshot/women-on-boards-where-the-us-ranks.
     html?_r=0 (accessed February 21, 2016); Judith Warner, "Women's Leadership Gap"
     (2016), Center for American Progress, www.americanprogress.org/issues/women
     /report/2015/08/04/118743/the-womens-leadership-gap/ (accessed February 21, 2016).

82. Credit Suisse Research Institute, "The CS Gender 3000: Women in Senior
     Management" (September 2014), https://publications.credit-suisse.com/tasks
     /render/file/index.cfm?fileid=8128F3C0-99BC-22E6-838E2A5B1E4366DF
     (accessed February 21, 2016).

83. M. Tarm, "Brokerage Giant Settles Discrimination Lawsuit," Associated Press (August
     28, 2013), http://bigstory.ap.org/article/brokerage-giant-settles-discrimination-lawsuit
     (accessed February 21, 2016); C. Suddath, "Hey Merrill Lynch, It's Not a Good Idea
     to Tell Women to 'Seduce the Boys' Club,'" *Bloomberg Businessweek* (July 29, 2013),
     www.businessweek.com/articles/2013-07-29/hey-merrill-lynch-its-not-a-good-idea-
     to-tell-women-to-seduce-the-boys-club (accessed February 21, 2016).

84. K. Weise, "Meet the Broker Who Made Merrill Pay for Racial Bias," *Bloomberg
     Businessweek* (December 3, 2013), www.bloomberg.com/news/2013-11-27/merrill-lynch-
     messed-up-my-career-says-broker-who-won-lawsuit.html (accessed February 21, 2016).

85. Daniel Seligman, "Up from Inscrutable," *Fortune* (April 6, 1992), note 24.

86. Clarence Thomas, *My Grandfather's Son* (New York: Harper Perennial, 2008),
     pp. 87–88; quoted in T. Loomis, "The 15-Cent Diploma: Clarence Thomas Says
     Affirmative Action Cheapened His Yale Law School Degree and Made It Almost
     Impossible for Him to Find a Law Firm Job," *American Lawyer* 30, no. 6 (2008).

87. General Motors, "Brief of General Motors as *Amicus Curiae* in Support of Defendants,"
     in *Gratz v. Bollinger,* 539 U.S. 244 (2003).

88. *Grutter v. Bollinger*, 539 U.S. 306 (2003).

89. See, for example, Stefanie K. Johnson, Kenneth E. Podratz, Robert L. Dipboye, and Ellie Gibbons, "Physical Attractiveness Biases in Ratings of Employment Suitability: Tracking Down the 'Beauty Is Beastly' Effect," *Journal of Social Psychology* 150, no. 3 (March 2010), pp. 301–318; Jennifer J. Argo, Darren W. Dahl, and Andrea C. Morales, "Positive Consumer Contagion: Responses to Attractive Others in a Retail Context," *Journal of Marketing Research* 45, no. 6 (2008), pp. 690–701.

90. N. Upton, "My Big, Fat Photo Spoof," *The Daily Beast* (September 9, 2011), www.thedailybeast.com/articles/2011/09/09/nancy-upton-on-her-american-apparel-plus-size-photo-spoof.html (accessed February 21, 2016).

91. A. Liptak, "Court Backs Michigan on Affirmative Action," *The New York Times* (April 22, 2014), www.nytimes.com/2014/04/23/us/supreme-court-michigan-affirmative-action-ban.html (accessed February 21, 2016).

Readings

Reading 6-1

Confessions of a Sweatshop Inspector

T. A. Frank

Presidential candidates are calling for tougher labor standards in trade agreements. But can such standards be enforced? Here's what I learned from my old job.

I remember one particularly bad factory in China. It produced outdoor tables, parasols, and gazebos, and the place was a mess. Work floors were so crowded with production materials that I could barely make my way from one end to the other. In one area, where metals were being chemically treated, workers squatted at the edge of steaming pools as if contemplating a sudden, final swim. The dormitories were filthy: the hallways were strewn with garbage—orange peels, tea leaves—and the only way for anyone to bathe was to fill a bucket with cold water. In a country where workers normally suppress their complaints for fear of getting fired, employees at this factory couldn't resist telling us the truth. "We work so hard for so little pay," said one middle-aged woman with undisguised anger. We could only guess how hard—the place kept no time cards. Painted in large characters on the factory walls was a slogan: "If you don't work hard today, look hard for work tomorrow." Inspirational, in a way.

I was there because, six years ago, I had a job at a Los Angeles firm that specialized in the field of "compliance consulting," or "corporate social responsibility monitoring." It's a service that emerged in the mid-1990s after the press started to report on bad factories around the world and companies grew concerned about protecting their reputations. With an increase of protectionist sentiment in the United States, companies that relied on cheap labor abroad were feeling vulnerable to negative publicity. They still are. (See "Disney Taking Heat Over China" in the *Los Angeles Times* this March.)

Today, labor standards are once again in the news. Barack Obama and Hillary Clinton have criticized trade deals such as NAFTA as unfair to American workers, and the new thinking is that trade agreements should include strict labor standards. Obama has cited a recent free trade agreement with Peru as an example of how to go forward. I hope he's right, but let's remember that NAFTA was also hailed, in its day, for including labor protections. Our solutions on paper have proved hard to enforce. Peru attempts to remedy some of the problems of NAFTA, but we're still advancing slowly in the dark.

In the meantime, as governments contemplate such matters on a theoretical level, what's happening on the ground is mostly in the hands of the private sector. Companies police themselves, often using hired outside help. That was the specialty of my company. Visit the website of almost any large American retailer or apparel manufacturer and you're likely to see a section devoted to "ethical sourcing" or "our compliance program." (Those are terms for making sure that your suppliers aren't using factories that will land you on the front page of the *New York Times*.) Read on and you'll often see that the company boasts of having a code of conduct that its suppliers must follow—a code of labor standards by which the factories in question will be regularly measured and monitored. Are they to be believed? Well, yes and no. Private

monitoring, if done properly, can do a lot of good. But it's a tricky thing.

A simplified story of Nike may be the best way to introduce the origins of the type of work I was in. In the 1960s, Nike (before it was named Nike) based its business on the premise that the company would not manufacture shoes—it would only design and market them. The physical goods would be produced by independent contractors in countries such as Japan or Taiwan, where labor was, at the time, cheap. In short, Nike would be offices, not factories. The idea was innovative and hugely profitable, and countless companies producing everything from sweaters to toys to exercise equipment have since adopted it. It is now standard.

The problem that arose for Nike and many other companies, however, was that the media, starting in the 1990s, began to run stories on terrible labor conditions in factories in Asia. When consumers started to get angry, Nike and many other companies were nonplussed. We're just buying these shoes, they said—it's not our business how Mr. X runs his factory. And they had a point. If, for example, I learned that my dry cleaner was paying his employees less than minimum wage, I might feel bad about it, but I doubt I'd spend hours vetting alternative dry cleaners for labor compliance. I've got too much else to worry about in life, including my shirts. But such musings hardly make for a great press release, and Nike's case included nasty allegations about child labor—twelve-year-old Americans playing with soccer balls sewn by twelve-year-old Pakistanis, that sort of thing. The company's stock value sank.

In this same period, the U.S. Department of Labor, led by Robert Reich, began cracking down on sweatshops within the United States and publicizing the names of firms who were their customers. Because of this, companies such as mine began to offer their services as independent, for-profit monitors of factory labor conditions. We would act as early-warning systems against shady suppliers who mistreated their workers. Based on the reports we provided, our clients could choose either to sever their relations with a given supplier or to pressure them to improve. Business at my old company is still going strong.

In Los Angeles, where small garment shops of, say, thirty employees were the main focus, we usually worked in pairs and did three inspections a day. Outside the country, where the factories were often quite large (several thousand employees) and made anything from toys to gym equipment, we worked alone or in pairs and did one or two a day. The procedures were similar, but the inspections were more thorough abroad. While one of us might tour the work floors to note all the health and safety violations (the gazebo factory, for instance, had no secondary exits, no guarding on machines, no first aid supplies, no eye protection—the list kept going), the other might review permits, employee files, and payroll records to see what shortcomings were apparent on paper alone.

Then we would begin interviewing employees in private, usually twenty or so, hoping to learn from them what our eyes wouldn't tell us. Did the factory confiscate personal documents, such as identity cards, and use them as ransom? (This was most common in the Gulf States, where foreign laborers from places like Bangladesh could find themselves effectively enslaved. But bosses sometimes confiscated national identification documents in China, too.) Were employees free to enter and leave the compound? How many hours a week did they *really* work—regardless of what the time cards might say?

Unfortunately, we missed stuff. All inspections do. And sometimes it was embarrassing. At one follow-up inspection of a factory in Bangkok at which I'd noted some serious but common wage violations, the auditors who followed me found pregnant employees hiding on the roof and Burmese import workers earning criminally low wages. Whoops. On the other hand, sometimes I was the one who uncovered what others had missed. A lot of it had to do with luck. Was the right document visible on the work floor? Did we choose the right employees for interviews—the ones who were willing to confide in outsiders? If we were working through a translator, was his manner of speaking to people soothing?

The major challenge of inspections was simply staying ahead of the factories we monitored. False time cards and payroll records, whole days spent coaching employees on how to lie during interviews, and even renaming certain factory buildings in order to create a smaller Potemkin village—all of these were techniques used by contractors to try to fool us. We were able to detect some of them. A collection of crisp time cards that showed every employee arriving within seconds of the next was easy to spot as having been punched by a single worker standing alone at the time clock. An employee whose recollection of hours worked differed markedly from her time sheet was another indication of shady bookkeeping. But others were hard to defeat. Employee coaching deserves special attention for its crude effectiveness. The following composite dialogue, in which every answer is a lie, is typical of the sort of thing we endured:

Me: How many days a week do you work?

Employee: Five.

Me: Any overtime?

Employee: Almost never. We get time and a half in pay for overtime.

Me: How much do you make per hour?

Employee: I don't know.

Me: How much did you get for your most recent pay period?

Employee: I can't remember.

Me: Rough idea?

Employee: I can't remember.

Me: How do you deal with the fumes from the glue?

Employee: It's no problem. We have masks. [Note: This was often true—harmful cotton masks that concentrated the fumes.]

Me: How much do you get paid for Sunday work?

Employee: We don't work on Sundays.

Me: Do you have any sort of worker representative here?

Employee: ?

Me: Someone who represents the workers and talks to your bosses?

Employee: ?

Me: What sort of accidents happen here—you know, people bumping themselves, or cutting themselves?

Employee: No accidents.

Such exchanges, needless to say, rarely produced killer testimony. Sometimes we could work around uncooperative interviewees, or we could get them to stumble over their own answers. However, just talking to employees was no guarantee of anything, no matter how gifted an interrogator you were.

Because any inspection misses something, there were factories that managed to embarrass everyone. In 2000, *BusinessWeek* published an expose about a factory in Guangdong, China, the Chun Si Enterprise Handbag Factory, which made bags for Wal-Mart. Titled "Inside a Chinese Sweatshop: 'A Life of Fines and Beating,'" the article described a nightmarish place in which nine hundred workers were locked in a walled compound all day, and security guards "regularly punched and hit workers for talking back to managers or even for walking too fast." The reporting, by Dexter Roberts and Aaron Bernstein, was superb. Unfortunately, that reporting led to the door of my company, which had been among the auditors monitoring the factory for Wal-Mart. While they had found excessive overtime work and insufficient pay, inspectors had missed the captive workers and physical abuse.

To be sure, the Chun Si Enterprise Handbag Factory episode was a debacle. (I have no inside account of the story, since it took place several years before my arrival.) I suspect, however, that the fault lay with Wal-Mart as much as with the inspectors. I say this because there's a broader point here: Monitoring by itself is meaningless. It only works when the company that's commissioning it has a sincere interest in improving the situation. In the case of Chun Si, inspectors visited five times, according to *BusinessWeek*, and kept finding trouble. Now, anyone in the business knows that when inspections uncover safety violations or wage

underpayment more than once or twice—let alone five times—it's a sign that bigger problems are lurking beneath. Companies rarely get bamboozled about this sort of thing unless they want to.

And many prefer to be bamboozled, because it's cheaper. While companies like to boast of having an ethical sourcing program, such programs make it harder to hire the lowest bidder. Because many companies still want to hire the lowest bidder, "ethical sourcing" often becomes a game. The simplest way to play it is by placing an order with a cheap supplier and ending the relationship once the goods have been delivered. In the meantime, inspectors get sent to evaluate the factory—perhaps several times, since they keep finding problems—until the client, seeing no improvement in the labor conditions, severs the bond and moves on to the next low-priced, equally suspect supplier.

For the half-assed company there are also half-assed monitoring firms. These specialize in performing as many brief, understaffed inspections as they can fit in a day in order to maximize their own profits. That gives their clients plausible deniability: problems undiscovered are problems avoided, and any later trouble can be blamed on the compliance monitors. It is a cozy understanding between client, monitoring company, and supplier that manages to benefit everyone but the workers.

While private monitoring can be misused, however, when it's done right it can really produce positive change. I've seen it. When companies make a genuine effort, the results can be impressive: safe factories that pay legal wages. That sounds modest, but it's actually hard to achieve in any country. Just visit a garment shop in Los Angeles.

At my company, I quickly figured out which clients cared. The first test was whether they conducted "pre-sourcing"—inspections of labor conditions before placing an order instead of after. This small step truly separates the top-rung companies from the pack, because to prescreen is to forgo the temptation of hiring the cheapest suppliers. (Those suppliers are the cheapest because they tend to break the rules, so they usually fail the preliminary inspection.) The second test was whether the company had a long-term relationship with its suppliers. Long-term commitments are what motivate both parties to behave: the supplier wants to preserve the relationship, and the customer wants to preserve its reputation. The third test was whether the company requested unannounced inspections as opposed to ones that were arranged in advance. The advantages of this are self-evident. And the final test was whether the company made inspection results public. This was almost never done.

Who, then, were the good actors of the trade? There are a number of them, actually, but here I'll just point out two that often surprise people. The first is Mattel, the same company that was tarnished last summer by a recall of toys that were found to have lead paint on them. Whatever the chemical flaws of their products, Mattel had a reputation among us monitors for earnestness in pressuring its suppliers to improve their labor practices. It also owned and operated a few factories in China—a country with dreadful factories—that were exemplary. These facilities were regularly inspected by independent monitors, and anyone who wants to know what they've found there can visit Mattel's website: the reports are public. The second unexpected company is Nike, which long ago took its bad press to heart and remade itself into a role model of how to carry out thoughtful labor monitoring. Nike has become such a leader in the field that its website may be the single best resource for those trying to understand the difficult business of international labor standards. Not only does Nike prescreen factories, it also discloses the name and address of every factory it uses and makes public much of its monitoring.

But let's not be confined to praise. You may get the sense that I'm not Wal-Mart's biggest fan. You'd be right. I betray no confidence here, since Wal-Mart wasn't a client of ours while I was at my company. Nevertheless, I still got to visit plenty of its supplier factories. That's because any given factory usually has more than one customer, and during an audit we would always ask the bosses to name their other customers. Wal-Mart was often one of them. And its suppliers were among the worst I saw—dangerous, nasty, and poorly paid even by local (usually Chinese) measures. I noticed that Wal-Mart claimed to require factories to maintain decent labor standards—but why did it seem to think it could find them among the lowest bidders?

Now, I know about good and bad actors mostly because I saw them directly. But ordinary consumers searching on company websites—Walmart. com, Nike.com, etc.—can find out almost everything they need to know just sitting at their desks. For instance, just now I learned from Wal-Mart's latest report on sourcing that only 26 percent of its audits are unannounced. By contrast, of the inspections Target conducts, 100 percent are unannounced. That's a revealing difference. And companies that do what Nike does—prescreen, build long-term relationships, disclose producers—make a point of emphasizing that fact, and are relatively transparent. Companies that don't are more guarded. (When in doubt, doubt.)

As for those who feel especially strongly about the issue and kick up a (peaceful) fuss about sweatshops, I think they're doing a valuable thing. Even when they take actions that are sometimes off-base—such as continuing to boycott Nike when its competitors are the bigger problem—the effect is still, overall, good: it scares businesses into taking compliance more seriously. Boycotts, protests, letters to Congress, saber-rattling lawmakers, media exposes—they do have an impact. And just imagine if members of Congress or the executive branch made an effort to praise or shame companies for their records with foreign suppliers and to encourage transparent monitoring in the private sector. I suspect it would do more for international labor standards in months than the most intricate trade agreements could do in years.

I don't pretend that everything monitoring brings about is for the best. An example: Mattel's factories in China are superb, but workers there often earn less than their peers in shadier factories because their employers confine them to shorter workweeks to avoid paying overtime. Another: You may rightly hate the idea of child labor, but firing a fourteen-year-old in Indonesia from a factory job because she is fourteen does nothing but deprive her of income she is understandably desperate to keep. (She'll find worse work elsewhere, most likely, or simply go hungry.) A third: Small village factories may break the rules, but they often operate in a humane and basically sensible way, and I didn't enjoy lecturing their owners about the necessity of American-style time cards and fifteen-minute breaks. But labor standards anywhere have a tendency to create such problems. They're enacted in the hope that the good outweighs the bad.

One final thought: If you're like me, part of you feels that Peru's labor standards are basically Peru's business. It's our job to worry about standards here at home. But that sort of thinking doesn't work well in an era of globalization. We are, like it or not, profoundly affected by the labor standards of our trading partners. If their standards are low, they exert a downward pressure on our own. That's

why monitoring and enforcement have such an important role to play. We don't expect developing nations to match us in what their workers earn. (A few dollars a day is a fortune in many nations.) But when a Chinese factory saves money by making its employees breathe hazardous fumes and, by doing so, closes down a U.S. factory that spends money on proper ventilation and masks, that's wrong. It's wrong by any measure. And that's what we can do something about if we try. It's the challenge we face as the walls come down, the dolls, pajamas, and televisions come in, and, increasingly, the future of our workers here is tied to that of workers who are oceans away.

Source: www.washingtonmonthly.com/features/2008/0804.frank.html.

T. A. Frank, an editor at the Washington Monthly, is an Irvine Fellow at the New America Foundation.

Reading **6-2**

Polishing Apple: *Fair Labor Association Gives Foxconn and Apple Undue Credit for Labor Rights Progress*

Scott Nova and Isaac Shapiro

On August 21, 2012, the Fair Labor Association (FLA) released an interim assessment of the progress made by Apple's largest supplier, Foxconn, in improving conditions for its factory workers in China. The assessment covered three Foxconn factories manufacturing Apple products in China: the Guanlan and Longhua factories in Shenzhen and the factory in Chengdu. In the report, *Foxconn Verification Status Report,* the FLA concludes that things are going very well:

> Foxconn and Apple are carrying out the robust remediation plan developed following FLA's investigation, published on March 28, 2012. Over the past three months, steady progress has been made at the three facilities . . . and all remediation items due within the timeframe have been

completed, with others ahead of schedule. (FLA 2012d).[1]

This briefing paper analyzes the FLA assessment and subsequent correspondence with the FLA's president. We also contrast the FLA's findings with recent independent assessments of working conditions at Foxconn and Apple's other suppliers in China, as well as with media reports regarding severe labor unrest and Foxconn's treatment of workers during iPhone 5 production.

We conclude that the FLA's rosy view of developments in Apple's supply chain is unfounded, for five reasons:

- Foxconn receives a perfect completion score from the FLA only because the FLA gives

Foxconn credit for reforms that are either incomplete or purely symbolic. For instance, the FLA grants Foxconn full credit for increasing the number of workers on a 32-person union leadership committee from two to "at least three"; the other 29 members can still be factory managers.

- Modest progress reported by the FLA in the early summer of 2012 in important areas such as excessive overtime and the use of coerced student labor was not sustained by at least some Foxconn factories by August/September, as labor practices predictably deteriorated when Foxconn ramped up production to meet iPhone 5 demand.

- One essential promise made by the FLA and Apple—that Foxconn workers would receive back pay for all cases in which overtime work had been illegally undercompensated—was broken, and the FLA's justification for this breach is wholly unpersuasive.

- The most fundamental remedies necessary to address Foxconn's ongoing violation of overtime laws, including ending violations of local law and ensuring that pay rates are increased so that there is no net loss of compensation as hours are reduced, have not occurred, and their completion is not even scheduled until July 2013. With fundamental changes in labor practices still only a promise, and still months away, it is clearly premature to express optimism about the nature of reforms.

- Independent reports paint a picture that contrasts sharply with the FLA's. The findings of a September 2012 report by the independent research group Students and Scholars Against Corporate Misbehaviour (SACOM),[2] based in Hong Kong, directly contradict key elements of the FLA report. Moreover, in September and October, Chinese media and major U.S. news outlets reported several disturbing developments, some of which are in the same areas where the FLA reports progress, including continued use of underage labor by Foxconn, involving workers as young as 14; forced overtime in the production of the iPhone 5, which

meant denial of leave for workers during a major Chinese national holiday that affords a rare opportunity for workers to return home to visit their families; and large-scale labor unrest and protests at two Foxconn factories.

It is important to note that the FLA report focuses on Foxconn alone. Reforms by Foxconn are essential, but they are hardly sufficient. A study by another independent group, China Labor Watch, released in late June, found that the deplorable working conditions found at Foxconn factories also prevail, sometimes in more severe form, at other Apple suppliers in China. Apple must ensure reforms by all of its suppliers before laudatory assessments of its labor practices will be justified.

It would be inaccurate to state that there have been no changes at Foxconn. For example, there appears to have been progress, albeit only partial and only at some Foxconn facilities, in providing compensation for certain overtime hours and also in reducing work hours overall. Relative to the size and scope of the labor abuses that have been exposed at Foxconn, however, these modest improvements are of limited significance and do not come close to establishing labor conditions that are consistent with applicable law and international labor rights norms.

The following sections address in detail the shortcomings in the FLA's assessment and contrast its findings with those of independent investigators and media reports.

"Perfect score" despite incomplete or purely symbolic improvements in essential areas

Meaningless changes in freedom of association are considered remedies

In a March 2012 press release (FLA 2012b), the FLA claimed it secured commitments to "establish a genuine voice for workers" at the Foxconn factories. Such a voice has been altogether lacking at these factories, as at virtually all factories in China; for example, so-called union leadership committees, theoretically representing the interests of workers, consist almost completely of management staff.

Here, though, the FLA applauds Foxconn for steps that do not represent progress. At the Guanlan factory, for example, the FLA (2012e) credits Foxconn for changing the composition of its union committee from 40 managerial staff and two workers (nominated by management) to 30 management representatives and 20 workers (who will purportedly be elected by workers starting in 2014). In other words, the FLA gives Foxconn credit for, and treats as an important step forward, a reform that would leave management in full control of the union leadership committee.

The credited reform at the Longhua factory would be even less meaningful. The current union leadership committee has two workers out of 32 members, the rest being managers. Under the "reform" for which the FLA (2012f) credits Foxconn and Apple, the ratio will be improved to at least three workers versus 29 managers.

In the absence of other avenues for defending their rights and protesting abusive conditions, it is not surprising that worker grievances are being expressed in more combative fashion. A September 2012 investigative report by SACOM (2012b) of Foxconn factories in Zhengzhou that produce iPhones found that workers have responded to their grievances with a series of strikes. And according to the workers interviewed by SACOM, "dispatched workers" who went on strike on September 5 were simply dismissed by Foxconn.

The FLA audits and progress reports did not focus on the Zhengzhou factories where SACOM interviewed workers; however, the FLA has repeatedly asserted that Foxconn is implementing FLA-recommended reforms at all of its facilities in China. For example, the FLA's March press release (2012b) says the implementation of reforms could benefit "more than 1.2 million Foxconn employees" (that is, all its employees in China). Thus, evidence from Zhengzhou and other major sites of Foxconn's Apple production are relevant to any assessment of Foxconn's labor practices.

The degree to which worker mistreatment played a role in the widely reported late September unrest at the dormitory of Foxconn's Taiyuan, China, plant is unclear. This riot of 2,000 workers was put down by 5,000 police officers. According to a Reuters report (Duncan and Jim 2012), Foxconn characterized the event as "a personal dispute in a dormitory that erupted into a mass brawl," but Internet postings by workers "accused factory guards of provoking the trouble by beating up workers." At minimum, the severity of the conflict demands that an independent investigation be undertaken, and it should give anyone pause before concluding that workers have been provided meaningful avenues to express their concerns and have them addressed.

Workers still would not be paid for all their work hours

In March, the FLA (2012c) reported that Foxconn would, as part of its corrective action plan, henceforth "ensure full payment of all hours of work including overtime (and fractions thereof). . . ." The purpose of this remedial action was to eliminate the common Foxconn management practice of illegally underpaying workers by paying those workers performing what the FLA calls "unscheduled overtime" in 30-minute increments, with no pay provided until and unless workers reach the 30-minute threshold on a given day. Thus, the FLA (2012a) explained that "29 minutes of overtime work results in no pay and 58 minutes results in only one unit of overtime pay." Unscheduled overtime could apply to the 14 percent of workers considered "indirect"; these workers "include quality control staff, mechanics, maintenance staff, guards, and so on."[3]

Here some progress was indeed made, but the FLA gave Foxconn full credit for a half measure. Rather than eliminating the practice of paying workers nothing until they have exceeded a threshold of overtime minutes, Foxconn merely reduced the threshold—from 30 minutes to 15. As the appendix covering conditions at the Longhua factory (FLA 2012f) states: "Based on workers' hours and payment records, working periods of less than 15 minutes were not paid, and working periods exceeding 15 but less than 30 minutes were paid as 15 minutes." The remedial action on this issue is then confirmed to be complete. The report also says that this is now the policy at all of the factories. It should be noted that this change is actually consistent with the FLA's recommendation, made at the time of its initial factory audits in March (2012a); however, this recommendation leaves in place a system that denies workers pay for time they have worked, in violation of applicable law and any reasonable standard of fairness.

Under this policy, many workers will continue to lose significant amounts of pay. For example, a worker who is asked on a regular basis to stay for 25 minutes after work will lose 10 minutes of pay per day, an hour's pay per six-day workweek, and 50 hours of pay over the course of a year.

Surveys and meetings are credited as reforms

The FLA repeatedly gives Foxconn credit for establishing surveys of workers or holding new meetings to receive their input. Such mechanisms are only meaningful, however, if this input is taken seriously, and in that regard the assessment is silent. For example, the FLA progress report (2012e) refers to factory health and safety committee meetings that have occurred and to the presence of worker representatives on those committees. But the report provides no information on the level of active worker participation in these meetings, what specific concerns the workers expressed, what proposals workers made for improvements, and what subsequent actions management took, based specifically on this worker input, to improve health and safety practices and procedures. Absent evidence that these meetings are having an actual impact, and given the pattern of management practices exhibited by Foxconn over the years, there is no basis for concluding that these meetings are meaningful tools for workers to influence labor practices.

Reported progress at Foxconn plants in early summer has not been sustained

The FLA report covered a period of "non-peak" production, in June and early July of this year, when it was presumably easier for Foxconn to adhere to improved labor practices, particularly those related to hours of work. The evidence suggests that, even if those improved practices did prevail during the period analyzed by the FLA, they were not sustained as iPhone 5 production intensified.

Several examples of this phenomenon stand out. For instance, the FLA asserted (2012d; 2012e) that all Foxconn employees were working no more than 60 hours per week, implying at most slightly more than 80 hours per month in overtime (a level that is still far above China's legal maximum of 36 overtime hours per month). SACOM's September investigation of Foxconn's Zhengzhou factories found otherwise. The group reports (2012b) that as iPhone production reached peak levels, overtime hours on some iPhone production lines reached 100 hours per month. SACOM also found that many workers were getting only one day off every 13 days; Chinese law requires at least one day off per week. This denial of rest days also contradicts what the FLA reported finding in early summer 2012.

The taxing physical work performed by Foxconn production workers makes regular ergonomic breaks essential to protect workers' health. The FLA progress report stated that Foxconn now ensures that all workers get ergonomic breaks during the day, but SACOM found that these breaks were not being provided.

The FLA report also said that Foxconn established a new policy to ensure that meetings and training would occur during regular work hours, and thus be paid, and to pay overtime if training has to occur outside regular hours (2012e). This new policy is important since the FLA found in March that Foxconn regularly—and illegally—failed to pay employees for pre- and post-shift meetings and for time spent in mandatory trainings. SACOM found that at least in Zhengzhou, this new group practice has not been implemented; workers there have to attend the daily work assembly meeting without payment. Also, on some production lines, workers must reach their work quota before they can stop working, even if that means working overtime without pay.

The FLA (2012d) also claimed "significant improvements were found regarding Foxconn's internship program" and that Foxconn's student interns now "understand that they are free to terminate the internship if and when they wish." These findings do not square with information, first reported by the Chinese media, that to make up for a worker shortfall, students in China have been coerced to work on iPhone 5 production. According to a Sept. 6, 2012, report in the *Shanghai Daily*:

> Thousands of students in an east China city are being forced to work at a Foxconn plant after classes were suspended at the beginning of the new semester, it has been revealed.
>
> Students from Huai'an in Jiangsu Province were driven to a factory in the city run by Taiwan's Foxconn Technology Company after the plant couldn't find sufficient workers for the production of Apple's much-anticipated iPhone 5, they said in online posts. (ShanghaiDaily.com 2012)

China National Radio reported similar findings (an unofficial English translation of this story is available upon request), and a *New York Times* report (Barboza and Duhigg 2012) covered this as well, noting the context that "[w]orker advocates say Foxconn is under intense pressure at critical moments—like leading up to the release of a new product, like the iPhone 5—to fill huge orders quickly." The *Shanghai Daily* story also revealed that the students were working six days a week, 12 hours a day. This is further confirmation that as iPhone 5 production ramped up, workweeks at Foxconn exceeded the 60-hour weekly limit the FLA claims has been achieved.

Retroactive pay promise has been broken

When the FLA reported in March that Foxconn had been systematically failing to pay workers for all their overtime hours, in violation of Chinese law, the organization simultaneously reported that Apple and Foxconn had pledged to provide back pay to all workers affected. The FLA publicly stated (2012b): ". . . FLA secured agreement from Foxconn and Apple to retroactively pay any worker due unpaid overtime. The companies are currently conducting an audit to determine the payments due. . . ." This was widely reported by media outlets.

The sums of money involved are meaningful to the poorly paid workers at Foxconn who make Apple products. Foxconn's failure to pay for all overtime hours was reported by independent investigators as early as 2009 (FinnWatch, SACOM, and SOMO 2009; SACOM 2010). As already noted, during its March 2012 audits, the FLA confirmed that Foxconn frequently failed to pay employees for pre- and post-shift meetings, for time spent in mandatory trainings, and for as much as 30 minutes of "unscheduled overtime" on any given day. The first two practices have affected a large percentage of Foxconn workers; the last, according to the FLA, potentially affected 14 percent of the workforce (the so-called indirect workers).

The FLA did not detail how many workers were affected and how much they were owed. Since these practices went on for at least several years, since there are high turnover rates at Foxconn, and since violations apparently occurred frequently, the company's illegal denial of overtime pay likely touched hundreds of thousands of current and former workers and involved tens of millions of dollars, possibly more.

The crucial and highly publicized commitment by Apple and Foxconn to provide back pay to all of these workers went unmentioned in the FLA's progress report, prompting the Worker Rights Consortium to write the FLA, inquiring why the issue was disregarded. The FLA confirmed in its reply that, contrary to the promise it made on behalf of Apple and Foxconn in March, no back pay has been provided and none is forthcoming. (Copies of the exchange are available from the Worker Rights Consortium.)

The FLA defended the failure of Apple and Foxconn to keep their back pay promise on two grounds: (1) it is "not possible" to provide back pay for uncompensated pre- and post-shift meetings because Foxconn did not keep records of the time workers spent in these meetings; and (2) the FLA itself did not find any workers who were denied pay for up to 30 minutes of unscheduled overtime. The FLA provided no explanation as to why back pay would not be provided for the third category of overtime pay violations—the failure to compensate workers for time spent in mandatory trainings.

The first justification is without merit. Foxconn's failure to keep proper records of workers' hours (itself a violation of official FLA standards) is the fault of Foxconn, not the workers, and the latter should not be penalized for the negligence or malfeasance of the former. Where proper records have not been kept by an employer, back pay can be estimated based on worker testimony as to the duration and frequency of the uncompensated work. The FLA's position that Foxconn should be absolved of financial responsibility because of its own failure to maintain proper records is an odd position for a labor rights organization to take; regardless, Foxconn's failure to maintain records is not a plausible justification for denying back pay legally owed, and publicly promised, to workers.

The second justification provided by the FLA, that it did not find, during its audits, cases of workers underpaid due to the 30-minute rule, has no bearing on the issue. As mentioned, the FLA (2012b) stated in March, "The companies [Apple and Foxconn] are currently conducting an audit to determine the payments due. . . ." There was no mention of an FLA role in identifying the affected workers, and there is no indication that the FLA conducted any sort of comprehensive review. Thus, what the FLA did or did not find is irrelevant.

What is relevant is the March FLA announcement that Apple and Foxconn were conducting an audit to identify "any worker" affected by this illegal policy. Apparently, Apple and Foxconn decided at some point to renege on this commitment. What is also relevant is that, as the FLA has reported,

Foxconn had a longstanding policy of not paying up to 30 minutes of "unscheduled" overtime, and 14 percent of Foxconn workers were subject to this policy; with just the three factories examined by the FLA employing nearly 300,000 workers (FLA 2012a) dedicated to Apple products, it is therefore virtually certain that tens of thousands of current and former workers are owed back pay for unscheduled overtime at these factories alone.

The promise of back pay by Apple and Foxconn, made public in March 2012 by the FLA, was not only one of the most significant reform pledges made by the companies; it was one of the most straightforward. The companies promised that they would identify all workers to whom money is owed and then pay them. Unlike issues that are harder to quantify—for example, the degree to which health and safety committee meetings actually serve as a meaningful vehicle for workers to influence factory practices—the back pay issue is one where progress can be measured very easily. Apple and Foxconn were either going to fulfill their back pay promise or break it. They broke it. Hopefully, they will reverse course, a result that will be more likely if the FLA does not continue to defend the companies' position.

Fundamental hour/pay remedies are not scheduled until July 2013

As previously mentioned, the March FLA report found that Foxconn workers frequently worked more than 60 hours a week, which means more than 80 overtime hours per month, far in excess of the legal limit of 36 per month. Compliance with this legal limit would require an average workweek of no more than 49 hours. The FLA progress report states that Foxconn is now meeting the interim goal, set by Apple, of limiting the workweek of all its employees to 60 hours (though, as discussed previously, independent groups and media investigations found that this reduced work schedule was dropped for at least some iPhone workers as production of the phone ramped up). But even if this standard is consistently followed, the standard itself is illegal, subjecting many workers to more than twice the maximum overtime hours allowed by Chinese law.

The FLA says that Apple and Foxconn should not be expected to achieve compliance with the law until July 2013. It is unclear on what basis the FLA deems it acceptable for Apple and Foxconn to continue to break the law on a massive scale for more than 15 months from the date of the FLA's March 2012 audits, particularly in light of the fact that both Apple and Foxconn have been promising to stop this behavior since 2006 (Apple 2006). To be sure, if Foxconn stops breaking the law now, this may cause substantial inconvenience for Apple in the form of delivery delays; however, there is no basis in Chinese law or any applicable code of conduct for temporarily exempting companies from their labor rights obligations based on convenience. Nor does the FLA recommend that Foxconn, or Apple, be penalized in any way, or workers be compensated in any way, for the companies' past and ongoing disregard for laws limiting the number of work hours— laws whose purpose, it is important to remember, are to protect workers from the physical and psychological damage that excessive work hours can cause.

Moreover, the FLA's interim report did not assess progress toward meeting the public commitment to protect the pay of workers when their overtime hours are cut. In March the FLA (2012b) stated, "More importantly, while employees will work fewer hours, Foxconn has agreed to develop a compensation package that protects workers from losing income due to reduced overtime." The FLA reports the reduction in overtime hours to no more than 60 hours a week but does not mention whether the hourly pay of these workers increased to offset the reduction in work hours, thereby protecting their monthly pay levels. Instead, the FLA (2012e) states that "addressing compensation given the reduced hours" is also a goal to be achieved by July 2013. Meanwhile, in May SACOM (2012a) found take-home pay has *fallen* due to the cut in overtime hours. Further, both SACOM and China Labor Watch have reported that, to the degree work hours have been reduced, the intensity of work has increased; that is, workers are expected to produce the same amount of goods in fewer hours (SACOM 2012a; CLW 2012b).

Independent investigations and press reports paint a different picture

In May 2012 SACOM released a report, based on research conducted over a brief period shortly after the FLA's investigative report came out in late March, on working conditions at Foxconn. The report covered some of the same facilities (Guanlan and Longhua) as the FLA audit. Beyond the already-mentioned reduction in take-home pay and the increased intensity of work in response to the reduction in overtime hours, SACOM found that "[t]he frontline management continue to impose humiliating disciplinary measures on workers, including forcing workers to write confession letters, reading out these confession letters, cleaning the toilets and manual labouring work." SACOM also reported that "workers do not know what kinds of chemicals they are using" (2012a).

SACOM's September report, covering a more recent and more intense production period than that covered by the FLA report, is even more troubling. As discussed, the SACOM report (2012b) indicates that in areas such as hours of overtime work, payment for all hours worked, and ergonomic breaks, the progress reported by the FLA does not accurately describe working conditions in Foxconn's Zhengzhou operations. (As noted, while Zhengzhou was not directly examined by the FLA, the FLA has repeatedly asserted that reforms would be implemented by Foxconn in all of its operations in China.)

SACOM also found that dehumanizing disciplinary practices, such as the use of confession letters, continue, and that, as noted, a series of strikes have occurred, demonstrating ongoing worker discontent. One cause of this discontent, according to SACOM, is arbitrary relocation of the workforce: In the rush to complete iPhone 5 orders, Foxconn is relocating workers from other provinces to the Zhengzhou operation. Workers may not have a choice in these transfers, do not always know how long they are going to stay in Zhengzhou, and, when they are given a schedule, sometimes have to stay long past the promised time.

SACOM's findings have been bolstered in recent weeks by a series of reports in Chinese and U.S. media concerning incidents at several Foxconn production facilities.

A new finding in early October, widely cited in U.S. news outlets and based on research by China Labor Watch (2012d), revealed the use of student interns as young as 14 at Foxconn's factory in Yantai, undercutting the FLA's findings. Foxconn has admitted this use of child labor. As the Associated Press reported on October 16 (McDonald 2012), "The Fair Labor Association, which was hired by Apple to audit working conditions at Foxconn factories, said in August that improvements it recommended in March were being carried out ahead of schedule. That included verifying the ages of student interns." If Foxconn is verifying the ages of student interns at some factories, it has clearly failed to do so at Yantai. Notably, Foxconn issued an unusual statement in response to the reports in which it denied that any Apple products are being made in Yantai; normally, Foxconn refuses any public comment concerning which customers' goods are produced at a given factory. There is no independent information available as to whether or not Apple products are in fact produced at Yantai.

China Labor Watch (CLW) also reported large-scale labor unrest at the Foxconn Zhengzhou factory on October 5, 2012. CLW (2012c) said that a strike involving 3,000 to 4,000 workers occurred there, driven by excessive quality control demands related to iPhone 5 production and the denial of vacation time for a national holiday. A precise picture of what actually occurred is difficult to obtain, but on October 14 the widely circulated *China Business Journal* (2012) published a story consistent with CLW's claims. CLW translated this story, which stated: "On October 5th, a massive strike of workers occurred at Zhengzhou Foxconn. . . . [T]here were several hundred workers directly involved with the conflict and another three to four thousand workers insisted not showing up for work as a protest. The whole strike lasted almost two days."

This strike comes on top of the already-discussed strikes documented by SACOM as well as the riot that occurred at the dormitory of the Foxconn Taiyuan plant. All these indications of labor unrest occurred in the last few months in Foxconn plants making Apple products, casting substantial doubt on the picture of major labor rights progress painted by the FLA interim report.

Protecting workers, or Apple's reputation?

Ever since the FLA released its investigative report of Foxconn in late March, with Apple agreeing to advance its remedies, the central question has been: Will Foxconn and Apple implement just enough reform to rehabilitate Apple's public image—or will labor practices be overhauled in a manner that decisively advances working conditions, remedies past abuses, and brings Foxconn into compliance with the law?

The theme of the FLA's progress report is that a genuine transformation is underway, with Foxconn and Apple implementing a broad range of meaningful reforms on an expedited basis and without a single instance in which the companies have come up short relative to their commitments.

But analysis of the FLA's findings and information from independent sources make clear that the broad portrait the FLA paints bears little resemblance to ongoing realities at Foxconn. In contrast to the FLA's glowing assessment, improvements in working conditions at Foxconn have in most cases been modest, fleeting, or purely symbolic, while some key reform pledges have been broken outright.

In closing, it must be emphasized that it is Apple that bears ultimate responsibility for the way the workers who make its products are treated. This responsibility is recognized by the FLA process itself, with the FLA's March report (2012a) noting, "As an affiliate of the Fair Labor Association, Apple has committed to ensuring that the FLA code standards are upheld in its supply chain."

Apple's responsibility is underscored by the reality that the company has profited greatly from a production system at Foxconn that has long been defined by low wages and harsh and illegal treatment of workers—a system that has in many ways been necessitated by the price pressures and production demands Apple imposes, especially when it is rolling out new products. As SACOM's most recent report (2012b) observes:

> It is ironic that Apple declared to the world that it would ensure that working hours and other working conditions would be improved, but would then push its major supplier Foxconn, and consequently its workers, to meet product schedules inconsistent with such improvements.

Apple has the power to bring an end to severe and chronic labor rights abuses in its supply chain. As a former Apple executive told the New York Times (Duhigg and Barboza 2012) early this year:

> We've known about labor abuses in some factories for four years, and they're still going on. . . . Why? Because the system works for us. Suppliers would change everything tomorrow if Apple told them they didn't have another choice. . . . If half of iPhones were malfunctioning, do you think Apple would let it go on for four years?

So the greatest responsibility for the lack of progress documented herein lies not with Foxconn or the FLA, but with Apple, the company with the largest market value and the most coveted consumer products in the world. The paramount issue remains whether Apple will ever choose to apply its legendary business prowess and spirit of innovation, and its enormous financial clout, to the goal of protecting the basic human rights of the people who make those products.

—*Scott Nova is executive director of the Worker Rights Consortium, a nonprofit labor rights–monitoring organization. WRC conducts independent investigations of working conditions in factories around the world. Its mission is to combat sweatshops and protect the rights of workers who make apparel and other products.*

—*Isaac Shapiro joined EPI in 2011 to direct work examining the economic effects of government regulation. He previously worked for nearly two decades at the Center on Budget and Policy Priorities, where he founded the center's International Budget Project; as a senior adviser at the Save Darfur Coalition; as special assistant to U.S. Secretary of Labor Robert Reich; and for a member of Congress.*

Source: Scott Nova and Isaac Shapiro, "Polishing Apple: Fair Labor Association Gives Foxconn and Apple Undue Credit for Labor Rights Progress," *Briefing Paper #352* (November 8, 2012), www.epi.org/publication/bp352-polishing-apple-fla-foxconn-labor-rights/ (accessed June 12, 2016).

Endnotes

1. The interim FLA report (FLA 2012d) relied on information collected from June 25, 2012, to July 6, 2012. Its aim was to assess implementation progress made since the remediation plans for these factories were established by the FLA in late March. These remediation plans set deadlines for reforms over the period from April 1, 2012, through July 1, 2013.

2. SACOM has been a vital source of information on working conditions at Foxconn and in China's electronics sector more broadly. Its research, which draws heavily on interviews with workers, documented violations at Foxconn years before the FLA commenced auditing at Apple's behest; many of the FLA's findings corroborated what SACOM had long been reporting. Of particular note, SACOM identified the combustion hazards at Foxconn's Chengdu production facility related to aluminum dust and warned Apple of the risks. Apple took no action until the massive aluminum dust explosion at Chengdu that killed four workers and injured dozens.

3. This description comes from a letter/email sent by FLA President and CEO Auret van Heerden to the Worker Rights Consortium on September 17, 2012. A copy is available upon request.

References

Apple. 2006. *Apple's Audit Report.* http://www.foxconn.com/ser/06110602_2.htm

Barboza, David, and Charles Duhigg. 2012. "China Contractor Again Faces Labor Issue on iPhones." *New York Times,* Sept. 10. http://www.nytimes.com/2012/09/11/technology/foxconn-said-to-use-forced-student-labor-to-make-iphones.html?pagewanted=all

China Business Journal. 2012. "The Mess at Foxconn Zhengzhou: Conflicts Triggered by Extensive Management," Oct. 14 [translated from Chinese to English by China Labor Watch]. http://www.chinalaborwatch.org/news/new-439.html

China Labor Watch (CLW). 2012a. *Beyond Foxconn: Deplorable Working Conditions Characterize Apple's Entire Supply Chain.* June 27. http://www.chinalaborwatch.org/pro/pro-show-176.html

China Labor Watch (CLW). 2012b, "Response to FLA's Progress Report on Apple." Aug. 21. http://www.chinalaborwatch.org/news/new-419.html

China Labor Watch (CLW). 2012c. "3000 to 4000 Workers Strike at Foxconn's China Factory." Oct. 5. http://chinalaborwatch.org/news/new-433.html

China Labor Watch (CLW). 2012d. "Foxconn Employs Interns Between 14 to 16." Oct. 15. http://www.chinalaborwatch.org/news/new-438.html

Duhigg, Charles, and David Barboza. 2012. "In China, Human Costs Are Built Into an iPad." *New York Times,* Jan. 25. http://www.nytimes.com/2012/01/26/business/ieconomy-apples-ipad-and-the-human-costs-for-workers-in-china.html?pagewanted=all&_r=0

Duncan, Maxim, and Clare Jim, 2012. "Foxconn China Plant Closed After 2,000 Riot." Reuters, Sept. 24. http://www.reuters.com/article/2012/09/24/us-hon-hai-idUSBRE88N00L20120924

Fair Labor Association (FLA). 2012a. "Independent Investigation of Apple Supplier, Foxconn Report Highlights."March. http://www.fairlabor.org/sites/default/files/documents/reports/foxconn_investigation_report.pdf

Fair Labor Association (FLA). 2012b. "Fair Labor Association Secures Commitment to Limit Workers' Hours, Protect Pay at Apple's Largest Supplier." March 29. http://www.fairlabor.org/blog/entry/fair-labor-association-secures-commitment-limit-workers-hours-protect-pay-apples-largest

Fair Labor Association (FLA). 2012c. "Independent Investigation of Apple Supplier, Foxconn Report Highlights. Appendix 1, Part 2." March.http://www.fairlabor.org/sites/default/files/documents/reports/appendix_1.2_sci_findings_longhua.pdf.pdf

Fair Labor Association (FLA). 2012d. *Foxconn Verification Status Report.* http://www.fairlabor.org/sites/default/files/documents/reports/foxconn_verification_report_final.pdf

Fair Labor Association (FLA). 2012e. "Foxconn Verification Status Report. Appendix 2, Foxconn Verification Tracker–Guanlan." Aug. 21. http://www.fairlabor.org/report/foxconn-remediation-verification

Fair Labor Association (FLA). 2012f. "Foxconn Verification Status Report. Appendix 3, Foxconn Verification Tracker–Longhua," Aug. 21. http://www.fairlabor.org/report/foxconn-remediation-verification

FinnWatch, SACOM, and SOMO. 2009. *Playing with Labour Rights: Music Player and Game Console Manufacturing in China.* http://german-watch.org/corp/it-labmus.pdf

Kan, Michael. 2012. "Apple Supplier Refutes Claim of Suicide at China Factory." *MacWorld,* Oct. 12. http://www.macworld.com/article/2011731/apple-supplier-refutes-claim-of-suicide-at-china-factory.html

McDonald, Joe. 2012. "Foxconn Admits to Underage Interns Working in Factories." Associated Press, Oct. 16. http://www.huffingtonpost.com/2012/10/16/foxconn-underage-interns_n_1969215.html?utm_hp_ref=business&ir=Business

SACOM. 2010. *Workers as Machines: Military Management in Foxconn.* http://sacom.hk/archives/740

SACOM. 2012a. *Sweatshops Are Good for Apple and Foxconn, But Not for Workers.* http://sacom.hk/archives/947

SACOM. 2012b. *New iPhone, Old Abuses: Have Working Conditions at Foxconn in China Improved?* http://sacom.hk/archives/960

ShanghaiDaily.com. 2012. "Students say they are forced to work on new iPhone 5." Sept. 6. http://www.shanghaidaily.com [available to subscribers only]

Tsukayama, Hayley. 2012. "Worker Commits Suicide at Apple Supplier Foxlink, Report Says." *Washington Post,* Oct. 11. http://www.washingtonpost.com/business/technology/worker-commits-suicide-at-apple-supplier-foxlink-report-says/2012/10/11/66d3c2d8-13ce-11e2-be82-c3411b7680a9_story.html

Reading **6-3**

What's So Bad about Apple's Factories?

Chris MacDonald

Like Nike and other big-name companies before it, Apple has been singled out for criticism with regard to working conditions at its factories in developing nations. Or rather, criticism over working conditions at factories run by its subcontractors. In particular, Apple has faced criticism with regard to pay and working conditions at the massive factories of its most important Chinese contractor, Foxconn. Critics have accused Foxconn (and, hence, Apple) of paying too little, of pushing workers too hard, of making workers work too much overtime, and for working conditions that they say have driven some workers to suicide.

But—even if we were to hold the company fully responsible for working conditions at a supplier's factories—it is far from clear that Apple has anything to be ashamed of. For starters, the Foxconn factories at which Apple's iPhones and iPads are made are nothing like the dire sweatshops to which some of the poorest of the poor in truly destitute countries are subjected. We ought not to confuse the two. No one at Foxconn's factories is chained to their workstations, and the wages paid are good by local standards. That's not to say, of course, that a Foxconn factory is any sort of workers' paradise. Violations have occurred—both violations of local laws and violations of Apple's own code of conduct. But reports suggest that improvements continue to be made.

As for accusations that standards are driving workers to suicide, those need to be examined carefully. For any workplace to drive employees to such extremes would be an alarming thing indeed. But it is not at all clear that Foxconn and Apple are responsible for any such thing. At least one author has pointed out that, given that Foxconn employs about a million people, a number of suicides by workers each year is virtually a statistical inevitability. In fact, suicide rates among Foxconn workers may actually be a little *lower* than the rate among the general Chinese population.[1] In this as in so many other cases, it is important to look beyond the most basic facts in order to compare them to other cases and to baseline statistics.

Indeed, far from being driven to suicide, all evidence suggests that Foxconn workers consider their jobs to be highly desirable ones. Foxconn has roughly 1.2 million employees, all of whom have actively sought out jobs at Foxconn's factories because those jobs represent opportunities not otherwise available to them. As for excessive overtime, it's worth pointing out that overtime at Foxconn, as in factories here in North America, is voluntary. And in fact journalists who have investigated conditions at Foxconn factories in depth report that one of the main complaints of workers there is that they aren't getting as much overtime as they would like to have![2] Of course, the fact that workers want more overtime doesn't in itself mean that their jobs are wonderful. Any employee can get employees to beg for overtime simply by keeping wages low enough. But Foxconn wages are not particularly low, and so we ought to think carefully before insisting that the company offer its employees less overtime when what they really wish for is more.

What about wages? Well, the fact is that Foxconn has actually raised wages several times over the last year. Indeed, one Chinese source says that Foxconn plans to *double* the minimum wage paid to its employees by the end of 2013.[3] Some might take this as a sign of moral progress on the part of Foxconn, even an admission that current wages are unconscionably low. But as Tim Worstall wrote for Forbes. com, the rise in wages, while certainly a wonderful thing, likely shouldn't be attributed to pressure from activist groups.[4] But the rise in wages isn't just good news for Foxconn workers. Higher wages at Foxconn is sure to put upward pressure on the wages paid by other Chinese workers. This is a concrete example of the general point made by many who defend labour standards like those found in Foxconn's factories. The flow of western money into those factories may not provide workers with the lives we all wish they could have, but it is nonetheless doing an awful lot of good.

Having said all of that, it remains true that working conditions at the Foxconn factories producing Apple's iPods and iPads are not ideal. In a perfect world, no one would have to work overtime at all, and everyone would be paid enough to enjoy the standard of living currently enjoyed by, say, middle-class North Americans. But the realities of economic development around the world, and in particular in places like China, simply do not permit that at present. So while it is good to keep an eye on companies like Foxconn, an important company with plenty of reason to want to cut corners, we need to examine the facts with a much more careful eye.

Endnotes

1. Tim Worstall, "The Apple Boycott: People Are Spouting Nonsense about Chinese Manufacturing," *Forbes.com* (January 29, 2012), www.forbes.com/sites/timworstall/2012/01/29/the-apple-boycott-people-are-spouting-nonsense-about-chinese-manufacturing/.

2. Tim Culpan, "Now Can We Start Talking about the Real Foxconn?" *Bloomberg.com* (March 20, 2012), http://go.bloomberg.com/tech-blog/2012-03-20-now-can-we-start-talking-about-the-real-foxconn/.

3. n.a., *WantChinaTimes.com*, May 27, 2012; "Foxconn to Double Salaries in China by End of 2013," *Want China Times*, www.wantchinatimes.com/news-subclass-cnt.aspx?id520120527000081& cid 51206&MainCatID512 (accessed August 9, 2012).

4. Tim Worstall, "Apple's Foxconn to Double Wages Again," *Forbes.com* (May 28, 2012), www.forbes.com/sites/timworstall/2012/05/28/apples-foxconn-to-double-wages-again/ (accessed August 9, 2012).

Reading **6-4**

A Tale of Two Agreements

Chris MacDonald

Agreement, Part I: May, 2013

It's easy to villainize a company like Walmart for being unwilling to sign an agreement seeking to improve safety for workers in Bangladesh. What's harder is to assess the company's actual motives, and its obligations.

Headlines recently blared that Walmart has refused to sign the new "Accord on Fire and Building Safety in Bangladesh,"[1] despite the fact that

24 other companies (including Europe's two largest clothing retailers, as well as American brand Tommy Hilfiger and Canada's Loblaw) had signed.

Other news sources avoided the Walmart-centric hysteria and pointed out that lots of retail chains have in fact opted not to sign, including Gap, J.C. Penney and Target. For its part, Walmart says that it plans to undertake its own plan to verify and improve conditions at its suppliers' factories in Bangladesh. Supporters of the accord, however, are skeptical about the effectiveness of company's proposed independent effort.

From the point of view of ethical responsibilities, could a well-intentioned company conscientiously decline to sign the pact?

It's worth looking at a few reasons why a company might choose not to sign a pact designed to improve, and even save, lives. Walmart presumably believes that its own effort will be sufficient, and perhaps even superior. The company's famous efficiency and notorious influence over suppliers lend some credibility to such a notion. Other companies have worried that signing the pact would bring new legal liabilities, which of course is precisely the point of a legally-binding document. (Gap, for instance, has said that it will sign only if language regarding arbitration is removed, a stance that effectively amounts to refusal.)[2]

There also may be worries about governance: the accord provides for the appointment of a steering committee "with equal representation chosen by the trade union signatories and company signatories"—equal, but to be chaired by a seventh member selected by the International Labour Organization (ILO). Perhaps some worry that the ILO-appointed chair won't really be neutral, giving unions an effective majority.

Other companies—including ones like Walmart, which is famous for its efficiency—may worry about the extra administrative burden implied by weaving this accord's regulatory apparatus into its own systems of supply-chain oversight.

Another worry might be the fact that the accord applies only to Bangladesh, and makes that country the subject of a separate set of procedures. The accord also commits signatories to expenditures specifically on safety in Bangladesh, when from a particular company's point of view Bangladesh might not be a priority. In the wake of the April factory collapse, it's worth pointing out that there are other places in the world with unsafe factories and crummy working conditions. It's not unreasonable for at least some companies to focus their efforts on places where conditions are equally bad, and that host even more of their suppliers.

None of this goes any distance toward excusing inaction. None of it condones apathy. The point is simply that while failure to sign a particular accord makes great headlines, we need to look carefully at reasons, as well as at a company's full range of obligations, if we are to make sense of such a decision.

Agreement, Part II: July, 2013

Workers in Bangladesh will be the beneficiaries of yet another massive effort to improve their lot. Will it work? And will it mean anything for workers in countries other than Bangladesh? It's a welcome move, but it also raises questions.

According to a press release, an alliance of leading North American retailers has committed to a new plan, The Bangladesh Worker Safety Initiative, intended to "dramatically improving factory safety conditions in Bangladesh."[3] This time, the coalition includes Walmart, Target, Canadian Tire, Gap, Hudson's Bay Company, and a dozen other major retailers. That means, according to the press release, that the Initiative covers the "overwhelming majority of North American apparel imports."

This new Initiative should not be confused with the earlier Accord on Fire and Building Safety in Bangladesh, a labour-led agreement that was announced in May, less than a month after the collapse of Bangladesh's 8-story Rana Plaza, a tragedy that eventually claimed 1,129 victims. Signatories to that Accord included Europe's two biggest clothing retailers, as well as Tommy Hilfiger, H&M, and Canada's Loblaw, but there were notable abstentions.

The new Initiative "sets aggressive timelines and accountability for inspections, training and worker empowerment." Of particular note: "Within one year, 100 percent of all factories that conduct work with an alliance member will be inspected," and members of the alliance have committed to refusing to do business with any factory deemed unsafe. And, in a worthy commitment to transparency, the alliance will make semi-annual progress reports public.

There is, of course, plenty of room for skepticism. Some will see this new Initiative as a PR move, albeit a rather expensive one. Members of the alliance have already committed $42 million, though of course that number has to be put into context by comparing it to the vast profit the alliance members derive from doing business in Bangladesh. The Bangladeshi garment industry is a $19 *billion*-a-year industry. (Quick math: that means the size of the Alliance budget amounts to roughly 0.2% of the size of the industry. That's not necessarily the most relevant comparison, but it gives you a sense of scale.)

Another source of skepticism, for some, is that this is an entirely business-driven initiative, unlike the May Accord, which was driven by labour and which will be guided by a Board that includes representatives of both corporate and labour interests. The Board of the new Initiative is perhaps less clearly unbiased: the 9-member board will consist of "four retailers, four stakeholders who provide specific expertise, and an independent board chair." Interestingly, however, the Initiative does include specific provisions not just to look after workers, in the paternalistic sense, but to empower them: it calls for members to support the election of Worker Participation Committees at all factories, along with the provision of anonymous worker hotlines to be administered by a third party.

I continue to wonder and worry that both the new The Bangladesh Worker Safety Initiative and May's Accord on Fire and Building Safety in Bangladesh represent a kind of Bangladeshi exceptionalism. Why are major retailers joining together in now two big agreements to improve conditions in Bangladesh, but in Bangladesh alone? Admittedly, Bangladesh is important—as far as the garment industry goes, it is second only to China among countries exporting Western brands. But still: it worries me that a factory collapse that could have happened in any number of developing nations has apparently drawn attention *only* to the fate of garment workers in one, admittedly needy, nation.

Discussion Questions

1. Why did Walmart take so much heat for choosing not to sign the May Accord, while others seemed to escape less scathed?

2. If Walmart has valid, credible concerns about the Accord, what might have been a more effective strategy it could have used in order to choose not to sign the Accord?

3. Why do you think some of the retailers did not sign the earlier May Accord, but did sign the July Bangladesh Worker Safety Initiative?

4. There seems to be criticism or, at least, skepticism of the second agreement, as well. If you were drafting an alternative agreement, how might you have modified the second agreement to have avoided this skepticism?

5. How might you answer author MacDonald's final query: "Why are major retailers joining together in now two big agreements to improve conditions in Bangladesh, but in Bangladesh alone?"

Endnotes

1. http://bangladeshaccord.org/.

2. www.washingtonpost.com/business/economy/most-us-clothing-chains-did-not-sign-pact-1f9_story.html.

3. http://bipartisanpolicy.org/news/press-releases/2013/07/alliance-leading-retailers-north-america-join-forces-comprehensive-five.

Reading **6-5**

Sexual Harassment: *An Asian Perspective*

G. Chan and G. Shenoy

For centuries men have dominated and controlled women, often in brutal ways. Asia is no exception in this respect. This cannot always be attributed to backwardness or ignorance. Even in industrialised Asian countries, harassment of women is a serious problem.[1] Most Asian countries have a missing women problem by which is meant that there is an imbalance between the number of men and women. This is an unfortunate indicator of the perception of Asian societies regarding the value of females. An explanation for the missing women problem has it that, because of the Asian preference for male children, pregnancies are terminated when the foetus is found to be female. Violence against women whether in the extreme form of so-called 'honour killings' or in the form of spousal or maid abuse is frequently reported in the press. Asia is also the continent where many low and medium skills-based factories are located. Most of the employees in these factories are women who come from far off villages with families dependent on their wages. Often, these women are the objects of abuse that includes forms of serious sexual harassment. Likewise, in the hospitality industry, which is an important segment of Asian economies, women play an important part and they are known to be harassed not only by colleagues and supervisors but also by customers of the establishment in which they work. Some Asian countries export female migrant labour who work as domestics in the Middle East and in affluent Asian countries such as Singapore. These migrant workers are the source of valuable foreign currency to their own countries.

Unfortunately, there have been credible reports of sexual and physical abuse of many women in the Middle East that go unchecked because their countries, relying on the remittances of these female workers, do not wish to protest to the governments of the host countries and jeopardise these inward remittances. Moreover, in some countries the practice of selling female children as domestic servants or *kamlaris* to middle-class and upper-class households still continues.[2]

Women, who have occupied traditional positions such as housewives and caregivers, are comparatively recent entrants into what used to be the male-dominated workplace. In the West, women have been in the workplace for a much longer period. Despite this, even in the West, women have not been free from unwanted advances from their male colleagues or their supervisors.

When considering male-female interaction in the workplace, it should be remembered that office romances are a fact of life. Any society wants to encourage marriage and many office workers meet their future life partners at the workplace. That said, a clear line should be drawn between an activity that would be regarded as legitimate courtship or dating conduct, on the one hand, and unwelcome conduct, on the other. The latter type of conduct, although commenced as an innocent flirtation, may at a particular point cross the line and become sexual harassment. It does not help that males and females may perceive conduct in different ways with females being less accepting of certain types of conduct than males. The phenomenon of 'acquaintance rape' is attributed to this 'misunderstanding' and psychologists have devised tests such as the Rape Myth Index[3] and the Sexual Harassment Attitude Scale to measure the different perceptions of males and females to certain types of behaviour.[4] The foregoing types of sexual harassment mainly consist of a request or demand for a type of sexual favour implicitly or explicitly made. However, there is another class of sexual harassment activity that does not involve sexual favours but relates to general workplace conditions that are so sexually charged that the employee's job performance is disrupted. This type of situation is referred to as a hostile working environment.

Sexual harassment in the workplace is illegal under the laws of most countries. According to the International Labour Organisation, more than 35 countries have laws that specifically prohibit sexual harassment in the workplace.[5] The United States played a pioneering role in addressing problems of sexual harassment and American law has influenced developments in other countries and shaped anti-sexual harassment initiatives of multinational companies. The term 'sexual harassment' itself was coined by a group studying at Cornell University and the nature of the conduct that gave rise to a workplace problem received wide publicity during the confirmation hearings of Justice Clarence Thomas when a former subordinate, Ms Anita Hill, accused him of sexual harassment.[6] Title VII of the Civil Rights Act of 1964 made illegal any employment discrimination based on sex but did not specifically mention sexual harassment. However, American courts held that sexual harassment was a form of illegal sex discrimination. Recently, an American court held that a business owner who alleged that a customer stopped buying from her when she refused his advances could sue his company for sexual harassment under anti-discrimination law.[7] In the United States, UK and Hong Kong, there has been increased resort to the courts to recover damages for such conduct. In India, the Supreme Court in the case of *Vishaka v State of Rajaslhan*[8] has held that sexual harassment violates the right to life and liberty granted to both men and women under Article 21 of the Indian Constitution and is therefore prohibited in India. The court went on to issue detailed guidelines on the subject. The court stated that it is a duty of the employer to prevent sexual harassment and to provide for procedures for the investigation and punishment of sexual harassment. It defined sexual harassment broadly as "unwelcome sexually determined behaviour" that included physical contact, sexually coloured remarks, and displays of pornography. In Malaysia, the Human Resources Ministry issued a Code of Practice and Eradication of Sexual Harassment in the Workplace in 1999. This is a voluntary code and contains practical guidelines for employers to combat sexual harassment in the workplace.[9] The Singapore Constitution does not explicitly protect the individual against sex discrimination and thus there are no specific constitutional guidelines on sexual harassment. Nevertheless, it should be borne in mind that employers and managers must be sensitive to the fact that Singapore is a multiethnic society where conduct, such as a male touching a female on the shoulder, that would be tolerated by one ethnic or religious group would be regarded as highly offensive by another.[10] Although Singapore, unlike Hong Kong, does not have a law specifically directed to sexual harassment in the workplace, the government has made it clear that its views certain sexual harassment practices as liable to prosecution under the Penal Code and the Miscellaneous Offences (Public Order and Nuisance) Act.[11] It is also an offence under Singapore law to use criminal force in order to outrage the modesty of another.[12]

International Standards and Ethical Standards

Article 11 of the Convention on the Elimination of All Forms of Discrimination Against Women[13] recognises the right of women to equality in employment, a right that will be undermined if women are subject to gender specific violence such as sexual harassment. In 1993, the UN General Assembly passed a resolution entitled Declaration on the Elimination of Violence Against Women'.[14] Article 2 of this resolution defines violence against women to include sexual harassment and intimidation at work. While the law may help define the boundaries of permissible and impermissible conduct and give some helpful pointers that we will consider later, it must be borne in mind that whether there is a specific law on the subject or not, sexual harassment is an unethical workplace practice. Why is this so?

Regardless of legal regulation, from an ethics standpoint, sexual harassment is morally repugnant. Society licenses people to do business through artificial entities like companies and thus limit personal liability so that these companies could produce goods and services for the benefit of the economy and thus for society. Implicit in this licence is the requirement that conduct that is unacceptable to society will not be engaged in by business. Violating human dignity through unwelcome sexual advances will transgress a basic societal norm relating to respecting the modesty of women and refraining from molestation. The employer-employee relationship viewed in the context of the principles of justice found in A *Theory of Justice*[15] requires that all employees must be given an equal opportunity to hold careers and advance in them without having to submit to unwelcome sexual advances. When a woman becomes an employee, she enters into an employment relationship that imposes mutual rights and obligations on both parties. As an employee, the woman must obey lawful instructions of the employer and must devote her time and energy during working hours in contributing to the success of the enterprise. But this does not mean that she must do whatever her manager tells her to do. She is not required to lie to customers or cheat them, or mislead government regulators. Likewise, she is not required to suffer sexually humiliating behaviour or submit to sexual advances. Kant's second principle requires that we treat people as ends and not as means. Slaves were treated as means because they were property of the master who could use them just like any other type of property. Even though terms such as "human resources" might seem to imply that employees are just like other resources, such as steel, bricks, and capital, that could be used in any way as an owner wishes, modern society recognises the dignity of labour. Respect for that dignity requires that employers treat all employees, including females, as human beings and not as chattels. They should not be exposed to unsafe working conditions, they should be allowed reasonable time for breaks, and not be penned up in locked dormitories at night.

This respect also extends to protecting employees from other threats in the workplace such as sexual harassment. Protecting employees from sexual harassment is a part of a larger duty of providing a safe working environment that also includes the duty not to expose employees to unsafe equipment or noxious fumes in the workplace. No employer will deny being under an obligation to keep employees protected from dangers, including physical violence, in the workplace. When sexual harassment is seen in its true light, it is a workplace hazard that the employer should monitor and eliminate.

The business case against sexual harassment becomes clear when one considers how sexual harassment affects the organisation. In most countries, sexual harassment is illegal, either as a crime or as a tort or both, and with the doctrine of vicarious liability in place, the employer is liable to pay damages for the harm caused by such conduct. The Mitsubishi Corporation paid US$34 million to 300 female employees of one of its factories in the United States.[16] A scandal involving the head of Toyota North America Inc. and his personal assistant who complained of harassment resulted in a reorganisation of its American operations.[17] Even a purely consensual romantic relationship between a boss and a subordinate could violate the organisation's code of ethics and lead to reprimands or a request for resignation. A former head of the World Bank and the head of the International Monetary Fund were both embroiled in public scandals involving inappropriate relationships in the workplace. Subordinates would be reluctant to work for a boss who has a reputation for sexual harassment. Time and energy that should be devoted to improving the company's profitability is wasted in sexual pursuits by the predator as well as the intended victim in fending off unwelcome advances or succumbing to them. Dissatisfaction and jealousies among other employees will grow as the boss will be seen as having favourites chosen on the basis of sexual favours and attraction rather than on merit. Where women are promoted, their achievements would be disparaged on the ground that they received these favours by granting sexual favours. A company that allows a sexually charged environment to exist would soon get a bad reputation especially in Asian cities where news spreads fast through word of mouth. This bad reputation would undoubtedly restrict the pool of job applicants because qualified women, mindful of their reputation, would not be willing to work in such a company. For employees, sexual harassment would distract and humiliate female staff whose focus on work would be disrupted. Finally, sexual harassment will infect the values of meritocracy of the enterprise and prevent it from reaching its highest potential.

Endnotes

1. Special terms such as *chikan* in Japan are used to describe people who engage in the practice of groping, and women-only train carriages have been created to protect women from these *chikan*.

2. See "Nepal Dad Sold Girl for $25, Paid in Installments," http://edition.cnn.com/2006/World/asiapcf/09/25/nepal.kamlari/index.html.

3. For a list of rape myths, see http://www.d.umn.edu/cla/faculty/jhamlin/3925/myths.html/.

4. DD Baker, DE Terpstra and BD Cutler, "Perceptions of Sexual Harassment: A Re-Examination of Gender Differences," *The Journal of Psychology* 124 (1990).

5. Nelian Haspels et al., *Action Against Sexual Harassment at Work in Asia and the Pacific* (Geneva, Switzerland: International Labour Office, 2001).

6. T Morrison (ed.), *Race-ing Justice, En-Gendering Power: Essays on Anita Hill, Clarence Thomas, and the Construction of Social Reality* (New York: Pantheon/Doubleday, 1992).

7. "Business-to-Business Sex Harassment? NJ Court Says It's Real," http://www.law.com/jsp/cc/PubArticleCC.jsp?id=1202437871667.

8. AIR 1997SC3011 (1992).

9. Lekha Laxman et al., *A Study of Sexual Harassment in Small and Medium Enterprises of Malaysia* (2003), http://eprints.utm.my/2682/.

10. Shu Li and Song Mei Lee-Wong, "A Study on Singaporeans' Perceptions of Sexual Harassment from the Cross Cultural Perspective?," *Journal of Applied Social Psychology* 35 (2005): 699.

11. "Sexual Harassment in the Workplace—Government Will Set a Positive Example to Other Employers in the Problem of Sexual Harassment," *Asia One* (26 August 2008). In Hong Kong, a legislator was accused of sexual harassment over allegations that he dismissed a female assistant who rejected his advances, "Pro-democracy Hong Kong lawmaker faces sexual harassment claims," http://www.topnews.in/prodemocracy-hong-kong-lawmacker-faces-sexual-harassment-claims-2222382.

12. Section 354 of the Penal Code (Chap. 224).

13. Convention on the Elimination of All Forms of Discrimination Against Women, December 18, 1979, 1249 **UNTS** 3. Popularly referred to as **"CEDAW,"** the text of the convention can be found at http://www.un.org.womenwatch/dwa/cedaw/. In 1995 Singapore became a party to this treaty. Most Asian countries are parties to this treaty.

14. Declaration on the Elimination of Violence Against Women, GA Res 48/104, UN Doc A/48/49/ (20 December 1993).

15. John Rawls, *A Theory of Justice* (Massachusetts: Belknap Press/Harvard University Press, 1972).

16. Paid pursuant to a consent decree dated 23 June 1998 that also required Mitsubishi to accept monitors who would oversee the remedial actions taken by Mitsubishi to combat sexual harassment. See "Monitors Say Mitsubishi in Compliance with **EEOC** Consent Decree," **EEOC** Press Release 9-6-00, 6 September 2000.

17. See "Toyota's Sex Harassment Lawsuit Could Set Standard," http://www.usatoday.com/money/companies/management/2006-08-07-toyota-settle-usat_x.htm/.

7

Ethical Decision Making: Technology and Privacy in the Workplace

This "telephone" has too many shortcomings to be seriously considered as a means of communication. The device is inherently of no value to us.

Western Union internal memo, 1876

People have really gotten comfortable not only sharing more information and different kinds, but more openly and with more people—and that social norm is just something that has evolved over time.

Mark Zuckerberg, cofounder and CEO of Facebook[1]

Things do not change; we change.

Henry David Thoreau

The CIO "has got this massively more complex job with fewer dollars, less disposable resources to meet that challenge and deliver on expectations to the business. . . . Technology has become the core fabric of how a company operates."

Tom Hogan, senior vice president of software, Hewlett-Packard[2]

One afternoon, your team is sitting in a client's conference room, pitching a new database system. This pitch concerns an important sale, so while a colleague presents your team's slides detailing the benefits of your system, you watch the client's team carefully and take detailed notes on your smartphone.

The client's chief information officer (CIO) and chief financial officer (CFO) are both present, and you are paying special attention to the CIO, watching her reaction to each feature mentioned during the presentation. By the end of the meeting, you have typed up a brief report that will help your team prepare for a follow-up visit that is planned for the following week.

When you get back to your own office, your boss—the head of sales—is waiting for you. "This deal is dead in the water," he says. "I just got a call from our client's CFO, and boy is she mad. She says you spent the entire meeting fiddling with your phone instead of paying attention. What on earth were you thinking?" While your boss is speaking, you feel your phone vibrating. You are expecting a call from another key client, one who does not like to be kept waiting. This is not a great moment to take a call. But it is not a good moment to lose a key client, either. You know the phone currently is set to ring with a sound after three vibrating alerts.

- Please list as many ethical issues as you can identify that are raised by the use of smartphones in the workplace.
- Did you do anything wrong this morning in the meeting?
- Recall that, clearly, your client was offended.
- At what point does impolite behavior—for instance, actions that might offend others, such as answering e-mails during a meeting or even playing games—the line into unethical behavior?
- What type of policy would you suggest for an organization regarding the use of smartphones in the workplace, if any?
- Should the rules be different for using smartphones during in-house meetings, on one hand, and during meetings with clients or suppliers, on the other?
- How might you have acted differently during the meeting described here to have achieved a different result with your client?
- What are you about to say to your boss?

 ## Chapter Objectives

After reading this chapter, you will be able to:

1. Explain and distinguish the two definitions of privacy.
2. Describe the ethical sources of privacy as a fundamental value.
3. Identify the three legal sources of privacy protection.
4. Discuss the concept of a "reasonable expectation of privacy."
5. Discuss recent developments in connection with employee monitoring.

6. Explain the risks involved in a failure to understand the implications of technology and its use.

7. Identify additional ethical challenges posed by technology use.

8. Enumerate the reasons why employers choose to monitor employees' work.

9. Discuss the ethics of monitoring as it applies to drug testing.

10. Discuss the ethics of monitoring as it applies to polygraphs, genetic testing, and other forms of surveillance.

11. Explain why monitoring might also pose some costs for the employer and for the employee.

12. Discuss the elements of a monitoring program that might balance the interests of the employee and the employer.

13. Explain the interests of an employer in regulating an employee's activities outside of work.

14. Discuss the implications of September 11, 2001, on privacy rights.

Introduction

In his best-selling book *The World Is Flat* Thomas Friedman describes the hastening pace of globalization and how significantly the business, economic, and political landscape has changed in just the first decade of the 21st century. Friedman employs the image of a "flat world" to convey the idea that neither distance, time, geography, nor national boundaries create artificial barriers to business and trade. In fact, 9 of the 10 forces that Friedman identifies as creating this flat world are the direct result of computer and Internet-related technologies. Even the 10th, the fall of the Berlin Wall and opening of Eastern Europe, is attributed in part to the information revolution that began in the years leading up to the fall of the wall. This is certainly not the first time we have faced the impact of technological changes on our personal privacy (see the Reality Check "Condemned to Repeat").

There can be no doubt that the business world today is global, or that a technological revolution is largely responsible for this fact. Not surprisingly, that technological revolution has brought with it as many challenges as opportunities. Many of these challenges raise ethical questions, particularly as this technology impacts employee and consumer privacy. You may recall in Chapter 1 that information threat, loss, or attack is one of the greatest concerns of executives worldwide.[3] One 2015 study found that, on average, U.S. companies lose $6.5 million annually from data breaches.[4] This chapter will review some of the key ethical issues of technology and privacy, with a particular focus on privacy in the workplace.

privacy
The right to be "let alone" within a personal zone of solitude, and/or the right to control information about oneself.

Privacy issues in the workplace raise ethical issues involving individual rights as well as those involving utilitarian consequences. Workplace privacy issues evoke an inherent conflict (or some might call it a delicate balance) between what some may consider to be a fundamental right of the employer to protect its interests and the similarly grounded right of the employee to be free from wrongful

Reality Check   *Condemned to Repeat*

How fast is technology changing? Are business organizations adapting fast enough to that change?

Technology blog writer Robert Kelly from *Wired* noted:

'[According to one 2014 study], only 41% of [chief marketing officers (CMOs)] feel that they share a common vision of how marketing and IT should work together. In addition, only 29% of them partner with [chief information officers (CIOs)] when procuring marketing technology. While the CMO typically can communicate the business case, they may not fully understand the technology implications across the enterprise and the company's enterprise architecture. On the flip side, the CIO needs to invest time and energy to truly understand the businesses that they support and align themselves with the business initiatives.'

Source: Robert Kelley, "Driving Digital Customer Engagement: Technology Bridges Gap between CMOs, CIOs," *Wired: Innovation Insights Blog* (April 21, 2014), http://insights.wired.com/profiles/blogs/technology-bridging-the-gap-between-cmos-and-cios-to-drive#ixzz3Ibddx3cO (accessed February 21, 2016).

intrusions into her or his personal affairs. This conflict can arise in the workplace environment through the regulation of personal activities or personal choices, or through various forms of monitoring. Some forms of monitoring, such as drug testing, may occur after a job offer has been made but even before the individual begins working. Other forms might also occur once the individual begins to work, such as electronic surveillance of e-mail. In Reading 7-5, "Letter from Lewis Maltby to Senator Chris Rothfuss (July 26, 2014)," Maltby, president of the National Workrights Institute, presents an articulation of these two perspectives, as well as a proposed middle ground.

Similarly, contrasting utilitarian arguments can be offered on the ethics of monitoring employees. The employer can argue that the only way to manage the workplace effectively and efficiently is to maintain knowledge about and control over all that takes place within it. The employee can simultaneously contend that she or he will be most productive in a supportive environment based on trust, respect, and autonomy. In any case, the question of balance remains—whose rights should prevail or which consequences take precedent?

This chapter will examine technology and its impact on these issues. We will explore the origins of the right to privacy as well as the legal and ethical limitations on that right. We will also explore the means by which employers monitor performance and the ethical issues that arise in connection with these *potential* technological invasions to privacy. We will then connect these issues of technology and privacy to the balance of rights and responsibilities between employers and employees.

Because of the extraordinary breadth of the technology's reach, this chapter could not possibly address all issues under its umbrella. We have therefore sought to limit our coverage in this chapter to issues of technology and privacy *in the workplace* and related arenas. For instance, the intersection between ethics, intellectual property, the law, and technology opens far too many doors for the survey anticipated by this text and will therefore not be examined within this overview.

Similarly, though a phone company's decision whether to comply with the government's request to turn over phone records certainly raises issues of both technology and privacy, it is not necessarily related to issues of employment, so we will not be examining that decision. However, readers should be aware of these issues and seek to apply the lessons of this chapter to wider issues of privacy and technology in business.

The Right to Privacy

privacy rights
The legal and ethical sources of protection for privacy in personal data.

Privacy is a surprisingly vague and disputed value in contemporary society. With the tremendous increase in computer technology in recent decades, calls for greater protection of **privacy rights** have increased. Yet there is widespread confusion concerning the nature, extent, and value of privacy. Some Western countries, for example, do not acknowledge a legal right to privacy as recognized within the United States, while others such as New Zealand and Australia seem far more sophisticated in their centralized and consistent approaches to personal privacy issues. Even within the United States there is significant disagreement about privacy. The U.S. Constitution makes no mention of a right to privacy and the major Supreme Court decisions that have relied on a fundamental right to privacy, *Griswold v. Connecticut* and *Roe v. Wade*, remain highly contentious and controversial.

OBJECTIVE

Defining Privacy

Two general and connected understandings of privacy can be found in the legal and philosophical literature on this topic: privacy as a *right to be "left alone"* within a personal zone of solitude, and privacy as the *right to control information* about oneself. It is valuable to consider the connection between these two senses of privacy. Certain decisions that we make about how we live our lives, as well as the control of personal information, play a crucial role in defining our own personal identity. Privacy is important because it establishes the boundary between individuals and thereby defines one's individuality. The right to control certain extremely personal decisions and information helps determine the kind of person we are and the person we become. To the degree that we value the inherent dignity of each individual and the right of each person to be treated with respect, we must recognize that certain personal decisions and information are rightfully the exclusive domain of the individual.

Many people believe that a right to be left alone is much too broad to be recognized as a moral right. It would be difficult for employees, for example, to claim that they should be totally left alone in the workplace. This has led some people to conclude that a better understanding focuses on privacy as involving the *control* of personal information. From this perspective, the clearest case of an invasion of privacy occurs when others come to know personal information about us, as when a stranger reads your e-mail or eavesdrops on a personal conversation. Yet, the claim that a *right* of privacy implies a right to control all personal information

TABLE 7.1

Legal Status of Employee Monitoring

Telephone calls	Monitoring is permitted in connection with quality control. Notice to the parties on the call is often required by state law, though federal law allows employers to monitor work calls without notice. If the employer realizes that the call is personal, monitoring must cease immediately.
E-mail messages	Under most circumstances, employers may monitor employee e-mails. Even in situations where the employer claims that it will not, it's right to monitor has been upheld. However, where the employee's reasonable expectation of privacy is increased (such as a password-protected account), this may impact the court's decision.
Voice-mail system messages	Though not yet completely settled, the law here appears to be similar to the analysis of e-mail messages.
Internet use	Where the employer has provided the equipment and/or access to the Internet, the employer may track, block, or review Internet use.

country maintains "adequate protections" of its own; in other words, protections equivalent to those the directive guarantees in EU countries.[19]

In 2015, European officials revised its data protection regulations, which provide European citizens with greater control over how their digital information is collected and managed. This new EU-wide data-protection law replaces a patchwork of 28 national laws, meant to bolster EU privacy rights, and will go into effect in 2017.

One of the more significant aspects of the revisions is the addition of the "right to be forgotten" into EU law. The revised law also requires companies to inform national regulators of breaches within three days of it being reported. Also, under the new law, national watchdogs can issue fines if companies misuse an individual's online data. Unlike the original directive, the new regulation also applies to organizations based outside the European Union if they process personal data of EU residents or have customers in that region, including companies that are not based in the EU.[20]

Because the United States would not qualify as having adequate privacy protections to satisfy many of the provisions in EU's original nor revised data protection laws, the U.S. Department of Commerce had negotiated a **Safe Harbor exception** for firms that maintained a certain level of protection of information. Under the exception, if a firm satisfied certain requirements, the directive allowed the firm to transfer the information. However, in October 2015 the Court of Justice of the European Union invalidated the Safe Harbor exception in *Schrems v. Data Protection Commissioner.*[21]

To replace the original safe harbor exemption, officials in the European Union and the United States reached a tentative agreement called the Data Privacy

Safe Harbor exception

Considered "adequate standards" of privacy protection for U.S.-based companies under the European Union's Data Protection Directive.

Accord. Under this agreement, U.S. companies must adhere to a detailed set of standards, which surpass what U.S. law typically requires. The "Privacy Shield" details more than a dozen privacy principles with which companies will have to comply in order to rely on the Privacy Shield as a means to legally transfer data from the EU.[22] (See Table 7.2.)

To gain a deeper understanding of additional differences between the European and American systems of privacy protection, see again the Reality Check "Privacy: Europe Compared to the United States."

Given the nature of the legal uncertainty or instability concerning these challenging areas of information gathering, perhaps the only source of an answer is ethics. Yet, "our laws, ethics rules, and codes of professional conduct have never been able to keep up with the pace of technology development. We update them from time to time, but such changes are always reactive, not proactive."[23] Still, as a court put it in regard to the legitimacy of police use of infrared thermal detection devices aimed at an individual's home without a warrant or notification,

> As technology races with ever increasing speed, our subjective expectations of privacy may be unconsciously altered . . . our legal rights to privacy should reflect thoughtful and purposeful choices rather than simply mirror the current state of the commercial technology industry.[24]

Perhaps the more personalized response of Northrup Grumman Corporation's former ethics officer, Frank Daly, sums it up better: "Can this characteristic of speed drive us and have a negative effect upon how we treat other people? You can't rush love or a soufflé."[25]

What are the implications of this definition or understanding of privacy for businesses and for business ethics analysis? In general, one would argue that personal

TABLE 7.2
The European Union Privacy Shield

Source: David Meyer, "Here's What U.S. Firms Will Have to Do under the EU Privacy Shield Deal" (February 29, 2016), http://fortune.com/2016/02/29/privacy-shield-details/ (accessed March 8, 2016).

Under the EU Privacy Shield:

- When using Europeans' data, U.S. intelligence services will have to adhere to the new limits and oversight mechanism.

- The U.S. State Department will have to employ a new watchdog to handle complaints about intelligence-related matters.

- Companies must self-certify compliance with the Privacy Shield and its stated principles. Certifications must be renewed annually.

- Companies must publicly display their privacy policies that show compliance with EU law.

- Companies will have to resolve complaints within 45 days of being filed.

- Companies will have to update their privacy policies to explain how people can access these services.

- Companies will face more restrictions on being able to forward Europeans' personal data to other companies.

The following information is sometimes requested on standard employment applications, though candidates might consider some of it to be private or personal. Which of the following items about an employee might an employer have a legitimate claim to know, and why?

- A job applicant's social security number
- An applicant's arrest record
- An employee's medical records
- An employee's marital status
- Whether a job applicant smokes
- An employee's political affiliation
- An employee's sexual orientation
- An employee's credit rating

- What facts are relevant to your decisions?
- What would the consequences be of refusing to answer any questions on an employment application?
- Are you basing your decision on particular rights of the employee or the employer?
- Are there people other than the employer and employee who might have a stake in what information is released to employers?

information should remain private unless a relationship exists between the business and the individual that legitimates collecting and using personal information about that individual. For example, to determine the range of employee privacy, we would have to specify the nature of the relationship between employer and employee. The nature of the employment relationship will help determine the appropriate boundary between employers and employees and therefore the information that ought to remain rightfully private within the workplace. (See the Decision Point "Inquiring Employers Want to Know" to consider information reasonably related to the job.) If we adopt something like a contractual model of employment, where the conditions and terms of employment are subject to the mutual and informed consent of both parties, then employee consent would become one major condition on what information employers can collect.

We can summarize our preceding examination by saying that employee privacy is violated whenever (1) employers infringe upon personal decisions that are not relevant to the employment contract (whether the contract is implied or explicit) or (2) personal information that is not relevant to that contract is collected, stored, or used without the informed consent of the employee. Further, since consent plays a pivotal role in this understanding, the burden of proof rests with the employer to establish the relevancy of personal decisions and information at issue.

Linking the Value of Privacy to the Ethical Implications of Technology

The advent of new technology challenges privacy in ways that we could never before imagine. For example, consider the implications of new technology on employee and employer expectations regarding the use of time; the distinction between work use and personal use of technology; the protection of proprietary information, performance measurement, and privacy interests; or accessibility issues related to the digital divide. Technology allows for in-home offices, raising extraordinary opportunities and challenges, issues of safety, and privacy concerns (there are now more than 30 million U.S. telecommuters[26]). Because each of us is capable of much greater production through the use of technology, technology not only provides benefits but also allows employers to ask more of each employee.

Though the following warning from the International Labour Office is more than a decade old, its cautions about the implications of the technology economy are as relevant today as the day they were issued:

> More and more, boundaries are dissolving between leisure and working time, the place of work and place of residence, learning and working. . . . Wherever categories such as working time, working location, performance at work and jobs become blurred, the result is the deterioration of the foundations of our edifice of agreements, norms, rules, laws, organizational forms, structures and institutions, all of which have a stronger influence on our behavioral patterns and systems of values than we are aware.[27]

New technology, however, does not necessarily impact our value judgments but instead simply provides new ways to gather the information on which to base them. Sorting through these issues is challenging nevertheless. Consider the impact of the attacks of September 11, 2001, on an employer's decision to share personal employee information or customer information with law enforcement. Private firms may be more willing—or less willing—today to share private information than they would have been previously.

Firms often experience, and often find themselves ill prepared for, the unanticipated challenges stemming from new technology. Consider the lesson one firm learned about how problems with Twitter use and abuse might extend beyond the end of the employment relationship. An employee with PhoneDog, a company that provides mobile device news and reviews, created a work-related Twitter account that amassed 17,000 followers.[28] When he left the company, he simply changed the user name of the account and kept it as his own, sending "tweets" that did not link back to or reference PhoneDog. The company sued to recover from the ex-employee the $2.50 per Twitter follower, per month, in revenue that it claims it has lost. The ex-employee claimed that the account belonged to him, not to PhoneDog.

Ultimately, PhoneDog and the ex-employee settled out of court and the former employee kept his Twitter account, along with its followers. We learn from this case that neither individual Twitter users nor a company can own their followers!

"No one 'owns' their followers as a matter of property," explain Kevin Werbach, Wharton professor of legal studies and business ethics. "I don't even know my followers; they can stop following me at any time. It's not that the company is doing something internally with the names [to generate more business.] It's not like the company's customer list." The lack of legislation or legal precedent means that social media disputes like PhoneDog's become a matter of contract law, says Andrea Matwyshyn, Wharton professor of legal studies and business ethics. "These are questions of contract law between the employee and the company," she notes. "You need to contract very carefully and in advance what social media practices are permissible in the workplace. If a transgression occurs before a written policy or agreement was put into place, the case stands or falls based on the facts around it." Issues addressed by this case did not go unnoticed by businesses; employers with policies governing social media use increased from 55 to 69 percent in the year following the case.[29]

Do we need "new ethics" for this "new economy"? Perhaps not, because the same values one held under previous circumstances should, if they are true and justified, permeate and relate to later circumstances.[30] However, the perspective one brings to each experience is impacted by the understanding and use of new technology and other advances. As economist Antonio Argandoña cautions, there has been a change in values "that may be caused by the opportunities created by the technology."[31] On the other hand, he points to the possibility that new technology may also do much good, including development of depressed regions, increased citizenship participation, defense of human rights, and other potential gains.

Information and Privacy

A business needs to be able to anticipate the perceptions of its stakeholders in order to be able to make the most effective decisions for its long-term sustainability. New technological advancements are often difficult for the public to understand and therefore ripe for challenge. How do you best manage the entrepreneurial passion for forward momentum with stakeholder comfort and security?

The motto at Google, the Internet-based search engine, is the deontological imperative: "don't be evil." Its founders describe that imperative by striving to "define precisely what it means to be a force for good—always do the right, ethical thing. Ultimately, 'don't do evil' seems the easiest way to summarize it."[32] For instance, Google does not allow gun ads, which admittedly upset the gun lobby, so one might expect that Google would be especially sensitive to stakeholder concerns as it develops new technology.

Google suggests that it is providing a value to society by offering its free "Gmail" e-mail system. However, in recent years Google has caused some controversy with its Gmail privacy policy. Google essentially mines a user's e-mail contents and search engine history to provide that user with targeted marketing and online advertising, specific to the user's interests. Many users were surprised when Google argued in a lawsuit about the issue that "Google's 425 million Gmail users have 'no reasonable expectation' that their communications are confidential."[33] However, perhaps as one economist wrote, "there is no such thing as a free lunch, and we must look carefully at the business motives behind these firms' generosity." But then how does that square with the same company that has told us in the past, "You should trust whoever is handling your email"?[34]

That trust is truly the crux of the issue with the introduction of new technology, isn't it? When consumers rely on technology provided by a business—from e-mail to Internet access and from cell phones to medical labs—they might easily assume that the business will respect their privacy. Most average e-mail users do not understand the technology behind the process. One would like to believe that those responsible for the technology are, themselves, accountable to the user. That would be the ideal.

Google previously has been in hot water over privacy violations. The Federal Trade Commission (FTC) accused the company of misrepresenting its policy of using "cookies," the small pieces of software that are used to track information on computers, to users of certain Internet browsers. Google agreed to pay $22.5 million, the largest civic penalty ever levied by the agency, for violating the terms of an earlier settlement regarding consumer privacy.[35] In a statement, Google asserted that the issue with cookies was inadvertent and had been repaired, adding that "We set the highest standards of privacy and security for our users."[36]

Despite this assertion, a new wave of litigation arose with the implementation of Google's new privacy policy. When Google announced the policy on data mining, it said that the policy did not apply to students using Google Apps for Education. Apps for Education is used by K–12 schools and institutions of higher education throughout the world to access free, online applications such as e-mail, calendar, word processing, and other services. However, Google later admitted that it does, indeed, data mine student e-mails for ad-targeting purposes outside of school, even when in-school ad serving is turned off. As a result, two students filed suit against Google in 2014, arguing that Google had no right to scan the e-mail of students who are required to use the apps. Joining this suit were seven other plaintiffs who argued that Google violated wiretap laws when it scanned e-mails sent from non-Google accounts in order to target ads to Gmail users. All plaintiffs argued that both the students and non-Gmail users had not accepted Google's terms of service.

While the suits remain ongoing, Google has since announced that all data mining from the Apps for Education application have been turned off, but the company also indicated that non-Gmail users sending e-mail to a Gmail user should have no "reasonable expectation of privacy."[37]

By failing to fully comprehend and plan for its stakeholders' perceptions of the program, Google not only breached ethical boundaries but also suffered public backlash. It did not anticipate concerns over privacy or the controversy its programs would engender. Critics argued that Google should have consulted with stakeholders, determined the best way to balance their interests, and then considered these interests as they introduced new programs, all of which might have precluded the negative impact on its reputation. The lesson learned is that, notwithstanding even reasonable justification (which remains arguable in this case),

Questions about using technology for "good" or "evil," from an anonymous web posting:

Management wants me to spy.

Management wants me to spy on a colleague. I'll be using [a spying program] that is 100% hidden, does screen captures, etc. Is there a document out there that I can have management sign to limit my liability? I want signatures from all management stating that they are authorizing me to spy. Thoughts? I have done this before, but this is the first time that they have asked me to compile data against a user for possible use in court. Thanks.

What are some of the questions or concerns you might bring up in an answer and what would you suggest this individual do to respond to them?

- What are the key facts relevant to your response?
- What is the ethical issue involved in peer spying in the workplace?
- Who are the stakeholders?
- What alternatives would you suggest to this individual, and what alternatives exist for employers who wish to gather information about employees surreptitiously?
- How do the alternatives compare; how do the alternatives affect the stakeholders?

people are simply not comfortable with an involuntary loss of control over these personal decisions. Google failed to consider the perspectives of its stakeholders, the impact of its decisions on those stakeholders, and the fundamental values its decisions implied. Consider the discomfort evidenced in the Decision Point "Technology Dilemmas."

Economist Antonio Argandoña contends that, if new technology is dependent on and has as its substance information and data, significant moral requirements should be imposed on that information. He suggests the following as necessary elements:

- **Truthfulness and accuracy:** The person providing the information must ensure that it is truthful and accurate, at least to a reasonable degree.

- **Respect for privacy:** The person receiving or accumulating information must take into account the ethical limits of individuals' (and organizations') privacy. This would include issues relating to company secrets, espionage, and intelligence gathering.

- **Respect for property and safety rights:** Areas of potential vulnerability, including network security, sabotage, theft of information, and impersonation, are enhanced and must therefore be protected.

- **Accountability:** Technology allows for greater anonymity and distance, requiring a concurrent increased exigency for personal responsibility and accountability.[38]

Imagine how firms may respond to this call for responsibility in the development, manufacturing, marketing, and service related to new production or other corporate activities. What ethical issues does Argandoña's proposal raise, and how will stakeholders be impacted if firms respond positively to this call?

Managing Employees through Monitoring

OBJECTIVE

One of the most prevalent forms of information gathering in the workplace, in particular, is monitoring employees' work, and technology has afforded employers enormous abilities to do so effectively at very low costs. If an employer has a rule about the use of technology, how can it ensure that employees are following that rule? For instance, according to a 2013–2014 survey of 120 multinational companies, 90 percent of firms use social networking for business purposes and more than 75 percent of businesses report having dealt with issues of employee misuse of social networks.[39] But, unless your supervisor is looking over your shoulder, it would be difficult to check on your access or personal use of technology without some advanced form of online monitoring.

CareerBuilder.com conducts an annual survey of more than 3,400 U.S. employees, along with over 2,000 hiring managers and human resource professionals, on the topics of both **e-mail monitoring** and also **Internet use monitoring** in the workplace. Its 2015 survey found that 21 percent of employers monitor employee e-mails and Internet usage, while 33 percent of employers block employees from accessing certain websites at work. With the rise of social media and social networking use in recent years, the role of the Internet in connection with monitoring is evolving. Fifty percent of employers restrict employees from posting on behalf of the company on social media, and 25 percent have adopted stricter policies in this regard over the past year.[40]

e-mail monitoring
The maintenance and either periodic or random review of e-mail communications of employees or others for a variety of business purposes.

Internet use monitoring
The maintenance and either periodic or random review of the use of the Internet by employees or others based on time spent or content accessed for a variety of business purposes.

We have come to expect that our e-mails are the property of—or at least subject to search by—our employers. For example, when a cheating scandal erupted at Harvard University in 2012, Harvard administrators secretly searched the e-mail accounts of 16 deans who had been responsible for handling the cheating case. The deans were neither informed nor asked to give consent.[41]

With the rise of social media and social networking use in recent years, Internet use monitoring also is evolving. A study completed in 2014 by PricewaterhouseCoopers predicted that data monitoring of employees will increase over the next decade as Generation Y is absorbed into the workforce. It concluded that, by 2020, approximately half of the global workforce will be between the ages of 18 and 32, and will bring different attitudes to work, technology, and personal data. The study also found that 31 percent of current workers would be happy to allow their employer to monitor their social media activity *if* it meant greater job security.[42]

OBJECTIVE

Unfortunately, many of the ethical issues that arise in the area of managing information are not readily visible. When we do not completely understand the technology, we might not understand the ethical implications of our decisions.

When that occurs, we are not able to protect our own information effectively because we may not understand the impact on our autonomy, the control of our information, our reciprocal obligations, or even what might be best for our personal existence. For example, do you always consider all the people who might see the e-mails you send? Can your employer read your e-mail? Your first response might be "no, my boss doesn't have my secret password." However, experts tell us that any system is penetrable. Employers have been known to randomly read e-mails to ensure that the system is being used for business purposes. Is this ethical? Does it matter if there is a company policy that systems must be used only for business purposes, or that the employees are given notice that their e-mail will be read?

How do you know that your boss will not forward your disparaging remarks about a colleague directly to that colleague? It can be done with the touch of a key. Are different issues raised by that concern from those that arose with a traditional written letter? People could always send or show your letter to someone. When we mistakenly believe that no one is watching, we may engage in activities that we would otherwise refrain from doing. For instance, you may believe that hitting the "delete" key actually deletes an e-mail message. But it does not always delete that message from the server, so it might be retrieved by your supervisor or have a negative impact in a lawsuit.

These ethical issues may be compounded by the fact that a knowledge gap exists between people who *do* understand the technology and others who are unable to protect themselves precisely because they *do not* understand. You might not expect to be fired for sending out an e-mail—but if you thought about it a bit, you might have known what to expect.

OBJECTIVE

Technology allows for access to information that was never before possible. Under previous circumstances, one could usually tell if someone had steamed open a letter over a teapot. Today, you usually cannot discover if someone reads the e-mail you sent yesterday to your best friend. Access can take place unintentionally as well. In doing a routine background check, a supervisor may unintentionally uncover information of an extremely personal nature that may bear absolutely no relevance to one's work performance.

Moreover, because technology allows us to work from almost anywhere on this planet, we are seldom out of the boundaries of our workplace. For instance, just because you are going to your sister's wedding does not mean that your supervisor cannot reach you. This raises a tough question: *Should* your supervisor try to reach you just because she has the ability to do so? Our total accessibility creates new expectations, and therefore conflicts. How long is reasonable to wait before responding to an e-mail? If someone does not hear from you within 24 hours of sending an e-mail, is it unreasonable for them to resend it? Should a text message be considered more urgent than an e-mail, or do the same answers apply? Continuous accessibility blurs the lines between our personal and professional lives. (See the Reality Check "Is Privacy Perception a Factor of Age?")

Another challenge posed by the new technology accessible in the workplace is the facelessness that results from its use. If we have to face someone as we

Reality Check   *Is Privacy Perception a Factor of Age?*

There's plenty of evidence that the "Facebook Generation" doesn't think of privacy quite the way their parents do.

Several studies have evaluated the differences in perception between the Millennial generation (defined as individuals between the ages of 18 and 29) and older generations when it comes to privacy concerns. Consider the following distinctions and whether you find your own perceptions aligned with those of your age group or older.

- **Definition of Privacy:** Baby Boomers (over 50 years) are 74 percent more likely to choose a traditional, offline description of privacy ("the right to be free from others watching me") and be less concerned with guarding their privacy in person. For example, Baby Boomers are 42 percent more likely to walk around naked in locker rooms. Millennials are 177 percent more likely to choose a modern, datacentric definition ("being able to delete anything about me online").[43]

- **Online Privacy Concerns:** Millennials are more interested in managing their online reputation among their peers, and in concealing private or incriminating information from authority figures such as their families, teachers, school administrators, college admissions officers, and potential employers. Older adults are more concerned with hiding their personal data from commercial interests, where almost half of Millennials in one survey think it is fair for corporations to gather personal information in exchange for a free service.[44]

- **Government Surveillance:** Nearly 60 percent of Millennials in another survey agreed with a former federal employee's decision to leak information about a U.S. National Security Agency spy program on citizens, while over half of adults 50 or older thought the decision was a criminal action. However, what is interesting is that a similar survey in 1971 after the Pentagon Papers were released showed that 75 percent of adults under 30 thought sharing those documents was the "right thing to do," while only half of those older than 50 agreed. Perhaps when you are born is not as important as how long you have been alive.[45]

make our decisions, we are more likely to care about the impact of that decision on that person. Conversely, when we do not get to know someone because we do not have to see that person in order to do our business, we often do not take into account the impact of our decisions on him or her. It is merely a name at the other end of a digital correspondence, rather than another human being's name. When people put something in writing, we assume that they mean what they say, and we hold them to it as a precise rendering of their intent. To the contrary, we consider e-mail, texting, and posting on social media sites to be more akin to conversation and treat them as such, lobbing notes back and forth, much as we would in a conversation, and permitting the idiosyncrasies that we would allow when speaking. Most forms of digital communication, in contrast, arose in the personal context as forms of spontaneous, casual, off-the-cuff communication. We do not think in advance and often write quickly without rereading before sending. We send things in writing now that we might only have chatted about before.

Given the ease and informality of electronic communications, we also often "say" (post, text, e-mail, and the like) things to each other that we would never say to someone's face, precisely because we do not have to consider the impact of what we are saying. We are more careless with our communications because they are easier to conduct—just hit a button and they are sent.

To address some of the ethical issues computers present, the Computer Ethics Institute has created "The Ten Commandments of Computer Ethics," which include these imperatives: "Thou shalt not snoop around in other people's computer files; Thou shalt think about the social consequences of the program you are writing or the system you are designing; and Thou shalt always use a computer in ways that ensure consideration and respect for your fellow humans." Of course, such guidelines have no enforcement mechanism and are little more than suggestions. To see the types of additional information available through other web services, see Table 7.3.

Why do firms monitor technology usage?

OBJECTIVE 8

A firm chooses to monitor its employees and collect the information discussed earlier for numerous reasons. Employers need to manage their workplaces to place workers in appropriate positions, to ensure compliance with affirmative action requirements, or to administer workplace benefits. Monitoring also allows the manager to ensure effective, productive performance by preventing the loss of productivity to inappropriate technology use. Research evidences a rise in personal use of technology; of the 6.8 billion people on the planet, 5.1 billion have access to a mobile phone, but only 4.5 billion have access to a toilet.[46] Nearly 90 percent of North Americans, 73 percent of Europeans, and a total of just over 45 percent of the world had Internet access in 2016.[47] More than 74 percent of the adult population on the Internet uses social media sites.[48] A 2015 survey found that, during a typical workday, 52 percent of employees are using their cell phones for personal use (such as calls or texts); 44 percent are conducting Internet searches unrelated to work; and 36 percent are checking personal social media accounts.[49]

Beyond the management of its human resources, monitoring offers an employer a method by which to protect its others resources. Employers use monitoring to protect proprietary information and to guard against theft, to protect their investment in equipment and bandwidth, and to protect against legal liability.[50]

More than 70 percent of businesses report taking disciplinary action against an employee for misuse of social media.[51] In addition, 24 percent have fired someone for using the Internet for non-work-related activity.[52] (See the

TABLE 7.3
Public Access to Personal Information

Source: InfoCheckUSA, "Pricing Guide" (2010), www.infocheckusa.com/background-check-pricing.htm (accessed February 23, 2016).

InfoCheck USA provides the following personal information at the listed prices, often instantaneously:

- General all-around background search, $249
- Countywide search for misdemeanors and felonies, $20
- Whether subject has ever spent time in state prison, $10
- Whether subject has ever served time in a federal prison, $20
- National search for outstanding warrants for subject, $20
- Countywide search for any civil filings filed by or against subject, $16
- Subject's driving record for at least three previous years, $15

Reality Check *Surfing Porn at Work*

In July 2011, it was widely reported that the head of Houston's public transit agency was suspended (for a week) for using the agency's Internet connection to view pornographic websites. This sort of conflict is likely to become increasingly common because some people joke that the only thing more common in office settings than boredom are high-quality Internet connections. But should the issue here really be porn, or instead should the issue be whether personal web surfing at the office is allowed at all? After all, there are all kinds of deviant, transgressive, and socially controversial materials on the web. What should be a company's policy?

A company might reasonably forbid use of company Internet for non-business-related purposes, just as most companies forbid use of corporate stationery or corporate premises by employees who are moonlighting. On the other hand, a company might reasonably allow a certain amount of personal usage. This "reasonable use" would compare to an employee being permitted the occasional personal call on a company phone. If it is company policy to prohibit any personal use of the Internet at all, there should be a clearly stated policy. Needless to say, simply because no policy might exist that prohibits surfing porn at work, it is not necessarily a good idea. It is generally pretty dumb, especially if there is any chance at all that co-workers are going to see and be offended.

Source: Adapted from Chris MacDonald, "Surfing Porn at Work," *Canadian Business* (August 1, 2011), www.canadianbusiness.com/blog/business_ethics/37233 (accessed February 23, 2016).

Reality Check "Surfing Porn at Work" for a discussion of these issues.) Without monitoring, how would they know what occurs? Moreover, as courts maintain the standard in many cases of whether the employer "knew or should have known" of wrongdoing, the state-of-the-art definition of "should have known" becomes all the more vital. If most firms use monitoring technology to uncover this wrongdoing, the definition of "should have known" will begin to include an expectation of monitoring.

Monitoring Employees through Drug Testing

OBJECTIVE

Drug testing is one area in which employers have had a longer history of monitoring employees than technology monitoring. The employer has a strong argument in favor of drug or other substance testing based on the law. Because the employer is often responsible for legal violations its employees committed in the course of their job, the employer's interest in retaining control over every aspect of the work environment increases. On the other hand, employees may argue that their drug usage is relevant only if it impacts their job performance. Until it does, the employer should have no basis for testing.

However, recent changes in the law, such as the legalization of marijuana in some jurisdictions for medical or recreational purposes, have made for complicated workplace dilemmas. The psychoactive ingredient in marijuana, THC, remains in one's system for as long as 30 days after use. Medical users may medicate throughout the day and therefore "likely will have to have a much higher blood-THC content than a casual user, but the casual user likely will be more impaired from a physical and mental standpoint than the chronic one."[53] Though most states do not protect marijuana users from terminations when they test positive, even if smoking pot is legal, Minnesota and Arizona do offer some protections. As long employees are not using the substance or impaired at work, they cannot be fired for testing positive—but testing for impairment is tough!

Consider the possibilities of incorrect presumptions in connection with drug testing. For instance, the National Council on Alcoholism and Drug Dependence suggests that the following behaviors may be warning signs of drug use:

Job Performance

- Inconsistent work quality
- Poor concentration and lack of focus
- Lowered productivity or erratic work patterns
- Increased absenteeism or on-the-job "presenteeism"
- Unexplained disappearances from the job site
- Carelessness, mistakes, or errors in judgment
- Needless risk taking
- Disregard for safety for self and others—on-the-job and off-the-job accidents
- Extended lunch periods and early departures

Workplace Behavior

- Frequent financial problems
- Avoidance of friends and colleagues
- Blaming of others for own problems and shortcomings
- Complaints about problems at home
- Deterioration in personal appearance or personal hygiene
- Complaints, excuses, and time off for vaguely defined illnesses or family problems[54]

On the other hand, it does not take a great deal of imagination to come up with other, more innocuous alternative possibilities. Yet, an employer may decide to test based on these "signs." Is it ethical to presume someone is guilty based on these signs? Does a person have a fundamental right to be presumed innocent? Or, perhaps, do the risks of that presumption outweigh the individual's rights in this situation and justify greater precautions?

A 2014 poll of more than 1,100 human resource professionals found that 58 percent of companies require job candidates to take a pre-employment drug test, 28 percent do not have such a requirement, and 14 percent test applicants only when required by state law or when the position is safety-sensitive. Large firms are more likely to require testing than smaller firms, with more than 62 percent of organizations with 4,000 employees or more requiring pre-employment drug tests.[55]

Though drug testing may provide a productivity benefit for companies, such policies may introduce legal and ethical challenges for employers. For example, a 2014 study by Quest Diagnostics, a popular provider of workplace drug tests, revealed that "the percentage of positive drug tests among American workers has increased for the first time in more than a decade [to 4.7 percent of those tested], fueled by a rise in marijuana and amphetamines."[56] The Americans with Disabilities Act prohibits employers from inquiring about an employee's use of prescription drugs unless the employer has a reasonable basis for believing that the worker poses a safety threat or is unable to do his or her job. "If somebody puts his head down on a desk, do you test him for drugs or not?" asks Dr. Robert DuPont, president of the Institute for Behavior and Health. "The first time you get an employee who says you're harassing them, you're not going to test anyone else even if they're passed out."[57]

In the seminal legal case on the issue, *Skinner v. Railway Labor Executives' Ass'n,*[58] the Court addressed the question of whether certain forms of drug and alcohol testing violate the Fourth Amendment. In *Skinner,* the defendant justified testing railway workers based on safety concerns "to prevent accidents and casualties in railroad operations that result from impairment of employees by alcohol or drugs." The court held that "the Government's interest in regulating the conduct of railroad employees to ensure safety, like its supervision of probationers or regulated industries, or its operation of a government office, school, or prison, likewise presents 'special needs' beyond normal law enforcement that may justify departures from the usual warrant and probable-cause requirements."

It was clear to the Court that the governmental interest in ensuring the safety of the traveling public and of the employees themselves "plainly justifies prohibiting covered employees from using alcohol or drugs on duty, or while subject to being called for duty." The issue then for the Court was whether, absent a warrant or individualized suspicion, the means by which the defendant monitored compliance with this prohibition justified the privacy intrusion. The Court concluded that the railway's compelling interests outweighed privacy concerns because the proposed testing "is not an undue infringement on the justifiable expectations of privacy of covered employees."

Where public safety is at risk, there is arguably a compelling public interest claim from a utilitarian perspective that may be sufficiently persuasive to outweigh any one individual's right to privacy or right to control information about oneself. However, what about jobs in which public safety is not at risk? Is it justifiable to test all employees and job applicants? Is the proposed benefit to the employer sufficiently valuable in your perspective to outweigh the employee's fundamental interest in autonomy and privacy? Should a utilitarian viewpoint govern or should deontological principles take priority? Should we consider a distributive justice perspective and the fairest result—does distributive justice apply under these circumstances?

Several major retail employers, including Home Depot, IKEA, and Walmart, have comprehensive drug-testing policies for both job applicants and employees. Many stores also promote their "drug-free" workplace policy as a marketing strategy. With just a few exceptions, such policies are legal throughout the United States. The question is, "Are they ethically appropriate?" The Decision Point "Limits on Personal Information in Hiring" explores these issues.

What limits should be placed on the reasons a job applicant can be denied employment? As we discussed earlier, the law prohibits denying someone a job on the basis of race, religion, ethnicity, gender, or disability. The law generally allows denial of a job on the basis of drug use. Like employment at will, the burden of proof lies with the job applicant to demonstrate that the denial was based on the prohibited categories; otherwise employers need no reason to deny someone a job. Suppose a business wanted to ensure not only a drug-free workplace but also an alcohol-free workplace. Would a business have the ethical right to deny a job, or dismiss an employee, for drinking alcohol? Courts have been asked to decide the legitimacy of dismissals for cigarette smoking, for political beliefs, and for having an abortion. Do you think any of these are legitimate grounds for dismissal? Between 60 and 70 percent of U.S. employers evaluate applicants' personalities with assessment tools.[59] Such tests ask many personal questions, including some that concern a person's sexual life. Would a business have an ethical right to deny employment to someone on the basis of the results of a personality test?

What are some of the questions or concerns you might have while trying to answer this challenge? What would you suggest a business do to respond to them?

- What are the key facts relevant to your response?
- What are the ethical issues involved in basing hiring decisions on personal information?
- Who are the stakeholders?
- What alternatives would you suggest to business in considering personal information in hiring, and what alternatives exist for employers?
- How do the alternatives compare for business and for the stakeholders?

Let us look at one company in particular and how it has navigated some of these issues. Xerox began using pre-employment personality tests in 2012. Recently, it began examining the results of the tests in connection with compassion factors, since data have demonstrated that applicants who score high on "empathy" tend to do better in customer service. However, Xerox stopped using the data that related to job applicants' commuting time even though it learned that customer-service employees who arrived at work more quickly were likely to retain their jobs at Xerox longer.

Why? Xerox managers decided that this information about commuting time potentially could place applicants from certain neighborhoods that were populated predominantly by minorities at a disadvantage in the hiring process. "There's some knowledge that you gain that you should stay away from when making a hiring decision," explains Teri Morse, Xerox's vice president of recruitment. Even though some of the information should not be used simply because good judgment tells you that it is not appropriate, Morse is surprised by how accurate the tests can be.[60]

Another consideration that is currently being investigated by the Equal Employment Opportunity Commission (EEOC) and in litigation based on the ADA is whether personality tests adversely impact individuals with certain mental illnesses such as depression or bipolar disorder. The EEOC is concerned because the tests ask respondents to answer questions honestly, such as "over the course of the day, I can experience many mood changes," and "if something very bad happens, it takes some time before I feel happy again."[61] Employers are watching and waiting for the EEOC's decision because a ruling against personality tests would "set a tremendous precedent," forcing companies and test makers to prove their tests are not discriminatory, says Marc Bendick, an economist and consultant who studies workforce diversity issues.[62]

- If you were researching this issue for the EEOC, would you conclude that these questions violate the ADA? Do the questions listed inappropriately ask these individuals to reveal a disability?
- Do you conclude that answering these questions may adversely impact their potential employment?
- If so, is there an alternative way of protecting against this discrimination while still retaining these assessments?
- How do the alternatives compare for business and for the stakeholders involved?

Other Forms of Monitoring

OBJECTIVE

Health Insurance Portability and Accountability Act (HIPAA) (Pub. L. 104-191)
HIPAA stipulates that employers cannot use "protected health information" in making employment decisions without prior consent. Protected health information includes all medical records or other individually identifiable health information.

Employers are limited in their collection of information through other various forms of testing, such as polygraphs or medical tests. Employers are constrained by a business necessity and relatedness standard or, in the case of polygraphs, by a requirement of reasonable suspicion. With regard to medical information specifically, employers' decisions are not only governed by the Americans with Disabilities Act but also restricted by the **Health Insurance Portability and Accountability Act (HIPAA).** HIPAA stipulates that employers cannot use "protected health information" in making employment decisions without prior consent. Protected health information includes all medical records or other individually identifiable health information.

In recent years polygraph and drug testing, physical and electronic surveillance, third-party background checks, and psychological testing have all been used as means to gain information about employees. More recently, electronic monitoring and surveillance are increasingly being used in the workplace. Where might this practice develop in the future? One area that is sure to provide new questions about privacy is genetic testing. Genetic testing and screening, of both employees and consumers, is another new technology that will offer businesses a wealth of information about potential employees and customers. The Genetic Information Non-Discrimination Act (GINA) 2008 became effective in November 2009 and prohibits discriminatory treatment in employment based on genetic information (disparate impact remains subject to the recommendation of an EEOC commission).

GINA presents interesting questions because it defines "genetic information" in a broader sense than one might imagine. Under GINA, your genetic information is not merely information about you, but also your family's medical history, including any disease or disorder or genetic test results of a family member. The term *family member* includes your dependents and relatives all the way to the fourth degree of kinship. In addition, GINA mandates that employers be extremely careful in terms of how they gather and manage employee genetic information as they are subject to similar conditions to the Americans with Disabilities Act.

GINA does provide for exceptions. For instance, an employer can collect genetic information in order to comply with the Family Medical Leave Act or to monitor the biological effects of toxic substances in the workplace. Also, though GINA contains a strict confidentiality provision, an employer may release genetic information about an employee under certain specific circumstances:

1. To the employee or member upon request;
2. To an occupational or other health researcher;
3. In response to a court order;
4. To a government official investigating compliance with this act if the information is relevant to the investigation;
5. In connection with the employee's compliance with the certification provisions of the Family and Medical Leave Act of 1993 or such requirements under state family and medical leave laws; or
6. To a public health agency.[63]

Finally, the EEOC issued clarifying guidelines in 2010 that include a "safe harbor" liability exception for employers that inadvertently receive genetic information in response to a lawful medical inquiry, so long as the employer has notified the respondent of her or his GINA rights.[64]

Coauthor of this textbook Chris MacDonald provides a helpful overview of the act, along with insights into areas of potential ethical vulnerabilities, in Reading 7-4, "Genetic Testing in the Workplace," at the end of the chapter. MacDonald contends that GINA represents a possible privacy intrusion not only into the individual employee's personal privacy, but also into the worker's family's information. However, MacDonald challenges his readers by asking whether discrimination based on genetic information could ever be an ethically justified basis for an employment decision. Consider your answer and then review his arguments.

Business Reasons to Limit Monitoring

OBJECTIVE

Notwithstanding these persuasive justifications for monitoring in the workplace, employee advocates suggest limitations on monitoring for several reasons. First, there is a concern that monitoring may create a suspicious and hostile workplace. By reducing the level of worker autonomy and respect, as well as workers' right to control their environment, the employer has neglected to consider the key stakeholder critical to business success in many ways—the worker. A second concern demonstrates the problem. Monitoring may arguably constrain effective performance since it can cause increased stress and pressure, negatively impacting performance and having the potential to cause physical disorders such as carpal tunnel syndrome.[65] One study found that monitored workers suffered more depression, extreme anxiety, severe fatigue or exhaustion, strain injuries, and neck problems than unmonitored workers. Stress might also result from a situation where workers do not have the opportunity to review and correct misinformation in the data collected. These elements will lead not only to an unhappy, disgruntled worker who perhaps will seek alternative employment but also to lower productivity and performance that will lead to higher costs and fewer returns to the employer. Finally, a third concern is that employees claim that monitoring is an inherent invasion of privacy that violates their fundamental human right to privacy.

Balancing Interests

Therefore, where should the line be drawn between employer and employee rights? Most of us would agree that installing video cameras in the washrooms of the workplace to prevent theft may be going a bit too far, but knowing where to draw the line before that might be more difficult. As long as technology exists to allow for privacy invasions, should the employer have the right to use it?

Consider whether monitoring could be made ethical or humane. One suggestion is to give due notice to employees that they will be monitored, plus the opportunity to avoid monitoring in certain situations. For instance, if an employer chooses to monitor random phone calls of its customer service representatives, it could notify the workers that certain calls may be monitored and these calls would be signified by a "beep" on the line during the monitoring. In addition, if workers make a personal call, they may use a nonmonitored phone to avoid a wrongful invasion of privacy.

However, such an approach may not solve all the concerns about monitoring. Suppose you are the employer and you want to make sure your service representatives handle calls in a patient, tolerant, and affable manner. By telling the worker which calls you are monitoring, your employees may be sure to be on their best behavior during those calls. This effect of employer monitoring is termed the "Hawthorne Effect": Workers are found to be more productive based on the psychological stimulus of being singled out, which makes them feel more important. In other words, merely knowing one is being studied might make one a better worker. Random, anonymous monitoring may better resolve your concerns (but not those of the worker).

Perhaps the most effective means to achieve monitoring objectives while remaining sensitive to the concerns of employees is to strive toward a balance that respects individual dignity while also holding individuals accountable for their particular roles in the organization.

OBJECTIVE

A monitoring program developed according to the mission of the organization (for example, with integrity), then implemented in a manner that remains accountable to the impacted employees, approaches that balance. Consider the following parameters for a monitoring policy that endeavors to accomplish the goals described earlier:

- No monitoring in private areas (e.g., restrooms).
- Monitoring limited to within the workplace.
- Employees should have access to information gathered through monitoring.

- No secret monitoring—advance notice required.
- Monitoring should only result in attaining some business interest.
- Employer may collect only job-related information.
- Agreement regarding disclosure of information gained through monitoring.
- Prohibition of discrimination by employers based on off-work activities.

These parameters allow the employer to effectively and ethically supervise the work employees do, to protect against misuse of resources, and to have an appropriate mechanism by which to evaluate each worker's performance, thus respecting the legitimate business interest of the employer. They are also supported by global organizations such as the International Labour Organization (ILO) (see Table 7.4).

Philosopher William Parent conceives the right to privacy more appropriately as a right to liberty and therefore seeks to determine the potential affront to liberty from the employer's actions. He suggests the following six questions to determine whether those actions are justifiable or have the potential for an invasion of privacy or liberty:

1. For what purpose is the undocumented personal knowledge sought?
2. Is this purpose a legitimate and important one?

TABLE 7.4
ILO Principles for Protecting Workers' Personal Data

Source: Adapted from International Labour Organization, Press Release, "ILO Meeting Adopts Draft Code of Practice on Protection of Workers' Data," ILO/96/29 (October 7, 1996), www.ilo.org/global/about-the-ilo/media-centre/press-releases/WCMS_008070/lang--en/index.htm (accessed March 6, 2016).

In 1997, the International Labour Organization published a Code of Practice on the Protection of Workers' Personal Data, and it remains in use today. Though not binding on employers, it serves to help codify ethical standards in connection with the collection and use of employee personal information.

The code explains that "personal data should be used lawfully and fairly, and only for reasons directly relevant to the employment of the worker."

Personal data should be used "only for the purposes for which they were originally collected."

The Draft Code emphasizes that "all persons . . . who have access to personal data, should be bound to a rule of confidentiality" in their handling of the data. It also says that "workers may not waive their privacy rights."

With respect to collection of personal data the code states that employers "should not collect personal data concerning a worker's sex life, political, religious or other beliefs or criminal convictions" unless "the data are directly relevant to an employment decision and in conformity with national legislation." In addition, "polygraphs, truth-verification equipment or any other similar testing procedure should not be used." Genetic screening "should be prohibited or limited to cases explicitly authorized by national legislation."

The code states that "Employers should ensure that personal data are protected by such security safeguards as are reasonable in the circumstances to guard against loss and unauthorized use, modification or disclosure." Personal data covered by medical confidentiality "should be stored only by personnel bound by rules on medical secrecy and should be maintained apart from all other personal data."

The code also states that "workers should have the right to be regularly notified of the personal data held about them and the processing of that data," and that they should have "access to all of their personal data."

3. Is the knowledge sought through invasion of privacy relevant to its justifying purpose?

4. Is invasion of privacy the only or the least offensive means of obtaining the knowledge?

5. What restrictions or procedural restraints have been placed on the privacy-invading techniques?

6. How will the personal knowledge be protected once it has been acquired?[66]

Both of these sets of guidelines may also respect the personal autonomy of the individual worker by providing for personal space within the working environment, by providing notice of where that "personal" space ends, and by allowing access to the information gathered, all designed toward achievement of a personal and professional development objective. Reading 7-2, "The Ethical Use of Technology in Business," by Tony Mordini walks us through the ethical decision-making process according to these balancing scenarios to demonstrate how they might be applied.

The following section will provide some guidance regarding how far the employer is permitted to go in directing the activities of its workers while they are *not at work*.

Regulation of Off-Work Acts

OBJECTIVE

The regulation of an employee's activities when she or he is away from work is an interesting issue, particularly in at-will environments. However, as discussed throughout this chapter, even employers of at-will employees must comply with a variety of statutes in imposing requirements and managing employees. For instance, New York's lifestyle discrimination statute prohibits employment decisions or actions based on four categories of off-duty activity: legal recreational activities, consumption of legal products, political activities, and membership in a union.

Across the nation, there are other less broad protections for off-work acts. A number of states have enacted protections about the consumption or use of legal products off the job, such as cigarettes.[67] These statutes originated from the narrower protection for workers who smoked off-duty. Currently, abstention from smoking cannot be a condition of employment in at least 29 states and the District of Columbia (and those states provide anti-retaliation provisions for employers who violate the prohibition). Some companies have sought to encourage non-smoking among employees by providing free smoking cessation programs and other wellness services. Others have chosen to use "the stick," rather than "the carrot," to promote nonsmoking. Under the Affordable Care Act (ACA), insurance companies are permitted to charge smokers and other tobacco users up to 50 percent more than nonsmokers for a health insurance policy. In response, large companies like Macy's and Walmart have instituted annual health care surcharges to employees who choose to smoke.[68]

On the other hand, only two states (Michigan and Nevada) and six cities ban discrimination on the basis of weight.[69] In all other U.S. regions, employers are not prohibited from making employment decisions on the basis of weight, as long as they are not in violation of the American with Disabilities Act (ADA) when they do so. The issue depends on whether the employee's weight is evidence of or results from a disability. The Equal Employment Opportunity Commission has defined morbid obesity as a disability and the American Medical Association has defined obesity as a disease, both of which increase the likelihood that courts will as well.[70]

If obesity is considered a disability, the employer then must explore whether the worker is otherwise qualified for the position. Under the ADA, the individual is considered "otherwise qualified" if she or he can perform the essential functions of the position with or without reasonable accommodations. If the individual cannot perform the essential functions of the position, the employer is not subject to liability for reaching an adverse employment decision. However, employers should be cautious because the ADA also protects workers who are not disabled but who are *perceived* as being disabled, a category into which someone might fall based on his or her weight.

Laws that protect against discrimination based on marital status exist in just under half of the states. However, though workers might be protected based on marital *status,* they are not necessarily protected against adverse action based on *the identity of the person* they married. For instance, some companies might have an antinepotism policy under which an employer refuses to hire or terminates a worker on the basis of the spouse's working at the same firm, or a conflict-of-interest policy under which the employer refuses to hire or terminates a worker whose spouse works at a competing firm.

Because 38 percent of workers have dated an office colleague, policies and attitudes on workplace dating have an especially strong potential impact.[71] Though only 28 percent of workplaces have policies addressing workplace dating,[72] a New York decision reaffirmed the employer's right to terminate a worker on the basis of romantic involvement. In *McCavitt v. Swiss Reinsurance America Corp.,*[73] the court held that an employee's dating relationship with a fellow officer of the corporation was not a "recreational activity," within the meaning of a New York statute that prohibited employment discrimination for engaging in such recreational activities. The employee argued that, even though his personal relationship with this fellow officer had no repercussions whatever for the professional responsibilities or accomplishments of either, and his employer, Swiss Re, had no written antifraternization or antinepotism policy, he was passed over for promotion and then discharged from employment largely because of his dating. The court, however, agreed with the employer that termination was permitted because dating was not a recreational activity, and therefore *not* protected from discrimination. While concerns about workplace dating used to surround issues of sexual harassment, they are more likely to involve apprehensions about claims of retaliation after a relationship is over. However, contrary to the court's holding in *McCavitt,* not everyone agrees that the most effective response to the discovery of an illicit relationship is termination of the individual in power. Consider the Decision Point "To Date or Not to Date."

What does a company do when its founder is socializing with an employee who is in a subordinate position? Google cofounder Sergey Brin became involved romantically with a Google employee and subsequently separated from his wife of six years. Complicating things further, Brin's former sister-in-law and former brother-in-law both have major positions at Google. Brin insists that nothing about his new (or former) relationship will impact Google; but some suspect that this story is only the beginning of a large problem for Google.

Google maintains an informal approach to workplace dating and its code of conduct does not prohibit dating between employees. The code states: "Romantic relationships between co-workers can, depending on the work roles and respective positions of the co-workers involved, create an actual or apparent conflict of interest. If a romantic relationship does create an actual or apparent conflict, it may require changes to work arrangements or even the termination of employment of either or both individuals involved."

Brin is an important and, some argue, vital part of the Google company and its research and development teams. He also has a controlling interest of Google stock. According to one article, Larry Page, the CEO and other cofounder, was extremely upset with Brin's relationship and they did not speak for a time. Further, some Google employees, especially women, were furious that Brin and his girlfriend were not more separated professionally.[74]

Under a utilitarian analysis, it might appear that the cost of Brin's alleged "errors" compared to the cost of his departure from Google might seem to weigh in favor of keeping Brin employed. Or would you argue that employee morale surrounding this situation is so damaging to the work environment that it outweighs Brin's current and future contributions?

Have you considered further challenges in this narrative? Who would be the one to make the decision to fire Brin from the company, given his position and stock holdings? Plus, should the girlfriend be fired? If so, on what basis? Is it possible for them to be professionally separated when one of them is the CEO? Does Google need a clearer policy on workplace romance?

Assume you are charged with drafting your organization's policy on workplace dating. In which direction will you tilt with regard to its management of this issue? Utilitarian, or more in line with the 28 percent of workplaces that simply prohibit workplace dating in order to have a clearer line of demarcation? If you opt for the former, what ethical issues do you anticipate and how do you plan to respond to them because planning ahead will help you to prepare most effectively and ethically? Who are your stakeholders and what options do you have in your responses to those stakeholders in order to best meet each of their interests and rights?

If you opt for a prohibition, how do you plan to enforce it? Are you willing to hire someone who is dating a current employee? Must they stop dating? What problems might arise as a result of your policy, in either direction?

The majority of states protect against discrimination on the basis of political involvement, though states vary on the type and extent of protection. Finally, lifestyle discrimination may be unlawful if the imposition of the rule treats one protected group differently than another. For instance, if an employer imposes a rule restricting the use of peyote in Native American rituals that take place during off-work hours, the rule may be suspect and may subject the employer to liability. Similarly, the rule may be unlawful if it has a different impact on a protected group than on other groups.

Most statutes or common-law decisions, however, provide for employer defenses for those rules that (1) are reasonably and rationally related to the employment activities of a particular employee; (2) constitute a "bona fide occupational requirement," meaning a rule that is reasonably related to that particular position; or (3) are necessary to avoid a conflict of interest or the appearance of conflict of interest.

The question of monitoring and managing employee online communications while the employee is *off work* is relevant to the issues of technology monitoring discussed earlier in this chapter; this question emerges as an astonishingly challenging area of conflict between employers and employees, and one without much legal guidance, demanding sensitive ethical decision making. For instance, consider the question of the off-duty use of social media sites, like Facebook.

As of January 2016, 72 percent of all adults online visted Facebook at least once a month, and usage encompassed 38 percent of the world.[75] Though Facebook and other social media sites may initially seem to offer a convenient environment in which employees can vent during office-work hours about their employment situation, imagine the impact when a posting goes viral. Corporate reputations are at stake and legal consequences can be severe. In one situation, an energy company employee in Detroit was fired after the employee grumbled on Facebook about customers who called the company with complaints about a lack of power after weekend storms.[76]

In another case, a vegan elementary school teacher posted a picture of a local farm with crates holding newborn calves that had been separated from their mothers. He commented that this practice was inhumane. The farm owners saw the picture and complained to the school, which then fired the teacher. The school explained that the farmer was afraid that someone might come and break the calf crates or free the cows. The school superintendent also explained to the teacher that the school was in an agricultural community and that a lot of money for the school comes from those particular residents.[77]

Today's youth begin accessing and posting to these sites long before they might anticipate ever being in front of a potential employer, so how far back in the past do we really wish to hold our prospective employees responsible? There is a potential here for a responsibility much deeper than that even imposed by the law. For some, this might seem quite reasonable while, for others, it is far beyond reason. Is it ethically justified? From an employee's perspective, they should probably beware.

In addition, while employers are legally prevented from asking candidates about their religion or prior illegal drug use during a job interview, is it ethical for them to seek out that information through online sources when the candidate voluntarily discloses it with no connection with work? For instance, in various individuals' profiles on Facebook, there may be posted, "Nothing is more important to me than the values I have learned from being a Seventh Day Adventist."

Another person might explain that he kicked a drug habit, got out of rehab, and is getting on with his life. The prospective employer could never access this information through the interview so is gathering it in this method any more appropriate?

As discussed earlier in the chapter, the laws on this matter vary from country to country and also from state to state. For instance, there are far greater limitations on the collection of personal information in Australia than in the United States.[78] Plus, as of 2016, fewer than half (22) of the states restricted employers from requiring social media passwords from prospective or current employees and at least eight more state legislatures have bills pending.[79]

In signing Illinois's legislation to prohibit employers from requiring job candidates or current employees to submit their social networking passwords, former Illinois governor Pat Quinn compared these passwords to ordinary house keys and said, "members of the workforce should not be punished for information their employers don't legally have the right to have. As use of social media continues to expand, this new law will protect workers and their right to personal privacy."[80] Avner Levin reviews the environment in Reading 7-3, "Hiring in a Social Media Age."

When comparing these restrictions across cultures, what ethical values should dictate? Should a single, universal value govern an employer's judgment, or should the employer's behavior also vary from country to country, if it is a global operation?

The Reality Check "The Employment Relationship Begins Pre-employment" provides an overview of the intersection of the discussions of the prior two sections in its evaluation of privacy, testing, and off-work acts. While our analysis to this point has addressed the regulation of behavior during employment, perhaps it is important to consider your choices before employment and the impact they will have on an employer's later decisions about hiring you. Alternatively, from the employer's perspective, it is important to understand when it is valuable to test prospective employees or why it might be effective to refrain from testing in the hiring process.

Uniting and Strengthening America by Providing Appropriate Tools Required to Intercept and Obstruct Terrorism (USA PATRIOT) Act of 2001
A U.S. statute designed to increase the surveillance and investigative powers of law enforcement agencies in the United States in response to the terrorist attacks of September 11, 2001. The act has been lauded as a quick response to terrorism (it was introduced less than a week after the attacks) and for implementing critical amendments to more than 15 important statutes; it also has been criticized for failing to include sufficient safeguards for civil liberties.

Privacy Rights since September 11, 2001

OBJECTIVE

The events of September 11, 2001, have had a major impact on privacy within the United States and on the employment environment in particular. The federal government has implemented widespread modifications to its patchwork structure of privacy protections since the terror attacks of September 11, 2001. In particular, proposals for the expansion of surveillance and information-gathering authority were submitted and, to the chagrin of some civil rights attorneys and advocates, many were enacted.

The most public and publicized of these modifications was the adoption and implementation of the **Uniting and Strengthening America by Providing Appropriate Tools Required to Intercept and Obstruct Terrorism (USA PATRIOT) Act of 2001.** The USA PATRIOT Act expanded states' rights with

Reality Check   *The Employment Relationship Begins Pre-employment*

Society has traditionally treated the employment relationship as beginning and ending with the start and end dates of the employment appointment. In fact, the relationship begins prior to hiring and ends, often, only with death.

PRE-EMPLOYMENT PRACTICES

The importance of the pre-employment relationship is commonly overlooked. In spite of this, pre-employees (i.e., job candidates) today have few if any legally recognized rights. This is becoming increasingly problematic because of widespread advances in technology and the virtual lack of respect afforded the personal privacy of job-tap seekers.

A number of companies have recently emerged and are taking advantage of new information-gathering technologies by offering these services to employers in the process of hiring new employees. These companies contract with organizations (and individuals) to gather personal information about potential new hires. They gather any information that is requested about job candidates—from credit histories to their driving records.

While collecting data on people prior to their employment is nothing new, the methods used today lack the transparency of the past and skew the balance of power even more toward the employer and away from the employee. Further, employers do not always ask permission or even inform job candidates that they are doing background checks and are often unwilling to reveal to applicants the specific information that has influenced their hiring decisions.

Firms support this sort of information gathering on the basis that it enables them to make better hiring decisions. Even so, the practice is not without serious drawbacks—even from the perspective of the hiring firms. For one reason, the accuracy of third-party information is not always assured. In addition, there are no guarantees that the data collected are complete. Background checks can result in inaccurate or downright erroneous candidate profiles. While employers assume they are finding out relevant information to enhance their hiring decisions, the reality is that the information they are obtaining might be distorted without their knowledge; instead of eliminating certain risky candidates, they might unknowingly be overlooking "diamonds in the rough."

From the perspective of job applicants, the practice of pre-employment information gathering is particularly insidious. Job candidates are not always given notice that they are being scrutinized and that the material being collected is highly personal. In addition, job candidates are generally not offered the opportunity to provide any sort of rebuttal to the reports generated by information-gathering agencies. This is especially problematic in situations where candidates are rejected on the basis of background checks.

IMPACT OF PRE-EMPLOYMENT PRACTICES

To see how this testing can have a negative impact on the hiring process, take the example of Maria, a fictitious job candidate. Maria applies for a job in marketing for a regional department store. She is asked to take a pre-screening drug test and, through this and the personal information she provides as part of a general background check, the potential employer gains access to Maria's credit report. This report reveals that she has a judgment pending against her. Fearing that Maria is an employment risk, the company decides not to hire her

While the credit report's data might be accurate, it does not tell the complete story about Maria. It does not indicate, for example, that Maria was the victim of identity fraud. In addition, the report might be inaccurate without her knowledge. While Maria should be aware of the credit information in her report, she has not looked at it in some time and the collecting agency has included some incorrect information. The fact that Maria has an unpaid debt does not provide information inherently relevant to the particular job for which she has applied.

The employer considering Maria's application might rationalize that the background check is necessary to assess her general suitability. Many employers consider this a legitimate purpose and argue that there is a relationship between a candidate's responsibility in handling client affairs and her manner of dealing with personal finances. Although such an argument is not without merit, the result seems somewhat excessive. Consider, for example, the relevance of the driving record of a candidate for a bus driver position: it would seem almost counterintuitive not to inquire into that sort of information. There are meaningful differences, however, between this situation and that of Maria. Where work is of a particularly sensitive nature or where the level of the open position is high within a company, background checks directly related to performance might be appropriate when linked to a legitimate business purpose. In addition, the type of company or potential liability for the company could also warrant specific checks. In Maria's situation, none of these circumstances are present.

ARGUMENTS AGAINST EXCESSIVE PRE-EMPLOYMENT TESTING

There are many arguments against pre-employment testing, particularly when used indiscriminately. Excessive pre-employment testing can be attacked on moral grounds. First, it undermines the dignity of the individual by strengthening the notion of the person as a mere factor of production. It effectively enables employers to treat people as a means to achieving profitable ends without regard for the individual as a person valuable in and of him- or herself. In addition, it creates a climate of suspicion that undermines trust and loyalty and encourages duplicity and insincerity. Finally, it affects the character of the companies and individuals who work there. Companies become secretive and manipulative through such information gathering and candidates, in turn, do what they can to conceal information they consider potentially unfavorable to their acceptance or advancement. This sort of behavior is to the detriment of the character of both employers and potential employees.

In addition to these sorts of ethical considerations, there are strong business arguments against excessive use of pre-employment testing. Unfettered collection of personal information disregards property interests associated with that personal information. Hiring practices involving background checks ignore a person's ownership of information about him- or herself. It also erodes the privacy expectations a person has in his or her personal information. Moreover, it creates a bad first impression for potential employees and detracts from general morale. During bad economic times this might not matter, but when times are good and employment rates are high, potential job candidates are likely to seek out opportunities with employers who do not utilize such intrusive methods. In addition, current employees—those who stay by necessity or choice—will see themselves in

a relationship with an employer who does not trust them or respect individual privacy. In other words, the practice used in hiring spills over and effectively becomes the tenor of the overall employment relationship, and this can prove demoralizing to employees and result in an underlying tone of distrust.

RESPONSIBLE USE OF PERSONAL INFORMATION

The availability of abundant information to employers does not mean that they have to use all of it. Ideally, personal information should remain personal and, at the very least, the individual should have the ability to determine who gains access to his or her personal information and to know when someone obtains that information. It is important here to keep in mind that the availability of access is not the same as the moral right to access information or to use that information in a hiring decision.

As employers consider how to use the information they gather, they should consider "legitimate business purpose" as a guiding principle. Where there is a legitimate business purpose (defined generally to be applied to job function, type of company, and so on) and an identifiable direct correlation between that information and the job candidate, it would then seem appropriate for personal information to be solicited.

At the same time and as Maria's situation illustrates, it now becomes incumbent upon individuals to keep better track of their personal information. Now that individuals are aware that credit checks can be performed and used against them, they need to make sure that the credit bureaus have accurate information. In addition, individuals need to be prepared to respond to anomalies that might exist in their personal information. It is no longer an issue of what is right and what is wrong, but what is going to happen. If we know that employers have access to this information, it is for us to determine what we are going to do about it for ourselves.

Source: Adapted for this publication and used by permission of the authors, Tara J. Radin and Martin Calkins.

regard to Internet surveillance technology, including workplace surveillance, and amended the Electronic Communications Privacy Act. The act also grants access to sensitive data with only a court order rather than a judicial warrant and imposes or enhances civil and criminal penalties for knowingly or intentionally aiding terrorists. In addition, the new disclosure regime increased the sharing of personal information between government agencies to ensure the greatest level of protection.

Title II of the act provides for the following enhanced surveillance procedures that have a significant impact on individual privacy and may impact an employer's effort to maintain employee privacy:

- Expands authority to intercept wire, oral, and electronic communications relating to terrorism and to computer fraud and abuse offenses.

- Provides roving surveillance authority under the Foreign Intelligence Surveillance Act (FISA) of 1978 to track individuals. (FISA investigations are not subject to Fourth Amendment standards but are instead governed by the requirement that the search serve "a significant purpose.")

- Allows nationwide seizure of voice-mail messages pursuant to warrants (i.e., without the previously required wiretap order).

- Broadens the types of records that law enforcement may obtain, pursuant to a subpoena, from electronic communications service providers.

- Permits emergency disclosure of customer electronic communications by providers to protect life and limb.

- Provides nationwide service of search warrants for electronic evidence.

These provisions allow the government to monitor anyone on the Internet simply by contending that the information is "relevant" to an ongoing criminal investigation. In addition, the act includes provisions designed to combat money laundering activity or the funding of terrorist or criminal activity through corporate activity or otherwise. All financial institutions must now report suspicious activities in financial transactions and keep records of foreign national employees, while also complying with the antidiscrimination laws discussed throughout this text.

The PATRIOT Act has been reauthorized three times, and elements have been amended, revised, and extended by several additional bills.[81]

Requests from businesses have become a topic of significant concern in recent years. The PATRIOT Act allows for and relies on requests from businesses to gather information. Recently, however, it also was revealed that the National Security Agency (NSA) was harvesting millions of e-mail and instant messaging contact lists, searching e-mail content, and tracking and mapping the location of cell phones, often with the cooperation of telecommunications companies.[82]

Through its PRISM program, the NSA was tapping into the data centers of companies like Yahoo! and Google to collect information from "hundreds of millions" of account holders worldwide on the basis of court-approved explicit access.[83] After this revelation, the large tech companies requested from the U.S. government the ability to be transparent with customers. A deal was brokered and four of the tech firms that participate in the NSA's PRISM program (Microsoft, Yahoo!, Google, and Facebook) released more information about the volume of data that the government demands they provide. Unfortunately, the government still does not allow these companies to itemize the data collected, so transparency remains relative.[84]

However, since that time all four companies plus many others have changed their privacy policies to state they will "notify users of requests for their information

Opening Decision Point Revisited
Being Smart about Smartphones

The Opening Decision Point asked you to consider the implications of using smartphones in business contexts. It might not have occurred to you previously that smartphones could be a source of ethical problems in the workplace because most people see a BlackBerry or iPhone simply as a source of productivity, allowing them to carry a powerful computer combined with a communications device in their pocket or handbag. The convenience of being able to access information, as well as to stay in touch with key clients and co-workers just about anywhere, typically is seen as a benefit rather than a problem. But, as the earlier box illustrated, smartphones—like many new technologies—also raise ethical questions.

Clearly, the Opening Decision Point involved miscommunication from the start. Using the ethical decision-making process, we are confronted with a scenario in which the stakeholders involved perceived the situation from entirely different perspectives. While you were entirely engaged in the meeting and working strenuously to produce the most effective result, your behavior left many involved with the perception that you were instead "checked out" and fiddling with your phone! Certainly, if you have known that was the impression you were likely to create, you would never have made the same decision. Instead, you would have . . . well? What would you have done?

That is the benefit of considering these scenarios at the outset. Not everyone will perceive your behavior from the same vantage point, nor with the same experiential background. You might be the type of person to take notes on your smartphone, while that option might never enter into someone else's mind. By understanding that perspective, you might have started the meeting by letting everyone know that you plan to record some bullet points directly into your phone so that you can upload them electronically the moment you return to your office. In that way, you will be best able to share them with the team in the most efficient manner immediately following the meeting. Everyone would have nodded and appreciated your thoughtfulness. To the contrary, you are left needing to explain the fiasco to your boss.

We should realize, of course, that sometimes it is not at all a matter of misunderstanding; some people actually may be playing games on their phones during meetings, texting with friends, or checking in on Facebook. To the extent that this activity means that they are paying less attention to what others in the meeting are saying, such activities are—at the very least—disrespectful. However, consider far worse implications for the workplace. A one-time offense arguably could be dismissed as simply rude; but ongoing behavior could demonstrate a pattern of rudeness, which implies a lack of overall respect for stakeholders. Respect for the personal dignity of others is a key element of ethical decision making.

Though there would be significant exceptions, of course, some disagreements over the use of smartphones in the workplace might also be generational. Some younger workers who have grown up with mobile phones and who are used to text messaging to keep in near constant contact with friends might see texting during a meeting as normal, and as implying no disrespect at all. Moreover, some of these workers might not even wear a watch anymore and often use their phone as their only method by which to check the time, so checking their phone is no more

(continued)

(concluded)   intrusive to them as someone else glancing at their wrist. To the contrary, some (be wary of generalizations here, again) older workers, even many of those who are comfortable using a smartphone, may see such devices more strictly in terms of their usefulness for a narrow range of essential business operations. To these workers, use of a smartphone during a meeting—even to check business-related e-mail—may cross a boundary of propriety.

- How might you respond if you observed a colleague texting in the middle of a meeting?
- Would it be different if the meeting involved just the two of you or other people? If the others were work colleagues or colleagues external to your firm?
- What would you do if you received a text from a colleague in the middle of a meeting (and the colleague is in the same meeting)?
- Are there new technologies other than smartphones that raise questions such as the ones discussed in this scenario? Does the use of a laptop during a business meeting raise the same or similar issues?
- Did it occur to you at the end of the Opening Decision Point that perhaps your boss might have given you the benefit of the doubt and asked whether you had been using your phone for note-taking? Does that perspective affect your response at all?
- When people differ with regard to the proper use of new technologies in the workplace, how should such differences be resolved? Should fans of new technologies be extra cautious? Or should those who resist new technologies be expected to "get with the times"?

prior to disclosure unless [they] are prohibited from doing so by statute or court order."[85] This statement does not necessarily protect users under the PRISM program, but it does protect them from other types of searches.

Many organizations previously turned over information requested by law enforcement without telling users. Now, however, most companies like Twitter, Facebook, and Google (plus many more) all notify users of requests for information prior to disclosure unless prohibited by statute or court order.[86]

Of course, the ultimate question is, if it were disclosed that your use could be monitored by the government, and you clicked "agree" to the terms of use when you began using the service, would you care enough to adjust your use?

Questions, Projects, and Exercises

1. Marriott Resorts had a formal company party for more than 200 employees. At one point during the party, the company aired a videotape that compiled employees' and their spouses' comments about a household chore they hated. However, as a spoof, the video was edited to make it seem as if they were describing what it was like to have sex with their partner. One employee's wife was very upset by the video and sued Marriott for invasion of privacy. Evaluate her argument, focusing on the ethical arguments for a violation of her rights.

2. Richard Fraser, an at-will independent insurance agent for Nationwide Mutual Insurance Company, was terminated by Nationwide and the parties disagree on the reason for Fraser's termination. Fraser argues that Nationwide terminated him because he filed complaints regarding Nationwide's allegedly illegal conduct, for criticizing Nationwide to the Nationwide Insurance Independent Contractors Association, and for attempting to obtain the passage of legislation in Pennsylvania to ensure that independent insurance agents could be terminated only for "just cause." Nationwide argues, however, that it terminated Fraser because he was disloyal. Nationwide points out that Fraser drafted a letter to two competitors saying that policyholders were not happy with Nationwide and asking whether the competitors would be interested in acquiring them. (Fraser claims that the letters were drafted only to get Nationwide's attention and were not sent.)

     When Nationwide learned about these letters, it claims that it became concerned that Fraser might also be revealing company secrets to its competitors. It therefore searched its main file server—on which all of Fraser's e-mail was lodged—for any e-mail to or from Fraser that showed similar improper behavior. Nationwide's general counsel testified that the e-mail search confirmed Fraser's disloyalty. Therefore, on the basis of the two letters and the e-mail search, Nationwide terminated Fraser's employment agreement. The search of his e-mail gives rise to Fraser's claim for damages under the Electronic Communications Privacy Act (ECPA) of 1986. Do you believe the employer was justified in monitoring the employee's e-mail and then terminating him? What ethical arguments do you believe either side could use in this case?

3. A customer service representative at an electronics store is surfing the Internet using one of the display computers. She accesses a website that shows graphic images of a crime scene. A customer in the store who notices the images is offended. Another customer service representative is behind the counter using the store's computer to access a pornographic site, and starts to laugh. A customer asks him why he is laughing. He turns the computer screen around to show her the images that are causing him amusement. Is there anything wrong with these activities?

4. The term *cybersquatting* refers to the practice of registering a large number of website domain names hoping to sell them at huge prices to others who may want the URL or who are prepared to pay to get rid of a potentially confusing domain name. For instance, People for the Ethical Treatment of Animals, which operates www.peta.org, was able to shut down www.peta.com, a pro-hunting website that dubbed itself "People Eating Tasty Animals." Cybersquatters often determine possible misspellings or slightly incorrect websites with the hopes that the intended website will pay them for their new domain. Others might simply hold onto a potentially extremely popular site name based on the expectation that someone will want it. For example, someone paid over $7 million for the address www.business.com. In one case, one day after a partnership was announced that would result in an online bookstore for the Toronto *Globe & Mail* newspaper, with the domain name www.chaptersglobe.com, Richard Morochove, a technology writer, registered the domain chapters-globe.com. When the partnership demanded that he stop using the name, he promptly agreed, as long as he received a percentage of the sales from the Chapters/Globe website. The case went to trial. In situations such as these, do you believe the cybersquatter is doing anything wrong? What options might the "intended website" owner have?

5. Spam, or spamming, refers to the use of mailing lists to blanket usenets or private e-mail boxes with indiscriminate advertising messages. Some people believe that spamming should be protected as the simple exercise of one's First Amendment right

to free speech while others view it as an invasion of privacy or even theft of resources or trespass to property, as Intel argued when a disgruntled ex-employee spammed more than 25,000 Intel employees with his complaints. In that case, the court agreed, considering his e-mail spamming equivalent to trespassing on Intel's property and recognizing that Intel was forced to spend considerable time and resources to delete the e-mail messages from its system.

It is amusing to note that the source of the term *spam* is generally accepted to be the Monty Python song "Spam spam spam spam, spam spam spam spam, lovely spam, wonderful spam. . . ." Like the song, spam is an endless repetition of worthless text. Others believe that the term came from the computer group lab at the University of Southern California, which gave it the name because it has many of the same characteristics as the lunchmeat Spam:

- Nobody wants it or ever asks for it.
- No one ever eats it; it is the first item to be pushed to the side when eating the entree.
- Sometimes it is actually tasty, like 1 percent of junk mail that is really useful to some people.[87]

Using stakeholder analysis, make an argument that spamming is either ethical or unethical.

6. Term papers on practically every subject imaginable are available on the Internet. Many of those who post the papers defend their practice in two ways: (1) These papers are posted to assist in research in the same way any other resource is posted on the web and should simply be cited if used; and (2) these papers are posted in order to encourage faculty to modify paper topics and/or exams and not to simply bring back assignments that have been used countless times in the past. Are you persuaded? Is there anything unethical about this service in general? If so, who should be held accountable, the poster, the ultimate user, or someone else?

7. A college provided its security officers with a locker area in which to store personal items. The security officers occasionally used the area as a dressing room. After incidents of theft from the lockers and reports that the employees were bringing weapons to campus, the college installed a video surveillance camera in the locker area. Did the employees have a reasonable expectation of privacy that was violated by the video surveillance? Explain.

8. While some companies block employee access to social networks such as Facebook and Twitter, others have a more permissive attitude. Explain several reasons a company might choose to *permit*—or be indifferent to—employee access to social networks.

9. You work as an accountant at large accounting firm where your job leaves you with a lot of down time at the office in between assignments. You spend this time on your office computer developing a program that can make your job even more efficient and it might even be a breakthrough in the industry. This new product could be a huge success and you could make a lot of money. You think of quitting your job and devoting all your time and resources to selling this new product. However, you have developed this product using company equipment and technology, and also used the time you were at work. Do these facts raise any red flags in terms of ethical issues? What should you do?

10. As you learned in this chapter, drug testing in the workplace is a somewhat controversial issue in terms of employer responsibilities and employee rights. Using sources from the web, discuss the pros and cons of these programs.

Key Terms

After reading this chapter, you should have a clear understanding of the following key terms. For a complete definition, please see the Glossary.

Electronic Communications Privacy Act (ECPA) of 1986, *p. 309*

e-mail monitoring, *p. 319*

European Union's Directive on Personal Data Protection, *p. 311*

Fourth Amendment protection, *p. 309*

Health Insurance Portability and Accountability Act (HIPAA), *p. 327*

hypernorms, *p. 306*

Internet use monitoring, *p. 319*

intrusion into seclusion, *p. 310*

moral free space, *p. 306*

personal data, *p. 311*

privacy, *p. 303*

privacy rights, *p. 305*

property rights, *p. 308*

reasonable expectation of privacy, *p. 311*

reciprocal obligation, *p. 306*

Safe Harbor exception, *p. 312*

Uniting and Strengthening America by Providing Appropriate Tools Required to Intercept and Obstruct Terrorism (USA PATRIOT) Act of 2001, *p. 335*

Endnotes

1. B. Johnson, "Privacy No Longer a Social Norm, Says Facebook Founder," *The Guardian* (January 10, 2010), www.guardian.co.u/technology/2010/jan/11/facebookprivacy (accessed February 21, 2016).

2. E. Sperling, "The CIO Squeeze," *Forbes* (January 5, 2009), http://www.forbes.com/2009/01/02/cio-squeeze-hogan-tech-cio-cx_es_0105hogan.html (accessed August 18, 2012).

3. A. Marshall, "Where Business Is Feeling the Heat," in P. Krielstra, Kroll and Economist Intelligence Unit, *Global Fraud Report* (2007/2008).

4. Poneman Institute, "2015 Cost of Data Breach Study: United States" (May 2015), www-03.ibm.com/security/data-breach/ (accessed March 2, 2016).

5. Ponemon Institute, J. Moore, "Your E-mail Trail: Where Ethics Meets Forensics," *Business and Society Review* 114, no. 2 (2009), pp. 273–293.

6. Patricia Werhane, *Persons, Rights, and Corporations* (Englewood Cliffs, NJ: Prentice Hall, 1985), p. 94.

7. Gerald Doppelt, "Beyond Liberalism and Communitarianism: Towards a Critical Theory of Social Justice," *Philosophy and Social Criticism* 14 (1988), pp. 271, 278.

8. Global Internet Liberty Campaign, "Privacy and Human Rights: An International Survey of Privacy Laws and Practice" (1998), www.gilc.org/privacy/survey/exec-summary.html (accessed February 21, 2016). For an up-to-date listing of international accords relating to privacy, see Electronic Frontier Foundation, "International Privacy Standards," www.eff.org/issues/international-privacy-standards (accessed February 21, 2016).

9. J. Whitman, "The Two Western Cultures of Privacy: Dignity versus Liberty," *Yale Law Journal* 113 (2004), p. 1151; A. Levin, "Dignity in the Workplace: An Enquiry into the Conceptual Foundation of Workplace Privacy Protection Worldwide," *ALSB Journal of*

Employment and Labor Law 11, no. 1 (Winter 2009), p. 63; Daniel Fisher, "Europe's 'Right to Be Forgotten' Clashes with U.S. Right to Know," *Forbes* (May 16, 2014), www.forbes.com/sites/danielfisher/2014/05/16/europes-right-to-be-forgotten-clashes-with-u-s-right-to-know/ (accessed February 21, 2016).

10. A. R. Levinson, "Industrial Justice: Privacy Protection for the Employed," *Cornell Journal of Law and Public Policy* 18, no. 3 (2009), http://papers.ssrn.com/sol3/papers.cfm?abstract_id=1269512 (accessed February 21, 2016); P. Kim, "Electronic Privacy and Employee Speech," *Chicago-Kent Law Review* 87, no. 901 (2012), http://ssrn.com/abstract=2049323 (accessed February 21, 2016).

11. Mike Brunker, "Cyberporn Nurse: I Feel Like Larry Flynt," *MSNBC,* July 16, 1999.

12. "Teacher Sacked for Posting Picture of Herself Holding Glass of Wine and Mug of Beer on Facebook," *Daily Mail* (February 7, 2011), www.dailymail.co.uk/news/article-1354515/Teacher-sacked-posting-picture-holding-glass-wine-mug-beer-Facebook.html#ixzz3J4QdZryi (accessed February 21, 2016.)

13. National Conference of State Legislatures, "Privacy Protections in State Constitutions" (December 11, 2013), www.ncsl.org/research/telecommunications-and-information-technology/privacy-protections-in-state-constitutions.aspx (accessed February 21, 2016).

14. *Lake v. Wal-Mart Stores, Inc.,* 582 N.W.2d 231 (Minn. 1998).

15. *City of Ontario v. Quon*, 130 S. Ct. 2619 (2010).

16. *Riley v. California,* 573 U.S. _ (2014), (Docket No. 13-132), (slip op., at 28); *Bakhit v. Safety Marking, Inc.,* D. Conn., No. 3:13-CV-1049, June 26, 2014.

17. National Conference of State Legislatures, "Employer Access to Social Media Usernames and Passwords" (February 2, 2016), www.ncsl.org/research/telecommunications-and-information-technology/employer-access-to-social-media-passwords-2013.aspx (accessed March 2, 2016); Aliah D. Wright, "More States Ban Social Media Snooping: Nearly 20 states Now Bar Employers from Requesting Access to Employees', Applicants' Social Media Posts" (August 12, 2014), www.shrm.org/hrdisciplines/technology/articles/pages/social-media-snooping.aspx#sthash.4XbI7Hj4.dpuf (accessed February 29, 2016).

18. Formally known as "Directive 95/46/EC of the European Parliament and of the Council of 24 October 1995 on the Protection of Individuals with Regard to the Processing of Personal Data and on the Free Movement of Such Data, Council Directive 95/46," 1995 O.J. (L281).

19. Formally known as "Directive 95/46/EC of the European Parliament and of the Council of 24 October 1995 on the Protection of Individuals with Regard to the Processing of Personal Data and on the Free Movement of Such Data, Council Directive 95/46," 1995 O.J. (L281) at arts, 25–26.

20. Mark Scott, "Europe Approves Tough New Data Protection Rules," *The New York Times* (December 15, 2015), www.nytimes.com/2015/12/16/technology/eu-data-privacy.html (accessed March 8, 2016).

21. *Schrems v. Data Protection Commissioner,* case C-362/14 [2015], Court of Justice of the European Union (delivered October 6, 2015).

22. Barnes & Thornburg LLP, "EU-U.S. Privacy Shield Set to Replace Safe Harbor: Smooth Sailing or Rough Waters Ahead?," *Lexology* (March 3, 2016), www.lexology.com/library/detail.aspx?g=fef184b7-4952-4b3c-af88-672eff0ce94e (accessed March 8, 2016).

23. J. Arden, "Techno-Ethics: Anti-Social Networking," *American Bar Association: GPSolo* 29, no. 3 (May/June 2012), www.americanbar.org/publications/gp_solo/2012/may_june/techno_ethics_anti_social_networking.html (accessed February 21, 2016).

24. *State of Washington v. Young,* 123 Wash.2d 173 (1994).

25. Frank Daly, "Reply, Delete . . . or Relate? IT's Human Dimension," Lecture as Verizon Professor in Business Ethics and Technology, Bentley College, March 31, 2004.

26. Kenneth Rapoza, "One in Five Americans Work from Home, Numbers Seen Rising over 60%," *Forbes* (February 8, 2013), www.forbes.com/sites/kenrapoza/2013/02/18/one-in-five-americans-work-from-home-numbers-seen-rising-over-60/ (accessed February 21, 2016).

27. U. Klotz, "The Challenges of the New Economy" (October 1999), cited in *World Employment Report 2001: Life at Work in the Information Economy* (Geneva: International Labour Office, 2001), p. 145.

28. *PhoneDog, LLC v. Kravitz,* case no. 3:2011cv03474 (filed July 15, 2011).

29. "Whom Do Social Media Followers Belong to—You, or Your Business?," Knowledge@Wharton, University of Pennsylvania (March 13, 2013), http://knowledge.wharton.upenn.edu/article/whom-do-social-media-followers-belong-to-you-or-your-business/ (accessed February 21, 2016); A. Fisher, "Who Owns Your Twitter Followers, You or Your employer?," *Fortune* (December 13, 2012), http://fortune.com/2012/12/13/who-owns-your-twitter-followers-you-or-your-employer/ (accessed February 21, 2016).

30. For a similar interpretation, see B. Kracher and C. Corritore, "Is There a Special E-Commerce Ethics?," *Business Ethics Quarterly* 14, no. 1 (2004), pp. 71–94.

31. Antonio Argandoña, "The New Economy: Ethical Issues," *Journal of Business Ethics* 44 (2003), pp. 3–22, 26.

32. Google S-1, filed with the Securities and Exchange Commission, www.sec.gov/Archives/edgar/data/1288776/000119312504139655/ds1a.htm, appendix B (2004) (accessed August 18, 2012).

33. Dominic Rushe, "Google: Don't Expect Privacy When Sending to Gmail," *The Guardian* (August 15, 2013), www.theguardian.com/technology/2013/aug/14/google-gmail-users-privacy-email-lawsuit (accessed February 21, 2016).

34. Jeff Gould, "Google Admits Data Mining Student Emails in Its Free Education Apps," *SafeGov.org* (February 21, 2016), http://safegov.org/2014/1/31/google-admits-data-mining-student-emails-in-its-free-education-apps (accessed November 23, 2014); Google S-1, filed with the Securities and Exchange Commission (August 3, 2004), www.sec.gov/Archives/edgar/data/1288776/000119312504139655/ds1a.htm (accessed August 17, 2012).

35. Federal Trade Commission, "Google Will Pay $22.5 Million to Settle FTC Charges It Misrepresented Privacy Assurances to Users of Apple's Safari Internet Browser," Press Release (August 9, 2012), http://ftc.gov/opa/2012/08/google.shtm (accessed February 21, 2016).

36. Claire Cain Miller, "F.T.C. Fines Google $22.5 Million for Safari Privacy Violations," *The New York Times: Bits Blog* (August 9, 2012), http://bits.blogs.nytimes.com/2012/08/09/f-t-c-fines-google-22-5-million-for-safari-privacy-violations/ (August 17, 2012).

37. Lisa Vaas, "Google Stops Data-mining Students' Email," *Naked Security* (April 30, 2014), https://nakedsecurity.sophos.com/2014/04/30/google-stops-data-mining-students-email/ (accessed February 21, 2016); Jeff Gould, "Google Admits Data Mining Student Emails in Its Free Education Apps," *SafeGov.org* (January 31, 2014), http://safegov.org/2014/1/31/google-admits-data-mining-student-emails-in-its-free-education-apps (accessed February 21, 2016).

38. Antonio Argandoña, "The New Economy: Ethical Issues," *Journal of Business Ethics* 44 (2003), pp. 3–22, 28.

39. Proskauer, "Social Media in the Workplace around the World 3.0: 2013/2014 Survey" (2014), www.proskauer.com/files/uploads/social-media-in-the-workplace-2014.pdf (accessed February 21, 2016).

40. CareerBuilder.com, "CareerBuilder Study Reveals Most Common and Strangest Productivity Killers at Work" (June 11, 2015), www.careerbuilder.com/share/aboutus/pressreleasesdetail.aspx?sd=6%2F11%2F2015&id=pr898&ed=12%2F31%2F2015 (accessed February 21, 2016).

41. Mary Carmichael, "Harvard Secretly Searched Deans' E-mail Chasing Leak in Cheating Scandal May Have Invaded Privacy," *The Boston Globe* (March 10, 2013), www.bostonglobe.com/metro/2013/03/10/harvard-university-administrators-secretly-searched-deans-email-accounts-hunting-for-media-leak/tHyFUYh2FNAa-G2w9wzcrLL/story.html (accessed March 9, 2016); see also L. V. Anderson, "Can Your Boss Read Your Email? In Most Cases, Employees Have Little Legal Right to Privacy," *Slate* (March 11, 2013), www.slate.com/articles/news_and_politics/explainer/2013/03/harvard_email_search_scandal_can_your_employer_read_your_private_messages.html (accessed March 9, 2016).

42. PricewaterhouseCoopers, "The Future of Work: A Journey to 2022" (2014), www.pwc.com/en_GX/gx/managing-tomorrows-people/future-of-work/assets/pdf/future-of-work-report-v23.pdf (accessed February 21, 2016).

43. Abine Report, "From Walking around Naked to Updating Facebook Privacy Settings, Younger Generation's Views on Privacy Are Changing," *PR Newswire* (April 23, 2013), www.prnewswire.com/news-releases/from-walking-around-naked-to-updating-facebook-privacy-settings-younger-generations-views-on-privacy-are-changing-204268481.html (accessed February 21, 2016).

44. Amanda Lenhert, "What Americans Think about Privacy, and Why Their Kids Think Differently," Lecture at Chautauqua Institution (July 10, 2014), http://chqdaily.com/2014/07/10/lenhart-adolescents-more-suspicious-of-government-less-suspicious-of-corporate-data-collection-online/ (accessed February 21, 2016).

45. Ibid.

46. Yue Wang, "More People Have Cell Phones Than Toilets, U.N. Study Shows," *Time* (March 25, 2013), http://newsfeed.time.com/2013/03/25/more-people-have-cell-phones-than-toilets-u-n-study-shows/ (accessed March 2, 2016).

47. "Internet Usage Statistics," *Internet World Stats* (2016), www.internet-worldstats.com/stats.htm (accessed February 21, 2016).

48. "Social Networking Fact Sheet," Pew Research Center (January 2014), www.pewinternet.org/fact-sheets/social-networking-fact-sheet/ (accessed March 2, 2016).

49. CareerBuilder.com, "CareerBuilder Study Reveals the Most Common and Strangest Productivity Killers at Work" (June 11, 2015), www.careerbuilder.com/share/aboutus

/pressreleasesdetail.aspx?sd=6%2F11%2F2015&id=pr898&ed=12%2F31%2F2015 (accessed February 21, 2016).

50. Robert Stroymeyer, "How to Monitor Your Employees' PCs without Going Too Far," *PCWorld* (March 22, 2011), www.pcworld.com/businesscenter/article/222169/how_to_monitor_your_employees_pcs_without_going_too_far.html (accessed August 17, 2011).

51. Proskauer, "Social Media in the Workplace around the World 3.0: 2013/2014 Survey" (2014), www.proskauer.com/files/uploads/social-media-in-the-workplace-2014.pdf (accessed February 21, 2016).

52. "Senior Executives More Likely Than Subordinates to Shop Online While at Work, Survey Says," *Chicago Business Journal* (November 25, 2014), www.bizjournals.com/chicago/news/2014/11/25/senior-executives-more-likely-than-subordinates-to.html (accessed February 21, 2016).

53. A. Taufen, "How Does Medical Marijuana Use Affect Employment?," *Benefits Pro* (August 12, 2014), www.benefitspro.com/2014/08/12/how-does-medical-marijuana-use-affect-employment?t=compliance&page=2&slreturn=1456427268 (accessed February 24, 2016).

54. National Council on Alcoholism and Drug Dependence, Inc., "Drugs and the Workplace" (n.d.), www.ncadd.org/index.php/learn-about-drugs/workplace/242-drugs-and-the-workplace (accessed August 17, 2012).

55. HireRight.com, "Employment Screening Benchmark Report: 2014 Edition" (2014), www.hireright.com/benchmarking/thank-you.php (accessed February 21, 2016).

56. Quest Diagnostic Drug Testing Index, "Workforce Drug Test Positivity Rate Increases for the First Time in 10 Years, Driven by Marijuana and Amphetamines, Finds Quest Diagnostics Drug Testing Index™ Analysis of Employment Drug Tests" (September 11, 2014), www.questdiagnostics.com/home/physicians/health-trends/drug-testing (accessed February 21, 2016).

57. Ibid.

58. 109 S. Ct. 1402 (1989).

59. S. Begley, J. Trankiem, and S. Hansel, "Employers Using Personality Tests to Vet Applicants Need Cautious 'Personalities' of Their Own," *Forbes.com* (October 30, 2014), www.forbes.com/sites/theemploymentbeat/2014/10/30/employers-using-personality-tests-to-vet-applicants-need-cautious-personalities-of-their-own/ (accessed February 21, 2016).

60. L. Weber and E. Dwoskin, "Are Workplace Personality Tests Fair? Growing Use of Tests Sparks Scrutiny amid Questions of Effectiveness and Workplace Discrimination," *The Wall Street Journal* (September 29, 2014), www.wsj.com/articles/are-workplace-personality-tests-fair-1412044257 (accessed February 21, 2016).

61. L. Weber and E. Dwoskin, "Are Workplace Personality Tests Fair? Growing Use of Tests Sparks Scrutiny amid Questions of Effectiveness and Workplace Discrimination," *The Wall Street Journal* (September 29, 2014), www.wsj.com/articles/are-workplace-personality-tests-fair-1412044257 (accessed February 21, 2016).

62. Ibid.

63. Genetic Information Nondiscrimination Act of 2008 (HR 493, P.L. No. 110-233), www.govtrack.us/congress/bills/110/hr493 (accessed February 21, 2016).

64. Equal Employment Opportunity Commission, "Genetic Information Discrimination" (n.d.), www.eeoc.gov/laws/types/genetic.cfm (accessed February 21, 2016).

65. W. Herbert and A. K. Tuminaro, "The Impact of Emerging Technologies in the Workplace: Who's Watching the Man (Who's Watching Me)?," *Hofstra Labor and Employment Law Journal* 5 (2009), p. 355; A. Bibby, "You're Being Followed: Electronic Monitoring and Surveillance in the Workplace" (2006), www.andrewbibby.com/pdf/Surveillance-en.pdf (accessed August 18, 2012).

66. M. Schulman, "Little Brother Is Watching You," *Issues in Ethics* 9, no. 2 (Spring 1998), www.scu.edu/ethics/publications/iie/v9n2/brother.html (accessed August 18, 2012).

67. Off-duty conduct statutes vary in which of the following three different levels of protection they provide: (1) use of tobacco only, (2) use of lawful products, and (3) any and all lawful activities. Jurisdictions that have enacted "tobacco only" statutes include Connecticut, District of Columbia, Indiana, Kentucky, Louisiana, Maine, Mississippi, New Hampshire, New Jersey, New Mexico, Oklahoma, Oregon, Rhode Island, South Carolina, South Dakota, Virginia, West Virginia, and Wyoming. States that protect the use of lawful products include Illinois, Minnesota, Missouri, Montana, Nevada, North Carolina, Tennessee, and Wisconsin. Four states offer statutory protection for employees who engage in lawful activities: California, Colorado, New York, and North Dakota. For a list of all state statutes, see National Conference of State Legislatures, "Discrimination Laws Regarding Off-Duty Conduct" (October 18, 2010), www.ncsl.org/issues-research/labor/discrimination-employment.aspx (accessed August 15, 2012).

68. Kytle Frye, "Can and Should You Link Health Insurance Rates and Smoking?," Society for Human Resource Management (February 20, 2014), www.shrm.org/legalIssues/federalresources/pages/link-health-insurance-rates-smoking.aspx (accessed February 21, 2016).

69. The following cities prohibit weight discrimination: Santa Cruz, CA; San Francisco, CA; Washington, DC; Urbana, IL; Binghamton, NY; and Madison, WI. See National Association to Advance Fat Acceptance (NAAFA), "Weight Discrimination Laws" (n.d.), www.naafaonline.com/dev2/education/laws.html (accessed March 2, 2016).

70. Michael Kraemer, "Is Obesity Considered a Disability under the ADA?," *Law.com* (November 11, 2014), www.law.com/sites/michaelkraemer/2014/11/11/is-obesity-considered-a-disability-under-the-ada/?slreturn=20141113174637 (accessed February 21, 2016); Martha Neil, "Obesity Is a Disease, AMA Says, Aiding Weight-Related Disability Claims," *ABA Journal* (July 23, 2013), www.abajournal.com/news/article/obesity_is_a_disease_ama_says_aiding_obesity-related_disability_claims2 (accessed February 21, 2016).

71. CareerBuilder.com, "Workers Name Their Top Office Romance Deal Breakers in New CareerBuilder Survey" (February 11, 2015), www.careerbuilder.com/share/aboutus/pressreleasesdetail.aspx?sd=2%2F11%2F2015&id=pr868&ed=12%2F31%2F2015 (accessed March 2, 2016).

72. Vault.com, "Vault Office Romance Survey 2014" (February 12, 2014), www.vault.com/blog/workplace-issues/love-is-in-the-air-vaults-2014-office-romance-survey/#slideshowAnchor (accessed February 21, 2016).

73. 37 237 F.3d 166 (2nd Cir. 2001).

74. Vanessa Grigoriadis, "O.K., Glass: Make Google Eyes," *Vanity Fair* (April 2014), www.vanityfair.com/society/2014/04/sergey-brin-amanda-rosenberg-affair# (accessed February 21, 2016).

75. "By the Numbers" (January 2016), http://expandedramblings.com/index.php/by-the-numbers-17-amazing-facebook-stats/ (accessed February 21, 2016); Statista.com, "Statistics and Facts about Facebook" (2016), www.statista.com/topics/751/facebook/ (accessed February 21, 2016).

76. Daniel Bean, "11 Brutal Reminders That You Can and Will Get Fired for What You Post on Facebook," *Yahoo.com* (May 6, 2014), www.yahoo.com/tech/11-brutal-reminders-that-you-can-and-will-get-fired-for-84931050659.html (accessed February 23, 2016).

77. *WGNTV.com,* "Vegan Teacher in Ohio Fired over Post" (December 13, 2014), http://wgntv.com/2014/12/13/vegan-teacher-in-ohio-fired-over-facebook-post/ (accessed February 23, 2016).

78. Michael Swinson, "Big Data Is Coming—and It's Getting Personal," Lexology.com (May 8, 2014), www.lexology.com/library/detail.aspx?g=5e0236a9-4fbd-4ad3-84cd-d7483a44560f (accessed February 23, 2016).

79. National Conference of State Legislatures, "Employer Access to Social Media Usernames and Passwords" (February 2, 2016), www.ncsl.org/research/telecommunications-and-information-technology/employer-access-to-social-media-passwords-2013.aspx (accessed March 2, 2016); Aliah D. Wright, "More States Ban Social Media Snooping: Nearly 20 states Now Bar Employers from Requesting Access to Employees', Applicants' Social Media Posts" (August 12, 2014), www.shrm.org/hrdisciplines/technology/articles/pages/social-media-snooping.aspx#sthash.4XbI7Hj4.dpuf (accessed February 29, 2016).

80. Illinois Government News Network, "Governor Quinn Signs Legislation to Protect Workers' Right to Privacy," Press Release (August 1, 2012), www3.illinois.gov/PressReleases/ShowPressRelease.cfm?SubjectID=2&RecNum=10442 (accessed February 21, 2016).

81. www.it.ojp.gov/default.aspx?area=privacy&page=1281.

82. Barton Gellman and Ashkan Soltani, "NSA Collects Millions of E-mail Address Books Globally," *The Washington Post* (November 1, 2013), www.washingtonpost.com/world/national-security/nsa-collects-millions-of-e-mail-address-books-globally/2013/10/14/8e58b5be-34f9-11e3-80c6-7e6dd8d22d8f_story.html (accessed February 23, 2016).

83. Barton Gellman and Ashkan Soltani, "NSA Infiltrates Links to Yahoo, Google Data Centers Worldwide, Snowden Documents Say," *The Washington Post* (October 30, 2013), www.washingtonpost.com/world/national-security/nsa-infiltrates-links-to-yahoo-google-data-centers-worldwide-snowden-documents-say/2013/10/30/e51d661e-4166-11e3-8b74-d89d714ca4dd_story.html (accessed February 23, 2016).

84. Spencer Ackerman and Dominic Rushe, "Microsoft, Facebook, Google and Yahoo Release US Surveillance Requests," *The Guardian* (February 3, 2014), www.theguardian.com/world/2014/feb/03/microsoft-facebook-google-yahoo-fisa-surveillance-requests (accessed February 23, 2016).

85. Electronic Frontier Foundation, "Who Has Your Back? 2014 Report" (2014), www.eff.org/who-has-your-back-2014 (accessed February 23, 2016).

86. Ibid.

87. www.webopedia.com/TERM/s/spam.html (accessed April 18, 2010).

Readings

Reading **7-1**

Drug Testing and the Right to Privacy: *Arguing the Ethics of Workplace Drug Testing*

Michael Cranford

In other work, author Cranford argues that drug testing is ethically justified within the terms of the employment agreement, and therefore does not amount to a violation of an employee's right to privacy. In the following article, which is an excerpt from a longer piece, "The Ethics of Privacy," he expands the contention to include an obligation to test in certain employment contexts.

Drug Testing and the Obligation to Prevent Harm

The argument over the ethical justification for drug testing takes a different turn when we consider drug testing, not as an employer's right under the terms of an employment contract, but as a means by which an employer may prevent harms committed by employees who abuse drugs. By "harms" I mean actual or probable dangers to the safety and health of employees (other than the one impaired by drugs) and of persons outside the workplace. At issue are two related arguments, either of which may provide adequate justification for workplace drug testing. The first argument assumes that an employer has a general obligation to prevent harm. This obligation requires an employer to utilize reasonable means to prevent or mitigate potential harms committed in connection with workplace activities. To the extent that drug testing is such a reasonable means, the employer is obligated to test for employee drug abuse.

A primary assumption in this argument is that employees who are drug users pose a threat to the safety and well-being of themselves and others. That alcohol and drug abuse are connected with significant work-related harms is reasonably established, however. For example, the National Transportation Safety Board found that marijuana used by a Conrail engineer was a major contributing factor to the Conrail-Amtrak collision in January 1987, which killed 16 people and injured 170. An earlier study by the Federal Railroad Administration (FRA) determined that between 1969 and 1979, 48 major train accidents, 37 deaths, and 80 injuries could be directly connected with alcohol and drug abuse. A similar study concluded that between 1975 and 1983 at least 45 significant train accidents, resulting in 34 fatalities, 66 injuries and over $28 million in property damage, could be directly linked to the errors of alcohol- and drug-impaired employees. Without the benefit of regular post-accident testing, these figures probably amount to less than half of the total drug- or alcohol-related accidents during that period.

The second argument is that employers have not only an obligation to prevent harm, but a responsibility for harms committed by their employees. This responsibility justifies an employer in obtaining information pertaining to employee drug abuse if by acquiring such information the employer can mitigate potential harms. It is this second phase of the argument that has drawn the greatest attention and criticism, though my analysis is ultimately grounded on the corporation's obligation to prevent harm.

Unlike the argument based on performance of contract, drug testing as a means to prevent harm does not entail a devaluation of human beings by considering them as means to purely economic ends. Rather, the purpose of drug testing affirms the essential value and dignity of human beings by subjugating technique and economic efficacy to human safety and well-being. The fact that preventing harms may also be in a company's best economic interests is a conclusion resulting from cost-benefit analysis that has no immediate bearing on a mandatory drug testing program.[1] Drug testing and employee assistance programs themselves place significant financial burdens on corporations that cannot always be rationalized as offsetting accident settlements that only *might* have been paid out.

Responsibility to Drug Test and Questions of Justification

Jennifer Moore addresses the second argument listed, that "because corporations are responsible for harms committed by employees while under the influence of drugs, they are entitled to test for drug use." She invokes Kant's "ought implies can" principle, which states that if a person is obligated to do X then they must have the capacity to do X (i.e., they must be free to do or not do X). In assigning corporations a responsibility for harms caused by employees who abuse drugs, it follows that they must have the capacity to prevent these harms. Specifically, they must have the freedom to

test for drug use. Moore then explores the meaning of the statement that corporations are "responsible" for harms committed by employees to determine if drug testing is, in fact, warranted.

Moore's first point is that, whatever is meant by "responsible," it cannot mean *legally* responsible. Legally, the doctrine of *respondeat superior* makes a corporation vicariously liable for an employee's action, regardless of whether or not the corporation was at fault. Legal liability, in this case, does not imply a capacity to have prevented harm. Moore concludes that holding corporations legally liable for harms committed by employees who abuse drugs while at the same time forbidding drug testing is not inconsistent.

Moore seems to think that just because legal liability applies when a corporation cannot prevent harm, a corporation should not attempt to prevent harm to the greatest degree possible, either on the basis of an obligation to beneficence or, in the very least, to minimize its liability. Certainly a corporation can be held liable when it is not at fault, but nothing follows from this with regard to its obligation to public safety when it *is* at fault. To the degree that a corporation *can* be at fault, it should be allowed the ability to prevent harms. Legal liability does imply a justification for drug testing.

Moore then addresses corporate responsibility as a *moral* obligation to prevent harm caused by employees who abuse drugs. The argument goes as follows:

1. If corporations have obligations, they must be capable of carrying them out, on the principle of "ought implies can."

2. Corporations have an obligation to prevent harm from occurring in the course of conducting their business.

3. Drug use by employees is likely to lead to harm.

4. Corporations must be able to take steps to eliminate (or at least reduce) drug use by employees.

5. Drug testing is an effective way to eliminate/reduce employee drug use.

6. Therefore corporations must be permitted to test for drugs.

Moore claims that this conclusion (6) does not follow, since it is not clear that the obligation to prevent harm justifies drug testing:

> Of course this does not necessarily mean that drug testing is *unjustified*. But it does mean that before we can determine whether it is justified, we must ask what is permissible for one person or group of persons to do to another to prevent harm for which they are responsible.

Moore offers a number of examples to show that the obligation to prevent harm cannot justify just any action. In none of her examples, however, does she actually counterpose the act of preventing harm with a right to privacy. For example, her first case is of a hostess who is responsible for a drunken guest leaving her party. Moore argues that she is perhaps allowed to take the guest's car keys away from her, but is not entitled to knock her out and lock her in the bathroom. Moore is relying on the difficulty in discerning between these actions to argue that drug testing is not obviously justified simply because it prevents harm.

While testing impairment by a battery of eye-hand coordination and reflex exercises might detect the most seriously impaired employees at the precise moment of testing, it would not detect employees who remained sober only during the time frame immediately preceding such tests. Such testing is also indeterminate, as anyone can vouch who has successfully passed a field sobriety test while legally intoxicated. Even if some degree of impairment were indicated, the employer is left with no means by which she may evaluate the significance of the employee's failure to pass the test. The difference between an employee who is impaired due to lack of sleep and an employee who is under the influence of an illegal substance is morally significant.[2]

Finally, testing impairment fails to detect habitual users of drugs who, while not noticeably impaired at the precise moment of testing, nonetheless may constitute a significant and ongoing risk. Consequently, testing for impairment is not "just more effective in all ways" than drug testing. Drug testing is not directed at identifying impairment, which (as I have pointed out) is rather difficult to quantify or detect by any means, but at (1) identifying employees who abuse drugs, and (2) deterring habitual users from becoming impaired at the workplace. Toward these ends, drug testing is the most effective and direct means currently available.

In response to Moore, I agree that drug testing is neither necessary nor sufficient for ridding the workplace of drug abuse. Consequently, she is correct in stating that the conclusion to the present argument (6) does not follow. But this is only if we allow her to define what it means for drug testing to be an "effective" way to eliminate or reduce employee drug abuse (5). If by "effective" we understand that drug testing prevents or eliminates harms that would not, in its absence, be prevented or eliminated by some other measure, then it follows that corporations must be permitted to test for drugs. Corporations must be permitted to undertake any reasonable measures for preventing workplace harms when no equally effectual measures are available. I will refer to all such measures as *measures of last resort*. In this understanding of "effective," the conclusion (6) does follow.

But in this case, however, our conclusion (6) is not strong enough. Referring back to our original argument, I asserted that an employer has a general obligation to prevent harm, and that this obligation requires an employer to utilize reasonable means to prevent or mitigate potential harms committed in connection with workplace activities. But if drug testing is necessary in that process as a measure of last resort, then it not only follows that corporations must be permitted to test for drugs, but that corporations are obligated to do so. It is for this reason that a corporation is responsible to take on the "Protector of Harms" role in its relationship with an employee even when such a role is not inherent in the employment contract.

The Kew Gardens Principle and the Obligation to Prevent Harm

There are two elements in my analysis to this point which I have offered without any accompanying substantiation. The first is the claim that an employer has a general obligation to prevent harm. The second is the claim that drug testing is a measure of last resort, as I have defined it. It is only if these assertions are reasonable that it would follow that corporations are obligated to test for drugs.

In defense of both these points I would like to introduce four criteria which together indicate a moral obligation to prevent harm. This combination of features governing difficult cases of assessing moral responsibility has elsewhere been termed the "Kew Gardens Principle."

1. *Need.* A corporation's responsibility to test for drugs, or take any other appropriate measures to reduce the occurrence of harms, is a function of the extent of the harms which may result. In cases where the other three factors are constant, increased need indicates increased responsibility. In reference to his engineering company, Lewis Maltby states that "a single Drexelbrook employee working under the influence of drugs could cause a disaster as tragic as occurred in Bhopal." If true, this would suggest a significant responsibility to prevent such harms.

2. *Proximity.* Proximity is less a function of distance and more a function of awareness. We hold a person blameworthy if she knows of a crisis or a potential crisis and does not do what she can to prevent it. "When we become aware of a wrongdoing or a social injury, we take on obligations that we did not have while ignorant." Greater responsibility exists in situations where one would expect a heightened awareness of need as a consequence of civic duty, duties to one's family, and so on. In other words, we

would hold a family member more blameworthy than a stranger for not being aware of a person's critical plight.

Proximity becomes important in the case of workplace drug abuse because the network of social relationships involved in a daily, cooperative setting, combined with the social and legal perception that an employer is responsible for the activities of her employees, entail a high degree of expectation that the employer not only will learn of a potential harm caused by drug abuse, but *should* learn of it. A corporation delegates its employees to act on its behalf and, in fact, acts only through its employees. This integral and intimate relationship whereby the employees act on behalf of the corporation obligates the corporation to become aware of potential dangers which could result from drug abuse.

While a variety of measures can and have been used that locate and address the problem of workplace drug abuse (such as direct observation of employees, hidden cameras, mandatory educational programs in dealing with drug abuse, and basic dexterity/reflexivity/judgment testing), none of these programs has the same certainty of screening out drug abusers as does drug testing. Direct observation and dexterity tests can be beaten (and are, routinely). While education is an effective counterpreventative, it does not screen out users who are resistant to receiving help—the individuals most likely to place others at risk. On the other hand, it can be argued that drug testing also is falsifiable. If given advance notice of testing, drug users can abstain long enough to pass the test. Or, they can procure a sample of "clean" urine from another individual and substitute it for their own.

At most, these examples argue against regularly scheduled testings—not against random, unannounced testings. These examples also overlook the fact that the time necessary for drug metabolites to become absent from the urine varies from individual to individual and from use to use. Serious and habitual users (who are the most likely to commit harms) would probably be unable to abstain from use long enough even to pass an announced test. And while drug testing is not unfalsifiable, it is more difficult to falsify than other options for testing. Consequently, while not a perfect instrument for the detection of drug abuse, drug testing has an effectiveness and specificity that remain unparalleled.

Since drug testing is the most effective technology currently available to make the employer aware of potential dangers by locating habitual users, and without which many such users will likely not be identified, use of drug testing is obligatory as a measure of last resort. Since no one other than the employer is more aware of the potential for an employee committing work-related harms, a significant moral responsibility to prevent such harms follows.

This responsibility could be mitigated if the employer has a reasonable certainty that an employee (or all employees) does not abuse drugs. Thus, drug testing is not only essential to the employer's obligation to come to know of potential harms, but it reduces a corporation's moral responsibility for harms committed by ruling out drug abuse as a contributing factor.

3. *Capability.* Even if there is a need to which someone has proximity, that person cannot be held morally responsible unless she has the capacity to meet the need. As I have discussed at length, not just any action offered to prevent a harm is necessarily reasonable. What is reasonable is that action which is least intrusive or harmful, most efficient and specific, and with the highest probability of achieving its goals (thus, my principles for what constitutes a reasonable means of coming to know private information). Drug testing, in combination with a counseling and rehabilitation program that relieves employees of hazardous duty, meets these criteria. In most cases, as will be noted below, no other agent has the capability of performing this combination of actions.

4. *Last Resort.* In situations where the other three features are present, one becomes more responsible the less likely it is that someone else will prevent the harm in question. While it is often difficult to assess whether one alone has knowledge of a potential harm, to the degree that one can be certain that one does, and that no one else has the proximity or capacity for intervening, significant responsibility is entailed.

In the case of harms caused by drug abuse, it is rarely the case that an agency outside the workplace will possess the means to either assess the potential for harm (thus need and proximity) or be able to prevent the harm from being realized (by possessing the capacity to locate and remove employees who abuse drugs from hazardous duty). When there is no agency beyond the employer which can effectively prevent harms, the employer becomes the agent of last resort. When there is no method of identifying drug abusers more effective than drug testing, it becomes a method of last resort in the process of preventing drug-related harms in the workplace. Consequently, the criterion of last resort, in connection with the other three features of the Kew Gardens Principle, assign a corporation a high degree of moral responsibility to prevent drug-related harms, and obligate it to make use of reasonable methods for identifying such harms, particularly when more effective methods are unavailable.

The actual degree of responsibility turns on the level of need (criterion #1), however. To the degree that harms are improbable or of little consequence to human life and safety, a corporation's obligation to prevent such harms is diminished. Drug testing is not justified under this argument if the condition it is testing for has little potential to result in any real danger. The difficulty arises in attempting a risk analysis when the effects of impairment remain hypothetical. For example, one might argue that the condition of increased need exists in the case of railroad engineers who control the velocity and breaking of high-speed locomotives. Similarly, a condition of increased need exists in the case of factory workers who operate heavy machinery in a crowded work setting. It is less clear, though, that a condition of increased need arises among clerks at the same railroad, who could potentially create disaster through an error in paper work that goes unnoticed by field operatives. Nor is it clear that a condition of increased need arises in the case of the janitorial staff at a factory, who might perhaps leave a bit too much water on the floor if they were impaired while mopping a hallway. Of these latter examples, the first is improbable, and the last is insignificant (or at least, not significant enough to justify drug testing the entire janitorial staff). While many cases can be cited that are problems in risk assessment, it is critical to note that nothing follows with regard to the obligation to prevent harms in cases that are not problematic. In such cases (like the two listed first), corporations can and should use reasonable means to prevent drug related harms.

Conclusions and Policy Recommendations

It is the position adopted in this paper that (1) a corporation is entitled to drug test its employees to determine employee capacity to perform according to the terms of the employment contract, and (2) a corporation is morally obligated to test employees for drug and alcohol abuse when a condition of impairment would place the safety and health of other human beings at risk. The first of these two justifications, I have argued, quantifies human beings under a measure of efficiency, treating them as means to a purely economic end (i.e., the corporation's profitability). Drug testing does not, in the large majority of cases, benefit the employee's best interests, and is therefore directed at effecting extrinsic goods only (as opposed to respecting the employee's intrinsic value and dignity). This criticism fails in the latter justification, however, since the ultimate end of drug testing *is* the preservation of human life as an intrinsic good. In this case, a corporation is not only entitled to use toxicological testing, but is obligated to do so, to the degree that a critical need to prevent drug-related harms is actually present.

Source: Adapted by permission of the author from his publication, "The Ethics of Privacy: Drug Testing, Surveillance, and Competing Interests in the Workplace," by Michael Cranford, PhD, University of Southern California, 2007, 292 pages; AAT 3291792.

Endnotes

1. Though it might have a bearing on a drug testing program that was only enacted for certain projects that were assessed as cost-prohibitive on the basis of potential harms. Consequently, drug testing will only be justified under this argument if it is effected uniformly and mandatorily without regard for such assessments.

2. My point here is best explained by way of an example. Let us say that a young employee dances all night for several nights in a row, and therefore shows up for work impaired due to lack of sleep. The difference between this individual and someone who is impaired because of substance abuse is at least that the latter admits of an addictive and increasingly significant (and ultimately self-destructive) condition, whereas the former is at worst compulsive, and is therefore unlikely to continue for more than a few nights (even the best of us

dancers eventually find ourselves nodding off). There is also the legality of purchasing and using illicit substances, not to mention driving under the influence of illicit substances. Breaking those laws is ethically significant,

whereas dancing all night is just dumb—but completely legal

Note: References were removed for publication here, but are available on the book website at www.mhhe.com/busethics4e.

Reading **7-2**

The Ethical Use of Technology in Business

Tony Mordini

Abstract

The business environment is dependent upon technology for a range of functions. The potential for communication, data management and business processes are endless but so too are the potential misuses of the technology. This poses problems which often require some ethical perspectives to be considered. In monitoring e-mail, phone and human traffic how much are we encroaching on personal space? In providing employees with technological tools such as lap top computers and cell phones what controls can we legitimately exercise on how they use them? In capturing data from staff and clients what safeguards need to be put in place to ensure information is not misused? There may not be a simple model that fits all contexts but the field of Applied Ethics provides research, frameworks and educational instruments that can help to maximize the ethical use of technology in business and help to articulate the issues, identify what is expected in particular contexts and propose appropriate ways to engender compliance.

Introduction

Technology is embedded in all aspects of our lives to the extent that we would find it difficult to conduct many of our day to day activities without it.

The business environment is no different. Technology is used in a myriad of ways including: communication; information and data capture, processing, analysis and storage; monitoring of business performance; electronic commerce; and surveillance.

The developments in information communication technology (ICT) have also resulted in the boundaries between individuals' private and public lives becoming significantly blurred. The cell phone means that people are contactable at almost any time, any where; wireless e-mail communication means faster response rates which can place pressure on individuals to not take a considered, metered approach in decision-making and like cell phones be able to send and receive e-mails almost anywhere and at any time; web-based social networking can create distractions for individuals in the workplace and surveillance of work sites, Internet traffic and phone usage provide rich data for employers but also present a privacy risk if data is misused.

Ethical Issues with Respect to the Use of Technology

The potential misuse of technology in the business environment is a real risk and presents many challenges for those leading and managing work sites and well as their employees. Technology is an integral business tool with the potential and capabilities to support a range of business functions and create value. However, technology also has the potential to invade individuals' personal lives, distract them from their work, cost businesses significantly if the technology resources are not deployed effectively and requires sound risk management to ensure data is not misappropriated. Some economic projections are explored in a case study that follows. These issues also represent some significant ethical questions for both employers and employees. The problem is that often the issues associated with the use of technology in business environments are not recognized as having potential risks nor that ethical frameworks need to be applied in relation to its use.

Looking at Issues Ethically

Jennifer Jackson (1996) proposes that the difficulties in ascertaining what is ethical and what isn't begins with the notions of *identification and compliance.* Specifically ascertaining what an individual's duties are in a particular situation, how they are expected to perform those duties and how the resources are expected to be deployed in executing those duties need to be articulated in the first instance. Subsequently, the employee needs to actually understand, appreciate and commit to actually doing what they know they ought to do.

Her foundational elements provide a basis for employer and employee to clearly communicate what is expected. Ostensibly employers (often and preferably in consultation with relevant stakeholders) need to work out and subsequently articulate what the job entails and how they expect it to be carried out and what the workplace "rules" will be.

Employees need to clearly understand the "rules" and how these are to be applied. The issue of compliance becomes difficult Jackson notes when the rules are not followed equitably. Where employees see different levels of application (for example, the VP has certain benefits that others don't have), they will at best accept apply the "rules" begrudgingly and at worst find surreptitious ways to "compensate themselves" (p.11).

How do employers work out how best to manage the technology and what frameworks can they use to ensure current and future technologies are approached appropriately? How can they foster an ethical culture in their workplace? Obviously each context needs to be examined on its own merits and models cannot be presumed to be all encompassing but from what has been examined in earlier chapters you have some useful frameworks that you can apply as long as you consider the elements in each case carefully. As John Haldane (1999), suggests that there is a "moral danger in applied ethics" (p. 726). Similar to the attack that Socrates made on the Sophists. The Sophists were seen as the "purveyors of moral and political wisdom in the Greek city-states in the fifth century BC." Haldane raises a cautionary note. It is risky to believe that some mechanical formula can be simply applied to all moral issues. Haldane argues it is "a disservice to philosophy" and could lead to a "spread of moral irrationalism" (ibid).

Thus we will proceed with a degree of caution and practicality but at the same time with a degree of confidence that to examine all that we do through an ethical framework has potential for positive personal, professional and business outcomes.

Looking at Business Issues Ethically

Case 1—Who Owns the Technology?

Miranda Rusden is a student liaison officer in the admissions office of a large university. Her main task is to attend to online and phone enquiries and relieve the receptionist when she needs to be away from her post. She has worked in this job for four years and although not overly challenged by the role is not interested in promotion. It suits her family and personal commitments because it is a "nine to five" job and it has few demands out of normal work hours. Furthermore, during semester breaks her days can be pretty quiet.

In the quiet times she will often use the time to catch up on personal e-mails, surf the web looking at online stores or connect to social networking sites. The university has policies in place on the use of the Internet but Miranda has justified the activity to herself as harmless. Furthermore, she feels that if she has done all that she has been asked to do or is able to answer any enquiries as they come in by phone, fax or e-mail she should be able to make use of the time this way. She feels that if she were to take any initiative to do additional tasks that it would bring attention to the fact that she is not overly challenged. If she is at her computer and appears to be hard at work people will leave her alone.

A recent audit of Internet usage has revealed that a number of university personnel are using work time to access online shopping and social networking. Miranda's manager, upon receiving the report from her Head of Division is amazed at the amount of time Miranda has spent on the Internet engaged in personal activities over the past month. She prepares to call her into a meeting and according to university policy, serve her with a formal written warning and advise her that a subsequent offence could result in a termination of her employment. She finds herself in a difficult situation as she gets on really well with Miranda but knows that it is strictly a business matter and hopes that Miranda will see it that way.

Ethical Analysis

The issues of work time and work equipment are critical factors in assessing and addressing a case like this. Individuals are often entrusted to do a job and act in good faith. Furthermore, the employer provides the "tools" to do the job and expects the employee to use these tools appropriately, and as they are intended to be used.

What Miranda did is common practice and many organizations would find similar evidence if they were to audit the Internet use of their employees. However, what would be even more telling would be if the audit was to also provide the costs of the lost productivity. Imagine for example, that Miranda is one of 3,000 staff and that 10% (300 staff) are chronic abusers of the technology and

the audit reveals that they spend approximately 1 hour a day on the Internet in private activities. That amounts to 5 hours of a 40 hour work week, thus 1/8th of the individual's time is not being used productively. If the average salary for an employee in this sector is $50,000, 300 employees cost $15 million in salaries alone and a loss of productivity of even 1 hour a day equates to $1,875,000 or the equivalent of 37.5 full time staff.

Time for Thinking

Individuals in organizations do not often consider their actions from an ethical perspective, nor do they often do the math as per the previous example to see the impact of such behavior when it is magnified several times over. Examples such as these can be a simple way for teams to work constructively to eradicate losses in productivity but also provide a means of engaging in dialogue that examines behavior from an ethical perspective.

Case 2—Private Lives in the Public Arena

Chat rooms and web-based social networking such as LinkedIn and Facebook connect individuals from all walks of life and with a myriad of interests. Such networks may have positive business outcomes. Matt Moore, Director of Innotecture, suggests that managed well, social networking and web-based tools such as wikis and blogs can be turned to an employer's advantage.

> 'If used well these tools allow participants to forge relationships with people they might never have found otherwise and do things they couldn't have done before. Social network analysis[1] allows individuals to better understand their own networks, as it also allows organizations to better understand the real complexity and power of the networks that form them' (2008, p. 38).

However, as Moore, rightly points out, Social Networking Analysis will not identify many of the qualitative aspects of web-based interactions. For example, how often is the approach a hindrance as opposed to a "helping hand"?

Another factor is that once connected to others in the public domain the lines between public and private become blurred. Blogging on a political site may make it clear what an individual's political leanings are. Participating in wikis means that any text a person writes in this space can be edited by others. Meeting people through web-based social networks may expose individuals to a variety of risks. In face to face interactions there are a number of visual and audio cues which are hard to pick up through chat rooms and e-mail communication. Nor do individuals have control over information which is in the public domain.

Consider the case of Jonathan, a young finance graduate working for an investment bank. Jonathan is eager to succeed, bright, seen by many of the senior managers as a young guy who will "go places."

Jonathan is reasonably circumspect about his personal life. When at work he is focused on the job. He steers clear of personal chit chat. Like many young gay men he uses social networking sites to keep abreast of events, contact mates and make new friends.

One night, one of the senior staff, Mitch Hendricks is at home surfing the City of Chicago website looking up some information on upcoming events. He notices some advertising for Chicago's Gay Pride Week with a photograph of a group of gay men and a hyperlink to the group's website. Jonathan is amongst the group of men in the photograph. Although it is not a work related matter, he is concerned of the possible career implications this could have for Jonathan. Many of the senior men in the firm are quite conservative family men. He doesn't know Jonathan that well but hopes that meeting over a coffee will help to map out a strategy should a situation arise that could put Jonathan in a difficult place.

Mitch sends Jonathan an e-mail that night and fortunately Jonathan is online. He responds to the message almost immediately and agrees to a coffee at 10:00 am the next day. Jonathan thinks nothing of it and assumes it is some routine assignment he is being asked to work on. Mitch is uncomfortable about the meeting as he is concerned Jonathan may

take it as an intrusion into his personal life. Mitch has grown up in a conservative Baptist family and except for his college years has not been exposed to a wide cross-section of the community. He is also a little anxious what others may deduce from their meeting.

Fortunately, for Mitch the meeting the next day is quite productive. Jonathan agrees with Mitch that although there should not be any problem with how he chooses to live his personal life, the firm and the sector he works in has some very conservative people and he may need to exercise careful judgment in how he balances his personal and professional lives and consider carefully how he might respond if a difficult situation was to arise.

For Mitch, the meeting also gave him a better understanding of how challenging things have been for Jonathan as he has come to terms with his identity and the potential problems it poses in the professional arena.

Ethical Analysis—Finding a Practical, Balanced and Responsible Position

Firms are rarely adequately prepared to respond to such issues. It is impossible to have one clear statement that covers all possible contingencies. Conventions such as freedom of association, freedom of speech, freedom of expression are constitutional rights. However, in practice, they can polarize people and create real tensions in the workplace or the community. Individuals' value systems particularly come into play on issues related to family responsibility, sexuality and religious beliefs and practices.

Workplaces need to be safe (in the broadest sense of the word—physically, emotionally, psychologically etc.). Rules need to be in place to ensure that individuals are not marginalized. Individuals however, need to be reminded that what is in the public arena, means exactly that, *information is public* and people can view material, make a range of assumptions based on what they view, can disseminate it as they please and use it in a way that we never intended it to be used.

The technologies associated with social networking sites and other web-based group activities can have positive outcomes providing networks and a means of accessing people but they can also expose individuals and their workplaces to various risks. However, firms may need to consider policies that clearly articulate their position. For example, institutions may need to consider disclaimers that enable them to clearly demarcate the boundaries between the individual's personal associations and their professional responsibilities. Notwithstanding this, in a number of professional areas such as teaching individuals may need to be reminded that their public and personal activity may impact adversely upon their professional life and that they may come under scrutiny by their employer if there appear to be any conflicts of interest or perceptions of moral impropriety.

Individuals may also need to be reminded that in public domain, web-based contexts they may be providing people who they don't know with more personal information than they realize and that once it is in the public domain, it will be impossible to control where it is disseminated and who will have access to it.

Case 3—Is Surveillance Always Legitimate?

Many firms have closed circuit television (CCTV) as a deterrent to theft and as a means of providing a safer working environment. For example, if issues arise in a customer service setting, the employee can use digital evidence to defend claims that they may have acted inappropriately.

However, the images captured through the recording of movements on a site need to be stored safely and appropriately. Organizations need to also consider a number of related factors including: how long images will be stored, where they will be stored, in what format and who has the right to view them.

Consider the following scenario. Murray is a rising star in a national retail chain. He has recently been appointed to a small regional centre to manage their store. This is his first management job and we wants to impress. He is very ambitious and sees this appointment as a stepping stone to a bigger role back on the East Coast where he has come from. He knows that head office is very keen to see productivity efficiencies and he is very keen to deliver them. Discussions with senior staff at the store have provided anecdotal evidence that a number of staff are not really pulling their weight and wasting time in certain areas of the business. He decides to use CCTV evidence as a mechanism to provide the metrics he needed to embarrass some staff who are not performing as well as he believes they should be.

Soon after he arrived at his new store he called the manager of the security company monitoring his building and asked if they could meet in a down town coffee shop. On the day they met he stressed that he did not want others to find out about the meeting and that any evidence had to be handed to him directly.

Ethical Analysis

The following week was determined as the week that a specific monitoring would take place. The loading bay and stores area was picked as the area to be placed under closer scrutiny. The evidence was gathered and handed to Murray. He analyzed it as soon as he got it and as he presumed, provided some telling evidence. His initial thought was to call the team of staff in. It was evident that there were some real inefficiencies and time wasting. Murray could use a hard hitting approach challenging the ethical behavior of employees and use it to censure them. He knew however, that this group was heavily unionized. Even if he could justify his actions, he anticipated it could really go against him and the legitimacy of his actions would be questioned.

Taking Action—a Considered Way Forward

He planned therefore, to use the surveillance data to map out a work plan and then take the group through it. By changing some of the rosters which he justified on the basis of the times that goods were delivered across the day, and clearly outlining tasks that could be done in quiet times when there was no stock to unload or process he was able to use the data to help him manage a very ineffectual situation. He was able to use inferences such as: "I assume that in between trucks arriving it might get a bit boring in the stores . . . this will give us a bit of time to do some other tidying up and sort out stock that needs to be returned because it is faulty or broken. . . . I have provided a check list of what we should be trying to achieve on a daily and weekly basis. . . ." There was some initial disquiet but Murray was correct in his comments that the group was not showing much initiative in the quiet times and that some clear direction would improve work output.

Some Concluding Remarks

In each of these case studies we see the potential and the possible pit falls of the technology. Used and managed appropriately it provides individuals and firms with the capacity to make better use of their time, network, research, analyze work flows, store information and improve efficiencies. However, technology may not always add value. Technology also increases risk for individuals and firms. Participating in the cyber world removes many barriers. Information in the public domain can injure the reputation of a firm or individual, misused or misappropriated data or information can create significant problems for people. Workplaces need to regularly review how they

manage this aspect of their workplace. It is difficult because of the rate at which technology use is developing to have an all embracing policy in place. Policies need to have some level of flexibility, need to be reviewed regularly and need to have a level of flexibility to deal with current, emerging and future issues.

Above all, workplaces need to be ethical work places and individuals need to be encouraged to work in a manner that is compliant and based on an understanding of what is considered appropriate workplace practice, what are appropriate ways to engage with the technology they are using in the workplace and how they can minimize the risks associated with the use of technology in their day to day lives especially in their personal activities if it could potentially marginalize them or injure their reputation or efficacy in the workplace.

Source: Used with permission of the author.

Endnotes

1. Social Network Analysis (SNA) is an instrument that has been used in Sociology since the 1930s to map relationships and collaborations between people. These maps help to illustrate the networks that exist in organizations and highlight areas where knowledge flow is poor or ineffective.

Note: References and additional notes have been removed for publication here, but are available on the book website at www.mhhe.com/busethics4e.

Reading 7-3

Hiring in a Social Media Age

Avner Levin

The number of organizations that rely on the information they collect through Google, Facebook and Spokeo is continuously on the rise.[1] Are current practices, of using online information for hiring decisions, ethical? May they be conducted ethically under certain conditions? This article will look at some common practices in order to address these questions.

Hiring Practices

Organizations display a wide range of hiring practices and policies regarding online information. One of the most common practices is the unauthorized use of such information in order to formulate a decision or an opinion about a candidate. In its simplest form this amounts to Googling a person, not by authorized human resources personnel but by someone such as a future immediate manager. In more sophisticated forms these unauthorized individuals embark on "fishing" expeditions on popular social media such as Facebook, taking advantage of unrestricted profiles or working through "friends" of "friends." Not all information about a candidate originates *with* the candidate, and organizations often discover such information on the social media platforms of others. The source of the information has ethical implications that are important to this discussion.

As use of online information increases so does the incorporation of this practice into formal organizational policy. Online sources may be accessed by human resources personnel, or by another party who has been contracted to provide such information. One popular example is Spokeo, an online business that aggregates information from a variety of online sources, including online social networks, and that offers subscriptions to its database.[2]

In an attempt to control the use of on-line media, firms may implement a practice that requires the candidate to be informed if on-line information is used in the hiring practice. This does not guarantee, however, that the practice is followed. Additionally, some organizations have taken the position that not disclosing such investigations is important to ensure that the information collected is authentic, and that hiring for certain sensitive positions, such as law enforcement positions, would be compromised otherwise.

Finally, it should be noted, that although they are a shrinking minority, there are organizations that have taken the position that they already have a hiring process that works for them and produces desirable candidates and that, in light of the success of their existing process, they see no need to take online information into consideration as part of their hiring decisions.

Ethical Implications and Considerations

Several other facts must be taken into consideration in light of the range of approaches to the use of online information. Individuals are comfortable posting large amounts of personal information online, but they generally do so while differentiating between destinations for this information. Individuals expect that information will not be shared between these destinations. This expectation is known as "network privacy."[3] Organizations, by and large, refuse to accept such network privacy concerns as valid, and adhere to the traditional approach by which personal information that is to be kept private must not be disclosed in the first place.[4]

The ethical question, therefore, is clear: should organizations use information that was not provided online with the intention of use by them? In light of current practice this may be a moot question, but it remains a question worth asking. Would organizations use information in the hiring process that would result in illegal discrimination? For example, is and, more importantly, should information about a candidate's race, national or ethnic origin, sexual preference or religion be used? How does this compare with the use of other information not intended to be received as part of an application for employment? There does not appear to be an easy answer to this question, but it is a pity that organizations are at least not considering its implications as they develop information-gathering policies and practices.

Organizations that use online information about candidates face additional ethical questions. Is it ethical to collect such information outside of the regular hiring process in for example, the performance evaluation process? Is it ethical not to disclose such collection either before or after it has occurred? And is it ethical to base hiring decisions on information that is derived from sources when you have no way of knowing whether or not they have biases against the candidate?

The answers to some of these questions appear easy enough. First, there does not seem to be either an ethical way or justification, for collecting, and then acting upon, information outside of an organization's defined hiring process. Unauthorized googling, for example, while perhaps irresistible, is unethical. Needless to say, more thorough unauthorized investigations into information online are all the more unethical and should not be condoned. Organizations that strive to operate ethically should, prior to any discussion on the merits of using online information, therefore prohibit such unauthorized practices and enforce them internally.

Second, except for a few, ultra-sensitive, positions, there appears to be no good reason not to disclose to a candidate that the hiring process will involve collection of online information. Organizations routinely disclose to candidates the extent and nature of other information that will be collected about them, through such means as background checks. They might easily include online sources in such a list—and indeed some organizations are beginning to do just that.

Third, although a process based on disreputable sources cannot in the end be ethical itself, not every external source is disreputable. Obviously sources will vary in terms of reliability. In this limited sense, it is more ethical to rely on information provided by the candidate than it is on information provided by others. True, it is possible for people that dislike the candidate to provide correct, even if unflattering, information about a candidate. If an organization were to verify such claims then it would probably be ethical to rely on such corroborated information as well. However, organizations that engage in such practices, let alone have such policies, are few and far between.

There is space here to raise one more ethical consideration which, is perhaps the most basic one, and was alluded to above. An organization must ask itself if its existing hiring process that does not rely on online information is broken. If it works well and selects candidates that go on to become successful, productive employees, then why would

it change current practices and, from an ethical perspective, there must very strong reasons for incorporating additional online information. Only if the existing process is broken will an organization look into revising the process, including perhaps, but not obviously, online information.

Recommendations and Conclusion

In the not too distant future every candidate may have an online digital record of his activities, hobbies, friends, political positions and basically, his life. If this information is provided to organizations, they will for the first time, have easy access to information about candidates that they have not traditionally collected. The boundaries between work and private life will blur to an extent that individuals will no longer be able to separate these parts of their life. To navigate this new terrain ethically organizations should consider the following recommendations:

- Develop an understanding of online social media and their role in the culture and communication behaviour of their candidates.

- Formulate, disclose to candidates, and enforce internally clear, transparent rules and guidelines about the use of social media for hiring purposes. Some examples:

  - If you look at online information—say so;

  - List your sources and let the candidate know in advance;

  - Ignore third parties with agendas that you do not share.

- Resist the temptation to seek unnecessary online information, and if such information is obtained, or unsolicited information is received, refrain from using it.

Hopefully, the suggestions and discussion above may lead to more ethical behaviour that future candidates will no doubt appreciate.

Source: Avner Levin, *Management Ethics*, Fall/Winter 2010, pp. 8–9.

Endnotes

1. For a comparison of how the landscape has changed take a look at the first survey conducted in Canada about this issue in 2008, and published by the Privacy Institute as "The Next Digital Divide: Online Social Network Privacy" (available at http://www.ryerson.ca/tedrogersschool/privacy/Ryerson_Privacy_Institute_OSN_Report.pdf) and compare it with Microsoft's comprehensive survey released earlier this year (available at http://www.microsoft.com/privacy/dpd/research.aspx).

2. http://www.spokeo.com.

3. For more on this see Levin, A., Sanchez Abril, P., "Two Notions of Privacy Online" *Vanderbilt Journal of Entertainment and Technology Law* 11 (4) 1001–1051 (2009).

4. The legal aspects of this issue are beyond the scope of this article.

Reading 7-4

Genetic Testing in the Workplace

Chris MacDonald

In October of 2005, I.B.M, one of America's leading corporations, announced to the world that, as a matter of policy, the company would *never* use genetic information in its hiring process, or in order to determine eligibility for its employee healthcare or benefits plans.[1] In a way, this was an odd proclamation: I.B.M. was swearing that it would never do . . . well, something few other firms seemed interested in doing anyway. That a major corporation should feel the need to make such a declaration is testament to the level of concern associated with genetic information, in general, and with genetic testing in particular.

As most readers will already know, DNA (deoxyribonucleic acid) is the chemical compound by means of which genetic information is stored in our cells; genes (in additional to being fundamental units of inheritance) are functional segments of DNA, stretches of DNA that do something—usually, they provide instructions for making one or another protein within the cell. Proteins, in turn, perform a vast range of functions within our cells (and indeed within the cells of all living things), including providing the basis for many cellular structures and catalyzing many intracellular chemical reactions. Since proteins play such a large role in how our bodies function, and since genes code

for proteins, examining genes can provide insight into how bodies function, or dysfunction, in the present, or are likely to function or dysfunction in the future.

Genetic *testing* is the process of examining an individual's DNA, typically to look for the presence or absence of a particular gene. Genetic testing typically involves obtaining a sample of blood for analysis, though any bodily substance containing cells can in principle be tested. Since the same genetic code is stored in every cell of our bodies,[2] we need only examine the genetic information stored in any one part (say, in our skin or blood) to learn about our genetic structure as a whole. *Workplace* genetic testing involves the testing of current or potential employees.

The idea of employers conducting genetic tests on employees has generated considerable controversy; indeed, the amount of controversy is somewhat surprising, given that relatively few employers seem to have expressed an interest in such use of genetic testing, and even fewer have used it. In May of 2002, the Burlington Northern Santa Fe Railroad settled a lawsuit filed by the U.S. Equal Employment Opportunity Commission under the Americans With Disabilities Act. The Railroad had been secretly testing employees who claimed disability due to carpal tunnel syndrome, in an attempt to establish that the employees' disability was genetic, and hence inherited, rather than work-related. This one case is cited in practically every scholarly paper and newspaper or magazine article on workplace genetic testing. Only a couple of other cases also get mentioned, perhaps illustrating that while scholars and labour activists are worried, we have yet to see significant usage of genetic testing in the workplace. But as the price of genetic testing continues to drop, it is to be expected that more employers will begin to find the technology attractive.

In early 2008, the U.S. government finally passed (after several failed attempts at passing similar legislation) the Genetic Information Non-discrimination Act[3] (GINA), which effectively prohibits discriminatory use of genetic information in the workplace (as well as in insurance). GINA is far-reaching legislation that may well serve to allay many of the concerns related to workplace genetic testing.[4] But the passage of that law did not eliminate all ethical questions related to genetic testing in the workplace. For starters, and most obviously, GINA only applies in the U.S., and not all jurisdictions have this kind of legislation. Canada, for example, has no specific legislation dealing with workplace genetic testing. Some, but not all, countries in the E.U. have such legislation, although the Council of Europe's Convention on Human Rights and Biomedicine states, in Article 12, that genetic tests are to be done "only for health purposes or for scientific research linked to health purposes"[5] (and, by implication, *not* for making decisions about insurance or employment). A large number of less-developed countries may not have such legislation in the foreseeable future. And generally the laws of developed nations don't apply to companies *working* overseas (i.e., American laws apply to American companies working in the U.S., though some American laws—such as the Americans With Disabilities Act—apparently also apply to the treatment by American companies of their *American employees* overseas).

But even in countries with clear and specific legislation, the ethical questions regarding workplace

genetic testing remain salient, for three reasons. First, there is the question of compliance. Even in the presence of legislation, companies still face the question of whether, and perhaps to what extent, to comply with the law. Second, ethical issues remain because there are question (and doubts) about the scope and adequacy of some of the existing legal protections. Third, there is the question of advocacy for legislative or regulatory change. The mere existence of a law does not mean that the law will never change; laws can be amended, rescinded, or augmented by legislatures. Thus, the mere existence of a law like GINA is far from obviating the ethical questions that surround workplace genetic testing. Workplace genetic testing remains an important ethical issue.

How Might Genetic Testing Be Used?

Workplace genetic testing can be divided into two major categories, based on the purpose for which the test is done: genetic *monitoring* and genetic *screening*. Genetic monitoring is the less controversial form of testing. The goal of genetic monitoring is to monitor and protect employee health: it tests for genetic damage that may have resulted from exposure to workplace toxins or radiation. Genetic screening, on the other hand, is used to detect either genes associated with hereditary diseases or genes associated with heightened susceptibility to workplace toxins. Screening is controversial because such information can in theory be used in decisions whether to hire or fire, and in promotion decisions.

Genetic screening involves looking for *inherited* genetic characteristics, rather than genetic damage acquired in the workplace. Genetic screening can further be broken down into two categories. The first type of genetic screening looks for genetic variations associated with heightened susceptibility to workplace toxins. Just as not all drugs are equally effective in all people, not all workplace toxins affect all people equally. At least some of the variability in individual response to workplace toxins is the result of individual genetic variability. This type of screening is less controversial, largely because it is aimed at keeping employees healthy.

The second, and more controversial, form of workplace genetic screening screens employees for genes associated with inherited illnesses, or illnesses in which inherited genes play a significant role. The case *for* such testing can be helpfully illustrated by an extreme, hypothetical example. Imagine a commercial airline finds out that the father of one of its pilots has died of Huntington's disease. Having one parent with Huntington's means that this pilot has a 50% chance of having inherited the genetic mutation that causes that disease. And, because the Huntington's mutation is highly "penetrant" (i.e., having the mutation *guarantees* the eventual arrival of the disease) the pilot herself has a 50% chance of developing the debilitating neurological symptoms associated with Huntington's Disease. If she does indeed have the mutation, at some point (probably somewhere between the age of 30 and 50), she will become unfit to fly and will pose a serious threat to her passengers. But the pilot also has a 50% chance of *not* having inherited the Huntington's mutation, and hence a 50% chance of *never* falling prey to the disease that first disabled, and then killed, her father. However, a simple genetic test will determine the truth. If she tests positive for the Huntington's mutation, she is destined eventually to succumb to the disease, and perhaps ought to stop flying planes; if she tests negative, then (provided she has no other relevant health problems) she can look forward to a long career of safe and healthy flying. In a situation like this, the case for genetic testing seems compelling. There is good prior reason (i.e., the family history of Huntington's) to motivate testing. Hundreds of lives (i.e., passengers) may be at stake. And a test is available that will tell, with great certainty, not just whether the pilot has the mutation in question but (because it is a highly penetrant mutation) whether serious illness will ensue. In such a situation, genetic testing is not just useful: implementing it might be ethically obligatory.

But the hypothetical example just given is far from typical. The Huntington's mutation is extremely unusual as genetic mutations go: it always results, with great certainty, in a devastating illness. Many genetic mutations are associated with less-dreadful diseases, and in most cases the link between mutation and disease is incomplete or simply unclear. Think, for example, of BRCA testing: women who test positive for a BRCA1 or BRCA2 mutations have a much higher than average chance of having breast or ovarian cancer *at some point* in their lives, but if it happens it could happen quite early or quite late in life. In particular—and this is crucial from an employer's point of view—breast cancer could happen either before or after retirement age (whereas Huntington's is very likely to begin to manifest itself prior to retirement). Also, breast and ovarian cancer are not uniformly lethal diseases: early detection is crucial, but in general breast cancer is treatable, and survival rates are reasonably good. Thus the BRCA test would be much less useful for employers than the test for Huntington's: an employee who tests positive is not guaranteed to develop breast cancer, and an employee who develops breast cancer is relatively likely to remain a productive employee. And the test for BRCA mutations is much more typical of genetic tests in this regard than is the test for Huntington's.

Thus the case for workplace genetic testing of the kind that screens for heritable diseases is not nearly as straightforward as the best-case-scenario for testing seems to suggest.

What Is at Stake in Workplace Genetic Testing

Genetic testing in the workplace raises two interconnected ethical issues. Those issues are privacy, on one hand, and discrimination on the other.

Privacy is an important human value, one that is important both intrinsically and for the freedom that it brings us. Most of us have strong objections to being observed and searched in ways that are not chosen by us. Though we sometimes choose to give up some of our privacy as a tradeoff for something we value (for example, submitting to airport security searches as part of the "cost" of air travel) for the most part we guard our privacy jealously, seeking to exercise as much control as we can over what information about our lives, our habits, and our bodies strangers gain access to.

Privacy in the workplace is particularly challenging. Limits to privacy in the workplace are many. Much of this lack of privacy is taken for granted, part of the inevitable tradeoff involved in leaving home to make a living. Other limits on workplace privacy have not been so easy to accept.[6] Some workplaces, for example, use closed-circuit cameras to observe employee behaviour and productivity. Others require employees to submit urine samples to be tested for narcotics and other drugs. Still others monitor employee phone calls, voice mail emails, and Internet usage.

Genetic testing represents a potential further limitation (or invasion) of privacy in the workplace. Genetic information is often regarded as highly private; the employer who seeks genetic information about an employee is, in some sense, seeking to know something very deep and personal. And, given that genes are shared within families, the employer seeking genetic knowledge of her employees is, at the same time, incidentally seeking knowledge about her employees' families. Thus the invasion of privacy involved in workplace genetic testing is an invasion not just of the worker's own privacy—a privacy which, after all, is very commonly limited in employment relationships—but also the privacy of the employee's *family*.

The other key ethical issue raised by workplace genetic testing is discrimination. Genetic testing in the workplace raises the specter of genetic discrimination because, after all, the whole point of most genetic tests is to allow someone (in the present case, an employer) to discriminate—that is, to tell the difference between people and to act on that knowledge. The ethical *worry,* of course, is that genetic testing will be used in the service of *discrimination* in the deeply pejorative sense in which that word is typically used. Discrimination in *that* sense means treating different people differently for no good reason, or indeed for ethically bad reasons. Discrimination in this sense is disrespectful of the fundamental human equality among workers, in that it turns ethically irrelevant differences (race, gender, sexual orientation, etc.) into ethically significant differences in opportunity and well-being.

What about discriminating based on health? Being in good health is a functional requirement for most jobs. Is health then a *bona fide* occupational requirement, one on the basis of which employers may rightly discriminate? That issue is too large to examine in detail here. Two points on this topic will suffice to illuminate our discussion of workplace genetic testing. First, it is relatively clear that, *if* it is fair to discriminate based on health, it is *only* fair to discriminate based on health issues that are directly related to one's performance as an employee. Emphysema, for example—a chronic lung disease that can seriously limit one's ability to engage in vigorous physical activity—is a health condition that would be directly relevant to one's ability to work as, say, a firefighter, but likely not directly relevant to one's ability to work as a file-clerk. Severe arthritis is likely to present serious difficulties for someone employed as a typist, but is much less of a workplace challenge for someone who sells cars for a living. The second point to make is that there is a subset of health conditions—namely, disabilities—that has often been singled out for special legal and ethical treatment. Discrimination based on disability is generally prohibited. In the U.S., the relevant legislation is the *Americans With Disabilities Act* (ADA) of 1990.[7] The ADA prohibits discrimination based on disability, which it defines as "physical or mental impairment that substantially limits a major life activity." Discrimination based on disability is particularly pernicious in part because it is a matter of, in a very real sense, adding insult to injury. Disability is, by its very nature, a limitation on what people can do, including on the ways available to them to make a living. Thus to further limit the options of persons living with disabilities by unjustly discriminating against them seems particularly morally problematic. Secondly, the health problems referred to as "disabilities" are socially distinct from other health problems in that, historically, persons with disabilities have been subject to serious marginalization and discrimination, both in and out of the workplace. Thus, for example, paraplegics, as a group, have been subject to discrimination in ways in which cancer patients, as a group, have not.

What about genes? Is genetic information ever a morally legitimate basis for discriminating among employees? To begin to get a grip on that question, we could start with asking whether a gene can interfere with an employee's ability to do her job. To be a pilot, one must have good eyesight. Good eyesight is a *bona fide* occupational requirement for pilots, and so in discriminating against the visually impaired an airline is not doing anything unfair. What about a gene such as the 'macular degeneration gene'? Macular degeneration is a progressive eye condition involving the deterioration of the central part of the retina, eventually resulting in blindness. In 2005 several teams of scientists each discovered a genetic mutation[8] strongly associated with Age-related Macular Degeneration ("AMD"). This opens up the possibility of a genetic test: someone who tests positive for this gene would be several times more likely than the average person to develop AMD, and hence eventually to go blind. Would it be fair to discriminate against— for example, by failing to hire or by firing—a pilot known to carry the AMD gene, but whose eyesight is, at present, 20/20? To begin, it is worth noting that such discrimination would likely be unwarranted *scientifically*. As with many genes, the gene associated with AMD is only loosely connected to the actual disease. Indeed, an editorial in a leading professional journal suggested that genetic testing for AMD would not be very useful: the mutation associated with AMD is much more common than the disease itself, which means that the presence of the mutation is a poor predictor.[9] Thus to fire (or refuse to hire) someone based on a positive test for the mutation associated with AMD seems unjustified. Of course, that is just one example, and there may be other tests that are sufficiently informative for employers to consider using them.

Is there an ethical case to be made in *favour* of workplace genetic testing? What reasons might employers? According to the American Medical Association's Council on Ethical and Judicial Affairs, there are three main reasons:

> "[E]mployers may not want to hire individuals with certain genetic risks for jobs that bear on the public's safety. Other justifications are based not on concerns about health but on concerns about costs, specifically the costs to the company of hiring workers with a genetic risk of disease. Individuals who have a heightened risk for certain illnesses may be less attractive as employees; on average, they may be able to spend fewer years in the work force, and they may impose greater health care costs on the employer."[10]

Each of these might constitute a reasonable justification. Certainly the safety of the public (as exemplified above by our example of a pilot with the Huntington's Disease mutation) and of co-workers is a laudable goal. Similarly, reducing operational costs and increasing efficiency is, other things being equal, a good thing. Indeed, running their business efficiently is an obligation that managers owe to share-holders. Further, to the extent that reducing costs and improving efficiency is conducive to sustaining the operations of the company, doing so could arguably be seen as an obligation owed by managers to other stakeholders as well, not just to shareholders. Thus, for example, a company's employees *as a group* have an interest (i.e., an employment interest) in the sustained operation of the company, and hence have-again, other things being equal—a shared interest in things management can do to reduce costs and maintain productivity. And that might well include genetic testing.

If employers have reasons to engage in testing, employees have reasons to want to *avoid* testing. After all, positive genetic tests might result in their not getting a job, or in their being fired. Employers' and employees' interests conflict in this regard. So given how interests conflict in this way, what should our view be of the ethics of workplace genetic testing? Three broad categories of answers present themselves.

The first, relatively permissive, approach is to argue that genetic testing in the workplace, and employment decisions made on that basis, are permissible because they are simply a matter of rational individuals choosing freely in the marketplace. Employment is, after all, a voluntary relationship between employer and employee. If you don't apply for a job, then you can't be subjected to any testing—it's all up to you! Seen this way, workplace genetic testing is a contractual matter between competent, consenting adults, and is generally undertaken by each party because each sees engaging in that contract as being in their best interests. Employees may not generally *like* submitting to genetic testing, but neither do they like lots of *other* aspects of employment. A loss of genetic privacy might be one more thing employees are willing to give up in exchange for employment.

A second approach to the ethics of genetic testing in the workplace is what might be referred to as a 'cautious' approach, according to which both genetic testing, and decision-making based on it, could be permitted in the workplace *only if* suitable safeguards are put in place. For example, in our 2002 paper, my colleague Bryn Williams-Jones and I argued that genetic testing could, in principle, play a legitimate role in the workplace, only requirements including the following are met:

- The genetic test must be scientifically sound: it must be highly specific and sensitive and must offer an acceptably low incidence of both false positives and false negatives;

- The test should be for a gene that is sufficiently penetrant for the test result to have some important health implication;

- Testing must be carried out by an independent lab, and results of genetic tests should be treated as confidential and given to workers directly, either by a geneticist or a genetic counsellor;

- Pre- and post-test genetic counselling must be available from a qualified health professional, at no cost to the employee;

- Where relevant, the employer must guarantee continued access to group insurance;

- The employer must ensure that if the employee chooses to reveal that she has tested positive, suitable policies are in place to ensure a reasonable degree of job security.[11]

If conditions such as these could be met, workplace genetic testing would be subject to relatively few objections. At present, it would likely be very difficult to meet the standard implied by such a list of conditions. But insisting on such standards at least constitutes a fairly cautious approach.

The third kind of answer to the ethical question posed by genetic testing in the workplace would go beyond mere caution, to proclaim such testing unjustifiable altogether. Some critics, for example, will argue that the *goals* typically sought through workplace genetic testing are objectionable. Such critics will argue that the main objective of workplace genetic testing would be unfairly to shift the costs of genetic illness[12] from employers to employees.

Others will argue that genetic testing constitutes an objectionable *means,* a way of achieving what might or might not be justifiable goals, and that those means are objectionable because they are inadequate to the task at hand. This criticism is grounded in the fact that, even in our best-case examples, genetic testing is not informative enough to provide reasonable grounds for action on the part of employers. Most genetic tests simply do not provide much concrete information about how healthy and productive a worker is going to be over the course of his or her career. This kind of critique probably goes some way towards explaining why workplace genetic testing is still relatively rare.

Finally, still other critics will argue that genetic testing is objectionable because it is an unethical process in and of itself. For example, such critics might argue that workplace genetic testing is unethical because employees do not (or cannot) give effective consent. After all, even if employees are technically "asked" to submit to testing, power imbalances between employers and employees may mean that workers have little choice but to accede to employers' requests that they undergo genetic testing. Employees may "consent," formally, but that consent may not be fully free. And it cannot be denied that genetic information may have consequences that are poorly understood, at this point, even by experts. To ask employees to agree to hand over such information is to ask them to do something the consequences of which they are unlikely to fully appreciate.

Conclusion

Workplace genetic testing clearly presents a range of complex ethical challenges, and this essay has perhaps raised more questions than it answers. As noted above, there's little evidence that employers are rushing to implement such testing. But the potential is certainly there. Scientists are developing more and more genetic tests every year, and the cost of genetic tests is dropping rapidly. If there is, as argued above, reason for doubt concerning the ethics of workplace genetic tests that are already possible, there is every reason to think that the genetic tests available for application in the workplace just 5 or 10 years from now will be even more problematic.

Endnotes

1. Steve Lohr, "I.B.M. to Put Genetic Data of Workers Of Limits," *New York Times.* October 10, 2005.

2. There are two important exceptions. Every sex cell (every sperm or egg) contain only half of our full genetic complement, and are thus not fully representative of our genome. Also, environmental factors (such as toxins and ultraviolet radiation) can cause mutations in individual cells during our lifetime, so that those cells are no longer accurate copies of our overall genome.

3. The Genetic Information Nondiscrimination Act of 2008, Public Law No. 110-233, 122 Stat. 881 (May 21, 2008)

4. It is worth noting that one of the main arguments made in favour of passing GINA was to prevent fear of discrimination from hindering scientific research. The idea was that if people are afraid of being discriminated against (either by employers or by insurers) they would be less likely to take part in studies that involve genetic tests.

5. Council of Europe, Convention for the Protection of Human Rights and Dignity of the Human Being with regard to the Application of Biology and Medicine: Convention on Human Rights and Biomedicine, 1997. (Online: http://conventions.coe.int/treaty/EN /Treaties/Html/164.htm)

6. For a stimulating discussion of the challenges of workplace privacy, see William S. Brown, "Ontological Security, Existential Anxiety and Workplace Privacy." *Journal of Business Ethics.* 23: 61–65, 2000.

7. Pub. L. 101-336, 104 Stat. 327, enacted July 26, 1990.

8. See papers by Haines et al; Edwards et al; and Klein et al; all in *Science,* April 15, 2005.

9. Albert O. Edwards, "Genetic Testing for Age-Related Macular Degeneration," *Ophthalmology* Vol. 113, No. 4, April 2006.

10. Council on Ethical and Judicial Affairs, American Medical Association. CEJA Report E—A-91: Genetic Testing by Employers. (Online: http:// www.ama-assn.org/ama1/pub/upload/mm/369 /ceja_ea91.pdf)

11. Chris MacDonald and Bryn Williams-Jones, "Ethics and Genetics: Susceptibility Testing in the Workplace," *Journal of Business Ethics* 35: 235–241, 2002.

12. Depending how you define things, somewhere between "most" and "all" illness has some genetic component, so it might make just as much sense here to speak more simply of shifting the costs of illness *per se* from employers to employees, rather than using the apparently more restrictive term "genetic illness."

Reading 7-5

Letter from Lewis Maltby to Senator Chris Rothfuss (July 26, 2014)

Lewis Maltby is president of the National Workrights Institute (formerly the ACLU's national employment rights project). He has been consulted by the sponsors of practically every major congressional privacy bill since 1990 and has testified before Congress numerous times. Senator Rothfuss was chair of the Task Force on Digital Information Privacy.

July 26, 2014

Senator Chris Rothfuss, Chairman
Task Force on Digital Information Privacy
Wyoming Legislative Service Office
213 State Capitol
Cheyenne, WY 82002

Dear Chairman Rothfuss:

Thank you for inviting me to share the National Workrights Institute's views on employment privacy with the task force.

The task force can make a vital contribution to privacy law in America. The core statute in this area, the Electronic Communications Privacy Act (ECPA) (18 U.S.C. 2510) was enacted in 1986. At that time, the primary method of communication was the telephone. Personal computers, e-mail, the Internet, and text messaging did not exist.

Communications technology has changed dramatically since 1986. But privacy law has not changed. There have been several attempts to update ECPA, but none of them has succeeded. We are trying to regulate 21st century communications technology with a law that was written before any of it was invented. The few state laws that have been enacted are reflexive responses to a specific incident.

It is high time to systematically examine modern methods of communications technology and create rules that are fair to both employers and employees. In creating the task force, Wyoming has initiated this critical and long overdue process.

Need for Employment Rules

Many people are legitimately concerned with the NSA's monitoring of personal communications. But monitoring by employers is far more common. While only limited information about the extent of federal government monitoring is available, the number of citizens affected is limited. The average person has little chance of having their personal communication monitored by the government.

Employment is entirely different. The Bentley Center for Business Ethics surveyed employers and found that 94% conduct electronic monitoring of employee communications. Other studies, including those conducted by the American Management Association, reach similar findings.

This does not mean that legislators should ignore government monitoring. But the first priority should be employer monitoring.

Employment Rules

The vital first step in this analysis is recognizing the need for different rules for employers and the government. The government generally monitors communications for the purpose of law enforcement. Employers are concerned with productivity, quality control, and compliance with company policies. Because the government and employers have different needs, they need different rules.

For example, the government generally needs a warrant to monitor a person's telephone or computer. To require employers to go to court every time they want to see an e-mail message sent by an employee on a company computer would be unfair and unworkable.

Current Paradigm

In the absence of statutory guidance, courts have been forced to develop common law to decide privacy disputes. The official standard that has emerged is whether an employee has a "reasonable expectation of privacy" in light of all the facts of her situation. Courts are to balance employees' need for privacy against the business needs of the employer.

In practice, the test is who owns the equipment involved in transmitting the communication. Courts have consistently held that employees have no reasonable expectation of privacy on company owned computers under any circumstances. In *Smyth v. Pillsbury Baking* (914 F. Supp. 97) the court held that an employee had no reasonable expectation in e-mail sent from a company computer even when the employer told employees it would not monitor. I have been following the caselaw in this area for 25 years and have never seen a single case holding that employees have any right to privacy on company owned equipment.

Harm to Employees

This paradigm is often unfair to employees. Initially, employers took the position that workplace computers were for business purposes only. Courts held that an employee who used her employer's computer for personal business in violation of company policy could not complain if her employer read the message. Employers quickly realized, however, that such a policy is unreasonable and unenforceable. In today's world, the once sharp line between work and personal life has been erased. People routinely log on to their company computer from home after they put their children to bed and return business calls from their cell phones on weekends. They also send personal e-mail from the workplace. The vast majority of employers (over 90%) have adopted policies that allow for reasonable personal use of employer communications technology.

But the legal rule has not changed. Even though employers now allow employees to send personal messages on company equipment, employees who do so are treated like trespassers who have no right to privacy. An employer can allow employees to use company equipment for personal matters, tell employees it will not monitor personal messages, and then deliberately read messages it knows are personal for no reason (or to learn about the employee's private life) without breaking the law. How is this reasonable or fair?

The loss of privacy is constant and serious. An employee's e-mail to her spouse, doctor, bank, and many others frequently contains extremely sensitive personal information. Monitoring the web sites an employee visits is possibly even more revealing. People visit the Internet for information and help about the most sensitive subjects imaginable. People seeking help with substance abuse, marital problems, unplanned pregnancy, psychiatric problems, or financial difficulties will often turn to the Internet. If you were trying to pry into someone's personal secrets, you couldn't find a better way than monitoring her Internet activity.

We now live in a world where people routinely communicate about personal matters while they are working with absolutely no privacy protection.

Harm to Employers

Employers are now beginning to experience difficulties with the ownership paradigm in privacy law. Increasingly, workplace communication takes place on equipment that the employer does not own. Many people download workplace information onto their personal computers so they can work at home. Sometimes this information includes important intellectual property. An employer could legitimately be concerned about how an employee uses this information.

But it is very difficult for employers to find out what employees do with downloaded business information. Because the computer involved belongs to the employee, courts are very reluctant to give employers access, even when employers have legitimate concerns. For example, in *Sabin v. Miller* (423 F. Supp. 2d 943), the court refused to give the employer access to an employee's personal computer, even though the employee had downloaded company documents and there was evidence of misconduct. In *Wyatt Technology v. Smithson* (2006 WL 5568246, C.D. Cal.), the court found the employer liable for violating the Computer Fraud and Abuse Act (18 U.S.C. 1030) when it accessed the computer of a former employee even though he was working for a competitor and the company had evidence that he was misusing its trade secrets.

Employers have the same problem regarding wireless communications. The Stored Communications Act (18 U.S.C. 121) provides that Internet Service Providers can reveal the contents of messages only to the parties. Employers are not considered parties to the message, even if they pay for the service. In *Quon v. Arch Wireless* (529 F.3d 892), the 9th circuit court of appeals held that the ISP violated SCA by disclosing the content of an employee's text messages to his employer. The court also held that the employer violated the act. The employer appealed other issues in this case to the Supreme Court, but did not appeal this ruling. This problem will grow more serious as more use of wireless communication grows.

New Paradigm

Both employers and employees would be better off if employer access to electronic information were determined by whether the employer has a legitimate interest in the information rather than whether it owns the equipment used to transmit/store the information.

This is the original paradigm for federal privacy law. The Electronic Communication Privacy Act (supra) allows employers to listen to employees' telephone conversations if they are work related, but not if they are personal. Both employers and employees receive fair treatment with this rule and courts had no difficulty implementing it.

The key to creating employment privacy legislation for the 21st century is returning to this paradigm for other forms of electronic communication.

Enforcement

Creating effective enforcement mechanisms for privacy laws has always been a challenge. Criminal penalties are not effective because law enforcement agencies are reluctant to divert resources from crimes against people or property to prosecuting violations of privacy law. Private civil actions are difficult to bring because violation of privacy laws seldom creates demonstrable economic harm.

These challenges can be met by providing successful plaintiffs with reasonable attorney's fees and the alternative of an administrative remedy.

Enforcement of employment laws is difficult because at will employees have little choice but to agree to waive their rights when their employers request it. This problem can be addressed by providing that rights created by a statute are not subject to waiver.

I look forward to speaking with you and the rest of the task force on July 30.

Sincerely yours.

Lewis L. Maltby
President
National Workrights Institute

Chapter

Ethics and Marketing

If you make customers unhappy in the physical world, they might each tell 6 friends. If you make customers unhappy on the Internet, they can each tell 6,000 friends.

Jeff Bezos, Amazon CEO

A magazine is simply a device to induce people to read advertising.

James Collins

I am the world's worst salesman; therefore, I must make it easy for people to buy.

F. W. Woolworth (1852–1919)

It is fair to say that marketing has undergone revolutionary changes in recent years as a result of digital technology. In the past, the primary media by which marketers reached their audience were television, radio, newspapers and magazines, direct mail, and billboards. These techniques were identified as indirect marketing because they relied on broad-based media that reached a general audience, a portion of which was thought to include potential customers. Because the audience was general, the ad content itself had to be fairly generic. As the marketing profession became more sophisticated, advertisers were able to rely on more direct marketing techniques to better identify potential customers and thereby direct more targeted and specific ad content to them.

With the explosion of digital technology and the Internet, the nature of the marketing function has changed dramatically. Digital technology has unimaginably increased the amount of information that marketers can compile about consumers; the speed at which that information can be collected, analyzed, and used; and the specificity of both who the consumers are and the details of their behavior and psychology.

Marketing firms have always conducted research on consumers to gather as much information as possible for understanding consumer wants, their dislikes, and their behavior. In just the recent past, market segments would be identified in terms of only a few general demographic variables: male/female, income level (often best estimated only by housing prices in the zip code associated with a consumer), education level, and the like. Today, digital technologies give marketers the ability to segment markets down to the level of individuals and their web browsing or shopping behavior of just the past few minutes.

Cell phone companies, search engines, Internet and cable providers, and social networks compile huge amounts of information on consumer behavior. They know what calls are being made, which Internet sites are being visited, what products have been viewed, and which programs are being watched. In many cases that information is only aggregated, overall data, but in other cases the data can be individualized and traced to individual mobiles, computers, or social network accounts. Typically, this tracking is done anonymously so that consumers seldom know that it is occurring and have little understanding of what information is being compiled and how it is being used.

Two factors in particular have contributed to this explosion of personal information being available for use by marketers. First is the tremendous increase in mobile devices, smartphones, and tablets. These devices do three things of value to marketers: they are typically associated with one unique individual; they are used by individuals almost constantly throughout the day and night precisely because they are mobile; and they are heavily reliant on apps, small self-contained programs that have proven to be unrivaled in delivering consumers to business, and advertisements to consumers.

The second, and related, factor is the global popularity of social networks such as Facebook, Twitter, and LinkedIn. The amount of personal information available about individuals now accessible by others because of social networking would have been inconceivable just a few years ago. Of course, the point of collecting this information is that it is a commodity that can be bought and sold, or "monetarized." While it might appear that the product of Google or Yahoo! is a search engine or the product of a Facebook is a social network, in fact searches are free and joining Facebook is free. As a business, search engines such as Google and social networks such as Facebook make their money by selling access to the wealth of information they collect to advertisers and others willing to pay for that access. (Compare to the quote from James Collins that opened this chapter: "A magazine is simply a device to induce people to read advertising.")

It is worth asking if the ethical principles and guidelines that were appropriate for evaluating traditional marketing techniques are still relevant in the age of digital marketing. Deception, manipulation, unfairness, and loss of privacy are some of the most common concerns raised against traditional advertising and marketing techniques. Consider how these concerns might apply to the following digital marketing activities.

Some issues closely parallel previous marketing practices. Deceptive or misleading product endorsements have always been part of marketing, as when actors portraying doctors endorse the alleged health benefits of a diet supplement or support one brand of acetaminophen over another. Today, consumers often research products by consulting user reviews on Internet sites such as TripAdvisor or Amazon, "likes" on social media sites such as Facebook, or reviews found in blogs, tweets, or on message boards. To add credibility, some sites such as Amazon will even identify product reviewers as a "verified purchaser," but consumers have no way of knowing that even these reviewers are truthful. What ethical issues are raised if these digital testimonials were placed by a marketing form hired to promote a particular product or service?

Companies can pay to have search results enhanced with their own ads that appear as a side banner or have their website appear first whenever consumers search for a product or a competitor's site. Consumers may believe that the first result to appear in a search is either random or that it simply reveals the most popular result. In fact, browser-based tacking cookies may have instantaneously identified the consumer's browsing history to a real-time auction among marketing firms and in milliseconds awarded the top-level banner ad to the auction winner.

Retailer companies use location-based services known as "beacons" to know when particular people enter their store. Beacon technology relies on low-powered Bluetooth signals that can be detected within a few hundred feet. A common use is to install this technology in a company's app, which like most apps regularly collects browsing and shopping information about the consumer. When that consumer is near the retail store, ads and enticements specifically targeted to that individual consumer based on past online behavior can be instantly sent to his or her mobile device.

- U.S. courts sometimes use the "expectation of privacy" as a test for limiting governmental monitoring. Thus, for example, the police can monitor your behavior without a warrant when you are in a public place, but not when you are talking on your phone. What expectations of privacy do you have when you are surfing the web? Ordering something from Amazon or Netflix? Spending time on Facebook?

- Physically stalking someone can be a crime. Are there parallels between physically stalking someone and regularly monitoring their activities on the web? How are they similar? How are they different?

- Most online tracking is done through the use of "cookies," small files stored on a computer or mobile device that provide information about past browsing history. Should consumers have a right to opt-out or should their explicit consent be required before cookies are installed?

- Information about your online behavior is a commodity that can be bought and sold. Who should own this personal information?

✳ CHAPTER OBJECTIVES

After reading this chapter, you will be able to:

1. Apply an ethical framework to marketing issues.
2. Describe the three key concerns of ethical analysis of marketing issues.
3. Describe two interpretations of "responsibility" and apply them to the topic of product safety.
4. Explain contractual standards for establishing business's responsibilities for safe products.
5. Articulate the tort standards for establishing business's responsibilities for safe products.
6. Analyze the ethical arguments for and against strict product liability.
7. Discuss how to evaluate both ethical and unethical means by which to influence people through advertising.
8. Explain the ethical justification for advertising.
9. Trace debates about advertising's influence on consumer autonomy.
10. Distinguish ethical from unethical target marketing, using marketing to vulnerable populations as an example.
11. Discuss business's responsibilities for the activities of its supply chain.

Introduction

marketing
Defined by the American Marketing Association as "an organizational function and a set of processes for creating, communicating, and delivering value to customers and for managing customer relationships in ways that benefit the organization and its stakeholders."

Some believe that the very purpose of business is found within the marketing function. The description of business's purpose offered by marketing scholar Theodore Levitt is a case in point. Levitt suggested that:

> The purpose of a business is to create and keep a customer. To do that you have to produce and deliver goods and services that people want and value at prices and under conditions that are reasonably attractive relative to those offered by others. . . .
> It was not so long ago that a lot of companies assumed something quite different about the purpose of business. They said quite simply that the purpose is to make money. But that is as vacuous as to say that the purpose of life is to eat. Eating is a prerequisite, not a purpose of life. . . . Profits can be made in lots of devious and transient ways. For people of affairs, a statement of purpose should provide guidance to the management of their affairs. To say that they should attract and hold customers forces facing the necessity of figuring out what people really want and value, and then catering to those wants and values. It provides specific guidance, and has moral merit.[1]

Similarly, the American Marketing Association defines **marketing** in a way that echos the stakeholder model of CSR describedin Chapter 5. According to the AMA, marketing is "an organizational function and a set of processes for creating, communicating, and delivering value to customers and for managing customer relationships in ways that benefit the organization and its stakeholders."[2]

The concept of an exchange between a seller and a buyer is central to the market economy and is the core idea behind marketing. Marketing involves all aspects of creating a product or service and bringing it to market where an exchange can take place. Marketing ethics therefore examines the responsibilities associated with bringing a product to the market, promoting it to buyers, and exchanging it with them. But this simple model of a seller bringing a product to the marketplace, and the ethics implicit within it, gets complicated fairly quickly.

Even before a product is created, a producer might first consider who, if anyone, is interested in purchasing it, or who can be influenced to want to purchase it. The product might then be redesigned or changed in light of what is learned about potential buyers from market research. Once the product is ready for market, the producer must decide on a price that will be mutually acceptable. At first glance, the minimal asking price should be the production cost plus some reasonable profit. But the producer might also consider who the buyers are and what they can afford, how price might influence future purchases, how the price might affect distributors and retailers, and what competitors are charging before settling on a price. The producer might also consider advertising the product to attract new potential purchasers and offer incentives to promote the product among buyers.

The producer must also consider how to bring the product to consumers and therefore consider hiring someone else, a salesperson, or delegating someone, a "retailer," to handle the actual exchange itself. Producers might be more concerned with cash flow than profit and therefore be willing to ask a price that is below production costs. They might consider where and under what conditions the product is sold, and they might decide that the best chance for a sale will occur only among certain people. The producer might also consider issues of volume and price the product in such a way to ensure profit only after certain sales targets are met. The producer might also consider how such factors as price, convenience, reliability, and service might contribute to sustaining an ongoing relationship with the customer. Finally, throughout this entire process the producer might conduct market research to gather information and use that information in production, pricing, promotion, and placement decisions.

This model gets even more complicated when we recognize the active role that retailers play in these relationships. In many cases, the actual producers are themselves passive participants who respond to decisions made by retailers and other marketing firms. Often the companies actually producing goods are simply hired by the marketing firm to produce a product that has already been fully vetted for the market.

All of these factors are elements of marketing. What, how, why, and under what conditions is something *produced*? What *price* is acceptable, reasonable, fair? How can the product be *promoted* to support, enhance, and maintain sales? Where, when, and under what conditions should the product be *placed* in the marketplace? These four general categories—*product, price, promotion, placement*—are sometimes referred to as the **"Four Ps" of marketing.**

"Four Ps" of marketing
Production, price, promotion, and placement.

Each of these elements raises important ethical questions. What responsibilities do companies have for the quality and safety of the products they produce and sell? Who is responsible for harms caused by a product? Are there some products that should not be produced, or does consumer demand decide all production questions? Is the consumer's willingness to pay the only ethical constraint on fair pricing? Do all customers deserve the same price, or can producers discriminate in favor of, or against, some consumers? Are deceptive or misleading ads ethical? What ethical constraints should be placed on sales promotions? Is the information gathered in market research the property of the business that conducts the research? What privacy protections should be offered for marketing data? Is it ethical to target vulnerable populations such as children or older people? What responsibilities do producers have to retailers? To competitors? To suppliers?

Marketing: An Ethical Framework

OBJECTIVE

We can take the simple model of a single exchange between two individuals as a useful way to introduce an ethical framework for marketing ethics (see Table 8.1). As in previous chapters, this framework will assist the decision maker in arriving at an ethical decision, but it will not definitively prove the "correct" decision as much as it will help reach a rationally responsible decision. In other words, it does not determine the right answer but instead the framework identifies rights, responsibilities, duties and obligations, causes and consequences.

This simple situation in which two parties come together and freely agree to an exchange is *prima facie* ethically legitimate. The rights-based ethical tradition described in chapter 3 would see it as upholding respect for individuals by treating them as autonomous agents capable of pursuing their own ends. This tradition presumes that each individual will abide by fundamental principles. The utilitarian ethical tradition would take the two parties' agreement as evidence that both are better off than they were prior to the exchange and thus conclude that overall happiness has been increased by any exchange freely entered into.

This assessment is only *prima facie* because, like all agreements, certain conditions must be met before we can conclude that autonomy has in fact been respected and mutual benefit has been achieved. Thus, for example, we would need to establish that the agreement resulted from an informed and voluntary consent, and that there was no fraud, deception, or coercion involved. When these conditions are violated, autonomy is not respected and mutual benefit is not attained. Furthermore, even when such conditions are met, other values may override the freedom of individuals to contract for mutually beneficial purposes. Thus, for example, the freedom of drug dealers to pursue mutually agreeable ends is overridden by society's concern to maintain law and order.

TABLE 8.1
Ethical Issues
in Marketing:
A Framework

Market exchange is *prima facie* ethically legitimate because of

- Respect for autonomy
- Mutual benefit

This ethical judgment is conditional because

- The transaction must be truly voluntary
- Informed consent is needed
- Benefits might not occur
- Other values might conflict

These four conditions imply the following four questions, each of which requires considering several factors:

1. Is exchange "voluntary"?

   - Real alternative choices available
   - Anxiety and stress in some purchasing situations
   - Price-fixing, monopolies, price gouging, etc.
   - Targeted and vulnerable consumers

2. Is consent to exchange really "informed"?

   - Lack of information
   - Deception
   - Complicated information

3. Are people truly benefited?

   - Impulse buying, "affluenza," consumerism
   - Injuries, unsafe products
   - "Contrived" wants

4. Competing values

   - Justice—e.g., "redlining" mortgages
   - Market failures (externalities)

OBJECTIVE

In general, therefore, it will be helpful to keep three concerns in mind as we approach any ethical issue in marketing:

- The rights-based ethical tradition would ask to what degree the participants are respected as free and autonomous agents rather than treated simply as means to the end of making a sale.
- The utilitarian tradition would want to know the degree to which the transaction provided actual as opposed to merely apparent benefits.
- Every ethical tradition would also wonder what other values might be at stake in the transaction.

Let us consider these three issues: the degree to which individuals freely participate in an exchange; the benefits and costs of each exchange; and other values that are affected by the exchange.

It is not always easy to determine if someone is being treated with respect in marketing situations. As a first approximation we might suggest two conditions.

First, the person must freely consent to the transaction. But how free is "free"? Surely transactions completed under the threat of force are not voluntary and therefore are unethical. But there are many degrees of voluntariness. For example, the more consumers need a product, the less free they are to choose and therefore the more protection they deserve within the marketplace. Consider the use of the Windows operating system by the overwhelming majority of computer users. How voluntary is the decision to use Windows as your computer's operating system? Do most people even make a decision to use Windows? Or, consider the anxiety and stress that many consumers experience during a car purchase. When an automobile dealer exploits that anxiety to sell extended warranty insurance or roadside assistance, it is not at all clear that the consumer has made a fully voluntary decision. More dramatic cases of price gouging, price-fixing, and monopolistic pricing clearly raise the issue of freedom in marketing. When a bank or an insurance company is "too big to fail," one must question if its consumers have any real bargaining power in the marketplace. Practices aimed at vulnerable populations such as children and the elderly also raise questions of voluntariness. Thus, an adequate analysis of marketing ethics challenges us to be sensitive to the many ways in which consumer choice can be less than fully voluntary. (To explore what it means to engage in "voluntary" purchasing decisions, see the Reality Check "Impulse Buying.")

A second condition for respect requires that the consent be not only voluntary, but also informed. Informed consent has received a great deal of attention in the medical ethics literature because patients are at a distinct informational disadvantage when dealing with health care professionals. But, similar disadvantages can occur in marketing situations. Outright deception and fraud clearly violate this condition and are unethical. A consumer's consent to purchase a product is not informed if that consumer is being misled or deceived about the product. But there can also be many more nuanced cases of deception and misleading marketing practices. (To explore what it means for a fully informed decision, see the Reality Check "GMO Labeling: Can Truthful Information Be Misleading?")

The complexity of many consumer products and services can mean that consumers may not fully understand what they are purchasing. Consider using two famous product safety cases as examples, all that would be involved for a consumer to determine which fuel tank design was safest for subcompact cars, or which tire design is least likely to cause blowouts. Consider also the many people who have very weak mathematical skills. Imagine such a person trying to decide on the economic benefits of whole-life versus term insurance, or a 48-month auto lease versus a five-year purchase loan at 2.9 percent financing. In general, while some businesses claim that an "informed consumer is our best customer," many others recognize that an uninformed consumer can be an easy target for quick profits.[3] Serious ethical questions should be raised whenever marketing practices either deny consumers full information or rely on the fact that they lack relevant information or understanding.

The second ethical concern looks to the alleged benefits obtained through market exchanges. Economics textbooks commonly assume that consumers benefit, almost by definition, whenever they make an exchange in the marketplace. But

Reality Check *Impulse Buying*

Though the cartoon pokes fun at the ability of marketing professionals to "make" us buy certain items, not everyone exercises similar levels of effective judgment necessary to protect themselves from poor decisions about credit and debt, good and bad spending choices. Young spenders in particular may not yet be sufficiently experienced—with shopping, spending, or responding to sophisticated marketing campaigns—to adequately protect themselves against strategies designed to encourage impulse buying.

Sales pitches that hype the latest and trendiest items, those that must be purchased today and worn tonight, are difficult to resist for some purchasers who buy in haste and perhaps regret it later. Marketing campaigns are also chastised for creating needs where the purchaser may originally have only sensed a desire. Purchases on impulse are often not reversible, but because they are often so hastily made that the purchaser fails to notice that the product is imperfect or does not match a personal style, they are perhaps most in need of later returns.

In the same way that a hungry person is more likely to buy groceries on impulse than one who has just had her or his meal, we are better off engaging in our purchasing efforts when we are capable of evaluating our options with a clear head (and a full stomach!).

Source: www.CartoonStock.com. Reprinted with permission.

this assumption won't bear up under close scrutiny. Many purchases do not result in actual benefit.

For example, impulse buying, and the many marketing techniques used to promote such consumer behavior, cannot be justified by appeal to satisfying consumer interests. (See the Reality Check "Impulse Buying.") The ever-increasing number of personal bankruptcies suggests that consumers cannot purchase happiness. Empirical studies provide evidence that suggests that greater consumption can lead to unhappiness, a condition called by some "affluenza."[4] So, if simple consumer satisfaction is not a conclusive measure of the benefits of market exchanges, one must always ask about the ends of marketing. What goods are attained by successfully marketing this product or service? How and in what ways are individuals and society benefited from the product?

Both parties to the marketing exchange are also not benefited in situations in which one party is injured by the product. Unsafe products do not further the utilitarian goal of maximizing overall happiness. It would also be the case that consumers are not benefited if the desires that they seek to satisfy in the market are somehow contrived or manipulated by the seller.

The third set of factors that must be considered in any ethical analysis of marketing are values other than those served by the exchange itself. Such primary social values as fairness, justice, health, and safety are just some of the values that can be jeopardized by some marketing practices. For example, a bank that offers lower mortgage rates in affluent neighborhoods than it does in inner-city neighborhoods might be involved only in deals that are mutually beneficial because they do not, in fact, sell mortgages in the inner city. But such contracts would violate important social norms of equal treatment and fairness.

There may be a very strong market for such things as body parts of endangered species. There is also, unfortunately, a market for children. But just because someone wants to buy something and someone else is willing to sell it does not mean that the transaction is ethically legitimate. An adequate ethical analysis of marketing must ask who else might be affected by the transaction. How, if at all, are the interests of these others represented? What social goods are promoted, and which are threatened, by marketing this product?

One must also ask what the true costs of production are. An adequate ethical analysis of marketing must consider externalities, those costs that are not integrated within the exchange between buyer and seller. Externalities show that even if both parties to the exchange receive actual benefits from the exchange, other parties external to the exchange might be adversely affected. One thinks of the environmental or health impact of marketing products such as SUVs, pesticides, and tobacco as examples in which a simple model of individual consumer exchange would ignore significant social costs. With these general issues in mind, we can now turn to a closer examination of several major aspects of marketing ethics.

Responsibility for Products: Safety and Liability

OBJECTIVE

Few issues have received as much scrutiny in law, politics, and ethics as has the responsibility of business for harms caused by its products. In general, business has an ethical responsibility to design, manufacture, and promote its products in ways that avoid causing harm to consumers.

It will be helpful to review here several different meanings of the word *responsibility* that were introduced in the discussion of corporate social responsibility in chapter 5. Recall that, in one sense, to be responsible is to be identified as the *cause* of something. Thus, we might say that Hurricane Katrina was responsible for millions of dollars in property damages in New Orleans. In another sense, responsibility involves accountability. When we ask who will be responsible for the damages caused by Katrina, we are asking who will pay for the damages. In many cases someone is held accountable because they were at fault, but not in all cases. For example, parents are held accountable for damage caused by their children, even if they were not at fault in causing the damage.

Both law and ethics rely on this framework when evaluating cases in which business products or services cause harm in the marketplace. Contract law, and the ethics implicit in contracts, is one legal approach to product safety. Contracts are a form of a promise and when a product is sold there is an implicit promise that it will perform as promised without hurting the user. Tort law provides a second legal approach to product safety. The law of torts recognizes that we all have a general duty not to cause harm to others. A third legal doctrine, strict liability, addresses questions of legal and ethical responsibility for cases in which no one is at fault but someone has been harmed.

Contractual Standards for Product Safety

OBJECTIVE

caveat emptor approach

Caveat emptor means "buyer beware" in Latin and this approach suggests that the burden of risk of information shall be placed on the buyer. This perspective assumes that every purchase involves the informed consent of the buyer and therefore it is assumed to be ethically legitimate.

It is fair to say that the standard of *caveat emptor* (let the buyer beware) is in the background to many discussions of product safety. The **caveat emptor approach** adopts a simple model of a contractual exchange between a buyer and seller. This model assumes that every purchase involves the informed consent of the buyer and therefore it is assumed to be ethically legitimate. Buyers have the responsibility to look out for their own interests and protect their own safety when buying a product. From this *caveat emptor* perspective, business's only legal and ethical responsibility is to provide a good or service at an agreed-upon price.

The social contract tradition in ethics holds that this contractual model is the best way to understand ethical responsibilities. From this perspective, the only duties that a person has are those freely taken on within a social contract. Individual contracts and promises are the basis of ethical duties. The implication of this within the business sphere is that unless a seller explicitly warrants a product as safe, unless, in other words, the seller promises otherwise, buyers are liable for any harm they suffer.

But even this simple model of a contractual market exchange would place ethical constraints on the seller. Sellers have a duty not to coerce, defraud, or deceive buyers, for example. Consumers who were injured by a product that was deceptively or fraudulently marketed would have legal recourse to recover damages from the seller. (To explore other ethical restraints on this contractual model see the Reality Check "*Caveat Emptor* in Buying Drugs.")

implied warranty of merchantability

Implied assurances by a seller that a product is reasonably suitable for its purpose.

In the United States, courts moved away from this *caveat emptor* approach and recognized an implicit promise, or implied warranty, that accompanies any product that is marketed. What the law refers to as the **implied warranty of merchantability** holds that in selling a product, a business implicitly offers assurances that the product is reasonably suitable for its purpose. Even without an explicit verbal or written promise or contract, the law holds that business has a duty to ensure that its products will accomplish their purpose.

The ethics implicit within the contract approach assumes that when consumers adequately understand products well enough, they can reasonably be expected to protect themselves. But consumers don't always understand products fully and they are not always free to choose not to purchase some things. In effect, the implied warranty standard shifts the burden of proof from consumers to producers by allowing consumers to assume that products were safe for ordinary use. By bringing goods and services to the market, producers were implicitly promising that their products were safe under normal use. The ethical basis for this decision is the assumption that consumers would not give

Reality Check *Caveat Emptor in Buying Drugs?*

Because some drugs are potentially very harmful, governments prevent consumers from purchasing them directly. Instead, physicians and other health care professionals act as gatekeepers and determine who can purchase drugs by issuing prescriptions to their clients. Assume that pharmaceutical companies continue to disclose all the potential side effects of using a drug;

would you favor eliminating the gatekeeper function from health care professionals? If consumers were provided with full information about a drug, should they be left free to decide for themselves whether or not to use it? Are there other products that you think should be treated similarly, or are pharmaceuticals in a unique category?

their consent to a purchase if they had reason to believe that they would be harmed by it when used in a normal way.

Of course, if law will hold business liable for implicit promises, a prudent business will seek to limit its liability by explicitly disowning any promise or warranty. Thus, many businesses will issue a disclaimer of liability (e.g., products are sold "as is"), or offer an expressed and limited warranty (e.g., the seller will replace the product but offers no other guarantees). Most courts will not allow a business to completely disclaim the implied warranty of merchantability.

Tort Standards for Product Safety

OBJECTIVE

negligence
Unintentional failure to exercise reasonable care not to harm other people. Negligence is considered to be one step below "reckless disregard" for harm to others and two steps below intentional harm.

The use of an implied warranty, and the ethics of contracts that underlies it, answered one set of questions of the responsibility for harms caused by products. But other problems remain. In particular, the ethics of contact law would not apply to the majority of business situations in which consumers do not have a contractual relation with the business that created or manufactured the product. **Negligence,** a concept from the area of law known as torts, provides a second avenue for consumers to hold producers responsible for their products.

The distinction between contract law and tort law calls attention to two different ways to understand ethical duties. Under a contract model, the only duties that a person owes are those that have been explicitly promised to another party. Otherwise, that person owes nothing to anyone. The ethical perspective that underlies tort law holds that we all owe other people certain general duties, *even if we have not explicitly and voluntarily assumed them.* Specifically, I owe other people a general duty not to put them at unnecessary and avoidable risk. Thus, for example, although I have never explicitly promised anyone that I will drive carefully, I have an ethical duty not to drive recklessly down the street.

Negligence is a central component of tort law. As the word suggests, negligence involves a type of ethical neglect, specifically neglecting one's duty to exercise reasonable care not to harm other people. Many of the ethical and legal issues surrounding manufacturers' responsibility for products can be understood as the attempt to specify what constitutes negligence in their design, production, and sale. What duties, exactly, do producers owe to consumers?

strict liability
A legal doctrine that holds an individual or business accountable for damages whether or not it was at fault. In a strict liability case, no matter how careful the business is in its product or service, if harm results from use, the individual or business is liable.

One can think of possible answers to this question as falling along a continuum. On one end of the continuum is the social contract answer: Producers owe only those things promised to consumers in the sales agreement. At the other end is something closer to **strict liability:** Producers owe compensation to consumers for any and all harms caused by their products. In between these extremes is a range of answers that vary with different interpretations of negligence.

Negligence can be characterized as a failure to exercise reasonable care or ordinary vigilance that results in an injury to another. In many ways, negligence simply codifies two fundamental ethical precepts: "ought implies can" (we cannot reasonably oblige someone to do what they cannot do) and "one ought not harm others." People have done an ethical wrong when they cause harm to others in ways that they can reasonably be expected to have avoided. One can be negligent by doing something that one ought not (e.g., speeding in a school zone) or by failing to do something that one ought to have done (e.g., neglecting to inspect a product before sending it to market).

Negligence involves the ability to foresee the consequences of our acts and failing to take steps to avoid the likely harmful consequences (see the Reality Check "Snapchat: When Is a Company's Product Responsible for Causing Injuries?"). The standards of what can be foreseen, however, raise interesting ethical challenges.

One standard would hold people liable only for those harms they actually foresaw occurring. Thus, for example, as happened in the famous Ford Pinto case, a company would be acting negligently if it brought to market a car that it knew, on the basis of engineering tests, had a fuel tank that would puncture and explode during crashes at speeds below 30 miles per hour.

But this standard of actual foreseeability is too narrow because it would imply that unthoughtful people cannot be negligent. By applying this standard, a person could escape liability by not actually thinking about the consequences of one's acts. "I never thought about that" would be an adequate defense if we used this standard of negligence. Yet this surely is not an ethically adequate excuse for harming innocent people.

A preferable standard would require people to avoid harms that they *should* have thought about. For example, in the Reality Check on Snapchat we might judge the company responsible even if we assume that the designers did not actually anticipate that customers would be using the speed filter to record driving at 100 mph. Had they thought about typical users and the fact that they often do unreasonable things, which they would have done had they acted reasonably, they could have foreseen such accidents. Moreover, the fact that Snapchat had received prior complaints about similar accidents suggests that a reasonable person would have concluded that this was a dangerous practice. This "reasonable person" standard is the one most often used in legal cases and seems to better capture the ethical goals of the very concept of negligence. People are expected to act reasonably and are held liable when they are not.

But even the reasonable person standard can be interpreted in various ways. On one hand, we expect people will act in ways that would be normal or average. A "reasonable" person does what we could expect the ordinary, average person to do. But, for example, the average person doesn't always read, or understand, warning

Reality Check   *Snapchat: When Is a Company's Product Responsible for Causing Injuries?*

Snapchat is a photo and video messaging app that sends images that the user can edit with numerous filters to distort or add doodles or commentary to the image before sending. One filter introduced by Snapchat allows the user to record the speed at which she or he was traveling when the image was recorded. Thus, for example, one could send out a selfie taken while flying in an airplane that shows the plane's speed superimposed on the photo. This filter includes a warning against using this filter when one is driving.

In September 2015, an 18-year-old Georgia girl crashed into the back of another car. News reports indicated that she was driving over 100 mph in a 55-mph speed zone and was using the Snapchat speed filter at the time. These news reports indicated that friends in her car had asked her to stop, but that she was intent on reaching the 100-mph mark. The driver of the other car was seriously injured, sustaining permanent brain injuries.

Lawyers for the injured driver sued both the girl and Snapchat, claiming that Snapshat should be held responsible for selling a product that it had reason to know would encourage reckless behavior. Months earlier an online petition was started to request Snapchat to remove the speed filter after reports of other similar accidents.

Snapchat denied responsibility for the accident, pointing out that its terms of service, the small print accompanying the app, advises users against unsafe practices. The terms of service document included the following:

"We also care about your safety while using our Services. So do not use our Services in a way that would distract you from obeying traffic or safety laws. And never put yourself or others in harm's way just to capture a Snap." The Snapchat terms of service statement runs for over 4,500 words, with 22 separate sections including sections on such topics as arbitration, severability, indemnity, disclaimers, limitation of liability, and venue. In reality, most users seldom read or understand the specifics of the terms of service. While in the ambulance on her way to the hospital, the girl who was driving sent out a Snapchat selfie of her bloody face with the caption "lucky to be alive."

- What liability, if any, should Snapchat have for the damages caused by this accident? No one denies that the driver bears primary responsibility, but did Snapchat also contribute to the harms caused?

- What uses could Snapchat have reasonably foreseen for this speed filter? What could Snapchat reasonably be expected to know about the users of its products?

- Was the advice contained in the terms of service sufficient warning to protect Snapchat from any misuse of its product?

- Do you think that the speed filter is a dangerous product? Was Snapchat negligent in marketing this product?

labels or terms of service. The average person standard when applied to consumers might exempt too many consumers from responsibility for their own acts. Especially when applied to producers, the average person standard sets the bar too low. We can expect more from a person who designs, manufacturers, and sells a product than average, especially if the product is intended to an adolescent or teen consumer.

These factors lead many to interpret the reasonable person standard as a standard of thoughtful, reflective, and judicious decision making. The problem with this, of course, is that we might be asking more of average consumers than they are capable of giving. Particularly if we think that vulnerable consumers (think of the teenage driver in the Snatchat case) deserve greater protection from harm, we might conclude that this sense of reasonable is too stringent a standard to be applied to consumer behavior. On the other hand, given the fact that producers do have more expertise than the average person, this stronger standard seems more appropriate when applied to producers than to consumers.

Strict Product Liability

OBJECTIVE

The negligence standard of tort law focuses on the sense of responsibility that involves someone being at fault. But there are also cases in which consumers can be injured by a product in which no negligence was involved. In such cases where no one was at fault, the question of accountability remains. Who should pay for damages when consumers are injured by products and no one is at fault? The legal doctrine of strict product liability holds manufacturers accountable in such cases and it raises unique ethical questions.

Ethical Debates on Product Liability

OBJECTIVE

Within the United States, calls to reform product liability laws, and in particular to ease or eliminate the strict product liability standard, have been common. But criticism of strict product liability has not been universal. The European Union, for example, has adopted clear strict liability standards. The EU concluded that "liability without fault [strict products liability] on the part of the producer is the sole means of adequately solving the problem, peculiar to our age of increasing technicality, of a fair apportionment of the risks inherent in modern technological production."[5]

It is fair to say that the business community in the United States is a strong critic of much of the legal standards of product liability. Liability standards, and the liability insurance costs in which they have resulted, have imposed significant costs on contemporary business. In particular, these critics single out the strict product liability standard as especially unfair to business because it holds business responsible for harms that were not the result of business negligence.

In fact, the rationale often used to justify strict product liability is problematic. Defenders of the strict product liability standard, including juries who decide in favor of injured consumers, often reply with two major claims. First, by holding business strictly liable for any harm their products cause, society creates a strong incentive for business to produce safer goods and services. Second, given that someone has to be accountable for the costs of injuries, holding business liable allocates the costs to the party best able to bear the financial burden. Each rationale is open to serious objections.

The incentive argument seems to misunderstand the nature of strict liability. Holding someone accountable for harm can provide an incentive only if the person could have done otherwise. But this means that the harm was foreseeable and the failure to act was negligent. Surely this is a reasonable justification for the tort standard of negligence. But strict liability is not negligence and the harms caused by such products as asbestos were not foreseeable. Thus, holding business liable for these harms cannot provide an incentive to better protect consumers in the future. See the Reality Check "Strict Liability as Risk Management."

The second rationale also suffers a serious defect. This argument amounts to the claim that business is best able to pay for damages. Yet, many businesses have been bankrupted by product liability claims.

If it is unfair to hold business accountable for harms caused by their products, it is equally (if not more) unfair to hold injured consumers accountable. Neither

---

Reality Check *Strict Liability as Risk Management*

Objections to the strict products liability standard often reference the unfairness of holding a business liable for something for which it was not at fault and which it could not control. Of course, exactly the same claim can be made on behalf of the consumer who is injured: It would seem equally unfair to make him or her bear the full costs of the injury caused through no fault of the individual.

Perhaps the problem lies in treating strict liability as involving fault at all. Perhaps strict liability is best understood not in terms of assigning responsibility, in the sense of assigning who is at fault, but in terms of allocating the risks involved in any product. As suggested by the quote from the European Union's standard on liability, we should recognize that all products, especially in an increasingly complicated and technological marketplace, carry some degree of risk.

Accidents and unforeseen harms are inevitable, and society must decide what the most ethical and economically sound method is to allocate risks. To do nothing is to make a decision by default: All costs and risks are borne by whomever happens to be the victim of the accident. Many observers believe this is unfair to the victim. Strict liability attempts to address this unfairness by allocating at last some of the costs to those who produced the product that caused the harm. Thus, the "costs" of the accident are shared by both the consumer, for whom the harm suffered is the primary cost, and the producer, who must pay financial damages for the harm.

---

party is at fault, yet someone must pay for the injuries. A third option would be to have government, and therefore all taxpayers, accountable for paying the costs of injuries caused by defective products. But this, too, seems unfair.

Another argument for holding business accountable might be more persuasive. Accountability, after all, focuses on those situations where no one is at fault, yet someone has to bear the burdens associated with the harm. But perhaps accountability is best understood as a matter of utilitarian efficiency rather than a matter of ethical principle of desert. When business is held accountable, the costs for injuries will eventually fall on those consumers who buy the product through higher costs, especially higher insurance costs to business. This amounts to the claim that external costs should be internalized and that the full costs of a product should be paid for by those who use the product. Products that impose a cost on society through injuries will end up costing more to those who purchase them. Companies that cannot afford to remain in business when the full costs of their products are taken into account perhaps ought not to remain in business.

Responsibility for Products: Advertising and Sales

OBJECTIVE

Along with product safety, advertising is a second area of marketing that has received significant legal and philosophical attention within business ethics. The goal of all marketing is the sale, the eventual exchange between seller and buyer. A major element of marketing is sales promotion, the attempt to influence the buyer to complete a purchase. (See the Decision Point "Advertising Drugs.") Target marketing and marketing research are two important elements of product placement, seeking to determine which audience is most likely to buy, and which audience is mostly likely to be influenced by product promotion.

There are, of course, ethically good and bad ways for influencing others. Among the ethically commendable ways to influence another are persuading, asking, informing, and advising. Unethical means of influence would include threats, coercion, deception, manipulation, and lying. Unfortunately, all too often sales and advertising practices employ deceptive or manipulative means of influence, or are aimed at audiences that are susceptible to manipulation or deception. The concept of manipulation, and its subset of deception, is central to the ethical issues explored in this chapter and can help organize the following sections.

To manipulate something is to guide or direct its behavior. Manipulation need not involve total control, and in fact it more likely suggests a process of subtle direction or management. Manipulating people implies working behind the scenes, guiding their behavior without their explicit consent or conscious understanding. In this way, manipulation is contrasted with persuasion and other forms of rational influence. When I manipulate someone, I explicitly do not rely on their own reasoned judgment to direct their behavior. Instead, I seek to bypass their autonomy (although successful manipulation can be reinforced when the person manipulated *believes* she acted of her own accord).

One of the ways in which we can manipulate someone is through deception, one form of which is an outright lie. I need not deceive you to manipulate you. We can manipulate someone without deception, as when I get my sons to mow the lawn by making them feel guilty about not carrying their share of family responsibilities. Or I might manipulate my students into studying more diligently by hinting that there may be a quiz during the next class. These examples raise a very crucial point because they suggest that the more I know about your psychology—your motivations, interests, desires, beliefs, dispositions, and so forth—the better able I will be to manipulate your behavior. Guilt, pity, a desire to please, anxiety, fear, low self-esteem, pride, and conformity can all be powerful motivators. Knowing such things about another person provides effective tools for manipulating her or his behavior.

We can see how this is relevant to marketing ethics. Critics charge that many marketing practices manipulate consumers. Clearly, many advertisements are deceptive, and some are outright lies. We can also see how marketing research plays into this. The more one learns about customer psychology, the better able one will be to satisfy their desires, but the better able one will also be to manipulate their behavior. Consider the cases of digital marketing described in the chapter's opening scenario for examples of how consumer information might be used to manipulate people. Critics also charge that some marketing practices target populations that are particularly susceptible to manipulation and deception.

Ethical Issues in Advertising

OBJECTIVE

The general ethical defense of advertising reflects both utilitarian and Kantian ethical standards. Advertising provides information for market exchanges and therefore contributes to market efficiency and to overall happiness. Advertising

According to Pew research, pharmaceutical companies spent $27 billion in 2012 promoting their drugs. All but one of the largest 10 firms spent more on marketing than they did on research and development. From 2012 to 2015, direct-to-consumer (DTC) marketing of drugs increased from $3.2 billion to almost $6 billion annually.

Advertisements promoting prescription drugs have increased significantly within the United States since the Food and Drug Administration (FDA) changed regulations in 1997 to allow DTC advertising. Among the most widely marketed drugs have been Lipitor, Zocor, Prilosec, Prevacid, Nexium, Celebrex, Vioxx, Zoloft, Paxil, Prozac, Viagra, Cialis, Levitra, Propecia, and Zyban. These drug names, literally household names today, were unheard of before the turn of the century; yet, together they accounted for over $20 billion in annual sales.

The medications mentioned here treat the following conditions: ulcers and acid-reflux (Prilosec, Prevacid, Nexium); high cholesterol (Lipitor, Zocor); arthritic pain (Celebrex, Vioxx); depression, panic attacks, and anxiety (Zoloft, Paxil, Prozac); "erectile dysfunction" (Viagra, Cialis, and Levitra); hair loss (Propecia); and cigarette and nicotine withdrawal (Zyban). Ads for these drugs often appeal to such emotional considerations as embarrassment; fear; shame; social, sexual, and romantic inferiority; helplessness; vulnerability; and vanity. Many of these drugs are heavily advertised in women's magazines or during televised sporting events and evening network news shows.

- Would you favor a ban on direct-to-consumer advertising for prescription drugs?
- What facts would you want to know before making a judgment about these ads?
- Which ads, if any, raise ethical questions?
- Who are the stakeholders in drug advertising? What are the potential benefits and potential harms of such advertising?
- Are customers for prescription drugs particularly vulnerable to manipulation?
- What ethical principles have you used in making your judgments?

information also contributes to the information necessary for autonomous individuals to make informed choices. But note that each of these rationales provides an ethical justification only if the information is true and accurate.

The principle-based tradition in ethics would have the strongest objections to manipulation. When I manipulate someone I treat him or her as a means to my own ends, as an object to be used rather than as an autonomous person in his or her own right. Manipulation is a clear example of disrespect for persons because it bypasses their own rational decision making. Because the evil rests with the intention to use another as a means, even unsuccessful manipulations are guilty of this ethical wrong.

As we might expect, the utilitarian tradition would offer a more conditional critique of manipulation, depending on the consequences. For example, there surely can be cases of paternalistic manipulation, in which someone is manipulated for his or her own good. But even in such cases, unforeseen harms can occur. Manipulation tends to erode bonds of trust and respect between persons. It can erode one's self-confidence and hinder the development of responsible choice

Reality Check   *GMO Labeling: Can Truthful Information Be Misleading?*

Free and informed consent is one of the fundamental ethical conditions on any exchange. Parties to the exchange must understand and give their voluntary consent in order for the exchange to be ethically responsible. By meeting this standard, the exchange will both respect the autonomy of the parties involved and meet utilitarian goals of providing mutual benefit. Product labeling for ingredients and nutritional value are two ways that food labeling serves this ethical goal by providing consumers with the information needed to make a fully informed decision. Should food that contains genetically modified organisms (GMOs) be required to carry a label that identifies them as GMO?

A number of reasons are offered to require GMO labeling. First, and perhaps most importantly, supporters cite a general consumer right to know what they are purchasing. Labels provide consumers with the information they require to make a truly informed decisions about food products. This information is particularly important for vegetarians and others who have health or religious reasons to avoid food containing animal products. Thus, labeling serves the ethical goals of mutual benefit and respect for autonomy. Second, label requirements will provide a disincentive for the use of GMO technology and thus reduce the use of herbicides and other chemicals in food production. Third, labeling provides a paper trail of information that can be used to track any potential problems that arise from the use of GMO foods. Finally, GMO labeling is thought to provide a check on the power of large agricultural and chemical corporations that own and control much of the GMO technology and products.

Those who oppose GMO labeling requirements argue that this would mislead and unduly alarm consumers. It is likely that consumers will perceive this as a warning label rather than simply an ingredient label and this will mislead consumers and discourage them from purchasing the product. Critics argue that there is no evidence that GMO foods are unsafe and, in fact, they add significantly to agricultural productivity. Thus, anything that discourages GMO foods will reduce the amount of food available for no health or nutritional reason. Critics also point out that they oppose only mandatory labeling, not voluntary labeling. Food producers are always free to label food as GMO-free, as organic food producers already do, thus consumers who desire GMO-free food already have a way to make informed food choices. Voluntary labeling allows the market to function as the means of meeting this consumer demand. If consumers demand GMO labeling, producers will have a financial incentive to provide it; if they are not demanding GMO labels, then requirements will unnecessarily raise the price of food products.

- Would you support mandatory labeling for all GMO food products?

- Besides the sellers and consumers, what other stakeholders should be considered in making this decision?

- How would you respond to the reasons offered by the side that disagrees with your views?

- Is it reasonable to expect that some consumers will interpret the label as a warning that GMO foods are unhealthy?

among those manipulated. In general, because most manipulation is done to further the manipulator's own ends at the expense of the manipulated, utilitarians would be inclined to think that manipulation lessens overall happiness. A general practice of manipulation, as critics claim often occurs in many sales practices, can undermine the very social practices (e.g., sales) that it is thought to promote as the reputation of sales is lowered.

A particularly egregious form of manipulation occurs when vulnerable people are targeted for abuse. Cigarette advertising aimed at children is one example that has received major criticism in recent years. Marketing practices targeted at older populations for such goods and services as insurance (particularly Medicare supplemental insurance), casinos and gambling, nursing homes, and funerals have been subjected to similar criticisms.

Reality Check *Does Digital Marketing Raise New Ethical Issues?*

Deception and manipulation are two ethical concerns that seem as relevant to digital marketing techniques as they do to traditional marketing. But digital marketing has the potential to raise concerns of consumer privacy that did not exist for traditional marketing techniques.

Tracking cookies are one common means by which digital businesses can collect information about consumers. In some cases, the use of cookies is explicitly detailed for consumers and they are allowed to opt-out of their use. In some cases, consumers are warned that by opting-out they risk losing functionality on the site they are visiting. In other cases, known as *stealth tracking,* consumers are unaware that their behavior is being tracked and recorded. Internet service providers (ISPs) and cell phone providers, for example, have the ability to track every online action and phone call. This information uniquely identifies the user and cannot be controlled by the user by deleting cookies or browsing history.

How tracking information is used raises other ethical questions. This information is regularly sold to third parties, most often companies interested in marketing to that user. But others might be interested as well. Already, potential employers have shown an interest in the social network sites of job applicants. Might they be as interested in browsing history?

For example, the dating site OKcupid allowed all registered users to access the personal information provided by users, including not only name, religion, and political sympathies, but also information about personal habits, alcohol and drug use, and sexual interests. All one needed to do to have access to this information was to register on the site and agree to OKcupid terms of service agreement. This did not prove a deterrent to some Dutch researchers who collected data from the site for a research project and made the data publicly available for others.

Another example involved the legal case *Valentine v. NebuAd.* This case involved a digital marketing company, NebuAd, that contracted with Internet service providers (ISPs) to install devices on their networks that monitored ISP subscribers' Internet activity and transmitted those data to NebuAd's California headquarters for analysis. The data were used to sell advertising tailored to subscribers' interests, which appeared in place of more generic advertisements on web pages visited by subscribers. In effect, NebuAd stepped into the communication between individuals and the browser they were using to substitute their client's ads for more generic ads that would otherwise have appeared. The advertising profits generated from this activity were split by NebuAd and its ISP partners.

ISP customers filed a class-action lawsuit against both NebuAd and their ISP providers alleging that this practice violated their federal and state privacy rights. The case was finally resolved after NebuAd entered bankruptcy and agreed to pay more than $2 million to settle the case.

- Identify as many ethical issues involved in these cases as you can. Are any of these issues unique to digital marketing?
- Who are the stakeholders in the OKcupid and NebuAd cases? Who was harmed by NebuAd?
- Who should own and control personal information collected by cookies? Are there any limits that should be placed on how that information is used and who has access to it?
- Does an individual relinquish all claims to privacy by posting personal information on a social network site?

We can suggest the following general guidelines. Marketing practices that seek to discover which consumers might already and independently be predisposed to purchasing a product are ethically legitimate. So, for example, contextual digital ads in which a banner ad for a Montreal hotel appears on your mobile screen immediately after you search for an airline flight to Montreal would seem legitimate.

Marketing practices that seek to identify populations that can be easily influenced and manipulated, on the other hand, are ethically questionable. Sales and marketing that appeal to fear, anxiety, or other nonrational motivations are ethically improper. For example, an automobile dealer who knows that an elderly woman is anxious about the purchase and who uses this anxiety as a way to sell extended warranty insurance, disability insurance, theft protection products, and the like is unethical. The manner in which this or other information is collected is also subject to ethical concerns. (To explore if consumer privacy might limit how information is collected, see the Reality Check "Does Digital Marketing Raise New Ethical Issues?")

Marketing research seeks to learn something about the psychology of potential customers. But not all psychological categories are alike. Some are more cognitive and rational than others. Targeting the considered and rational desires of consumers is one thing; targeting their fears, anxiety, and whims is another. (To explore another way in which even truthful ads might mislead consumers, go back to the Reality Check "GMO Labeling: Can Truthful Information Be Misleading?")

Marketing Ethics and Consumer Autonomy

OBJECTIVE

Defenders of advertising argue that despite cases of deceptive practices, overall advertising contributes much to the economy. The majority of advertisements provide information to consumers, information that contributes to an efficient function of economic markets. These defenders argue that over time, market forces will weed out deceptive ads and practices. They point out that the most effective counter to a deceptive ad is a competitor's ad calling attention to the deception.

Beyond this question of what advertising does *for* people, a second important ethical question asks what advertising specifically and marketing in general do *to* people. People may well benefit from business's marketing of its products. People learn about products they may need or want, they get information that helps them make responsible choices, they even sometimes are entertained. But marketing also helps shape culture and the individuals who are socialized within that culture, some would say dramatically so. Marketing can have direct and indirect influence on the very persons we become. How it does that, and the kind of people we become as a result, is of fundamental ethical importance. Critics of such claims either deny that marketing can have such influence or maintain that marketing is only a mirror of the culture of which it is a part.

The initial proposal in this debate was offered by economist John Kenneth Galbraith in his 1958 book *The Affluent Society*. Galbraith claimed that advertising and marketing were creating the very consumer demand that production then aimed to satisfy. Dubbed the "dependence effect," this assertion held that consumer demand depended on what producers had to sell. This fact had three major and unwelcome implications.

First, by creating wants, advertising was standing the "law" of supply and demand on its head. Rather than supply being a function of demand, demand turns out to be a function of supply. Second, advertising and marketing tend to create irrational and trivial consumer wants and this distorts the entire economy. The "affluent" society of consumer products and creature comforts is in many ways worse off than so-called undeveloped economies because resources devoted to contrived, private consumer goods are therefore denied to more important public goods and consumer

Reality Check *New Challenges to Old Problems: From Redlining to E-lining*

by Tara J. Radin, Martin Calkins, and Carolyn Predmore

Today, nearly two decades since the Internet became widely and publicly available, we still lack consensus about the degree of ownership and acceptable limits of data gathering and use. In fact, Richard De George's 1999 remark is arguably more valid now than previously: "The U.S. is schizophrenic about information privacy, wanting it in theory and giving it away in practice."[6] Such schizophrenia is problematic in itself, but it has been exacerbated by the questionable applications of data collection that have occurred. E-lining (electronic redlining) represents one glaring example of how data gathering crosses moral boundaries.

Redlining is the practice of denying or increasing the cost of services to residents of certain geographic locations. In the United States, it has been deemed illegal when the criteria involve race, religion, or ethnic origin. The term came to prominence with the discussions that led to the Housing Act of 1934, which established the Federal Housing Authority, which later became the Department of Housing and Urban Development. It occurs when financial institutions (banks, brokerages, and insurance companies) literally draw red lines on maps to distinguish between creditworthy and financially risky neighborhoods.

Although illegal, redlining has not died out completely. It reemerged recently when MCI removed international long-distance service via calling cards from pay phones in poorer communities in the suburbs of Los Angeles. It reappeared also in retail sales when Victoria's Secret allegedly tailored its catalog prices along customer demographics (specifically, ethnicity). In this case, two sisters living in different parts of town discovered price differences when discussing items from seemingly identical catalogs. As the two compared prices on the phone, they found that the cost of some items varied by as much as 25 percent. A subsequent and more thorough investigation revealed that Victoria's Secret had been engaging in an extensive practice of price variation according to gender, age, and income. In the end, although Victoria's Secret was vindicated in the court of law, it lost in the court of public opinion.

Finally, it resurfaced when Kozmo.com, an online provider of one-hour delivery services, used zip codes to refuse to deliver merchandise to customers in predominantly black neighborhoods. In all of these cases, companies (to different degrees) "exclude[d] classes of individuals from full participation in the marketplace and the public sphere."

E-lining differs from these more traditional forms of redlining by not drawing a red line on a map, but by using information that Internet users unwittingly leave behind as they surf websites. E-liners use "spyware" programs embedded in web pages to collect information surreptitiously and with little or no outside oversight. They are able to "spy on" surfers in this way without much challenge because, at present, there are few limits on what companies can do with the information they gather.

In recent years companies have used customer information to direct customers to particular products or services. In this way, they have used information in much the same way high-end clothing stores use a Rolodex of customer phone numbers to alert customers about newly arrived items that match or complement prior purchases. At other times, businesses have not acted so benevolently. They have used the data they collected in a discriminatory way to direct customers to particular products or services that fit a profile based on demographics. Amazon has received significant criticism for its use of historical purchase information to tailor web offerings to repeat customers. Amazon allegedly used data profiling in order to set prices. In September 2000, Amazon customers determined that they were charged different prices for the same CDs. Although Amazon claimed that the price differentiation was part of a randomized test, the result was price discrimination that appeared to be based on demographics.

This sort of discrimination and deprivation of financial opportunities according to demographics is exactly what the rules against redlining are intended to prevent. The absence of comparable rules against e-lining is not, as some firms might like to argue, an indication that this sort of behavior is acceptable in e-commerce, but, rather, is a reflection of the lag in time it is taking for the legal infrastructure to catch up with e-commerce. Our current legal infrastructure, particularly in the United States, which is aimed almost exclusively toward brick-and-mortar enterprises, does not account for the tremendous amount of information available through e-commerce or for the numerous ways in which e-merchants are able to exploit customers through misuse of that information. The unfortunate reality is that there is not a clear distinction between acceptable and unacceptable forms of information gathering, use, and market segmentation, and e-commerce provides a cloak that insulates from detection many firms engaging in inappropriate behavior.

There are few if any obstacles to firms engaging in questionable e-commerce business practices in the first place. Public outcries are generally short-lived and do not appear to have a significant impact on e-shopping. If anything, e-commerce continues to attract an increasing number of customers. In the meantime, few generally agreed-upon standards exist regarding the acceptable limits of information gathering via the Internet. Instead, businesses are shaping the expectations of web users and society in general as they implicitly set standards to guide future marketers through their irresponsible behavior. They are sending the message "Internet user beware!" to Internet surfers and potential e-customers. As long as the legal infrastructure remains underdeveloped, society remains vulnerable to an increasing number of potential electronic abuses.

Source: Adapted by the authors with permission from work copyrighted © by Tara J. Radin, Martin Calkins, and Carolyn Predmore. All rights reserved by the authors.

needs. Taxpayers deny school districts small tax increases to provide essential funding while parents drop their children off at school in $50,000 SUVs. A society that cannot guarantee vaccinations and minimal health care to poor children spends millions annually for cosmetic surgery to keep its youthful appearance. Finally, by creating consumer wants, advertising and other marketing practices violate consumer autonomy. Consumers who consider themselves free because they are able to purchase what they want are not in fact free if those wants are created by marketing. In short, consumers are being manipulated by advertising. (To explore another means by which consumer behavior might be influenced, see the Reality Check "New Challenges to Old Problems: From Redlining to E-lining.")

Ethically, the crucial point is the assertion that advertising violates consumer autonomy. The law of supply and demand is reversed and the economy of the affluent society is contrived and distorted, only if consumer autonomy can be violated by advertising's ability to create wants. But can advertising violate consumer autonomy and, if it can, does this occur? Consider the annual investment in this effort (see the Reality Check "Advertising Spending"). Given this investment, what does advertising do *to* people and *to* society?

An initial thesis in this debate claims that advertising controls consumer *behavior.* Psychological behaviorists and critics of subliminal advertising, for example, would claim that advertising can control consumer behavior by controlling their choices. But this is an empirical claim and the evidence suggests that it is false. For example, some studies show that more than half of all new products introduced in the market fail, a fact that should not be true if consumer behavior could be controlled by marketing. Consumers certainly don't seem controlled by advertising in any obvious sense of that word.

But consumer autonomy might be violated in a subtler way. Rather than controlling behavior, perhaps advertising creates the wants and desires on the basis of which consumers act. The focus here becomes the concept of *autonomous desires* rather than *autonomous behavior.* This is much closer to the original assertion by Galbraith and other critics of advertising. Consumer autonomy is violated by advertising's ability to create non-autonomous desires.

Reality Check *Advertising Spending*

Total spending in the United States on advertising in all media for 2015 was estimated by one group of analysts to exceed $198 billion. Worldwide, advertising was a $600 billion industry—a number that was up about 4 percent from the previous year. China was the second-largest advertising market accounting for $73 billion worth of ads.[7]

In terms of digital and mobile advertising alone companies spent nearly $230 billion globally in 2015, with predictions that digital and mobile ads will surpass all other media by 2017.

Source: "Advertisers Will Spend Nearly $600 Billion Worldwide," *eMarketer* (December 10, 2014), www.emarketer.com/Article/Advertisers-Will-Spend-Nearly-600-Billion-Worldwide-2015/1011691 (accessed May 24, 2016).

A helpful exercise to understand how desires might be non-autonomous is to think of the many reasons people buy the things they buy and consume the things they do, and why, in general, people go shopping. After certain basic needs are met, there is a real question of why people consume the way they do. People buy things for many reasons, including the desire to appear fashionable, for status, to feel good, because everyone else is buying something, and so forth. The interesting ethical question at this point is where *these* desires originated, and how much marketing has influenced these nonnecessity purchases. These questions and issues are raised in the Reality Check "Advertising for Erectile Dysfunction."

Marketing to Vulnerable Populations

OBJECTIVE

Consider two examples of target marketing. In one case, based on market research supplied by the manufacturer, an automobile retailer learns that the typical customer is a single woman, between 30 and 40 years old; she has an annual income over $30,000, and she enjoys outdoor sports and recreation. Knowing this information, the dealer targets advertising and direct mail to this audience. Ads depict attractive and active young people using their product and enjoying outdoor activities. A second targeted campaign is aimed at selling an emergency call device to older widows who live alone. This marketing campaign depicts an elderly woman at the bottom of a stairway crying out "I've fallen and can't get up!" These ads are placed in media that older women are likely to see or hear. Are these marketing campaigns on an equal ethical footing?

The first marketing strategy appeals to the considered judgments which consumers, presumably, have settled on over the course of their lives. People with similar backgrounds tend to have similar beliefs, desires, and values and often make similar judgments about consumer purchases. Target marketing in this sense is simply a means for identifying likely customers based on common beliefs and values. On the other hand, there does seem to be something ethically offensive about the second case. This campaign aims to sell the product by exploiting the real fear and anxiety that many older people experience. This marketing strategy tries to manipulate people by appealing to nonrational factors such as fear or anxiety rather than relying on straightforward informative ads. Is there anything to the claim that elderly women

Reality Check *Advertising for Erectile Dysfunction*

Perhaps few marketing campaigns have received as much critical attention as the Viagra, Cialis, and Levitra campaign to counteract erectile dysfunction. Much of the criticism has focused on the ad placements, particularly in places where young children would see them such as during prime-time television and during high-profile sporting events. Other criticisms suggest that although these drugs can be used to treat real medical conditions, they are being marketed as little more than recreational drugs and sex toys. Erectile dysfunction can be a problem for older men and especially for men recovering from such medical treatments as prostate surgery. But for younger and otherwise healthy men, the primary causes of erectile dysfunction are alcohol consumption, obesity, lack of exercise, smoking, and the use of other prescription drugs. All these causes are either easily addressed without reliance on pharmaceuticals or, as is the case with alcohol abuse, erectile dysfunction drugs are potentially unsafe.

Arguments in support of direct-to-consumer marketing of prescription drugs are that it provides information to consumers, respects consumer choice, encourages those who are reluctant to seek medical care to do so, gets more people into the health care system, addresses real public health issues, and increases competition and efficiency in the pharmaceutical industry. Opponents claim that these ads increase the unnecessary use of drugs; increase public harms because all drugs have harmful side effects; increase reliance on pharmaceutical health care treatments and discourage alternative therapies and treatments, many of which have fewer side effects; manipulate and exploit vulnerable consumers; often provide misleading and incomplete information; alienate patients from physicians by bypassing the gatekeeper function of medical professionals; and treat social and behavior problems with medical and chemical solutions.

What is your judgment about the ethics of advertising Viagra, Cialis, and Levitra? Do the reasons for advertising prescription drugs in general apply equally well to these three drugs?

- What alternatives exist for marketing prescription drugs?
- Who are the stakeholders of drug marketing?
- What are the consequences of alternative marketing strategies?
- What rights and duties are involved?

Reality Check *Targeting Vulnerable People?*

An important case of marketing drugs to targeted populations involves the drug Strattera, Eli Lilly's prescription medication that controls attention deficit/hyperactivity disorder (ADHD) in children. The ad ran in magazines such as *Family Circle* (September 2003) under the simple title "Welcome to Ordinary." The ad pictured two boys holding up a model airplane that they had finished building, a challenging task for a child with ADHD. The ad reads: "4:30 P.M. Tuesday. He started something you never thought he'd finish. 5:20 P.M. Thursday. He's proved you wrong." The ad suggests that, if a child with ADHD is not "ordinary," it is the parents who are "wrong" because all it would take would be Strattera to solve their problem. The same issue of *Family Circle* contained ads for McNeil Pharmaceutical's Concerta and Shire Pharmaceutical's Adderall, the two major competitors to Strattera.

Are these marketing practices ethically responsible?

- What facts would you want to know before deciding this case?
- What alternative marketing practices were open to these companies?
- Who are the stakeholders of your decision? What is the impact of each alternative decision on each stakeholder you have identified?
- What rights and duties are involved?
- How would you decide the case? Would you primarily consider consequences, or are important principles involved?

living alone are more "vulnerable" than younger women and that this vulnerability creates greater responsibility for marketers? In general, do marketers have special responsibility to individuals who are vulnerable?

Are older people living alone particularly vulnerable? The answer to this depends on what we mean by particularly vulnerable. In one sense, a person is vulnerable as a consumer by being unable in some way to participate as a fully informed and voluntary participant in the market exchange. Valid market exchanges make several assumptions about the participants: They understand what they are doing, they have considered their choice, they are free to decide, and so forth. What we can call *consumer vulnerability* occurs when a person has an impaired ability to make an informed consent to the market exchange. A vulnerable consumer lacks the intellectual capacities, psychological ability, or maturity to make informed and considered consumer judgments. Children would be the paradigmatic example of consumer vulnerability. (See the Reality Check "Targeting Vulnerable People?") The harm to which such people are susceptible is the harm of not satisfying one's consumer desires and/or losing one's money.

There is a second sense of vulnerability in which the harm is other than the financial harm of an unsatisfactory market exchange. Elderly people living alone are susceptible to injuries from falls, from medical emergencies, from expensive health care bills, from loneliness. Alcoholics are susceptible to alcohol abuse, the poor are susceptible to bankruptcy, single women walking alone at night are vulnerable to sexual assault, accident victims are susceptible to high medical expenses and loss of income, and so forth. What we can call *general vulnerability* occurs when someone is susceptible to some specific physical, psychological, or financial harm.

From this we can see that there can be two types of marketing that targets vulnerable populations. Some marketing practices might target those consumers who are likely to be uninformed and vulnerable as consumers. Marketing aimed at children, for example, aims to sell products to customers who are unable to make thoughtful and informed consumer decisions. Other marketing practices might target populations that are vulnerable in the general sense as when, for example, an insurance company markets flood protection insurance to homeowners living in a river's floodplain. Are either, or both, types of targeting ethically legitimate?

As an initial judgment, we must say that marketing that is targeted at those individuals who are vulnerable as consumers is unethical. This is a case of taking advantage of someone's frailty and manipulating it for one's own advantage. Clearly a portion of marketing and sales targets people who are vulnerable as consumers. Just as clearly such practices are wrong.

One way that this issue plays out involves groups who are vulnerable in both senses. Oftentimes people can become vulnerable as a consumer *because* they are vulnerable in some more general sense. The vulnerability that many older adults have with respect to injuries and illness might cause them to make consumer choices based on fear or guilt. A family member grieving over the death of a loved one might make choices in purchasing funeral services based on guilt or sorrow, rather than on a considered judgment. A person with a medical condition or disease is vulnerable, and the anxiety or fear associated with this vulnerability can lead to uninformed consumer choices. An inner-city resident who is poor, unedu-cated, and chronically unemployed is unlikely to weigh the full consequences of the choice of alcoholic beverage.

A number of marketing campaigns seem to fit this model. The most abhorrent (and stereotypical) example is the ambulance-chasing attorney seeking a client for a personal-injury lawsuit. An accident victim is vulnerable to many harms and, while experiencing the stress of this situation, is unlikely to make a fully informed choice about legal representation. Marketing campaigns that target elderly individuals for such products as supplemental medical insurance, life insurance, emergency call devices, funeral services, and insurance often play on the fears, anxiety, and guilt that many older people experience. (See again the Reality Check "Targeting Vul-nerable People?" to consider examples of marketing to specific populations.)

But just as people can be made vulnerable as consumers because they are vulner-able to other harms, there can also be cases in which people become vulnerable to other harms because they are vulnerable as consumers. Perhaps this strategy is the most abhorrent case of unethical marketing. Certain products—tobacco and alcohol are the most obvious examples—can make an individual vulnerable to a wide range of health risks. Marketing campaigns for products that target people who are vulnerable as consumers seem ethically repugnant. This explains the particular public outrage directed at tobacco and alcohol companies that target young people. Companies that market alcoholic beverages in poor inner-city neighborhoods must take this ethical guideline into account. Marketing malt beverages, fortified wines, and other alcoholic drinks to poor inner-city residents must acknowledge that many people in such situ-ations are not fully autonomous consumers. Many people in such situations drink to get drunk; they drink to escape; they drink because they are alcoholics. (For an exam-ination of online marketing that targets children, see Reading 8-2, "First Analysis of Online Food Advertising Targeting Children," by the Kaiser Family Foundation.)

One final form of marketing to a vulnerable population involves potentially all of us as consumer targets. We are each vulnerable when we are not aware that we are subject to a marketing campaign. This type of campaign is called **stealth or undercover marketing** and refers to those situations where we are subject to directed commercial activity without our knowledge. Certainly we are subjected to numerous communications on a regular basis without paying much attention, such as the billboards at which we might glance sideways as we speed past on a high-way. That is not undercover marketing. Instead, undercover marketing is an inten-tional effort to hide the true marketing element of the interaction. For example, Sony Ericsson Mobile Communications hired 60 actors to pose as tourists in New York City's Empire State Building. The actors were supposed to pretend they were tourists and ask passersby if they would mind taking their pictures. In doing so, the unsuspecting passersby had a chance to see how easy the new Ericsson mobile phone cameras were to operate. The actors praised the phones and said how much they loved them, and the passersby left having had a good experience with the new product, unaware they were just involved in a product test!

With the advent of blogs, stealth marketing has hit the Internet as well. Internet users reading a product review cannot know if the individual posting the review is

stealth or undercover marketing
Marketing campaigns that are based on envi-ronments or activities where the subject is not aware that she or he is the target of a market-ing campaign; those situations where one is subject to directed com-mercial activity without knowledge or consent.

a user, the product's manufacturer, or even a competitor posting a negative review just to sway consumers away from the product. "Buzz marketing," where people are paid to create a "buzz" around a new product by using it or discussing it in ways that create media or other attention, also creates the potential for unspoken conflicts of interest. For an extensive exploration of these marketing techniques and the implications of technology on the ethics involved, see Reading 8-1, "The Friendship of Buzz, Blog and Swag," by Kalynne Hackney Pudner.

Marketing experts consider stealth marketing extraordinarily effective because the consumer's guard is down; she is not questioning the message as she might challenge a traditional advertising campaign. Consumers do not seek out the communicator's vested interest; they see the communication as more personal and often tend to trust the communicator much more than they would trust an advertisement or other marketing material.

These practices would seem unethical on both principle and utilitarian grounds. As a matter of ethical principle, there is a violation of trust in the communication and the intent would appear to be to deceive or manipulate the consumer. The consumer is no longer being treated as an end in itself but instrumentally only as a means to the manufacturer's end. Utilitarian analysis also does not support these types of practices. Any deceptive practice undermines the mutual benefit that should result from market exchanges. Further, when a consumer cannot trust the company's communication, the consumer may also lose faith in the company as a whole and will choose to purchase products and services elsewhere.

Supply Chain Responsibility

OBJECTIVE

In creating a product, promoting it, and bringing it to the market, the marketing function of business involves a wide range of relationships with other commercial entities. Much of the discussion in this chapter has assumed a simple model of a consumer–business relationship. In recent decades, however, the ethical spotlight has focused on the responsibility that a firm has for the activities of these other entities, what we shall refer to as supply chain responsibility. Few businesses have received as much attention in this regard as Nike.

Nike is the world's largest athletic shoe and apparel maker. In 1999, Nike held over 30 percent of the world's market share for athletic footwear, and along with Adidas (15 percent) and Reebok (11 percent) controls more than half of the world market. Nike began business in 1964 as Blue Ribbon Sports, an importer and marketer of low-priced Japanese sport shoes. As sales increased, the company began to design its own line of shoes and subcontract the manufacturing of the shoes to Japanese firms, eventually changing its name to Nike. Nike's website described its business philosophy decades later in the following words: "Our business model in 1964 is essentially the same as our model today: We grow by investing our money in design, development, marketing and sales and then contract with other companies to manufacture our products."

In the late 1990s, as discussed in chapter 6, Nike was subjected to intense international criticism for the working conditions in the factories where its products were manufactured. Critics charged that Nike relied on child labor and sweatshops in producing its shoes. They charged that workers in these factories were paid pennies a day; were subjected to cruel, unhealthy, and inhumane working conditions; were harassed and abused; and were prohibited from any union or collective bargaining activities.

Nike initially seemed to ignore the critics and deflect any criticism by denying responsibility for the behavior of its suppliers. If local manufacturers treated their workers poorly, that was beyond Nike's responsibility. At one point, Nike's vice president for Asia claimed that Nike did not "know the first thing about manufacturing. We are marketers and designers." Nike soon learned that the public was not persuaded by this response.

Ordinarily, we do not hold a person responsible for the actions of someone else; we believe that each person is responsible for her or his own actions. But this is not always the case. There is a legal parallel to the idea that a business should be held responsible for the actions of its suppliers. The doctrine of *respondent superior,* Latin for "let the master answer," holds a principal (e.g., an employer) responsible for the actions of an agent (e.g., an employee) when that agent is acting in the ordinary course of his or her duties to the principal.[8] Thus, in the standard example, an employer can be held liable for damages caused by an accident involving an employee driving the company car on company business.

The justification for doing what might otherwise be considered unfair is that the agent is acting on the principal's behalf, at the principal's direction, and that the principal has direct influence over the agent's actions. Thus, if someone is doing something for you, at your direction, and under your influence, then you must take at least some responsibility for that person's actions. Most of the ethical rationale for business's responsibility for the actions of its suppliers stems from two of these conditions: Suppliers often act at the direction of business, and business often exercises significant influence over the actions of its suppliers.

However, in the multinational apparel and footwear industry, historically the corporate brands accepted responsibility only for their own organizations and specifically did not regard themselves as accountable for the labor abuses of their contractors. This conception changed as multinationals and others became more aware of working conditions in these factories and the lack of legal protections for workers. Today, multinationals customarily accept this responsibility and use their leverage to encourage suppliers to have positive working environments for workers. The new concept of responsibility travels far deeper throughout the entire supply chain system, as is depicted in Figure 8.1.

Each element of what should strike you as a tremendously complicated set of interrelationships is based on the potential to influence or exercise leverage throughout the system. The question, however, relates back to our earlier discussion of responsibility. How far down—or across—the supply chain should responsibility travel? Should a firm like Nike truly be responsible for the entire footwear and apparel system? If not, where would you draw the line as a consumer, or where would you draw the line if you were the corporate responsibility vice president for Nike? What response will most effectively protect the rights of those involved while creating the most appropriate incentives to achieve profitable, ethical results? In today's increasingly complicated, globalized multinational systems, stakeholders have yet to resolve this challenging dilemma.

FIGURE 8.1
Multiple Lines of Responsibility to Diverse Stakeholders

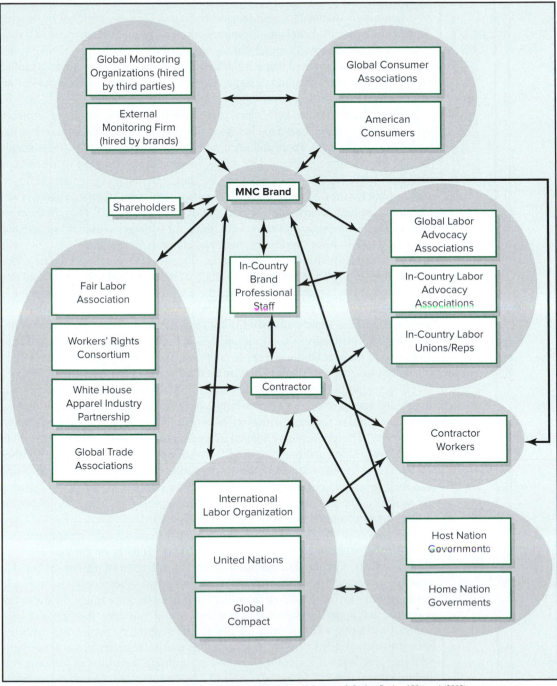

Source: D. Arnold and L. Hartman, "Moral Imagination and the Future of Sweatshops," *Business & Society Review* 108, no. 4 (2003).

In the United States, the Federal Trade Commission (FTC) has the primary responsibility for regulating sales and advertisements. Traditionally, the FTC has relied on two major criteria in establishing standards: deception and unfairness. The two criteria are related in that a marketing technique that deceives a consumer has, at the same time, proven unfair to competitors who now have to compete for that consumer with an undeserved disadvantage. With the advent of digital marketing techniques, the FTC is working, some would say struggling, to establish standards that can keep pace with the rapidly changing environment.

In 2009, the FTC issued a report that cited four basic principles to govern online marketing. Three of the four clearly fit the ethical model traditionally employed. The FTC asserted the importance of "transparency and consumer control," and required "affirmative consent" for any changes in a company's privacy policy and for the use of sensitive personal information (e.g., medical records, financial information) collected about consumers. These standards plainly derive from the ethical standards of autonomy as free and informed consent. The fourth standard recognized the changing role of collecting consumer information and asserted that businesses had a responsibility to "reasonable security" for data collected about consumers.

As if to acknowledge the fast pace of change in digital marketing, only three years later the FTC issued a new report that highlighted five goals for regulating digital marketing. The FTC recommended the development of more effective "Do Not Track" mechanisms to allow consumers to easily opt-out of online tracking. It also emphasized the need to include the rapidly expanding mobile technologies under the same regulatory umbrella as computer technologies. Third, it argued for inclusion of third-party "data brokers" in the regulatory scheme and called on these companies to make their operations more transparent to consumers. Fourth, the FTC let it be known that ISPs will face increased government attention in the effort to protect consumer privacy. Fifth, perhaps in recognition that government regulation was lagging behind this rapidly evolving technology, the FTC encouraged all of the relevant stakeholders to "develop industry-specific codes of conduct" and acknowledged that these codes would likely provide the basis for future governmental regulation.

- How big a role do you think that governmental regulation should play in digital marketing?
- Are there any laws or regulations that you would like to see applied to digital marketing?
- Do you think that voluntary self-regulation in the form of industry codes of conduct can effectively protect consumers from unethical practices?
- Would you favor a "Do Not Track" option that tracks unless a consumer opts-out, or an alternative that would require companies to first obtain positive permission before tracking?

Questions, Projects, and Exercises

1. Are some products too dangerous to be marketed in any circumstance? What regulations, if any, would you place on marketing cigarettes? Handguns? Prescription drugs?

2. Conduct a classroom debate on the well-known McDonald's spilt coffee case. Conduct an Internet search for the case *Liebeck v. McDonald's* to find both legal and journalistic comments on the case. One-third of the class should play the role of Mrs. Liebeck's attorneys, one-third the role of McDonald's attorneys, and one-third the role of the judge and jury.

3. Research the case *Pelman v. McDonald's* in which it was alleged that McDonald's was partially responsible for the health problems associated with the obesity of children who eat McDonald's fast food. Should McDonald's and other fast-food restaurants be judged negligent for selling dangerous products, failing to warn consumers of the dangers of a high-fat diet, and using deceptive advertising?

4. The Federal Trade Commission regulates advertising on the basis of two criteria: deception and unfairness. How can an ad be unfair? Can you think of examples of an unfair ad? Who gets hurt by deceptive advertising?

5. Collect several sample prescription drug ads from magazines, newspapers, and television. On the basis of location of the ad, what do you think is the intended target audience? Are the ads in any way misleading? Are the required side-effect warnings deceptive in any way? Do you believe that health care professionals provide adequate screening to ensure that prescription drugs are not misused?

6. Many salespeople are compensated predominantly on a commission basis. In other words, though the salesperson receives a small base hourly rate, most of her or his compensation derives from a percentage of the price of items sold. Because the salesperson makes money only if you buy something and he or she makes more money if you spend more money, do you ever trust a salesperson's opinion? What would make you more likely to trust a commission-based salesperson, or less likely? Is there anything a commissioned salesperson could do to get you to trust her or him? Best Buy, the consumer electronics store, communicates to consumers that it does *not* pay its salespeople on the basis of commissions in order to encourage objectivity. Are you more likely to go to Best Buy as a result?

Key Terms

After reading this chapter, you should have a clear understanding of the following key terms. For a complete definition, please see the Glossary.

caveat emptor approach, *p. 385*	implied warranty of merchantability, *p. 385*	stealth or undercover marketing, *p. 401*
"Four Ps" of marketing, *p. 379*	marketing, *p. 378*	strict liability, *p. 387*
	negligence, *p. 386*	

Endnotes

1. The Levitt quote is taken from Theodore Levitt, "Marketing and the Corporate Purpose: The Purpose Is to Create and Keep a Customer," a speech delivered at New York University, March 2, 1977, available from Vital Speeches of the Day. Similar claims can be found in Theodore Levitt, "Marketing and the Corporate Purpose," chapter 1 of *The Marketing Imagination* (New York: Free Press, 1983), pp. 5 and 7.

2. The American Marketing Association definition is taken from its website: www.marketingpower.com/ (accessed April 17, 2010).

3. An informal Internet search found more than a hundred companies advertising with this slogan. They ranged from real estate companies to antique dealers, and from long-distance phone providers to water filtration systems dealers. Presumably those who disagree do not advertise that fact.

4. See, for example, the PBS video *Affluenza,* produced by KCTS/Seattle and Oregon Public Broadcasting. See also Juliet Shor, "Why Do We Consume So Always?," the Clemens Lecture at St. John's University, in *Contemporary Issues in Business Ethics,* Joseph DesJardins and John McCall, eds. (Belmont, CA: Wadsworth, 2005); Jim Pooler, *Why We Shop: Emotional Rewards and Retail Strategies* (Westport, CT: Praeger, 2003).

5. "European Economic Community Adopted the Product Liability Directive," 85/374/EEC, 1985.

6. References have been removed but are available from the authors.

7. McCann-Erickson U.S. Advertising Volume Reports and Bob Coen's Insider's Report for December 2005, www.mccann.com/news/pdfs/insiders05.pdf (accessed June 6, 2006).

8. This parallel is explained in Michael Santoro, *Profits and Principles: Global Capitalism and Human Rights in China* (Ithaca, NY: Cornell University Press, 2000), p. 161, and is cited as well by Denis Arnold and Norman Bowie, "Sweatshops and Respects for Persons," *Business Ethics Quarterly* 13, no. 2 (2003), pp. 221–242

Readings

Reading **8-1**

The Friendship of Buzz, Blog and Swag

Kalynne Hackney Pudner

Word-of-mouth (WOM) is arguably the biggest trend in advertising since the television commercial. This is not because it is a novel form of disseminating product information (it is rather the oldest), but because the Internet has magnified its reach beyond the most optimistic marketer's imaginings. Where WOM was once restricted by the logistics of proximity and cost, the Internet enables "word explosion," the simultaneous, potentially global transmission of a single message to dozens, hundreds, or even thousands of other Internet users through e-mail, postings, or links; search engines multiply the effect exponentially.[1] Unsurprisingly, the marketing industry is eager to harness this explosive power.

What, precisely, is WOM? The Word of Mouth Marketing Association (WOMMA), the self-appointed industry standard and watchdog, defines it as "the act of consumers providing information to other consumers"; word-of-mouth marketing, then, consists of "giving people a reason to talk about your products and services, and making it easier for that conversation to take place."[2] Fundamentally, WOM is a marketing strategy that utilizes pre-existing relationships between someone who will advocate the marketer's product (the "advocate") and the marketer's targeted consumers (the "target").

Authentic WOM unhitches the marketing message from control of the marketer, which allows the message to reach targets who may have thrown up a barrier between themselves and the marketer (what one commentator calls a "no-marketing zone"), but which also removes the message from the marketer's direct control.[3] It might be expected that this combination of features places the targeted consumer in a position of vulnerability, particularly toward fraud or deception. For this reason, WOMMA has undertaken to set and informally enforce ethical standards for the practice of WOM. While it also addresses the engagement of minors and respect for venue rules, WOMMA's ethics initiative focuses on transparency, or what it calls "Honesty ROI." It urges WOM marketers and their advocates to be honest and open regarding their *Relationship;* it urges advocates to express only honest and open *Opinions;* and it urges advocates to be honest and open in disclosing their *Identity.*

The intuitive appeal of disclosure is understandable. The ethical red flags were flying high when "Wal-Marting Across America" was exposed as the fake blog ("flog") of a professional journalist couple under paid contract by Edelman, Wal-Mart's public relations firm. Even worse, a second blog called "Paid Critics," which bashed public officials and others who oppose Wal-Mart's expansion and operating practices, was exposed as a flog authored by two full-time Edelman employees.[4] The original flog's web address, www.forwalmart.com, now bears the Wal-Mart logo and a message reading, "Please check back soon for a new site brought to you by Wal-Mart. For now, please visit Wal-Mart Facts." WOMMA's Code of Conduct would have required the Wal-Mart tour couple to fully disclose their relationship with Edelman, and Edelman's relationship with Wal-Mart, as well as the "Paid Critics" blog authors' identity as Edelman employees. Here, transparency would have benefited readers, the WOM industry and—in light of the scathingly negative publicity backlash—Wal-Mart and Edelman.

WOMMA's disclosure requirement extends beyond blogging and flogging to other forms of word-of-mouth promotion. Think of traditional, person-to-person WOM. The Edelman employees would be required to identify themselves as such before recommending the ten-cent spiral notebooks at Wal-Mart's Back to School extravaganza. This is intuitively odd. Not only is it irrelevant, but it could be off-putting, a superfluous and affected authority claim.

The intuitive oddness may be ascribed to the presupposition that the target either is already aware of the advocate's connection to the marketer, or has reason to trust the advocate's assessment independently of any such connection. I think this is an important observation. But it isn't sufficient to dispel the intuition of awkwardness, because the disclosure would be similarly awkward where there is no such presupposition about the advocate-target relationship. Ditto for the casual acquaintance who urges others to try this tea or that hand cream. To render already-presumed motivation explicit is to render it dubious, it seems, and thereby less effective WOM.

What these considerations suggest is that transparency is not panacea to the ethical tensions of WOM, but rather serves a particular function that varies in importance relative to the particular context of the practice. I would argue that transparency is a subsidiary, and potentially deflecting, aspect of the real crux of the ethical issue: the pre-existing relationship on which WOM seeks to capitalize. If I am correct, then WOMMA's calls for advocate transparency are well-intentioned but misdirected. The relationship that must be made transparent to the target is not that between the advocate and the marketer, but between the advocate and him/ herself, the target.

This hypothesis can be supported by comparing the pre-existing relationships utilized by three different forms of WOM: buzz, blog and swag.

Buzz

Departing slightly from WOMMA's usage, the term "buzz" refers here to traditional word-of-mouth communication between particular individuals, regardless of catalyst (advertising, product experience, marketer direction), and regardless of medium (face-to-face, telephone, print or electronic). The essential feature of buzz is that the pre-existing relationship between advocate and target is determinate, between particular and identified individuals.

True buzz (as opposed to the spontaneous product referral it seeks to imitate) is frequently accompanied by product seeding, defined by WOMMA as "placing the right product into the right hands at the right time, providing information or samples to influential individuals." Advocates are given free samples of the marketer's product, to use personally and sometimes to distribute to target consumers as well. BzzAgent (www.bzzagent.com), which bills itself as the leading WOM media network, directs its advocates, or "agents," to disclose to targets that they are receiving free product in exchange for their advocacy.

Note that the very transparency WOMMA thinks will enhance the advocate's credibility actually seems to damage it. The act of disclosure redirects the target's attention from the product, and to the advocacy message itself. Does my friend feel an implicit obligation, grounded on reciprocity or gratitude, to promote this product insincerely? Of course, such promotion would be unethical. But disclosing the receipt of free product doesn't fix the problem.

In addition to raising suspicion of insincerity, buzz transparency raises that of hyperbole; research has established that self-generated advertisements show a marked tendency to exaggerate the positive experience of product use, and that this tendency is recognized and severely discounted by its audience.[5] Even if the disclosure itself is negative ("I'm not getting anything for this"), the very fact that the advocate feels the disclosure is necessary casts aspersion on the reliability of the testimony. Instead, the disclosure raises the question whether product mention is part of an advertising strategy unless explicitly stated otherwise. Nor do the questions stop with product-oriented messages; the target may be led to wonder about the sincerity and motivation of other communication by the advocate, and indeed, about the basis of their relationship itself.

Swag

I want to jump now to the opposite end of the relational spectrum, to "swag." Swag refers in its central cases to free product and other items given by marketers to journalists, editors and public personalities, in the hope that they may be induced to use their regular media platforms to disseminate a positive product message. In some cases, swag is of considerable monetary value, even extravagant.[6] The obvious concern is that the media message not appear to be "purchased," and thus presumably biased. Still, there is a practical argument in favor of swag: how are products supposed to be reviewed unless the reviewer is given no-cost access to the product?[7]

Swag distribution is not limited to product seeding, however, and marketers have strong incentive to pursue positive media coverage by whatever means they can devise. It's almost an advertising truism that negative news can do more harm than the most expensive, expansive advertising campaign can do good. In fact, the downward pull of negative media coverage is so pronounced that subsequent advertising has been shown to be wasted, even if it is an explicit counter to the coverage.[8] Conversely, positive publicity followed by a surge of traditional advertising elicits a stronger, more positive response by consumers than either the publicity or the advertising alone.[9] Because consumers discount positive publicity when it is known to be paid advertising, marketers covet what politicians term "earned media," and swag has proven itself a viable option for generating it, Of course, the value of earned media is imparted by the perception of unbiased, objective, un-self-interested reporting, and this perception is precisely what is compromised when the media is motivated by a sense of obligation to repay the benefit of swag received, or by the hope of future swag. So while a media review of the Kindle is valuable to consumers only if the writer has personal experience with a Kindle, it is considerably less valuable if the writer also has personal experience of, say, the Paris Air Show at Amazon's expense.

In swag WOM, then, advocate transparency does serve the target, and by reinforcing the presumption of unbiased reporting, it serves the marketer as well. Even if stating the obvious ("I was given a free cup of shaved ice to taste before writing this review"), the disclosure does not cloud the advocate-target relationship in the same way it does in buzz. Why? I would suggest this is because transparency is a natural feature of the relationship itself. As in the case of buzz, swag utilizes a pre-existing relationship between the advocate and the target; but unlike buzz, this relationship is non-particular, generally unidentified, and often invisible. Unlike buzz, the advocate-target relationship in swag consists essentially of one-way dissemination of messages to an indeterminate audience; also unlike buzz, these messages are presumed to be impartial. The target's assumption that the advocate's messages are unbiased, objective, and un-self-interested is necessary for the relationship to work. Transparency is a condition of this assumption.

Blog

Occupying a vast, variegated and ever-evolving relational middle ground between buzz and swag is "blog," in which a particular individual or group of individuals (named or pseudonymous) uses the Internet to disseminate messages to a non-particular, generally unidentified and qualifiedly invisible audience that ordinarily has feedback capability. Although blogs have been around since the mid-90s, they have burgeoned in popularity primarily since 2005, due in large part to the free, user-friendly sites designed to host them. The Pew Internet and American Life Project reports that as of 2006, eight percent of Internet users, approximately 12 million American adults, kept a blog; thirty-nine percent, or 57 million, read them regularly.[10] Although the statistics will certainly have grown further by the time this paper is published, it is projected that the ratio of blog consumption to production will remain constant in the vicinity of 80/20.[11] Marketers who wish to utilize the blogger-audience relationship for WOM are advised to identify bloggers who are passionate about their product or product type, and therefore likely to talk about the product in strong and positive terms, rather than to aim for broader but shallower message dissemination.[12]

One of the more extensive studies on blog activity and the people who engage in it finds that blogs "may function as a personal diary, a daily pulpit, a collaborative space, a political soapbox, a collection of links, or a set of memos to the world."[13] It follows from this range of purpose that the character of blog messages and blogger-audience relationship is anything but standard, and the implications of this variation for blog WOM are enormous. But two generalizations about blogger-audience relationships can be made: first, they are usually derived from contiguous blogger-audience relationships; and second, they are independently defined by the audience.

The overwhelming volume of blog content on the World Wide Web tends to limit the reader's exposure to blog content, as paradoxical as this may sound. The few sites that offer thematically-grouped lists of blogs can be cumbersome as well as vague, and the prospect of browsing for new, relevant and engaging blogs can be daunting.[14] Thus most blog visits are generated by links from other websites, especially other blogs. Blogrolls and linked comment sections act as letters of introduction from one blog to another, creating jaggedly overlapping virtual communities of bloggers and their regular, shared readers. The virtual community phenomenon can also be overtly created, as when a blogger links to another blog with explicit instructions to "go here"; and commentators who do so ordinarily credit the referring blog in their feedback.

As I have argued elsewhere, the relationship between blogger and audience, in the absence of further relationship unmediated by electronic communication, is indeterminate, leaving the audience to interpret it as she chooses in order to contextualize both incoming and outgoing messages.[15] This may tip the blogger-audience relationship toward buzz, as it seems to do in the case of "mommy bloggers," or it may tip it toward swag, as in (for example) the blogs of reporter Jeff Jarvis or the Chronicle of Higher Education.[16] Relationship interpretation online is also subject to radical revision, from personal to impersonal, or vice versa.[17]

Just as advocate-target relationships vary across the blog universe, so does the function of advocate transparency. The target is imaginatively constructing the advocate's personality by filling in gaps between advocate disclosures (both related and unrelated to the marketer and its product), and then crafting a relationship with this constructed personality; therefore, the meaning and importance of the transparent information also will be determined solely by the target. Where the advocate-target relationship in blog may be buzz-like, transparency is likely to be disruptive; where swag-like, it is likely to be an asset. But since the relationship is interpreted, frequently revised, and sometimes unilaterally discontinued by the target, transparency's likely effect is ultimately unpredictable.

The Ethics of Transparency

What these comparisons suggest is that the ethical importance of transparency is not intrinsic to WOM as a marketing strategy, but to the relationships that WOM constitutionally employs. As these vary according to WOM type, so does the importance of transparency.

The most intuitively unethical cases of WOM are those in which the target is deliberately and actively deceived, as with the Wal-Mart flogs.

Passive deception ("don't ask, don't tell") is marginally better, but still problematic. And the ethical problem is a straightforward one: deception undermines the autonomy of the moral agent at whom it is directed. Intentionally deceptive WOM, whether active or passive, leaves the target with incomplete or erroneous information on which to base his choice; he is therefore not in a position to make his purchase decision autonomously. Transparency, then, protects target autonomy: in Kantian terms, it helps prevent the advocate from using the target as a mere means instead of as an end-in-himself.

All marketing, and indeed much of life, involves using other persons as means: employees are means to profit for owners, teachers are means to learning for students, professional athletes are means to the vicarious thrills of victory and agonies of defeat for inactive spectators. We say that these relationships between employees and owners, teachers and students, athletes and couch potatoes have instrumental value. Yet they are not inherently unethical, as long as each party respects the autonomy of the other, instead of using her as a mere, subhuman, non-autonomous means.

If transparency functions as a kind of ethical insurance policy for the target's autonomy, then its value for swag is obvious. Of all the WOM relationships, swag is the most impersonal and carries the greatest potential for both advocate and target to use each other as mere means. But it is also carries the least potential for alternative relational reward, so the target values his ability to make autonomous decisions about the advocate's message above any personal connection with the advocate. The smart advocate values the target's autonomy as well: the target can just as easily choose not to receive the advocate's publicly disseminated messages, and when a media personality's audience wanes, so does the media personality.

Buzz is very different. The advocate-target relationship is personal, particular and identified, and as such, mitigates against using each other as mere means. Autonomy is generally respected as an integral component of the valued other's personality, and to adopt transparency as an ethical insurance policy introduces the question of its need where it may rightfully be assumed no need exists. Moreover, the relationship itself may require that none exists, and to insert it would change the character of the relationship. What kind of relationship is this, where transparency as a guarantee of autonomy introduces a conceptual third wheel? In a word, friendship.

Friendship and Self-Disclosure

Friendship is a difficult concept to pin down, prompting one contemporary author to recommend abandoning the attempt in favor of a post-modernist "family resemblance" approach. Still, philosophical tradition from Aristotle to Kant and beyond concurs on certain features, notably esteem, well-wishing, and mutuality or reciprocity.[18] These features themselves presume identified particularity: esteem is esteem for someone in particular, mutuality is between particular persons. Note the neat correspondence with our observations of buzz, blog and swag; central cases of buzz occur between friends, and blog relationships that are interpreted by the audience as virtual friendships lend themselves to buzz strategies, while those that are interpreted as public media lend themselves to swag strategies.

Can the necessarily instrumental relationships of WOM be considered friendships in the philosophical sense? Yes, as long as the instrumentality is subordinate to, and constrained by, the necessary features of, friendship properly understood. The philosophical tradition makes a definite (if not altogether clear) distinction between what Neera Badhwar calls "instrumental friendships" and "end friendships," but both types qualify as friendship. That is, they lie within the parameters of esteem, well-wishing and mutuality. On Badhwar's account, instrumental as well as end friendship esteems (i.e., values) the friend as a particular individual, wishes the friend well for his own particular sake, and enjoys the reciprocation of that particular individual; it is "instrumental" only in the sense that it is "based on features that are in some sense *tangential* or *accidental* to the friend

and is motivated primarily by each friend's independently defined goals."[19] In an "end friendship," by contrast, it is a connection with the other's own "self" (with all the history, plans, projects, virtues, etc. that this entails) that is one's end.

J. M. Cooper's well-known reading of Aristotle's classification of pleasure-friendship, utility-friendship and virtue-friendship corroborates this view. The charge that friendship can consist of mutual use for pleasure or other self-seeking advantage misconstrues Aristotle, according to Cooper; pleasure, utility and virtue distinguish friendships not by function, but rather by the character and original source of the relationship's bond.[20] It is the friendship itself, and not the friend, that provides the occasion for pleasure, utility or virtue. The friend is always valued and wished well for his own sake, and never as a mere means. "[I]f one is someone's friend one wants that person to prosper, achieve his goals, be happy, and so on, in the same sort of way in which he wishes these things for himself, whatever else one may want as well, and whatever explains one's having this desire."[21]

Applying this analysis to the pre-existing personal relationship of buzz, for example, it would be consistent with morally sound friendship for the advocate to want to benefit herself by connecting her friend with a marketer's product (whatever form this benefit might take) and at the same time want her friend to benefit from the product. Her relationship with the marketer is a means of benefiting her friend at the same time as it is a means of benefiting herself. But both benefits are subordinate to, and constrained by, the necessary features of the friendship between herself and the target, even if this subordination and constraint is not made explicit. Indeed, to make the subordinate and constrained activity explicit is to draw it larger than the relationship to which it is subordinate and by which it is constrained.

We might say that friendship, like politics and sausage-making, is best experienced without poking about behind the scenes. As Christine Korsgaard notes of Aristotle, friendship requires trust in the goodness of the other; but it need not require full transparency of the other's state of mind.[22] Kant, whose conception of friendship is in many ways parallel to Aristotle's, also acknowledges that "men are not transparent to each other," that not every end, reason or intention of one friend can or need be revealed to the other.[23]

Kant concurs with Aristotle, also, that authentic friendship can have varied bases, such as need, taste, or moral attitude.[24] The duties of friendship are complementary love and respect, where love is a practical decision instead of an emotional response (since the emotions, not being subject to the will, are outside the reach of Kant's concept of morality and therefore duty). The positive demands of love, to pursue the friend's good, and negative demands of respect, to refrain from acting in such a way that compromises the friend's autonomy, act in tension of simultaneous attraction and repulsion, keeping persons at the morally appropriate distance.[25]

Kant explicitly addresses transparency in the context of friendship, though perhaps not consistently. In the *Lectures on Ethics,* Kant cautions against fully revealing oneself to a friend, even a moral friend of complete communion, for fear that the friend—who is, after all, only human and subject to changing attitudes—may someday become an enemy. In his later *Metaphysical Principles of Virtue,* he extols the love and trust of moral friendship which allay this fear, thus enabling "complete communion."[26] The very core of this highest form of friendship seems to consist in the mutual confidence of two persons to disclose their most secret thoughts—what Kant calls "free intercourse of mind with mind." But to remain free, mental intercourse must submit to the demands of respect for autonomy, and full revelation of one's thoughts, attitudes, etc. could contravene this respect. In this case, too, friendship itself sets the boundaries of self-disclosure.

Conclusion

The ethical rough edges that transparency is intended to smooth are more clearly visible through the lens of friendship. Whether the advocate's relationship with the marketer ought to be disclosed to the target depends on the advocate's relationship with the target. Transparency may be either a help or a hindrance to the advocate's pre-existing relationship with the target. If the advocate-target relationship is instrumentally valuable to the advocate's WOM intentions, rather than the WOM intentions being merely incidental to the relationship—then transparency will help the target to recognize that instrumentality. Instrumentally valuable relationships, remember, do not necessarily entail one party treating the other as a mere means; they entail an intention to use the relationship itself as a means. This is not necessarily bad. A given relationship may well be a means—to profit, to free product, to social advancement; but also to spiritual fulfilment, to a richer appreciation of art, to a heightened sensitivity to the plight of the poor. It is only when the other party is under the illusion that the relationship is intrinsically valuable, or instrumental to a different sort of end, that the ethical red flags are unfurled. Even then, the illusion may not be anyone's ethical fault so much as a simple misunderstanding.

A "disconnect" between friends in the roles of advocate and target may or may not involve the marketer/advocate relationship. When it does, advocate transparency will improve the situation; when not, not. The dialectic of mutual response in friendship mitigates against this kind of disconnect, as an ongoing series of adjustments maintains equilibrium between advocate and target and their respective perceptions of the relationship. In its highest form, friendship will entail a shared understanding of ends and reasons, of intellectual and moral principles. Not every friendship need adopt this highest form as its goal, but Kant's complementary constraints of love and respect urge every friendship toward a mutual understanding of the friendship itself.

At the other end of the spectrum, the one-way, one-size-fits-all media transmission of swag is ordinarily recognized as such by both parties, and while advocate transparency can be valuable, it is very often unnecessary. The danger of mismatched perception is greatest in blog, where the relationship between blogger and reader is inherently indeterminate and requires reader construction.

In summary, there is no doubt that WOM is appropriately subjected to ethical analysis and can benefit from clearly articulated ethical standards. WOMMA's efforts in this regard are laudable. But they are also somewhat off-target. The ethics of utilizing pre-existing relationships in marketing strategy must first direct attention to the pre-existing relationships themselves, and examine the place of marketing activities within their context.

Source: WOMMA.org, reprinted with permission of WOMMA.org.

Endnotes

1. Andrea Wojnicki, "Word-of-Mouth and Word-of-Web: Talking About Products, Talking About Me," *Advances in Consumer Research* 33 (2006): 575.

2. http://www.womma.org/wom101/.

3. Mike Hofman, "Lies, Damn Lies and Word of Mouth," in *Business Ethics Annual Edition 07/08,* edited by John Richardson (Dubuque: McGraw-Hill, 2008), 162–165.

4. CNNMoney.com, "PR FirmAdmits It's Behind WalMart Blogs," http://money.cnn.com/2006/10/20/news/companies/walmart_blogs/index.htm. See also Angelo Fernando, "Transparency under Attack," *Communication World* 24 (2007): 9–11.

5. Terence Shimp, Stacy Wood, and Laura Smarandescu, "Self-Generated Advertisements: Testimonials and the Perils of Consumer Exaggeration," *Journal of Advertising Research* 47 (2007): 459f.

6. David Weddle, "Swagland" (*Business Ethics Annual Edition 07/08.* 178–183).

7. Joshua Trupin, "Bring On the Swag," *MSDN Magazine,* March 2007, http://msdn2.microsoft.com/en-us/magazine/cc163458.aspx.

8. "Thunder-stealing," proactive admission of the negative news item and announcement of a planned remedy, is the exception to this rule.

May-May Meijer and Jan Kleinnijenhuis, "News and Advertisements: How Negative News May Reverse Advertising Effects," *Journal of Advertising Research* 47 (December, 2007): 516.

9. Marsha Loda and Barbara Carrick Coleman, "Sequence Matters: A More Effective Way to Use Advertising and Publicity," *Journal of Advertising Research* 45 (December, 2005): 370.

10. Amanda Lenhart and Susannah Fox, "Bloggers: A Portrait of the Internet's New Storytellers," *Report of the Pew Internet and American Life Project* (Washington: Pew Foundation), 7/19/2006, http://www.pewinternet.org/pdfs/PIP%20Bloggers%20Report%20July%2019%202006.pdf.

11. See also Clay Shirky, *Here Comes Everybody* (New York: Penguin, 2008).

12. Cate Riegner, "Word of Mouth on the Web: The Impact of Web 2.0 on Consumer Purchase Decisions," *Journal of Advertising Research* 47 (December, 2007): 447.

13. Chun-Yao Kuang et al., "'Bloggers' Motivations and Behaviors: A Model," *Journal of Advertising Research* 47 (December, 2007): 473.

14. One site that has addressed the problem of sifting through overwhelming amounts of content in search of worthwhile blogs is Stumble-Upon (www.stumbleupon.com), which allows users to identify categories of interest, under which the site has bookmarked blogs and other pages recommended by users with similar interests.

15. "MySpace Friends and the Kingdom of Ends," *Philosophy of Education Society Yearbook 2007:* 273–281. I also find fascinating the phenomenon whereby members of the same blog community are motivated to meet in person, defining and concretizing their relationships (see for example coverage of "BlogHer 2008," a conference of mommy bloggers held in San Francisco in July of that year, at http://www.blogher.com/blogher_conference/conf/2/general/1).

16. Jeff Jarvis' blog is found at http://www.buzzmachine.com/ (note the "disclosures"

link, following "about me"); the CHE blog is at http://chronicle.com/news/. The tone of the comments on these blogs is sharply different than those on either of Meehan's.

17. See also Anna Lund Jepson, "Information Search in Virtual Communities: Is It Replacing Use of Off-Line Communication?" *Journal of Marketing Communication* 12 (2006): 248.

18. A. Sandra Lynch, *Philosophy and Friendship* (Edinburgh: Edinburgh University Press, 2005), 21.

19. Neera Badhwar, "Friendship: A Philosophical Reader" (Ithaca: Cornell University Press, 1993), 3. Emphasis in original.

20. John Cooper, "Aristotle on the Forms of Friendship," *Review of Metaphysics* 30 (1977): 633.

21. "Aristotle on the Forms of Friendship" 622 (fn 7); 626f.

22. Christine Korsgaard, *Creating the Kingdom of Ends* (Cambridge: Cambridge University Press, 1996), 190.

23. "Lectures on Ethics," quoted in Pakaluk, 216.

24. Immanuel Kant, "Lectures on Ethics," in Michael Pakaluk, *Other Selves: Philosophers on Friendship* (Indianapolis: Hackett Publishing, 1991), 214. Here, Kant describes friendship of taste as "pseudo-friendship."

25. See H. J. Paton, "Kant on Friendship," in Badhwar, 139–141.

26. Andrea Veltman, "Aristotle and Kant on Self-Disclosure in Friendship," *Journal of Value Inquiry* 38 (2004), 231f.

Note: References were removed for publication here, but are available on the book website at connect.mheducation.com.

Reading 8-2

First Analysis of Online Food Advertising Targeting Children

The Kaiser Family Foundation

Food company websites feature advergames, viral marketing, TV ads, and incentives for product purchases.

Washington, D.C.—Concerned about the high rates of childhood obesity in the U.S., policymakers in Congress, the Federal Trade Commission, and agencies such as the Institute of Medicine have explored a variety of potential contributing factors, including the marketing and advertising of food products to children. One area where policymakers have expressed interest, but have also noted a lack of publicly available data, is in the realm of online food marketing to children. In order to help fill this gap, the Kaiser Family Foundation today released the first comprehensive analysis of the nature and scope of online food advertising to children, to help

inform the decision making process for policymakers, advocates, and industry.

The report, *It's Child's Play: Advergaming and the Online Marketing of Food to Children,* found that more than eight out of ten (85%) of the top food brands that target children through TV advertising also use branded websites to market to children online. Unlike traditional TV advertising, these corporate-sponsored websites offer extensive opportunities for visitors to spend an unlimited amount of time interacting with specific food brands in more personal and detailed ways. For instance, the study documents the broad use of "advergames" (online games in which a company's product or brand characters are featured, found on 73% of the websites) and viral marketing (encouraging children to contact their peers about a specific product or brand, found on 64% of sites). In addition, a variety of other advertising and marketing tactics are employed on these sites, including sweepstakes and promotions (65%), memberships (25%), on-demand access to TV ads (53%), and incentives for product purchase (38%).

"Online advertising's reach isn't as broad as that of television, but it's much deeper," said Vicky Rideout, vice president and director of Kaiser's Program for the Study of Entertainment Media and Health, who oversaw the research. "Without good information about what this new world of advertising really looks like, there can't be effective oversight or policymaking, whether by the industry or by government," she noted. The advertising industry has announced that it is developing more detailed voluntary guidelines for online marketing to children, expected to be released shortly.

The study included detailed analysis of 77 websites, including more than 4,000 unique web pages. Based on data from Nielsen NetRatings, these sites received more than 12.2 million visits from children ages 2–11 in the 2nd quarter of 2005.

About three-quarters (73%) of the websites in the study included advergames, ranging from one to more than 60 games per site. In total, the sites in the study contained 546 games featuring one or more food brands, such as the Chips Ahoy Soccer Shootout, Chuck E. Cheese's Tic Tac Toe, the M&M's Trivia Game, and the Pop-Tart Slalom. For example, on Kellogg's FunKtown children can "race against time while collecting delicious Kellogg's cereal," and at the Lucky Charms site they can play Lucky's Magic Adventure and "learn the powers of all eight charms" found in Lucky Charms cereal. To encourage additional time spent at the website, many of the games promote repeat playing (71%), offer multiple levels of play (45%), or suggest other games the visitor might enjoy (22%).

Almost two-thirds (64%) of sites in the study use viral marketing, in which children are encouraged to send e-mails to their friends about a product, or invite them to visit the company's website. For example, at juicyfruit.com users were encouraged

to "Send a friend this fruitylicious site!" and told that if they "send this site to 5 friends" they would get a code that could then be used to access additional features on the site. Other sites encourage young users to invite friends to help them "redecorate" their online "rooms," challenge them to play an advergame on the site, or send them an "e-card" featuring the company's brand or spokes characters. For example, on Keebler's Hollow Tree website, children are invited to send a friend some "Elfin Magic" in a birthday or seasonal greeting.

The report was released today at a forum in Washington, D.C., that featured food industry leaders, government health officials, and consumer advocates. The study was conducted for Kaiser by Elizabeth Moore, associate professor of marketing at the University of Notre Dame. A web cast of the session is available.

The following are additional key findings from the survey:

Television Advertising Online

- Half (53%) of all sites in the study have television commercials available for viewing. On Kellogg's FunKtown site, children can earn stamps by viewing commercials in the "theater." On the Lucky Charms and Frootloops sites, serialized "webisodes" unveil animated stories featuring brand characters and products. On Skittles.com, users are told they can watch the ads "over and over right now" instead of having to wait for them to appear on TV.

Nutrition Information

- Half of sites (51%) included nutritional information such as that found on a product label, and 44% included some type of nutritional claim, such as "good source of vitamins and minerals."

- Twenty-seven percent of all sites have information about eating a healthy diet, such as the number of servings of fruits and vegetables that should be eaten daily. For example, the Kellogg's site nutritioncamp.com included such features as "nuts about nutrition" and "decipher the secrets of the Food Pyramid."

Incentive for Product Purchases

- Almost four in ten sites (38%) have incentives for the user to purchase food so they can collect brand points or stamps that they can then exchange for premiums (such as gaining access to new games or purchasing brand-related clothing). For example, children are encouraged to purchase specially-marked packages of Bubble Tape gum and then enter the codes online to get free Nintendo game tips.

Memberships, Registration, and Marketing Research

- One in four (25%) sites offer a "membership" opportunity for children age 12 or younger. Children who sign up on websites may be proactively informed about new brands, exclusive offers, and new television commercials available for viewing. Thirteen percent require parental permission, while 12% do not.

- Thirteen percent of sites include polls or quizzes, some of which were used to ask visitors their opinions on products or brand-related items. For example, on cuatmcdonalds.com, visitors are asked to vote for "the dollar menu item you crave the most" and for "your favorite McDonald's IM icon character."

Extending the Online Experience Offline

- Three out of four (76%) websites studied offered at least one "extra" brand-related option for children, such as screensavers or wallpaper for a child's computer, printable coloring pages, branded CD covers, or brand logos or characters that can "live" on the child's computer desktop.

Educational Information

- Thirty-five percent of sites offer some type of educational content, ranging from historical facts about dinosaurs to astronomy, sports or geography.

- A third (33%) of sites include what the study has dubbed "advercation," a combination of advertising and education, such as using a brand character to present educational topics, or covering topics such as the history of how chocolate is made on hersheys.com.

Web Site Protections for Children

- Almost all (97%) of the sites in the study provided some information explicitly labeled for parents, such as what type of information is to be collected from children on the site (93%), legal disclaimers (88%), a "contact us" link (87%), statements about the use of "cookies" (81%), and statements of compliance with the Children's Online Privacy Protection Act (COPPA) (74%), or adherence to Children's Advertising Review Unit's (CARU) guidelines (46%).

- On all websites where personal data was requested (beyond a first name, screen name or e-mail address for one-time use), mechanisms were in place to ensure that children age 12 and under did not submit any information without parental permission.

- Although CARU's guidelines state that "advertising content should be clearly identified as such" on product-driven websites, only 18% of the websites studied included any kind of "ad break" or other notice to children that the content on the site included advertising.

Sweepstakes & Promotions

- Two-thirds (65%) of all brands in the study have promotions in which children may participate in some way. They include sweepstakes (such as the chance to win a Nintendo Game

Cube system on bubbletape.com or a trip to Nickelodeon studios on pfgoldfish.com), or the chance to get free merchandise related to the food product.

Methods

The study was designed by staff of the Kaiser Family Foundation in collaboration with Elizabeth Moore, Ph.D., associate professor of marketing at the University of Notre Dame. Professor Moore and her colleagues collected and analyzed the data, and she authored the report to the Foundation on the findings. All websites were accessed and content was coded during the period from June through November 2005.

Using data from Competitive Media Reports, researchers identified the top food brands advertised to children on TV, and then searched for corporate or brand websites for those food products. Any child-oriented brand that was in the top 80% of television advertising spending in its product category was included in the study. A total of 96 brands were identified through this process.

Websites for these brands were included in the study if they had content for children age 12 and under. In most cases, these were sites whose primary audience was children; in some cases, the primary audience appeared to be either teens or all ages, with content or separate sections likely to appeal to children. Only websites sponsored by a food manufacturer and dealing with the branded products identified through the process described above were included; food ads on sites such as nick.com or neopets.com were not included.

A total of 77 unique websites were identified through this process. Every page of these websites was reviewed and coded by two trained coders (more than 4,000 unique web pages in total), and more than 400 advergames were played. Screenshots were captured for all pages on each website

Source: This information was reprinted with permission from the Henry J. Kaiser Family Foundation. The Kaiser Family Foundation, a leader in health policy analysis, health journalism and communication, is dedicated to filling the need for trusted, independent information on the major health issues facing our nation and its people. The Foundation is a nonprofit private operating foundation, based in Menlo Park, California.

Reading 8-3

Fortune at the Bottom of the Pyramid

C. K. Prahalad and Stuart L. Hart

With the end of the Cold War, the former Soviet Union and its allies, as well as China, India, and Latin America, opened their closed markets to foreign investment in a cascading fashion. Although this significant economic and social transformation has offered vast new growth opportunities for multinational corporations (MNCs), its promise has yet to be realized.

First, the prospect of millions of "middle-class" consumers in developing countries, clamouring for products from MNCs, was wildly oversold. To make matters worse, the Asian and Latin American financial crises have greatly diminished the attractiveness of emerging markets. As a consequence, many MNCs worldwide slowed investments and began to rethink risk–reward structures for these markets. This retreat could become even more pronounced in the wake of the terrorist attacks in the United States last September.

The lackluster nature of most MNCs' emerging market strategies over the past decade does not change the magnitude of the opportunity, which is in reality much larger than previously thought. The real source of market promise is not the wealthy few in the developing world, or even the emerging middle-income consumers: It is the billions of *aspiring poor* who are joining the market economy for the first time.

This is a time for MNCs to look at globalization strategies through a new lens of inclusive capitalism. For companies with the resources and persistence to compete at the bottom of the world economic pyramid, the prospective rewards include growth, profits, and incalculable contributions to humankind. Countries that still don't have the modern infrastructure or products to meet basic human needs are an ideal testing ground for developing environmentally sustainable technologies and products for the entire world.

Furthermore, MNC investment at "the bottom of the pyramid" means lifting billions of people out of poverty and desperation, averting the social decay, political chaos, terrorism, and environmental meltdown that is certain to continue if the gap between rich and poor countries continues to widen.

Doing business with the world's 4 billion poorest people—two-thirds of the world's population—will require radical innovations in technology and business models. It will require MNCs to reevaluate price–performance relationships for products and services. It will demand a new level of capital efficiency and new ways of measuring financial success. Companies will be forced to transform their understanding of scale, from a "bigger is better" ideal to an ideal of highly distributed small-scale operations married to world-scale capabilities.

In short, the poorest populations raise a prodigious new managerial challenge for the world's wealthiest companies: selling to the poor and helping them improve their lives by producing and distributing products and services in culturally sensitive, environmentally sustainable, and economically profitable ways.

Four Consumer Tiers

At the very top of the world economic pyramid are 75 to 100 million affluent Tier 1 consumers from around the world. (See Reading exhibit 8.1.) This is a cosmopolitan group composed of middle- and upper-income people in developed countries and the few rich elites from the developing world. In the middle of the pyramid, in Tiers 2 and 3, are poor customers in developed nations and the rising middle classes in developing countries, the targets of MNCs' past emerging-market strategies.

Now consider the 4 billion people in Tier 4, at the bottom of the pyramid. Their annual per capita income—based on purchasing power parity in U.S. dollars—is less than $1,500, the minimum considered necessary to sustain a decent life. For well over a billion people—roughly one-sixth of humanity—per capita income is less than $1 per day.

Even more significant, the income gap between rich and poor is growing. According to the United Nations, the richest 20 percent in the world accounted for about 70 percent of total income in 1960. In 2000, that figure reached 85 percent. Over the same period, the fraction of income accruing to the poorest 20 percent in the world fell from 2.3 percent to 1.1 percent.

This extreme inequity of wealth distribution reinforces the view that the poor cannot participate

READING EXHIBIT 8.1

The World Economic Pyramid

Source: U.N. World Development Reports.

Annual Per Capita Income*	Tiers	Population in Millions
More Than $20,000	1	75–100
$1,500–$20,000	2 & 3	1,500–1,750
Less Than $1,500	4	4,000

* Based on purchasing power parity in U.S.$

in the global market economy, even though they constitute a majority of the population. In fact, given its vast size, Tier 4 represents a multitrillion-dollar market. According to World Bank projections, the population at the bottom of the pyramid could swell to more than 6 billion people over the next 40 years, because the bulk of the world's population growth occurs there.

The perception that the bottom of the pyramid is not a viable market also fails to take into account the growing importance of the informal economy among the poorest of the poor, which by some estimates accounts for 40 to 60 percent of all economic activity in developing countries. Most Tier 4 people live in rural villages, or urban slums and shanty-towns, and they usually do not hold legal title or deed to their assets (e.g., dwellings, farms, businesses). They have little or no formal education and are hard to reach via conventional distribution, credit, and communications. The quality and quantity of products and services available in Tier 4 is generally low. Therefore, much like an iceberg with only its tip in plain view, this massive segment of the global population—along with its massive market opportunities—has remained largely invisible to the corporate sector.

Fortunately, the Tier 4 market is wide open for technological innovation. Among the many possibilities for innovation, MNCs can be leaders in leapfrogging to products that don't repeat the environmental mistakes of developed countries over the last 50 years. Today's MNCs evolved in an era of abundant natural resources and thus tended to make products and services that were resource-intensive and excessively polluting. The United States' 270 million people—only about 4 percent of the world's population—consume more than 25 percent of the planet's energy resources. To re-create those types of consumption patterns in developing countries would be disastrous.

We have seen how the disenfranchised in Tier 4 can disrupt the way of life and safety of the rich in Tier 1—poverty breeds discontent and extremism. Although complete income equality is an ideological pipe dream, the use of commercial development to bring people out of poverty and give them the chance for a better life is critical to the stability and health of the global economy and the continued success of Western MNCs.

The Invisible Opportunity

Among the top 200 MNCs in the world, the overwhelming majority are based in developed countries. U.S. corporations dominate, with 82; Japanese firms, with 41, are second, according to a list compiled in December 2000 by the Washington, D.C.–based Institute for Policy Studies. So it is not surprising that MNCs' views of business are conditioned by their knowledge of and familiarity with Tier 1 consumers.

Perception of market opportunity is a function of the way many managers are socialized to think and the analytical tools they use. Most MNCs automatically dismiss the bottom of the pyramid because they judge the market based on income or selections of products and services appropriate for developed countries.

To appreciate the market potential of Tier 4, MNCs must come to terms with a set of core assumptions and practices that influence their view of developing countries. We have identified the following as widely shared orthodoxies that must be reexamined:

- Assumption #1—The poor are not our target consumers because with our current cost structures, we cannot profitably compete for that market.
- Assumption #2—The poor cannot afford and have no use for the products and services sold in developed markets.
- Assumption #3—Only developed markets appreciate and will pay for new technology. The poor can use the previous generation of technology.
- Assumption #4—The bottom of the pyramid is not important to the long-term viability of our business. We can leave Tier 4 to governments and nonprofits.
- Assumption #5—Managers are not excited by business challenges that have a humanitarian dimension.
- Assumption #6—Intellectual excitement is in developed markets. It is hard to find talented managers who want to work at the bottom of the pyramid.

Each of these key assumptions obscures the value at the bottom of the pyramid. It is like the story of the person who finds a $20 bill on the sidewalk. Conventional economic wisdom suggests if the bill really existed, someone would already have picked it up! Like the $20 bill, the bottom of the pyramid defies conventional managerial logic, but that doesn't mean it isn't a large and unexplored territory for profitable growth. Consider the drivers of innovation and opportunities for companies in Tier 4. (See Reading exhibit 8.2.) MNCs must recognize that this market poses a major new challenge: how to combine low cost, good quality, sustainability, and profitability.

Furthermore, MNCs cannot exploit these new opportunities without radically rethinking how they go to market. Reading exhibit 8.3 suggests some (but by no means all) areas where an entirely new perspective is required to create profitable markets in Tier 4.

READING EXHIBIT 8.2
Innovation and MNC Implications in Tier 4

Drivers of Innovation	Implications for MNCs
Increased access among the poor to TV and information	Tier 4 is becoming aware of many products and services and is aspiring to share the benefits
Deregulation and the diminishing role of governments and international aid	More hospitable investment climate for MNCs entering developing countries and more cooperation from nongovernmental organizations
Global overcapacity combined with intense competition in Tiers 1, 2, and 3	Tier 4 represents a huge untapped market for profitable growth
The need to discourage migration to overcrowded urban centers	MNCs must create products and services for rural populations

READING EXHIBIT 8.3
New Strategies for the Bottom of the Pyramid

Price Performance	Views of Quality
• Product development • Manufacturing • Distribution	• New delivery formats • Creation of robust products for harsh conditions (heat, dust, etc.)
Sustainability	**Profitability**
• Reduction in resource intensity • Recyclability • Renewable energy	• Investment intensity • Margins • Volume

Tier 4 Pioneers

Hindustan Lever Ltd. (HLL), a subsidiary of Great Britain's Unilever PLC and widely considered the best managed company in India, has been a pioneer among MNCs exploring markets at the bottom of the pyramid. For more than 50 years, HLL has served India's small elite who could afford to buy MNC products. In the 1990s, a local firm, Nirma Ltd., began offering detergent products for poor consumers, mostly in rural areas. In fact, Nirma created a new business system that included a new product formulation, low-cost manufacturing process, wide distribution network, special packaging for daily purchasing, and value pricing.

HLL, in typical MNC fashion, initially dismissed Nirma's strategy. However, as Nirma grew rapidly, HLL could see its local competitor was winning in a market it had disregarded. Ultimately, HLL saw its vulnerability and its opportunity: In 1995, the company responded with its own offering for this market, drastically altering its traditional business model.

HLL's new detergent, called Wheel, was formulated to substantially reduce the ratio of oil to water in the product, responding to the fact that the poor often wash their clothes in rivers and other public water systems. HLL decentralized the production, marketing, and distribution of the product to leverage the abundant labor pool in rural India, quickly creating sales channels through the thousands of small outlets where people at the bottom of the pyramid shop. HLL also changed the cost structure of its detergent business so it could introduce Wheel at a low price point.

Today, Nirma and HLL are close competitors in the detergent market, with 38 percent market share each, according to IndiaInfoline.com, a business intelligence and market research service. Unilever's own analysis of Nirma and HLL's competition in the detergent business reveals even more about the profit potential of the marketplace at the bottom of the pyramid. (See Reading exhibit 8.4.)

Contrary to popular assumptions, the poor can be a very profitable market—especially if MNCs change their business models. Specifically, Tier 4 is not a market that allows for the traditional pursuit of high margins; instead, profits are driven by volume and capital efficiency. Margins are likely to be low (by current norms), but unit sales can be extremely high. Managers who focus on gross margins will miss the opportunity at the bottom of the pyramid; managers who innovate and focus on economic profit will be rewarded.

Nirma has become one of the largest branded detergent makers in the world. Meanwhile, HLL, stimulated by its emergent rival and its changed business model, registered a 20 percent growth in revenues per year and a 25 percent growth in profits per year between 1995 and 2000. Over the same period, HLL's market capitalization grew to $12 billion— a growth rate of 40 percent per year. HLL's parent company, Unilever, also has benefited from its subsidiary's experience in India. Unilever transported HLL's business principles (not the product or the brand) to

READING EXHIBIT 8.4

Nirma vs. HLL in India's Detergent Market (1999)

Source: Presentation by John Ripley, senior vice president, Unilever, at the Academy of Management Meeting, August 10, 1999.

	Nirma	HLL (Wheel)	HLL (High-End Products)
Total Sales ($ Million)	150	100	180
Gross Margin (%)	18	18	25
ROCE (%)	121	93	22

create a new detergent market among the poor in Brazil, where the Ala brand has been a big success. More important, Unilever has adopted the bottom of the pyramid as a corporate strategic priority.

As the Unilever example makes clear, the starting assumption must be that serving Tier 4 involves bringing together the best of technology and a global resource base to address local market conditions. Cheap and low quality products are not the goal. The potential of Tier 4 cannot be realized without an entrepreneurial orientation: The real strategic challenge for managers is to visualize an active market where only abject poverty exists today. It takes tremendous imagination and creativity to engineer a market infrastructure out of a completely unorganized sector.

Serving Tier 4 markets is not the same as serving existing markets better or more efficiently. Managers first must develop a commercial infrastructure tailored to the needs and challenges of Tier 4. Creating such an infrastructure must be seen as an investment, much like the more familiar investments in plants, processes, products, and R&D.

Further, contrary to more conventional investment strategies, no firm can do this alone.

Multiple players must be involved, including local governmental authorities, nongovernmental organizations (NGOs), communities, financial institutions, and other companies. Four elements—creating buying power, shaping aspirations, improving access, and tailoring local solutions—are the keys to a thriving Tier 4 market. (See Reading exhibit 8.5.)

Each of these four elements demands innovation in technology, business models, and management processes. And business leaders must be willing to experiment, collaborate, empower locals, and create new sources of competitive advantage and wealth.

Creating Buying Power

According to the International Labour Organization's *World Employment Report 2001*, nearly a billion people—roughly one-third of the world's work force—are either underemployed or have such low-paying jobs that they cannot support themselves

READING EXHIBIT 8.5
The Commercial Infrastructure at the Bottom of the Pyramid

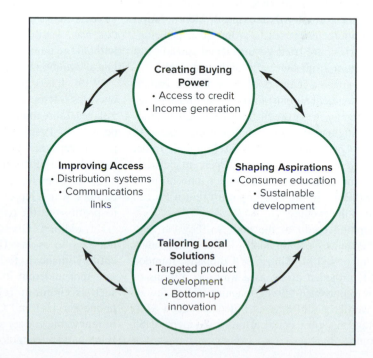

or their families. Helping the world's poor elevate themselves above this desperation line is a business opportunity to do well and do good. To do so effectively, two interventions are crucial—providing access to credit, and increasing the earning potential of the poor. A few farsighted companies have already begun to blaze this trail with startlingly positive results.

Commercial credit historically has been unavailable to the very poor. Even if those living in poverty had access to a bank, without collateral it is hard to get credit from the traditional banking system. As Peruvian economist Hernando de Soto demonstrates in his pathbreaking work, *The Mystery of Capital: Why Capitalism Triumphs in the West and Fails Everywhere Else,* commercial credit is central to building a market economy. Access to credit in the U.S. has allowed people of modest means to systematically build their equity and make major purchases, such as houses, cars, and education.

The vast majority of the poor in developing countries operate in the "informal" or extralegal economy, since the time and cost involved in securing legal title for their assets or incorporation of their microenterprises is prohibitive. Developing countries have tried governmental subsidies to free the poor from the cycle of poverty, with little success. Even if the poor were able to benefit from government support to start small businesses, their dependence on credit from local moneylenders charging usurious rates makes it impossible to succeed. Local moneylenders in Mumbai, India, charge interest rates of up to 20 percent per day. This means that a vegetable vendor who borrows Rs.100 ($2.08) in the morning must return Rs.120 ($2.50) in the evening.

Extending credit to the poor so they can elevate themselves economically is not a new idea. Consider how I.M. Singer & Company, founded in 1851, provided credit as a way for millions of women to purchase sewing machines. Very few of those women could have afforded the steep $100 price tag, but most could afford a payment of $5 per month.

The same logic applies on a much larger scale in Tier 1. Consider the experience of the Grameen Bank Ltd. in Bangladesh, one of the first in the world to apply a microlending model in commercial banking. Started just over 20 years ago by Muhammad Yunus, then a professor in the Economics Department at Chittagong University, Bangladesh, Grameen Bank pioneered a lending service for the poor that has inspired thousands of microlenders, serving 25 million clients world-wide, in developing countries and wealthy nations, including the United States and Great Britain.

Grameen Bank's program is designed to address the problems of extending credit to lowest-income customers—lack of collateral, high credit risk, and contractual enforcement. Ninety-five percent of its 2.3 million customers are women, who, as the traditional breadwinners and entrepreneurs in rural communities, are better credit risks than men. Candidates for loans must have their proposals thoroughly evaluated and supported by five nonfamily members of the community. The bank's sales and service people visit the villages frequently, getting to know the women who have loans and the projects in which they are supposed to invest. In this way, lending due diligence is accomplished without the mountain of paperwork and arcane language common in the West.

With 1,170 branches, Grameen Bank today provides microcredit services in more than 40,000 villages, more than half the total number in Bangladesh. As of 1996, Grameen Bank had achieved a 95 percent repayment rate, higher than any other bank in the Indian subcontinent. However, the popularity of its services has also spawned more local competitors, which has cut into its portfolio and shrunk its profits over the past few years.

In addition, Grameen Bank's rate of return is not easy to assess. Historically, the bank was an entirely manual, field-based operation, a structure that undercut its efficiency. Today, spin-offs such as Grameen Telecom (a provider of village phone service) and Grameen Shakti (a developer of renewable energy sources) are helping Grameen Bank build a technology infrastructure to automate its processes. As the bank develops its online business model, profitability should increase dramatically, highlighting the importance of information technology in the acceleration of the microcredit revolution.

Perhaps the most pertinent measure of Grameen Bank's success is the global explosion of institutional interest in microlending it has stimulated around the world. In South Africa, where 73 percent of the population earns less than R5,000 ($460) per month, according to a 2001 World Bank study, retail banking services for low-income customers are becoming one of the most competitive and fast-growing mass markets. In 1994, Standard Bank of South Africa Ltd., Africa's leading consumer bank, launched a low-cost, volume-driven e-banking business, called AutoBank E, to grow revenue by providing banking services to the poor. Through the use of 2,500 automated teller machines (ATMs) and 98 AutoBank E-centres, Standard now has the largest presence in South Africa's townships and other underserviced areas of any domestic bank. As of April 2001, Standard served nearly 3 million low-income customers and is adding roughly 60,000 customers per month, according to South Africa's *Sunday Times.*

Standard does not require a minimum income of customers opening an AutoBank E account, although they must have some regular income. People who have never used a bank can open an account with a deposit of as little as $8. Customers are issued an ATM card and shown how to use it by staff who speak a variety of African dialects. A small flat fee is charged for each ATM transaction. An interest-bearing "savings purse" is attached to every account to encourage poor customers to save. Interest rates on deposits are low, but superior to keeping cash in a jar. The *Sunday Times* also reported that Standard Bank is considering a loan program for low-income clients.

Computerization of microlending services not only makes the overall operation more efficient, but also makes it possible to reach many more people—lending money to individuals with no collateral and no formal address. Since there is lower overhead and little paperwork, AutoBank's costs are 30 to 40 percent lower than those at traditional branches.

At the 1999 Microcredit Summit, the United Nations, in conjunction with several major MNCs, such as Citigroup Inc. and Monsanto Company, set a goal of making basic credit available to the 100 million poorest families in the world by the year 2005. Unfortunately, the success of this undertaking has been slowed by high transaction costs, a lack of automation, and poor information and communications infrastructures in rural areas.

To address these issues and accelerate the development of microlending, French banker Jacques Attali, the founding president of the European Bank for Reconstruction and Development and a former chief aide of French President François Mitterand during the 1980s, has created PlaNet Finance. Its website, www.planetfinance.org, links thousands of microcredit groups worldwide into a network to help microbanks share solutions and lower costs.

Ultimately, the development of an automated solution for tracking and processing the millions of small loans associated with microlending should be possible. If processing and transaction costs can be reduced enough, they can then be bundled together and sold in the secondary market to multinational financial institutions like Citigroup. This would greatly expand the capital available for microlending beyond the current pool from donors and governments.

In the United States, microlending has also taken root over the past decade in poor urban neighborhoods. For example, the ShoreBank Corporation, formerly South Shore Bank, has demonstrated the profitability of banking for the poor in Chicago's troubled South Side. Project Enterprise, a Grameen-like program based in New York City, is aimed at minority entrepreneurs.

Several multinational banks are beginning to offer microbanking services in developing countries. Citigroup, for instance, is experimenting in Bangalore, India, with 24/7 services for customers with as little as a $25 on deposit. Initial results are very positive.

Shaping Aspirations

Sustainable product innovations initiated in Tier 4, and promoted through consumer education, will not only positively influence the choices of people at the bottom of the pyramid, but may ultimately reshape the way Americans and others in Tier 1 live. Indeed, in 20 years, we may look back to see that Tier 4 provided the early market pull for disruptive technologies that replaced unsustainable technologies in developed countries and advanced the fortunes of MNCs with foresight.

For example, Unilever's HLL subsidiary has tackled the lack of practical, inexpensive, low-energy-consuming refrigeration in India. HLL's laboratories developed a radically different approach to refrigeration that allows ice cream to be transported across the country in standard non-refrigerated trucks. The system allows quantum reductions in electricity use and makes dangerous and polluting refrigerants unnecessary. As a bonus, the new system is cheaper to build and use.

Electricity, water, refrigeration, and many other essential services are all opportunities in developing countries. A U.S.-based NGO, the Solar Electric Light Fund (SELF), has creatively adapted technology and applied microcredit financing to bring electrical service to people in remote villages in Africa and Asia who otherwise would spend money to burn hazardous kerosene, candles, wood, or dung for their light and cooking. SELF's rural electrification system is based on small-scale on-site power generation using renewable resources. A revolving loan fund gives villagers the financial means to operate these electrical systems themselves, also creating jobs. Since its founding in 1990, SELF has launched projects in China, India, Sri Lanka, Nepal, Vietnam, Indonesia, Brazil, Uganda, Tanzania, South Africa, and the Solomon Islands.

The success of SELF and other NGOs focused on small-scale distributed energy solutions has begun to attract the attention of Western companies such as the U.S.'s Plug Power Inc. (fuel cells) and Honeywell Inc. (microturbines). They see the logic in moving into a wide-open market in Tier 4 rather than trying to force their technology prematurely into applications for the developed markets, where incumbents and institutions stand in their way. With several billion potential customers around the world, investments in such innovations should be well worth it.

Improving Access

Because Tier 4 communities are often physically and economically isolated, better distribution systems and communication links are essential to development of the bottom of the pyramid. Few of the large emerging market countries have distribution systems that reach more than half of the population. (Hence the continued dependence of the poorest consumers on local products and services and moneylenders.) As a consequence, few MNCs have designed their distribution systems to cater to the needs of poor rural customers.

Creative local companies, however, lead the way in effective rural distribution. In India, for instance, Arvind Mills has introduced an entirely new delivery system for blue jeans. Arvind, the world's fifth-largest denim manufacturer, found Indian domestic denim sales limited. At $40 to $60 a pair, the jeans were not affordable to the masses, and the existing distribution system reached only a few towns and villages. So Arvind introduced "Ruf & Tuf" jeans—a ready-to-make kit of jeans components (denim, zipper, rivets, and a patch) priced at about $6. Kits were distributed through a network of thousands of local tailors, many in small rural towns and villages, whose self-interest motivated them to market the kits extensively. Ruf & Tuf jeans are now the largest-selling jeans in India, easily surpassing Levi's and other brands from the U.S. and Europe.

MNCs can also play a role in distributing the products of Tier 4 enterprises in Tier 1 markets, giving bottom-of-the-pyramid enterprises their first links to international markets. Indeed, it is possible through partnerships to leverage traditional knowledge bases to produce more sustainable, and in some cases superior, products for consumption by Tier 1 customers.

Anita Roddick, CEO of The Body Shop International PLC, demonstrated the power of this strategy in the early 1990s through her company's "trade not aid" program of sourcing local raw material and products from indigenous people.

More recently, the Starbucks Corporation, in cooperation with Conservation International, has pioneered a program to source coffee directly from farmers in the Chiapas region of Mexico. These farms grow coffee beans organically, using shade, which preserves songbird habitat. Starbucks markets the product to U.S. consumers as a high-quality, premium coffee; the Mexican farmers benefit economically from the sourcing arrangement, which eliminates intermediaries from the business model. This direct relationship also improves the local farmers' understanding and knowledge of the Tier 1 market and its customer expectations.

Information poverty may be the single biggest roadblock to sustainable development. More than half of humanity has yet to make a single phone call. However, where telephones and Internet connections do exist, for the first time in history, it is possible to imagine a single, interconnected market uniting the world's rich and poor in the quest for truly sustainable economic development. The process could transform the "digital divide" into a "digital dividend."

Ten years ago, Sam Pitroda, currently chairman and CEO of London-based Worldtel Ltd., a company created by a telecommunications union to fund telecom development in emerging markets, came to India with the idea of "rural telephones." His original concept was to have a community telephone, operated by an entrepreneur (usually a woman) who charged a fee for the use of the telephone and kept a percentage as wages for maintaining the telephone. Today, from most parts of India, it is possible to call anyone in the world. Other entrepreneurs have introduced fax services, and some are experimenting with low-cost e-mail and Internet access. These communication links have dramatically altered the way villages function and how they are connected to the rest of the country and the world.

With the emergence of global broadband connections, opportunities for information-based business in Tier 4 will expand significantly. New ventures such as CorDECT in India and Celnicos Communications in Latin America are developing information technology and business models suited to the particular requirements of the bottom of the pyramid. Through shared-access models (e.g., Internet kiosks), wireless infrastructure, and focused technology development, companies are dramatically reducing the cost of being connected. For example, voice and data connectivity typically costs companies \$850 to \$2,800 per line in the developed world; CorDECT has reduced this cost to less than \$400 per line, with a goal of \$100 per line, which would bring telecommunications within reach of virtually everyone in the developing world.

Recognizing an enormous business and development opportunity, Hewlett-Packard Company has articulated a vision of "world e-inclusion," with a focus on providing technology, products, and services appropriate to the needs of the world's poor. As part of this strategy, HP has entered into a venture with the MIT Media Lab and the Foundation for Sustainable Development of Costa Rica—led by former President Jose Maria Figueres Olsen—to develop and implement "telecenters" for villages in remote areas. These digital town centers provide modern information technology equipment with a high-speed Internet connection at a price that is affordable, through credit vehicles, at the village level.

Bringing such technology to villages in Tier 4 makes possible a number of applications, including tele-education, telemedicine, microbanking, agricultural extension services, and environmental monitoring, all of which help to spur microenterprise, economic development, and access to world markets. This project, named Lincos, is expected to spread from today's pilot sites in Central America and the Caribbean to Asia, Africa, and Central Europe.

Tailoring Local Solutions

As we enter the new century, the combined sales of the world's top 200 MNCs equal nearly 30 percent of total world gross domestic product. Yet these same corporations employ less than 1 percent of the world's labor force. Of the world's 100 largest economies, 51 are economies internal to corporations. Yet scores of Third World countries have suffered absolute economic stagnation or decline.

If MNCs are to thrive in the 21st century, they must broaden their economic base and share it more widely. They must play a more active role in narrowing the gap between rich and poor. This cannot be achieved if these companies produce only so-called global products for consumption primarily by Tier 1 consumers. They must nurture local markets and cultures, leverage local solutions, and generate wealth at the lowest levels on the pyramid. Producing in, rather than extracting wealth from, these countries will be the guiding principle.

To do this, MNCs must combine their advanced technology with deep local insights. Consider packaging. Consumers in Tier 1 countries have the disposable income and the space to buy in bulk (e.g., 10-pound boxes of detergent from superstores like Sam's Club) and shop less frequently. They use their spending money to "inventory convenience." Tier 4 consumers, strapped for cash and with limited living space, shop every day, but not for much. They can't afford to stock up on household items or be highly selective about what they buy; they look for single-serve packaging. But consumers with small means also have the benefit of experimentation.

Unburdened by large quantities of product, they can switch brands every time they buy. Already in India, 30 percent of personal care products and other consumables, such as shampoo, tea, and cold medicines, are sold in single-serve packages. Most are priced at Rs. 1 (about 1¢). Without innovation in packaging, however, this trend could result in a mountain of solid waste. Dow Chemical Company and Cargill Inc. are experimenting with an organic plastic that would be totally biodegradable. Such packaging clearly has advantages in Tier 4, but it could also revolutionize markets at all four tiers of the world pyramid.

For MNCs, the best approach is to marry local capabilities and market knowledge with global best practices. But whether an initiative involves an MNC entering Tier 4 or an entrepreneur from Tier 4, the development principles remain the same: New

business models must not disrupt the cultures and lifestyles of local people. An effective combination of local and global knowledge is needed, not a replication of the Western system.

The development of India's milk industry has many lessons for MNCs. The transformation began around 1946, when the Khira District Milk Cooperative, located in the state of Gujarat, set up its own processing plant under the leadership of Verghese Kurien and created the brand Amul, today one of the most recognized in the country.

Unlike the large industrial dairy farms of the West, in India, milk originates in many small villages. Villagers may own only two to three buffaloes or cows each and bring their milk twice a day to the village collection center. They are paid every day for the milk they deliver, based on fat content and volume. Refrigerated vans transport the milk to central processing plants, where it is pasteurized. Railroad cars then transport the milk to major urban centers.

The entire value chain is carefully managed, from the village based milk production to the world-scale processing facilities. The Khira District cooperative provides such services to the farmers as veterinary care and cattle feed. The cooperative also manages the distribution of pasteurized milk, milk powder, butter, cheese, baby food, and other products. The uniqueness of the Amul cooperative is its blending of decentralized origination with the efficiencies of a modern processing and distribution infrastructure. As a result, previously marginal village farmers are earning steady incomes and being transformed into active market participants.

Twenty years ago, milk was in short supply in India. Today, India is the world's largest producer of milk. According to India's National Dairy Development Board, the country's dairy cooperative network now claims 10.7 million individual farmer member–owners, covers 96,000 village-level societies, includes 170 milk producer unions, and operates in more than 285 districts. Milk production has increased 4.7 percent per year since 1974. The per capita availability of milk in India has grown from 107 grams to 213 grams per day in 20 years.

Putting It All Together

Creating buying power, shaping aspirations, improving access, and tailoring local solutions—the four elements of the commercial infrastructure for the bottom of the pyramid are intertwined. Innovation in one leverages innovation in the others. Corporations are only one of the actors; MNCs must work together with NGOs, local and state governments, and communities. Yet someone must take the lead to make this revolution happen. The question is, Why should it be MNCs?

Even if multinational managers are emotionally persuaded, it is not obvious that large corporations have real advantages over small, local organizations. MNCs may never be able to beat the cost or responsiveness of village entrepreneurs. Indeed, empowering local entrepreneurs and enterprises is key to developing Tier 4 markets. Still, there are several compelling reasons for MNCs to embark on this course:

- Resources. Building a complex commercial infrastructure for the bottom of the pyramid is a resource- and management-intensive task. Developing environmentally sustainable products and services requires significant research. Distribution channels and communication networks are expensive to develop and sustain. *Few local entrepreneurs have the managerial or technological resources to create this infrastructure.*

- Leverage. MNCs can transfer knowledge from one market to another—from China to Brazil or India—as Avon, Unilever, Citigroup, and others have demonstrated. Although practices and products have to be customized to serve local needs, *MNCs, with their unique global knowledge base, have an advantage that is not easily accessible to local entrepreneurs.*

- Bridging. MNCs can be nodes for building the commercial infrastructure, providing access to knowledge, managerial imagination, and financial resources. Without MNCs as catalysts, well-intentioned NGOs, communities, local governments, entrepreneurs, and even multilateral development agencies will continue to flounder in their attempts to bring development to the bottom. *MNCs are best positioned to unite the range of actors required to develop the Tier 4 market.*

- Transfer. Not only can MNCs leverage learning from the bottom of the pyramid, but they also have the capacity to transfer innovations upmarket all the way to Tier 1. As we have seen, Tier 4 is a testing ground for sustainable living. *Many of the innovations for the bottom can be adapted for use in the resource- and energy-intensive markets of the developed world.*

It is imperative, however, that managers recognize the nature of business leadership required in the Tier 4 arena. Creativity, imagination, tolerance for ambiguity, stamina, passion, empathy, and courage may be as important as analytical skill, intelligence, and knowledge. Leaders need a deep understanding of the complexities and subtleties of sustainable development in the context of Tier 4. Finally, managers must have the interpersonal and intercultural skills to work with a wide range of organizations and people.

MNCs must build an organizational infrastructure to address opportunity at the bottom of the pyramid. This means building a local base of support, reorienting R&D to focus on the needs of the poor, forming new alliances, increasing employment intensity, and reinventing cost structures. These five organizational elements are clearly interrelated and mutually reinforcing.

- *Build a local base of support.* Empowering the poor threatens the existing power structure. Local opposition can emerge very quickly, as Cargill Inc. found in its sunflower-seed business in India. Cargill's offices were twice burned, and the local politicians accused the firm of destroying locally based seed businesses. But Cargill persisted. Through Cargill's investments in farmer education, training, and supply of farm inputs, farmers have significantly improved their productivity per acre of land. Today, Cargill is seen as the friend of the farmer.

Political opposition has vanished. To overcome comparable problems, MNCs must build a local base of political support. As Monsanto and General Electric Company can attest, the establishment of a coalition of NGOs, community leaders, and local authorities that can counter entrenched interests is essential. Forming such a coalition can be a very slow process. Each player has a different agenda; MNCs have to understand these agendas and create shared aspirations.

In China, this problem is less onerous: The local bureaucrats are also the local entrepreneurs, so they can easily see the benefits to their enterprise and their village, town, or province. In countries such as India and Brazil, such alignment does not exist. Significant discussion, information sharing, the delineation of benefits to each constituency, and sensitivity to local debates is necessary.

- *Conduct R&D focused on the poor.* It is necessary to conduct R&D and market research focused on the unique requirements of the poor, by region and by country. In India, China, and North Africa, for example, research on ways to provide safe water for drinking, cooking, washing, and cleaning is a high priority. Research must also seek to adapt foreign solutions to local needs. For example, a daily dosage of vitamins can be added to a wide variety of food and beverage products. For corporations that have distribution and brand presence throughout the developing world, such as Coca-Cola Company, the bottom of the pyramid offers a vast untapped market for such products as water and nutritionals.

Finally, research must identify useful principles and potential applications from local practices. In Tier 4, significant knowledge is transmitted orally from one generation to the next. Being respectful of traditions but willing to analyze them scientifically can lead to new knowledge. The Body Shop's creative CEO, Ms. Roddick, built a business predicated on understanding the basis for local rituals and practices. For example, she observed that some African women use slices of pineapple to cleanse their skin. On the surface, this practice appears to be a meaningless ritual. However, research showed active ingredients in pineapple that cleared away dead skin cells better than chemical formulations. MNCs must develop research facilities in emerging markets such as China, India, Brazil, Mexico, and Africa, although few have made a big effort so far. Unilever is an exception; it operates highly regarded research centers in India, employing more than 400 researchers dedicated to the problems of "India-like markets."

- *Form new alliances.* MNCs have conventionally formed alliances solely to break into new markets; now they need to broaden their alliance strategies. By entering into alliances to expand in Tier 4 markets, MNCs gain insight into developing countries' culture and local knowledge. At the same time, MNCs improve their own credibility. They may also secure preferred or exclusive access to a market or raw material. We foresee three kinds of important relationships: Alliances with local firms and cooperatives (such as the Khira District Milk Cooperative); alliances with local and international NGOs (like Starbucks's alliance with Conservation International in coffee); and alliances with governments (e.g., Merck & Company's recent alliance in Costa Rica to foster rain forest preservation in exchange for bioprospecting rights). Given the difficulty and complexity of constructing business models dependent on relationships with national or central governments (e.g., large infrastructure development), we envision more alliances at the local and regional level. To succeed in such alliances, MNC managers must learn to work with people who may not have the same agenda or the same educational and economic background as they do. The challenge and payoff is how to manage and learn from diversity—economic, intellectual, racial, and linguistic.

- *Increase employment intensity.* MNCs accustomed to Tier 1 markets think in terms of capital intensity and labor productivity. Exactly the opposite logic applies in Tier 4. Given the vast number of people at the bottom of the pyramid, the production and distribution approach must provide jobs for many, as in the case of Ruf & Tuf jeans from Arvind Mills: It employed an army of local tailors as stockers, promoters, distributors, and service providers, even though the cost of the jeans was 80 percent below that of Levi's. As Arvind demonstrated, MNCs need not employ large numbers of people directly on their payroll, but the organizational model in Tier 4 must increase employment intensity (and incomes) among the poor and groom them to become new customers.

- *Reinvent cost structures.* Managers must dramatically reduce cost levels relative to those in Tier 1. To create products and services the poor can afford, MNCs must reduce their costs significantly—to, say, 10 percent of what they are today. But this cannot be achieved by fine-tuning the current approaches to product development, production, and logistics. The entire business process must be rethought with a focus on functionality, not on the product itself. For example, financial services need not be distributed only through branch offices open from 9 A.M. to 5 P.M. Such services can be provided at a time and place convenient to the poor consumer—after 8 P.M. and at their homes. Cash-dispensing machines can be placed in safe areas—police stations and post offices. Iris recognition used as a security device could substitute for the tedious personal-identification number and card for identification.

Lowering cost structures also forces a debate on ways to reduce investment costs. This will inevitably lead to greater use of information technology to develop production and distribution systems. As noted, village-based phones are already transforming the pattern of communications throughout the developing world. Add the Internet, and we have a whole new way of communicating and creating economic development in poor, rural areas. Creative use of IT will emerge in these markets as a means to dramatically lower the costs associated with access to products and services, distribution, and credit management.

A Common Cause

The emergence of the 4 billion people who make up the Tier 4 market is a great opportunity for MNCs. It also represents a chance for business, government, and civil society to join together in a common cause. Indeed, we believe that pursuing strategies for the bottom of the pyramid dissolves the conflict between proponents of free trade and global capitalism on one hand, and environmental and social sustainability on the other.

Yet the products and services currently offered to Tier 1 consumers are not appropriate for Tier 4, and accessing this latter market will require approaches fundamentally different from those even in Tiers 2 and 3. Changes in technology, credit, cost, and distribution are critical prerequisites. Only large firms with global reach have the technological, managerial, and financial resources to dip into the well of innovations needed to profit from this opportunity.

New commerce in Tier 4 will not be restricted to businesses filling such basic needs as food, textiles, and housing. The bottom of the pyramid is waiting for high-tech businesses such as financial services, cellular telecommunications, and low-end computers. In fact, for many emerging disruptive technologies (e.g., fuel cells, photovoltaics, satellite-based telecommunications, biotechnology, thin-film microelectronics, and nanotechnology), the bottom of the pyramid may prove to be the most attractive early market.

So far, three kinds of organizations have led the way: local firms such as Amul and Grameen Bank; NGOs such as the World Resources Institute, SELF, The Rainforest Alliance, The Environmental Defense Fund, and Conservation International, among others; and a few MNCs such as Starbucks, Dow, Hewlett-Packard, Unilever, Citigroup, DuPont, Johnson & Johnson, Novartis, and ABB, and global business partnerships such as the World Business Council for Sustainable Business Development. But to date, NGOs and local businesses with far fewer resources than the MNCs have been more innovative and have made more progress in developing these markets.

It is tragic that as Western capitalists we have implicitly assumed that the rich will be served by the corporate sector, while governments and NGOs will protect the poor and the environment. This implicit divide is stronger than most realize. Managers in MNCs, public policymakers, and NGO activists all suffer from this historical division of roles. A huge opportunity lies in breaking this code—linking the poor and the rich across the world in a seamless market organized around the concept of sustainable growth and development.

Collectively, we have only begun to scratch the surface of what is the biggest potential market opportunity in the history of commerce. Those in the private sector who commit their companies to a more inclusive capitalism have the opportunity to prosper and share their prosperity with those who are less fortunate. In a very real sense, the fortune at the bottom of the pyramid represents the loftiest of our global goals.

Note: Notes and references were removed for publication here, but are available on the book website at connect. mheducation.com.

Reading **8-4**

POM Wonderful

Chris MacDonald

The makers of the POM Wonderful fruit juice seem to want consumers to use their hearts, not their brains, in deciding whether to buy their product.

The makers of POM, the trendy pomegranate juice sold in a distinctive curvy bottle, are embroiled in a legal and public-relations battle with the U.S. Federal Trade Commission. At the heart of that battle is the company's insistence on stating—or sometimes just implying—that its product has beneficial health effects. One ad boasts of POM's "incredible healing powers" while another refers to it as "good medicine." Things came to a head on May 21st [2012], when an FTC judge found that at least some of POM's ads made "false and misleading" claims.

Not surprisingly, it looks like POM will appeal the decision. What *is* surprising is that the company has struck back at the FTC with a new set of ads that make the judge seem to support the company's health claims. One ad quotes the judge's reference to "[c]ompetent and reliable scientific evidence" for the healthful effects of pomegranate juice, but leaves out his follow-up, which notes that the "greater weight of the persuasive expert testimony" failed to back POM's claims.

The tagline for these ads is "*FTC v. POM:* You be the judge." On the surface, that sounds like POM wants you to think for yourself. And who could complain about that? But context matters. So when the company is pushing back against the FTC's assertion (and the court's finding) that the health claims made on behalf of its juice just don't stand up to scientific scrutiny, the implied message is that yes, you the consumer should decide, but you shouldn't use your *head* in doing so. After all, if you used your head and thought it through rationally, you would want to look at the evidence. And, well, the evidence doesn't look so good for POM. But the makers of POM, it seems, would rather you look inward instead of looking at the evidence. *C'mon, you've tasted it. It's delicious. It must be good for you. And you, dear customer, are smart enough to know that, right? Forget what the science says.*

The key issues here are clearly about truthfulness, and about who gets to determine the truth about complex product characteristics. The makers of POM are prepared to make grand claims on behalf of their product, and they don't think consumers should let scientists or courts get in the way of believing those claims. But to fully appreciate the significance of this, you need first to understand something about the ethical significance of markets.

Markets are all about providing value. When they work well, they make the world a better place by giving literally everyone involved the things they value, things they couldn't readily have obtained otherwise. That's the basic ethical argument in favour of free markets. Now, strictly speaking, the economic theory underlying market capitalism is "value-neutral"—that is, it is agnostic about whether people's particular desires are in any sense "good" ones. This neutrality results from the fact that finding a rationally defensible universal metric by which to judge people's preferences is a notoriously hard philosophical problem. Some people like chocolate ice cream while others like vanilla. When it comes to entertainment, some people like poetry readings or foreign films, while some like mixed martial arts. And it's tough to argue that one is better than the other, in some rational, objective way. So from a market point of view, we tend to avoid this problem altogether by focusing on satisfying people's desires, rather than judging those desires. As long as you're providing stuff that people truly value, all is fair as far as the market goes.

But this way of looking at things assumes that people have the information needed to figure out whether a product they're considering buying really is likely to satisfy their desires. A market functioning according to a principle of "complete disclosure" may be an impossible ideal, but at the very least companies should not attempt to mislead their customers. They also ought not to interfere when responsible third parties—including regulators like the FTC—attempt to help consumers stay informed.

Companies should also be able to demonstrate a degree of modesty in the face of scientific uncertainty and the public's inability to evaluate such evidence. There's nothing wrong with well-informed consumers pinning their hopes on fancy fruit juice: that's a choice they should be free to make. But there is plenty wrong with a company fostering such implausible hopes through dodgy science.

But POM's insistence on claiming health benefits has an effect beyond the relationship between buyer and seller. By bending the facts and inflating certain bits of truth, POM is polluting the commercial atmosphere of truth-telling on which the market relies. The company is making it harder for consumers to know whom to trust, and hence making it harder for well-intentioned companies to sell their products. In effect, the company isn't just letting down its customers; it's undermining the market itself.

Sources: Based in part on Chris MacDonald, "POM Wonderful," *Canadian Business* (July 16, 2011), p. 17; Chris MacDonald, "POM Wonderful and Hearts vs. Brains," *Canadian Business* (May 28, 2012), www.canadianbusiness.com/blog/business_ethics/85667 (accessed August 12, 2012).

Chapter 9

Business and Environmental Sustainability

A thing is right when it tends to preserve the integrity, stability and beauty of the biotic community. It is wrong when it does otherwise.

Aldo Leopold

Growth for the sake of growth is the ideology of the cancer cell.

Edward Abbey

Waste equals food.

William McDonough

Environmental regulation is a signal of design failure.

William McDonough

Food security can be defined in terms of the availability of adequate nutritious food and the ability of people to have access to that food. Global food security raises a multitude of ethical issues concerning the relationship between individuals, business, government, and the natural environment. Perhaps rivaled only by the decisions we make about energy, our food choices have a profound impact on the environment. And as in the case with energy, the choices we have as consumers are greatly shaped by what happens in business.

At first glance, one might think that food should be treated like any other economic commodity, produced and distributed according to market demand. From this perspective, business has no unique ethical responsibilities regarding food. But two factors in particular suggest that there are good ethical reasons for paying close attention to the business of food. First, unlike most other economic goods, food is an essential human need; a case can be made that food is something for which all people have a basic human right. It would be difficult to judge any economic system as ethically adequate if it failed to meet this basic human need for food. Second, food production and distribution can have a profound impact on the earth's biosphere and the long-term productive capacity of the natural environment to provide for human needs. How food is produced—something deeply influenced by business—greatly impacts the ongoing capacity of the earth's biosphere to support life.

These factors are captured in the well-known definition of sustainable development offered by the World Commission on Environment and Development (the "Brundtland Report") in 1987. This definition states that sustainable development "meets the needs of the present without compromising the ability of future generations to meet their own needs." The Brundtland Report concluded that the standard model of economic development, and the role played by business within that model, was failing to meet the needs of large portions of the present human population and was operating in such a way that the ability of future generations to meet their own needs was at risk.

The food business continues to have a deep connection with a wide range of ethical and environmental issues. What we eat, the availability of food, how food is produced, the nutritional quality of food, food safety, who produces food, how food products are processed, and the environmental and social consequences of agriculture all raise important ethical questions.

It seems fair to say that the most important ethical issue concerning food is the fact that hundreds of millions of people do not have enough of it. In 2015, the United Nations Food and Agricultural Organization reported that some 800 million people globally were undernourished. In some areas of sub-Saharan Africa and Southeast Asia, as much as one-third of the population lacks adequate nutritional food. But the same UN report also points out that despite a growing global population, the number of people lacking adequate nutritional food has decreased by 200 million since 1990. Increased agricultural productivity created by modern farming techniques has played a major role in this decrease.

In the past 200 years, observers have often argued that global population growth was outpacing food supply and continued growth was likely to lead to major food shortages and mass starvation. In the early 19th century, Thomas Malthus famously claimed that because population grows exponentially and food growth increases only arithmetically, population size will inevitably outgrow food availability. In the

1960s, Paul Erhlich's book *The Population Bomb* similarly predicted that continued population growth was leading to an imminent global food crisis.

In both cases, food crises were avoided because of improved agricultural productivity that resulted from shifts toward a more centralized and industrial model of agriculture. In the 19th century, the food collapse predicted by Malthus was avoided by technological advances produced by the Industrial Revolution, advances that greatly increased both the amount of land that could be turned to agriculture and the efficiency and productivity of that land. In the late 20th century and continuing today, technological advances in machinery, irrigation, pesticides, fertilizers, plant and animal breeding, and genetically modified organisms have greatly increased food production across the globe.

Critics charge that many of these modern agricultural practices, including the very model of industrial agriculture itself, contribute to a range of health, safety, social, and environmental problems. Intensive farming techniques threaten soil fertility, deplete groundwater supplies, poison soil and water with pesticide residue, disrupt ecosystems, threaten biodiversity, and jeopardize the ongoing productivity of the earth's biosphere. Many critics also claim that the model of contemporary agribusiness has placed significant political, economic, and social power into the hands of a few giant multinational corporations.

Food shortages can also be explained by wider market forces. The type of food that is produced and the uses to which it is put are determined at least as much by market demand as by what people need. Market demand, understood as what someone is willing to pay for, explains why agricultural resources in some of the world's most productive lands are used to produce feed crops for animals rather than food for humans. In 2014, a *National Geographic* story pointed out that almost half of the world's crops are used as animal feed (36 percent) or for fuel or industrial products (9 percent).[1]

Modern agriculture accounts for 25 percent of greenhouse gas emissions and more than 70 percent of groundwater extraction. In the United States, 75 percent of global corn production is used for animal feed, ethanol production, or sweeteners such as high fructose corn syrup. As societies become more affluent, as happened in Europe and North America and as is happening in China and India, increased demand for beef, dairy products, poultry, and pork diverts an even larger percentage of crops away from fulfilling direct human needs. In terms of pollution, greenhouse gas emissions, and water usage, producing beef, poultry, dairy, and pork products has a much higher environmental toll than grain production.

Of course, agribusiness and food production has an even more direct effect on the natural environment with its treatment of animals. Many critics argue that there are serious ethical issues involved in animal agriculture beyond problematic human health and environmental consequences. Specifically, chickens and turkeys are bred to be overweight flightless animals with little resemblance to their natural species. Animals are kept in overcrowded facilities, prevented from any form of exercise, fed unnatural diets, dosed with antibiotics and growth hormones, separated from their offspring, mutilated to prevent natural behaviors like flight or pecking, and then slaughtered in brutal, mechanized ways. According to critics, all this is done in the name of market efficiency and profit.

(continued)

(concluded)   The food industry itself, including agriculture, retail food suppliers, and restaurants, often defends its practices on market demand grounds. From this perspective, the global demand for food could not be met without the industrial techniques used in modern agriculture. The type and quality of food available is also dependent on consumer demand. If the market demanded smaller serving sizes, less beef, more fresh fruits and vegetables, and less convenient and inexpensive processed foods, then business would provide it. But, according to the food industry, asking business to do these things without the market demand will result in business failures and food shortages.

- What food choices have you made today? In what ways were your choices shaped or influenced by business decisions and business practices?
- In what ways and on what grounds does the fast-food restaurant industry compete for customers? What are the environmental and ethical impacts of fast food?
- In what ways might your food choices shape the way the food industry, including both agriculture and restaurants, interacts with the natural environment?

 ## Chapter Objectives

After reading this chapter, you will be able to:

1. Explain how environmental challenges can create business opportunities.
2. Describe a range of values that play a role in environmental decision making.
3. Explain the difference between market-based and regulatory-based environmental policies.
4. Describe business's environmental responsibilities that flow from each approach.
5. Identify the inadequacies of sole reliance on a market-based approach.
6. Identify the inadequacies of regulatory-based environmental policies.
7. Define and describe sustainable development and sustainable business.
8. Highlight the business opportunities associated with a move toward sustainability.
9. Describe the sustainable principles of eco-efficiency, biomimicry, and service.
10. Explain how marketing can be used both to support and detract from the goals of sustainable business.

Introduction

There is a tendency to believe that environmental challenges *always* create a burden on business and that environmental and business interests are *always* in conflict. While environmental regulations can add costs to business operations and restrict business choice, environmental considerations can also provide opportunities for business. Where one automobile manufacturer sees government-mandated fuel efficiency standards as a burden on its ability to sell large sport-utility vehicles (SUVs), another company sees it as an opportunity to market fuel-efficient hybrids. While one agricultural business sees restrictions on pesticide use as a burden, another sees the opportunity to market organic products.

Many observers believe we have entered the sustainability revolution, an age in which the race to create environmentally and economically sustainable products and services is creating unlimited business opportunities. As happened in the Industrial Revolution, there will be winners and losers in this sustainability revolution and, according to supporters, the economic winners will be the firms and industries that do the most environmental good.

As described by geographer Jarad Diamond in the best-selling book *Collapse,* human history provides many examples of societies that have run up against the environmental limits of their lifestyles. But the Industrial Revolution of the 18th and 19th centuries brought with it the ability to degrade the natural environment to a greater extent and at a faster rate than ever before. The industrial model of growth and productive efficiency and seemingly unlimited energy supply continued along almost unchecked by environmental regulation until the latter half of the 20th century. As in most other industries, this model reshaped the food and agriculture business (see the Opening Decision Point "The Business of Food").

By the start of the 21st century, the earth is experiencing the greatest period of species extinction since the end of the dinosaurs 65 million years ago. Humans are also threatened by global climate change. These monumental environmental events are largely due to human activity, and specifically to our present arrangements of modern industrial society. Simply put, the way we have done business over the last two centuries has brought us up against the biophysical limits of the earth's capacity to support all human life, and it has already crossed those limits in the case of countless other forms of now-extinct life. Thus, the major ethical question of this chapter is what responsibilities contemporary businesses have regarding the natural environment.

It is fair to say that throughout the history of industrial economies, business most often looked at environmental concerns as unwanted burdens and barriers to economic growth. Nonetheless, the sustainable business and sustainable economic development seek to create new ways of doing business in which business success is measured in terms of economic, ethical, and environmental sustainability, often called the *triple bottom line* approach. (For a critical perspective on the triple bottom line, see Reading 9-2, "Getting to the Bottom of 'Triple Bottom Line,'" by Wayne Norman and Chris MacDonald.) The sustainability paradigm sees environmental responsibilities as a fundamental part of basic business practice. Indeed, sustainable business ventures may find that environmental considerations offer creative and entrepreneurial businesses enormous opportunities.

OBJECTIVE

The environmental research and consulting group The Natural Step uses an image of a funnel, with two converging lines, to help business understand the opportunities available in the age of sustainability. The resources necessary to sustain life are on a downward slope. While there is disagreement about the angle of the slope (are we at the start with only a mild slope, or further along with a sharper downward slope?), there is widespread consensus that available resources are in decline. The second line represents aggregate worldwide demand, accounting for both population growth and the increasing demand of consumerist lifestyles. Barring an environmental catastrophe, many but not all industries will emerge through the narrowing funnel into an era of sustainable living. Businesses unable to envision that sustainable future will hit the narrowing wall. Innovative and entrepreneurial business will find their way through. The Natural Step's funnel is illustrated in Figure 9.1.

backcasting
The Natural Step challenges businesses to imagine what a sustainable future must hold. From that vision, creative businesses then look backward to the present and determine what must be done to arrive at that future.

The Natural Step then challenges business to "backcast" a path toward sustainability. We are all familiar with forecasting, in which we examine present data and predict the future. **Backcasting** examines what the future will be when we emerge through the funnel. Knowing what the future must be, creative businesses then look backward to the present and determine what must be done to arrive at that future. In simple terms, sustainable business must use resources and produce wastes at rates that do not jeopardize human well-being by exceeding the earth's capacity to renew the resources and absorb the wastes. Businesses that do so will succeed in moving through the funnel and emerge as successful in the age of sustainability. The "business case" for sustainability will be examined in more detail in the next section.

FIGURE 9.1
The Natural Step's Funnel

RESOURCES
Life supporting resources are decreasing...

... Demand for resources is increasing.

DEMAND

Through innovation, creativity, and the unlimited potential for change we can open the walls of the funnel.

Source: Reprinted with permission.

This chapter will introduce a range of ethical issues that have set the stage for this transition to an environmentally sustainable future. Environmental issues are no longer at the periphery of business decisions, as burdens to be managed if not avoided altogether; nor are they external regulatory constraints in managerial decision making. (To explore how some business leaders are thinking about the centrality of sustainability, see the Reality Check "What Do Business Leaders Think?") Environmental sustainability must accompany financial sustainability for business to survive in the 21st century. For reasons of both rights and duties and for promoting the overall social good, sustainable business is the wave of the future.

Business Ethics and Environmental Values

OBJECTIVE

The opening chapters of this text introduced ethics in terms of practical reasoning. Deciding what we should do is the ultimate goal of practical reason and our values are those standards that encourage us to act one way rather than another. Given this objective, which values and decisions are supported by a concern with the natural environment? Why should we act in ways that protect the natural environment from degradation? Why should business be concerned with, and value, the natural world?

Human self-interest is the most obvious answer to these questions. Environmental concerns are relevant to business because human beings, both presently living humans and future generations of humans, depend on the natural environment in order to survive. Humans need clean water to drink, healthy air to breathe, fertile soil and oceans to produce food, an ozone layer to screen out solar radiation, and a biosphere that maintains the delicate balance of climate in which human life can exist. Two aspects of contemporary environmental realities underscore the importance of self-interested reasoning.

As documented in *Collapse,* past human societies have often run up against the limits of the local environment's ability to sustain human life. In these historical cases, environmental degradation has been localized to a particular region and has seldom affected more than a generation. In contrast, some contemporary environmental issues have the potential to adversely affect the entire globe and change human life forever. Global climate change, species extinction, soil erosion and desertification, and nuclear wastes will threaten human life into the indefinite future.

Second, the science of ecology and its understanding of the interrelatedness of natural systems have helped us understand the wide range of human dependence on ecosystems. Where once we might have thought that buried wastes were gone forever, we now understand how toxins can seep into groundwater and contaminate drinking water across time and great distances. We now understand how pesticides accumulate throughout the food chain and pose greatest dangers not only to top predators such as bald eagles, but to human beings as well. (Consider the basic issue of the environment's impact on breast milk, discussed in the Reality Check "Breast Milk Toxins.") Where once we thought that ocean fisheries were inexhaustible and the atmosphere

Reality Check *Breast Milk Toxins*

Pollutants in the biosphere will tend to accumulate in the fatty tissue of species at the top of the food chain. In mammals, fatty tissue is broken down as a source of energy during lactation. As a result, breast milk is a particularly significant resource for studying toxins that the body has absorbed. The following is a list of synthetic toxins that one study found in human breast milk:

- Chlordane (a compound used in pesticides)
- DDT (a pesticide that has been banned in the United States for decades)
- Dieldrin, Aldrin, and Endrin (insecticides)
- Hexachlorobenzene (a pesticide and an industrial chemical)
- Hexachlorocyclohexane (insecticide)
- Heptachlor (insecticide)
- Mirex (insecticide)

- Nitro musks (used as a fragrance in household products such as detergents and soaps)
- Toxaphene (agricultural insecticide)
- Dioxins and furans (any of a number of polychlorinated compounds produced as by-products from industry and combustion)
- PBDEs (used as flame retardants in clothes and other fabrics)
- PCBs (no longer manufactured, but persistent toxins that were used for a wide variety of industrial purposes)
- Solvents (any of a number of chemical compounds used to dissolve or stabilize other complex chemical compounds)
- Lead, mercury, cadmium, and other metals (can be especially toxic to the developing brain)

too big to be changed by humans, we now understand that a delicate environmental balance is necessary to maintain life-supporting systems.

By the late 19th century, humans came to recognize the self-interested reasons for protecting the natural environment. The conservation movement, the first phase of modern environmentalism, advocated a more restrained and prudent approach to the natural world. From this perspective, the natural world was still valued as a resource, providing humans with both direct benefits (air, water, food), and indirect benefits (the goods and services produced by business). Conservationists argued against the exploitation of natural resources as if they could provide an inexhaustible supply of material. They made the case that business had good reasons for conserving natural resources, reasons that paralleled the rationale to conserve financial resources. The natural world, like capital, had the productive capacity to produce long-term income but only if managed and used prudently.

Besides these self-interested reasons to protect human life and health, the natural environment is essential and valuable for many other reasons. Often, these other values conflict with the more direct instrumental value that comes from treating the natural world as a resource. The beauty and grandeur of the natural world provide great aesthetic, spiritual, and inspirational value. Many people view the natural world as a manifestation of religious and spiritual values. Parts of the natural world can have symbolic value, historical value, and such diverse psychological values as serenity and exhilaration. These values can clearly conflict with the use of the earth itself as a resource to physically, as opposed to spiritually, sustain those who live on it.

Is the market, what people are most willing to pay, the best means to determine land and resource use? Consider the case of a proposed development in Virginia.

The city of Manassas is today a suburb of Washington, DC, in northern Virginia. During the U.S. Civil War it was the site of two historic battles, the first and second Battle of Bull Run. Thousands of soldiers were killed during these battles and many more thousands injured. Today, Manassas Battlefield National Park and several Civil War cemeteries are located at the site.

In the late 1980s developers announced plans to build a large shopping mall on the land that had once served as Robert E. Lee's headquarters during the battle. Significant public opposition led to a public purchase of the land and its incorporation into the national park. A few years later, Disney Company announced plans to develop a large theme park called Disney's America on land adjacent to the national park. Disney's America would have included a theme park that would be a tribute to the Civil War, as well as residential subdivisions and commercial developments including hotels and restaurants. Eventually, the national park would have been surrounded by commercial development.

The plan met with vociferous opposition from a coalition of environmentalists, preservationists, historians, and Civil War authorities. Although it was convinced that the project would have been a tremendous commercial success, Disney eventually abandoned its plans to develop this site. Should the company have abandoned these plans?

- What facts would be helpful to know before making a decision?
- What values are in conflict in this case? Take a look at Disney's environmental mission statement: http://thewaltdisneycompany.com/citizenship/policies/environmental-policy (it now calls it an environmental policy). How might its mission guide its decisions or present conflicts in a dilemma similar to the Manassas case?
- Who are the stakeholders in this case?
- What would be the consequences if all public land uses were decided by the market?
- What are the rights and duties involved in this case?

Aesthetic and inspirational values often play out in public debates about economic development. The 1970s song "Big Yellow Taxi" captured this sentiment with the well-known lyric "they paved paradise and put up a parking lot." Many critics fault business for destroying natural beauty and replacing it with strip malls, neon signs, fast-food restaurants and, yes, parking lots. Consider these debates as you review the Decision Point "Commercialize a Historic Civil War Site?"

A final set of values that we will consider involves the moral status of animals and other living beings, an environmental value that has raised some of the most widely publicized ethical challenges to business. Variously referred to as the animal rights, animal liberation, or animal welfare movement, this approach attributes a moral standing to animals. According to many people, animals, and perhaps all

Reality Check Treatment of Animals in Agriculture

As mentioned in the Opening Decision Point "The Business of Food," some animal farming practices, especially within large-scale industrial factory farms, have been criticized as cruel and heartless. Calves are prevented from exercising and intentionally malnourished so that consumers can enjoy tender and pink veal. Chickens are tightly packed in cages with their beaks cut off to prevent them from pecking each other. Cattle are raised in giant feed lots where they spend their time walking in their own manure.

As part of this effort, McDonald's now has a system for auditing suppliers to ensure adherence to the company's animal welfare standards.

Auditing Animal Welfare Practices

McDonald's requires all processing facilities used by our beef suppliers to adhere to our animal welfare principles, designed to ensure that animals are free from cruelty, abuse and neglect. In addition, abattoirs used by our suppliers are required to be audited by external experts every year. In 2009, 100% of facilities were audited and 100% passed their audits. Facilities that do not pass their audits on the first or second try are given a defined period to make improvements or they will be removed from our supply chain.

Source: McDonald's Corporation, "Worldwide Corporate Responsibility Report 2010," www.aboutmcdonalds.com/content/dam/AboutMcDonalds /Sustainability/Sustainability%20Library/2010-CSR-Report.pdf.

other living things, deserve to be respected and treated with dignity. Such a status would create a wide variety of distinctive ethical responsibilities concerning how we treat animals and would have significant implications for many businesses.

To defend this perspective, some argue that many animals, presumably all animals with a central nervous system, have the capacity to feel pain. Reminiscent of the utilitarian tradition described in chapter 3, this view asserts an ethical responsibility to minimize pain. Inflicting unnecessary pain is taken to be an ethical wrong; therefore, acts that inflict unnecessary pain on animals are ethically wrong. Raising and slaughtering animals for food, particularly in the way industrial farming enterprises raise poultry, hogs, and cattle, would be an obvious case in which business would violate this ethical responsibility, as one side argues in the Reality Check "Treatment of Animals in Agriculture."

A second approach argues that at least some animals have the cognitive capacity to possess a conscious life of their own. Reminiscent of the Kantian ethical tradition described in chapter 3, this view asserts that we have a duty not to treat these animals as mere objects and means to our own ends. Again, businesses that use animals for food, entertainment, or pets would violate the ethical rights of these animals.

Business's Environmental Responsibility: The Market Approach

While debate continues to surround some environmental values, an overwhelming consensus exists about the self-interested and prudential reasons for protecting the natural environment—humans have a right to be protected from undue harm. What controversy remains has more to do with the best means for achieving this goal. Historically, this debate has focused on whether efficient markets or government regulation is the most appropriate means for meeting the environmental responsibilities of business. Each of these two approaches has significant implications for business.

OBJECTIVE

From one perspective, if the best approach to environmental concerns is to trust them to efficient markets, then the responsible business manager simply ought to seek profits and allow the market to allocate resources efficiently. By doing this, business fills its role within a market system, which in turn serves the greater overall (utilitarian) good. On the other hand, if government regulation is a more adequate approach, then business ought to develop a compliance structure to ensure that it conforms to those regulatory requirements.

A market-based approach to resolving environmental challenges is reminiscent of the narrow, economic view of CSR described in chapter 5. Defenders of this market approach contend that environmental problems are economic problems that deserve economic solutions. Fundamentally, environmental problems involve the allocation and distribution of limited resources. Whether we are concerned with the allocation of scarce nonrenewable resources such as gas and oil, or with the earth's capacity to absorb industrial by-products such as CO_2 or PCBs, efficient markets can address environmental challenges.

OBJECTIVE

Consider the implications of this model for pollution and resource conservation. In his well-known book *People or Penguins: The Case for Optimal Pollution,* William Baxter argued that there is an optimal level of pollution that would best serve society's interests.[2] This optimal level is best attained, according to Baxter, by leaving it to a competitive market.

Denying that there is any "natural" or objective standard for clean air or water (as this view would deny there is an objective state of perfect health), Baxter begins with a goal of "safe" air and water quality, and translates this goal to a matter of balancing risks and benefits. Society *could* strive for pure air and water, but the costs (lost opportunities) that this would entail would be too high. A more reasonable approach is to aim for air and water quality that is safe enough to breathe and drink without costing too much. This balance, the "optimal level of pollution," can be achieved through competitive markets. Society, through the activities of individuals, will be willing to pay for pollution reduction as long as the perceived benefits outweigh the costs.

The free market also provides an answer for resource conservation. From a strict market economic perspective, resources are "infinite." Julian Simon, for example, has argued that resources should not be viewed as material objects but simply as any means to our ends.[3] History has shown that human ingenuity and incentive have always found substitutes for any shortages. As the supply of any resources decreases, the price increases, thereby providing a strong incentive to supply more or provide a less costly substitute. In economic terms, all resources are "fungible." They can be replaced by substitutes, and in this sense resources are infinite. Resources that are not being used to satisfy consumer demand are being wasted.

A similar case can be made for the preservation of environmentally sensitive areas. Preservation for preservation's sake would be wasteful because it would use resources inefficiently. Thus, to return to the Manassas Battlefield development plan described previously, preserving open space surrounding the area rather than developing the land as a theme park should be done only if people are willing to pay more for open space than for a park. Because the Disney plan would have been financially very profitable, leaving it undeveloped would be wasting these valuable resources.

OBJECTIVE 5

Challenges to this narrow economic view of corporate social responsibility are familiar to both economists and ethicists. A variety of market failures, many of the best known of which involve environmental issues, point to the inadequacy of market solutions. One example is the existence of externalities, the textbook example of which is environmental pollution. Because the "costs" of such things as air pollution, groundwater contamination and depletion, soil erosion, and nuclear waste disposal are typically borne by parties "external" to the economic exchange (e.g., people downwind, neighbors, future generations), free-market exchanges cannot guarantee optimal results.

A second type of market failure occurs when no markets exist to create a price for important social goods. Endangered species, scenic vistas, rare plants and animals, and biodiversity are just some environmental goods that typically are not traded on open markets (or, when they are, they are often traded in ways that seriously threaten their viability as when rhinoceros horns, tiger claws, elephant tusks, and mahogany trees are sold on the black market). Public goods such as clean air and ocean fisheries also have no established market price. With no established exchange value, the market approach cannot even pretend to achieve its own goals of efficiently meeting consumer demand. Markets alone fail to guarantee that such important public goods are preserved and protected.

A third way in which market failures can lead to serious environmental harm involves a distinction between individual decisions and group consequences. We can miss important ethical and policy questions if we leave policy decisions solely to the outcome of individual decisions. Consider the calculations that an individual consumer might make regarding the purchase of a large SUV and the consequences of that decision on global warming. The additional CO_2 that would be emitted by a single large SUV is miniscule enough that an individual would likely conclude that her decision will make no difference. However, if every consumer made exactly the same decision, the consequences would be significantly different.

corporate average fuel economy (CAFE) standards
Established by the Energy Policy Conservation Act of 1975, corporate average fuel economy (CAFE) is the sales-weighted average fuel economy, expressed in miles per gallon (mpg), of a manufacturer's fleet of passenger cars or light trucks. The U.S. federal government establishes CAFE standards as a means of increasing fuel efficiency of automobiles.

This example demonstrates that the overall social result of individual calculations might be significant increases in pollution and such pollution-related diseases as asthma and allergies. A number of alternative policies (e.g., restricting large SUV sales, increasing taxes on gasoline, treating SUVs as cars instead of light trucks in calculating **corporate average fuel economy [CAFE] standards**) that could address pollution and pollution-related disease would never be considered if we relied only on market solutions. Because these are important ethical questions, and because they remain unasked from within market transactions, we must conclude that markets are incomplete (at best) in their approach to the overall social good. In other words, what is good and rational for a collection of individuals is not necessarily what is good and rational for a society.

Such market failures raise serious concerns for the ability of economic markets to achieve a sound environmental policy. Defenders of a narrow economic view of corporate social responsibility have responses to these challenges of course. Internalizing external costs and assigning property rights to unowned goods such as wild species are two responses to market failures. But there are good reasons for thinking that such ad hoc attempts to repair market failures are environmentally inadequate. One important reason is what has been called the first-generation problem. Markets can work to prevent harm only through information supplied by the existence of market failures. Only when fish populations in the North Atlantic collapsed, for example, did we learn that free and open competition among the world's fishing industry for unowned public goods failed to prevent the decimation of cod, swordfish, Atlantic salmon, and lobster populations. That is, we learn about market failures and thereby prevent harms in the future only by sacrificing the "first generation" as a means of gaining this information. When public policy involves irreplaceable public goods such as endangered species, rare wilderness areas, and public health and safety, such a reactionary strategy is ill advised.

Business's Environmental Responsibility: The Regulatory Approach

OBJECTIVE

A broad consensus emerged in the United States in the 1970s that unregulated markets are an inadequate approach to environmental challenges. Instead, governmental regulations were seen as the better way to respond to environmental problems. Much of the most significant environmental legislation in the United States was enacted during the 1970s. The Clean Air Act of 1970 (amended and renewed in 1977), Federal Water Pollution Act of 1972 (amended and renewed as the Clean Water Act of 1977), and the Endangered Species Act of 1973 were part of this national consensus for addressing environmental problems. Each law was originally enacted by a Democratic Congress and signed into law by a Republican president.

These laws share a common approach to environmental issues. Before this legislation was enacted, the primary legal avenue open for addressing environmental concerns was tort law. Only individuals who could prove that they had been harmed by pollution could raise legal challenges to air and water pollution. That legal approach placed the burden on the person who was harmed and, at best, offered compensation for the harm only after the fact. Except for the incentive provided by the threat of compensation, U.S. policy did little to prevent the pollution in the first place. Absent any proof of negligence, public policy was content to let the market decide environmental policy. Because endangered species themselves had no legal standing, direct harm to plant and animal life was of no legal concern and previous policies did little to prevent harm to plant and animal life.

The laws enacted during the 1970s established standards that effectively shifted the burden from those threatened with harm to those who would cause the harm. Government established regulatory standards to try to prevent the occurrence of pollution or species extinction rather than to offer compensation after the fact. We can think of these laws as establishing minimum standards to ensure air and water quality and species preservation. Business was free to pursue its own

Reality Check *Cap and Trade—a Mixed Approach?*

One strategy that combines elements of both market and regulatory approaches is the so-called cap and trade model that has been proposed in the United States as part of legislation to address carbon emissions. Under the cap and trade model, government sets an overall annual target, or "cap," on the amount of CO_2 emissions nationally. Companies then buy government-issued permits to emit pollution. The permits limit the total overall amount of pollution to the national cap. Individual businesses are free to buy or sell their permits in such a way that an efficient company that emits less pollution than its permits allow can sell its remaining pollution credits to a less efficient company. By thus creating a market for pollution credits, government regulation creates an incentive for individual businesses to reduce their own pollution. Government can then slowly reduce the overlap pollution target annually to achieve its public policy goal.

Defenders see this approach as a powerful way to use market incentives to reduce pollution. Critics see it as government issuing a "license to pollute."

goals as long as it complied with the side constraints these minimum standards established.

The consensus that emerged was that society had two opportunities to establish business' environmental responsibilities. As consumers, individuals could demand environmentally friendly products in the marketplace. As citizens, individuals could support environmental legislation. As long as business responded to the market and obeyed the law, it met its environmental responsibilities. If consumers demand environmentally suspect products, such as large gas-guzzling SUVs, and those products are allowed by law, then we cannot expect business to forgo the financial opportunities of marketing such products.

OBJECTIVE

Several problems suggest that this approach will prove inadequate over the long term. First, it underestimates the influence that business can have in establishing the law. The CAFE standards mentioned previously provide a good example of how this can occur. A reasonable account of this law suggests that the public very clearly expressed a political goal of improving air quality by improving automobile fuel efficiency goals (and thereby reducing automobile emissions). However, the automobile industry was able to use its lobbying influence to exempt light trucks and SUVs from these standards. It should be no surprise that light trucks and SUVs at the time represented the largest-selling, and most profitable, segment of the auto industry.

Second, this approach also underestimates the ability of business to influence consumer choice. To conclude that business fulfills its environmental responsibility when it responds to the environmental demands of consumers is to underestimate the role that business can play in shaping public opinion. Advertising is a $200 billion a year industry in the United States alone. It is surely misleading to claim that business passively responds to consumer desires and that consumers are unaffected by the messages that business conveys. Assuming that business is not going to stop advertising its products or lobbying government, this model of corporate environmental responsibility is likely to prove inadequate for protecting the natural environment.

Further, if we rely on the law to protect the environment, environmental protection will extend only as far as the law extends. Yet, most environmental issues, pollution problems especially, do not respect legal jurisdictions. New York State might pass strict regulations on smokestack emissions, but if the power plants are located downwind in Ohio or even further west in the Dakotas or Wyoming, New York State will continue to suffer the effects of acid rain. Similarly, national regulations will be ineffective for international environmental challenges. While hope remains that international agreements might help control global environmental problems, the failure of the international community to reach enforceable carbon emission standards suggests that this might be overly optimistic.

sustainable development
Development that meets the needs of the present without compromising the ability of future generations to meet their own needs as defined by the Brundtland Commission in 1987.

Finally, and perhaps most troubling from an environmental standpoint, this regulatory model assumes that economic growth is environmentally and ethically benign. Regulations establish side constraints on business's pursuit of profits and, as long as they remain within those constraints, accept as ethically legitimate whatever road to profitability management chooses. What can be lost in these discussions is the very important fact that there are many different ways to pursue profits within the side constraints of law. Different roads toward profitability can have very different environmental consequences, as is discussed in the Reality Check "Cap and Trade—a Mixed Approach?"

Business's Environmental Responsibilities: The Sustainability Approach

OBJECTIVE

sustainable business practice
A model of business practice in which business activities meet the standards of sustainability.

three pillars of sustainability
Three factors that are often used to judge the adequacy of sustainable practices. Sustainable development must be (1) economically, (2) environmentally, and (3) ethically satisfactory.

Beginning in the 1980s, a new model for environmentally responsible business began to take shape, one that combines financial opportunities with environmental and ethical responsibilities. The concept of **sustainable development** and **sustainable business practice** suggests a radically new vision for integrating financial and environmental goals, compared to the growth model that preceded it (as explored in the Reality Check "Why Sustainability?"). These three goals, economic, environmental, and ethical sustainability, are often referred to as the **three pillars of sustainability.** Assessing business activity along these three lines is often referred to as the triple bottom line. (For a critical perspective on the triple bottom line, see Reading 9-2, "Getting to the Bottom of 'Triple Bottom Line,'" by Wayne Norman and Chris MacDonald.)

The concept of sustainable development can be traced to a 1987 report from the United Nations' World Commission on Environment and Development (WCED), more commonly known as the Brundtland Commission, named for its chair Gro Harlem Brundtland. The commission was charged with developing recommendations for paths toward economic and social development that would not achieve short-term economic growth at the expense of long-term environmental and economic sustainability. The Brundtland Commission offered what has become the standard definition of sustainable development. Sustainable development is "development that meets the needs of the present without compromising the ability of future generations to meet their own needs."

Reality Check *Why Sustainability?*

Three factors are most often cited to explain and justify the need for a model of economic development that stresses sustainability rather than growth.

First, billions of human beings live in severe poverty and face real challenges on a daily basis for meeting their basic needs for food, water, health care, and shelter. Addressing these challenges will require significant economic activity.

Second, world population continues to grow at a disturbing rate, with projections of an increase from 7 billion shortly after 2010 and 8 billion before 2030. Most of this population growth will occur within the world's poorest regions, thereby only intensifying the first challenge. Even more economic activity will be needed to address the needs of this growing population.

Third, all of this economic activity must rely on the productive capacity of the earth's biosphere. Unfortunately, there is ample evidence that the type and amount of economic activity practiced by the world's economies have already approached if not overshot the earth's ability to support human life.

Given these realities, citizens within developed economies have three available paths. First, we can believe that developing economies in places such as China, India, and Indonesia cannot, will not, or should not strive for the type of economic lifestyle and prosperity enjoyed in developed economies. Second, we could believe, optimistically, that present models of business and economic growth can be extended across the globe to an expanding population without degrading the natural environment beyond its limits. Third, we can search for new models of economic and business activity that provide for the needs of the world's population without further degrading the biosphere. Sustainable development and the connected model of sustainable business choose this third path.

Economist Herman Daly has been among the leading thinkers who have advocated an innovative approach to economic theory based on the concept of sustainable development. Daly makes a convincing case for an understanding of economic *development* that transcends the more common standard of economic *growth.* Unless we make significant changes in our understanding of economic activity, unless quite literally we change the way we do business, we will fail to meet some very basic ethical and environmental obligations. According to Daly, we need a major paradigm shift in how we understand economic activity.

We can begin with the standard understanding of economic activity and economic growth found in almost every economics textbook. What is sometimes called the "circular flow model" (Figure 9.2) explains the nature of economic transactions in terms of a flow of resources from businesses to households and back again. Business produces goods and services in response to the market demands of households, then ships the goods and services to households in exchange for payments back to business. These payments are in turn sent back to households in the form of wages, salaries, rents, profits, and interests. Households receive the payments in exchange for the labor, land, capital, and entrepreneurial skills business uses to produce goods and services.

Two aspects of this circular flow model are worth noting. First, it does not differentiate natural resources from the other factors of production. This model does not explain the origin of resources. They are simply owned by households from which they, like labor, capital, and entrepreneurial skill, can be sold to business. Economist Julian Simon has argued, "As economists or consumers, we are interested in the particular services that resources yield, not in the resources themselves." Those

FIGURE 9.2
The Circular Flow Model

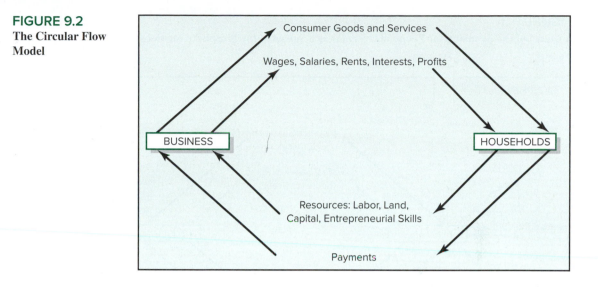

services can be provided in many ways and by substituting different factors of production. In Simon's terms, resources can therefore be treated as "infinite."

A second observation is that this model treats economic growth as both the solution to all social ills and also as boundless. To keep up with population growth, the economy must grow. To provide for a higher standard of living, the economy must grow. To alleviate poverty, hunger, and disease, the economy must grow. The possibility that the economy cannot grow indefinitely is simply not part of this model.

The three points summarized in the Reality Check "Why Sustainability?" suggest why this growth-based model will be inadequate. According to some estimates, the world's economy would need to grow by a factor of 5- to 10-fold over the next 50 years to bring the standard of living of present populations in the developing world into line with the standard of living in the industrialized world. Yet, within those 50 years the world's population will increase by more than 3 billion people, most of them born in the world's poorest economies. Of course, the only source for all this economic activity is productive capacity of the earth itself.

Daly argues that neoclassical economics, with its emphasis on economic growth as the goal of economic policy, will inevitably fail to meet these challenges unless it recognizes that the economy is but a subsystem within earth's biosphere. Economic activity takes place within this biosphere and cannot expand beyond its capacity to sustain life. All the factors that go into production—natural resources, capital, entrepreneurial skill, and labor—ultimately originate in the productive capacity of the earth. In light of this, the entire classical model will prove unstable if resources move through this system at a rate that outpaces the productive capacity of the earth and the earth's capacity to absorb the wastes and by-products of this production. Thus, we need to develop an economic system that uses resources only at a rate that can be sustained over the long term and that recycles or reuses

FIGURE 9.3

A Model of the Economy (or Economic System) as a Subset of the Biosphere (or Ecosystem)

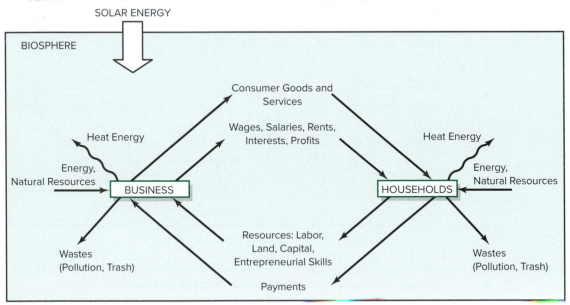

both the by-products of the production process and the products themselves. A model of such a system, based on Daly's work, is presented in Figure 9.3.

Figure 9.3 differs from Figure 9.2 in several important ways. First, the sustainable model recognizes that the economy exists within a finite biosphere that encompasses a band around the earth that is little more than a few miles wide. From the first law of thermodynamics (the conservation of matter/energy), we recognize that neither matter nor energy can truly be "created," it can only be transferred from one form to another. Second, energy is lost at every stage of economic activity. Consistent with the second law of thermodynamics (entropy increased within a closed system), the amount of usable energy decreases over time. "Waste energy" is continuously leaving the economic system and thus new low-entropy energy must constantly flow into the system. Ultimately, the only source for low-entropy energy is the sun. Third, this model no longer treats natural resources as an undifferentiated and unexplained factor of production emerging from households. Natural resources come from the biosphere and cannot be created ex nihilo. Finally, it recognizes that wastes are produced at each stage of economic activity and these wastes are dumped back into the biosphere.

The conclusion that should be drawn from this new model is relatively simple. Over the long term, resources and energy cannot be used, nor waste produced, at rates at which the biosphere cannot replace or absorb them without jeopardizing its ability to sustain (human) life. These are what Daly calls the "biophysical limits to growth."[4] The biosphere can produce resources indefinitely, and it can absorb wastes indefinitely, but only at a certain rate and with a certain type of economic activity. This is the goal of sustainable development. Finding this rate and type of economic activity, and thereby creating a sustainable business practice, is the ultimate environmental responsibility of business.

The "Business Case" for a Sustainable Economy

OBJECTIVE 8

While the regulatory and compliance model tends to interpret environmental responsibilities as constraints upon business, the sustainability model is more forward looking and may present business with greater opportunities than burdens. Indeed, it offers a vision of future business that many entrepreneurial and creative businesses are already pursuing. Many observers argue that a strong economic and financial case can be made for the move toward a sustainable future (but also see the Reality Check "Should Every Business Be Sustainable?").

First, sustainability is a prudent long-term strategy. As the Natural Step's funnel image suggests, business will need to adopt sustainable practices to ensure long-term survival. Firms that fail to adapt to the converging lines of decreasing availability of resources and increasing demand risk their own survival. One can look to the ocean fishing industry as an example.

Second, the huge unmet market potential among the world's developing economies can only be met in sustainable ways. Enormous business opportunities exist in serving the billions of people who need, and are demanding, economic goods and services. The base of the economic pyramid represents the largest and fastest-growing economic market in human history. Yet, the sheer size of these markets alone makes it impossible to meet this demand with the environmentally damaging industrial practices of the nineteenth and twentieth centuries. For example, if China were to consume oil at the same rate as the United States, it alone would consume more than the entire world's daily production and would more than triple the emission of atmospheric carbon dioxide. It is obvious that new sustainable technologies and products will be required to meet the Chinese demand.

Third, significant cost savings can be achieved through sustainable practices. Business stands to save significant costs in moves toward eco-efficiency. Savings on energy use and materials will reduce not only environmental wastes, but spending wastes as well. Minimizing wastes makes sense on financial grounds as well as on environmental grounds.

Fourth, competitive advantages exist for sustainable businesses. Firms that are ahead of the sustainability curve will both have an advantage serving environmentally conscious consumers and enjoy a competitive advantage attracting workers who will take pride and satisfaction in working for progressive firms.

Finally, sustainability is a good risk management strategy. Refusing to move toward sustainability offers many downsides that innovative firms will avoid. Avoiding future government regulation is one obvious benefit. Firms that take the initiative in moving toward sustainability will also likely be the firms that set the standards of best practices in the field. Thus, when regulation does come, these

Reality Check   *Should Every Business Be Sustainable?*

The idea of *sustainability* is everywhere in contemporary business, with virtually all business divisions including management, marketing, investing, accounting, strategy, and operations claiming sustainable models and practices. It is difficult to find a major corporation that does not issue an annual sustainability report; by one account 95 percent of the Global 250 issue annual sustainability reports.[5] Countless other firms have supplemented, if not replaced, their annual financial report with a broader annual sustainability report.

As originally used by the Brundtland Commission, "sustainable development" was clearly an ethical concept, suggesting an ethical norm to guide practical decision making. Sustainable development was understood as economic activity that met human needs without exploiting the productive capacity of the natural environment. But this demonstrates that the ethical force of sustainable development as envisioned by the Brundtland Report comes from the noun *development*, not from the modifier *sustainable*. That is, the ethical goal is economic development that

meets human needs and, because this is an ethically desirable goal, we should seek to achieve this in ways that are environmentally sustainable.

Implicit in this observation is the fact that the words *sustainable* and *sustainability* have no ethical meaning in themselves. To describe something as sustainable is simply to describe it as capable of continuing long term. Not everything that is sustainable is ethically good. We could easily imagine any number of unethical business practices, from deceptive advertising and fraudulent investment schemes to racial discrimination and marketing of dangerous products, as being sustainable.

So we should be wary anytime we hear the words *sustainable* or *sustainability* used without specifying what it is that should be sustained. We should always ask: "What is being sustained?" "Should it be sustained?" "How would we contribute to the long-term economic productivity of the global environment by sustaining this organization or this practice?"

firms will likely play a role in determining what those regulations ought to be. Avoiding legal liability for unsustainable products is another potential benefit. As social consciousness changes, the legal system may soon begin punishing firms that are now negligent in failing to foresee harms caused by their unsustainable practices. Consumer boycotts of unsustainable firms are also a risk to be avoided.

We can summarize these previous sections by reflecting on the ethical decision-making model used throughout this text. The facts suggest that the earth's biosphere is under stress and that much of this comes from the type of global economic growth that has characterized industrial and consumerist societies. The ethical issues that develop from these facts include fairness in allocating scarce resources, justice in meeting the real needs of billions of present and future human beings, and the values and rights associated with environmental conservation and preservation. The stakeholders for these decisions include, quite literally, all life on earth. Relying on our own moral imagination, we can envision a future in which economic activity can meet the real needs of present generations without jeopardizing the ability of future generations to meet their own needs. Sustainability seems to be just this vision. The next section describes directions in which business might develop toward this sustainable model. (To consider how the idea of sustainability might also mislead business, see the Reality Check "Triple Bottom Line: A Trojan Horse?")

Principles for a Sustainable Business

OBJECTIVE

Figure 9.3 provides a general model for understanding how firms can evolve toward a sustainable business model. In the simplest terms, resources should not enter into the economic cycle from the biosphere at rates faster than they are replenished. Ideally, waste should be eliminated or, at a minimum, not produced at a rate faster than the biosphere can absorb it. Finally, the energy to power the economic system should be renewable, ultimately relying on the sun, the only energy that is truly renewable.

The precise implications of sustainability will differ for specific firms and industries, but three general principles will guide the move toward sustainability. Firms and industries must become more efficient in using natural resources; they should model their entire production process on biological processes; and they should emphasize the production of services rather than products.

eco-efficiency
Doing more with less. Introduced at the Rio Earth Summit in 1992, the concept of eco-efficiency is a way business can contribute to sustainability by reducing resource usage in its production cycle.

Versions of the first principle, sometimes called **eco-efficiency,** have long been a part of the environmental movement. "Doing more with less" has been an environmental guideline for decades. On an individual scale, it is environmentally better to ride a bike than to ride in a bus, to ride in a fuel-cell or hybrid-powered bus than in a diesel bus, to ride in a bus than to drive a personal automobile, and to drive a hybrid car than an SUV. Likewise, business firms can improve energy and materials efficiency in such things as lighting, building design, product design, and distribution channels. Some estimates suggest that with present technologies alone, business could readily achieve at least a fourfold increase in efficiency and perhaps as much as a tenfold increase. Consider that a fourfold increase, called "Factor Four" in the sustainability literature, would make it possible to achieve double the productivity from one-half the resource use.[6] When applied to the additional costs for buildings associated with Leadership in Energy and Environmental Design (LEED) standards, for example, such a return on investment means that companies can quickly recoup this environmental investment.

The second principle of business sustainability can be easily understood by reference to Figure 9.3. Imagine that the waste leaving the economic cycle is being turned back into the cycle as a productive resource. "Closed-loop" production seeks to integrate what is presently waste back into production. In an ideal situation, the waste of one firm becomes the resource of another, and such synergies can create eco-industrial parks. Just as biological processes such as photosynthesis cycle the "waste" of one activity into the resource of another, this

biomimicry ("closed-loop" production)
Seeks to integrate what is presently waste back into production in much the way that biological processes turn waste into food.

principle is often referred to as **biomimicry ("closed-loop" production).**

The ultimate goal of biomimicry is to eliminate waste altogether rather than reducing it. If we truly mimic biological processes, the end result of one process (e.g., leaves and oxygen produced by photosynthesis) is ultimately reused as the productive resources (e.g., soil and water) of another process (plant growth) with only solar energy added.

The evolution of business strategy toward biomimicry can be understood along a continuum. The earliest phase has been described as "take-make-waste."

Reality Check   *Triple Bottom Line: A Trojan Horse?*

The original idea of sustainable development is now often replaced by calls for a more general and vague goal of "social sustainability." When this happens, we should avoid a type of "reverse greenwashing" in which unrelated social concerns are smuggled into the call for sustainable development. John Elkington, the originator of the triple bottom line concept, seems to have done just that. In a 2008 interview with a reporter from the magazine *Mother Jones*, Elkington responded to a question about how he developed the idea of triple bottom line:

> I think quite a number of multinational corporations, in particular US corporations, were quite spooked by the whole social agenda and actively steering away from it.

So" "triple bottom line" was very consciously business language, trying to get under the guard of business people. It's almost a Trojan horse trying to give them a sense that this was something that they wanted to play with and subscribe to. Once they started to use the language and commit to it to some degree, we could then define it in ways that could stretch their imaginations a little. That's how it went down.

In other words, it was justifiable to mislead and manipulate business for the greater good of some unspecified social agenda.

Source: Jesse Finfrock, *Mother Jones*, November/December 2008.

Business takes resources, makes products out of them, and discards whatever is left over. A second phase envisions business taking responsibility for its products from "cradle to grave." Sometimes referred to as "life-cycle" responsibility, this approach has already found its way into both industrial and regulatory thinking. Cradle-to-grave or life-cycle responsibility holds that a business is responsible for the entire life of its products, including the ultimate disposal even after the sale. Thus, for example, a cradle-to-grave model would hold a business liable for groundwater contamination caused by its products even years after they had been buried in a landfill.

cradle-to-cradle responsibility
Holds that a business should be responsible for incorporating the end results of its products back into the productive cycle.

Cradle-to-cradle responsibility extends this idea even further and holds that a business should be responsible for incorporating the end results of its products back into the productive cycle. This responsibility, in turn, would create incentives to redesign products so that they could be recycled efficiently and easily.

The environmental design company McDonough and Braungart, founded by architect William McDonough and chemist Michael Braungart, has been a leader in helping businesses reconceptualize and redesign business practice to achieve sustainability. Their book *Cradle to Cradle* traces the life cycle of several products, providing case studies of economic and environmental benefits attainable when business takes responsibility for the entire life cycle of products. Among their projects is the redesign of Ford Motor Company's Rouge River manufacturing plant. McDonough and Braungart provide greater details about their design principles in Reading 9-1, "The Next Industrial Revolution," at the end of this chapter.

Beyond eco-efficiency and biomimicry, a third sustainable business principle involves a shift in business model from products to services. Traditional economic and managerial models interpret consumer demand as the demand for products— washing machines, carpeting, lights, consumer electronics, air conditioners,

service-based economy
Interprets consumer demand as a demand for services, for example, for clothes cleaning, floor covering, cool air, transportation, or word processing, rather than as a demand for products such as washing machines, carpeting, air conditioners, cars, and computers.

cars, computers, and so forth. A **service-based economy** interprets consumer demand as a demand for services—for clothes cleaning, floor covering, illumination, entertainment, cool air, transportation, word processing, and so forth.

The book *Natural Capitalism* provides examples of businesses that have made such a shift in each of these industries.[7] This change produces incentives for product redesigns that create more durable and more easily recyclable products.

One well-known innovator in this area is Interface Corporation and its CEO, Ray Anderson. Interface has made a transition from selling carpeting to leasing floor-covering services. On the traditional model, carpet is sold to consumers who, once they become dissatisfied with the color or style or once the carpeting becomes worn, dispose of the carpet in landfills. There is little incentive here to produce long-lasting or easily recyclable carpeting. Once Interface shifted to leasing floor-covering services, it created incentives to produce long-lasting, easily replaceable and recyclable carpets. Interface thereby accepts responsibility for the entire life cycle of the product it markets. Because the company retains ownership and is responsible for maintenance, Interface now produces carpeting that can be easily replaced in sections rather than in its entirety, that is more durable, and that can eventually be remanufactured. Redesigning carpets and shifting to a service lease has also improved production efficiencies and reduced material and energy costs significantly. Consumers benefit by getting what they truly desire at lower costs and fewer burdens.

Sustainable Marketing

OBJECTIVE

sustainable or green marketing
Sustainable or green marketing is the marketing of products on the basis of their environmentally friendly nature.

"Sustainability" was introduced in chapter 5 as an approach to corporate social responsibility that is gaining influence in all areas of business. **Sustainable or green marketing** is one aspect of this approach that already has changed how many firms do business. The four characteristics (Four Ps) of marketing introduced earlier in chapter 8—product, price, promotion, and placement—are a helpful way to structure an understanding of sustainable, green marketing.

Product

The most significant progress toward sustainability will depend on the sustainability of products themselves. Discovering what the consumer "really wants" and developing products to meet those wants have always been among the primary marketing challenges. Meeting the real needs of present and future generations within ecological constraints can be understood simply as a refinement of this traditional marketing objective.

Consider, for example, the business differences between marketing the physical pieces of computer hardware and marketing computing services. Should Dell or HP be in the business of selling computer components, or are they selling the service to provide consumers with up-to-date computer hardware, software, and data storage? A later section will examine the distinction between products and service in more depth, but the marketing department should be at the forefront of identifying the real needs of consumers so that a business can develop the long-term relationships with consumers that will ensure both financial and ecological sustainability.

Another aspect of marketing involves the design and creation of products. William McDonough (see Reading 9-1 at the end of this chapter) has often described environmental regulation as a design problem; a product or production process that pollutes and wastes resources is a poorly designed product or process. Regulatory mandates usually result when business has a poorly designed product or process. Marketing departments therefore should also be involved in the design of products, finding ways to build sustainability into the very design of each product.

Finally, marketing professionals have an opportunity to influence the packaging of products. Overpackaging and the use of petroleum-based plastics are packaging issues already under environmental scrutiny. Imagine the marketing opportunities if a major soft-drink bottler such as Coke or Pepsi turned to corn-based biodegradable plastics for their bottles. Imagine what the marketing department of major mail-order companies such as Lands' End or L.L.Bean could do if their catalogs were printed on recycled paper. Imagine the marketing opportunities, and responsibilities, of a company such as Procter & Gamble moving toward recycled cardboard for its packaging.

These three areas come together clearly within the context of extended producer responsibility and take-back legislation in which a firm is held responsible to take back and recycle all the products it introduces into the marketplace. These regulatory developments, now taking hold especially in Europe, will be seen as barriers to profit by some firms. But more creative firms will see opportunities here for generating entire new markets. Take-back legislation provides strong incentives for redesigning products in ways that make it easier to reuse and recycle. Marketing services rather than products, of course, will be the most efficient means for accomplishing this objective.

Price

A second aspect of marketing is price. Sustainability asks us to focus on the environmental costs of resources, the "natural capital" on which most firms rely, and points out that environmental costs are seldom factored into the price of most products. Marketing professionals should play a role in setting prices that reflect a product's true ecological cost.

At first glance, this might seem a peculiar area in which to expect business to move. Internalizing environmental externalities sounds like a polite way of suggesting that business ought to raise its prices. Such a strategy would seem, at best, unrealistic. Government regulation, rather than voluntary action, is more likely to move business in this direction. Without government mandates across the board for an industry, internalizing the costs of natural capitalism into its products will put a company at a comparative disadvantage.

On the other hand, setting prices in such a way that more sustainable products are priced competitively with other products is a more reasonable strategy for sustainable marketing. Ordinarily, we might think that pricing is a straightforward and objective process. One starts with the costs of producing a product, adds a

Marketing to the Base of the Pyramid

In his landmark book (and in Reading 8-3 with coauthor Stuart L. Hart) business scholar C. K. Prahalad details the business opportunities that exist for firms that are creative and resourceful enough to develop markets among the world's poorest people.[8]

Done correctly, marketing to the 4 billion people at the base of the global economic pyramid would employ market forces in addressing some of the greatest ethical and environmental problems of the 21st century.

Obviously, helping meet the needs of the world's poorest people would be a significant ethical contribution. The strategy involves another ethical consideration as well: A market of this size requires environmentally sustainable products and technologies. If everyone in the world used resources and created wastes at the rate Americans do, the global environment would suffer immeasurably. Businesses that understand this fact face a huge marketing opportunity.

Accomplishing such goals will require a significant revision to the standard marketing paradigm. Business must, in Prahalad's phrase, "create the capacity to consume" among the world's poor. Creating this capacity to consume among the world's poor would create a significant win–win opportunity from both a financial and an ethical perspective.

Prahalad points out that the world's poor do have significant purchasing power, albeit in the aggregate rather than on a per capita basis. Creating the capacity to consume among the world's poor will require a transformation in the conceptual framework of global marketing and some creative steps from business. Prahalad mentions three principles as key to marketing to the poor: affordability, access, and availability.

Consider how a firm might market such household products as laundry soap differently in India than in the United States. Marketing in the United States can involve large plastic containers, sold at a low per-unit cost. Trucks transport cases from manufacturing plants to wholesale warehouses to giant big-box retailers where they can sit in inventory until purchase. Consumers wheel the heavy containers out to their cars in shopping carts and store them at home in the laundry room.

The aggregate soap market in India could be greater than the market in the United States, but Indian consumers would require smaller and more affordable containers. Prahalad therefore talks about the need for single-size servings for many consumer products. Given longer and more erratic work hours and a lack of personal transportation, the poor often lack access to markets. Creative marketing would need to find ways to provide easier access to their products. Longer store hours and wider and more convenient distribution channels could reach consumers otherwise left out of the market.

So, too, can imaginative financing, credit, and pricing schemes. Microfinance and microcredit arrangements are developing throughout less developed economies as creative means to support the capacity of poor people to buy and sell goods and services. Finally, innovative marketing can ensure that products are available where and when the world's poor need them. Base-of-the-pyramid consumers tend to be cash customers with incomes that are unpredictable. A distributional system that ensures product availability at the time and place when customers are ready and able to make the purchase can help create the capacity to consume. Prahalad's

(continued)

approach—tied to moral imagination discussed previously responds both to the consumers and to the corporate investors and other for-profit multinational stakeholders.

- Do you think that business firms and industries have an ethical responsibility to address global poverty by creating the capacity to consume among the world's poor? Do you think that this can be done? What responsibilities, ethical and economic, do firms face when marketing in other countries and among different cultures? Imagine that you are in the marketing department of a firm that manufacturers a consumer product such as laundry detergent or shampoo. Describe how it might be marketed differently in India.
- What are the key facts relevant to your judgment?
- What ethical issues are involved in a firm's decision to market its products among the world's poor by creating the capacity to consume?
- Who are the stakeholders?
- What alternatives does a firm have with regard to the way in which it markets its products?
- How do the alternatives compare; how do the alternatives you have identified affect the stakeholders?

reasonable rate of return, and the result is the asking price. Ultimately, the actual price is whatever buyer and seller agree on. However, this simple model misses some important complexities. To understand some of the complexities of price, and the role of marketing in this, consider the example of hybrid automobiles.

Like any new product, a hybrid automobile required investments in research, design, production, and marketing long before it could be brought to market. For such a complex product as a hybrid automobile, these investments were substantial, well into the hundreds of millions of dollars for each automaker that produces a hybrid. Setting a price for this product involves a complicated process of projecting sales, markets, and a product's life cycle. In one sense, the very first hybrid cost millions of dollars to manufacture, well beyond an affordable and marketable price. Businesses normally take a loss on a new product until such time as economies of scale kick in to lower costs and market share develops sufficiently to produce a revenue stream that can begin to pay down the initial investment and generate profits. Marketing professionals who are aware of sustainability concerns have much to contribute in establishing prices that protect sustainable products from short-term cost–benefit analyses.

Consider also how price functions with such business practices as sales, manufacturer's rebates, cash-back incentives to consumers, bonuses to sales staff, and the use of loss leaders in retailing. Obviously price is often manipulated for many marketing reasons, including promotion to help gain a foothold in a market. Short-term losses are often justified in pricing decisions by appeal to long-term considerations. This seems a perfect fit for sustainable marketing goals.

Perhaps nowhere is price a more crucial element of marketing than it is in marketing to the base of the economic pyramid. Small profit margins and efficient distribution systems within large markets, as demonstrated so clearly by large retailers like Walmart, can prove to be a highly successful business model. An ethically praiseworthy goal would be to export this marketing ingenuity to serve the cause of global sustainability. The Decision Point "Marketing to the Base of the Pyramid" explains the mechanics of this process, and in chapter 8 Reading 8-3 by Prahalad and Hart offers a classic discussion of its marketing analysis.

Promotion

A third aspect of marketing, of course, is the promotion and advertising of products. Marketing also has a responsibility to help shape consumer demand, encouraging consumers to demand more sustainable products from business. Without question, marketing has already shown how powerful a force it can be in shaping consumer demand. Marketing has played a major role in creating various social meanings for shopping and buying. Sustainable marketing can help create the social meanings and consumer expectations supportive of sustainable goals. An often overlooked aspect of advertising is its educational function. Consumers learn from advertising and marketers have a responsibility as educators. Helping consumers learn the value of sustainable products, helping them become sustainable consumers, is an important role for sustainable marketing. For example, see the Reality Check "Terra Choice's Seven Sins of Greenwashing" as one effort in consumer education.

Certainly one aspect of product promotion will involve the "green labeling." Just as ingredient labels, nutrition labels, and warning labels have become normal and standardized, environmental pressure may well create a public demand for environmental and sustainable labeling. But, history has shown a tendency for some firms to exploit green labeling initiatives and mislead consumers. "Greenwashing" is the practice of promoting a product by misleading consumers about the environmentally beneficial aspects of the product. Labeling products with such terms as *environmentally friendly, natural, eco, energy efficient, biodegradable,* and the like can help promote products that have little or no environmental benefits. Take a look at the Decision Point "Examples of Greenwashing?" to see if you can distinguish the greenwashing claims from the sincere ones.

Placement

The final aspect of marketing involves the channels of distribution that move a product from producer to consumer. Professor Patrick Murphy suggests two directions in which marketing can develop sustainable channels.[9] As typically understood, marketing channels involve such things as transportation, distribution, inventory, and the like. Recent advances in marketing have emphasized just-in-time (JIT) inventory control, large distribution centers, and sophisticated transportation schemes. Murphy foresees new sustainability options being added to this model that emphasize fuel efficiency and alternative fuel technologies used in transportation, more localized and efficient distribution channels, and a greater reliance on electronic rather than physical distribution. More efficient distribution channels can also serve the underserved base of the pyramid consumers.

Reality Check Terra Choices Seven Sins of Greenwashing

SIN OF THE HIDDEN TRADE-OFF

A claim suggesting that a product is "green" based on a narrow set of attributes without attention to other important environmental issues. Paper, for example, is not necessarily environmentally preferable just because it comes from a sustainably harvested forest. Other important environmental issues in the paper-making process, such as greenhouse gas emissions, or chlorine use in bleaching, may be equally important.

SIN OF NO PROOF

An environmental claim that cannot be substantiated by easily accessible supporting information or by a reliable third-party certification. Common examples are facial tissues or toilet tissue products that claim various percentages of post-consumer recycled content without providing evidence.

SIN OF VAGUENESS

A claim that is so poorly defined or broad that its real meaning is likely to be misunderstood by the consumer. "All natural" is an example. Arsenic, uranium, mercury, and formaldehyde are all naturally occurring, and poisonous. "All natural" isn't necessarily "green."

SIN OF WORSHIPING FALSE LABELS

A product that, through either words or images, gives the impression of third-party endorsement where no such endorsement exists; fake labels, in other words.

SIN OF IRRELEVANCE

An environmental claim that may be truthful but is unimportant or unhelpful for consumers seeking environmentally preferable products. "CFC-free" is a common example because it is a frequent claim despite the fact that CFCs are banned by law.

SIN OF LESSER OF TWO EVILS

A claim that may be true within the product category, but that risks distracting the consumer from the greater environmental impacts of the category as a whole. Organic cigarettes could be an example of this sin, as might the fuel-efficient sport-utility vehicle.

SIN OF FIBBING

Environmental claims that are simply false. The most common examples are products falsely claiming to be Energy Star certified or registered.

Consider, as an example, how the publishing industry has evolved its channels of distribution. Originally, books, magazines, catalogs, or newspapers were printed in one location and then distributed via truck, rail, or air across the country. More modern practices piloted by such companies as *USA Today* and the *Wall Street Journal* send electronic versions of the content to localized printers who publish and distribute the final product locally. Textbook publishers do a similar thing when they allow users to select specific content and create a custom-published book for each use. As subscriptions to hard-copy publications decline, many newspapers, magazines, and catalogs are taking this a step further by moving toward online publishing.

Murphy also describes a second aspect of the channel variable in marketing that promises significant sustainability rewards. "Reverse channels" refers to the growing marketing practice of taking back one's products after their useful life. The life-cycle responsibility and "take-back" models described previously will likely fall to marketing departments. The same department that is responsible for sending a product out into the marketplace should expect the responsibility for finding ways to take back that product to dispose, recycle, or reuse it.[10]

Which of the following corporate marketing initiatives would you describe as an example of greenwashing?

- An ad for the GM Hummer that describes the truck as "thirsty for adventure, not gas." The Hummer was rated at 20 mpg on the highway.
- A major rebranding of the oil company British Petroleum by renaming itself "BP" for "beyond petroleum."
- An "eco-shaped" bottle for the bottle water brand Ice Mountain. For that matter, any bottled water described as "natural," "pure," or "organic."

Which of the following examples, all taken from the Federal Trade Commission, are cases of misleading greenwashing?

- A box of aluminum foil is labeled with the claim "recyclable," without further elaboration. Unless the type of product, surrounding language, or other context of the phrase establishes whether the claim refers to the foil or the box, the claim is deceptive if any part of either the box or the foil, other than minor, incidental components, cannot be recycled.
- A trash bag is labeled "recyclable"" without qualification. Because trash bags will ordinarily not be separated out from other trash at the landfill or incinerator for recycling, they are highly unlikely to be used again for any purpose.
- An advertiser notes that its shampoo bottle contains "20 percent more recycled content." The claim in its context is ambiguous. Depending on contextual factors, it could be a comparison either to the advertiser's immediately preceding product or to a competitor's product.
- A product wrapper is printed with the claim "Environmentally Friendly." Textual comments on the wrapper explain that the wrapper is environmentally friendly because it was not chlorine bleached, a process that has been shown to create harmful substances. The wrapper was, in fact, not bleached with chlorine. However, the production of the wrapper now creates and releases to the environment significant quantities of other harmful substances.
- A product label contains an environmental seal, either in the form of a globe icon, or a globe icon with only the text *Earth Smart* around it. Either label is likely to convey to consumers that the product is environmentally superior to other products.
- A nationally marketed bottle bears the unqualified statement that it is "recyclable." Collection sites for recycling the material in question are not available to a substantial majority of consumers or communities, although collection sites are established in a significant percentage of communities or available to a significant percentage of the population.
- The seller of an aerosol product makes an unqualified claim that its product "Contains no CFCs." Although the product does not contain CFCs, it does contain HCFC-22, another ozone-depleting ingredient.

Consumer demand plays a powerful, yet ambiguous, role in the food industry. There clearly is a market demand for super-sized, high-salt, high-fat, sugary, highly processed food. But legitimate questions can be raised about the consumer's understanding of their own needs, and their ability to influence food production.

In a 2015 report, the United States Centers for Disease Control and Prevention found that childhood obesity in the United States nearly tripled between 1980 and 2012, resulting in a wide range of serious health problems including heart disease, high blood pressure, and diabetes. In this sense, millions of people are eating too much of the wrong type of food. Oversized portions of high-calorie, high-fat, and sugary food products directly contribute to significant health problems for children and adults.

In addition to obesity, many other health issues can be traced to what we eat. Artificial food colorings; artificial sweeteners; food additives such as monosodium glutamate, trans fats, nitrates, and high fructose corn syrup; and artificial preservatives such as sodium benzoate have all been linked to human health problems. All of these products are added to food by the food industry.

Defenders of the food industry will point out that business is only responding to consumer demand in providing "super-sized" portions and tasty, inexpensive, and convenient food products. Many additives are included to increase shelf-life of food, to make it more tasty and attractive, or to lower costs.

In 2015, for example, General Mills announced that it would be phasing out the use of synthetic artificial dyes and flavors in its breakfast cereals. In explaining its decision, General Mills claimed that "people eat with their eyes" and want cereals that are "fun" and have "vibrant colors" and "fruity flavor."[11] Assuming this market demand as a given, General Mills still had the discretion to change how they would meet that demand and chose to reduce the health risks posed by artificial colors and flavors.

But, of course, the consumer demand for colorful, sugary breakfast treats is itself something over which General Mills has at least some influence. Childhood obesity is a major health problem and marketing high-sugar breakfast treats to children cannot be said to be meeting needs, although it seems to meet consumer preferences. A business also cannot escape responsibility for failing to meet needs for nutritional foods by claiming that it is merely responding to what consumers want if it has spent hundreds of millions of dollars creating and promoting colorful high-sugar treats as "part of a complete breakfast."

Yet, in other ways consumer demand is changing the nature of the food industry. Organic food sales in the United States have grown by an average of 14 percent annually since the year 2000. Globally, the organic food sales volume almost doubled, from $57 billion to $104 billion between 2010 and 2015. Major retailers such as Whole Foods, Walmart, Kroger, and Costco actively promote organic and sustainably grown food products. Major food producers such as General Mills and Unilever have moved aggressively into the organic and sustainable food market.

- To what degree should the movement toward organic and sustainably raised food be left to the market? What role, if any, should government regulation play in this regard? What responsibilities does the food industry, including restaurants and grocers, have?

- Many food products are marketed as "natural." Can you think of any such products that raise ethical problems? Is everything that is natural also good?

- Sustainable products should be designed to meet the needs of present and future generations. Who decides what people need? Can every product be sustainable?

Questions, Projects, and Exercises

1. As a research project, choose a product with which you are familiar (one with local connections is best) and trace its entire life cycle. From where does this product originate? What resources go into its design and manufacture? How is it transported, sold, used, and disposed of? Along each step in the life cycle of this product, analyze the economic, environmental, and ethical costs and benefits. Consider if a service could be exchanged for this product. Some examples might include your local drinking water, food items such as beef or chicken, any product sold at a local farmer's market, or building materials used in local projects.

2. Conduct a web search for ecological footprint analysis. You should be able to find a self-administered test to evaluate your own ecological footprint. If everyone on earth lived as you do, how many earths would be required to support this lifestyle?

3. Research corporate sustainability reports. How many corporations can you find that issue annual reports on their progress toward sustainability? Can you research a company that does not and explore why not (perhaps through its critics), or whether it has plans to change?

4. A movement within the European Union requires that a business take back its products at the end of their useful life. Can you learn the details of such laws? Discuss whether or not you believe such a law could be passed in the United States. Should the United States have similar laws?

5. Apply the concept of sustainability to a variety of businesses and industries. What would sustainable agriculture require? What are sustainable energy sources? What would sustainable transportation be? What would be required to turn your hometown into a sustainable community?

6. Investigate what is involved in an environmental audit. Has such an audit been conducted at your own college or university? In what ways has your own school adopted sustainable practices? In what ways would your school need to change to become more sustainable?

7. Do you believe that business has any direct ethical duties to living beings other than humans? Do animals, plants, or ecosystems have rights? What criteria have you used in answering such questions? What is your own standard for determining what objects count, from a moral point of view?

8. Investigate LEED (Leadership in Energy and Environmental Design) building designs. If possible, arrange a visit to a local building designed according to LEED principles. Should all new buildings be required by law to adopt LEED design standards and conform to the LEED rating system?

Key Terms

After reading this chapter, you should have a clear understanding of the following key terms. For a complete definition, please see the Glossary.

backcasting, *p. 440*

biomimicry ("closed-loop" production), *p. 455*

corporate average fuel economy (CAFE) standards, *p. 446*

cradle-to-cradle responsibility, *p. 456*

eco-efficiency, *p. 455*

service-based economy, *p. 457*

sustainable business practice, *p. 449*

sustainable development, *p. 449*

sustainable or green marketing, *p. 457*

three pillars of sustainability, *p. 449*

Endnotes

1. Jonathan Foley, "Feed the World," *National Geographic,* May 2014.

2. William Baxter, *People or Penguins: The Case for Optimal Pollution* (New York: Columbia University Press, 1974).

3. Julian Simon, *The Ultimate Resource* (Princeton, NJ: Princeton University Press, 1983).

4. Herman Daly, *Beyond Growth* (Boston: Beacon Press, 1996), 33–35

5. Ernst Ligteringen, keynote speech at the GRI Global Conference on Sustainability and Reporting, May 22, 2013, as reported in *Sustainability Reporting: The Time Is Now,* Ernst & Young, p. 13, (www.ey.com/Publication/vwLUAssets/EY-Sustainability-reporting-the-time-is-now/$FILE/EY-Sustainability-reporting-the-time-is-now.pdf (accessed October 14, 2014).

6. For the Factor Four claim, see Ernst von Weizacker, Amory B. Lovins, L. Hunter Lovins, and Kogan Page, "Factor Four: Doubling Wealth—Halving Resource Use: A Report to the Club of Rome" (Earthscan/James & James, 1997); for Factor 10, see Friedrich Schmidt-Bleek, Factor 10 Institute, www.factor10-institute.org/ (accessed April 22, 2010).

7. Paul Hawken, Amory Lovins, and Hunter Lovins, *Natural Capitalism* (Boston: Little Brown, 1999).

8. C. K. Prahalad, *The Fortune at the Bottom of the Pyramid* (Upper Saddle River, NJ: Wharton, 2005).

9. Patrick E. Murphy, "Sustainable Marketing," Business and Environmental Sustainability Conference, Carlson School of Management, Minneapolis, MN, 2005.

10. Sustainable marketing seems a growing field within both business and the academic community. Two of the earliest books in this field, both of which remain very helpful, are: *Environmental Marketing: Strategies, Practice, Theory, and Research,*

Michael J. Polonsky and Alma T. Mintu-Wimsatt, eds. (Binghampton, NY: Haworth Press, 1995); Donald Fuller, *Sustainable Marketing: Managerial-Ecological Issues* (Thousand Oaks, CA: Sage, 1999). A particularly helpful essay in the Polonsky book is by Jagdish N. Seth and Atul Parvatiyar, "Ecological Imperatives and the Role of Marketing," pp. 3–20. Seth and Parvatiyar are often credited with coining the term *sustainable marketing* in this essay.

11. James Hamblen, "Lucky Charms, the New Superfood," *The Atlantic,* June 23, 2015.

Readings

Reading **9-1**

The Next Industrial Revolution

William McDonough and Michael Braungart

In the spring of 1912 one of the largest moving objects ever created by human beings left Southampton and began gliding toward New York. It was the epitome of its industrial age—a potent representation of technology, prosperity, luxury, and progress. It weighed 66,000 tons. Its steel hull stretched the length of four city blocks. Each of its steam engines was the size of a townhouse. And it was headed for a disastrous encounter with the natural world.

This vessel, of course, was the *Titanic*—a brute of a ship, seemingly impervious to the details of nature. In the minds of the captain, the crew, and many of the passengers, nothing could sink it. One might say that the infrastructure created by the Industrial Revolution of the nineteenth century resembles such a steamship. It is powered by fossil fuels, nuclear reactors, and chemicals. It is pouring waste into the water and smoke into the sky. It is attempting to work by its own rules, contrary to those of the natural world. And although it may seem invincible, its fundamental design flaws presage disaster. Yet many people still believe that with a few minor alterations, this infrastructure can take us safely and prosperously into the future.

During the Industrial Revolution resources seemed inexhaustible and nature was viewed as something to be tamed and civilized. Recently, however, some leading industrialists have begun to realize that traditional ways of doing things may not be sustainable over the long term. "What we thought was boundless has limits," Robert Shapiro, the chairman and chief executive officer of Monsanto, said in a 1997 interview, "and we're beginning to hit them."

The 1992 Earth Summit in Rio de Janeiro, led by the Canadian businessman Maurice Strong, recognized those limits. Approximately 30,000 people from around the world, including more than a hundred world leaders and representatives of 167 countries, gathered in Rio de Janeiro to respond to troubling symptoms of environmental decline. Although there was sharp disappointment afterward that no binding agreement had been reached at the summit, many industrial participants touted a particular strategy: eco-efficiency. The machines of industry would be refitted with cleaner, faster, quieter engines. Prosperity would remain unobstructed, and economic and organizational structures would remain intact. The hope was that eco-efficiency would transform human industry from a system that takes, makes, and wastes into one that integrates economic, environmental, and ethical concerns. Eco-efficiency is now considered by industries across the globe to be the strategy of choice for change.

What is eco-efficiency? Primarily, the term means "doing more with less"—a precept that has its roots in early industrialization. Henry Ford was adamant about lean and clean operating policies; he saved his company money by recycling and reusing materials, reduced the use of natural resources, minimized packaging, and set new standards with his timesaving assembly line. Ford wrote in 1926, "You must get the most out of the power, out of the material, and out of the time"—a credo that could hang today on the wall of any eco-efficient factory. The linkage of efficiency with sustaining the environment was perhaps most famously articulated in *Our Common Future,* a report published in 1987 by the United Nations' World Commission on Environment and Development. *Our Common Future* warned that if pollution control were not intensified, property and ecosystems would be threatened, and existence would become unpleasant and even harmful to human health in some cities. "Industries and industrial operations should be encouraged that are more efficient in terms of resource use, that generate less pollution and waste, that are based on the use of renewable rather than nonrenewable

resources, and that minimize irreversible adverse impacts on human health and the environment," the commission stated in its agenda for change.

The term "eco-efficiency" was promoted five years later, by the Business Council (now the World Business Council) for Sustainable Development, a group of 48 industrial sponsors including Dow, Du Pont, ConAgra, and Chevron, who brought a business perspective to the Earth Summit. The council presented its call for change in practical terms, focusing on what businesses had to gain from a new ecological awareness rather than on what the environment had to lose if industry continued in current patterns. In *Changing Course,* a report released just before the summit, the group's founder, Stephan Schmidheiny, stressed the importance of eco-efficiency for all companies that aimed to be competitive, sustainable, and successful over the long term. In 1996 Schmidheiny said, "I predict that within a decade it is going to be next to impossible for a business to be competitive without also being 'eco-efficient'—adding more value to a good or service while using fewer resources and releasing less pollution."

As Schmidheiny predicted, eco-efficiency has been working its way into industry with extraordinary success. The corporations committing themselves to it continue to increase in number, and include such big names as Monsanto, 3M, and Johnson & Johnson. Its famous three *R*s—reduce, reuse, recycle—are steadily gaining popularity in the home as well as the workplace. The trend stems in part from eco-efficiency's economic benefits, which can be considerable: 3M, for example, has saved more than $750 million through pollution-prevention projects, and other companies, too, claim to be realizing big savings. Naturally, reducing resource consumption, energy use, emissions, and wastes has implications for the environment as well. When one hears that Du Pont has cut its emissions of airborne cancer-causing chemicals by almost 75 percent since 1987, one can't help feeling more secure. This is another benefit of eco-efficiency: it diminishes guilt and fear. By subscribing to eco-efficiency, people and industries can be less "bad" and less fearful about the future. Or can they?

Eco-efficiency is an outwardly admirable and certainly well-intended concept, but, unfortunately, it is not a strategy for success over the long term, because it does not reach deep enough. It works within the same system that caused the problem in the first place, slowing it down with moral proscriptions and punitive demands. It presents little more than an illusion of change. Relying on eco-efficiency to save the environment will in fact achieve the opposite—it will let industry finish off everything quietly, persistently, and completely.

We are forwarding a reshaping of human industry—what we and the author Paul Hawken call the Next Industrial Revolution. Leaders of this movement include many people in diverse fields, among them commerce, politics, the humanities, science, engineering, and education. Especially notable are the businessman Ray Anderson; the philanthropist Teresa Heinz; the Chattanooga city councilman Dave Crockett; the physicist Amory Lovins; the environmental-studies professor David W. Orr; the environmentalists Sarah Severn, Dianne Dillon Ridgley, and Susan Lyons; the environmental product developer Heidi Holt; the ecological designer John Todd; and the writer Nancy Jack Todd. We are focused here on a new way of designing industrial production. As an architect and industrial designer and a chemist who have worked with both commercial and ecological systems, we see conflict between industry and the environment as a design problem—a very big design problem.

Any of the basic intentions behind the Industrial Revolution were good ones, which most of us would probably like to see carried out today: to bring more goods and services to larger numbers of people, to raise standards of living, and to give people more choice and opportunity, among others. But there were crucial omissions. Perpetuating the diversity and vitality of forests, rivers, oceans, air, soil, and animals was not part of the agenda.

If someone were to present the Industrial Revolution as a retroactive design assignment, it might sound like this: Design a system of production that

- Puts billions of pounds of toxic material into the air, water, and soil every year.
- Measures prosperity by activity, not legacy.
- Requires thousands of complex regulations to keep people and natural systems from being poisoned too quickly.
- Produces materials so dangerous that they will require constant vigilance from future generations.
- Results in gigantic amounts of waste.
- Puts valuable materials in holes all over the planet, where they can never be retrieved.
- Erodes the diversity of biological species and cultural practices.

Eco-efficiency instead

- Releases *fewer* pounds of toxic material into the air, water, and soil every year.
- Measures prosperity by *less* activity.
- *Meets or exceeds* the stipulations of thousands of complex regulations that aim to keep people and natural systems from being poisoned too quickly.
- Produces *fewer* dangerous materials that will require constant vigilance from future generations.
- Results in *smaller* amounts of waste.
- Puts *fewer* valuable materials in holes all over the planet, where they can never be retrieved.
- Standardizes and homogenizes biological species and cultural practices.

Plainly put, eco-efficiency aspires to make the old, destructive system less so. But its goals, however admirable, are fatally limited.

Reduction, reuse, and recycling slow down the rates of contamination and depletion but do not stop these processes. Much recycling, for instance, is what we call "downcycling," because it reduces the quality of a material over time. When plastic other than that found in such products as soda and water bottles is recycled, it is often mixed with different plastics to produce a hybrid of lower quality, which is then molded into something amorphous and cheap, such as park benches or speed bumps. The original high-quality material is not retrieved, and it eventually ends up in landfills or incinerators.

The well-intended, creative use of recycled materials for new products can be misguided. For example, people may feel that they are making an ecologically sound choice by buying and wearing clothing made of fibers from recycled plastic bottles. But the fibers from plastic bottles were not specifically designed to be next to human skin. Blindly adopting superficial "environmental" approaches without fully understanding their effects can be no better than doing nothing.

Recycling is more expensive for communities than it needs to be, partly because traditional recycling tries to force materials into more lifetimes than they were designed for—a complicated and messy conversion, and one that itself expends energy and resources. Very few objects of modern consumption were designed with recycling in mind. If the process is truly to save money and materials, products must be designed from the very beginning to be recycled or even "upcycled"—a term we use to describe the return to industrial systems of materials with improved, rather than degraded, quality.

The reduction of potentially harmful emissions and wastes is another goal of eco-efficiency. But current studies are beginning to raise concern that even tiny amounts of dangerous emissions can have disastrous effects on biological systems over time. This is a particular concern in the case of endocrine disrupters—industrial chemicals in a variety of modern plastics and consumer goods which appear to mimic hormones and connect with receptors in human beings and other organisms. Theo Colborn, Dianne Dumanoski, and John Peterson Myers, the authors of *Our Stolen Future* (1996), a groundbreaking study on certain synthetic chemicals and the environment, assert that "astoundingly small quantities of these hormonally active compounds can wreak all manner of biological havoc, particularly in those exposed in the womb."

On another front, new research on particulates—microscopic particles released during incineration and combustion processes, such as those in power plants and automobiles—shows that they can lodge in and damage the lungs, especially in children and the elderly. A 1995 Harvard study found that as many as 100,000 people die annually as a result of these tiny particles. Although regulations for smaller particles are in place, implementation does not have to begin until 2005. Real change would be not regulating the release of particles but attempting to eliminate dangerous emissions altogether—by design.

Applying Nature's Cycles to Industry

"Produce more with less," "Minimize waste," "Reduce," and similar dictates advance the notion of a world of limits—one whose carrying capacity is strained by burgeoning populations and exploding production and consumption. Eco-efficiency tells us to restrict industry and curtail growth—to try to limit the creativity and productiveness of humankind. But the idea that the natural world is inevitably destroyed by human industry, or that excessive demand for goods and services causes environmental ills, is a simplification. Nature—highly industrious, astonishingly productive and creative, even "wasteful"—is not efficient but *effective*.

Consider the cherry tree. It makes thousands of blossoms just so that another tree might germinate, take root, and grow. Who would notice piles of cherry blossoms littering the ground in the spring and think, "How inefficient and wasteful"? The tree's abundance is useful and safe. After falling to the ground, the blossoms return to the soil and become nutrients for the surrounding environment. Every last particle contributes in some way to the health of a thriving ecosystem. "Waste equals food"—the first principle of the Next Industrial Revolution.

The cherry tree is just one example of nature's industry, which operates according to cycles of nutrients and metabolisms. This cyclical system is powered by the sun and constantly adapts to local circumstances. Waste that stays waste does not exist.

Human industry, on the other hand, is severely limited. It follows a one-way, linear, cradle-to-grave manufacturing line in which things are created and eventually discarded, usually in an incinerator or a landfill. Unlike the waste from nature's work, the waste from human industry is not "food" at all. In fact, it is often poison. Thus the two conflicting systems: a pile of cherry blossoms and a heap of toxic junk in a landfill.

But there is an alternative—one that will allow both business and nature to be fecund and productive. This alternative is what we call "eco-effectiveness." Our concept of eco-effectiveness leads to human industry that is regenerative rather than depletive. It involves the design of things that celebrate interdependence with other living systems. From an industrial-design perspective, it means products that work within cradle-to-cradle life cycles rather than cradle-to-grave ones.

Waste Equals Food

Ancient nomadic cultures tended to leave organic wastes behind, restoring nutrients to the soil and the surrounding environment. Modern, settled societies simply want to get rid of waste as quickly as possible. The potential nutrients in organic waste are lost when they are disposed of in landfills, where they cannot be used to rebuild soil; depositing synthetic materials and chemicals in natural systems strains the environment. The ability of complex, interdependent natural ecosystems to absorb such foreign material is limited if not nonexistent. Nature cannot do anything with the stuff *by design:* many manufactured products are intended not to break down under natural conditions. If people are to prosper within the natural world, all the products and materials manufactured by industry must after each useful life provide nourishment for something new. Since many of the things people make are not natural, they are not safe "food" for biological systems. Products composed of materials that do not biodegrade should be designed as technical nutrients that continually circulate within closed-loop industrial cycles—the technical metabolism.

In order for these two metabolisms to remain healthy, great care must be taken to avoid cross-contamination. Things that go into the biological metabolism should not contain mutagens, carcinogens, heavy metals, endocrine disrupters, persistent toxic substances, or bio-accumulative substances. Things that go into the technical metabolism should be kept well apart from the biological metabolism.

If the things people make are to be safely channeled into one or the other of these metabolisms, then products can be considered to contain two kinds of materials: *biological nutrients* and *technical nutrients.*

Biological nutrients will be designed to return to the organic cycle—to be literally consumed by microorganisms and other creatures in the soil. Most packaging (which makes up about 50 percent by volume of the solid-waste stream) should be composed of biological nutrients—materials that can be tossed onto the ground or the compost heap to biodegrade. There is no need for shampoo bottles, toothpaste tubes, yogurt cartons, juice containers, and other packaging to last decades (or even centuries) longer than what came inside them.

Technical nutrients will be designed to go back into the technical cycle. Right now anyone can dump an old television into a trash can. But the average television is made of hundreds of chemicals, some of which are toxic. Others are valuable nutrients for industry, which are wasted when the television ends up in a landfill. The reuse of technical nutrients in closed-loop industrial cycles is distinct from traditional recycling, because it allows materials to retain their quality: high-quality plastic computer cases would continually circulate as high-quality computer cases, instead of being down-cycled to make soundproof barriers or flowerpots.

Customers would buy the *service* of such products, and when they had finished with the products, or simply wanted to upgrade to a newer version, the manufacturer would take back the old ones, break them down, and use their complex materials in new products.

First Fruits: A Biological Nutrient

A few years ago we helped to conceive and create a compostable upholstery fabric—a biological nutrient. We were initially asked by Design Tex to create an aesthetically unique fabric that was also ecologically intelligent—although the client did not quite know at that point what this would mean. The challenge helped to clarify, both for us and for the company we were working with, the difference between superficial responses such as recycling and reduction and the more significant changes required by the Next Industrial Revolution.

For example, when the company first sought to meet our desire for an environmentally safe fabric, it presented what it thought was a wholesome option: cotton, which is natural, combined with PET (polyethylene terephthalate) fibers from recycled beverage bottles. Since the proposed hybrid could be described with two important eco-buzzwords, "natural" and "recycled," it appeared to be environmentally ideal. The materials were readily available, market-tested, durable, and cheap. But when the project team looked carefully at what the manifestations of such a hybrid might be in the long run, we discovered some disturbing facts. When a person sits in an office chair and shifts around, the fabric beneath him or her abrades; tiny particles of it are inhaled or swallowed by the user and other people nearby. PET was not designed to be inhaled. Furthermore, PET would prevent the proposed hybrid from going back into the soil safely, and the cotton would prevent it from re-entering an industrial cycle. The hybrid would still add junk to landfills, and it might also be dangerous.

The team decided to design a fabric so safe that one could literally eat it. The European textile mill chosen to produce the fabric was quite "clean" environmentally, and yet it had an interesting problem: although the mill's director had been diligent about reducing levels of dangerous emissions, government regulators had recently defined the trimmings of his fabric as hazardous waste. We sought a different end for our trimmings: mulch for the local garden club. When removed from the frame after the chair's useful life and tossed onto the ground to mingle with sun, water, and hungry microorganisms, both the fabric and its trimmings would decompose naturally.

The team decided on a mixture of safe, pesticide-free plant and animal fibers for the fabric (ramie and wool) and began working on perhaps the most difficult aspect: the finishes, dyes, and other processing chemicals. If the fabric was to go back into the soil safely, it had to be free of mutagens, carcinogens, heavy metals, endocrine disrupters, persistent toxic substances, and bio-accumulative substances. Sixty chemical companies were approached about joining the project, and all declined, uncomfortable with the idea of exposing their chemistry to the kind of scrutiny necessary. Finally one European company, Ciba-Geigy, agreed to join.

With that company's help the project team considered more than 8,000 chemicals used in the textile industry and eliminated 7,962. The fabric—in fact, an entire line of fabrics—was created using only 38 chemicals.

The director of the mill told a surprising story after the fabrics were in production. When regulators came by to test the effluent, they thought their instruments were broken. After testing the influent as well, they realized that the equipment was fine—the water coming out of the factory was as clean as the water going in. The manufacturing process itself was filtering the water. The new design not only bypassed the traditional three-R responses to environmental problems but also eliminated the need for regulation.

In our Next Industrial Revolution, regulations can be seen as signals of design failure. They burden industry by involving government in commerce and by interfering with the marketplace. Manufacturers in countries that are less hindered by regulations, and whose factories emit *more* toxic substances, have an economic advantage: they can produce and sell things for less. If a factory is not emitting dangerous substances and needs no regulation, and can thus compete directly with unregulated factories in other countries, that is good news environmentally, ethically, and economically.

A Technical Nutrient

Someone who has finished with a traditional carpet must pay to have it removed. The energy, effort, and materials that went into it are lost to the manufacturer; the carpet becomes little more than a heap of potentially hazardous petrochemicals that must be toted to a landfill. Meanwhile, raw materials must continually be extracted to make new carpets.

The typical carpet consists of nylon embedded in fiberglass and PVC. After its useful life a manufacturer can only downcycle it—shave off some of the nylon for further use and melt the leftovers. The world's largest commercial carpet company, Interface, is adopting our technical-nutrient concept with a carpet designed for complete recycling. When a customer wants to replace it, the manufacturer simply takes back the technical nutrient—depending on the product, either part or all of the carpet—and returns a carpet in the customer's desired color, style, and texture. The carpet company continues to own the material but leases it and maintains it, providing customers with the *service* of the carpet. Eventually the carpet will wear out like any other, and the manufacturer will reuse its materials at their original level of quality or a higher one.

The advantages of such a system, widely applied to many industrial products, are twofold: no useless and potentially dangerous waste is generated, as it might still be in eco-efficient systems, and billions of dollars' worth of valuable materials are saved and retained by the manufacturer.

Selling Intelligence, Not Poison

Currently, chemical companies warn farmers to be careful with pesticides, and yet the companies benefit when more pesticides are sold. In other words, the companies are unintentionally invested in wastefulness and even in the mishandling of their products, which can result in contamination of the soil, water, and air. Imagine what would happen if a chemical company sold intelligence instead of pesticides—that is, if farmers or agro-businesses paid pesticide manufacturers to protect their crops against loss from pests instead of buying dangerous regulated chemicals to use at their own discretion. It would in effect be buying crop insurance. Farmers would be saying, "I'll pay you to deal with boll weevils, and you do it as intelligently as you can."

At the same price per acre, everyone would still profit. The pesticide purveyor would be invested in *not* using pesticide, to avoid wasting materials. Furthermore, since the manufacturer would bear responsibility for the hazardous materials, it would have incentives to come up with less-dangerous ways to get rid of pests. Farmers are not interested in handling dangerous chemicals; they want to grow crops. Chemical companies do not want to contaminate soil, water, and air; they want to make money.

Consider the unintended design legacy of the average shoe. With each step of your shoe the sole releases tiny particles of potentially harmful substances that may contaminate and reduce the vitality of the soil. With the next rain these particles will wash into the plants and soil along the road, adding another burden to the environment.

Shoes could be redesigned so that the sole was a biological nutrient. When it broke down under a pounding foot and interacted with nature, it would nourish the biological metabolism instead of poisoning it. Other parts of the shoe might be designed as technical nutrients, to be returned to industrial cycles. Most shoes—in fact, most products of the current industrial system—are fairly primitive in their relationship to the natural world. With the scientific and technical tools currently available, this need not be the case.

Respect Diversity and Use the Sun

The leading goal of design in this century has been to achieve universally applicable solutions. In the field of architecture the International Style is a good example. As a result of the widespread adoption of the International Style, architecture has become uniform in many settings. That is, an office building can look and work the same anywhere. Materials such as steel, cement, and glass can be transported all over the world, eliminating dependence on a region's particular energy and material flows. With more energy forced into the heating and cooling system, the same building can operate similarly in vastly different settings.

The second principle of the Next Industrial Revolution is "Respect diversity." Designs will respect the regional, cultural, and material uniqueness of a place. Wastes and emissions will regenerate rather than deplete, and design will be flexible, to allow for changes in the needs of people and communities. For example, office buildings will be convertible into apartments, instead of ending up as rubble in a construction landfill when the market changes.

The third principle of the Next Industrial Revolution is "Use solar energy." Human systems now rely on fossil fuels and petrochemicals, and on incineration processes that often have destructive side effects. Today even the most advanced building or factory in the world is still a kind of steamship, polluting, contaminating, and depleting the surrounding environment, and relying on scarce amounts of natural light and fresh air. People are essentially working in the dark, and they are often breathing unhealthful air. Imagine, instead, a building as a kind of tree. It would purify air, accrue solar income, produce more energy than it consumes, create shade and habitat, enrich soil, and change with the seasons. Oberlin College is currently working on a building that is a good start: it is designed to make more energy than it needs to operate and to purify its own wastewater.

Equity, Economy, Ecology

The Next Industrial Revolution incorporates positive intentions across a wide spectrum of human concerns. People within the sustainability movement have found that three categories are helpful in articulating these concerns: equity, economy, and ecology.

Equity refers to social justice. Does a design depreciate or enrich people and communities? Shoe companies have been blamed for exposing workers in factories overseas to chemicals in amounts that exceed safe limits. Eco-efficiency would reduce those amounts to meet certain efficiency would reduce those amounts to meet certain standards; eco-effectiveness would not use a potentially dangerous chemical in the first place.

What an advance for humankind it would be if no factory worker anywhere worked in dangerous or inhumane conditions.

Economy refers to market viability. Does a product reflect the needs of producers and consumers for affordable products? Safe, intelligent designs should be affordable by and accessible to a wide range of customers, and profitable to the company that makes them, because commerce is the engine of change.

Ecology, of course, refers to environmental intelligence. Is a material a biological nutrient or a technical nutrient? Does it meet nature's design criteria: Waste equals food, Respect diversity, and Use solar energy?

The Next Industrial Revolution can be framed as the following assignment: Design an industrial system for the next century that

- Introduces no hazardous materials into the air, water, or soil.

- Measures prosperity by how much natural capital we can accrue in productive ways.

- Measures productivity by how many people are gainfully and meaningfully employed.

- Measures progress by how many buildings have no smokestacks or dangerous effluents.

- Does not require regulations whose purpose is to stop us from killing ourselves too quickly.

- Produces nothing that will require future generations to maintain vigilance.

- Celebrates the abundance of biological and cultural diversity and solar income.

Albert Einstein wrote, "The world will not evolve past its current state of crisis by using the same thinking that created the situation." Many people believe that new industrial revolutions are already taking place, with the rise of cybertechnology, biotechnology, and nanotechnology. It is true that these are powerful tools for change. But they are only tools—hyperefficient engines for the steamship of the first Industrial Revolution. Similarly, eco-efficiency is a valuable and laudable tool, and a prelude to what should come next. But it, too, fails to move us beyond the first revolution. It is time for designs that are creative, abundant, prosperous, and intelligent from the start. The model for the Next Industrial Revolution may well have been right in front of us the whole time: a tree.

Source: Published in the *Atlantic Monthly,* October 1998. Reproduced with permission of the authors. See www.mcdonough.com.

Source: Published in the *Atlantic Monthly,* October 1998. Reproduced with permission of the authors. See www.mcdonough.com.

Reading **9-2**

Getting to the Bottom of "Triple Bottom Line"

Wayne Norman and Chris MacDonald

Introduction

The notion of "Triple Bottom Line" (3BL) accounting has become increasingly fashionable in management, consulting, investing, and NGO circles over the last few years. The idea behind the 3BL paradigm is that a corporation's ultimate success or health can and should be measured not just by the traditional financial bottom line, but also by its social/ethical and environmental performance. Of course, it has long been accepted by most people in and out of the corporate world that firms have a variety of obligations to stakeholders to behave responsibly. It is also almost a truism that firms cannot be successful in the long run if they consistently disregard the interests of key stakeholders. The apparent novelty of 3BL lies in its supporters' contention that the overall fulfilment of obligations to communities, employees, customers, and suppliers (to name but four stakeholders) should be measured, calculated, audited and reported—just as the financial performance of public companies has been for more than a century. This is an exciting promise. One of the more enduring clichés of modern management is that "if you can't measure it, you can't manage it." If we believe that ethical business practices and social responsibility are important functions of corporate governance and management, then we should welcome attempts to develop tools that make more transparent to managers, shareholders and other stakeholders just how well a firm is doing in this regard.

In this article we will assume without argument both the desirability of many socially responsible business practices . . . and the potential usefulness of tools that allow us to measure and report on performance along these dimensions. . . . These are not terribly controversial assumptions these days. Almost all major corporations at least pay lip service to social responsibility—even Enron had an exhaustive code of ethics and principles—and a substantial percentage of the major corporations are now issuing annual reports on social and/or environmental performance. We find controversy not in these assumptions, but in the promises suggested by the 3BL rhetoric.

The term "Triple Bottom Line" dates back to the mid 1990's, when management think-tank Accountability coined and began using the term in its work. The term found public currency with the 1997 publication of the British edition of John Elkington's *Cannibals With Forks: The Triple Bottom Line of 21st Century Business.* There are in fact very few references to the term before this date, and many (including the man himself) claim that Elkington coined it. In the last three or four years the term has spread like wildfire. The Internet search engine, Google, returns roughly 25,200 web pages that mention the term. The phrase "triple bottom line" also occurs in 67 articles in the *Financial Times* in the year preceding June 2002. Organisations such as the Global Reporting Initiative and Accountability have embraced and promoted the 3BL concept for use in the corporate world. And corporations are listening. Companies as significant as AT&T, Dow Chemicals, Shell, and British Telecom, have used 3BL terminology in their press releases, annual reports and other documents. So have scores of smaller firms. Not surprisingly, most of the big accounting firms are now using the concept approvingly and offering services to help firms that want to measure, report or audit their two additional "bottom lines." Similarly, there is now a sizable portion of the investment industry devoted to screening companies on the basis of their social and environmental performance, and many of these explicitly use the language of 3BL. Governments, government departments and political parties (especially Green parties) are also well represented in the growing documentation of those advocating or accepting 3BL "principles." For many NGOs and activist organisations 3BL seems to be pretty much an article of faith. Given the rapid uptake by corporations, governments, and activist groups, the paucity of academic analysis is both surprising and worrisome.

In this paper, we propose to begin the task of filling this academic lacuna. We do this by seeking answers to a number of difficult questions. Is the intent of the 3BL movement really to bring accounting paradigms to bear in the social and environmental domains? Is doing so a practical possibility? Will doing so achieve the goals intended by promoters of the 3BL? Or is the idea of a "bottom line" in these other domains a mere metaphor? And if it is a metaphor, is it a useful one? Is this a form of jargon we should embrace and encourage?

Our conclusions are largely critical of this "paradigm" and its rhetoric. Again, we are supportive of some of the aspirations behind the 3BL movement, but we argue on both conceptual and practical grounds that the language of 3BL promises more than it can ever deliver. That will be our bottom line on Triple Bottom Line.

What Do Supporters of 3BL Believe?

There are two quick answers to the question in the above section heading: first, different supporters of 3BL seem to conceive of the 3BL in a variety of ways; and second, it is rarely clear exactly what most people mean when they use this language or what claims they are making on behalf of "taking the 3BL seriously." Despite the fact that most of the documents by advocates of 3BL are explicitly written to introduce readers to the concept and to sell them on it, it is difficult to find anything that looks like a careful definition of the concept, let alone a methodology or formula (analogous to the calculations on a corporate income statement) for calculating one of the new bottom lines. In the places where one is expecting a definition the most that one usually finds are vague claims about the aims of the 3BL approach. We are told, for example, that in the near future "the world's financial markets will insist that business delivers against" all three bottom lines. If "we aren't good corporate citizens"— as reflected in "a Triple Bottom Line that takes into account social and environmental responsibilities along with financial ones"—"eventually our stock price, our profits and our entire business could suffer." 3BL reporting "defines a company's ultimate worth in financial, social, and environmental terms." Such reporting "responds to *all* stakeholder demands that companies take part in, be accountable for, and substantiate their membership in society." Further, 3BL is "a valuable management tool—that is, an early warning tool that allows you to react faster to changes in stakeholders' behaviour, and incorporate the changes into the strategy before they hit the [real?] bottom line." Many claims on 3BL's behalf are very tepid indeed, suggesting little more than that the concept is "an important milestone in our journey toward sustainability," or an approach that "places emphasis" on social and environmental aspects of the firm, along with economic aspects, and that "should move to the top of executives' agendas."

From these many vague claims made about 3BL it is possible to distil two sets of more concrete propositions about the meaning of the additional bottom lines and why it is supposed to be important for firms to measure and report on them. (For the sake of brevity. . . , from this point on we will look primarily at the case of the so-called social/ethical bottom line. But most of the conceptual issues we will explore with this "bottom line" would apply equally to its environmental sibling.)

A. What does it mean to say there are additional bottom lines?

- (*Measurement Claim*) The components of "social performance" or "social impact" can be measured in relatively objective ways on the basis of standard indicators. . . . These data can then be audited and reported.

- (*Aggregation Claim*) A social "bottom line"— that is, something analogous to a net social "profit/loss"—can be calculated using data from these indicators and a relatively uncontroversial formula that could be used for any firm.

B. Why should firms measure, calculate and (possibly) report their additional (and in particular their social) bottom lines?

- (*Convergence Claim*) Measuring social performance helps improve social performance, and firms with better social performance tend to be more profitable in the long-run.

- (*Strong Social-obligation Claim*) Firms have an obligation to maximise . . . their social bottom line—their net positive social impact—and accurate measurement is necessary to judge how well they have fulfilled this obligation.

- (*Transparency Claim*) The firm have obligations to stakeholders to disclose information about how well it performs with respect to all stakeholders.

In short, 3BL advocates believe that social (and environmental) performance can be measured in fairly objective ways, and that firms should use these results in order to improve their social (and environmental) performance. Moreover, they should report these results as a matter of principle, and in using and reporting on these additional "bottom lines"

firms can expect to do better by their financial bottom line in the long run.

We will not examine each of these claims in isolation now. Rather we will focus on some deeper criticisms of the 3BL movement by making reference to these five central claims about the project and its aims. . . .

* * * *

What Is Sound about 3BL Is Not Novel

[M]any uses of "Triple Bottom Line" are simply synonymous with "corporate social responsibility" (CSR)—for example, when the CEO of VanCity (Canada's largest credit union) defines "the 'triple bottom line' approach to business" as "taking environmental, social and financial results into consideration in the development and implementation of a corporate business strategy". . . .

Now it might be argued that what is new about the 3BL movement is the emphasis on measurement and reporting. But this is not true either. Those who use the language of 3BL are part of a much larger movement sometimes identified by the acronym SEAAR: social and ethical accounting, auditing and reporting. This movement . . . has grown in leaps and bounds over the past decade, and has produced a variety of competing standards and standard-setting bodies, including the Global Reporting Initiative (GRI), the SA 8000 from Social Accountability International, the AA 1000 from Account Ability, as well as parts of various ISO standards. . . . [I]t would be safe to say that anyone supporting the SEAAR movement would endorse at least four of the five 3BL claims listed above—and certainly the Measurement and Transparency Claims. . . . But only the Aggregation Claim is truly distinctive of a "bottom line" approach to social performance, and this claim is definitely not endorsed by any of the major social-performance standards to date. . . .

One often has the impression that 3BL advocates are working with a caricature that has traditional "pre-3BL" or "single-bottom-line" firms and managers focussing exclusively on financial data. . . . But obviously, even a pure profit-maximiser knows that successful business cannot be run like this. Indeed, most of the data to be reported on the so-called social-bottom-line is already gathered by the standard departments in any large organisation. For example, Human Resource departments will typically keep records on employee turnover, employee-demographic information by gender and/or ethnicity, and various measures of employee satisfaction; good Marketing and Sales departments will try to track various measures of customer satisfaction; Procurement departments will monitor relationships with suppliers; Public Relations will be testing perceptions of the firm within various external communities, including governments; the Legal department will be aware of law suits from employees, customers or other stakeholders; and so on. . . .

In short, if there is something distinctive about the 3BL approach, it cannot be merely or primarily that it calls on firms and senior managers to focus on things besides the traditional bottom line; it has never been possible to do well by the bottom line without paying attention elsewhere, especially to key stakeholder groups like employees, customers, suppliers and governments. . . .

* * * *

What Is Novel about 3BL Is Not Sound

The keenest supporters of the 3BL movement tend to insist . . . that firms have social and environmental bottom lines *in just the same way* that they have "financial" or "economic" bottom lines. We submit that the only way to make sense of such a claim is by formulating it (roughly) in the way we have with the Aggregation Claim, above. That is, we cannot see how it could make sense to talk about a bottom line analogous to the bottom line of the income statement unless there is an agreed-upon methodology that allows us, at least in principle, to add and subtract various data until we arrive at a net sum.

Probably the most curious fact about the 3BL movement . . . is that none of the advocates of so-called 3BL accounting ever actually proposes, presents or even sketches a methodology of the sort implied by the Aggregation Claim. In other words, for all the talk of the novelty of the 3BL idea, and for the importance of taking all three "bottom lines" seriously, nobody . . . has actually proposed a way to use the data on social performance to calculate some kind of a net social bottom line. . . .

If it makes sense to say that there is a bottom line for performance in some domain, x, that is directly analogous to the financial bottom line, then it makes sense to ask what a given firm's x-bottom line is. And there should be a relatively straight forward answer to this question, even if we do not yet know what that answer is. So we might reasonably ask of firms like The Body Shop, or British Telecom, or Dow Chemical—all companies that have claimed to believe in the 3BL—what their social bottom line actually was last year. . . .

* * * *

. . . We may not be sure what the right answer should look like, but this kind of answer, even (or especially?) if it were expressed in monetary units, just does not seem right. So it is worth reflecting for a moment about what *would* look like a plausible answer to the question of what some particular firm's social bottom line is. We can have good grounds for thinking that one firm's social performance (say, BP's) is better than another's (say, Enron's); or that a given firm's social/ethical performance improved (Shell) or declined (Andersen) over a five-year period. And indeed, our judgments in these cases would be at least partly based on, or reflected in, the kind of indicators that various proposed social standards highlight—including, for example, charitable donations, various measures of employee satisfaction and loyalty, perceptions in the community, and so on. But this is still a long way from saying that we have any kind of systematic way of totting up the social pros and cons, or of arriving at some global figure for a firm's social performance.

The problem with [the] alleged analogy between the "traditional" bottom line and social or environmental bottom lines runs deeper still. The traditional bottom line, of course, is the last line of the income statement indicating net income (positive or negative). Net income is arrived at by subtracting the expenses incurred by the organisation from the income earned by it within a given period. We have just suggested that we are not sure what the social version of this "line" should look like, or in what sort of units it should be expressed. But we are also puzzled when we look for conceptual analogies *above* the bottom line, so to speak. What are the ethical/social equivalents or analogues of, say, revenue, expenses, gains, losses, assets, liabilities, equity, and so on? The kinds of raw data that 3BL and other SEAAR advocates propose to collect as indications of social performance do not seem to fit into general categories, analogous to these, that will allow for a straightforward subtraction of "bads" from "goods" in order to get some kind of net social sum.

With reference to typical SEAAR criteria we could imagine a firm reporting that:

(a) 20% of its directors were women,

(b) 7% of its senior management were members of "visible" minorities,

(c) it donated 1.2% of its profits to charity,

(d) the annual turnover rate among its hourly workers was 4%, and

(e) it had been fined twice this year for toxic emissions.

Now, out of context—e.g., without knowing how large the firm is, where it is operating, and what the averages are in its industrial sector—it is difficult to say how good or bad these figures are. Of course, in the case of each indicator we often have a sense of whether a higher or lower number would generally be better, from the perspective of social/ethical performance. The conceptual point, however, is that these are quite simply not the sort of data that can be fed into an income-statement-like calculation to produce a final net sum. . . . Again, we are not disputing that these are relevant considerations in the evaluation of a firm's level of social responsibility; but it does not seem at all helpful to think of this evaluation as in any way analogous to the methodology of adding and subtracting used in financial accounting.

An Impossibility Argument

Ultimately, we argue, there are fundamental philosophical grounds for thinking that it is impossible to develop a sound methodology for arriving at a meaningful social bottom line for a firm. . . .

We can begin by expressing this . . . argument in the . . . terminology of accountancy. One of the three basic assumptions underlying the methodologies of the standard financial statements, including the income statement, is the so-called "unit of measure" assumption—that all measures for revenue, expenses, assets, and so on, are reducible to a common unit of currency. What is lacking in the ethical/social realm is an obvious, and obviously measurable, common "currency" (whether in a monetary or non-monetary sense) for expressing the magnitude of all good and bad produced by the firm's operations and affecting individuals in different stakeholder groups.

* * * *

. . . We could also consider the challenge of comparing good to good and bad to bad. For example, would a firm do more social good by donating one-million dollars to send underprivileged local youths to college, or by donating the same amount to the local opera company? How should we evaluate the charitable donation by a firm to a not-for-profit abortion clinic, or to a small fundamentalist Christian church? Examples like these make it clear that although there are many relevant and objective facts that can be reported and audited, any attempt to "weigh" them, or tot them up, will necessarily involve subjective value judgments, about which reasonable people can and will legitimately disagree. . . .

The power of this illustration does not rest on acceptance of any deep philosophical view about whether all value judgments are ultimately subjective or objective; it rests only on a realistic assessment of the open-ended nature of any attempt to make a global assessment of a firm's social impact given the kind of data that would go into such an evaluation. In the language of moral philosophers, the various values involved in evaluations of corporate behaviour are "incommensurable"; and reasonable and informed people, even reasonable and informed moral philosophers, will weigh them and trade them off in different ways. To say they are incommensurable is to say that there is no overarching formula that can be appealed to in order to justify all of these trade-offs. . . .

Conclusion: What Use Bottom Lines without a Bottom Line?

We cannot help but conclude that there is no meaningful sense in which 3BL advocates can claim there is a social bottom line. (Again, we believe that analogous arguments would undermine the idea of an environmental bottom line. . . .) This piece of jargon is, in short, *inherently misleading:* the very term itself promises or implies something it cannot deliver. This raises two issues worth reflecting upon. First, why has the idea spread so quickly, not just among Green and CSR activists, but also among the top tier of multinational corporations? And secondly, should we be concerned about the use, and propagation of the use, of jargon that is inherently misleading?

There is no simple answer to the first question, and certainly no general explanation for why so many different kinds of individuals and groups have found the language of 3BL so attractive. There are no doubt many conflicting motivations at play here, and by and large we can do no more than speculate about the mental states of different key actors. For many grassroots activists it is likely that the metaphor of bottom lines captured perfectly their long-held sense that social responsibility and environmental sustainability are at least as important as profitability when evaluating the performance and reputations of firms. . . . For some of the initiators and early adopters of the concept within activist circles . . . it is likely that there were also perceived rhetorical advantages to

borrowing from the "hard-headed" language and legitimacy of accountancy. Perhaps senior executives would find it easier to take seriously the fuzzy notions of CSR and sustainability if they could be fit into more familiar paradigms with objective measures and standards. Many of these early movers . . . were also offering large corporations consulting and auditing services that were built, at least in part, around the 3BL paradigm; and they would soon be joined, as we noted at the outset, by some of the most powerful "mainstream" accounting and consulting firms. Paid consultants have, of course, mixed motives for promoting and legitimising something like the 3BL paradigm: on the one hand, they can be committed to the utility for the clients of collecting, auditing, and reporting social and environmental data . . . but on the other, they cannot be blind to the fact that this opens up a market niche that might not otherwise have existed. . . .

More fanciful leaps of speculation are necessary for explaining the motivations of some of the early adopters of 3BL rhetoric and principles among multinational corporations. As we have noted already, there are a number of corporations that have long prided themselves on their traditions of social responsibility and good corporate citizenship. Having succeeded despite putting principles ahead of short-term profits is part of the lore in the cultures of companies like Johnson & Johnson, Levi Strauss, Cadbury's, and IKEA. And in the cultures of many smaller or more recent firms, from The Body Shop to your local organic grocer, CSR and green principles have often served as the organisation's very *raison d'être*. For many of these firms, social and environmental reporting provides an opportunity to display their clean laundry in public, so to speak. They have long sought to improve their social and environmental performance, so they can be confident that reporting these achievements publicly will cause little embarrassment. . . .

* * * *

[S]hould we be concerned about the use, and propagation of the use, of 3BL jargon that is inherently misleading? From an abstract normative point of view the answer clearly has to be Yes. If the jargon of 3BL implies that there exists a sound methodology for calculating a meaningful and comparable social bottom line, the way there is for the statement of net income, then it is misleading; it is a kind of lie. . . . But there is another more serious concern that should trouble the most committed supporters of CSR and sustainability principles who have embraced the 3BL.

The concept of a Triple Bottom Line in fact turns out to be a "Good old-fashioned Single Bottom Line plus Vague Commitments to Social and Environmental Concerns." And it so happens that this is exceedingly easy for almost any firm to embrace. By committing themselves to the principles of the 3BL it sounds like companies are making a *more* concrete, verifiable commitment to CSR and sustainability. And no doubt many are. But it also allows them to make almost no commitment whatsoever. Without any real social or environmental bottom lines to have to calculate, firms do not have to worry about having these "bottom lines" compared to other firms inside or outside of their sector; nor is there likely to be any great worry about the firm being seen to have declining social and environmental "bottom lines" over the years or under the direction of the current CEO. At best, a commitment to 3BL requires merely that the firm report a number of data points of its own choosing that are potentially relevant to different stake-holder groups. . . . From year to year, some of these results will probably improve, and some will probably decline. Comparability over time for one firm is likely to be difficult and time-consuming for anybody without a complete collection of these reports and handy filing system. The firm can also change the indicators it chooses to report on over time, perhaps because it believes the new indicators are more relevant (. . . or perhaps to thwart comparability). And comparability across firms and sectors will often be impossible. At any rate, such comparisons will be on dozens or hundreds of data points, not on any kind of global figure like profit/loss, cash flow, return-on-investment, or earnings-per-share. . . . In short, because of its inherent emptiness and vagueness, the 3BL paradigm makes it as easy as possible for a cynical firm to appear to be committed to social responsibility and ecological sustainability. Being vague about this commitment hardly seems risky when the principal propagators of the idea are themselves just as vague.

Once again, we do not wish by these remarks to be casting aspersions on any particular firm that has adopted 3BL rhetoric and issued some form of 3BL report. We have tried to emphasize that there can be many non-cynical motivations for doing this. A careful reading of these reports is often sufficient to judge a firm's real level of commitment to the principles. If activists interested in propagating the rhetoric of Triple Bottom Line are not troubled by its inherently misleading nature (perhaps because they feel the ends justify the means), they should at the very least be concerned with the fact that it is potentially counterproductive. . . .

* * * *

Source: Wayne Norman and Chris MacDonald, "Getting to the Bottom of 'Triple Bottom Line,'" *Business Ethics Quarterly* 14, no. 2 (2003), pp. 243–262.

Beyond Corporate Responsibility: *Social Innovation and Sustainable Development as Drivers of Business Growth*

Patrick Cescau, Group Chief Executive of Unilever

It is a long time since I graduated from INSEAD. I return older but, I hope, a little wiser. Of course when I was here in the early seventies, the subjects I will talk about today—corporate responsibility and sustainable development—barely existed. The green movement that was emerging at that time was the province of politics and protest not business.

The idea that companies had responsibilities to society beyond making a few charitable donations did not really start to take shape until a decade later. A lot has changed since then—and I'm not just talking about my appearance! This agenda is no longer about protest and philanthropy, although both still have their place. And businesses and NGOs are no longer automatic adversaries. In many areas, they are partners working together to achieve common goals.

Today social responsibility and environmental sustainability are core business competencies, not fringe activities. We have come a long way since the early eighties when the godfather of free market economics Milton Friedman proudly proclaimed that the only obligation which business had to society was "to make a profit and pay its taxes."

This change has come about for a variety of reasons. Certainly the political context has altered. The laissez faire economics which characterised the Reagan/Thatcher era have been superseded by a more realistic assessment of what the invisible hand of the market can achieve acting alone.

Today there is a growing recognition that the social and environmental challenges facing us in the 21st century are so complex and so multidimensional that they can only be solved if government, NGOs and industry work together effectively. It is difficult, for example, to imagine a problem like climate change being addressed without the active participation of Shell, BP and Toyota. Likewise it is hard to see an issue like poor nutrition being effectively tackled without the involvement of the world's major food companies.

Slowly but surely both governments and NGOs are accepting that business has a role to play in the development agenda and that we can be trusted. But perhaps the biggest catalyst for change has been the increasing awareness within business itself that many of the big social and environmental challenges of our age, once seen as obstacles to progress, have become opportunities for innovation and business development.

I believe that we have come to a point now where this agenda of sustainability and corporate responsibility is not only central to business strategy but will increasingly become a critical driver of business growth. I would go further: I believe that how well and how quickly businesses respond to this agenda will determine which companies succeed and which will fail in the next few decades.

I realise that is a bold assertion but it is based on three key premises that I will explore today: Firstly, economic development. Developing and emerging markets will be the main source of growth for many multinational companies in the years to come. Those that make a positive contribution to economic development and poverty reduction in these countries will be better placed to grow than those that do not. I will use the example of Unilever's businesses in Indonesia, Africa and India to illustrate my arguments.

Secondly, social innovation. I will look at how heightened consumer concerns about social justice, poverty and climate change are raising expectations that companies should do more to tackle such issues. The brands that see these challenges as opportunities for innovation, rather than risks to be mitigated will be the successful brands of the future. The examples I will use here are two of our global brands—Dove and Ben & Jerry's.

Thirdly, sustainability. As globalisation accelerates, and as the limits of the planet's resources are reached, large companies and brands will increasingly be held to account on the sustainability of their business practices. The companies that succeed will be those that reduce their environmental impacts and increase the sustainability of their supply chains now, rather than wait until either legislation or public outcry forces them to do so.

First some background about Unilever. Unilever is one of the world's leading consumer goods companies:

- We have operations in around 100 countries and sales in over 150.

- Our products are present in half the households on the planet.

- 160 million times a day, someone somewhere will buy a Unilever brand.

- Our €40 billion turnover is spread across 400 Foods and Home & Personal Care brands.

Corporate responsibility is deeply coded into Unilever's DNA. You can trace its origins to our British and Dutch founders—William Hesketh Lever, Anton Jurgens and Simon van den Bergh— all of whom had an innate sense of social responsibility towards their employees and consumers.

It is from them that we have inherited two enduring principles which have guided our approach to doing business. The first is that the health and prosperity of our business is directly linked to the health and prosperity of the communities we serve. Lever gave substance to this belief by building a garden village for his workforce at Port Sunlight and by his determination to tackle the appalling standards of hygiene and sanitation in late Victorian Britain. He did this by the simple mechanism of making available to millions of people good quality, low cost soap.

The second principle that has been handed down is the simple notion that a successful business is a responsible business. Or if you prefer "doing well and doing good." Central to this is the idea that we can create social benefits through our brands and through the impact which our business activities have on society and, very importantly, still make a good return for our shareholders.

Our commitment to address social and environmental issues has been strengthened over the years by our deep roots in developing and emerging countries. Over 40% of Unilever's business is now in these markets. That makes them bigger for us than Europe and sales there are growing much faster. By 2012 more of our business will come from Asia, Africa and Latin America than from the developed markets of Europe and the USA. Doing business responsibly has served Unilever well. If you look at our share price over the past 25 years and compare it with the S&P 500 you can see that "doing good" and "doing well" are not mutually exclusive.

The Role of Business in Economic Development and Poverty Reduction

Multinational companies can, and do, play a significant role in the development agenda. They stimulate economic growth through international trade and facilitate social progress through the development of human capital. But the positive role of business is rarely talked about in the media. If brands are mentioned at all, it tends to be the ones that have not behaved responsibly, rather than those who have. Part of the problem is that companies do not normally measure their social, economic and environmental footprint in the markets in which they operate and, as we all know, communication without facts is tough. So Unilever has been trying to find out what impacts its operations have in the developing world.

In 2003 we joined forces with Oxfam—an unlikely bedfellow—to research the question. Together we embarked on a project to analyse the impacts of our business in one of our largest markets. The country we chose was Indonesia—a country where I have seen the damaging effects of poverty at first hand.

The report we jointly produced highlighted a number of interesting things. Firstly, it demonstrated that most of the cash value Unilever creates in Indonesia stays in the local economy. This challenges head on the perception which some NGOs have that multinationals are mere extractors of wealth, who make large profits locally that are then immediately remitted to shareholders in London and New York, without benefiting the local economy.

Secondly, the report looked at the impact of our upstream supply chain. It found that some 84% of our raw and packaging materials were sourced from local suppliers thereby creating not just jobs but technology transfer from other Unilever factories around the world.

Finally, our report revealed the extent to which our operations in Indonesia have a major "multiplier effect" on job creation. While Unilever Indonesia itself employs only 5,000 employees, the business supports the full time equivalent of 300,000 jobs, more than half of them in the distribution and retail chain.

Impressive though these figures are, the exercise did also reveal the very limited impact which our operations had in helping the farmers and shopkeepers at the furthest ends of the value chain to lift themselves out of poverty.

Nevertheless, the evidence from Indonesia is that a global company like Unilever with embedded local operations—what we call a multi-local multinational—can have a very positive effect on developing economies.

Encouraged by the Indonesian exercise we have initiated a second study; this time in Africa. Working with Ethan Kapstein—Professor of Sustainable Development here at INSEAD—we are investigating the social, economic and environmental impacts of Unilever's operations in South Africa. Professor Kapstein's report, which will be published later this year, will take the work that we did in Indonesia to a higher level. He will not only measure our footprint in quantitative terms but he will also seek to capture and analyse our "soft" impacts. By soft I mean such intangibles as:

- training and skills transfer;
- support for government capacity building;
- black empowerment initiatives; and
- environmental standard setting.

In a very real sense Ethan is getting a measure of the contribution which Unilever is making to develop a healthy and prosperous South Africa.

Let me give you some examples of how Unilever's presence in the emerging economies of Asia and Africa is contributing to the development agenda. I shall do this under three headings:

- capacity building;
- new business models to generate economic activity at the base of the pyramid; and
- product innovation which addresses specific social needs.

Capacity Building

Capacity building is the jargon that economists use to describe the creation of the skills, physical infrastructure, public health and administrative frameworks that are so necessary for developing countries to prosper. Capacity can be built at both the macro level of the state and at the micro level of individual companies and communities. In Africa, Unilever engages at both levels.

A good example of an intervention at the macro level is the work that Unilever is doing to facilitate cross border trade on the continent. We were one of the founder members of the Investment Climate Facility, a new public private partnership that aims to address some of the structural bottlenecks holding back investment in Africa. We have committed €1m to getting this going and are concentrating our efforts on working with African governments to rethink their approach to customs and border controls. This is something they have traditionally approached with a revenue mindset rather than a trade mindset.

If Africa is to develop as an economic region there need to be fewer restrictions on crossborder trade. These not only discourage foreign direct investment but also stifle intraregional trade—an important driver of economic growth. In ASEAN, for example, 60% of trade is between neighbours. In Africa it's more like 10–15%.

An example of capacity building at the micro or community level in Africa is Business Action against Chronic Hunger—an initiative we helped to launch last year. This is a programme orchestrated by the World Economic Forum and involving The Millennium Villages Project—a UN initiative pioneered by Professor Jeffrey Sachs. Our shared aim is to help communities lift themselves out of poverty through sustainable income generation.

The pilot programme is in Western Kenya. Agriculture is the primary livelihood there but the land available for farming is less than half a hectare per household—insufficient to produce enough food for the average family. As a result 60 to 70% of the population live below the poverty line.

Agronomists from Unilever's Kenyan tea plantations are helping farmers to convert their small-holdings from commodities like maize to higher value crops—specifically sunflowers and herbs and spices. The land was prepared in January and February. The seeds—which we provided—were planted in March. And in September, they will be harvested.

We have guaranteed to buy their crop at market prices. The sunflower oil will be used in Blue Band margarine and the herbs in Royco—a local brand of bouillon stock cubes. Our aim is for the farmers to make enough money in the first year to be able to feed themselves and to make a surplus for next year. In return for help with training and start-up costs, the farmers have agreed to put 10% of the value of any surplus they make in future years into community projects.

We are in the embryonic phase of this project but plan to scale it up from 30 farmers to 4,000—benefiting some 20,000 people. Again our objectives are clear. We want to work with others to make Kenya a healthy, prosperous society in which businesses like ours can flourish.

New Business Models

Capacity building of this kind is critical for long-term economic development. Of more immediate impact, however, is the ability of the private sector to create new business models. Some of these are designed to reach down towards what C. K. Prahalad has described as "the fortune at the bottom of the pyramid."

An excellent example of this is our Shakti initiative in India. At the end of the 1990's Hindustan Unilever realised that if they were to maintain their growth trajectory then they would need to find a way of selling their products to the rural poor. One in eight people on the planet lives in an Indian village. There are some 650,000 of them. All very isolated. Very few of them served by a retail distribution network.

The solution that we came up with to reach these consumers was to tap into existing networks of women's self-help groups which had grown up on the back of micro-credit schemes. From these groups we recruited and trained our Shakti entrepreneurs who became our local sales representatives. Their role was to go door to door selling our products.

Of course it was not our standard range. We had to re-engineer our products in such a way that they were affordable to people on desperately low incomes. More often than not this implied small pack formats—mainly sachets—which could be sold at prices as low as one or two rupees.

Shakti is at the intersection between social responsibility and business strategy. The social benefits of the scheme are obvious. It creates economic activity at the very bottom of the pyramid. It gives poor people access to products that address their basic needs for hygiene and nutrition. It gives dignity and a sense of empowerment to a large number of rural women.

At the same time the business benefits are huge. Today we have 30,000 Shakti entrepreneurs operating in 100,000 villages serving nearly 100 million consumers. The revenues generated are now close to $100 million per annum and the margins are very similar to those we achieve through our mainstream distribution channels. Make no mistake. Shakti is not a philanthropic activity. It is a serious and profitable business proposition.

Routes to market like Shakti enable Unilever to serve the needs of first time consumers. In turn this gives us the opportunity to address some of the nutrition and hygiene needs of some of the poorest people on the planet.

Products that meet the social needs in the D&E world.

Two examples to illustrate this—one from India and one from Africa. The Indian example is Lifebuoy soap. Every ten seconds a child dies from diarrhoea somewhere in the world. One-third of these deaths are in India. Most are children under five. Yet according to the World Bank, something as mundane and simple as washing hands with soap can reduce diarrhoeal diseases by half.

Lifebuoy has been India's leading soap brand for decades. In the late 1990's it launched the largest rural health and hygiene education programme ever undertaken in India. It is called Swasthya Chetna—which means "Health Awakening" in Sanskrit. Piggy backing on the infrastructure created by Shakti, Lifebuoy health education teams visit thousands of schools and communities to teach children about the existence of germs and the importance of washing hands with soap.

Marketing activity of this kind is a classic "win-win." The education programme has a measurable impact on public health. The benefits for Lifebuoy come through in an expanding market for soap which allows strong sales growth—nearly 10% in 2006.

The second example, this time from Africa and from the foods side of our business, is the fortification of basic foodstuffs with micro-nutrients. One of the biggest nutritional challenges in Africa is the absence of certain nutrients in the diet. Iodine deficiency is a case in point. It affects millions of people and can cause mental retardation and brain damage.

In Ghana, for example, simply adding iodine to our Annapurna salt brand helped to nearly double iodine consumption to over half the population.

Here our impact was amplified by partnering with UNICEF to create and implement a programme of social marketing. Again this was a win-win. UNICEF and the Ghanaian Ministry of Health achieved their public health goals of increasing iodine consumption. Unilever Ghana was able to open up a new market.

Let me conclude this section by summarising the role which business can play in economic development and poverty alleviation. Unilever's experience is that business can:

- help build human and institutional capacity through activities such as the customs project in West Africa and training subsistence farmers in Kenya;
- develop new business models such as Shakti which allow the creation of profitable economic activity at the very bottom of the pyramid;
- use its R&D and marketing skills to tackle public health problems in areas like nutrition (fortified salt in Ghana) and hygiene (hand wash education in India).

What does business get in return? If it is smart it gets:

- access to new markets;
- new opportunities for innovation and growth;
- new partners;
- and over the long term, it earns the trust and confidence of the community—something without which sustainable growth is impossible.

Social Innovation

By social innovation I mean finding new products and services that meet not only the functional needs of consumers for tasty food or clean clothes but also their wider aspirations as citizens. To some degree both Lifebuoy soap in India and Annapurna salt in Ghana are examples of social innovation.

But in the developed markets of Europe and the United States the opportunities are just as broad. Here we are observing new patterns of consumption. They are being driven by the emergence of what has become known as the "conscience consumer." These are consumers who are worried about social and environmental issues and realise they can influence change through the brands they choose to either buy or boycott.

For Unilever this trend fits neatly with our Vitality mission, which is about feeling good, looking good and getting more out of life. Our market research is telling us that consumers want the benefits of "vitality" products—but not at any price. A growing number, when making their purchasing decision, want to be reassured that the brands they buy will benefit society and the planet, not harm them. In other words, they want brands that not only make them feel good and look good but that also do good. This movement is gathering momentum. In fact we believe this trend has all the hallmarks of ushering in a new age of marketing and branding.

40 years ago brands were all about functional benefits—whether, for example, Persil washed whiter than Ariel. Then advertising agencies, influenced by the social sciences like psychology and anthropology started building in emotional benefits—wash with Lux, the soap the stars prefer, and some of Hollywood's glamour will rub off on you. Now there's a new dimension—brands with social benefits that appeal to consumers as citizens.

I should explain, for those of you who may not be aware, that Dove is a brand whose social mission is to change people's stereotypical views of female beauty. Research shows that 90% of women are not happy with the way they look. Much of the problem lies with the unrealistic way women are portrayed in advertising, fashion and the media. Through the Dove Self-Esteem Fund, Dove is helping women, and young women in particular, to see through the artifice that permeates the world of fashion and, in doing so, build their self-esteem and become more confident about the way they look.

Incidentally it was neither pressure from the NGO world nor legislation that drove the Dove team towards the Campaign for Real Beauty. It was consumer insight. Intelligent interpretation of market research highlighted that this issue resonated strongly with women of all ages around the world. The team realised that by championing the cause they would not only be doing something worthwhile but at the same time strengthening the loyalty of their consumers to the brand. Today we are reaping the benefits of this in rapid rates of growth for Dove all around the world.

Another Unilever brand with strong campaigning credentials is Ben & Jerry's. We acquired the business in 2000 but the values of their eponymous founders, Ben Cohen and Jerry Greenfield, remain the values of the company today. One of Ben & Jerry's key concerns is the environment and, in particular, the devastating effect global warming is having on the earth's polar ice-caps. As Ben Cohen and Jerry Greenfield like to say: "Listen to two old ice cream guys—if it's melted, it's ruined." Their Lick Global Warming campaign and the Climate Change College, which they set up in partnership with WWF, are outstanding examples of how you can make a complex subject accessible to people and relevant to their everyday lives. Last week Ben & Jerry's announced their intention to become a "climate neutral brand"—the first big European food brand to do so.

The examples of Ben & Jerry's with climate change and Dove with its Campaign for Real Beauty are good illustrations of brands picking up issues of concern to millions of people and starting to take meaningful action to raise awareness and change behaviour. Both brands have the credibility to make a difference at a societal level. Both brands, by championing these causes, will cement the loyalty of their consumers. Both are classic examples of brands that are "doing well by doing good."

Sustainability

For Unilever, sustainability covers not just environmental but also social and economic considerations. This is an area we have been addressing with systematic rigour since the early 1990's with programmes to improve the sustainability of our operations and our supply chain.

With over two-thirds of our raw materials coming from agriculture we have had an active programme of sustainable agriculture for more than a decade. Teams of agronomists have been beavering away to learn how to grow crops like tomatoes, tea, palm, peas and spinach without using too much water and with minimal use of pesticide and fertiliser.

But until recently this valuable work never aroused the interest of our brand teams. Now they are beginning to understand that this is an area where there is a convergence between our long-standing expertise in sustainability and consumers' concerns as citizens.

Let me give you an example. Many consumers are increasingly worried about the welfare of the people in developing countries who grow and harvest the food and drink they enjoy. This is behind the phenomenal growth of the fair trade movement. Until now this has largely been the preserve of niche operators. A couple of large companies like Starbucks and Nestlé have dipped a toe in the water. Both have introduced Fairtrade versions of their coffees. But these represent just a small fraction of the total volumes they buy.

Coffee companies are not the only ones trying to capitalise on consumer concerns in this area. Countless brands are jumping on the eco-ethical bandwagon. This is an agenda where you are judged by your actions, not by your press releases. Consumers are quick to spot the difference between those brands that are authentic and those that aren't. Companies that try to promote themselves as being ethical in one aspect of their business but who tolerate bad practice in another will come unstuck.

At Unilever we believe this agenda offers huge potential for innovation and brand development. But we believe it will only work for us if it is fully integrated into our way of doing business. To help us do this, we have developed a diagnostic tool called Brand Imprint. It helps our brands take a 360° look at their impacts on society and the environment and gain deep insights into the external forces shaping this agenda.

A number of our global brands have started to use this tool and the first fruits of their work are starting to come through. In fact I can today announce that Unilever has decided to commit to purchasing all its tea from sustainable sources and has asked the Rainforest Alliance, the international NGO, to start auditing the estates from which we buy our tea, including our own in Kenya. Unilever is the world's largest tea company and Lipton is the world's favourite tea brand. We aim to have all Lipton Yellow Label and PG Tips tea bags sold in Western Europe certified as sustainable by 2010 and all Lipton tea bags sold globally certified by 2015.

It is the first time a major tea company has committed to introducing sustainably produced tea on such a large scale and the first time the Rainforest Alliance, better known for coffee certification, will audit tea farms. I have no doubt this decision will transform the global tea industry, which has been suffering for many years from over capacity and falling prices. The decision has the potential to improve the crops, incomes and livelihoods of nearly 1 million tea growers and pluckers in Africa. Eventually, up to 2 million people around the world could benefit— nearly all of them in developing countries, and many of them living on or below the poverty line.

Again this is a win-win. Our consumers will have the reassurance that the tea they enjoy is both sustainably grown and traded fairly. Subsistence farmers will get a better price. Tea pluckers will be better off. The environment will be better protected. And we expect to sell more tea.

This is the way forward for business and brands. At one level it is very simple. It's about:

- brands continuing to provide consumers the functional benefits they seek;
- while at the same time maximising the social benefits and minimising the environmental impacts.

In reality, finding the sweet spot between meeting the needs of society, the needs of the planet, and the needs of consumers as citizens is complex. But it will be a real differentiator for those who do it well and do it with integrity.

So, to summarise, there have been six key themes to my presentation.

- Business can play an effective role in development and poverty reduction, as demonstrated by our subsidiaries in South Africa, Indonesia and Kenya.
- New business models such as Shakti can reach the poorest of the poor and at the same time produce rapid rates of growth at good levels of profitability.
- Brands can be agents of positive social change. Look at Annapurna, Lifebuoy and Dove. Each in its separate way is tackling a social issue—malnutrition, diarrheal disease and women's self-esteem.
- "The conscience consumer" is here to stay. It is a movement that is gathering momentum and will change the face of business and brands. Companies that grasp the opportunity this agenda presents in a genuine and sustainable way will be the ones that succeed in the 21st century.
- Business has to become genuinely sustainable. This is a win-win opportunity. Our decision to buy tea from sustainable sources is good news for farmers, good news for consumers, good news for the environment and makes good business sense.
- Finally and most importantly there is no dichotomy between business doing good and doing well. In fact the two go hand in hand. All of the brands I have talked about are growing rapidly. All are profitable. If they weren't their social and environmental initiatives would not be sustainable. Both parties—business and society—need to benefit.

Conclusion

I started this presentation by saying that social responsibility and sustainable development are no longer fringe activities but are central to our business. And, just as this agenda has become core to business, so it should also become core to management education. It must be moved to the heart of the curriculum. Business schools generally need to give much more prominence to this subject than they

have historically. Some are beginning to do so. But many are being slow to integrate this agenda.

Doing business in the 21st century is a much more subtle and complex process than some MBA courses would lead one to believe. Of course there is a place for the financial modelling, the DCF calculations and yield curves. But in the end the big decisions in business are about culture and consumers. It is clear that many business schools are waking up to this. A survey conducted in 2005 found that 54% of schools required one or more courses in corporate social responsibility, sustainability, or business and society, up from 34% four years earlier. This is progress, but not yet enough. The same survey, conducted for the Aspen Institute, found that while students in the top 30 schools covered social and environmental issues in roughly 25% of their coursework, the figure for students in the remaining schools was a disappointing 8%.

From a Unilever perspective, we are already giving increased attention to this in our recruitment policy—and we will continue to do so. Those who come to us with a deep understanding of the area will be at a significant advantage.

So let me finish by offering members of this forum the following advice: For those of you now studying for your MBA, I would say this: get to know this agenda. Understand how it can be a driver of business growth. Build it into your professional skill set. The business world will very soon be divided into those that recognised its potential early on and those who woke up to it too late. Make sure you are an early adopter. For those of you with MBAs who, like me, didn't cover this subject as part of your course, I am sure that you are already grappling with these issues in your various industry sectors. I hope this talk will have stimulated your thinking a little. As was once famously said: "a company that makes only money is a poor company."

Source: This reading is taken from a speech delivered at the 2007 INDEVOR Alumni Forum in INSEAD, Fontainebleau, France, May 25, 2007.

10

Ethical Decision Making: Corporate Governance, Accounting, and Finance

It astounds me how little senior management gets a basic truth: If clients don't trust you they will eventually stop doing business with you. It doesn't matter how smart you are.

Greg Smith, former Goldman Sachs executive director

Whenever an institution malfunctions as consistently as boards of directors have in nearly every major fiasco of the last forty or fifty years, it is futile to blame men. It is the institution that malfunctions.

Peter Drucker

Earnings can be as pliable as putty when a charlatan heads the company reporting them.

Warren Buffett

In September 2015, the U.S. Environmental Protection Agency (EPA) announced that it was ordering a recall for more than 500,000 Volkswagens sold in the United States. The EPA reported that VW's diesel engine cars contained software code that manipulated emission tests and allowed the cars to meet required emission standards. The software "defeat devices" activated emission controls only while the car was undergoing testing; however, while driving under normal conditions the cars emitted nitrous oxide pollution that was more than 30 times higher than what was allowed by law. Investigations followed in other countries and eventually some 11 million vehicles were recalled globally. Within days, Volkswagen's stock price had dropped almost 40 percent. By mid-2016, estimates were that VW would pay out $18 billion in repairs, fines, and legal settlements as a result of the scandal. This figure does not include lost sales, nor the heavy financial losses suffered by thousands of independent VW dealers and suppliers.

For at least one year prior to the EPA announcement, VW and the EPA had discussed apparent discrepancies in the testing data, which VW initially dismissed as the result of testing anomalies. Only after the EPA took steps to withhold approval for all the upcoming 2016 VW diesel cars did VW acknowledge that a real problem existed. Upon the EPA recall announcement in September, VW officials admitted that the problem involved intentional fraud and took responsibility for the scandal.

Volkswagen CEO Martin Winterkorn apologized for "the terrible mistakes of a few people" and, while denying any knowledge of or involvement, resigned within weeks. In a statement accompanying his resignation, Winterkorn said, "I am stunned that misconduct on such a scale was possible in the Volkswagen Group, I am not aware of any wrongdoing on my part." Testifying before the U.S. Congress soon after the EPA announcement, VW of America's president Michael Horn admitted that "Our company was dishonest with the EPA, and the California Air Resources Board and with all of you." Horn resigned in March 2016.

Initial reports coming from VW placed responsibility with a small number of engineers, acting under managerial pressure to meet corporate goals for both engine performance and fuel efficiency. But later evidence suggested that as early as 2006 VW management had indications that they were not able to achieve emission standards within established cost targets.

For decades, government regulators across the world have worked with automobile manufacturers to develop environmental and fuel-efficiency standards that would meaningfully improve air quality by reducing pollution, yet still be technologically achievable. Manufacturers chose various strategies to meet these standards. Technological and design advances in engines, body aerodynamics, pollution control devices, and materials all contributed to increasingly fuel-efficient cars. Some manufacturers chose to develop smaller cars, some moved in the direction of hybrids and electric vehicles, and others, like VW, worked to improve diesel technology.

The scandal struck at the heart of the VW brand. Improved diesel engines had become a hallmark of the VW brand of "German engineering." Diesels have always had performance benefits over gas-powered engines. Diesel engines last longer, get better fuel mileage, provide more torque and power, and are more dependable than gasoline engines. Yet, historically they emitted more pollution, especially nitrous oxides and particulate matter (the black soot often seen coming from truck or bus exhaust). VW, a brand long promoted for its engineering skill, marketed its turbocharged direct injection (TDI) engines as a new generation of "smart diesels," able to maintain all the high-performance benefits of diesels while also meeting stringent new environmental standards.

Given the centrality of the new-generation diesels to the VW brand and to its global sales, many observers found it difficult to believe that a widespread fraud involving such a crucial element of its key product could have resulted from "the terrible mistakes of a few people." How could a major scandal involving the fraudulent design and promotion of a core product, especially a product that everyone knew would be subjected to extensive governmental testing and regulation, occur? Even if the decision to insert the defeat device rested with only a few engineers, the scandal could only have occurred if there were widespread failures of oversight and control at every level, from the shop floor to the corporate board room. In the opinion of many, this widespread failure of oversight and control, especially at the management and board level, was as great a corporate failing as the fraud itself. Where was the oversight and supervision?

A plausible description of the realities leading up to this scandal is that engineers were expected to achieve a balance among three factors that were in tension: They were to develop a diesel engine that met high performance standards while also meeting environmental emission standards. Importantly, they were expected to accomplish this while also meeting cost targets. Later evidence revealed that earlier proposals that would have achieved this balance had been rejected by management because they would have added costs of a few hundred dollars to each vehicle. One option, of course, would have been for management to conclude that this balance could not therefore be achieved. However, by most reports the VW corporate culture was such that there was little tolerance for work teams that failed to meet goals and little willingness among management to encourage questions or challenges to their decisions.

Professional codes of ethics can sometimes function to shield engineers from pressures to compromise professional standards in order to meet employer or client goals. Professionals such as lawyers, accountants, and engineers have ethical duties that should override the demands of one's employer. But engineers in Germany do not have the level of professional licensing and training requirements as engineers face in Canada and the United States, for example. In any case, there is little evidence that any VW engineer, the individuals who had direct and firsthand experience of the fraud, stepped forward to take a stand against the fraud. There have been no reported cases of whistle-blowing by anyone within the organization.

VW management would have had many opportunities to prevent the fraud, mitigate its damage, or at the very minimum acknowledge and report it sooner. Senior executives failed across the board in their oversight responsibilities. They failed employees by setting unfeasible expectations and being inflexible in the face of evidence that these were unattainable. VW had no internal mechanisms that encouraged or even allowed reporting of malfeasance.

As the scandal unfolded, VW's largest union criticized management for having a "rigid hierarchy" that was authoritarian and unwilling to listen to bad news. Matthias Müller, Volkswagen's new chief executive appointed after the Winterkorn resignation, acknowledged problems with the previous managerial style and promised a more open management style.

(continued)

(continued)

One might expect the VW board to have set high expectations and to have held management to them. But, according to press reports, the relationship between the VW board and senior executives had been contentious for a long time. As the scandal became public, board members criticized Winterkorn for failing to keep them informed. Three board members, including government officials and union representatives, revealed that they learned of the scandal only by reading about it in the media. Critics pointed out that either senior executives were unaware of the fraud, in which case they failed in their managerial duties, or they did know and neither fixed the problem nor kept the board informed, in which case they failed other duties.

In a statement released after VW admitted the fraud, Stephan Weil, a board member who is also prime minister of the German state Lower Saxony, where Volkswagen is based, claimed that "Talks took place for a full year before Volkswagen admitted the deception. This confession should clearly have occurred much earlier." Weil described the failure of senior executives to inform the board "a grave mistake."

Despite these criticisms, the VW board had extended Winterkorn's contract as CEO just two weeks before the public recall announcement from the EPA. Winterkorn certainly knew of the pending EPA action at this point, but most board members claimed that they did not.

But there is evidence that the VW board was in disarray at this time. Winterkorn's contract extension came just four months after a failed attempt to oust him by board chair Ferdinand Piech. Piech, the grandson of VW founder Ferdinand Porsche and often described as the "patriarch" of VW, had held senior leadership positions including CEO or board chair for decades. Peich was well known for his authoritarian management style, which had resulted in similar dismissals of other senior executives. When the attempt to oust Winterkorn failed, Peich resigned as board chair and stepped away from all other roles with VW.

But there were other structural issues with the VW board that might also help explain some of the governance disarray. In the United States and Canada, for example, corporations are governed by a single board of directors, which has the ultimate legal fiduciary responsibility to company shareholders. In Germany, however, corporations are governed by two boards, a supervisory board with general oversight responsibility and a managerial board, which is comprised of senior executives who are responsible for operational oversight. Further, the German workplace democracy model of codetermination legally requires that half the board seats go to representatives of workers.

The VW board is comprised of 20 members. The board chair is former VW corporate finance director. Ten of the remaining 19 seats are hold by representatives of VW's union workers. Four other seats are reserved for members of the Porsche and Piech families, who own 52 percent of the corporate stock. Prior to the failed attempt to oust Winterkorn, Ferdinand Piech and his wife Ursala held two of the four family board memberships. Two seats are held by representatives of the German state of Lower Saxony, the region in which the VW plant is located and holder of 20 percent of the corporate stock. Two seats are reserved for representatives of the country of Qatar, which owns 17 percent of VW stock.

Thus, only 10 percent of this publicly traded company's stock is freely floating in the marketplace. Of the 20-person supervisory board, only 1 member could be classified as independent. Critics suggest that this structure is at the root of VW's

(continued)

(concluded)

dysfunctional governance. Members of the supervisory board have split loyalties that can conflict with the duties for corporate transparency and integrity. For example, the VW facility is reputed to be a highly inefficient production plant. It manufactures slightly more cars than its competitor Toyota, but employs almost twice as many workers to do it. It would be difficult, for example, to get approval for job cuts or production transfers from a board with 60 percent of its membership in the hands of unions and local governments. The split board system can also shield management from oversight from the supervisory board.

In April 2016, in anticipation of its annual stockholders meeting, the VW supervisory board announced that investigations had concluded that VW's executive management was not responsible for the fraud. As a result, the board would recommend that executives receive end-of-year bonuses for 2015. It was also revealed that Martin Winterkorn had received $8 million in compensation for 2015, only half of his 2014 compensation. Union leaders angrily denounced these recommendations, pointing out that employees would be receiving little or no bonuses for 2015 due to the financial losses associated with the scandal.

- How would you assign responsibility for the VW scandal? What should have been done differently and by whom?
- Who are the stakeholders in this case? How were the interests of each stakeholder represented?
- Is it fair to expect any employees, including professionals such as engineers and accountants, to confront management over directives that they believe are unethical?
- What changes to the VW board would you recommend that might help prevent future scandals?
- The codetermination principle was created to ensure that employees have a role in managerial decision making, thus creating a more democratic workplace. What are the benefits of this model? What are the disadvantages?
- What do you understand by "independent" board member? Who or what should an independent board member represent that would be different from other board members?

Chapter Objectives

After reading this chapter, you will be able to:

1. Explain the role of accountants and other professionals as "gatekeepers."
2. Describe how conflicts of interest can arise for business professionals.
3. Outline the requirements of the Sarbanes-Oxley Act.
4. Describe the COSO framework.
5. Define the "control environment" and the means by which ethics and culture can impact that environment.
6. Discuss the legal obligations of a member of a board of directors.
7. Explain the ethical obligations of a member of a board of directors.

8. Highlight conflicts of interest in financial markets and discuss the ways in which they may be alleviated.

9. Describe conflicts of interest in governance created by excessive executive compensation.

10. Define insider trading and evaluate its potential for unethical behavior.

Introduction

The first edition of this textbook was written in 2006, soon after a wave of major corporate scandals had shaken the financial world. Recall those companies involved in the ethical scandals during the early years of this century: Enron, WorldCom, Tyco, Rite Aid, Sunbeam, Waste Management, Health-South, Global Crossing, Arthur Andersen, Ernst & Young, KPMG, J.P. Morgan, Merrill Lynch, Morgan Stanley, Citigroup, Salomon Smith Barney, Marsh & McLennan, Credit Suisse First Boston, and even the New York Stock Exchange itself. At the center of these scandals were fundamental questions of corporate governance and responsibility. Significant cases of financial fraud, mismanagement, criminality, and deceit were not only tolerated, but in some cases were endorsed by those people in the highest levels of corporate governance who should have been standing guard against such unethical and illegal behavior.

Sadly, the very same issues are as much alive today as they were several years ago. Consider the rash of problems associated with the financial meltdown in 2007–2008 and the problems faced by such companies as AIG, Countrywide, Lehman Brothers, Merrill Lynch, and Bear Stearns, and of the financier Bernard Madoff. More recent ethical scandals, many described in this latest edition, have been alleged against such corporations as Volkswagen, Goldman Sachs, Barclays Bank, Walmart, HSBC, Mitsubishi Motors, UBS, and Wells Fargo. Once again, we have witnessed financial and ethical malfeasance of historic proportions and the inability of internal and external governance structures to prevent it.

At the heart of many of the biggest ethical and business failures of the past decade were aspects of financial and accounting misconduct, ranging from manipulating special purpose entities to defraud lenders, to cooking the books, to instituting questionable tax dodges, to allowing investment decisions to warp the objectivity of investment research and advice, to Ponzi schemes, to insider trading, to excessive pay for executives, to dicey investments in sub-prime mortgages and hedge funds, to risky credit default swaps, to fraudulent reporting of loan rates. Ethics in the governance and financial arenas has been perhaps the most visible issue in business ethics during the first decades of the new millennium. Accounting and investment firms that were once looked upon as the guardians of integrity in financial dealings have now been exposed as corrupt violators of the fiduciary responsibilities entrusted to them by their stakeholders.

Many analysts contend that this corruption is evidence of a complete failure in **corporate governance** structures. As we reflect on the ethical corruption and financial failures of the past decade, some fundamental questions should be asked.

corporate governance
The structure by which corporations are managed, directed, and controlled toward the objectives of fairness, accountability, and transparency. The structure generally will determine the relationship between the board of directors, the shareholders or owners of the firm, and the firm's executives or management.

What happened to the internal governance structures within these firms that should have prevented these disasters? In particular, why did the boards, auditors, accountants, lawyers, and other professionals fail to fulfill their professional, legal, and ethical duties? Could better governance and oversight have prevented these ethical disgraces? Going forward, can we rely on internal governance controls to provide effective oversight, or are more effective external controls and government regulation needed?

Professional Duties and Conflicts of Interest

Enron Corporation
An energy company based in Houston, Texas, that *Fortune* magazine named America's most innovative company for six consecutive years before it was discovered to have been involved in one of the largest instances of accounting fraud in world history. In 2001, with over 21,000 employees, it filed the largest bankruptcy in United States history and disclosed a scandal that resulted in the loss of millions of dollars, thousands of jobs, the downfall of Big Five accounting firm Arthur Andersen LLP, at least one suicide, and several trials and convictions, among other consequences. Enron remains in business today as it continues to liquidate its assets.

OBJECTIVE

The watershed event that brought the ethics of finance to prominence at the beginning of the 21st century was the collapse of **Enron Corporation** and its accounting firm Arthur Andersen. The Enron case "has wreaked more havoc on the accounting industry than any other case in U.S. history,"[1] including the demise of Arthur Andersen. Of course, ethical responsibilities of accountants were not unheard of prior to Enron, but the events that led to Enron's demise brought into focus the necessity of the independence of auditors and the responsibilities of accountants like never before.

Accounting is one of several professions that serve very important functions within the economic system itself. Remember that even a staunch defender of free-market economics such as Milton Friedman believes that markets can function effectively and efficiently only when certain rule-based conditions are met. It is universally recognized that markets must function within the law and they must be free from fraud and deception. The LIBOR rate scandal described in the Decision Point is a case of how fraud can undermine the integrity of an entire financial system. Some argue that only government regulation can ensure that these rules will be followed. Others argue that enforcement of these rules is the responsibility of important internal controls that exist within market-based economic systems. Several important business professions, for example, attorneys, auditors, accountants, and financial analysts, function in just this way. Just as the game of baseball requires umpires to act with integrity and fairness, business and economic markets require these professionals to operate in a similar manner by enforcing the rules and attesting to the fundamental fairness of the system.

These professions can be thought of as **gatekeepers** or "watchdogs" in that their role is to ensure that those who enter into the marketplace are playing by the rules and conforming to the very conditions that ensure the market functions as it is supposed to function. Recall from chapter 3 the importance of role identities in determining ethical duties of professionals. These roles provide a source for rules from which we can determine how professionals ought to act. In entering into a profession, we accept responsibilities based on our roles.

These professions can also be understood as intermediaries, acting between the various parties in the market, and they are bound to ethical duties in this role as well. All the participants in the market, especially investors, boards, management, and bankers, rely on these gatekeepers. Auditors verify a company's financial statements so that investors' decisions are free from fraud and deception.

On June 27, 2012, as part of a U.S. Department of Justice Investigation, Barclays Bank admitted to manipulating and reporting fraudulent interest rates used in international financial markets. Barclays, a multinational financial services and banking firm headquartered in London, was fined more than $450 million (U.S.) by regulators in both the United Kingdom and the United States. Within a week, Marcus Agius, board chair, Bob Diamond, chief executive officer, and Jerry del Missier, chief operating officer, all resigned.

Evidence showed that Barclays had regularly manipulated the LIBOR (London Inter-Bank Offered Rate) interest rate since at least 2005 in order both to profit from large trades and to falsely portray the bank as financially stronger than it was.

The LIBOR is the rate at which major London banks report that they are able to borrow. This rate then serves as the benchmark at which interest rates are set for countless other loans, ranging from credit cards to mortgages and interbank loans. It also acts as a measure of market confidence in the bank; if a bank must pay a higher rate than others to borrow, then markets must have less confidence in the institution's financial strength.

The LIBOR is established in a surprisingly simple manner. Each morning at 11 A.M. London time, members of the British Bankers Association (BBA) report to the financial reporting firm of Thomson Reuters the rates they would expect to pay for loans from other banks. Discarding the highest and lowest quartiles, Thomson Reuters then calculates a daily average, which becomes the daily LIBOR benchmark. Within an hour, Thomson Reuters publicizes this average worldwide, along with all of the individual rates reported to the firm. This benchmark is then used to settle short-term interest rates as well as futures and options contracts. By one estimate, the LIBOR is used to set interest rates for global financial transactions worth more than $500 trillion. The individual rates also provide an indirect measure of the financial health of each reporting institution: the lower their rates, the stronger their financial position.

Evidence shows that as early as 2007, before the major financial collapse of Lehman Brothers and the economic meltdown that followed, regulators in both the United States and the United Kingdom were aware of allegations that Barclays was underreporting its rates. In the early days of the 2008 financial collapse, the *Wall Street Journal* published a series of articles that questioned the integrity of LIBOR reporting and suggested that banks were intentionally misreporting rates to strengthen public perception of their financial health. Timothy Geithner, U.S. secretary of treasury under President Obama, acknowledged that in 2008 when he was chair of the New York Federal Reserve Bank, he recommended that British regulators change the process for setting the LIBOR. In testimony to the U.S. Congress in July 2012, Geithner said, "We were aware [in 2008] of the risks that the way this was designed created not just the incentive to underreport, but also the opportunity to underreport."

Internal documents and e-mails, acknowledged by Barclays during the investigation, showed that traders, compliance officers, and senior management were aware of and approved the underreporting. An e-mail sent from a Barclays employee to his supervisor in 2007 said: "My worry is that we are being seen to be contributing patently false rates. We are therefore being dishonest by definition and are at risk of damaging our reputation in the market and with the regulators. Can we discuss urgently please?"

- What ethical issues are involved in this case?
- Who are the stakeholders in this case? Who was hurt by rate fixing?
- What responsibilities did senior executives at Barclays have to prevent fraud in circumstances that, in Timothy Geithner's words, created both the incentive and opportunity for fraud?
- What sort of internal controls might the Barclays board of directors have instituted to prevent such fraud?

Sources: Sources for this Decision Point, as well as detailed summaries of the ongoing LIBOR scandal, can be found at the websites for the *Financial Times,* www.ft.com/indepth/libor-scandal (accessed December 27, 2012); and the BBC, www.bbc.co.uk/news/business-18671255 (accessed December 27, 2012).

gatekeepers
Some professions, such as accountant, that act as "watchdogs" in that their role is to ensure that those who enter into the marketplace are playing by the rules and conforming to the conditions that ensure the market functions as it is supposed to function.

conflict of interest
A conflict of interest exists where a person holds a position of trust that requires that she or he exercise judgment on behalf of others, but where her or his personal interests and/or obligations conflict with those of others.

OBJECTIVE

fiduciary duties
A legal duty to act on behalf of or in the interests of another.

Analysts evaluate a company's financial prospects or creditworthiness so that banks and investors can make informed decisions. Attorneys ensure that decisions and transactions conform to the law. As suggested by the VW case in the Opening Decision Point, engineers can also have a role to ensure products are safe and legal. Indeed, even boards of directors can be understood in this way. Boards function as intermediaries between a company's stockholders and its executives and should guarantee that executives act on behalf of the stockholders' interests.

The most basic ethical issue facing professional gatekeepers and intermediaries in business contexts involves conflicts of interest. A **conflict of interest** exists where a person holds a position of trust that requires that she or he exercise judgment on behalf of others, but where her or his personal interests and/or obligations conflict with those of others. For instance, a friend knows that you are heading to a flea market and asks if you would keep your eyes open for any beautiful quilts you might see. She asks you to purchase one for her if you see a "great buy." You are going to the flea market to buy your mother a birthday present. You happen to see a beautiful quilt at a fabulous price, the only one at the market. In fact, your mother would adore the quilt. You find yourself in a conflict of interest—your friend trusted you to search the flea market on her behalf. Your personal interests are now in conflict with the duty you agreed to accept on behalf of your friend.

Conflicts of interest can also arise when a person's ethical obligations in her or his professional duties clash with personal interests. Thus, for example, in the most egregious case a financial planner who accepts kickbacks from a brokerage firm to steer clients into certain investments fails in her or his professional responsibility by putting personal financial interests ahead of client interest. Such professionals are said to have **fiduciary duties**—a professional and ethical obligation—to their clients, duties rooted in trust that override their own personal interests. (See the Decision Point "How to Solve the 'Agency Problem.'")

Unfortunately, and awkwardly, many of these professional intermediaries are paid by the businesses over which they keep watch, and perhaps are also employed by yet another business. For example, David Duncan was the principal accounting professional employed by Arthur Andersen and assigned to work at Enron. As the

Arthur Andersen case so clearly demonstrated, this situation can create real conflicts between a professional's responsibility and his or her financial interests. Certified *public* accountants (CPAs) have a professional responsibility to the public. But they work for clients whose financial interests are not always served by full, accurate, and independent disclosure of financial information. Even more dangerously, they work daily with and are hired by a management team that itself might have interests that conflict with the interests of the firm represented by the board of directors. Thus, real and complex conflicts can exist between professional duties and a professional's self-interest. We will revisit conflicts in the accounting profession later in the chapter. (See Figure 10.1 for an overview of potential conflicts of interest for CPAs.)

FIGURE 10.1

Conflicts of Interest in Public CPA Activity

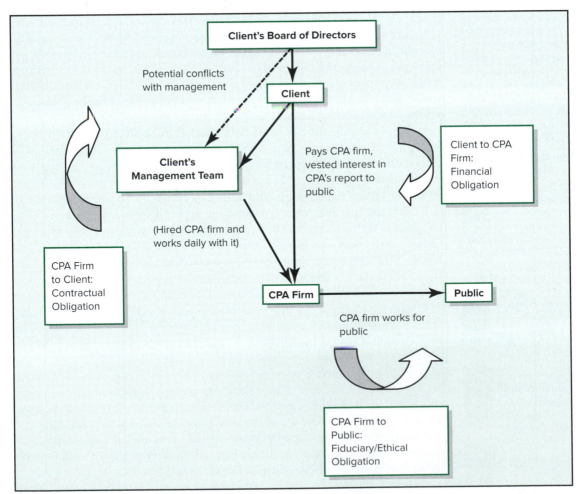

Decision Point

How to Solve the
"Agency Problem"

According to many observers, there is a deep problem at the heart of modern capitalist economies. Modern economies rely on individuals, legally known as "agents," who work for the best interests of others, the "principals." For the system to work, agents must be loyal representatives of their principal's interests, even in those situations when their own personal interest is at stake. For example, a member of a board of directors acts as an agent for the stockholders, executives act as agents for the boards, and attorneys and accountants act as agents for their clients. This agent–principal model assumes that individuals *can* put their own interests on hold and be sufficiently motivated to act on behalf of another. But this would seem to run counter to a view of human nature that is assumed by much of modern economic theory: individuals are self-interested—thus, the "agency problem." How can we trust self-interested individuals to act for the well-being of others in cases where by doing so their own self-interest must be sacrificed?

Many of the ethical failures described in this chapter can be seen as examples of the agency problem. These are precisely those situations where boards have failed to protect the interests of stockholders; executives have failed to serve their boards; and accountants, lawyers, and financial analysts have failed to act on behalf of their clients.

Economics and management theorists have offered several solutions to the agency problem. Some argue that the best solution is to create incentives that connect the agent's self-interest with the self-interest of the principal. Linking executive compensation to performance by making bonuses contingent on stock price means that an executive gains only when stockholders gain. Placing representatives of major stockholders on corporate boards, as happens at Volkswagen, is another approach to align corporate interests with stockholder interests.

Another approach is to create structures and institutions that restrict an agent's actions. Strict legal constraints would be the most obvious version of this approach. Agents have specific legal duties of loyalty, confidentiality, and obedience and face criminal punishments if they fail to uphold those duties. Professional or corporate codes of conduct and other forms of self-regulation are also versions of this approach.

These two most common answers share a fundamental feature: the agency problem can be solved by connecting motivation to act on the principal's behalf back to the agent's own self-interest. In the first case, motivation is in the form of the "carrot" and the agent benefits by serving the principal; in the second case, motivation is in the form of the "stick," and the agent suffers if she fails to serve her principal.

A third answer to the agency problem denies that there truly is a problem by denying that self-interest dominates human motivation. This third approach points out that, in fact, humans regularly act from loyalty, trust, and altruism. Human relationships are built on trust and reliability; and these motivations are just as basic, just as common, as self-interest. Thus, this approach would encourage corporations to look to moral character and corporate culture to develop policies and practices that reinforce, shape, and condition people to want to do the right thing.

(continued)

(concluded)

- Can you think of examples in your own experience where someone is required to work as an agent for another, or when you were involved as an agent? How is the agent motivated in this particular case?
- If you were asked to design a policy that would provide a solution to the agency problem in the company that you work, where would you begin?
- Review the section on virtue ethics in chapter 3 and explain how the agency problem would be viewed from that perspective.
- Under what circumstances, or for what kinds of tasks, do you think agency problems are most likely to be a challenge?

In one sense, the ethical issues regarding such professional responsibilities are clear. Because professional gatekeeper duties are necessary conditions for the fair and effective functioning of economic markets, they should trump other responsibilities to one's employer. David Duncan's professional responsibilities as an auditor should have overridden his role as an Andersen employee in large part because he was hired *as* an auditor. But knowing one's duties and fulfilling those duties are two separate issues. Consider the conflict of interest involved in the Decision Point "When Does Financial Support Become a Kickback?"

Agency responsibilities generate many ethical implications. If we recognize that the gatekeeper function is necessary for the very functioning of economic markets, and if we also recognize that self-interest can make it difficult for individuals to fulfill their gatekeeper duties, then society has a responsibility to create institutions and structures that will minimize these conflicts. For example, as long as auditors are paid by the clients on whom they are supposed to report, there will always be an apparent conflict of interest between their duties as auditors and their personal financial interests. This conflict is a good reason to make structural changes in how public accounting operates. Perhaps boards rather than management ought to hire and work with auditors because the auditors are more likely reporting on the management activities rather than those of the board. Perhaps public accounting somehow ought to be paid by public fees. Perhaps legal protection or sanctions ought to be created to shield professionals from conflicts of interests. These changes would remove both the apparent and the actual conflicts of interest created by the multiple roles—and therefore multiple responsibilities—of these professionals. From the perspective of social ethics, certain structural changes would be an appropriate response to the accounting scandals of recent years.

Possibly the most devastating aspect of the banking industry meltdown of the first decade of this century was the resulting deterioration of trust that the public has in the market and in corporate America. Decision makers in large investment banks and other financial institutions ignored their fiduciary duties to shareholders, employees, and the public in favor of personal gain, a direct conflict of interest leading to extraordinary personal ruin and the demise of some of the largest investment banks in the world, and contributing to a major economic crisis that

Consider the case of what is referred to as "soft money" within the securities industry. According to critics, a common practice in the securities industry amounts to little more than institutionalized kickbacks. Soft money payments occur when financial advisors receive payments from a brokerage firm to pay for research and analyst recommendations that, in theory, should be used to benefit the clients of those advisors. Such payments can benefit clients *if* the advisor uses them to improve the advice offered to the client. Conflicts of interest can arise when the money is used instead or also for the personal benefit of the advisor.

In 1998, the Securities and Exchange Commission released a report that showed extensive abuse of soft money. Examples included payments used for office rent and equipment, personal travel and vacations, memberships at private clubs, and automobile expenses. If you learned that your financial advisor received such benefits from a brokerage, could you continue to trust the financial advisor's integrity or professional judgment?

- What facts do you need to know to better judge this situation?
- Who are the stakeholders involved and what values are at stake in this situation? Who is harmed when a financial advisor accepts payments from a brokerage? What are the consequences?
- For whom does a financial advisor work? To whom does she have a professional duty? What are the sources of these obligations?
- Does accepting these soft money payments violate any individual's rights? What would be the consequence if this practice were allowed and became commonplace?
- Can you think of any public policies that might prevent such situations? Is this a matter for legal solutions and punishments?
- Compare this situation with the practice, as described in chapter 8, of pharmaceutical companies supplying physicians with small gifts and promotional items. In what ways are they similar? Dissimilar? Are physicians gatekeepers? The pharmaceutical industry voluntarily banned such gifts; should the brokerage industry do the same?

harms millions. The fact is that major federal legislation enacted after Enron to provide regulatory checks on such behavior failed to prevent it from happening.

Critics contend that government regulatory rules alone will not rid society of the problems that led to this crisis. (To explore further how government might have failed in its regulatory role, see the Decision Point: Crony Capitalism: Is Government–Business Partnership the Answer?") Instead, they argue, extraordinary executive compensation and conflicts within the accounting and financial industries have created an environment where the watchdogs have little ability to prevent harm. Executive compensation packages based on stock options create huge incentives to artificially inflate stock value. (Review Reading 10-4, "How Much Compensation Can CEOs Permissibly Accept?," by Jeffrey Moriarty to

Decision Point *Crony Capitalism: Is Government–Business Partnership the Answer?*

Crony capitalism refers to economic situations in which economic winners and losers are determined by collusion between business and government officials. In contrast, the standard democratic understanding of business and government is that the role of government is to ensure that the public interest is served by an economic system in which participants are motivated by self-interest. On this standard model, the political power of government serves as a counterbalance to the economic power of business and industry. Government acts as a neutral arbitrator and judge to ensure that every economic competitor plays by the rules and conflicts are resolved fairly.

Crony capitalism corrupts this system when government officials conspire with their business partners, or "cronies," to use governmental authority to provide them with illegitimate and unearned benefits. The result is a rigged system in which political power and economic power are combined rather than balanced, and governmental authority serves the private rather than public interests.

Crony capitalism can occur on many levels, ranging from systemic to individual corruption. On a systemic level, entire countries have been characterized by cronyism. For example, a ruling political party or regime might grant government contracts or licenses only to members of their own party, religion, or region, as regularly happens in nondemocratic oligarchies and plutocracies. Cronyism can be less systemic but still widespread as when campaign donations and lobbyists gain favored status for particular industries or firms. Cronyism can even exist on the individual level as when a government official grants a friend a favored status in attaining some governmental benefit.

In contemporary settings critics alleged many causes of crony capitalism. Critics from the left assert that cronyism is an inevitable result of the concentration of power in the hands of a wealthy minority. Some critics claim that the United States Supreme Court decision in *Citizens United,* which ruled that political spending by corporations was a protected form of free speech under the First Amendment, institutionalized crony capitalism within the political process by allowing undue corporate influence in politics.

Critics from the political right assert that crony capitalism is an inevitable corruption by a growing governmental involvement in the market. From this perspective, it is a mistake to assume that government regulators can escape their own personal interests to make decisions in the public interest. (See again the Decision Point "How to Solve the 'Agency Problem'" for a discussion of a similar issue.) A similar situation occurs in cases of "regulatory capture," alleged to be a common situation in which the close working relationship between business and government regulators. By working so closely with the firms that are charged with regulating, and inevitably relying on those firms for much of the information required to do their job, government regulators get co-opted, or "captured," by the regulated. The result is that regulators become more of an advocate for, rather than a check upon, industry.

Both sides agree that a "revolving door" between government work and private enterprise results in too many former government officials entering private industry after leaving office and using their former political influence on behalf of their new employers. Conversely, to fill government positions, administrations recruit candidates from the very industries that they will oversee. Critics on both the left and the right agree that crony capitalism results in unfair market disadvantages for those firms and industries that play by the rules.

An ethical critique of crony capitalism appeals to some of the most basic values of democratic capitalism. Equal rights are denied when some firms received unfair advantages. The public interest is corrupted for private gain. The utilitarian and efficiency goals of the market vanish when winners and losers result from manipulated markets. Government authority loses legitimacy and gets replaced by power and influence.

The reality of crony capitalism leaves those firms and industries that do play by the rules in a dilemma. On one hand, if they continue to play by the rules as a matter of ethical integrity, they risk losing in the marketplace because of undeserved disadvantages. On the other hand, the cost of succeeding in a corrupt system is to compromise your integrity.

Sarbanes-Oxley Act (Public Accounting Reform and Investor Protection Act of 2002)

Implemented on July 30, 2002, and administered by the Securities and Exchange Commission to regulate financial reporting and auditing of publicly traded companies in the United States. SOX or SarbOx (popular shorthands for the act) was enacted very shortly following and directly in response to the Enron scandals of 2001. One of the greatest areas of consternation and debate

examine this issue in more detail.) Changes within the accounting industry stemming from the consolidation of major firms and avid "cross-selling" of services such as consulting and auditing within single firms have virtually institutionalized conflicts of interest.

Answers to these inherent challenges are not easy to identify. Imagine that an executive is paid based on how much she or he impacts the share price and will be ousted if that impact is not significantly positive. A large boost in share price—even for the short term—serves as an effective defense to hostile takeovers and boosts a firm's equity leverage for external expansion. In addition, with stock options as a major component of executive compensation structures, a higher share price is an extremely compelling quest to those in leadership roles. That same executive, however, has a fiduciary duty to do what is best for the stakeholders in the long term, an obligation that is often at odds with that executive's personal interests. This is not the best environment for responsible, or even for basically decent, decision making.

The Sarbanes-Oxley Act of 2002

that has emerged surrounding SOX involves the high cost of compliance and the challenging burden therefore placed on smaller firms. Some contend that SOX was the most significant change to the corporate landscape to occur in the second half of the 20th century.

The string of corporate scandals since the beginning of the millennium took its toll on investor confidence. Because reliance on corporate boards to police themselves did not seem to be working, the U.S. Congress passed the Public Accounting Reform and Investor Protection Act of 2002, commonly known as the **Sarbanes-Oxley Act,** which is enforced by the Securities and Exchange Commission (SEC). The act applies to more than 15,000 publicly held companies in the United States and some foreign issuers. (To consider how the European Union addressed similar issues, see the Reality Check: Global Consistencies: The European Union 8th Directive.") In addition, a number of states have enacted legislation similar to Sarbanes-Oxley that apply to private firms,

Reality Check *Global Consistencies: The European Union 8th Directive*

The **European Union 8th Directive,** effective in 2005 (though member states have two years to integrate it into law), covers many of the same issues as Sarbanes-Oxley but applies these requirements and restrictions to companies traded on European Union exchanges. The directive mandates external quality assurances through audit committee requirements and greater auditing transparency.

The directive also provides for cooperation with the regulators in other countries, closing a gap that previously existed. However, contrary to Sarbanes-Oxley, the directive does not contain a whistle-blower protection section, does not require similar reporting to shareholders, and has less detailed requirements compared to Sarbanes-Oxley's section 404.

OBJECTIVE

European Union 8th Directive

Covers many of the same issues as Sarbanes-Oxley but applies these requirements and restrictions to companies traded on European Union exchanges. The updates to the directive in 2005 clarified required duties, independence, and ethics of statutory auditors and called for public oversight of the accounting profession and external quality assurance of both audit and financial reporting processes. In addition, the directive strives to improve cooperation between EU oversight bodies and provides for effective and balanced international regulatory cooperation with oversight bodies outside the EU regulatory infrastructure (e.g., the U.S. Public Company Accounting Oversight Board).

and some private for-profits and nonprofits have begun to hold themselves to Sarbanes-Oxley standards even though they are not necessarily subject to its requirements.

Sarbanes-Oxley responded to the scandals by regulating safeguards against unethical behavior. Because one cannot necessarily predict each and every lapse of judgment, no regulatory "fix" is perfect. However, the act is intended to provide protection where oversight did not previously exist. Some might argue that protection against poor judgment is not possible in the business environment but Sarbanes-Oxley seeks instead to provide oversight in terms of direct lines of accountability and responsibility. The following provisions have the most significant impact on corporate governance and boards:

- *Section 201:* Services outside the scope of auditors (prohibits various forms of professional services that are determined to be consulting rather than auditing).
- *Section 301:* Public company audit committees (requires independence), mandating majority of independents on any board (and all on audit committee) and total absence of current or prior business relationships.
- *Section 307:* Rules of professional responsibility for attorneys (requires lawyers to report concerns of wrongdoing if not addressed).
- *Section 404:* Management assessment of *internal controls* (requires that management file an internal control report with its annual report each year in order to delineate how management has established and maintained effective internal controls over financial reporting).
- *Section 406:* Codes of ethics for senior financial officers (required).
- *Section 407:* Disclosure of audit committee financial expert (requires that they actually have an expert).

Sarbanes-Oxley includes requirements for certification of the documents by officers. When a firm's executives and auditors are required to literally *sign off* on these statements, certifying their veracity, fairness, and completeness, they are more likely to personally ensure their truth.

The Internal Control Environment

internal control
A process, effected by an entity's board of directors, management, and other personnel, designed to provide reasonable assurance regarding the achievement of objectives in the following categories: effectiveness and efficiency of operations, reliability of financial reporting, and compliance with applicable laws and regulations.

Committee of Sponsoring Organizations (COSO)
COSO is a voluntary collaboration designed to improve financial reporting through a combination of controls and governance standards called the Internal Control–Integrated Framework. It was established in 1985 by five of the major professional accounting and finance associations originally to study fraudulent financial reporting and later developed standards for publicly held companies. It has become one of the most broadly accepted audit systems for internal controls.

Sarbanes-Oxley and the European Union 8th Directive are external mechanisms that seek to ensure ethical corporate governance by establishing regulations enforced by external bodies and laws. **Internal control** mechanisms are processes established internally, by boards and management, to ensure compliance with financial reporting laws and regulations. One way that many firms ensure appropriate controls within the organization is to utilize a framework advocated by the **Committee of Sponsoring Organizations (COSO).** COSO is a voluntary collaboration of professional audit and accounting organizations that seeks to improve financial reporting through a combination of controls and governance standards called the Internal Control–Integrated Framework. It was established in 1985 by five of the major professional accounting and finance associations, originally to study fraudulent financial reporting and later to develop standards for publicly held companies. COSO describes "control" as encompassing "those elements of an organization that, taken together, support people in the achievement of the organization's objectives."[2] The elements that comprise the control structure will be familiar as they are also the essential elements of culture discussed in chapter 4. They include:

- *Control environment*—the tone or culture of a firm: "the control environment sets the tone of an organization, influencing the control consciousness of its people."
- *Risk assessment*—risks that may hinder the achievement of corporate objectives.
- *Control activities*—policies and procedures that support the control environment.
- *Information and communications*—directed at supporting the control environment through fair and truthful transmission of information.
- *Ongoing monitoring*—to provide assessment capabilities and to uncover vulnerabilities.

Control environment refers to cultural issues such as integrity, ethical values, competence, philosophy, and operating style. Many of these terms should be reminiscent of issues addressed in chapter 4 during our discussion of corporate culture. COSO is one of the first efforts to address corporate culture in a quasi-regulatory framework in recognition of its significant impact on the satisfaction of organizational objectives. Control environment can also refer to more concrete elements (that can better be addressed in an audit) such as the division of authority, reporting structures, roles and responsibilities, the presence of a code of conduct, and a reporting structure. It will be helpful to review the Opening Decision Point on VW as you consider the COSO definition.

The COSO standards for internal controls moved audit, compliance, and governance from a *numbers orientation* to concern for the *organizational environment*. The discussion of corporate culture in chapter 4 reminds us that both

control environment
One of the five elements that comprise the control structure, similar to the culture of an organization, and support people in the achievement of the organization's objectives. The control environment "sets the tone of an organization, influencing the control consciousness of its people."

internal factors as the COSO controls and external factors such as the Sarbanes-Oxley requirements must be supported by a culture of accountability. In fact, these shifts impact not only executives and boards; internal audit and compliance professionals also are becoming more accountable for financial stewardship, resulting in greater transparency, greater accountability, and a greater emphasis on effort to prevent misconduct. All the controls one could implement have little value if there is no unified corporate culture to support it or mission to guide it. It is reasonable to think that the "rigid hierarchy" of authoritarian management described at VW prevented any internal efforts from preventing the fraud.

More recently, COSO developed a new system, Enterprise Risk Management–Integrated Framework, to serve as a framework for management to evaluate and improve their firms' prevention, detection, and management of risk. This system expands on the prior framework in that it intentionally includes "objective setting" as one of its interrelated components, recognizing that both the culture and the propensity toward risk are determined by the firm's overarching mission and objectives. Enterprise risk management, therefore, assists an organization or its governing body in resolving ethical dilemmas based on the firm's mission, its culture, and its appetite and tolerance for risk.

Going beyond the Law: Being an Ethical Board Member

duty of care
Involves the exercise of reasonable care by a board member to ensure that the corporate executives with whom she or he works carry out their management responsibilities and comply with the law in the best interests of the corporation.

As suggested previously, the corporate failures of recent years would seem to suggest a failure on the part of corporate boards, as well as a failure of government to impose high expectations of accountability on boards of directors. After all, it is the board's fiduciary duty to guard the best interests of the firm itself. However, in many cases boards and executives operated well within the law. For instance, it is legal for boards to vote to permit an exception to a firm's conflicts of interest policy, as happened in the Enron case. These actions may not necessarily have been ethical or in the best interests of stakeholders, but they were legal nonetheless. The law offers some guidance on minimum standards for board member behavior, *but is the law enough?*

Legal Duties of Board Members

OBJECTIVE

U.S. law imposes three clear duties on board members: the duties of care, good faith, and loyalty. The **duty of care** involves the exercise of reasonable care by a board member to ensure that the corporate executives with whom she or he works carry out their management responsibilities and comply with the law in the best interests of the corporation. Directors are permitted to rely on information and opinions only if they are prepared or presented by corporate officers, employees, a board committee, or other professionals the director believes to be reliable and competent in the matters presented. Board members are also directed to use their "business judgment as prudent caretakers": the director is expected to be disinterested and reasonably informed, and to rationally believe the decisions made are in the firm's best interest. The bottom line is that a director does not need to be an expert or actually run the company!

duty of good faith
Requires obedience, compelling board members to be faithful to the organization's mission. In other words, they are not permitted to act in a way that is inconsistent with the central goals of the organization.

duty of loyalty
Requires faithfulness; a board member must give undivided allegiance when making decisions affecting the organization. This means that conflicts of interest are always to be resolved in favor of the corporation.

The **duty of good faith** is one of obedience, which requires board members to be faithful to the organization's mission. In other words, they are not permitted to act in a way that is inconsistent with the central goals of the organization. Their decisions must always be in line with organizational purposes and direction, strive toward corporate objectives, and avoid taking the organization in any other direction.

The **duty of loyalty** requires faithfulness; a board member must give undivided allegiance when making decisions affecting the organization. This means that conflicts of interest are always to be resolved in favor of the corporation. A board member may never use information obtained through her or his position as a board member for personal gain, but instead must act in the best interests of the organization.

Board member conflicts of interest present issues of significant challenges, however, precisely because of the alignment of their personal interests with those of the corporation. Don't board members usually have *some* financial interest in the future of the firm, even if it is only through their position and reputation as a board member? Consider whether a board member should own stock. If the board member does own stock, then her or his interests may be closely aligned with other stockholders, removing a possible conflict there. Once again, the VW case shows a board comprised of all major stockholders. However, if the board member does not hold stock, perhaps he or she is best positioned to consider the long-term interests of the firm in lieu of a sometimes enormous windfall that could occur as the result of a board decision. In the end, a healthy board balance is usually sought.

The Federal Sentencing Guidelines (FSG), promulgated by the U.S. Sentencing Commission and (since a 2005 Supreme Court decision) discretionary in nature, do offer boards some specifics regarding ways to mitigate eventual fines and sentences in carrying out these duties by paying attention to ethics and compliance. In particular, the board must work with executives to analyze the incentives for ethical behavior. It must also be truly knowledgeable about the content and operation of the ethics program. The FSG also suggest that the board exercise "reasonable oversight" with respect to the implementation and effectiveness of the ethics/compliance program by ensuring that the program has adequate resources, appropriate level of authority, and direct access to the board. In order to assess their success, boards should evaluate their training and development materials, their governance structure and position descriptions, their individual evaluation processes, their methods for bringing individuals onto the board or removing them, and all board policies, procedures, and processes, including a code of conduct and conflicts policies. It would be an interesting exercise to imagine how the VW scandal might have evolved if Germany had something comparable to the FSG expectations.

Beyond the Law, There Is Ethics

OBJECTIVE

One question we would expect the law to answer, but that instead remains unclear, is whom the board represents. Who are its primary stakeholders? By law, the board of course has a fiduciary duty to the owners of the corporation—the stockholders.

Reality Check *The Basics*

Bill George, former chair and CEO of Medtronic and a recognized expert on governance, contends that there are 10 basic tenets that boards should follow to ensure appropriate and ethical governance:

1. *Standards:* There should be publicly available principles of governance for the board created by the independent directors.

2. *Independence:* Boards should ensure their independence by requiring that the majority of their members be independent.

3. *Selection:* Board members should be selected based not only on their experience or the role they hold in other firms but also for their value structures.

4. *Selection, number 2:* The board's governance and nominating committees should be staffed by independent directors to ensure the continuity of independence.

5. *Executive sessions:* The independent directors should meet regularly in executive sessions to preserve the authenticity and credibility of their communications.

6. *Committees:* The board must have separate audit and finance committees that are staffed by board members with extensive expertise in these arenas.

7. *Leadership:* If the CEO and the chair of the board are one and the same, it is critical that the board select an alternative lead director as a check and balance.

8. *Compensation committee outside expert:* The board should seek external guidance on executive compensation.

9. *Board culture:* The board should not only have the opportunity but be encouraged to develop a culture including relationships where challenges are welcomed and difference can be embraced.

10. *Responsibility:* Boards should recognize their responsibility to provide oversight and to control management through appropriate governance processes.[3]

However, many scholars, jurists, and commentators are not comfortable with this limited approach to board responsibility and instead contend that the board is the guardian of the firm's social responsibility as well. (For one perspective on a board's additional, *ethical* responsibilities, see the Reality Check "The Basics.")

Some executives may ask whether the board even has the legal right to question the ethics of its executives and others. If a board is aware of a practice that it deems to be unethical but that is completely within the realm of the law, on what basis can the board require the executive to cease the practice? The board can prohibit actions to protect the long-term sustainability of the firm. Notwithstanding the form of the unethical behavior, unethical acts can negatively impact stakeholders such as consumers or employees, who can, in turn, negatively impact the firm, which could eventually lead to a firm's demise. (And good governance can have the opposite effect—see the Reality Check "The Concerns of Corporate Directors.") It is in fact the board's fiduciary duty to protect the firm and, by prohibiting unethical acts, it is doing just that.

Fortune journalists Ram Charan and Julie Schlosser[4] suggest that board members have additional responsibilities beyond the law to explore and to investigate the organizations that they represent, and they suggest that an open conversation is the best method for understanding, not just what board members know, but also what they do not know. They suggest that board members often ignore even the most basic questions such as how the firm actually makes its money and whether customers and clients truly do pay for products and services. That is rather basic,

Reality Check *The Concerns of Corporate Directors*

Here are the top five concerns expressed by Canadian corporate directors, as drawn from research conducted by the Clarkson Centre for Business Ethics and Board Effectiveness:

Strategic Planning/Risk Management A Board's role in strategic planning is key to the long term success of a corporation. Many Directors believe that their Boards do not allocate enough time to strategy in Board meetings to ensure effective strategic planning. In addition, many Boards do not have the skills and expertise to fully understand the business /industry and drive strategy. . . .

Board Independence In order for shareholders' interests to be optimally represented by the Board of Directors, individual Directors must be able to act independently from the interests of management, and independently from the other Directors on the Board. Material relationships with management increase the potential risk that a Director will put executive interests before those of the shareholder. Optimizing Board independence helps to mitigate the effects of conflicts of interests between management and the Board and better aligns the Board's decisions with shareholder interests.

Top Executive Compensation Boards of Directors are solely responsible for the compensation of the CEO. In order to best align the interests of management and shareholders, compensation must be linked to the company's financial performance. . . . With increased scrutiny by markets and investors since 2008, many Boards are struggling to design pay packages that can attract and retain top management, while ensuring ongoing confidence among the investing public.

Top Executive Succession Planning Many Directors insist that the hiring and firing of the CEO is a Board's most important responsibility. Boards often do not have formal, ongoing plans in place for the succession of the CEO, either in normal or in unexpected circumstances. Sometimes Boards feel a lack of urgency because their current CEO is highly effective. In other cases, Boards find it culturally awkward to broach the subject of a CEO's departure. Regardless of the cause, however, Directors are experiencing increasing internal and external pressures to formalize the CEO succession process.

Board Renewal/Diversity A formal Board renewal process provides Boards with an effective tool for Boards to understand whether and when turnover is needed, as well as whether or not the current balance of skills on the Board is appropriate. . . . The primary goal of Board renewal is to maintain an effective and passionate Board. Formal processes for Board renewal are a powerful tool to enable the achievement of this goal. Boards are facing increased scrutiny from shareholders/stakeholders to increase gender and ethnic diversity. Directors have expressed that increased Board diversity can increase the effectiveness of Board decisions. However, Boards struggle to increase gender and ethnic diversity when seeking the best available candidate to fill the Board seat.

Source: Clarkson Centre for Business Ethics and Board Effectiveness, "Top 5 Director Concerns of Corporate Directors," http://clarksoncentre.wordpress.com/2012/08/21/top-5-concerns-of-corporate-directors/.

but the truth is that the financial flow can explain a lot about what moves the firm. Board members should also be critical in their inquiries about corporate vulnerabilities—what could drag the firm down and what could competitors do to help it along that path? Ensuring that information about vulnerabilities is constantly and consistently transmitted to the executives and the board creates effective prevention. Board members need to understand where the company is heading and whether it is realistic that it will get there. This is less likely if it is not living within its means or if it is paying out too much of its sustainable growth dollars to its chief executives in compensation.

Failing in any of these areas creates pressures on the firm and on the board to take up the slack, to manage problems that do not have to exist, to be forced to make decisions that might not have had to be made if only the information systems were working as they should. It is the board members' ultimate duty to provide oversight, which is impossible without knowing the answers to the preceding questions.

Conflicts of Interest in Accounting and the Financial Markets

OBJECTIVE

Conflicts of interest, while common in many situations among both directors and officers as discussed previously, also extend beyond the board room and executive suite throughout the financial arena. In fact, trust is an integral issue for all involved in the finance industry. After all, what more can an auditor, an accountant, or an analyst offer than her or his integrity and trustworthiness? There is no real, tangible product to sell, nor is there the ability to "try before you buy." Therefore, treating clients fairly and building a reputation for fair dealing may be a finance professional's greatest assets. Conflicts—real or perceived—can erode trust and often exist as a result of varying interests of stakeholders. As discussed earlier in this chapter, public accountants are accountable to their stakeholders—the stockholders and investment communities who rely on their reports—and therefore should always serve in the role of independent contractor to the firms whom they audit. In that regard, companies would love to be able to direct what that outside accountant says because people believe the "independent" nature of the audit. On the other hand, if accountants were merely rubber stamps for the word of the corporation, they would no longer be believed or considered "independent."

Accounting is often defined as "the process by which any business keeps track of its financial activities by recording its debits and credits and balancing its accounts." Accounting offers us a system of rules and principles that govern the format and content of financial statements. Accounting, by its very nature, is a system of principles applied to present the financial position of a business and the results of its operations and cash flows. It is hoped that adherence to these principles will result in fair and accurate reporting of this information. Now, would you consider an accountant to be a watchdog or a bloodhound? Does an accountant stand guard or instead seek out problematic reporting? The answer to this question may depend on whether the accountant is employed internally by a firm or works as outside counsel.

Linking public accounting activities to those conducted by investment banks and securities analysts creates tremendous conflicts between one component's duty to audit and certify information with the other's responsibility to provide guidance on future prospects of an investment. Perhaps the leading example of the unethical effects of conflicts of interest is manifested in the shocking fact that 10 of the top investment firms in the country had to pay fines in 2005 for actions that involved conflicts of interest between research and investment banking.

Companies that engaged in investment banking pressured their research analysts to give high ratings to companies whose stocks they were issuing, whether those ratings were deserved or not.

The ethical issues and potential for conflicts surrounding accounting practices go far beyond merely combining services. They may include underreporting income, falsifying documents, allowing or taking questionable deductions, illegally evading income taxes, and engaging in fraud. In order to prevent accountants from being put in these types of conflicts, the American Institute of CPAs publishes professional rules. In addition, accounting practices are governed by generally accepted accounting principles (GAAP) established by the Financial Accounting Standards Board that stipulate the methods by which accountants gather and report information. Accountants are also governed by the American Institute of Certified Public Accountants's (AICPA) Code of Professional Conduct. The code relies on the judgment of accounting professionals in carrying out their duties rather than stipulating specific rules.

But can these standards keep pace with readily changing accounting and financing activities in newly emerging firms such as what occurred with the evolution of the dot.coms of a decade or more ago and as occurred in investment banks on recent years? In complex cases such as these it can take regulators, legislature, and courts years to catch up with the changing practices in business. In any case, would regulatory standards be enough? The answers to ethical dilemmas are not always so easily found within the rules and regulations governing the industry. Scholar Kevin Bahr identifies a number of causes for conflicts in the financial markets that may or may not be resolved through simple rule-making:

1. *The financial relationship between public accounting firms and their audit clients:* Because audits are paid for by audited clients, there is an inherent conflict found simply in that financial arrangement.

2. *Conflicts between services offered by public accounting firms:* Because many public accounting firms offer consulting services to their clients, there are conflicts in the independence of the firm's opinions and incentives to generate additional consulting fees.

3. *The lack of independence and expertise of audit committees.*

4. *Self-regulation of the accounting profession:* Because the accounting industry has historically self-regulated, oversight has been lax, if any.

5. *Lack of shareholder activism:* Given the diversity of ownership in the market based on individual investors, collective efforts to manage and oversee the board are practically nonexistent.

6. *Short-term executive greed versus long-term shareholder wealth:* Executive compensation packages do not create appropriate incentive systems for ethical executive and board decision making. "Enron paid about $681 million in cash and stock to its140 senior managers, including at least $67.4 million to former chairman and chief executive Kenneth Lay, in the year prior to December 2, 2001, when the company filed for bankruptcy. Not bad for a company that saw

its stock decline from $80 in January of 2001 to less that $1 when filing for bankruptcy."

7. *Executive compensation schemes:* Stock options and their accounting treatment remain an issue for the accounting profession and the investment community because, though meant to be an incentive to management and certainly a form of compensation, they are not treated as an expense on the income statement. They also tend to place the incentives, again, on short-term growth rather than long-term sustainability.

8. *Compensation schemes for security analysts:* Investment banking analysts have an interest in sales; this is how they generate the commissions or fees that support their salaries. However, the sale is not always the best possible transaction for the client, generating potential conflicts.[5]

Similarly, scholar Eugene White contends that, in part based on the preceding challenges, markets are relatively ineffective and the only possible answer is additional regulation. Though Bahr argues that there may be means by which to resolve the conflicts, such as due notice and separation of research and auditing activities, White instead maintains that these conflicts cannot in fact be eliminated.[6] "Financial firms may hide relevant information and disclosure may reveal too much proprietary information." There remains no perfect solution; instead the investment community has no choice but to rely in part on the ethical decision making of the agent who acts within the market, constrained to some extent by regulation. Moreover, there is not simply just one solution. Consider how the financial community needed to reply on the honesty of individuals reporting their lending rates for the LIBOR benchmark. It is difficult to imagine an adequate response to this scandal that did not include everything from individual integrity to government regulation, both nationally and internationally.

Executive Compensation

Few areas of corporate governance and finance have received as much public scrutiny in recent years as executive compensation. A *Fortune* cover exclaimed "Inside the Great CEO Pay Heist," and the article inside detailed how many top corporate executives now receive "gargantuan pay packages unlike any seen before." In the words of *Fortune*'s headline: "Executive compensation has become highway robbery—we all know that."[7] (A sophisticated ethical analysis of executive compensation is offered in Reading 10-4, "How Much Compensation Can CEOs Permissibly Accept?," by Jeffrey Moriarty.)

In 1960, the after-tax average pay for corporate chief executive officers (CEOs) was 12 times the average pay earned by factory workers. By 1974 that factor had risen to 35 times the average, but by 2000 it had risen to a high of 525 times the average pay received by factory workers! (See the Reality Check "Average CEO to Average Worker Compensation Ratio.") Even after a decline following the recession of 2008, this ratio remained high. In 2010 it was 343 times the average salary, and in 2011 it reached 380 times average. Importantly, these numbers address only

Reality Check *Average CEO to Average Worker Compensation Ratio*

In May 2012 the Economic Policy Institute (EPI), a nonpartisan economic think tank, reported that from 1978 to 2014 CEO compensation in the United States grew more than 997 percent. Average worker compensation during the same period increased by only 5.7 percent. EPI also reported that the CEO-to-worker compensation ratio had changed from 18.3:1 to an all-time high of 411.3:1 in 2000, and settled at 300:1 in 2015.

Source: www.epi.org/publication/top-ceos-make-300-times-more-than-workers-pay-growth-surpasses-market-gains-and-the-rest-of-the-0-1-percent/.

Reality Check *AIG's Bonuses*

One strategy to avoid the agency problem and motivate executives to act for the best interests of their company is to connect compensation with performance. In a 2012 article, *The Economist* reported on a study by financial research firm Obermatt that indicated that, at least among America's largest companies, CEO pay is not correlated at all with either performance or market capitalization. The data presented included a calculation of "excess pay"—basically a measure of how much a CEO is paid compared to his or her demonstrated contribution to the firm's success. The data showed, for example, that between 2008 and 2010, Ray Irani, CEO of Occidental Petroleum, earned an amount nearly eight times as much as his value to the company.[8]

But few cases of executive compensation have caused as much cynicism about the connection between pay and performance as the AIG case introduced in chapter 3. After accepting $180 billion in U.S. federal government bailout money to avoid bankruptcy, AIG announced that it was paying $165 million in bonuses to 400 top executives in its financial division, the very unit that was at the heart of the company's collapse. These bonuses came less than a year after former AIG CEO Martin Sullivan resigned as AIG's financial troubles intensified. As his company headed toward bankruptcy, Sullivan received a $47 million severance package when he retired.

the *average* pay; the differences would be more dramatic if we compared the top salary for CEOs and minimum-wage workers. In two of the more well-publicized cases in recent years, Sandy Weill, the CEO of Travelers Insurance, received more than $230 million in compensation for 1997, and Michael Eisner of Walt Disney received $589 million in 1998. These numbers continue to rise. In 2005, total direct compensation for CEOs rose by 16 percent to reach a median figure of $6.05 million, not including pensions, deferred compensation, and other perks.[9]

Forbes reported that the CEOs of 800 major corporations received an average 23 percent pay raise in 1997 while the average U.S. worker received around 3 percent. The median total compensation for these 800 CEOs was reported as $2.3 million. Half of this amount was in salary and bonuses, and 10 percent came from such things as life insurance premiums, pension plans and individual retirement accounts, country club memberships, and automobile allowances. Slightly less than half came from stock options.

Compensation packages paid to the top executives of ExxonMobil drew harsh public criticism amid rising gas prices and soaring profits. ExxonMobil CEO Lee Raymond received total compensation of $28 million, including $18 million in stock in 2003 and $38 million, of which $28 million was in ExxonMobil stock, in 2004. In 2005, the year in which he retired, Raymond received $51 million in salary. The interest alone on this three-year salary would, at a modest 5 percent rate of return, forever produce $5.85 million annually. Apparently this was not sufficient for Raymond's needs because he also received an additional retirement package with a combined worth of $400 million. When he succeeded Raymond, new CEO Rex Tillerson's salary increased 33 percent to a total of $13 million including $8.75 million in stock. The combined compensation just for these two executives in 2004 and 2005 was in excess of $500 million. During the same period ExxonMobil also achieved record profits, earning more than $25 billion in 2004 and $36 billion in 2005. A few years later the bonuses of AIG executives came under scrutiny, as you saw see in the Reality Check "AIG's Bonuses."

These gaps continue to increase. For the decade ending in 2000, the U.S. minimum wage increased 36 percent, from $3.80 per hour to $5.15 per hour. The median household income in the United States increased 43 percent, from $29,943 to $42,680. The average annual salary for a tenured New York City teacher increased 20 percent, from $41,000 to $49,030. During this same decade the total compensation for the Citicorp CEO increased 12,444 percent, from $1.2 million to $150 million annually. General Electric CEO Jack Welch's salary increased 2,496 percent, from $4.8 million to $125 million.

Skyrocketing executive compensation packages raise numerous ethical questions. Greed and avarice are the most apt descriptive terms for the moral character of such people from a virtue ethics perspective. Fundamental questions of distributive justice and fairness arise when these salaries are compared to the pay of average workers or to the billions of human beings who live in abject poverty on a global level. Consider Tyco's Dennis Kozlowski's justification of his salary in the Reality Check "How Do Salaries Motivate?"

OBJECTIVE

But serious ethical challenges are raised against these practices even from within the business perspective. Both *Fortune* and *Forbes* magazines have been vocal critics of excessive compensation while remaining staunch defenders of corporate interests and the free market. Beyond issues of personal morality and economic fairness, however, excessive executive compensation practices also speak to significant ethical issues of corporate governance and finance.

In theory, lofty compensation packages are thought to serve corporate interests in two ways: They provide an incentive for executive performance (a consequentialist justification), and they serve as rewards for accomplishments (a deontological justification). In terms of ethical theory, they have a utilitarian function when they act as incentives for executives to produce greater overall results, and they are a matter of ethical principle when they compensate individuals on the basis of what they have earned and deserve.

In practice, reasonable doubts exist about both of these rationales. First, as suggested by Moriarty's essay (Reading 10-4), and the *Forbes* story mentioned previously, there is much less correlation between pay and performance than one would expect. At least in terms of stock performance, executives seem to reap large rewards regardless of business success. Of course, it might be argued that in difficult financial times an executive faces greater challenges and therefore perhaps deserves his salary more than in good times. But the corollary of this is that in good financial times, as when ExxonMobil earns a $30 billion profit, the executives have less to do with the success.

More to the point of governance, there are several reasons why excessive compensation may evidence a failure of corporate boards to fulfill their fiduciary duties. First, as mentioned, is the fact that in many cases there is no correlation between executive compensation and performance. Second, there is also little evidence that the types of compensation packages described earlier are actually needed as incentives for performance. The fiduciary duty of boards ought to involve approving high enough salaries to provide adequate incentive, but not more than what is needed. Surely there is a diminishing rate of return on incentives beyond a certain level. Does a $40 million annual salary provide twice the incentive of $20 million, four times the incentive of $10 million, and 40 times the return of a $1 million salary?

Another crucial governance issue is the disincentives that compensation packages, and in particular the heavy reliance on stock options, provide. When executive compensation is tied to stock price, executives have a strong incentive to focus on short-term stock value rather than long-term corporate interests. One of the fastest ways to increase stock price is through layoffs of employees. This may not always be in the best interests of the firms, and there is something perverse about basing the salary of an executive on how successful he or she can be in putting people out of work.

Further, a good case can be made that stock options have also been partially to blame for the corruption involving managed earnings. Two academic studies concluded that there is a strong link between high levels of executive compensation and the likelihood of misstating or falsely reporting financial results.[11] When huge amounts of compensation depend on quarterly earning reports, there is a strong incentive to manipulate those reports in order to achieve the money.

Excessive executive compensation can also involve a variety of conflicts of interests and cronyism. The board's duties should include ensuring that executives are fairly and not excessively paid. They also have a responsibility to evaluate the executive's performance. However, all too often the executive being evaluated and paid also serves as chair of the board of directors. The board is often comprised of members hand-selected by the senior executives. In addition, the compensation board members receive is determined by the chief executive officer, creating yet another conflict of interest. (See Figure 10.2.)

The cronyism does not end at the boardroom door. One of the larger concerns to have arisen in recent years has been the cross-fertilization of boards. The concern spawned a website called www.theyrule.net, which allows searching for

FIGURE 10.2
Duties of the Board and Senior Executives That May Give Rise to Conflicts of Interest

links between any two given companies. A search for a connection, for instance, between Coca Cola and PepsiCo uncovers within seconds the fact that PepsiCo board member Robert Allen sits on the Bristol-Myers Squibb board alongside Coca-Cola board member James D. Robinson III. Though sitting on a board together does not necessarily mean Pepsi's board member will gain access to Coke's secret recipe, it does lend itself to the appearance of impropriety and give rise to a question of conflicts.

In another case involving lesser-known companies, three individuals served on the boards of three companies, with each serving as CEO and chair of one of the companies, Brocade, Verisign, and Juniper. Unfortunately, the companies were found to have backdated stock options, and each firm found itself subject to either Securities and Exchange Commission inquiries or criminal or civil legal proceedings. Cronyism or basic occurrences of overlapping board members might occur, of course, simply because particular individuals are in high demand as a result of their expertise. However, where the overlap results in a failure of oversight and effective governance—the primary legal and ethical responsibility of board members—the implications can be significant to all stakeholders involved.

insider trading
Trading of securities by those who hold private inside information that would materially impact the value of the stock and that allows them to benefit from buying or selling stock.

Insider Trading

OBJECTIVE

No discussion of the ethics of corporate governance and finance would be complete without consideration of the practice of **insider trading** by board members, executives, and other insiders. The issue became front-page news in the 1980s when financier Ivan Boesky was sent to prison for the crime of insider trading. Though it certainly has not left the business pages in the intervening years, it once again gained iconic status when Ken Lay and his colleagues at Enron were accused of insider trading when they allegedly dumped their Enron stock, knowing of the inevitable downturn in the stock's worth, while encouraging others to hold on to it. More recent cases involved financiers and bankers such as Raj Rajaratnam, the billionaire founder of the hedge fund Galleon Group (discussed later), and Fidelity Investments employee David K. Donovan Jr., who was convicted in 2009 for giving his own mother inside information on which she then traded.

The definition of insider trading is trading by shareholders who hold private inside information that would materially impact the value of the stock and that allows them to benefit from buying or selling stock. Illegal insider trading also occurs when corporate insiders provide "tips" to family members, friends, or others and those parties buy or sell the company's stock based on that information. "Private information" would include privileged information that has not yet been released to the public. That information is deemed material if it could possibly have a financial impact on a company's short- or long-term performance or if it would be important to a prudent investor in making an investment decision.

The Securities and Exchange Commission defines insider information in the following way:

> "Insider trading" refers generally to buying or selling a security, in breach of a fiduciary duty or other relationship of trust and confidence, while in possession of material, nonpublic information about the security. Insider trading violations may also include "tipping" such information, securities trading by the person "tipped" and securities trading by those who misappropriate such information. Examples of insider trading cases that have been brought by the Commission are cases against: corporate officers, directors, and employees who traded the corporation's securities after learning of significant, confidential corporate developments; friends, business associates, family members, and other "tippees" of such officers, directors, and employees, who traded the securities after receiving such information; employees of law, banking, brokerage and printing firms who were given such information in order to provide services to the corporation whose securities they traded; government employees who learned of such information because of their employment by the government; and other persons who misappropriated, and took advantage of, confidential information from their employers.[12]

Because insider trading undermines investor confidence in the fairness and integrity of the securities markets, the commission has treated the detection and prosecution of insider trading violations as one of its enforcement priorities.[13] Accordingly, if an executive gets rid of a stock he knows is going to greatly decrease in worth because of bad news in the company that no one knows except a few insiders, he takes advantage of those who bought the stock from him without full disclosure.

Insider trading may also be based on a claim of unethical misappropriation of proprietary knowledge, that is, knowledge only those in the firm should have, knowledge owned by the firm and not to be used by abusing one's fiduciary responsibilities to the firm. The law surrounding insider trading therefore creates a responsibility to protect confidential information, proprietary information, and intellectual property. That responsibility also exists based on the fiduciary duty of "insiders" such as executives. Misappropriation of this information undermines

Where does a private investor find information relevant to stock purchases? Barring issues of insider trading, do all investors actually have equivalent access to information about companies?

- What are the ethical issues involved in access to corporate information?
- Where do private investors go to access information about stock purchases? On whose opinion do they rely? Does everyone have access to these same opinions? If not, what determines access to information in an open market? Instead, is there equal opportunity to have access to information?
- Who are the stakeholders involved in the issue of access? Who relies on information relevant to stock purchases?
- Who has an interest in equal access to information?
- What alternatives are available when considering access to information? How can we perhaps best ensure equal access?
- How do the alternatives compare, and how do the alternatives affect the stakeholders?

the trust necessary to the proper functioning of a firm and is unfair to others who buy the stock. Though one might make the argument that, in the long run, insider trading is not so bad because the inside information will be discovered shortly and the market will correct itself, this contention does not take account of the hurt to those who completed the original transactions in a state of ignorance.

Insider trading is considered patently unfair and unethical because it precludes fair pricing based on equal access to public information. If market participants know that one party may have an advantage over another via information that is not available to all players, pure price competition will not be possible and the faith upon which the market is based will be lost.

On the other hand, trading on inside information is not without its ethical defense. If someone has worked very hard to obtain a certain position in a firm and, by virtue of being in that position, the individual is privy to inside information, isn't it just for that person to take advantage of the information because she or he has worked so hard to obtain the position? Is it really wrong? Unethical? Consider an issue that might be closer to home. If your brother has always been successful in whatever he does in the business world, is it unethical to purchase stock in the company he just acquired? Others don't know quite how successful he has been, so are you trading on inside information? Would you tell others? What about officers in one company investing in the stocks of their client companies? No legal rules exist other than traditional SEC rules on insider trading, but is there not something about this that simply feels "wrong"? Consider the ethical issues surrounding access to information in the Decision Point "The Know-It-Alls."

Some people do seem to have access to more information than others, and their access does not always seem to be fair. Consider how Martha Stewart found herself in jail. Stewart was good friends with Sam Waksal, who was the founder and CEO of a company called ImClone. Waksal had developed a promising new cancer drug and had just sold an interest in the drug to Bristol-Myers Squibb for $2 billion.

In evaluating the causes of the Enron debacle and its implications for change, scholar Lisa Newton analyzes the possible responses we could utilize as a society.[14] Contemplate her arguments that some responses *will not work* and consider whether you agree or disagree:

More regulation: "The people who are making the money eat regulations for breakfast. You can't pass regulations fast enough to get in their way." Regulations are bad for business, she states; they do not have sufficient foresight; and virtual and global business leaves us with little to grasp in terms of regulation.

Business ethics courses: Newton contends that they are ineffective in guiding future action, and they do not sufficiently impact motivations.

Changes in corporate cultures: "What the company's officers do, when they act for good or (more likely) evil, does not *proceed from* the corporate culture, as if the corporate culture *caused* their actions. . . . What people do, habitually, just *is* their character, which they create by doing those things. What a corporation does, through its officers, just *is* its culture, created by that behavior. To say that if we change the culture we'll change the behavior is a conceptual mistake—trivial or meaningless."

Does anything work? "Back to those other eras: this is not the first time that, up to our waists in the muck of corporate dishonesty, we have contemplated regulations and ethics classes and using large rough weapons on the corporate culture. And nothing we did in the past worked."

Instead, Newton posits, "Capitalism was always known not to contain its own limits; the limits were to be imposed by the democratic system, whose representatives were the popularly elected watchdogs of the economy." Business crime comes not from "systemic capitalist contradictions" or sin; instead it

. . . arises from a failure of the instruments of democracy, which have been weakened by three decades of market fundamentalism, privatization ideology and resentment of government. Capitalism is not too strong; democracy is too weak. We have not grown too hubristic as producers and consumers [as if the market were, when working right, capable of governing itself]; we have grown too timid as citizens, acquiescing to deregulation and privatization (airlines, accounting firms, banks, media conglomerates, you name it) and a growing tyranny of money over politics.[15]

Newton then explains that we need, as Theodore Roosevelt well knew (20 years before his cousin presided over the aftermath of the 1929 disaster), democratic oversight of the market, or it will run amok. As it has.

Her conclusion? "Ultimately, our whining and hand-wringing about corporate culture, or executive incentives, or other technicalities of the way businesses run themselves, is useless. Business was never supposed to run itself, at least not for long. We the people were supposed to be taking responsibility for its operations as a whole. We have evaded this responsibility for almost a quarter of a century now, and that's long enough. It is time to remember that we have a public responsibility hat as well as a private enterprise hat, to put it on and put the country back in order."

Is taking public responsibility the answer to ethical lapses in business?

- What else might you need to know in order to effectively evaluate Professor Newton's conclusion?
- What ethical issues are involved in the challenges she addresses?
- Who are the stakeholders?

(continued)

- What do you think about her evaluation of the preceding alternatives?
- How do the alternatives compare? How do the alternatives affect the stakeholders?

Source: Elements adapted by the authors with permission of Dr. Lisa Newton.

Unfortunately, though everyone thought the drug would soon be approved, Waksal learned that the Food and Drug Administration had determined that the data were not sufficient to allow the drug to move to the next phase of the process. When this news became public, ImClone's stock price was going to fall significantly.

On learning the news (December 26, 2001), Waksal contacted his daughter and instructed her to sell her shares in ImClone. He then compounded his violations by transferring 79,000 of his shares (worth almost $5 million) to his daughter and asking her to sell those shares, too. Though the Securities and Exchange Commission would likely uncover these trades, given the decrease in share price, it was not something he seemed to consider. "Do I know that, when I think about it? Absolutely," says Waksal. "Did I think about it at the time? Obviously not. I just acted irresponsibly."[16] Waksal eventually was sentenced to more than seven years in prison for these actions.

How does Martha Stewart fit into this picture? The public trial revealed that Stewart's broker ordered a former Merrill Lynch & Co. assistant to tell her that Waksal was selling his stock, presumably so that she would also sell her stock. Stewart subsequently sold almost 4,000 shares on December 27, 2001, one day after Waksal sold his shares and one day prior to the public statement about the drug's failed approval.

Stewart successfully avoided prison for several years, and on November 7, 2003, she explained that she was scared of prison but "I don't think I will be going to prison." Nevertheless she was convicted on all counts except securities fraud and sentenced to a five-month prison term, five months of home confinement, and a $30,000 fine, the minimum the court could impose under the Federal Sentencing Guidelines.

During the trial the public heard the testimony of Stewart's friend, Mariana Pasternak, who reported that Stewart told her several days after the ImClone sale that she knew about Waksal's stock sales and that Stewart said, "Isn't it nice to have brokers who tell you those things?" So, to return to the issue with which we began this tale, it appears that some investors do seem to have access to information not necessarily accessible to all individual investors.

A similar, but more far-ranging situation was revealed in November 2009 when the FBI and U.S. Attorneys announced arrests stemming from a large insider-trading operation at the hedge fund Galleon Group. The Securities and Exchange Commission accused the billionaire Raj Rajaratnam and dozens of others associated with the Galleon Group of insider trading that resulted in more than $33 million in profit. They were accused of trading on secret details of corporate takeovers and quarterly earnings leaked to them by company insiders.

Though Stewart, Waksal, Rajaratnam, and others involved in these stories were caught and charged with criminal behavior, many believe they were identified and later charged because they were in the public eye. If others are not in the public eye and also engage in this behavior, can the SEC truly police all inappropriate transactions?

Opening Decision Point Revisited
Government Regulation and the VW Scandal

Many people and institutions have responsibility for corporate oversight and control. The Opening Decision Point considered most of the key stakeholders: professional employees, management, boards. But government also plays a role, and it is worth considering how government regulators functioned in this case.

It was the responsibility of government regulators to set environmental emission standards. Given the well-established economic problems associated with externalities and the commons, it would be difficult to imagine environmental standards voluntarily emerging from either automobile manufacturers or consumers, especially when these standards add costs to the price of a car. But in establishing these standards, this case shows how governments worked cooperatively with manufacturers, sometimes over decades, to establish meaningful and achievable standards. Government regulators also worked with VW for a year or more to determine the validity of testing results. Despite denials and attempts by VW to mislead regulators, government agencies succeeded in uncovering the fraud and taking strong steps to end the sale of the offending diesel cars. Investigations were extended to include other manufacturers and, while the exact circumstances were different, Mitsubishi Motors admitted in April 2016 that it had manipulated mileage and emission tests on hundreds of thousands of cars for decades.

If anything, critics charged that government regulators were too slow or ineffectual in addressing the problems. In 2012 both Hyundai and Kia were fined for manipulating their fuel economy tests. Critics point out that in the desire to treat manufacturers fairly, and given inadequate funding, government regulators too often leave all testing and reporting responsibility to the manufacturers themselves.

Once the VW fraud was established, other government agencies stepped in to assess the damage, adjudicate disputes, and ensure that consumers and dealers who were deceived received adequate compensation. Thus, government regulated to prevent harms, and enforced compensation for those cases where the harms had occurred. By most measures, government was the only agency that fulfilled its oversight duties.

- Do you believe that government agencies fulfilled their responsibilities in this case?
- What else could government do to better create and enforce environmental standards?
- Are there government policies or actions that could have encouraged better oversight within the VW corporate setting and prevented this from occurring?

Is there a sufficient deterrent effect to discourage insider trading in our markets today? If not, what else can or should be done? Or, to the contrary, is this simply the nature of markets, and those who have found access to information should use it to the best of their abilities? What might be the consequences of this latter, perhaps more Darwinian, approach to insider trading, and whose rights might be violated if we allow it?

Consider whether we might have learned anything from the experiences of the past decade, and how we might most effectively proceed, as you review the Decision Point "The Winds of Change."

Questions, Projects, and Exercises

1. You have been asked by the board of a large corporation to develop a board assessment and effectiveness mechanism, which could be a survey, interviews, an appraisal system, or other technique that will allow you to report back to the board on both individual and group effectiveness. What would you recommend?

2. You have been asked to join the board of a medium-sized charitable organization. What are some of the first questions that you should ask, and what are the answers that you are seeking?

3. You have been asked to join the board of a large corporation. What are some of the first questions that you should ask and what are the answers that you are seeking?

4. Scholars have made strong arguments for required representation on boards by stakeholders that go beyond stockholders, such as employees, community members, and others, depending on the industry. What might be some of the benefits and costs of such a process?

5. You are an executive at a large nonprofit organization. Some of your board members suggest that perhaps the company should voluntarily comply with Sarbanes-Oxley. What are some of the reasons the company might consider doing so or not doing so?

6. You are on the compensation committee of your board and have been asked to propose a compensation structure to be offered to the next CEO. Explore some of the following websites on executive compensation and then propose a structure or process for determining CEO compensation at your corporation: archive.aflcio.org/corporatewatch /paywatch/; www.rileyguide.com/execpay.html; www.sec.gov/news/speech/spch120304cs .htm; www.eri-executive-compensation.com/?TrkID=5479-82; www.directorship.com /a-fresh-look-at-executive-pay-dynamics/

7. A press release has a significant negative impact on your firm's stock price, reducing its value by more than 50 percent in a single day of trading! You gather from conversations in the hallway that the company's fundamentals remain strong, aside from this one-time event. You see this as a great opportunity to buy stock. Is it appropriate to act on this and to purchase company stock? Does it make a difference whether you buy 100 shares or 1,000 shares? Is it OK to discuss the "dilemma" with family members and friends? What should you do if you do mention it to family and friends but then later feel uncomfortable about it?

8. Modify slightly the facts of the previous question. Assume that you are also privy to the annual forecast of earnings, which assures you that the fundamentals remain strong. Stock analysts and investors are also provided this same information. Do your answers change at all?

9. In connection with the two previous questions, assume instead that you think something significant is about to be made public because all officers have consistently stayed late, a special board meeting has been called, you and your boss have been advised to be on call throughout the weekend, and various rumors have been floating throughout the company. You are not aware of the specifics, but you can reasonably conclude that it's potentially good or bad news. You decide to call a friend in the accounting department who has been staying late to find out what she knows. In this situation, do your answers about what you might do change? Is it appropriate to partake in the "rumor mill"? Is it appropriate to discuss and confide your observations with family and friends? Is it appropriate to buy or sell company stock based on these observations (you may rationalize that it is only speculation and you do not know the facts)?

10. Have you ever been in, or are you familiar with, a conflict of interest situation? How was it resolved? Can you think of any rules or any practices that could have prevented the situation from occurring? Can you think of any initiatives, structures, or procedures that could make it easy to avoid such conflicts in the future?

Key Terms

After reading this chapter, you should have a clear understanding of the following key terms. For a complete definition, please see the Glossary.

Committee of Sponsoring Organizations (COSO), *p. 507*

conflict of interest, *p. 499*

control environment, *p. 507*

corporate governance, *p. 496*

duty of care, *p. 508*

duty of good faith, *p. 509*

duty of loyalty, *p. 509*

Enron Corporation, *p. 497*

European Union 8th Directive, *p. 506*

fiduciary duties, *p. 499*

gatekeepers, *p. 497*

insider trading, *p. 518*

internal control, *p. 507*

Sarbanes-Oxley Act (Public Accounting Reform and Investor Protection Act of 2002), *p. 505*

Endnotes

1. C. William Thomas, "The Rise and Fall of Enron," *Journal of Accountancy,* April 2002, p. 7.
2. Committee of Sponsoring Organizations, Board Guidance on Control, www.coso.org/guidance.htm (accessed December 27, 2012).
3. William W. George, "Restoring Governance to Our Corporations," address given to the Council of Institutional Investors, September 23, 2002, www.bus.wisc.edu/update/fall02/ten_step.htm (accessed April 10, 2010).
4. Ram Charan and Julie Schlosser, "Ten Questions Every Board Member Should Ask; And for That Matter, Every Shareholder Too," *Fortune,* November 10, 2003, p. 181.
5. Kevin Bahr, "Conflicts of Interest in the Financial Markets" (Stevens Point, WI: Central Wisconsin Economic Research Bureau, 2002), www.uwsp.edu/business/cwerb/4thQtr02/SpecialReportQtr4_02.htm (accessed April 10, 2010).
6. Eugene White, "Can the Market Control Conflicts of Interest in the Financial Industry?," presentation at the International Monetary Fund (June 4, 2004), www.imf.org/external/np/leg/sem/2004/cdmfl/eng/enw.pdf (accessed April 10, 2010).
7. Geoffrey Colvin, "The Great CEO Pay Heist," *Fortune,* June 25, 2001, p. 64.
8. "Focus: Executive Pay and Performance," *The Economist Online* (February 7, 2012), www.economist.com/blogs/graphicdetail/2012/02/focus-0.
9. Carol Hymowitz, "Sky-High Payouts to Top Executives Prove Hard to Curb," *The Wall Street Journal,* June 26, 2006, p. B1.
10. William Shaw, "Justice, Incentives, and Executive Compensation," in *The Ethics of Executive Compensation,* ed. Robert Kolb (Malden, MA: Blackwell, 2006), p. 93.
11. J. Harris and P. Bromiley, "Incentives to Cheat: Executive Compensation and Corporate Malfeasance," paper presented at the Strategic Management Society International Conference, Baltimore, MD, 2003; O'Conner et al., "Do CEO Stock Options Prevent or Promote Corporate Accounting Irregularities?" as quoted in Jared Harris, "How Much Is Too Much?" in *The Ethics of Executive Compensation,* ed. Robert Kolb (Malden, MA: Blackwell, 2006), pp. 67–86.
12. U.S. Securities and Exchange Commission, "Key Topics: Insider Trading," www.sec.gov/answers/insider.htm (accessed April 24, 2010).

13. U.S. Securities and Exchange Commission, "Insider Trading," www.sec.gov/divisions /enforce/insider.htm (accessed April 10, 2010).

14. Adapted and quoted from Lisa Newton, "Enron and Andersen: Guideposts for the Future," presentation to the Society for Business Ethics, Annual Meeting, August 2002. Elements adapted by the authors with permission of Dr. Lisa Newton.

15. Benjamin Barber, "A Failure of Democracy, Not Capitalism," *The New York Times,* July 29, 2002, Op-Ed, p. A19.

16. *CBS News,* "Sam Waksal: I Was Arrogant" (June 27, 2004), www.cbsnews.com /stories/2003/10/02/60minutes/main576328.shtml (accessed April 10, 2010).

Readings

Reading 10-1: "The Cultural Dependence of Corporate Governance," by Bob Tricker

Reading 10-2: "Libor and Capitalist Moral 'Decay,'" by Chris MacDonald

Reading 10-3: "How Much Compensation Can CEOs Permissibly Accept?," by Jeffrey Moriarty

Reading 10-1

The Cultural Dependence of Corporate Governance

Bob Tricker

(From comments presented September 2011 at an international corporate governance conference hosted jointly by the Corporate Secretaries International Association [CSIA] and the Shanghai Stock Exchange.)

A decade or so ago, it was widely thought that corporate governance practices around the world would gradually converge on the United States model. After all, the U.S. Securities and Exchange Commission had existed since 1934, sound corporate regulation and reporting practices had evolved, and American governance practices were being promulgated globally by institutional investors. But that was before the collapse of Enron, Arthur Andersen, the sub-prime financial catastrophe, and the ongoing global economic crisis. A decade ago it was also believed that the world would converge with U.S. practices because the world needed access to American capital. That is no longer the case.

So the convergence or differentiation question remains unanswered.

Forces for Convergence

Consider first some forces that are leading corporate governance practices around the world to convergence.

Corporate governance codes of good practice around the world have a striking similarity, which is not surprising given the way they influence each other. Though different in detail, all emphasise corporate transparency, accountability, reporting, and the independence of the governing body from management, and many now include strategic risk assessment and corporate social responsibility. The codes published by international bodies, such as the World Bank, the Commonwealth of Nations, and OECD, clearly encourage convergence. The corporate governance policies and practices of major corporations operating around the world also influence convergence.

Securities regulations for the world's listed companies are certainly converging. The International Organisation of Securities Commissions (IOSCO), which now has the bulk of the world's securities regulatory bodies in membership, encourages convergence. For example, its members have agreed to exchange information on unusual trades, thus making the activities of global insider trading more hazardous.

International accounting standards are also leading towards convergence. The International Accounting Standards Committee (IASC) and the International Auditing Practices Committee (IPAC) have close links with IOSCO and are further forces working towards international harmonization and standardization of financial reporting and auditing standards. U.S. General Accepted Accounting Principles (GAAP), though some way from harmonization, are clearly moving in that direction.

In 2007, The U.S. Securities and Exchange Commission announced that U.S. companies could adopt international accounting standards in lieu of U.S. GAAPs. However, American accountants and regulators are accustomed to a rule-based regime and international standards are principles-based requiring judgment rather than adherence to prescriptive regulations.

Global concentration of audit for major companies in just four firms, since the demise of Arthur Andersen, encourages convergence. Major corporations in most countries, wanting to have the name of one of the four principal firms on their audit reports, are then inevitably locked into that firm's world-wide audit, risk analysis and other governance practices.

Globalisation of companies is also, obviously, a force for convergence. Firms that are truly global in strategic outlook, with world-wide production, service provision, added-value chain, markets and customers, which call on international sources of finance, whose investors are located around the world, are moving towards common governance practices.

Raising capital on overseas stock exchanges also encourages convergence as listing companies are required to conform to the listing rules of that market. Although the governance requirements of stock exchanges around the world differ in detail, they are moving towards internationally accepted norms through IOSCO.

International institutional investors, such as CalPers [the California Public Employees' Retirement System], have explicitly demanded various corporate governance practices if they are to invest in a specific country or company. Institutional investors with an international portfolio have been an important force for convergence. Of course, as developing and transitional countries grow, generate and plough back their own funds, the call for inward investment will decline, along with the influence of the overseas institutions.

Private equity funding is changing the investment scene. Owners of significant private companies may decide not to list in the first place. Major investors in public companies may find an incentive to privatise. Overall the existence of private equity funds challenges boards of listed companies by sharpening the market for corporate control.

Cross-border mergers of stock markets could also have an impact on country-centric investment dealing and could influence corporate governance expectations; as could the development of electronic trading in stocks by promoting international securities trading.

Research publications, international conferences and professional journals can also be significant contributors to the convergence of corporate governance thinking and practice.

Forces for Differentiation

However, despite all these forces pushing towards convergence, consider others which, if not direct factors for divergence, at least cause differentiation between countries, jurisdictions and financial markets.

Legal differences in company law, contract law and bankruptcy law between jurisdictions affect corporate governance practices. Differences between the case law traditions of the U.S., UK and Commonwealth countries and the codified law of Continental Europe, Japan, Latin America and China distinguish corporate governance outcomes.

Standards in legal processes, too, can differ. Some countries have weak judicial systems. Their courts may have limited powers and be unreliable. Not all judiciaries are independent of the legislature. The state and political activities can be involved in jurisprudence. In some countries bringing a company law case can be difficult and, even with a favourable judgment, obtaining satisfaction may be well nigh impossible.

Stock market differences in market capitalisation, liquidity, and markets for corporate control affect governance practices. Obviously, financial markets vary significantly in their scale and sophistication, affecting their governance influence.

Ownership structures also vary between countries, with some countries having predominantly family-based firms, others have blocks of external investors who may act together, whilst some adopt complex networked, leveraged chains, or pyramid structures.

History, culture and ethnic groupings have produced different board structures and governance practices. Contrasts between corporate governance in Japan with her *keiretsu,* Continental European countries, with the two-tier board structures and worker co-determination, and the family domination of overseas Chinese, even in listed companies in countries throughout the Far East, emphasise such differences. Views differ on ownership rights and the basis of shareholder power.

The concept of the company was Western, rooted in the notion of shareholder democracy, the stewardship of directors, and trust—the belief that directors recognise a fiduciary duty to their company. But today's corporate structures have outgrown that simple notion. The corporate concept is now rooted in law, and the legitimacy of the corporate entity rests on regulation and litigation. The Western world has created the most expensive and litigious corporate regulatory regime the world has yet seen. This is not the only approach; and certainly not necessarily the best. The Asian reliance on relationships and trust in governing the enterprise may be closer to the original concept. There is a need to rethink the underlying idea of the corporation, contingent with the reality of power that can (or could) be wielded. Such a concept would need to be built on a pluralistic, rather than an ethnocentric, foundation if it is to be applicable to the corporate groups and strategic alliance networks that are now emerging as the basis of the business world of the future.

Around the world, the Anglo-Saxon model is far from the norm. A truly global model of corporate governance would need to recognise alternative concepts including:

- the networks of influence in the Japanese keiretsu
- the governance of state-owned enterprises in China, where the China Securities and Regulatory Commission (CSRC) and the State-owned Assets Supervision and Administration Commission (SASAC) can override economic objectives, acting in the interests of the people, the party, and the state, to influence strategies, determine prices, and appoint chief executives
- the partnership between labour and capital in Germany's co-determination rules
- the financially-leveraged chains of corporate ownership in Italy, Hong Kong and elsewhere
- the power of investment block-holders in some European countries
- the traditional powers of family-owned and state-owned companies in Brazil
- the domination of spheres of listed companies in Sweden, through successive generations of a family, preserved in power by dual-class shares
- the paternalistic familial leadership in companies created throughout Southeast Asia by successive Diaspora from mainland China
- the governance power of the dominant families in the South Korean chaebol, and
- the need to overcome the paralysis of corruption from shop floor, through boardroom, to

government officials in the BRIC and other nations.

The forces for convergence in corporate governance are strong. At a high level of abstraction some fundamental concepts have already emerged, including the need to separate governance from management, the importance of accountability to legitimate stakeholders, and the responsibility to recognise strategic risk. These could be more widely promulgated and adopted. But a global convergence of corporate governance systems at any greater depth would need a convergence of cultures and that seems a long way away.

Source: Bob Tricker, "The Cultural Dependence of Corporate Governance," *Corporate Governance*, November 7, 2011, http://corporategovernanceoup.wordpress.com/2011/11/07/the-cultural-dependence-of-corporate-governance/.

Reading **10-2**

Libor and Capitalist Moral "Decay"

Chris MacDonald

Is the collapse of capitalism upon us? Are we facing a moral Armageddon in the marketplace? Is every scandal-driven headline another sign of impending apocalypse in the world of business? You could be forgiven for thinking so, if you read enough editorials.

Just look at the opinion pieces carried by major news outlets recently. Eduardo Porter editorialized in *The New York Times* (July 10, 2012) about "The Spreading Scourge of Corporate Corruption." *The Atlantic* carried a piece (July 13, 2012) called "The Libor Scandal and Capitalism's Moral Decay," by Pulitzer Prize–winner David Rohde. Even business school professors are down with the effort to convince you the end is nigh: *Bloomberg* just recently featured a piece by Professor Luigi Zingales (July 16, 2012) who went to the apparent heart of the matter by asking, "Do business schools incubate criminals?"

But do editorials of that sort really bring to bear any solid evidence that things in the world of business are getting worse? Not as far as I can see.

I've argued before that the evidence for a real moral crisis in business is pretty scarce. Headlines don't count as evidence. And pointing to the fact that people don't *trust* business is putting the cart before the horse. People have been wringing their hands about moral decay and longing for the "good old days" at least since the time of the ancient Greeks. So as far as I can see, things just are not all that bad. I've even argued that we are currently enjoying a sort of golden age of business ethics. Business today is, in many ways, more accountable and better behaved than ever before in history.

But maybe the two sides of this debate are really arguing past each other, due to differences in focus. Perhaps critics like Porter and Rohde and Zingales are focused on the personal ethics of various business people, where I'm focusing on the behaviour of capitalism as a whole. If so, this difference is itself instructive. For it is crucially important to recognize a difference between our ethical evaluation of capitalists, on one hand—such as the bank employees accused of manipulator Libor—and our ethical evaluation of capitalism itself, on the other. After all, one of the major virtues of the capitalist system is that it is supposed to be able to produce good outcomes even if participants aren't always squeaky clean. In no way does it assume that all the players will be of the highest virtue.

It is worth noting that Adam Smith himself took a pretty dim view of businessmen. In *The Wealth of Nations,* Smith wrote: "People of the same trade seldom meet together, even for merriment and diversion, but the conversation ends in a conspiracy against the public." And yet despite his dim view of capitalists, Smith remained a great fan of capitalism—or rather (since the term "capitalism" hadn't been coined yet) a fan of what he referred to as "a system of natural liberty." And history has vindicated Smith's optimism: capitalism, for all its flaws, has had an enormously positive impact on standards of living across the globe.

The lesson here is that evidence (such as it is) of low moral standards at our financial institutions shouldn't make us panic. Perhaps it should make us shrug, and say, "Such is human nature." Of course, that's an exaggeration. We shouldn't be complacent about attempts by major financial institutions to rig the system in their own favour. But rather than focus on the moral failings of individuals, we ought to look to institutional failings—failings like, for example, relying on what was obviously a badly flawed Libor system.

For those not already acquainted with the term, "Libor" is short for the London Inter-Bank Offered Rate, which is the name of the most important single number in the world of finance. It is essentially a benchmark indicating the interest rate at which various banks are willing to lend money to each other. Importantly, Libor isn't established by government, but by the banking industry itself. The number is established by averaging the numbers submitted by various banks; the numbers submitted are supposed to indicate the rate at which various banks believe they can borrow from other banks. Libor is critically important because it is used as a reference point for establishing interest rates for various financial instruments. The problem at the heart of the Libor scandal is the fact that there is no external verification of the numbers submitted by various banks. And because Libor affects actual interest rates for so many financial instruments, banks can sometimes enhance profits, or reduce losses, by fudging their own numbers in ways calculated to affect the final Libor calculation. In other words, Libor is a system that relies on people being honest, in situations in which their basic motivations point in another direction altogether. A saner system would base the Libor on something more concrete and less open to self-serving manipulation, such as numbers based on the interest rates that participating banks actually get charged by other banks.

The challenge for capitalist markets, more broadly, is to devise systems that take the crooked timber of humanity and mould it in constructive ways. Governments need to take corporate motives as they are and devise regulations that encourage appropriate behaviour. And executives need to take the motives of their employees as they are and devise corporate structures—hierarchies, teams, incentive plans—that motivate those employees in constructive ways. In both cases, while the players should of course look inward at what motivates them, the rest of us should focus not on the players, but on the game.

So on the question of moral decay, let's call it a draw, and focus instead on what's really important. The question isn't whether moral standards in business are higher or lower than they were at some point in the past. The point is whether they're currently high enough. And, assuming the answer to that question is "no," the next question is what to do about it.

And there's plenty of work to do. To begin, we need to keep working to find the right balance of regulatory carrots and sticks to encourage good corporate behaviour. And we need to figure out the right corporate governance policies and structures to foster good behaviour *within* corporations as well. And to the extent that bad behaviour in the corporate arena—as in every other area of life—is unavoidable, we need to think hard about the appropriate mechanisms to mitigate and remediate the effects of such behaviour. All of this requires a good deal of humility, of course, and a willingness to tolerate, even foster, a degree of creative experimentation.

But one thing is certain. Rather than wasting time worrying about whether the world is coming to an end, our energy would be better spent figuring out how to make it better.

Source: Based in part on Chris MacDonald, "Debating Capitalist Moral Decay," *Canadian Business*, July 17, 2012, www.canadianbusiness.com/blog/business_ethics/91413; Chris MacDonald, "Ethics on Wall Street: Hate the Player, Not the Game," *Canadian Business*, July 11, 2012, www.canadianbusiness.com/blog/business_ethics/90576.

How Much Compensation Can CEOs Permissibly Accept?

Jeffrey Moriarty

Executive compensation has received a great deal of attention. This is due, in part, to the large amounts of pay executives, especially CEOs, receive. In 2006, the median total compensation of the top 150 U.S. CEOs was $10.1 million. This is 314 times the $32,142 earned by the median full-time private industry worker in the U.S. that year. This paper examines some moral aspects of executive compensation. It is not the first to do so, but it engages the issue from a new perspective. I focus on the duties *executives themselves* have with respect to *their own* compensation, and argue that CEOs' fiduciary duties place a moral limit on how much compensation they can seek or accept from their firms. Accepting excessive compensation leaves the beneficiaries of their duties (e.g., shareholders) worse off, and thus is inconsistent with observing those duties. Like others who write on executive compensation, I am primarily interested in chief executive officer compensation. By 'executive', then, I mean principally 'CEO'. However, most of what I say applies, with minor modifications, to the pay of other top executives.

1. The CEO's Fiduciary Duty

I begin with the common assumption that executives are fiduciaries. What does this mean? Marcoux explains, "[t]o act as a fiduciary means to place the interests of [a] beneficiary ahead of one's own interests and, obviously, those of third parties, with respect to the administration of some asset(s) or project(s)" (2003: 3). In the CEO's case, the asset or project is the firm. So, CEOs are required insofar as they are fiduciaries to place one party's interests ahead of their own and others' when managing the firm. That is, they have a *fiduciary duty* to do so.

According to some writers, CEOs are fiduciaries for shareholders (Boatright, 1994; Marcoux, 2003). According to others, they are fiduciaries for all stakeholders (Evan & Freeman, 2005). The moral limit I identify exists if CEOs are fiduciaries for *anyone* who stands to lose when CEOs accept excessive compensation. This includes shareholders, stakeholders, and certain other parties. To fix ideas, however, I assume that CEOs are fiduciaries for shareholders.

I further assume that CEOs are fiduciaries in a *moral,* not merely *legal,* sense. To determine whether CEOs' fiduciary duties in law have implications for their pay negotiations with directors, all that is required is to look at the relevant law. My goal is to determine to what, if any, implications CEOs' moral fiduciary duties have for their negotiations with directors.

Assuming that CEOs have fiduciary duties in the moral sense (hereafter, I drop this qualifier), what follows about how they should manage their firms? It is standardly assumed that shareholders want to maximize the monetary value of their investments. Thus, in his classic defense of shareholder theory, Friedman says that a CEO is obligated "to conduct the business in accordance with [his employers'] desires, which generally will be to make as much money as possible" (2005: 8). Let us assume that shareholder value is maximized when firm value, which Jensen defines as "the market values of the equity, debt, and any other contingent claims outstanding on the firm" (2002: 239), is maximized. If so, then executives should manage the firm so as to maximize its value. Managing the firm this way has implications for how much compensation a CEO can permissibly seek or accept from it.

Compensation produces value for the firm by attracting and retaining talented employees, and motivating them to do their best. But compensation is a cost. Other things equal—where "other things" includes the firm's performance—the lower this cost is, the better. It is widely believed that directors have a duty to minimize this cost. I claim that *CEOs themselves* do too. Suppose a compensation package worth $10 million is sufficient to induce a CEO to do his best for the firm, i.e., to maximize its value, so far as he is able. But suppose that the CEO would also do his best if he were paid only $9 million. Then he should refuse the larger package in favor of the smaller one. Now suppose that, if the CEO were paid $8 million, he would not do his best, and the firm would be worse off by more than $1 million. In this case, the CEO is justified in accepting the $9 million package. In general, the optimum amount of compensation for a CEO is the amount that maximizes firm value, taking into account the cost of the compensation. Of course, a CEO is unlikely to work, or work hard, for free.[1] She will require some, perhaps even a lot, of pay. And shareholders are willing to pay for talent. Hiring a talented but expensive CEO, and properly motivating her, produces more net value for the firm than hiring an untalented but inexpensive one, or failing to properly motivate her. But still what is best for shareholders is that they pay the (talented) CEO no more than is necessary to attract, retain, and motivate her. The CEO's fiduciary duty prohibits her from accepting more than this amount.

Let us call this amount—i.e., the minimum necessary to attract, retain, and motivate the CEO to maximize firm value—her *minimum effective compensation,* or MEC. This amount is *effective* because it succeeds in attracting, retaining, and motivating the CEO, and *minimum* because no less would do. Let us further assume, as is standard, that the CEO is motivated exclusively by self-interested considerations, i.e., she is not intrinsically motivated by shareholders' interests. (Later in the paper I examine the implications of relaxing this assumption.) Finally, let us define "excessive compensation" for a CEO as compensation in excess of her MEC.

In economic terms, a CEO's MEC is her "reservation wage" for the job, i.e., the amount necessary for her to accept and retain it, unless, as is often the case,

extra pay (e.g., in the form of performance-based incentives) would motivate her to produce an amount of extra revenue for the firm that exceeds the amount of the extra compensation. In this case, the CEO's MEC includes the *minimum amount* necessary to produce that extra revenue. A CEO's MEC will be a function of her next best alternative, including working for another firm, or not working at all. This in turn will depend on her talents, preferences, and market conditions. Note that the CEO's MEC is *not* defined in terms of what she is "worth," understood as how much revenue she adds to the firm (compared to the next most effective available candidate). So it is possible for an amount of compensation to be more than a CEO's MEC but less than her worth. However, the more revenue the CEO adds to the firm, the better alternative offers she will have. So her MEC and worth will tend to converge in a free market.

As I have suggested, the CEO's fiduciary duty entails not only a duty not to *seek* more than her MEC in negotiation, but a duty not to *accept* more than her MEC if it is offered. To illustrate: Richard Grasso, former head of the New York Stock Exchange (NYSE), famously was awarded a $187 million compensation package. In his defense, Grasso said he never had a "two-way dialogue" with the NYSE's directors about his pay. Assuming that $187 million was more than necessary to attract, retain, and motivate Grasso, this does not excuse his behavior. CEOs do not avoid blame by simply staying out of the pay setting process, as they would in a standard conflict-of-interest situation. They are required by their fiduciary duty to be proactive about ensuring that they do not receive excessive pay.

2. Objections and Replies

I have argued for a new moral limit on CEO compensation: CEOs should not accept excessive compensation—i.e., more than their MECs—from their firms. In this section, I defend it against objections.

Objection 1. This moral limit is moot: a CEO will never accept excessive compensation, because it will never be offered to her. Directors will make sure she gets paid no more than is necessary to attract, retain, and motivate her. Market pressures will aid directors in this effort.

Response. This objection assumes that directors are highly powerful and knowledgeable with respect to the CEO. Against this, first, many writers have argued that pay negotiations between CEOs and directors are not carried out at arm's-length, and in particular, that directors do not aggressively represent shareholders' interests at the bargaining table (Bebchuk & Fried, 2004). Second, even if they have the will to achieve the optimal result, directors are likely to be ignorant of what it is. Knowing, as they often do, the average compensation of CEOs of comparable firms does not tell them the precise minimum effective compensation of their *particular* CEO. Thus, we have reason to believe that it is possible for executives to receive excessive pay, and hence that it is worth determining whether or not they are morally permitted to.

Objection 2. When a CEO negotiates her compensation, she is not yet a member of the firm. The employment agreement through which she becomes a fiduciary has not been made. So, she does not yet have a fiduciary duty to the firm's shareholders and, as a result, is not yet forbidden to accept excessive compensation.

Response. This objection does not apply to CEOs who are negotiating *subsequent* compensation packages with their firms. Nor does it apply to CEOs negotiating their *first* compensation packages with a firm who are promoted to the CEO's position from within the firm's top management. Both kinds of CEO are already top managers in their firms, and so have fiduciary duties to their firms' shareholders. The objection applies, then, only to CEOs who come from outside the firm, and only when they are negotiating their first compensation packages. Although the number of outsider CEOs has increased in recent years, approximately 75% of new CEOs are insiders (Jensen, Murphy, & Wruck, 2004). In addition, at least half of CEOs engage in subsequent compensation negotiations

while in office. Thus, the substantial majority of CEO compensation negotiations are immune from this objection.

Even given its limited target, however, the objection fails. Whether or not *some* CEOs lack fiduciary duties to shareholders when they negotiate their compensation packages (e.g., because they are outsiders), *all* CEOs have these duties when they receive them. This effectively prevents all CEOs from seeking in negotiation, or accepting, more than their MECs. Consider an example. C, an outsider, is soon to become the CEO of firm F. C negotiates her compensation package before she starts working for F. Call this time T1. She begins to receive the agreed upon compensation once she starts work. Call this time T2. Because C is not a member of F at T1, C does not have fiduciary duties to F's shareholders at T1. However, C will be a member of F at T2, and will have fiduciaries duties to F's shareholders at that time. Thus, at T2, C cannot accept more than her MEC. Given that C will receive the agreed upon compensation at T2, it would be wrong for her to seek more than her MEC at T1.

I am not claiming that, if a person has a duty at T2, and T2 is later than T1, then she has that duty at T1. This claim is easily refuted. Suppose a person who is now 30 will be a parent when she is 31. At 31, she will have a duty to care for her child. But it doesn't follow that she has a duty to care for her (or any) child now, when she is 30. Nevertheless, the fact that the 30 year old *will have* a duty to care for her child at 31 constrains what she can do at 30. She cannot at 30 promise a friend to devote all of her resources and attention when she is 31 to political activism in a distant nation, for she will be obligated, and knows she will be obligated, to care for her child at that time. In the same way, since C is negotiating at T1 the nature of an event that will occur at T2, the duties she will have at T2 constrain her actions at T1.

Objection 3. CEOs are not required *always* to act so as to maximally benefit shareholders. They are only required to do so when they are acting *as managers,* i.e., managing the firm. So, for example, when they are acting *as parents,* i.e., raising their children, they need not act so as to maximally benefit shareholders by, say, trying to persuade their children to buy their firms' products. The same goes for when CEOs are acting as players on a softball team or members of a neighborhood watch. On this objection, when CEOs are negotiating their pay, they are not acting as managers. Put another way, this is not something they need be concerned with in their role as managers. Here they can act *as private citizens:* they are free of the fiduciary duty to shareholders, and so are free to accept excessive compensation.

Response. The claim that CEOs are required to maximize shareholder return only insofar as they are acting as managers is correct. It would be absurd to suppose that they are required to do so in every facet of their lives. However, the claim that, when they are negotiating the terms of their compensation, they are free to act as private citizens and not as managers, is wrong. Surely, the question of how much to pay a firm's workers is a business decision. Attracting, retaining, and motivating talented workers—while not overpaying them—is crucial to a firm's success. So, the CEO's fiduciary duty to shareholders to maximize firm value requires that she concern herself, at some level, with the compensation of the firm's employees. But the CEO is an employee too, so it follows that she must concern herself, *as a manager,* with her own compensation. In examining the firm's payroll to determine whether any cuts can be made to boost firm value, she cannot exclude her own pay from consideration. Much as she might like to be free of the duty not to accept excessive compensation, she is not.

Objection 4. A party to whom a duty is owed can waive its performance, wholly or in part. If they do, the party who owes the duty is not obligated to perform it. I can release you from your duty to drive me wherever I want with respect to, say, driving me to the airport. According to this objection, shareholders—or their representatives, the directors—have done something similar with respect to the CEO's fiduciary duty. While

generally leaving it in place, they have waived it in the context of determining the CEO's pay. They have not done so explicitly, by declaring the duty to be waived, but they have done so implicitly, by employing a negotiation to set the CEO's pay. Employing an *adversarial* process signals that, in this context, the CEO's fiduciary duties are suspended: directors are safeguarding the firm's interests, and the CEO can do as she pleases, including accept excessive compensation.

Response. To be clear, the issue is not whether the CEO and directors (merely) *recognize* the application of the CEO's fiduciary duty to the pay setting process. This duty can apply even if it is not thought to apply. The issue is whether directors have *waived* its observance. The objection claims that they have.

In response, it is not clear, first, that directors *can* waive executives' fiduciary duties. Just because one is owed a duty—in the sense that one is the beneficiary of it—does not mean one has the power to waive it. I cannot waive your duty not to enslave me, though I benefit from your observance of it. If your duty to me is based on a contract we have entered into, then I can waive its performance. Thus, if the foundation of your duty to drive me wherever I want is that you have promised me to do so, then I can waive your duty. But it is not clear that the CEO's fiduciary duty to shareholders is contractually based. Boatright, for example, argues that the reason executives owe fiduciary duties to shareholders (as opposed to others) is that this is "the most socially beneficial system of economic organization" (1994: 401). If he is right, then *directors* cannot waive CEOs' fiduciary duties. It does not follow, of course, that they cannot be waived *simpliciter.* But if anyone can waive them, it is society as a whole.

For the sake of argument, however, let us suppose that directors can waive CEOs' fiduciary duties. According to the objection, the evidence that they have done so in the context of setting the CEO's pay is that the process used to determine it is adversarial in nature. This is poor evidence. At present, the CEOs' duties not to accept more than their MECs is not widely recognized, so it would be foolish for directors to allow them a free hand in setting their own pay. Even if this duty were recognized, directors might still wish to retain the negotiation as a way to protect the firm. CEOs will be tempted to seek excessive compensation, even if they know they should not.

Objection 5. According to commonsense morality, while people are sometimes required to benefit others at their own expense, they are not required to make enormous sacrifices for them. For example, this morality would have us give some—perhaps even a substantial amount—of our wealth to the poor, but not so much that we end up impoverished ourselves. Prohibiting the CEO from accepting excessive compensation, according to this objection, places too great a burden on him—i.e., it is too demanding—and cannot be justified by his fiduciary duty.

Response. This is simply implausible. Recall that excessive compensation is compensation in excess of the CEO's MEC, which is in turn of a function of his next best option. Since a CEO's MEC depends on his particular talents and preferences, it is difficult or even impossible to identify what any given CEO's MEC is. But few deny that CEOs are (at least perceived to be) highly talented individuals who can command considerable premiums for their labor. As a result, every CEO is likely to have at least one other very high-paying option for work. This means that their MECs will be very high—far higher than the compensation of the average worker. Given this, it is implausible to suppose that prohibiting the CEO from accepting excessive compensation is too demanding. To be sure, a CEO who refuses to accept more than his MEC might have to refuse a large sum of money. But it doesn't follow that the burden he is under is heavy, given how high his MEC is likely to be.

Objection 6. The prohibition against accepting more than one's MEC discriminates against steward CEOs, i.e., CEOs who are intrinsically motivated by shareholders' interests (Davis, Schoorman, & Donaldson, 1997). Because of this motivation,

it takes less compensation, other things equal, to attract, retain, and motivate a steward CEO than an agent CEO, i.e., one who is motivated only by self-interested considerations (Wasserman, 2006). So it seems that the steward CEO accepts more than his MEC at a lower compensation level than the agent CEO. But intuitively, the former is more virtuous than the latter. The prohibition against accepting more than one's MEC thus punishes the steward CEO for his virtue.

Response. This objection misunderstands the definition of MEC. I said that a CEO accepts more than his MEC when he accepts more pay than is necessary to attract, retain, and motivate him to maximize firm value, *assuming he is acting on self-interested motives only.* This assumption is not an empirical conjecture but a normative standard. The MEC is defined relative to the compensation demands of the agent CEO. So, a steward CEO who seeks more than he *actually needs* to be attracted, retained, and motivated does not accept more than his MEC, if that is not more than what he *would need* if he were acting on self-interested motives only.

It is nevertheless true that whether a CEO accepts more than his MEC is in large part a personal matter. It depends on the CEO's particular situation—whether he, given his preferences and options, would work just as hard for the firm for less. This has two important implications. First, one CEO's MEC may be less than another's, even when all else, besides their preferences and options, is equal. One CEO's preference for leisure might be stronger than the other's. Second, it will be difficult or impossible to tell "from the outside" whether a CEO is accepting more than her MEC. The prospects, then, for enforcing a ban on doing so is dim. Some might regard this as problematic for my argument. It might be if my claim were that there should be a *law* against accepting more than one's MEC, so that violators should be subject to civil or criminal penalties. But my claim is that CEOs have a *moral duty* to accept no more than their MECs. The validity of a moral rule does not depend on its enforceability.

3. How Low Should CEOs Go?

Objection 6 raises an important issue which we have so far bracketed. We have measured the CEO's MEC by a partly objective standard, viz., that of the agent CEO. It is the minimum necessary to attract, retain, and motivate him to maximize firm value *assuming he is acting on self-interested motives only.* But, it might be said, while it is desirable to have *some* objective standard for measuring the CEO's MEC, why choose this one? Instead of pegging it to the motivational set of the agent CEO, why not peg it to the motivational set of the steward CEO, i.e., the CEO who is intrinsically motivated by shareholders' interests?

If we adopt the steward CEO as our standard, the prohibition on driving a hard bargain becomes more burdensome. As seen, because they are intrinsically motivated by their fiduciary duties, steward CEOs need less money to maximize firm value, other things equal, than agent CEOs (Wasserman, 2006). The more weight the fiduciary duty gets in the CEO's motivational set—i.e., the more of a steward he is—the less money he needs. At the limit, if we choose as our standard the maximally "steward-like" CEO, then it seems the CEO can permissibly accept very little, or even no, pay.

We see now why it makes sense to start, as we did, with the assumption that CEOs are agents. This minimizes the burden imposed on the CEO by the prohibition against accepting excessive pay. If this weak burden cannot be justified, then no stronger one can be. But since the former is justified, it makes sense to inquire into whether the latter can be. Our question is, how much weight should the CEO give to his fiduciary duty in his motivational set, as compared to self-interested considerations? To what extent should he do what is best for shareholders (viz., accept less and less pay), and to what extent can he do what is best for himself (viz., accept more and more pay)? Answering this question requires weighing the force of the CEO's fiduciary duty against moral considerations on the other side.

The CEO's fiduciary duty is thought to have considerable weight. It is appealed to to justify laying off workers and moving plants to foreign countries, despite the burdens these actions impose on employees and communities. It is also thought to justify prohibiting CEOs from shirking, hiring unqualified friends, and empire-building, despite the burdens these prohibitions impose on CEOs.

But if we take seriously, as many do, the idea that morality doesn't require people to take on *enormous* burdens in order to do what is right, then there is a limit to this duty's force. Having to accept a job as a CEO on the condition that one accepts very little compensation is a heavy burden not only on the CEO, but on his family. It is unlikely that the CEO's fiduciary duty requires this level of sacrifice.

Moreover, it is probable that what is best for the firm is not that the CEO accept *very* little compensation. There must be incentives for others, both inside and outside the firm, to aspire to the CEO's position. One such incentive is high pay for the CEO. This is stressed by tournament theory, according to which employees in the firm work hard to win the "prize" of being CEO. In this way, the CEO may be *required* by her fiduciary duty to receive a large amount of compensation. This is not to say that in some cases the CEO is justified in accepting more than her MEC, but that in some cases her MEC, which she may be required to accept, may be de-coupled from the minimum amount necessary to attract, retain, and motivate *her.* The "effectiveness" of compensation is a function of its effects on firm value. We have assumed, consistently with firms' own justifications of their executive compensation packages, that the utility of these packages results from their attracting, retaining, and motivating the very persons who receive them. But if their utility results from motivating *others,* then this must be taken into account in determining the most effective amount of pay.

Finally, it may be good not only for individual firms but for society as a whole if CEOs negotiate in their self-interest, at least to an extent. If CEO compensation is too low, few people will want to become CEOs. They will seek work as, e.g., lawyers or investment advisors. But society as a whole benefits when talented people occupy these important and demanding positions (Jensen & Murphy, 1990). One way to make it more likely that they do is for CEOs to be highly paid. And one way to promote this is to encourage self-interested negotiation by CEOs.[2]

In sum, while the CEO's fiduciary duty exerts downward pressure on her compensation by encouraging selfless negotiation over compensation, it is unlikely to tell in favor of her receiving very little pay. And other considerations tell in favor of (permitting) more self-interested negotiation and thus higher compensation. Determining where the balance of considerations lies—i.e., how self-interestedly the CEO can and should act when negotiating her pay—is a complex inquiry lying outside the scope of this paper. It will be important in this inquiry to identify the foundational moral values that justify the CEO's fiduciary duty, and evaluate the extent to which they are promoted or thwarted by selfless negotiation over

compensation. Whatever the outcome, my more modest conclusions seem safe, viz., that CEOs' fiduciaries duties apply in the pay setting context, and imply (minimally) that they should accept no more than their MECs, assuming that they are acting on self-interested motives only. Most people believe only that directors have a duty not to award CEOs excessive pay; I have argued that CEOs also have a duty not to accept excessive pay.

Endnotes

1. But, it might be said, *shouldn't* she? After all, this would be *best* for shareholders. I explore this suggestion below.

2. But if this is the reason for high(er) CEO pay, one might wonder why its cost should fall entirely on shareholders, as opposed to the general public.

Note: References have been removed from publication here, but are available on the book website at connect. mheducation.com.

Glossary

A

affirmative action A policy or a program that strives to redress past discrimination through the implementation of proactive measures to ensure equal opportunity. In other words, affirmative action is the intentional inclusion of previously excluded groups. Affirmative action efforts can take place in employment environments, education, or other arenas.

autonomy From the Greek for "self-ruled," autonomy is the capacity to make free and deliberate choices. The capacity for autonomous action is what explains the inherent dignity and intrinsic value of individual human beings.

B

backcasting The Natural Step challenges businesses to imagine what a sustainable future must hold. From that vision, creative businesses then look backward to the present and determine what must be done to arrive at that future.

biomimicry ("closed-loop" production) Seeks to integrate what is presently waste back into production in much the way that biological processes turn waste into food.

C

categorical imperative An imperative is a command or duty; "categorical" means that it is without exception. Thus a categorical imperative is an overriding principle of ethics. Philosopher Immanual Kant offered several formulations of the categorical imperative: act so as the maxim implicit in your acts could be willed to be a universal law; treat persons as ends and never as means only; treat others as subjects, not objects.

caveat emptor **approach** *Caveat emptor* means "buyer beware" in Latin and this approach suggests that the burden of risk of information shall be placed on the buyer. This perspective assumes that every purchase involves the informed consent of the buyer and therefore it is assumed to be ethically legitimate.

change blindness A decision-making omission that occurs when decision makers fail to notice gradual changes over time.

character The sum of relatively set traits, dispositions, and habits of an individual. Along with rational deliberation and choice, a person's character accounts for how she or he makes decisions and acts. Training and developing character so that it is disposed to act ethically is the goal of virtue ethics.

child labor Though the term literally signifies children who work, it has taken on the meaning of exploitative work that involves some harm to a child who is not of an age to justify his or her presence in the workplace. The elements of that definition—harm, age of the child, justification to be in the workplace relative to other options—remain open to social and economic debate. UNICEF's 1997 State of the World's Children Report explains, "Children's work needs to be seen as happening along a continuum, with destructive or exploitative work at one end and beneficial work—promoting or enhancing children's development without interfering with their schooling, recreation and rest—at the other. And between these two poles are vast areas of work that need not negatively affect a child's development."

code of conduct A set of behavioral guidelines and expectations that govern all members of a business firm.

Committee of Sponsoring Organizations (COSO) COSO is a voluntary collaboration designed to improve financial reporting through a combination of controls and governance standards called the Internal Control–Integrated Framework. It was established in 1985 by five of the major professional accounting and finance associations originally to study fraudulent financial reporting and later developed standards for publicly held companies. It has become one of the most broadly accepted audit systems for internal controls.

common-law agency test A persuasive indicator of independent contractor status that provides the employer the ability to control the manner in which the work is performed. Under the common-law agency approach, the employer need not actually control the work, but must merely have the right or ability to control the work for a worker to be classified an employee.

compliance-based culture   A corporate culture in which obedience to laws and regulations is the prevailing model for ethical behavior.

conflict of interest   A conflict of interest exists where a person holds a position of trust that requires that she or he exercise judgment on behalf of others, but where her or his personal interests and/or obligations conflict with those of others.

consequentialist theories   Ethical theories, such as utilitarianism, that determine right and wrong by calculating the consequences of actions.

control environment   One of the five elements that comprise the control structure, similar to the culture of an organization, and support people in the achievement of the organization's objectives. The control environment "sets the tone of an organization, influencing the control consciousness of its people."

corporate average fuel economy (CAFE) standards   Established by the Energy Policy Conservation Act of 1975, corporate average fuel economy (CAFE) is the sales-weighted average fuel economy, expressed in miles per gallon (mpg), of a manufacturer's fleet of passenger cars or light trucks. The U.S. federal government establishes CAFE standards as a means of increasing fuel efficiency of automobiles.

corporate governance   The structure by which corporations are managed, directed, and controlled toward the objectives of fairness, accountability, and transparency. The structure generally will determine the relationship between the board of directors, the shareholders or owners of the firm, and the firm's executives or management.

corporate social responsibility (CSR)   The responsibilities that businesses have to the societies within which they operate. In various contexts, it may also refer to the voluntary actions that companies undertake to address economic, social, and environmental impacts of their business operations and the concerns of their principal stakeholders. The European Commission defines CSR as "a concept whereby companies decide voluntarily to contribute to a better society and a cleaner environment." Specifically, CSR suggests that a business identify its stakeholder groups and incorporate its needs and values within its strategic and operational decision-making process.

corporate sustainability report   Provides all stakeholders with financial and other information regarding a firm's economic, environmental, and social performance.

cradle-to-cradle responsibility   Holds that a business should be responsible for incorporating the end results of its products back into the productive cycle.

culture   A shared pattern of beliefs, expectations, and meanings that influences and guides the thinking and behaviors of the members of a particular group.

D

descriptive ethics   As practiced by many social scientists, provides a descriptive and empirical account of those standards that actually guide behavior, as opposed to those standards that should guide behavior. Contrast with *normative ethics*.

diversity   Diversity refers to the presence of differing cultures, languages, ethnicities, races, affinity orientations, genders, religious sects, abilities, social classes, ages, and national origins of the individuals in a firm. When used in connection with the corporate environment, it often encompasses the values of respect, tolerance, inclusion, and acceptance.

downsize   The reduction of human resources at an organization through terminations, retirements, corporate divestments, or other means.

due process   The right to be protected against the arbitrary use of authority. In legal contexts, due process refers to the procedures that police and courts must follow in exercising their authority over citizens. In the employment context, due process specifies the conditions for basic fairness within the scope of the employer's authority over its employees.

duties   Those obligations that one is bound to perform, regardless of consequences. Duties might be derived from basic ethical principles, from the law, or from one's institutional or professional role.

duty of care   Involves the exercise of reasonable care by a board member to ensure that the corporate executives with whom she or he works carry out their management responsibilities and comply with the law in the best interests of the corporation.

duty of good faith   Requires obedience, compelling board members to be faithful to the organization's mission. In other words, they are not permitted to act in a way that is inconsistent with the central goals of the organization.

duty of loyalty   Requires faithfulness; a board member must give undivided allegiance when making decisions affecting the organization. This means that conflicts of interest are always to be resolved in favor of the corporation.

E

eco-efficiency   Doing more with less. Introduced at the Rio Earth Summit in 1992, the concept of eco-efficiency is a way business can contribute to sustainability by reducing resource usage in its production cycle.

economic model of CSR   Limits a firm's social responsibility to the minimal economic responsibility of producing goods and services and maximizing profits within the law.

economic realities test   A test by which courts consider whether the worker is economically dependent on the business or, as a matter of economic fact, is in business for himself or herself.

egoism   As a psychological theory, egoism holds that all people act only from self-interest. Empirical evidence strongly suggests that this is a mistaken account of human motivation. As an ethical theory, egoism holds that humans ought to act for their own self-interest. Ethical egoists typically distinguish between one's perceived best interests and one's true best interests.

Electronic Communications Privacy Act (ECPA) of 1986   The U.S. statute that establishes the provisions for access, use, disclosure, interception, and privacy protections relating to electronic communications.

e-mail monitoring   The maintenance and either periodic or random review of e-mail communications of employees or others for a variety of business purposes.

employment at will (EAW)   The legal doctrine that holds that, absent a particular contractual or other legal obligation that specifies the length or conditions of employment, all employees are employed "at will." Unless an agreement specifies otherwise, employers are free to fire an employee at any time and for any reason. In the same manner, an EAW worker may opt to leave a job at any time for any reason, without offering any notice at all; so the freedom is *theoretically* mutual.

Enron Corporation   An energy company based in Houston, Texas, that *Fortune* magazine named America's most innovative company for six consecutive years before it was discovered to have been involved in one of the largest instances of accounting fraud in world history. In 2001, with over 21,000 employees, it filed the largest bankruptcy in United States history and disclosed a scandal that resulted in the loss of millions of dollars, thousands of jobs, the downfall of Big Five accounting firm Arthur Andersen LLP, at least one suicide, and several trials and convictions, among other consequences. Enron remains in business today as it continues to liquidate its assets.

ethical decision-making process   Requires a persuasive and rational justification for a decision. Rational justifications are developed through a logical process of decision making that gives proper attention to such things as facts, alternative perspectives, consequences to all stakeholders, and ethical principles.

ethical relativism   An important perspective within the philosophical study of ethics that holds that ethical values and judgments are ultimately dependent on, or relative to, one's culture, society, or personal feelings. Relativism denies that we can make rational or objective ethical judgments.

ethical values   Those properties of life that contribute to human well-being and a life well lived. Ethical values would include such things as happiness, respect, dignity, integrity, freedom, companionship, and health.

ethics   Derived from the Greek word *ethos,* which refers to those values, norms, beliefs, and expectations that determine how people within a culture live and act. Ethics steps back from such standards for how people *do* act, and reflects on the standards by which people *should* live and act. At its most basic level, ethics is concerned with how we act and how we live our lives. Ethics involves what is perhaps the most monumental question any human being can ask: How *should* we live? Following from this original Greek usage, ethics can refer to both the standards by which an individual chooses to live her or his own personal life, and the standards by which individuals live in community with others (see also *morality*). As a branch of philosophy, ethics is the discipline that systematically studies questions of how we ought to live our lives.

ethics officers   Individuals within an organization charged with managerial oversight of ethical compliance and enforcement within the organization.

European Union 8th Directive   Covers many of the same issues as Sarbanes-Oxley but applies these requirements and restrictions to companies traded on European Union exchanges. The updates to the directive in 2005 clarified required duties, independence, and ethics of statutory auditors and called for public oversight of the accounting profession and external quality assurance of both audit and financial reporting processes. In addition, the directive strives to improve cooperation between EU oversight bodies and provides for effective and balanced international regulatory cooperation with oversight bodies outside the EU regulatory infrastructure (e.g., the U.S. Public Company Accounting Oversight Board).

European Union's Directive on Personal Data Protection   EU legislation seeking to remove potential obstacles to cross-border flows of personal data, to ensure a high level of protection within the European Union, and to harmonize protections across the European continent and with those countries with whom EU countries do business.

F

Federal Sentencing Guidelines for Organizations (FSGO)   Developed by the United States Sentencing Commission and implemented in 1991, originally as mandatory parameters for judges to use during organizational sentencing cases. By connecting punishment to prior business practices, the guidelines establish legal norms for ethical business behavior. However, since a 2005 Supreme Court decision, the FSG are now considered to be discretionary in nature and offer some specifics for organizations about ways to mitigate eventual fines and sentences by integrating bona fide ethics and compliance programs throughout their organizations.

fiduciary duties   A legal duty to act on behalf of or in the interests of another.

"Four Ps" of marketing   Production, price, promotion, and placement.

Fourth Amendment protection   The U.S. Constitution's Fourth Amendment protection against unreasonable search and seizure extends privacy protections to the public-sector workplace through the Constitution's application to state action.

G

gatekeepers   Some professions, such as accountant, that act as "watchdogs" in that their role is to ensure that those who enter into the marketplace are playing by the rules and conforming to the conditions that ensure the market functions as it is supposed to function.

H

Health Insurance Portability and Accountability Act (HIPAA) (Pub. L. 104-191)   HIPAA stipulates that employers cannot use "protected health information" in making employment decisions without prior consent. Protected health information includes all medical records or other individually identifiable health information.

human rights   Those moral rights that individuals have simply in virtue of being a human being. Also called *natural rights* or *moral rights*.

hypernorms   Values that are fundamental across culture and theory.

I

implied warranty of merchantability   Implied assurances by a seller that a product is reasonably suitable for its purpose.

inattentional blindness   If we happen to focus on or are told specifically to pay attention to a particular element of a decision or event, we are likely to miss all of the surrounding details, no matter how obvious.

insider trading   Trading of securities by those who hold private inside information that would materially impact the value of the stock and that allows them to benefit from buying or selling stock.

integrative model of CSR   For some business firms, social responsibility is fully integrated with the firm's mission or strategic plan.

internal control   A process, effected by an entity's board of directors, management, and other personnel, designed to provide reasonable assurance regarding the achievement of objectives in the following categories: effectiveness and efficiency of operations, reliability of financial reporting, and compliance with applicable laws and regulations.

Internet use monitoring   The maintenance and either periodic or random review of the use of the Internet by employees or others based on time spent or content accessed for a variety of business purposes.

intrusion into seclusion   The legal terminology for one of the common-law claims of invasion of privacy. Intrusion into seclusion occurs when someone intentionally intrudes on the private affairs of another when the intrusion would be "highly offensive to a reasonable person."

IRS 20-factor analysis   A list of 20 factors to which the IRS looks to determine whether someone is an employee or an independent contractor.

J

just cause   A standard for terminations or discipline that requires the employer to have sufficient and fair cause before reaching a decision against an employee.

M

marketing   Defined by the American Marketing Association as "an organizational function and a set of processes for creating, communicating, and delivering value to customers and for managing customer relationships in ways that benefit the organization and its stakeholders."

mission statement   A formal summary statement that describes the goals, values, and institutional aim of an organization.

moral free space   That environment where hypernorms or universal rules do not govern or apply to ethical decisions but instead culture or other influences govern decisions, as long as they are not in conflict with hypernorms. In other words, as long as a decision is not in conflict with a hypernorm, it rests within moral free space and reasonable minds may differ as to what is ethical.

moral imagination   When one is facing an ethical decision, the ability to envision various alternative choices, consequences, resolutions, benefits, and harms.

morality   Sometimes used to denote the phenomena studied by the field of ethics. This text uses *morality* to refer to those aspects of ethics involving personal, individual decision making. "How should I live my life?" or "What type of person ought I be?" are taken to be the basic questions of morality. Morality can be distinguished from questions of *social justice*, which address issues of how communities and social organizations ought to be structured.

multiculturalism   Similar to diversity, refers to the principle of tolerance and inclusion that supports the co-existence of multiple cultures, while encouraging each to retain that which is unique or individual about that particular culture.

N

negligence   Unintentional failure to exercise reasonable care not to harm other people. Negligence is considered to be one step below "reckless disregard" for harm to others and two steps below intentional harm.

normative ethics   As a *normative* discipline, ethics deals with norms and standards of appropriate and proper (normal) behavior. Norms establish the guidelines or standards for determining what we should do, how we should act, what type of person we should be. Contrast with *descriptive ethics*.

normative myopia   The tendency to ignore, or the lack of the ability to recognize, ethical issues in decision making.

norms   Those standards or guidelines that establish appropriate and proper behavior. Norms can be established by such diverse perspectives as economics, etiquette, or ethics.

O

Occupational Safety and Health Administration (OSHA)   The United States Occupational Safety and Health Administration, an agency of the federal government that publishes and enforces safety and health regulations for U.S. businesses.

P

perceptual differences   Psychologists and philosophers have long recognized that individuals cannot perceive the world independently of their own conceptual framework. Experiences are mediated by and interpreted through our own understanding and concepts. Thus, ethical disagreements can depend as much on a person's conceptual framework as on the facts of the situation. Unpacking our own and others' conceptual schema plays an important role in making ethically responsible decisions.

personal and professional decision making   Individuals within a business setting are often in situations in which they must make decisions both from their own personal point of view and from the perspective of the specific role they fill within an institution. Ethically responsible decisions require an individual to recognize that these perspectives can conflict and that a life of moral integrity must balance the personal values with the professional role-based values and responsibilities.

personal data   Any information relating to an identifiable person, directly or indirectly, in particular by reference to one or more factors specific to her or his physical, physiological, mental, economic, cultural, or social identity.

personal integrity   The term *integrity* connotes completeness of a being or thing. Personal integrity, therefore, refers to individuals' completeness within themselves, often derived from the consistency or alignment of actions with deeply held beliefs.

practical reasoning   Involves reasoning about what one ought to do, contrasted with *theoretical reasoning*, which is concerned with what one ought to believe. Ethics is a part of practical reason.

principle-based framework   A framework for ethics that grounds decision making in fundamental principles such as justice, liberty, autonomy, and fairness. Principle-based ethics typically assert that individual rights and duties are fundamental and thus can also be referred to as a rights-based or duty-based (deontological) approach to ethics. Often distinguished from consequentialist frameworks, which determine ethical decisions based on the consequences of our acts.

principles   Ethical rules that put values into action.

privacy   The right to be "let alone" within a personal zone of solitude, and/or the right to control information about oneself.

privacy rights   The legal and ethical sources of protection for privacy in personal data.

property rights   The boundaries defining actions that individuals can take in relation to other individuals regarding their personal information. If one individual has a *right* to her or his personal information, someone else has a commensurate duty to observe that right.

R

reasonable expectation of privacy   The basis for some common-law claims of invasion of privacy. Where an individual is notified that information will be shared or space will not be private, there is likely no reasonable expectation of privacy.

reciprocal obligation   The concept that, while an employee has an obligation to respect the goals and property of the employer, the employer has a *reciprocal obligation* to respect the rights of the employee as well, including the employee's right to privacy.

reputation management   The practice of caring for the "image" of a firm.

reverse discrimination   Decisions made or actions taken against those individuals who are traditionally considered to be in power or the majority, such as white men, or in favor of a historically nondominant group.

risk assessment   A process to identify potential events that may affect the entity, and manage risk to be within its risk appetite, to provide reasonable assurance regarding the achievement of entity objectives.

S

Safe Harbor exception   Considered "adequate standards" of privacy protection for U.S.-based companies under the European Union's Data Protection Directive.

Sarbanes-Oxley Act (Public Accounting Reform and Investor Protection Act of 2002)   Implemented on July 30, 2002, and administered by the Securities and Exchange Commission to regulate financial reporting and auditing of publicly traded companies in the United States. SOX or SarbOx (popular shorthands for the act) was enacted very shortly following and directly in response to the Enron scandals of 2001. One of the greatest areas of consternation and debate that has emerged surrounding SOX involves the high cost of compliance and the challenging burden therefore placed on smaller firms. Some contend that SOX was the most significant change to the corporate landscape to occur in the second half of the 20th century.

service-based economy   Interprets consumer demand as a demand for services, for example, for clothes cleaning, floor covering, cool air, transportation, or word processing, rather than as a demand for products such as washing machines, carpeting, air conditioners, cars, and computers.

social ethics   The area of ethics that is concerned with how we should live together with others and how social organizations ought to be structured. Social ethics involves questions of political, economic, civic, and cultural norms aimed at promoting human well-being.

stakeholder   In a general sense, a stakeholder is anyone who can be affected by decisions made within a business. More specifically, stakeholders are considered to be those people who are necessary for the functioning of a business.

stakeholder model of CSR   The view that business exists within a web of social relationships. The stakeholder model views business as a citizen of the society in which it operates and, like all members of a society, business must conform to the normal range of ethical duties and obligations that all citizens face.

stakeholder theory   A model of corporate social responsibility that holds that business managers have ethical responsibilities to a range of stakeholders that go beyond a narrow view that the primary or only responsibility of managers is to stockholders.

stealth or undercover marketing   Marketing campaigns that are based on environments or activities where the subject is not aware that she or he is the target of a marketing campaign; those situations where one is subject to directed commercial activity without knowledge or consent.

strict liability   A legal doctrine that holds an individual or business accountable for damages whether or not it was at fault. In a strict liability case, no matter how careful the business is in its product or service, if harm results from use, the individual or business is liable.

sustainable business practice   A model of business practice in which business activities meet the standards of sustainability.

sustainable development   Development that meets the needs of the present without compromising the ability of future generations to meet their own needs as defined by the Brundtland Commission in 1987.

sustainable or green marketing   Sustainable or green marketing is the marketing of products on the basis of their environmentally friendly nature.

sweatshops   A term that remains subject to debate. Some might suggest that all workplaces with conditions that are below standards in more developed countries are sweatshops because all humans have a right to equally decent working conditions. (See the discussion in chapter 6 and D. Arnold and L. Hartman, "Beyond Sweatshops: Positive Deviancy and Global Labor Practices," *Business Ethics: A European Review* 14, no. 3 [July 2005].) In this text we use the following definition: any workplace in which workers are typically subject to two or more of the following conditions: systematic forced overtime, systematic health and safety risks that stem from negligence or the willful disregard of employee welfare, coercion, systematic deception that places workers at risk, underpayment of earnings, and income for a 48-hour workweek less than the overall poverty rate for that country (one who suffers from overall poverty lacks the income necessary to satisfy one's basic nonfood needs such as shelter and basic health care).

T

theoretical reasoning   Involves reasoning that is aimed at establishing truth and therefore at what we ought to believe. Contrast with practical reasoning, which aims at determining what is reasonable for us to do.

three pillars of sustainability   Three factors that are often used to judge the adequacy of sustainable practices. Sustainable development must be (1) economically, (2) environmentally, and (3) ethically satisfactory.

U

United States Sentencing Commission (USSC)   An independent agency in the United States judiciary created in 1984 to regulate sentencing policy in the federal court system.

Uniting and Strengthening America by Providing Appropriate Tools Required to Intercept and Obstruct Terrorism (USA PATRIOT) Act of 2001   A U.S. statute designed to increase the surveillance and investigative powers of law enforcement agencies in the United States in response to the terrorist attacks of September 11, 2001. The act has been lauded as a quick response to terrorism (it was introduced less than a week after the attacks) and for implementing critical amendments to more than 15 important statutes; it also has been criticized for failing to include sufficient safeguards for civil liberties.

utilitarianism   An ethical theory that tells us that we can determine the ethical significance of any action by looking to the consequences of that act. Utilitarianism is typically identified with the policy of "maximizing the overall good" or, in a slightly different version, of producing "the greatest good for the greatest number."

V

values   Those beliefs that incline us to act or to choose in one way rather than another. We can recognize many different types of values: financial, religious, legal, historical, nutritional, political, scientific, and aesthetic. Ethical values serve the ends of human well-being in impartial, rather than personal or selfish, ways.

values-based culture   A corporate culture in which conformity to a statement of values and principles rather than simple obedience to laws and regulations is the prevailing model for ethical behavior.

virtue ethics   An approach to ethics that studies the character traits or habits that constitute a good human life, a life worth living. The virtues provide answers to the basic ethical question "What kind of person should I be?"

W

whistle-blowing   A practice in which an individual within an organization reports organizational wrongdoing to the public or to others in position of authority.

Index